Advanced corporate legal procedures

Elizabeth A. Gillis

2004
EMOND MONTGOMERY PUBLICATIONS LIMITED
TORONTO, CANADA

Printed in Canada.

Edited, designed, and typeset by WordsWorth Communications, Toronto.
Cover design by John Vegter, CBC Art Department.

We acknowledge the financial support of the Government of Canada through the Book Publishing Industry Development Program (BPIDP) for our publishing activities.

The events and characters depicted in this book are fictitious. Any similarity to actual persons, living or dead, is purely coincidental.

Disclaimer. Although every effort has been made to ensure the completeness and accuracy of the material contained in this work, there is no warranty, express or implied, that the user will achieve the desired end. The publisher, and the authors and editors, disclaim any liability for loss, whether direct or indirect, flowing from the use of the procedures, precedents, and other materials contained in this work.

National Library of Canada Cataloguing in Publication Data

Gillis, Elizabeth A. (Elizabeth Anne), 1948–
    Advanced corporate legal procedures / Elizabeth A. Gillis.

Includes index.
ISBN 1-55239-031-4

    1. Corporation law—Ontario—Textbooks. 2. New business enterprises—Ontario—Textbooks. 3. Incorporation—Ontario—Textbooks. I. Title.

KE1345.G54 2004   346.713'066   C2004-902115-X
KF1355.G54 2004

To Millie, Hank, Ray, and Alanna
Thank you for all you have taught me and for always believing in me

Contents

PART IV
NOT-FOR-PROFIT CORPORATIONS

Preface

This book is written for law clerks. It is not a book on corporate law. It is a concise and comprehensive book about corporate procedures. It identifies, in simple terms, the legal issues that law clerks should be aware of to perform their responsibilities under the ultimate direction and guidance of lawyers. It does not concentrate heavily on precedents because most firms will have their own precedents, and if they do not, there are precedent sources available both in hard copy and on the Internet.

All of the precedents used in this book, unless otherwise indicated, are provided courtesy of Miller Thomson LLP.

The book is intended to be used by students of law clerk or paralegal courses and by students taking the Institute of Law Clerks of Ontario Associate level corporate course. After reading and learning the material provided in the book, students should be able to assist lawyers in the corporate practice area adequately.

The book is also intended as a reference manual for existing law clerks and lawyers who need to complete the corporate legal procedures discussed in the book.

Finally, the material in the book is accurate, subject to any errors and omissions, at the date of writing. The law, regulations, and policies and procedures are constantly changing. It is important to ensure that the procedures you are following are up to date at the time they are being used.

Elizabeth A. Gillis
Toronto, April 2004

Acknowledgments

The knowledge to write this book has been gained over my 30-year career in the Ontario legal profession from certain pivotal people. I was driven to author this book to share that knowledge and the standards that have been modelled to me by these mentors.

My career started at the law firm of Fraser & Beatty in the early 1970s at the encouragement of John Fuke. He suggested that I take a law clerk course, which I did. I owe my grounding as a law clerk in corporate law to the patience of Fraser & Beatty lawyers' Larry Hynes, John Elder, Bill Corbett, David Hasley, Harry Sutherland, Jack Whiteside, and many others at that firm who graciously accepted me into the team. It was also at Fraser & Beatty that I, an honest Scots woman, was introduced to "softball" and exposed to coaches of the Frasby Legals Softball team such as Ross Freeman and Ross King. It was due to David Waugh, initially an associate lawyer with Fraser & Beatty, that I received experience as a law clerk in real estate, corporate, wills and estates, and the many aspects of small firm administration with the firms of Jones & Waugh and Jones, Waugh, Yates & Kitamura. But it was Jim Matthews at Aird & Berlis who gave me my true grounding in corporate procedures. He always had faith in my abilities and encouraged me to take on more responsibility. When I ultimately moved to Miller Thomson LLP, I believe I hit the apex of my career. With expert guidance from Wayne Gray, I developed a technical appreciation for the nuances of the corporate statutes and corporate procedures.

In addition to the influences that many lawyers have had on my career over the years, I must also acknowledge the wealth of experience I gained through my volunteer work with the Institute of Law Clerks of Ontario (ILCO) and the Legal Assistant Management Association (LAMA). As a director, secretary, and ultimately president of ILCO and as editor of the *LAMA Manager*, chair of the LAMA Marketing Committee, LAMA Toronto Chapter chair, and co-chair of the 1998 LAMA Annual Conference, I had the opportunity to work with many accomplished and successful law clerks both in Canada and the United States of America.

My community college involvement has also shaped my knowledge. As a member of the Advisory Committee for the Legal Assistant Program at Durham College, I was part of an ad hoc committee that reviewed and recommended improvements to the program. At Seneca College, I taught ILCO's Associate Level Corporate Course and learned skills in teaching adults through Seneca's "Excellence in Adult Education" courses. With the constant encouragement of Barbara Silvers, I developed my course notes into the basis of this book. To my students at Humber College and Seneca College, thank you for giving me the opportunity to make my foray into teaching.

The journey of writing a book is like the journey of running a marathon, or building a house, both of which I have also undertaken. It requires the making of many decisions, consistent organization, unfailing commitment to the goal, and pain. As with the marathon, there are many people who have helped me along the journey and without whom the end of this book would never have been achieved.

Brenda Taylor, Catherine Vena, Patricia Hicks, Nicoletta Monachino, David Savarie, Dawn McKevitt, Vanessa Bonomo, and Robert Shipcott responded to my requests for advice, information, and ideas.

Brenda Taylor of Miller Thomson LLP contributed part IV of the text on not-for-profit corporations, for which I am grateful.

Judson Whiteside, chair and chief executive officer of Miller Thomson LLP, believed in my abilities and allowed me the opportunity to write this book.

Richard Leblanc, Tom Tower, and Jeff Woodlock, associate lawyers with Miller Thomson LLP, read the chapters for legal content.

Monica Thom Umpleby, who took on the huge task of organizing the text and preparing it for the publisher, helped me in ways I cannot count. I would not have done the book without her.

Paul Emond, Jim Black, and David Stokaluk of Emond Montgomery Publications and Jim Lyons, Nancy Ennis, and Paula Pike of WordsWorth Communications were supportive and professional over the whole long course of production and made the book better than I thought it would be.

My running buddies put up with me throughout the writing of the book.

Finally, and most importantly, I am grateful to my family — my husband Ray, my daughter Alanna, and my parents, all of whom have supported my commitment to the roles of employee, teacher, association worker, and writer. Without their understanding and generosity, I could not have begun, continued, or finished this book.

Abbreviations

References to statutes, government ministries, and government officials are listed throughout the text. The abbreviations that are most frequently used in the text are listed below.

SOURCE	ABBREVIATION
Statutes	
Business Corporations Act (Ontario), RSO 1990, c. B.16, as amended	OBCA
Business Names Act (Ontario), RSO 1990, c. B.17, as amended	BNA
Canada Business Corporations Act, RSC 1985, c. C-44, as amended	CBCA
Corporations Information Act (Ontario), RSO 1990, c. C.39, as amended	CIA
Extra-Provincial Corporations Act (Ontario), RSO 1990, c. E.27, as amended	EPCA
Income Tax Act (Canada), RSC 1985, c. 1 (5th Supp.), as amended	ITA
Limited Partnerships Act (Ontario), RSO 1990, c. L.16, as amended	LPA
Partnerships Act (Ontario), RSO 1990, c. P.5	PA
Government ministries and officials	
Canada Revenue Agency	CRA
Companies and Personal Property Security Branch of the Ontario Ministry of Consumer and Business Services (amalgamation of Companies Branch and Personal Property Security Registration Branch effective January 1, 2002)	Ontario Companies Branch or CPPSB
Director appointed under the CBCA	Federal Director
Director appointed under the OBCA	Ontario Director
Ontario Business Connects	OBC
Ontario Ministry of Consumer and Business Services	MCBS or Ontario ministry

PART I

An overview of the different types of business entities

CHAPTER 1

Legal structures for carrying on business and other activities

CHAPTER OVERVIEW

A person who decides to start up a business can choose from a number of forms of business organizations. This chapter discusses the various legal structures for carrying on business or other activities — for example, sole proprietorship, partnership, co-ownership, joint venture, limited liability corporation (LLC), franchise, and unincorporated association. The chapter highlights the major advantages and disadvantages of each structure and outlines any government filing requirements. It also includes a broad outline of the various types of corporations, both profit and not-for-profit.

CHAPTER OBJECTIVES

After completing this chapter, you should be able to:

1. List the various structures for carrying on business and other activities and discuss the advantages and disadvantages of each.

2. Identify when a particular structure is appropriate.

3. Complete the requisite forms to register a sole proprietorship and an extra-provincial LLC in Ontario.

4. Describe government filings required for the various activities discussed in the chapter.

INTRODUCTION

Individuals and corporations wishing to start a new business or not-for-profit venture have a number of options to choose from. In this chapter we consider the different forms of carrying on business with and without a "view to profit" and learn how to recognize the appropriate choice for a given set of circumstances. Given the space allowed in this text, it is not possible to give each topic more than a cursory glance — for example, "partnership" could be the subject of an entire book. Others have written books on this subject and other subjects covered in this chapter. At the end of this chapter, you will find a list of these texts for your reference.

SOLE PROPRIETORSHIP

Definition of sole proprietorship

sole proprietorship
the carrying on of business for profit by an individual without other owners

A **sole proprietorship** is the carrying on of business for profit by an individual without other owners.

Characteristics of sole proprietorship

The sole proprietorship is the simplest form of business in Canada. A sole proprietor is an individual. This individual can use his or her own name or a business name to identify the business. The sole proprietor may have employees, but he or she is the sole owner of the business.

All income or loss derived from the business is included in the personal income tax return for the sole proprietor, which is filed for the tax year ending December 31 by April 30 of the following year. The rate of income tax is based on the rate applicable to the individual for the year of filing.

A sole proprietor is personally responsible for all the obligations of the business. These obligations include all losses and liabilities, including those arising from wrongful acts of the sole proprietor or those of his or her employees. The sole proprietor also receives all the benefits of the business, including all profits.

Should one of the sole proprietor's customers or business associates decide to sue the business, the claim is made against the individual sole proprietor personally. All business and personal assets of the sole proprietor may be seized by an order of the court to satisfy debts and obligations of the sole proprietorship. Subject to the business name registration requirements set out below, the *Rules of Civil Procedure* allow a sole proprietor carrying on business in a name other than the individual's own name to sue and be sued in the name of the sole proprietorship.

It may be possible for a sole proprietor to reduce personal liability by purchasing insurance and by implementing creditor-proofing strategies on the advice of its legal and financial advisers.

Registration under the Business Names Act (Ontario)

Although there are few legal restrictions to carrying on business as a sole proprietor in Ontario, there are some registration and licensing processes that the sole proprietor may need to follow.

If a sole proprietor chooses to carry on business using a name other than the individual's own name, the business must be registered under the *Business Names Act* (Ontario) (BNA) (s. 2.(2)). Registration is accomplished by filing Form 1 under the BNA with the Ministry of Consumer and Business Services (MCBS) and paying the appropriate fee by cash, money order, or cheque. Form 1 must be filed before using the business name, although there is no penalty for late registration, which corrects any default. Upon completion of registration, the sole proprietor receives a **master business licence (MBL)** and a business identification number is assigned by the registrar. This number must be quoted on all subsequent amendments and renewals and on cancellation. The MBL can be used as proof of business name registration at financial institutions and to facilitate any other business-related registration with the Ontario government. It is intended that this one licence will eventually replace many of the government forms, licences, and certificates held by a business or businesses.

The following information must be printed on the form "clearly in capital letters":

1. The name to which the form relates. Each square provided on the form represents a letter of the alphabet. If the name you are registering exceeds the number of squares on one form, you can use additional forms. All items must be completed on the additional forms and the number of the additional pages completed in the top right-hand corner of each form.

2. An indication whether the form is for a new registration or a renewal, amendment, or cancellation of a registration.

3. If the individual has a place of business in Ontario,

    a. the mailing address of the individual set out in item 3 of the form; and

    b. the address of the individual's principal place of business in Ontario, including the municipality, street and number, if any, and postal code set out in item 4 of the form.

4. If the individual does not have a place of business in Ontario, the address of the individual's principal place of business outside Ontario, including the municipality, street and number, if any, and postal code set out in item 3 of the form. Item 4 of the form should be completed with the words "not applicable."

5. A description, which must not exceed 40 characters, of the activity being carried out under the name to which the form relates. The 40 characters include punctuation marks and spaces.

6. An indication that the individual is carrying out the activity in sole proprietorship.

7. The name of the individual, including first given name, initial of the second given name, if any, and surname.

8. The address of the individual, including the municipality, the street and number, if any, and the postal code. A post office box number is not acceptable.

master business licence (MBL)
a licence issued by the Ministry of Consumer and Business Services upon registration of a sole proprietorship, partnership, limited partnership, or business name that can be used as proof of business name registration at financial institutions and to facilitate any other business-related registration with the Ontario government

9. The name of the individual, if he or she has not authorized an attorney to submit the form.

10. If the individual has authorized an attorney to submit the form, the name of the attorney.

The form does not require a signature and can be submitted by any person (including a solicitor or a corporation) acting under a power of attorney that authorizes the person to submit the form on behalf of the individual.

The form can be filed by any of the methods illustrated in table 1.1.

If a sole proprietorship is registered under a different name from that of the owner, the name of the owner must be set out in full in all contracts, invoices, negotiable instruments, and orders involving goods or services issued or made by the sole proprietor.

When registering through Ontario Business Connects (OBC), you can also complete forms for electronic registration for Ontario retail sales tax vendor permit, employer health tax, and Workplace Safety and Insurance Board premiums.

The purpose of filing is to enable members of the public dealing with the sole proprietorship to find out the business owner's name by conducting a search of the business names public record at the Ontario Companies Branch. You will be able to obtain:

1. a certified copy of the record for any name registered; or

2. if the name searched is not registered, a certificate to that effect.

Sections 4(2) and (3) of the BNA and O. reg. 122/91 contain restrictions with respect to the use of permitted names under the BNA. Read these carefully to become familiar with the requirements, particularly since O. reg. 122/91 sets out certain words — for example, "college," "institute," or "university" — that may not be included in the name. The registrar appointed under the BNA is not permitted to accept a name that does not comply with the prescribed requirements. You may wish to conduct a search of the public record of business names and/or obtain a new upgraded automated name search (NUANS) report to see whether someone is already using the name you are about to register or whether there are other similar names. The process for obtaining a NUANS report is discussed in chapter 6. The NUANS database is a Canada-wide corporate and business name registry that will show corporations, business names, and trademarks similar to the name you are searching.

A registration made under the BNA is valid for five years and is renewable on an ongoing basis for periods of five years. There is provision for a late renewal within 60 days after expiration, provided that an additional late renewal fee is paid. To date, however, late renewal fees have not been prescribed by regulation.

If there is a change in the information that is filed, an amended registration must be made within 15 days of the change. There is no fee for filing an amendment.

When a sole proprietor ceases to carry on business under the registered name, a further Form 1 should be registered indicating "cancellation." There is no fee for filing a cancellation.

TABLE 1.1 INFORMATION FOR FILINGS UNDER THE BUSINESS NAMES ACT AND THE LIMITED PARTNERSHIPS ACT IN ONTARIO

Method of delivery	Filing fee
• By paper copy and attending in person at the Ministry of Consumer and Business Services (MCBS), Companies and Personal Property Registration Branch at 393 University Avenue, 2nd Floor, Toronto, M5G 2M2. A paper copy of Form 1 can be obtained from the MCBS or printed from the Ontario Business Connects (OBC) Web site at www.cbs.gov.on.ca/obc. You will receive the master business licence (MBL) during your visit.	$80.00 payable by cash or cheque to the Minister of Finance
• By mailing a paper copy together with the appropriate fee to the MCBS in Toronto. You will receive the MBL in the mail in 6 to 8 weeks.	$80.00 payable by cheque or money order payable to the Minister of Finance
• Online through one of the 140 dedicated self-help workstations operated by OBC services. To inquire about a location near you, call 416-314-9151. You will receive the MBL during your visit.	$60.00 payable by American Express, MasterCard or Visa
• Online through the OBC services at www.cbs.gov.on.ca/obc. You will receive the MBL in the mail in approximately 2 weeks. It will be mailed to the address shown on the form.	$60.00 payable by American Express, Master Card or Visa
• Electronically through Business Registration Online (BRO) available at Canada Revenue Agency (CRA) offices across the country. You will receive the MBL within 10 days.	$60.00 payable by American Express, Master Card or Visa
• Electronically through one of the MCBS's service providers — Cyberbahn Inc. and OnCorp Direct Inc. — if you have established an account with them. The MBL will be faxed to you within 3 hours. The original will then be mailed and should be received within a week.	$60.00 plus a service fee (approximately $32.10)

Note:

1 Renewals, amendments, or cancellations of sole proprietorships or partnerships cannot be processed online.
2 Filings for limited partnerships and limited liability partnerships cannot be processed online.

Penalties for non-compliance

A sole proprietor who does not comply with the BNA is deemed incapable of maintaining a proceeding in a court in Ontario in connection with that business except with leave of the court (s. 7(1)). This penalty is not too onerous, because the sole proprietor can register at any time and correct the default. Dollar penalties for non-compliance may be enforced through a summary offence notice procedure under the *Provincial Offences Act*. Fines of not more than $2,000 may be levied upon conviction; if the person is a corporation, the fine may not be more than $25,000 (s. 10).

Licensing

It may be necessary for an individual carrying on business to obtain a licence. Consider the following.

MUNICIPAL LICENCE

A local business or municipal licence may be required by plumbers, electricians, restaurants, taxi cabs, masseurs, cigar stores, and driving schools and for various other activities. This information is available from the municipal government.

PROVINCIAL LICENCE

Certain provincial laws may require a licence — for example, employment and personnel agencies, car dealers, real estate brokers, and securities dealers.

FEDERAL LICENCE

Examples of businesses requiring a federal licence include interprovincial carriers and businesses involving the use of aircraft.

Other provinces in Canada also have registration requirements for sole proprietorships. Ask the particular province for information regarding registration procedures.

PARTNERSHIP

The most popular method of carrying on business other than by way of sole proprietorship has historically been by way of partnership. This is generally due to the fact that incorporation has been available only since the mid-19th century.[1] It is believed that the concept of business "partnership" existed in Roman law and has developed slowly over the years. A "partnership" is basically a "contract" between parties. A large body of law developed in England dealing with every aspect of a partnership. However, it was not always easy to decipher the broader principles from the many detailed decisions. To deal with this situation, the British Parliament passed the *Partnership Act* in 1890, which codified all the major principles concerning partnerships.

There have not been many changes to this statute over the years, largely due to the fact that the law was well established when the statute was written.

Definition of partnership

The *Partnerships Act* (Ontario) (PA), which is modelled on the British *Partnership Act*, defines partnership as follows:

> **Partnership** is the relation that subsists between persons carrying on a business in common with a view to profit.

The definition in the PA goes on to exclude corporations: "but the relation between the members of a company or association that is incorporated by or under the authority of any special or general Act in force in Ontario or elsewhere, or registered as a corporation under any such Act, is not a partnership within the meaning of this Act."

Of key importance to determining whether a partnership exists is that the activity be carried on with "a view to profit." There are many court decisions that have interpreted "a view to profit."

General characteristics of a partnership

In Ontario there are three basic types of partnerships:

1. **general partnership** — a partnership in which each partner is liable for the debts and other obligations of all partners to an unlimited degree;

2. **limited partnership** — a partnership in which there are one or more general partners who are liable for the debts and other obligations of the other partners to an unlimited degree and one or more limited partners whose liability is limited to the amount that such limited partner has contributed to the partnership business; and

3. **limited liability partnership** — a partnership in which each partner is jointly and severally liable for all the debts and obligations of the partnership except for liabilities arising from professional negligence, which remain those of the partner whose acts or omissions or whose subordinates' acts or omissions resulted in the professional liability.

We take a more detailed look at the characteristics and registration requirements of partnerships in chapter 2.

CORPORATIONS

The most popular method of carrying on business today is by way of a corporation. A **corporation** has a separate legal identity from that of its principals and is brought into existence by filing a document — for example, articles of incorporation — under the appropriate statute or special statute of the jurisdiction in which the corporation carries on business. This might be a federal statute, a provincial statute, or a federal or provincial special act. Corporations have perpetual existence and cease to exist only when their charter is cancelled either voluntarily or for failure to comply with the requirements of their governing statute.

The following is a summary of the different types of "corporations," some of which are discussed in more depth in other chapters in this book:

---

partnership
the relation that subsists between persons carrying on a business in common with a view to profit

general partnership
a partnership in which each partner is liable for the debts and other obligations of all partners to an unlimited degree

limited partnership
a partnership in which there are one or more general partners who are liable for the debts and other obligations of the other partners to an unlimited degree and one or more limited partners whose liability is limited to the amount that such limited partner has contributed to the partnership business

limited liability partnership
a partnership in which each partner is jointly and severally liable for all the debts and obligations of the partnership except for liabilities arising from professional negligence, which remain those of the partner whose acts or omissions or whose subordinates' acts or omissions resulted in the professional liability

corporation
an entity with a separate legal identity from that of its principals, which is brought into existence by filing a document under the appropriate statute or special statute of the jurisdiction in which the corporation carries on business

1. ***Share capital corporations*** *with limited liability for their owners.*
   These corporations can be "closely held" — for example, a small family-owned
   business — or "offering"— for example, a corporation that lists its shares on a
   recognized stock market.

2. *Share capital corporations with unlimited liability for their owners.* Nova
   Scotia unlimited liability corporations (NSULCs) are often attractive to
   Canadian subsidiaries of US-based corporations. This is due to the fact that the
   US Internal Revenue Service treats them as "partnerships" and not as
   corporations, which may under certain circumstances be beneficial to the US
   corporation from a tax perspective.

3. *Professional corporations.* On November 1, 2001, the schedule to Bill 152,
   Balanced Budgets for Brighter Futures Act, 2000, came into force. This
   amended the *Law Society Act* to allow Ontario lawyers to carry on the practice
   of law through a corporation. The Ontario *Business Corporations Act* (OBCA)
   (s. 3(1)) provides for the incorporation of professional corporations. These are
   corporations that hold a valid certificate of authorization or other authorizing
   document issued under an act governing a profession. If the practice of a
   profession is governed by an act, a professional corporation may practise the
   profession if

   a. that act expressly permits the practice of the profession by a corporation
      and subject to the provisions of that act; or

   b. the profession is governed by an act named in schedule 1 of the *Regulated
      Health Professions Act, 1991*, one of the following acts, or a prescribed act:

      i. *Certified General Accountants Association of Ontario Act, 1983*;

      ii. *The Chartered Accountants Act, 1956*;

      iii. *Law Society Act*;

      iv. *Social Work and Social Service Work Act, 1998*; and

      v. *Veterinarians Act.*

   Every professional corporation is required to meet the following provisions
   of the OBCA (s. 3.2(1)):

   1. All of the issued and outstanding shares of the corporation shall be legally
   and beneficially owned, directly or indirectly, by one or more members of the
   same profession.

   2. All officers and directors of the corporation shall be shareholders of the
   corporation.

   3. The name of the corporation shall include the words "Professional Corporation" or "Société professionnelle" and shall comply with the rules respecting the
   names of professional corporations set out in the regulations and with the rules
   respecting names set out in the regulations or by-laws made under the Act governing the profession.

   4. The corporation shall not have a number name.

---

5. The articles of incorporation of a professional corporation shall provide that the corporation may not carry on a business other than the practice of the profession but this paragraph shall not be construed to prevent the corporation from carrying on activities related to or ancillary to the practice of the profession, including the investment of surplus funds earned by the corporation.

4. *Not-for-profit corporations.* These corporations do not issue share capital and are typically formed for social, community, or charitable purposes — for example, a service club could be incorporated as a not-for-profit corporation. The business of a not-for-profit corporation is limited to its stated objects and is carried on for purposes other than the financial gain of its members.

5. *Not-for-profit charitable corporations.* These are not-for-profit corporations with charitable objects — for example, a "foundation," which collects, invests, and distributes money to needy individuals and other charities, and a "charitable organization," which provides services directly to its target group by operating programs itself. These corporations are registered as charities with Canada Revenue Agency (CRA) to benefit from special tax status.

6. *Co-operative corporations.* A **co-operative** is defined as "a type of member-owned organization in which people with common interests and goals join forces to advance a cause such as providing housing assistance or promoting the interests of workers."[2]

    Co-operatives may be incorporated in Ontario under the *Co-operative Corporations Act*.

    Co-operative corporations are required to file returns pursuant to s. 2(1) of the *Corporations Information Act* (CIA).

> **co-operative**
> a type of member-owned organization in which people with common interests and goals join forces to advance a cause such as providing housing assistance or promoting the interests of workers

7. *Condominium corporations.* A **condominium** is defined as "a method of land ownership in which the entire property is owned by a corporation, which is in turn owned by the owners of individual units within the condominium; the ownership of the units is registered separately from the ownership of the complex as a whole."[3]

    In Ontario, condominium corporations are incorporated under the *Condominium Act, 1998.* This statute contains many provisions that, among others, govern:

    a. registration and creation of condominium corporations,

    b. the condominium declaration and description,

    c. ownership,

    d. officers and directors,

    e. owners,

    f. bylaws and rules,

    g. auditors and financial statements,

    h. sale and lease of units,

> **condominium**
> a method of land ownership in which the entire property is owned by a corporation, which is in turn owned by the owners of individual units within the condominium; ownership of units is registered separately from ownership of the complex as a whole

    i.   operation of the condominium corporation, including common expenses and repair and maintenance,

    j.   amalgamation, and

    k.   termination.

Condominium corporations are required to file returns pursuant to s. 2(1) of the CIA.

8. *Other special types of corporations.* The above list is not exhaustive of the different types of corporations. For example, many corporations are formed and governed by a special act of Parliament, such as CN Railways, loan and trust corporations, certain hospitals, religious organizations and other charities, and Crown corporations, both federal and provincial.

In addition, s. 2(3) of the OBCA states that it does not apply to:

- corporations within the meaning of the *Loan and Trust Corporations Act*, except as provided by that act;

- a corporation to which the *Co-operative Corporations Act* applies;

- a corporation to which the *Credit Unions and Caisses Populaires Act* applies;

- a corporation that is an insurer within the meaning of s. 141(1) of the *Corporations Act*; and

- railways operating under the *Railways Act*.

Section 3 of the *Canada Business Corporations Act* (CBCA) provides that no corporation shall carry on the business of

- a bank — banks are regulated by the federal *Bank Act*;

- a company to which the *Insurance Companies Act* applies; or

- a company to which the *Trust and Loan Companies Act* applies.

Except for corporations subject to the federal *Bank Act*, if the above companies are carrying on business in Ontario, they are required under the CIA to file Form 2 within 60 days of commencing their business.

LIMITED LIABILITY CORPORATIONS

Limited liability corporations (LLCs) are popular in the United States and other parts of the world and are included here because you may have to deal with them as shareholders of a corporate client or register them to carry on business in Canada. There is no standard LLC law in the United States and each state has its own rules. Generally, an LLC is a type of business that is an alternative to traditional corporations, general partnerships, and limited partnerships. Like general partnerships, LLCs have the advantage of "flowthrough" taxation — that is, the LLC's profits and losses flow through to the LLC members — and flexibility in management and other matters. Like corporations, LLCs have limited liability for their investing members or shareholders.

limited liability corporation (LLC) an alternative to a traditional corporation, general partnership, and limited partnership; like a general partnership, an LLC has the advantage of flowthrough taxation — that is, the LLC's profits and losses flow through to the LLC members — and flexibility in management and other matters; like a corporation, an LLC has limited liability for its investing members or shareholders

Although Ontario has no law under which an LLC can be created, effective February 15, 2001, the BNA provides that "no 'extra-provincial limited liability company' can carry on business in Ontario unless it has registered its company name" (BNA s. 2.1(2)).

The BNA defines **extra-provincial limited liability company** as an unincorporated association, other than a partnership, formed under the laws of another jurisdiction that grants to each of the members limited liability with respect to the liabilities of the association.

To date, it must carry on business in its registered name and cannot use a different business name.

Registration is made on Form 6 under the BNA and the process is the same as for a sole proprietor described above except that the information required is as follows:

1. The name of the company, including the words or abbreviations identifying the company as a limited liability company as required under the laws of the jurisdiction under which the company is formed.

2. An indication whether the form is for a new registration or a renewal, amendment, or cancellation of a registration.

3. If the company has a place of business in Ontario,

   a. the mailing address of the company; and

   b. the address of the principal place of business of the company in Ontario, including the municipality, the street and number, if any, and the postal code.

4. If the company does not have a place of business in Ontario, the address of the principal place of business of the company outside Ontario, including the municipality, the street and number, if any, and the postal code.

5. A description of the activity being carried on under the company name. The description shall not exceed 40 characters, including punctuation marks and spaces.

6. An indication that the company is an extra-provincial limited liability company.

7. The jurisdiction under whose laws the company is formed.

8. The name of the person submitting the form on behalf of the company. The form can be submitted on behalf of the LLC by

   • a general manager or representative of the LLC; or

   • an attorney acting under a power of attorney that authorizes the attorney to submit the form on behalf of the LLC.

JOINT VENTURE

A **joint venture**[4] is a commercial business activity that is carried on by two or more parties for a common purpose in compliance with established terms and

extra-provincial limited liability company
an unincorporated association, other than a partnership, formed under the laws of another jurisdiction that grants to each of the members limited liability with respect to the liabilities of the association

joint venture
a commercial business activity carried on by two or more parties for a common purpose in compliance with established terms and conditions

conditions. Joint ventures are usually created for a specific purpose or time period to share resources, profits, and losses. A "joint venture agreement" will set out the rights of the parties.

There are two forms of joint venture:

1. equity joint ventures, and

2. contractual joint ventures.

Equity joint ventures constitute a separate legal entity pursuant to a contribution of capital by the parties. The agreed form of ownership interest generally entitles each party to participate in the control of the business and share in the profits. Examples of an equity joint venture include a corporation, partnership, and limited partnership. An example of a well-known equity joint venture is that of MacMillan Bloedel and Bathurst Paper, which in 1983 decided to operate a joint venture under the name MacMillan Bathurst Inc. The vehicle they used was a corporation.

In an equity joint venture, the legal form of the joint venture will determine the form of the joint venture agreement. For example, if the joint venture is a corporation, the agreement will be a shareholder agreement; if the legal form is a partnership, the agreement will be a partnership agreement.

Contractual joint ventures include strategic alliances, partnerings, teaming arrangements, co-ownerships, licensing and distribution arrangements, and franchising systems. In these cases, a joint venture agreement that deals with the same basic legal issues as the shareholder agreement and the partnership agreement is used.

It is sometimes difficult to distinguish a contractual joint venture relationship from that of a partnership. The following steps will assist in making the distinction:

1. Establish the degree of separation among the joint venturers of the interests in and ownership of the property of the joint venture.

2. Determine the restrictions on the ability of a co-venturer to dispose of its own property.

3. Establish that decisions taken by members of the joint venture are unanimous.

4. Determine how gross revenues and expenses are allocated to each of the co-venturers as opposed to the calculation of profit or loss at the "venture" level.

The joint venture agreement should state that the parties do not intend to form a partnership.

The following are some of the basic provisions that should be included in the joint venture agreement:

- the objectives of the joint venture activity, including the scope of the activity and the consequences of failure to meet the objectives;

- the relationship between the parties;

- capital contributions and financing;

- other contributions such as personnel, expertise, and technology;

- patents, trademarks, and other intellectual property including, for example, ownership and cost of protection;

- allocations and distributions — that is, how each co-venturer will share in the profits and losses;

- management of the joint venture;

- book and record keeping and maintenance of financial information;

- transfer of ownership;

- rights upon default;

- resignation and withdrawal of the parties;

- exit strategies;

- termination of the joint venture activity; and

- dispute resolution procedures to be used.

FRANCHISES AND LICENCES

Both licences and franchise agreements provide a means of conveying information or intellectual property rights from one person to another to enable the receiver to carry on a commercial activity.[5]

A **franchise** is an arrangement formed by a written agreement whereby one person — the franchisor — grants a right to another person — the franchisee — to use a trademark or trade name in connection with the supply of goods or services by the franchisee. A franchise agreement requires the franchisee to conduct its business in accordance with operating methods and procedures developed and controlled by the franchisor — for example, McDonald's restaurants. The degree of sophistication of the procedures and the control of the franchisor vary widely according to the specific franchise. The franchisor has a continuing right to receive compensation from the franchisee through royalty fees, lease payments, or its sale of products to the franchisee for resale.

A **licence** is a contractual arrangement whereby the owner of certain property such as a trademark, copyright, or patent — the licensor — grants to another person — the licensee — the right to use such property for a royalty fee. Usually, the licensor has little control over the operation of the licensee's business.

Both franchisees and licensees are independent from the franchisor or licensor, and are not their employees.

Some advantages to operating a franchise include:

- the benefit of the goodwill of the franchisor,

- reduction of risk in going into business, and

- available knowledge of the franchisor.

The major disadvantages to the franchisee are the degree of control exercised by the franchisor over the franchisee's business and the continuing compensation that must be paid by the franchisee to the franchisor.

From the franchisor's perspective, the ability to expand the business by using the financial resources of the franchisee is a plus. A negative is the unknown suc-

franchise
an arrangement formed by a written agreement whereby one person — the franchisor — grants a right to another person — the franchisee — to use a trademark or trade name in connection with the supply of goods or services by the franchisee and requires the franchisee to conduct its business in accordance with operating methods and procedures developed and controlled by the franchisor

licence
a contractual arrangement whereby the owner of certain property such as a trademark, copyright, or patent — the licensor — grants to another person — the licensee — the right to use such property for a royalty fee

cess of the franchisee's business and the effect this may have on the franchisor's cash flow.

CO-OWNERSHIP

Co-ownership generally refers to a number of persons holding title to property. The key point to note is that the parties' relative interests remain separate and they are free to dispose of their interest without the consent of the other co-owners, subject to any agreement that the parties may have entered into. When drafting such an agreement, care must be taken to ensure that the terms of the agreement do not present the relationship between the parties as that of a partnership. The distinction between co-owner and partner is an important one to make because of the different legal rights attaching to partners — for example, the fact that the acts of one partner bind all the partners jointly and severally.

One advantage of co-ownership over partnership is the ability of the parties to claim capital cost allowance (CCA), or depreciation, at different times and at different rates. In a partnership, CCA must be reported at the partnership level, which requires that the partners agree on whether and how much CCA will be claimed in each year.

The PA sets out rules in s. 3 for determining the existence of a partnership and makes it clear that even if the co-owners share in profits generated by a property, such relationship alone does not create a partnership:

> 1. Joint tenancy, tenancy in common, joint property, common property, or part ownership does not of itself create a partnership as to anything so held or owned, whether the tenants or owners do or do not share any profits made by the use thereof.

UNINCORPORATED ASSOCIATIONS

Unincorporated associations are associations of persons carrying on a not-for-profit activity without the protection of incorporation. Like not-for-profit corporations, they may have charitable or non-charitable objects. Typically, members formulate a "constitution" or "memorandum of association" that sets out the purpose, management, and other rules of the association. Many associations are the forerunners of not-for-profit corporations.

There are no registration requirements for unincorporated not-for-profit associations. If the association has charitable objects, its members may apply to the CRA for charitable status registration and, if the association deals with property situated in Ontario, its members must file certain prescribed information with the Public Guardian and Trustee.

KEY TERMS

condominium

co-operative

co-ownership

corporation

extra-provincial limited liability
   company

franchise

general partnership

joint venture

licence

limited liability corporation (LLC)

limited liability partnership

limited partnership

master business licence (MBL)

partnership

share capital corporation

sole proprietorship

unincorporated association

REFERENCES

Business Corporations Act (Ontario) (OBCA), RSO 1990, c. B.16, as amended.

Business Names Act (Ontario) (BNA), RSO 1990, c. B.17, as amended.

Canada Business Corporations Act (CBCA), RSC 1985, c. C-44, as amended.

Condominium Act, 1998 (Ontario), SO 1998, c. 19.

Co-operative Corporations Act (Ontario), RSO 1990, c. C.35.

Corporations Information Act (Ontario) (CIA), RSO 1990, c. C.39, as amended.

Institute of Law Clerks of Ontario Corporate Syllabus 2002.

Law Society of Upper Canada, *Business Law*, Bar Admission Course Materials
   (Toronto: LSUC, 2001).

Partnerships Act (Ontario) (PA), RSO 1990, c. P.5, as amended.

Van Duzer, J. Anthony, *The Law of Partnerships and Corporations* (Toronto: Irwin
   Law, 1997).

FORMS AND PRECEDENTS

Figure 1.1: Form 1, *Business Names Act*

Figure 1.2: Form 6, *Business Names Act*

NOTES

1   J.E. Smyth, D.A. Soberman, and A.J. Easson, *The Law and Business Administration in Canada*, 9th ed. (Toronto: Prentice-Hall, 2001), 580.

2   Mark Walma and Patricia McCann-Smith, *The Fundamentals of Corporate Law and Procedure* (Toronto: Emond Montgomery, 2000), 34.

3   Mark W. Walma, *Advanced Residential Real Estate Transactions*, 2d ed. (Toronto: Emond Montgomery, 2003), 279.

4   Miller Thomson LLP, Mergers and Acquisitions Group, "Notes for Presentation on Strategic Alliances," April 10, 2001.

5   Law Society of Upper Canada, *Methods of Carrying On Business*, Business Law Reference Materials (Toronto: LSUC, 2000), 1–17.

REVIEW QUESTIONS

1. Explain briefly the significant features of the following methods of carrying on business:

    a.   sole proprietorship

    b.   partnership

    c.   co-ownership

    d.   joint venture

    e.   franchise

    f.   licence

    g.   corporation

2. Describe the circumstances under which an individual carrying on business as a sole proprietor would be required to register and give the statutory authority for doing so.

3. List three ways in which a sole proprietorship can be registered.

4. List the information that is required to complete a sole proprietorship registration.

5. When must the registration be made?

6. Can lawyers in Ontario incorporate? Explain your answer.

7. What restrictions would you find in the articles of a professional corporation?

8. List four items you would find in a joint venture agreement and explain them briefly.

9. List three types of partnerships in Ontario and briefly describe the significance of each.

10. Why is an NSULC attractive, and to whom?

11. What is an LLC? Where would you most likely find one: Ontario, Canada, or Delaware?

CASE STUDIES

Case study 1.1: Registration of a sole proprietorship

Hailey Hanberry has a small business designing freestyle routines and appropriate music for dressage riders riding the Kur (freestyle dressage ridden to music). She wants to call her business "Klassic Kur Designs" and has asked your firm for some advice regarding registration of the name. You explain that since she will be carrying on business in a name other than her own, she must register the business name pursuant to s. 2(2) of the *Business Names Act* (Ontario) by filing Form 1 under the Act prior to commencing business.

See figure 1.1 at the end of this chapter.

Case study 1.2: Registration of an LLC

Your firm is acting for a Delaware LLC called Glamour Beauty Products LLC, which wants to carry out its direct selling business in Ontario. It has established an office in Toronto that it will use as the address of the principal place of business in Ontario. Ronald D. Smith, the general manager, will authorize the registration. You are asked to complete the registration under s. 2.2(1) of the *Business Names Act* (Ontario) by preparing Form 6 under the Act.

See figure 1.2 at the end of this chapter.

FIGURE 1.1   FORM 1, BUSINESS NAMES ACT

 **Ontario**

Ministry of
Consumer and
Business Services

Ministère des Services
aux consommateurs
et aux entreprises

Registration   Form 1
under the Business Names Act - Sole Proprietorship / Partnership
Enregistrement   Formule 1
en vertu de la *Loi sur les noms commerciaux*
(Entreprise personnelle / société en nom collectif)

INSTRUCTIONS

It is important to read these notes before completing the attached form.

Print all information clearly in CAPITAL LETTERS using black ink.

Complete all sections of the form. Incomplete forms will be returned.

Fees: • there is a fee payable for new registrations and renewals;
• fees may be paid in cash, money order or cheque;
• payable to the **Ontario Minister of Finance;**
• do not send cash in the mail;
• a handling fee will be charged for a non-negotiable cheque.

Please forward both copies of the enclosed form to the Ministry of
Consumer and Business Services. The Client copy will no longer
be certified consistent with Ontario Regulation 175 / 94 Section 4.
The Client copy will be **returned**, with a validation in the bottom right-hand corner.

Return completed forms to: Ministry of Consumer and Business Services
Companies and Personal Property Security Branch
393 University Ave., Suite 200
Toronto ON M5G 2M2

Please do not separate the form.

Refer to these notes while completing form.

1. Registration Type - Check the appropriate box:
New   (Fee payable)
• a new registration is the first filing of the business name
• a change of business name, sole proprietor, or a complete change of partners, is considered a new registration
Renewal (Fee payable)
• a registration expires in five years and must be renewed
Amendment (No fee payable)
• an amendment should be filed whenever there is a change in address or change of activity
Cancellation (No fee payable)
• a cancellation should be submitted if you stop using the business name
BIN
For renewal, amendment or cancellation, enter "Business Identification No.".

2. Business Name - Please print the business name. This is the name you are registering. The business name must be set out in Block Capital Letters in the squares provided and must commence on the first line of the 'grid' in the first square. Each square of the grid represents a letter of the alphabet, a punctuation mark, or a space. If there is not sufficient space on the grid for the name, please use additional form(s). Please complete all items on additional form(s) and note the number of each additional page in the top right-hand corner of each form.

3. Mailing Address - Include street number, name, municipality and postal code. Your copy of the registration will be mailed to this address.

4. Address of Principal Place of Business in Ontario - Include street, number, name, municipality and postal code. A post office box is not acceptable in a business address. If there is more than one place of business, select one as the principal place. Where the business address is outside Ontario, set out the words "Not Applicable" in item 4. If this is the case, please ensure that Item 3, the mailing address, includes the street address of the principal place of business outside of Ontario, as a post office box is not acceptable.

5. Activity - Include a brief description of the activity being performed.

6. Type of Registrant - Check the appropriate box. If you are registering a partnership with more than 10 partners, you may set out the name and address of a designated partner(s), and check the box marked "More than 10 Partners". Information on all partners carrying on business in Ontario must be kept and made available to the public at the partnership business address.

7/8. Registrant Information - include the full name and residential address or address for service of the sole proprietor, each partner, or designated partner(s). A post office box is not acceptable. For partnerships with more than two partners, please fill out and attach another form(s) with the additional names and addresses.

Additional Information - If the registrant is **not** an individual, enter the name of the business or corporation in "Additional Information". Also enter the address of the business or corporation in item 8. If the registrant is a corporation, enter the corporation number in the space titled "Ontario Corporation No."

9. Print the name of the person authorizing this registration, (either a sole proprietor, or a partner, or a person acting under a power of attorney).

Additional Information: If the person authorizing the registration is not an individual, (e.g. corporation, trust, syndicate) set out the name in "Additional Information" and do not complete the boxes for the last, first and middle names.

en français au verso

07219 (03/2003)

FIGURE 1.1   CONCLUDED

Ministry of
Consumer and
Business Services

Ministère des Services
aux consommateurs
et aux entreprises

Registration   Form 1
under the Business Names Act - Sole Proprietorship / Partnership
Enregistrement   Formule 1
en vertu de la *Loi sur les noms commerciaux*
(Entreprise personnelle / société en nom collectif)

Print clearly in CAPITAL LETTERS /
Écrivez clairement en LETTRES MAJUSCULES

1.   Registration Type /
Type d'enregistrement

If B, C, or D enter "Business Identification Number" /
En cas de B, C ou D, inscrivez le n° d'identification de l'entreprise.

Page 1 of / de 1

A ☑ New
Nouvel

B ☐ Renewal
Renouvellement

C ☐ Amendment
Modification

D ☐ Cancellation
Révocation

BIN Business Identification No./
NIE le n° d'identification de l'entreprise

2.
Business Name /
Nom commercial

KLASSIC KUR DESIGNS

3.
Mailing Address /
Adresse postale

Street No./ N° de rue Street Name / Nom de la rue	Suite No. / Bureau n°
203 FERRIS LANE 6	
City / Town / Ville Province / Province	Postal Code / Code postal
MARKVILLE ON L5Y 1W1	
Country / Pays	
CANADA	

4.   Address of principal place of business in Ontario (*P.O. Box not acceptable*) /
Adresse de l'établissement principal en Ontario (*Case postale non acceptée*)

☑ Same as above / comme ci-dessus

Street No. / N° de rue Street Name / Nom de la rue	Suite No. / Bureau n° City / Town / Ville
203 FERRIS LANE	6 MARKVILLE
Province / Province	Country / Pays	Postal Code / Code postal
ON	CANADA	L5Y 1W1

5.   Give a brief description of the ACTIVITY being carried out under the business name./
Résumez brièvement le genre d'ACTIVITÉ exercée sous le nom commercial.

MUSIC PRODUCTION

6.   Type of Registrant /
Type de personne enregistrée

A ☑ Sole proprietorship /
Entreprise personnelle

B ☐ Partnership /
Société en nom collectif

☐ More than 10 Partners:
records at business address /
Plus de 10 associés :
dossiers à l'adresse d'affaires

7.   Registrant Information /
Renseignements sur la personne enregistrée

| Last Name / Nom de famille | First Name / Prénom | Middle Initial / initiale 2° prénom |
| HANBERRY | HAILEY | |

8.

Street No. / N° de rue Street Name / Nom de la rue	Suite No. / Bureau n° City / Town / Ville
203 FERRIS LANE	MARKVILLE
Province / Province	Country / Pays	Postal Code / Code postal
ONTARIO	CANADA	L5Y 1W1

Additional Information. Only complete if the registrant is not an individual. See instructions 7/8 on the form. /
Renseignements supplémentaires. À remplir uniquement si la personne enregistrée n'est pas un particulier.
Voir les instructions 7 et 8 sur le formulaire.

Ont. Corporation No. / (*For Corporate Partners Only*)
N° matricule de la personne morale en Ontario *Pour les personnes morales associées seulement*

7.

| Last Name / Nom de famille | First Name / Prénom | Middle Initial / initiale 2° prénom |
| | | |

8.

Street No. / N° de rue Street Name / Nom de la rue	Suite No. / Bureau n° City / Town / Ville
Province / Province	Country / Pays	Postal Code / Code postal

Additional Information. Only complete if the registrant is not an individual. See instructions 7/8 on the form. /
Renseignements supplémentaires. À remplir uniquement si la personne enregistrée n'est pas un particulier.
Voir les instructions 7 et 8 sur le formulaire.

Ont. Corporation No. / (*For Corporate Partners Only*)
N° matricule de la personne morale en Ontario *Pour les personnes morales associées seulement*

9.   Print name of person authorizing this registration / (*either the sole proprietor, a partner or a person acting under a power of attorney*)
If the person is a corporation, complete **additional information** below only. /
Indiquez en lettres majuscules le nom de la personne autorisant l'enregistrement / (*propriétaire unique, associé, ou personne habilitée en vertu d'une procuration*). (Si c'est une personne morale qui autorise l'enregistrement, compléter les **renseignements supplémentaires** ci-dessous).

| Last Name / Nom de famille | First Name / Prénom | Middle Initial / initiale 2° prénom |
| HANBERRY | HAILEY | |

If person authorizing the registration is not an individual (eg. corporation, trust, syndicate), print name below and do not complete last, first and middle names above. /
Si la personne qui autorise l'enregistrement n'est pas un individu (c'est-à-dire une personne morale, un trust ou syndicat) ne pas remlir le nom de famille, prénom et 2° prénom.

MINISTRY USE ONLY - RÉSERVÉ AU MINISTÈRE

Additional Information / Renseignements supplémentaires

07219 (03/2003)

FIGURE 1.2 FORM 6, BUSINESS NAMES ACT

 Ontario

Ministry of
Consumer and
Business Services

Ministère des Services
aux consommateurs
et aux entreprises

Registration Form 6
under the *Business Names Act* -
Ontario Limited Liability Partnership
Extra-Provincial Limited Liability Partnership
Extra-Provincial Limited Liability Company
Enregistrement Formule 6
en vertu de la Loi sur les noms commerciaux
Société à responsabilité limitée de l'Ontario
Société à responsabilité limitée extraprovinciale
Société de capitaux extraprovinciale

INSTRUCTIONS

It is important to read these notes before completing the attached form.

Print all information clearly in CAPITAL LETTERS using black ink.

Complete all sections of the form. Incomplete forms will be returned.

Fees: • there is a fee payable for new registrations and renewals;
• fees may be paid in cash, money order or cheque;
• payable to the **Ontario Minister of Finance;**
• do not send cash in the mail;
• a handling fee will be charged for a non-negotiable cheque.

Please forward both copies of the form to the Ministry of
Consumer and Business Services. The Client copy will no longer
be certified consistent with Ontario Regulation 175 / 94 Section 4.
The Client copy will be **returned**, with a validation in the bottom right-hand corner.

Return completed forms to: Ministry of Consumer and Business Services
Companies and Personal Property Security Branch
393 University Ave., Suite 200
Toronto ON M5G 2M2

Please do not separate the form.

Refer to these notes while completing form.

1. **Registration Type** - Check the appropriate box:

   New *(Fee payable)*
   • a new registration is the first filing of the business
   name
   • a change of business name, or a complete change of
   partners is considered a new registration
   Renewal *(Fee payable)*
   • a registration expires in five years and must be renewed
   Amendment *(No fee payable)*
   • an amendment should be filed whenever there is a
   change in address or change of activity
   Cancellation *(No fee payable)*
   • a cancellation should be submitted if you stop using the
   business name

   BIN
   For renewal, amendment or cancellation, enter "Business
   Identification No.".

2. **Business Name** - The name must contain the legal element
   which identifies the entity, for example; Limited Liability
   Partnership, LLP, Limited Liability Company, LLC or the
   equivalent French or other similar terms required under the law
   where the entity was formed. Please print the business name
   in Block Capital Letters in the squares provided, commencing
   on the first line of the "grid" in the first square. Each square of
   the grid represents a letter of the alphabet, a punctuation mark
   or a space. If there is not sufficient space on the grid for the
   name, please use additional form(s) and write the number of
   each additional page in the top right-hand corner of each form.

3. **Mailing Address** - Include street number, name, municipality
   and postal code. Your copy of the registration will be mailed
   to this address.

4. **Address of Principal Place of Business in Ontario** -
   Include street, number, name, municipality and postal code.
   A post office box is not acceptable in a business address. If
   there is more than one place of business, select one as the
   principal place. For an Extra-Provincial Limited Liability
   Partnership or an Extra-Provincial Limited Liability Company
   where the business address may be outside of Ontario, set
   out the words "Not Applicable" in item 4. If this is the case,
   please ensure that item 3, the mailing address, includes the
   street address of the principal place of business outside of
   Ontario, as a post office is not acceptable.

5. **Activity** - Include a brief description of the activity being
   performed.

6. **Type of Registrant** - Check the appropriate box. If you are
   registering an Ontario Limited Liability Partnership or an
   Extra-Provincial Limited Liability Partnership with more than
   10 partners, you may set out the name and address of a
   designated partner(s) and check the box marked "More than
   10 Partners". Information on all partners carrying on
   business in Ontario must be kept and made available to the
   public at the Limited Liability Partnership's business address
   in Ontario.

7. **Jurisdiction of Formation** - Enter the name of the jurisdiction
   in which the Ontario Limited Liability Partnership, the Extra-
   Provincial Limited Liability Partnership or the Extra-Provincial
   Limited Liability Company was formed. Please do not use
   abbreviations.

8/9. **Registrant Information** - This item applies only to an Ontario
   Limited Liability Partnership or to an Extra-Provincial Limited
   Liability Partnership (*it is not required for an Extra-Provincial
   Limited Liability Company*). Include the full name and
   residential address or address for service of each partner or
   designated partner(s). A post office box is not acceptable. If
   there are more than two partners, please fill out and attach
   another form(s) with the additional names and addresses.

   Additional Information - If the registrant is **not** an individual,
   enter the name of the business or corporation in "Additional
   Information". Also enter the address of the business or
   corporation in item 9. If the registrant is a corporation, enter
   the Ontario Corporation No.

10. **Print the name of the person authorizing this registration,**
   *(either a partner for a Limited Liability Partnership,
   a general manager/representative for a Limited Liability
   Company or a person acting under power of attorney).*

   Additional Information: If the person authorizing the
   registration is not an individual, *(e.g. corporation, trust,
   syndicate),* **set out the name, together with the name of
   the individual authorized to sign on that person's
   behalf,** in "Additional Information", and do not complete the
   space above. Eg:

   xxxx Limited
   Authorized to Sign: Last and First Name

en français au verso

07193 (03/2004)

FIGURE 1.2   CONCLUDED

| Ontario | Ministry of Consumer and Business Services | Ministère des Services aux consommateurs et aux entreprises | **Registration   Form 6**
under the *Business Names Act* -
Ontario Limited Liability Partnership
Extra-Provincial Limited Liability Partnership
Extra-Provincial Limited Liability Company
Enregistrement   Formule 6
en vertu de la Loi sur les noms commerciaux
Société à responsabilité limitée de l'Ontario
Société à responsabilité limitée extraprovinciale
Société de capitaux extraprovinciale |

Print clearly in CAPITAL LETTERS
Écrivez clairement en LETTRES MAJUSCULES

1. Registration Type
Type d'enregistrement

If B, C, or D enter "Business Identification Number"
En cas de B, C ou D, inscrivez le n° d'identification de l'entreprise.

Page 1 ____ of / de 1 ____

| A ☑ New *Nouveau* | B ☐ Renewal *Renouvellement* | C ☐ Amendment *Modification* | D ☐ Cancellation *Révocation* | BIN Business Identification No.
NIE N° d'identification de l'entreprise |

2.
Business Name
Nom commercial

GLAMOUR BEAUTY PRODUCTS LLC

3.
Mailing Address
Adresse postale

Street No. / N° de rue   Street Name / Nom de la rue   Suite No. / Bureau n°
123 ELM STREET 100

City / Town / Ville   Province / Province   Postal Code / Code postal
CARMEL CALIFORNIA   87619

Country / Pays
U.S.A.

4. Address of principal place of business in Ontario *(P.O. Box not acceptable)*
Adresse de l'établissement principal en Ontario (Case postale non acceptée)   Same as above *comme ci-dessus* ☐

| Street No. / N° de rue
120 | Street Name / Nom de la rue
EDWARD AVENUE | Suite No. / Bureau n°
1 | City / Town / Ville
TORONTO |
| Province / Province
ONTARIO | | Postal Code / Code postal
H5Z 2Y1 | Country / Pays
CANADA |

5. Give a brief description of the ACTIVITY being carried out under the business name.
Résumez brièvement le genre d'ACTIVITÉ exercée sous le nom commercial.

DIRECT SALES OF BEAUTY PRODUCTS

6. Type of Registrant
Type d'entité enregistrée   ☐ More than 10 Partners: records at business address / *Plus de 10 associés : dossiers à l'adresse d'affaires*

| A ☐ Ontario Limited Liability Partnership
Société à responsabilité limitée de l'Ontario **OU** | B ☑ Extra-Provincial Limited Liability Partnership
Société à responsabilité limitée extraprovinciale **OU** | C ☐ Extra-Provincial Limited Liability Company
Société de capitaux extraprovinciale |

8. Registrant Information *(P.O. Box not acceptable)*
Renseignements sur la personne enregistrée (Case postale non acceptable)

7. Jurisdiction of Formation / *Territoire d'origine*
DELAWARE

9. Last Name / *Nom de famille* — First Name / *Prénom* — Middle Initial / *Initiale 2e prénom*

Street No. / N° de rue   Street Name / Nom de la rue   Suite No. / Bureau n°   City / Town / Ville

Province / Province   Postal Code / Code postal   Country / Pays

Additional Information. Only complete if the registrant is not an individual. See instructions 8/9 on the form.
Renseignements supplémentaires. *À remplir uniquement si la personne enregistrée n'est pas un particulier. (Voir Instructions, art. 8 /9)*

Ont. Corporation No.
N° matricule de la personne morale en Ontario

8. Last Name / *Nom de famille* — First Name / *Prénom* — Middle Initial / *Initiale 2e prénom*

9. Street No. / N° de rue   Street Name / Nom de la rue   Suite No. / Bureau n°   City / Town / Ville

Province / Province   Postal Code / Code postal   Country / Pays

Additional Information. Only complete if the registrant is not an individual. See instructions 8/9 on the form.
Renseignements supplémentaires. *À remplir uniquement si la personne enregistrée n'est pas un particulier. (Voir Instructions, art. 8 /9)*

Ont. Corporation No.
N° matricule de la personne morale en Ontario

10. Print name of person authorizing this registration *(either a partner (for LLP), a general manager/representative (for LLC) or a person acting under power of attorney).*
Indiquez en lettres majuscules le nom de la personne autorisant l'enregistrement (associé (s.r.l.), directeur général / représentant (s.c.), ou personne habilitée en vertu d'une procuration).

| Last Name / *Nom de famille*
SMITH | First Name / *Prénom*
RONALD | Middle Initial / *Initiale 2e prénom*
D |

Additional Information: If the person authorizing the registration is not an individual, *(e.g. corporation, trust, syndicate),* **set out the name,** together with the name of the individual authorized to sign on that person's behalf, in "Additional Information", and do not complete the space above. Eg:
   xxxx Limited
   Authorized to Sign: Last and First Name

Renseignements supplémentaires :
Si l'enregistrement est autorisé par une entreprise (personne morale, société de fiducie, consortium, etc.), **indiquez** *ci-dessous la raison sociale de l'entité et le nom de la personne habilitée à signer (voir Instructions, art. 10).*

MINISTRY USE ONLY - *RÉSERVÉ AU MINISTÈRE*

Additional Information *(name)* / *Renseignements supplémentaires (raison sociale)*

Authorized to Sign / *Signataire autorisé*
Last Name / *Nom de famille*   First Name / *Prénom*

07193 (03/2004)

CHAPTER 2

Carrying on business in partnership

CHAPTER OVERVIEW

This chapter reviews the provisions of the *Partnerships Act* and how they relate to general partnerships and limited liability partnerships and the provisions of the *Limited Partnerships Act* and how they relate to limited partnerships and extra-provincial limited partnerships. It also discusses how to register general partnerships under the *Business Names Act* and limited partnerships under the *Limited Partnerships Act*.

CHAPTER OBJECTIVES

After completing this chapter, you should be able to:

1. Differentiate between general partnerships, limited liability partnerships, limited partnerships, and extra-provincial limited partnerships in Ontario.

2. Apply the provisions of the statutes governing partnerships in Ontario.

3. Identify the filings required to register the different types of partnerships in Ontario.

4. List other filings required in connection with partnerships in Ontario.

INTRODUCTION

Two or more persons who come together to carry on business with a view to profit may agree to carry on business in partnership. Each member of the partnership, whether an individual or corporation, is called a "partner." Partnership is similar to sole proprietorship in that the individuals carry on business in their own right. A partnership is not considered a separate legal entity. Partnerships are a common legal structure for small businesses but they can also be used by large corporations on a joint venture basis.

In Ontario, there are three types of partnerships:

1. *General partnerships.* In a general partnership, each partner is liable for the debts and other obligations of all partners to an unlimited degree.

2. *Limited liability partnerships.* A limited liability partnership (LLP) is a type of general partnership that is applicable only to the practice of a profession governed by the *Partnerships Act*. It must be registered in order to exist. In an LLP, the partners have limited protection against the professional negligence of other partners.

3. *Limited partnerships.* In a limited partnership, there are one or more general partners who are liable for the debts and other obligations of the other partners to an unlimited degree, and one or more limited partners whose liability is limited to the amount that the limited partner has contributed to the partnership business.

GENERAL PARTNERSHIPS
Characteristics

In Ontario, the statute that governs partnerships is the *Partnerships Act* (PA). The provisions of the PA are short and much of the law governing partnerships is based on the contractual arrangements between the partners and precedent established by **common law**. As well, there is a large body of case law that will be considered when interpreting statutory provisions or contracts between the parties. In addition, s. 45 of the PA provides that the "rules of equity and of common law applicable to partnership continue in force, except so far as they are inconsistent with the express provisions of this Act." Rules of equity were developed in England to ensure that justice and equity were used to complement the technical provisions of the law.

common law
the body of recognized legal principles that is derived from case law and judicial precedent

This discussion on general partnerships follows the layout of the PA and covers the following:

1. defining the nature of a partnership,

2. relation of partners to persons dealing with them,

3. relation of partners to one another,

4. dissolution of general partnerships.

Following the discussion of the provisions of the PA we examine the registration requirements for general partnerships as set out in the *Business Names Act* (BNA).

DEFINING THE NATURE OF A PARTNERSHIP (ss. 2–5)

Section 2 of the PA reads:

Partnership is the relation that subsists between persons carrying on a business in common with a view to profit, but the relation between the members of a company or association that is incorporated by or under the authority of any special or general Act in force in Ontario or elsewhere, or registered as a corporation under any such Act, is not a partnership within the meaning of this Act.

This definition provides three criteria for the existence of a partnership:

1. The partners must be "carrying on a business" — the definition of "business" under the PA is broad and includes every trade, occupation, and profession. Section 3 helps to clarify the meaning by providing rules for determining the existence of a partnership. These include:

    1. Joint tenancy, tenancy in common, joint property, common property, or part ownership does not of itself create a partnership as to anything so held or owned, whether the tenants or owners do or do not share any profits made by the use thereof.

    2. The sharing of gross returns does not of itself create a partnership, whether the persons sharing such returns have or have not a joint or common right or interest in any property from which or from the use of which the returns are derived.

    3. The receipt by a person of a share of the profits of a business is proof, in the absence of evidence to the contrary, that the person is a partner in the business, but the receipt of such a share or payment, contingent on or varying with the profits of a business, does not of itself make him or her a partner in the business.

    Section 3 continues with a number of circumstances where receipt of a share in profits does not constitute carrying on business.

2. There must be "a view to making a profit." Therefore, a not-for-profit association such as a club will not be considered a "partnership." In addition, note s. 3.2 of the PA, which provides that the "sharing of gross returns does not of itself create a partnership." In other words, an author is not considered to be in partnership with the publisher just because the author receives royalties from the sale of the author's book.

3. Finally, the partners must have agreed to be "carrying on business in common." They can agree orally or in writing, or it may be evident from their conduct.

It is not always easy to determine whether a partnership relation exists. In arriving at a decision, the courts will look at the parties' intent set out in the agreement, if any, or their conduct. Generally, therefore, it is better for those carrying on business in partnership to enter into a written agreement or describe themselves as partners and behave as such by carrying on business in common, contributing property or services to the business, sharing in its net profits, sharing in its losses, and being involved in the affairs of the business.

Use of the word "firm"

The members of a partnership are called "partners." For the purposes of the PA, partners collectively are called a "firm" and the name under which the partners' business is carried on is called the firm name (PA s. 5).

Separate entity

As in a sole proprietorship, in a general partnership the partners carry on business themselves directly. A partnership is not a "legal entity" separate from its partners. At one stage lawsuits could only be brought by or against the partners. Now, the *Rules of Civil Procedure* permit a registered partnership to sue or be sued in the firm name.

A person cannot be both a partner and an employee of the partnership because no person can enter into a contract with himself or herself.

RELATION OF PARTNERS TO PERSONS DEALING WITH THEM (ss. 6–19)

The PA contains provisions regarding the relation of partners to third persons. These provisions cannot be varied by agreement of the partners.

Power of a partner to bind the firm

One of the important factors of partnership law with respect to the relations of partners to third parties is the fact that each partner is an agent of the partnership and the other partners when acting in the normal course of the business of the partnership. Thus, one partner's actions bind all the partners (the law of principal and agent). A partner does not bind the firm when it is obvious that the partner is not acting within the scope of the partnership business or when a third party knows that the partner has no authority to bind the firm (s. 6).

Each partner is liable with all the other partners to the full extent of such partner's personal assets for all debts and other obligations incurred by the firm while such person is a partner. This is a joint liability, which means that a judgment against or release of one partner bars action against the others.

Even after death, a partner's estate remains severally liable for partnership debts and obligations, to the extent that they remain unsatisfied, subject to the prior payment of the partner's individual debts.

In the case of tortious liability, the firm is liable and each partner is jointly and severally liable, to the same extent as the partner committing the wrongdoing, for any penalty, loss, or injury caused to a non-partner acting in the ordinary course of the firm's business or with the authority of the other partners (s. 11).

If a partner, acting within the scope of the partner's authority, receives property of a third person and misapplies it, or if a partner misapplies property of a third person received by the firm in the course of its business, the firm is liable and each partner is jointly and severally liable to make good the loss (s. 12).

A person is not liable to the creditors of the firm for anything done before becoming a partner.

A retired partner remains liable for partnership debts or obligations incurred before retirement unless such partner is discharged by an agreement between the partner, the remaining partners, and the firm's creditors. A retired partner is not liable for the obligations of the firm if the partner is not known to the person dealing with the firm to be a partner. Under the PA, a retired partner can achieve this status with persons who had not had dealings with the firm before he retired by publishing an advertisement in the *Ontario Gazette* regarding his retirement. Other persons who did deal with the firm when the retired partner was a partner should be given notice of the partner's retirement (ss. 18 and 36).

RELATION OF PARTNERS TO ONE ANOTHER (ss. 20–31)

The PA contains provisions regarding the relation of partners to one another. These may be varied according to agreement among the partners.

Rights, duties, and obligations of partners (s. 20)

General partnerships are by law presumed to be based on the mutual trust and confidence of each partner, not only with respect to that partner's skill and knowledge but also in the integrity of every other partner. Although this principle is not specifically set out in the PA, it is implied by ss. 29 and 30:

1. Section 29 requires a partner to account to the firm for any benefit derived without the consent of the other partners from a transaction relating to the partnership or partnership property.

2. Section 30 prohibits a partner from carrying on a business competing with that of the firm without the consent of the other partners.

Partnership property (ss. 21–23)

Unless the contrary can be shown, any property that the partners have contributed to the partnership or purchased in the course of business belongs to the partnership and is known as partnership property.

A partner has a right to a division of the profits on an equal basis or as agreed on by the partners. A partner is entitled to the sale and division of the proceeds of partnership property only on dissolution of the partnership, after the discharge of all the partners' liabilities (s. 39).

DISSOLUTION OF GENERAL PARTNERSHIPS (ss. 32–44)

Unless an agreement exists to the contrary, a partnership is dissolved upon any of the events set out in the PA.

Dissolving events

A partnership is dissolved:

1. on the expiration of the term fixed for its existence;

2. at the termination of the single adventure or undertaking for which it was entered into;

3. if entered into for an undefined time, by a partner giving notice to the other partners of that partner's intention to dissolve the partnership on the date mentioned in the notice or, if no date is given, on the date of the notice's communication; and

4. by the death or insolvency of a partner.

Illegality of business

In addition, a partnership is immediately dissolved by the occurrence of any event that makes it unlawful for the business of the firm to be carried on or for the members of the firm to carry it on in partnership.

General dissolution by the court

On application by a partner, a court may order dissolution of the partnership in the circumstances provided in s. 35 of the PA, which include:

- mental incompetence;

- incapacity to perform the partnership contract;

- conduct prejudicial to the business;

- persistent breach of the partnership agreement or other conduct by a partner that makes it impracticable for the other partner or partners to continue in partnership with such partner;

- when the partnership can only be carried on at a loss; or

- where in the opinion of the court it is just and equitable that a partnership be dissolved.

LIMITED LIABILITY PARTNERSHIPS (ss. 44.1–44.4)

The PA was amended in 1998 to allow limited liability partnerships (LLPs). Their business is limited by s. 44.2 to carrying on business for the purpose of practising a profession governed by an act and only if

1. that act expressly permits an LLP to practise the profession;

2. the governing body of the profession requires the partnership to maintain a minimum amount of liability insurance; and

3. the partnership complies with the registration requirements of the PA under the BNA.

Examples of LLPs include many law firms and accounting firms.

The main difference between a general partnership and an LLP is the partner's exposure to liability. Section 10(2) of the PA provides that a partner in an LLP is not liable, by means of indemnification, contribution, assessment, or otherwise, for debts, obligations, and liabilities of the partnership or any partner arising from negligent acts or omissions that another partner or an employee, agent, or representative of the partnership commits in the course of the partnership business. A partner is still liable for the partner's own negligence or the negligence of a person under the partner's direct supervision or control.

Unlike general partnerships, but similar to limited partnerships, LLPs come into existence when two or more persons enter into a written agreement that designates the partnership as an LLP and states that the PA governs the agreement.

The PA provides for an existing partnership to continue as an LLP if all the partners enter into an agreement setting out the matters as above. If there is an existing partnership agreement, the partners can amend the agreement to provide as above. Thus, once the Law Society of Upper Canada amended the *Solicitors Act* to allow for lawyers in Ontario to practise their profession by way of an LLP, many law firms amended their partnership agreements in accordance with these provisions of the PA.

LLPs formed in other jurisdictions can carry on business in Ontario provided that they register under the BNA. The laws of the jurisdiction where the extra-provincial LLP is registered govern the organization, internal affairs, and liability of its partners for debts, obligations, and liabilities of or chargeable to the partnership or any of its partners.

REGISTRATION OF GENERAL PARTNERSHIPS AND LIMITED LIABILITY PARTNERSHIPS IN ONTARIO

Section 2(3) of the BNA reads:

> No persons associated in partnership shall carry on business or identify themselves to the public unless the firm name of the partnership is registered by all of the partners.

Section 2(3.2) exempts a corporation that carries on business or identifies itself to the public by a name other than its corporate name from the registration requirements of the BNA if the name is registered as a partnership under the BNA or as a limited partnership under the *Limited Partnerships Act*.

As a result of BNA s. 2(3.2), if you are asked to register a partnership consisting of two corporations under the BNA, you need to make only one registration under the BNA — the partnership registration on Form 1 (see chapter 1).

Section 2(3.3) states that the BNA does not apply to prohibit persons associated in a limited partnership from carrying on business in accordance with the LPA.

A partnership is not, however, required to be registered if the partnership identifies itself or carries on business under a name that is composed of the names of the partners (s. 2(4)).

Section 2(3.1) allows a partnership to carry on business or identify itself to the public under a name other than the firm name — that is, a "business name" — provided that the partnership is registered under the BNA and the business name is also registered under the BNA. The form required to register a business name for a partnership is Form 5.

Under s. 2(6) of the BNA, the partnership must set out both the partnership name and the registered business name in all contracts, invoices, negotiable instruments, and orders involving goods or services issued or made by the partnership.

Registration procedures

Registration of a partnership is made by filing Form 1 under the BNA. This is the same form required to register a sole proprietorship and the procedure is identical. Refer to table 1.1 in chapter 1 for the different methods of registration.

Registration must be made before commencing business, although late registration corrects any default. Registration is valid for a period of five years, after which it can be renewed on an ongoing basis for further periods of five years.

The information required to complete the form is set out in s. 2(1) of O. reg. 121/91, as amended:

1. The firm name followed by

   a. the words "limited liability partnership" or "société à responsabilité limitée" or the abbreviations "L.L.P." or "s.r.l." as required by s. 44.3(3) of the PA (if the partnership is an LLP as defined in the PA, formed under the laws of Ontario); or

   b. the words or abbreviations, if any, that identify the partnership as an LLP and that are required by the laws of the jurisdiction under which the partnership is formed (if the partnership is an extra-provincial LLP as defined in the PA).

2. An indication whether the form is for a new registration or a renewal, amendment, or cancellation of a registration.

3. If the partnership has a place of business in Ontario,

   a. the mailing address of the partnership, and

   b. the address of the principal place of business of the partnership in Ontario, including the municipality, the street and number, if any, and the postal code.

4. If the partnership does not have a place of business in Ontario, the address of the principal place of business of the partnership outside Ontario, including the municipality, the street and number, if any, and the postal code.

5. A description of the activity being carried out under the firm name. This description should not exceed 40 characters, including punctuation marks and spaces.

6. The name of each partner — that is, the first given name, the initial of the second given name, if any, and the surname — if the partner is an individual; the Ontario corporation number, if the partner is a corporation.

7. The address of each partner who is an individual, including the municipality, the street and number, if any, and the postal code.

8. The address for service of each partner that is not an individual, including the municipality, the street and number, if any, and the postal code.

9. The name of the person submitting the form on behalf of the partnership.

10. In the case of an LLP as defined in the PA,

    a. an indication whether it is an LLP formed under the laws of Ontario or an extra-provincial LLP as defined in the Act, and

    b. the jurisdiction under whose laws the partnership is formed.

The form can be submitted on behalf of the partnership by

1. one of the partners, or

2. an attorney acting under a power of attorney that authorizes the attorney to submit the form on behalf of the partnership.

A partner who submits a form on behalf of a partnership with more than 10 partners and a principal place of business in Ontario is known as a **designated partner**.

If the designated partner maintains a record of partners, other than with respect to his or her own information, the designated partner may omit items 6, 7, and 8 above — that is, the name of each partner, the address of each partner who is an individual, and the address for service of each partner that is not an individual — from the registration form. In order to do this, the designated partner must comply with O. reg. 121/91 ss. 3(3), (4), (5), (6), and (7).

The record of partners, which on request and without charge is open to inspection by any person during the normal business hours of the partnership, must show:

1. the persons associated in the partnership who carry out the business of the partnership in Ontario;

2. the name of each partner, the address of each partner that is an individual, and the address for service of each partner that is not an individual; and

3. the date on which each partner became associated in the partnership.

The record must also show:

1. the persons who were associated in the partnership on or after May 1, 1991 who carried out the business of the partnership in Ontario and who subsequently left the partnership, and

2. the period during which each person was associated in the partnership.

The designated partner may delete information regarding a person who has left the partnership when six years have elapsed after the departure.

O. reg. 121/91 prescribes restrictions with respect to the name to be used. These restrictions resemble the restrictions under the company statutes but are more flexible. The BNA provides that a person who suffers damages by reason of the registration of a name that is the same as or deceptively similar to another person's registered name is entitled to recover compensation from the registrant for damages suffered because of registration up to the greater of $500 and the actual amount of damages incurred.

In view of the foregoing, it is recommended that before registering any business or partnership name, you conduct searches to determine whether there are any similar names registered. See chapter 6 for a complete discussion on the different types of searches.

Change to information registered (BNA s. 4(4))

If there is a change in information set out in a registration, an amended registration showing the change and signed by any one partner must be registered within 15 days after the change. This change too is registered using Form 1 of the BNA. There is no filing fee for registering a declaration of change.

designated partner
a partner in a partnership with more than 10 partners and a principal place of business in Ontario who submits a form on behalf of the partnership for registration under the *Business Names Act*

Cancelling registration (BNA s. 4(7))

When the partnership no longer exists, a cancellation may be registered by once again completing Form 1 and checking the appropriate box at item 4D. There is no filing fee for registering a cancellation.

Renewal of registration (BNA s. 5)

A registration may be renewed before it expires by paying the prescribed fee. A registration may also be renewed within 60 days after it expires by paying a late renewal fee. To date, late renewal fees have not been prescribed by regulation. The renewal is effective on the day immediately following the expiration day of the registration that is being renewed.

Penalties for non-compliance

A person who does not comply with the BNA is deemed incapable of maintaining a proceeding in a court in Ontario in connection with the business except with leave of the court (s. 7(1)). Dollar penalties for non-compliance may be enforced through a summary offence notice procedure under the *Provincial Offences Act*. Fines of not more than $2,000, or if the person is a corporation, $25,000, may be levied on conviction (s. 10).

As with the late registration of a sole proprietorship, a partnership may be registered at any time without a late filing penalty, and this filing corrects any default.

Searching public records

At the time the registration is made, the information is uploaded into the Ontario Business Information System (ONBIS) with the Ontario Companies and Personal Property Security Branch ("Ontario Companies Branch"). The purpose of the registration system is to make available sufficient information about the partnership and the firm to enable a plaintiff to serve each partner with notice of an action. It is also helpful to prospective creditors or other suppliers in checking the accuracy of information provided by a member of the partnership concerning the membership of the firm. Any member of the public may attend at the offices of the Ontario Companies and Personal Property Security Branch, at 375 University Avenue in Toronto, or order an electronic search through one of the ministry's service providers and for a small fee obtain either a document replica of the registration or a business names and limited partnerships (BNLP) document list. If the search reveals that the partnership has more than 10 partners and a designated partner has registered the declaration, it will be necessary to contact the designated partner in order to inspect the record of partners. This is provided for under s. 3(6) of O. reg. 121/91 as amended by O. reg. 579/91 and O. reg. 332/92.

History of partnership registrations

Before the BNA came into force on May 1, 1991, the statute governing the registration of partnerships was the *Partnerships Registration Act*. This was repealed by the BNA. The BNA includes businesses in the professional and service sectors. Previously, only businesses engaged in trading, manufacturing, or mining activities were required to register. The BNA consolidated registration requirements for business names, sole proprietorships, and partnerships under the one statute.

Taxation of partnerships

The income or loss of the business carried on in partnership is determined at the partnership level and then allocated to the members of the partnership. The partnership itself is *not* a taxable entity.

Expenditures, capital cost allowance, and other deductions are subtracted from the income of the partnership to determine whether the partnership has a net income or loss. The resulting income or loss is divided among the partners and pro-rated to each partner's contribution. Each partner's share of the income or loss is included in the calculation for that partner's income from all sources for tax purposes.

If the partner is an individual, the partner is taxed at the rates applicable to individuals under the *Income Tax Act*, as is a sole proprietor.

A corporate partner is taxed on its share of the partnership income at the applicable corporate tax rates.

A partnership is treated as a separate person for the purposes of the goods and services tax (GST) under the *Excise Tax Act*. The partnership must register for GST and collect and remit GST as required.

PARTNERSHIP AGREEMENTS

Although many small businesses operate without a partnership agreement, it is often wise to put such an agreement in place before a dispute occurs or if the partners wish to deviate from any of the provisions of the PA with regard to their internal relationships. In any event, larger partnerships will generally have a partnership agreement.

There are many important considerations for drafting an agreement, each of which will be specific to the particular circumstances. A good knowledge of the provisions in the PA is essential. There are several different approaches to drafting a partnership agreement. Some practitioners start with a good precedent and adapt it to meet the circumstances. Another approach is to work from a checklist and make an outline of the areas to be included in the agreement. If there is an appropriate precedent available, this can be adapted, or it may be necessary to draft the bulk of the agreement. There are also certain standard items to be included.

If you are asked to draft a partnership agreement, ask the lawyer you are working with for a precedent. This will provide a starting point, but you will need to read all the provisions in the precedent carefully to decide which ones apply in your particular circumstance.

The following is a brief discussion of some of the sections you are likely to find in a partnership agreement. It is not intended to be a full instruction on how to draft partnership agreements. Many legal issues that must be considered are beyond the scope of this book. This discussion is intended as an introduction to the non-lawyer of some of the basic parts of an agreement. It is neither inclusive nor legally based.

Usually, the body of the agreement is divided into parts and the parts are further subdivided into sections, subsections, paragraphs, subparagraphs, and clauses, which are given numbers. This facilitates reference and ensures consistency.

Typically, the divisions of an agreement are named and given headings that describe the subject matter of their content. Usually, the type size and face of the headings is styled.

The divisions of an agreement should be numbered consecutively. There is a wide variety of choice — for example, 1.0, 1.1, 1.2, 2.0, and so on, or 1, (a), (i), etc.

The major parts of an agreement include:

1. *Heading*

   The heading, which sets out the name of the agreement.

2. *Parties*

   An individual is usually identified by name and place of residence, while a corporation is identified by name and governing statute. Usually the parties are given a short definition or acronym, which is then used throughout the agreement to avoid repetition of the full names of parties every time reference is made to them.

3. *Recitals*

   Recitals are often used to describe the background leading up to the making of the agreement.

4. *Consideration*

   The majority of agreements contain a statement that consideration or a dollar value has been given by each of the parties. The argument for this is that it binds the promise contained in the terms of the agreement.

5. *Body*

   The body of the agreement contains its operative provisions and varies according to the agreement's requirements.

   The following are only a few of the possible areas for inclusion in the body of a partnership agreement. For a broader list of considerations, see the Partnership Agreement Checklist on page 37.

   a. Definitions

      Often the first division of an agreement is a list of defined words used in the agreement. It is customary to capitalize the first letter of a defined word when it is used in the body of the agreement.

   b. Definition of the business

      A partnership agreement should always describe the full extent of the partnership's activities. This limits the scope or liability of one partner for the acts of others. It also helps define where partnership income will come from given the requirement of s. 29 of the PA, which provides that every partner must account to the firm for any benefit derived from any use of the partnership names, property, or business connection. Further, s. 30 of the PA requires an accounting for all profits of a competing business carried on by a partner and for the partner to pay over to the firm all profits made by the partner in that business. It is not uncommon for agreements to state that each partner will devote the partner's full time to the partnership business and will not engage in any other business.

PARTNERSHIP AGREEMENT CHECKLIST

The following issues should be considered when deciding the terms of a partnership agreement:

1. Who are the partners?
   - list the names
2. Where will the partnership be situated?
   - under what laws — for example, the province of Ontario — will the agreement be made?
3. What are the terms of the partnership?
   - date of commencement of business as well as a termination date if applicable
4. Which name will be used for carrying on business?
   - legal name and what is to be done with this name once the partnership is terminated
5. Purpose of the business
   - proposed business activities
   - provisions for limitations on the business activity and for changes in the activity
6. Location of the business
   - registered office as well as area to be covered by the business
7. Proportion of ownership
8. Division of profits and losses among the partners
9. Fiscal year for the business
10. Percentage and form of contribution by each partner
    - value
    - interest
    - policy on loans
11. Restriction on partnership
    - prohibitions against a partner borrowing for the partnership
    - restrictions on partners giving bonds, guarantees, etc., against the partnership
12. Bank, branch, signing authority, and borrowing authority
13. Who will be the lawyer, accountant/auditor, and other professional appointments for the partnership?
14. Insurance
15. Partners' liability
16. How to amend a partnership agreement
17. Management and decision making
    - delegating responsibility to a partner or appointing a manager
    - division of functions
    - procedure for business meetings
    - policies
    - description of roles of each partner
    - voting procedures, one vote per partner or otherwise
    - majority rule or unanimity
18. Limitations on power of partners
    - policies concerning a partner who leaves the business
    - restrictions on engaging in non-partnership business
    - prohibiting partners from engaging in competing business
19. Provisions for admitting new partners
    - majority or unanimous
    - qualifications
    - function of new partner
20. Provisions for selling one's interest in a partnership
    - right to sell or provisions for compelling purchase by other partners
    - when is sale permitted
    - restrictions, if any, on who may purchase
21. Removing a partner
    - reasons for expelling a partner
    - majority vote or unanimous
22. Dispute resolution process

c. Firm name

If the name of the partnership includes one of the names of the partners, you may wish to include a clause providing that if the person whose name is used withdraws from the partnership, the name of the partnership will be changed. This is because the name forms part of the goodwill of the partnership and may be used by each partner on dissolution.

d. Restrictions on carrying on a competing business
The effects of s. 30 of the PA generally restrict partners from carrying on a business in competition with the partnership business. With regard to the restrictions continuing after the partner withdraws, it appears that the courts will enforce such a provision only if it is reasonable with respect to area and time.

e. Admission of new partners
Section 24 of the PA provides, among other things, that "[n]o person may be introduced as a partner without the consent of all existing partners." Often a partnership agreement will provide qualifications for new partners. You might also consider whether provisions for the transfer of partnership interests are to be included in the agreement.

f. Control or management of the partnership
The PA provides that each partner may take part in the management of the partnership business. Differences with respect to ordinary matters connected with the partnership business may be decided by a majority of the partners, but no change in the nature of the partnership business can be made without the consent of all partners. This provision may be modified in the agreement according to each partner's economic interest.

g. Capital inputs and distribution of capital
A partnership, like any other business, requires working capital in order to pay its overheads such as rent, salaries, and other expenses. This may come from capital contributed by the partners or it may come from borrowed money. Often, the required capital contribution to a partnership will be in the same ratio as the distribution of profits from the partnership. A partner may also contribute property other than cash, such as real estate or equipment. Consider also initial and continuing capital contributions and distribution of capital.

h. Retirement and dissolution
The requirements of s. 33(1) of the PA are that the partnership is dissolved by the death or insolvency of any partner, unless there is an agreement to the contrary. The partnership agreement should therefore set out what will happen to the partnership should one of these circumstances arise. It is probably desirable that the partnership continue and, if this is the case, the agreement should provide for some method of compensating the withdrawing partner for contributions to the partnership, goodwill, work in progress, and increase in the value of the basic assets of the partnership.

Other factors to consider include whether the partnership will purchase insurance on the life of each partner, to be payable to the partner's estate for the protection of the partner's wife and children, with premiums taken from the partner's draw; the age at which partners must retire from the partnership; and whether there will be a retirement allowance or registered retirement savings plan (RRSP) contributions.

i. Division of profits

The PA provides that all partners share equally, but because the division of profits is usually in the same ratio as the capital contributions to the partnership, it is probably important to make some other provisions by way of agreement. In addition to considering the amount of capital contributed, also consider, for example, the amount of working time on partnership business, past contributions, ability to encourage team work, and the ability to enhance the partnership's reputation. Many of these considerations are difficult to quantify and often various formulas are included, depending on the items that are considered of importance to the partnership.

j. Work in progress

Because work in progress is a constantly changing factor, it may be desirable to include a method for determining its allocation to partners.

k. Standard clauses

Standard clauses that might be included in the agreement relate to:

i. the agreement being the entire agreement between the parties;

ii. where to give notice to each of the parties;

iii. time being of the essence;

iv. the fact that the agreement enures to the benefit of the parties and their respective heirs, executors, administrators, successors, and permitted assigns.

6. *Execution*

The last part of the agreement is execution by all the parties to the agreement. If a partner is a corporation, the authorized signatory for the corporation will sign the agreement. If a partner is an individual, the individual's signature is usually witnessed.

LIMITED PARTNERSHIP

Limited partnerships evolved in the 1800s, the main purpose for their development being to provide a structure for the raising of capital while maintaining the partnership structure required by many businesses.

The statute governing limited partnerships is the *Limited Partnerships Act* (LPA). Unlike a general partnership, a limited partnership is formed when a declaration (Form 3 under the LPA) is filed with the registrar in accordance with the LPA (s. 3(1)).

The major factor distinguishing a limited partnership from other partnerships is that there must be one or more general partners — that is, partners with unlimited liability — and one or more partners with limited liability — that is, a liability limited to the amount contributed in cash or property by each partner as capital to the limited partnership as stated in the record of limited partners (s. 9). (See the discussion of record of limited partners below.) A limited partnership may carry on any business that a general partnership may carry on.

A limited partnership combines some of the characteristics of both corporations and general partnerships. The limited liability of limited partners is similar to that granted shareholders of a corporation. However, shareholders of a corporation are able to take part in the activities of the corporation whereas limited partners of a limited partnership are not allowed to take part in the activities of the limited partnership.

Record of limited partners (s. 4)

A current record of limited partners must be kept by the general partners of the limited partnership at the limited partnership's principal place of business in Ontario and may be inspected and copied free of charge by any person during normal business hours.

The following information must be kept for each limited partner:

1. If the partner is an individual, the partner's surname, the given name by which the partner is commonly known, the first letters of the partner's other given names, and the partner's residential address or address for service, including municipality, street and number, if any, and postal code.

2. If the partner is not an individual, the partner's name and address or address for service, including municipality, street and number, if any, and postal code, and the partner's Ontario corporation number, if any.

3. The amount of money and the value of other property contributed or to be contributed by the partner to the limited partnership.

Role of a limited partner

A limited partner may contribute money and other property to the limited partnership, but may not contribute services (s. 7(1)). A limited partner is, therefore, a passive investor.

A limited partner has the same right as a general partner to inspect the limited partnership books and to demand information concerning all limited partnership matters (s. 10).

A limited partner may look into the state and progress of the limited partnership business and may give advice as to its management; but a limited partner may not take part in the control of the business (ss. 12(2) and 13(1)). If a limited partner takes part in the control of the business, he or she may be deemed to be a general partner and may lose the protection of limited liability. Generally, if a limited partner acts as a passive investor, he or she will not be perceived as being a principal in the business's activity. Certain activities are more likely than others to affect the degree of control — for example, the manner in which general partners are removed should be provided in the partnership agreement because limited partners cannot remove general partners unless the agreement so provides.

A person may, however, be a general partner and a limited partner in the same limited partnership. Such a person has the rights and powers and is subject to the restrictions and liabilities of a general partner. But with respect to the partner's contribution as a limited partner, the partner has the same rights against the other partners as other limited partners. The degree to which a limited partner participates in the running of the business must be closely examined so as not to jeopardize the partner's limited liability status. Such special relationships should be clearly set out in the limited partnership agreement.

Restrictions on firm name

The surname or a distinctive part of the corporate name of a limited partner may not be part of the firm name of the limited partnership unless it is also the surname or a distinctive part of the corporate name of one of the general partners (s. 6(1)).

Where the surname or a distinctive part of the corporate name of a limited partner appears in the firm name contrary to s. 6(1), the limited partner is liable as a general partner to any creditor of the limited partnership who has extended credit without actual knowledge that the limited partner is not a general partner (s. 6(2)).

The word "limited" may be used in the firm name, but only in the expression "limited partnership" (s. 6(3)). Although it is common to include the words "limited partnership" in the name, it is not necessary to do so.

Rights of general partners

A general partner in a limited partnership has all the rights and powers and is subject to all the restrictions and liabilities of a partner in a partnership without limited partners. However, s. 8 of the LPA provides some protection for the limited partner by restricting the general partner from doing certain acts without the written consent or ratification of the specific act by all the limited partners, including:

1. doing any act in contravention of the partnership agreement;

2. doing any act that makes it impossible to carry on the ordinary business of the limited partnership;

3. consenting to a judgment against the limited partnership;

4. possessing limited partnership property, or assigning any rights in specific partnership property, for other than a partnership purpose;

5. admitting a person as a general partner;

6. admitting a person as a limited partner, unless the right to do so is given in the partnership agreement; and

7. continuing the business of the limited partnership on the death, retirement, or mental incompetence of a general partner or dissolution of a corporate general partner, unless the right to do so is given in the partnership agreement (s. 8).

Rights of a limited partner to a return of contributions and a share of profits

A limited partner is entitled to a share in the profits of a limited partnership by way of income in proportion to the limited partner's contribution. However, subject to an agreement to the contrary, no payment will be made if that payment reduces the assets of the limited partnership to an amount insufficient to discharge the liabilities of the limited partnership to persons who are not general or limited partners (s. 11).

A limited partner may loan money to and transact other business with the limited partnership, and will rank equally with general creditors with respect to claims arising from such loans or transactions. A limited partner may not hold any limited partnership property as collateral security for a loan to the limited partnership. A limited partner may not receive any payment ahead of a creditor that is not a partner if the assets are insufficient to discharge the liabilities of the limited partnership to such creditors (s. 12(1)).

A limited partner has the right to demand and receive the return of his or her contribution

1. upon the dissolution of the limited partnership;

2. when the time specified in the partnership agreement for the return of the contribution occurs;

3. after the limited partner has given six months' notice in writing to all other partners, if no time is specified in the partnership agreement for the return of the contribution or for the dissolution of the limited partnership; or

4. when all the partners consent to the return of the contribution (s. 15(1)).

This cannot happen, however, until all liabilities to third parties have been paid or there remains sufficient limited partnership assets to pay them, and the partnership agreement is terminated or amended, if necessary, to reflect the withdrawal or reduction of the contribution (s. 15(2)). Furthermore, unless the limited partnership agreement provides otherwise or all the partners consent, the return of the contribution is restricted to payments of money as opposed to return of property (s. 15(3)).

Limited partners' rights as between themselves

Subject to any agreement made between the limited partners, limited partners, in relation to one another, share in the limited partnership assets

1. for the return of contributions, and

2. for profits or other compensation by way of income on account of their contributions

in proportion to the respective amounts of money and other property actually contributed by the limited partners to the limited partnership.

Limited partner's liability to partnership

Section 16 of the LPA renders a limited partner liable to the limited partnership for any difference between the value of his or her actual contribution and the value stated in the limited partnership declaration. Furthermore, a limited partner is deemed to hold as trustee for the limited partnership specific property stated in the partnership agreement to be that limited partner's contribution, when either it has not been contributed or it has been returned in contravention of the LPA, and money or other property conveyed to the limited partner contrary to the statute. Even when his or her contribution has been returned, a limited partner is liable to creditors to the extent of the amount returned with interest if the creditors' claims arose before the return of the contribution.

Admission of additional limited partners

Additional limited partners may be admitted by amending the record of limited partners (s. 17). No additional filings are required.

Assignment of limited partner's interest (s. 18)

A limited partner's interest is assignable and the assignee may become a substituted limited partner. A substituted limited partner is a person entitled to all the rights and powers of a limited partner who has died or who has assigned his or her interest in the limited partnership. An assignee may become a substituted limited partner

1. if all the partners, except the assignor, consent in writing to the substitution; or

2. if the assignor, being so authorized in the partnership agreement, designates the assignee as a substituted limited partner.

An assignee, who is entitled to become a substituted limited partner, becomes a substituted limited partner when the record of limited partners is amended.

A substituted limited partner has all the rights and powers and is subject to all the restrictions and liabilities of his or her assignor, but is not subject to any liability that he or she did not have notice of at the time he or she became a substituted limited partner and that could not be ascertained from the partnership agreement, the declaration, or the record of limited partners.

An assignee who does not become a substituted limited partner has no right to inspect the limited partnership books or to be given any information about matters affecting the limited partnership or an account of the partnership affairs. He or she is, however, entitled to receive the share of the profits or other compensation by way of income or the return of the contribution to which the assignor would otherwise be entitled.

The legal representative of a deceased limited partner has all the rights and powers of a limited partner for the purposes of settling the estate and whatever power the limited partner had under the partnership agreement to designate his or her assignee as a substituted limited partner. The estate is liable for all the liabilities of the deceased limited partner as a limited partner (s. 22).

Dissolution of limited partnership

The retirement, death, or mental incompetence of a general partner or dissolution of a corporate general partner dissolves a limited partnership unless the business is continued by the remaining general partners

1. pursuant to a right to do so contained in the partnership agreement, *and*

2. with the consent of all the remaining limited and general partners (s. 21).

A limited partner is entitled to have the limited partnership dissolved and its affairs wound up where

1. the limited partner is entitled to the return of his or her contribution but, upon demand, the contribution is not returned to him or her; or

2. the other liabilities of the limited partnership have not been paid or the limited partnership assets are insufficient for their payment and the limited partner seeking dissolution would otherwise be entitled to the return of his or her contribution (s. 15(4)).

A limited partner also has the same right as a general partner to obtain dissolution of the limited partnership by court order (s. 10).

Settling accounts on dissolution (s. 24)

When a limited partnership is dissolved, the liabilities of the limited partnership to creditors, except to limited partners on account of their contributions and to general partners, are paid first. Then, unless the partnership agreement or a subsequent agreement provides otherwise, payments are made in the following order:

1. to limited partners in respect of their share of the profits and other compensation by way of income on account of their contributions;

2. to limited partners in respect of their contributions;

3. to general partners other than for capital and profits;

4. to general partners in respect of profits; and

5. to general partners in respect of capital.

Access to documents (s. 33)

Every limited partnership is required to keep at its principal place of business in Ontario

1. a copy of the partnership agreement;

2. a copy of the declaration and a copy of each declaration of change amending the declaration;

3. a copy of any court order requiring compliance with the LPA;

4. a copy of any written authority to any other person to sign on his or her behalf given by a general or limited partner (power of attorney); and

5. in the case of an extra-provincial limited partnership, a copy of the power of attorney filed with the registrar.

These documents are open to inspection by any partner during the normal business hours of the partnership and are often kept in a minute book or document book maintained for the limited partnership.

Maintaining records for a limited partnership

In addition to maintaining records for any corporate general partner, it is also common to maintain records for the limited partners. For example, minutes of the meetings of limited partners, held from time to time, are kept in a minute book. If you are responsible for maintaining the minute book, ensure that the minutes of the limited partners do not include any discussion relating to the general management of the partnership.

Penalties

No limited partnership that has unpaid fees or penalties or that has not filed a declaration as required by the LPA, and no member of such a limited partnership, can maintain a proceeding in a court in Ontario with respect to the business carried on by the limited partnership except with leave of the court (s. 20(1)).

Where a limited partnership declaration contains a false or misleading statement, any person suffering loss as a result of relying on such a statement may hold liable

1. every general partner who knew when the declaration was signed that the statement was false or misleading, and

2. every general partner who became aware after signing the declaration that the statement was false or misleading and failed within a reasonable time to file a declaration of change (s. 29).

Where a record of limited partners contains a false or misleading statement, any person suffering loss as a result of relying on such a statement may hold liable

1. every general partner, and

2. every limited partner who became aware that the statement was false or misleading and who failed within a reasonable time to take steps to cause the record of limited partners to be corrected (s. 30).

Offences

Every person who contravenes the LPA or its regulations or makes a false statement, etc., is guilty of an offence and, on conviction, is liable to a fine of not more than $2,000 or, if such person is a corporation, to a fine of not more than $20,000. Where a corporation is guilty of an offence, every director or officer of such corporation, and where the corporation is an extra-provincial corporation, every person acting as its representative in Ontario who authorized, permitted, or acquiesced in such an offence is also guilty of an offence and on conviction is liable to a fine of not more than $2,000 (s. 35).

EXTRA-PROVINCIAL LIMITED PARTNERSHIPS

Provision is made in the *Limited Partnerships Act* for an **extra-provincial limited partnership**, a limited partnership organized under the laws of a jurisdiction other than Ontario (s. 1).

extra-provincial limited partnership
in Ontario, a limited partnership organized under the laws of a jursidiction other than Ontario

An extra-provincial limited partnership is deemed to carry on business in Ontario if

1. it solicits business in Ontario;

2. its name is listed in a telephone directory for any part of Ontario;

3. its name is included in any advertisement in which an address in Ontario is given for the limited partnership;

4. it has a resident agent or representative or a warehouse, office, or place of business in Ontario;

5. it owns real property situated in Ontario;

6. it effects a distribution of securities in Ontario by way of a prospectus or offering memorandum in compliance with the *Securities Act* and its regulations; or

7. it otherwise carries on business in Ontario (s. 25(2)).

In the absence of legislation respecting the status of a limited partnership organized in one province and carrying on business in another province, it may be unclear whether the limited partners retain their limited liability in the other province. At present, all provinces other than Manitoba and Quebec have partnership legislation that provides that if an extra-provincial limited partnership is registered in the province, the limited partners continue to enjoy limited liability. If an Ontario limited partnership carries on business in Manitoba or Quebec, it is unclear whether the limited partners retain their limited liability in that province.

According to s. 27:

(1) A limited partner of an extra-provincial limited partnership is not liable in Ontario as a general partner of the extra-provincial limited partnership by reason only that it carries on business in Ontario without filing the declaration and power of attorney required by this Act.

(2) The laws of the jurisdiction under which an extra-provincial limited partnership is organized govern its organization and internal affairs and the limited liability of its limited partners.

Except with leave of the court, an extra-provincial limited partnership that has not filed the required declaration and power of attorney is not capable of maintaining a proceeding in a court in Ontario with respect to the business carried on by it. Subsequent registration, however, corrects any default in this regard.

In addition to the record of limited partners, an extra-provincial limited partnership is required to maintain the documents listed in s. 33 at its principal place of business in Ontario. If an extra-provincial limited partnership does not have a principal place of business in Ontario, the documents must be kept by an attorney and representative in Ontario at the address stated in the power of attorney filed with the registrar appointed under the BNA. (See Form 3 at item 8.)

Any person may inspect the record of limited partners during the normal business hours of the limited partnership or the limited partnership's attorney and representative and may make copies of and take extracts from it.

Any partner may inspect any of the documents required under s. 33 during normal business hours, and any person who has a business relationship with the partnership may inspect these documents — with the exclusion of the partnership agreement — during normal business hours.

The same penalties apply to an extra-provincial limited partnership as apply to regular limited partnerships except that the attorney and representative in Ontario may also be found guilty of an offence.

REGISTRATION OF LIMITED PARTNERSHIPS AND EXTRA-PROVINCIAL LIMITED PARTNERSHIPS

Section 3(1) of the LPA provides that a limited partnership is formed when a declaration is filed with the registrar. All the general partners must sign the declaration. At the time of writing, the form to file is Form 3 under the LPA and the filing fee is $210.

Section 25(1) of the LPA provides that extra-provincial limited partnerships must file a declaration with the registrar as well as execute a power of attorney appointing a person resident in Ontario or a corporation having its head or registered office in Ontario to be its attorney and representative in Ontario. See item 8 in Form 3, LPA.

If the extra-provincial limited partnership is formed in another Canadian jurisdiction and has an office or other place of business in Ontario, it does not need to sign a power of attorney.

Section 32 makes provision for a general or limited partner to give written authority to any other person to sign on the partner's behalf any documents under the LPA. This authority must be indicated on Form 3 at item 7.

Every declaration filed expires five years after its date of filing unless the declaration is cancelled by filing a declaration of dissolution or the declaration is replaced by filing a new declaration before the expiry date (s. 3(3)). A limited partnership is not dissolved if a declaration expires, but an additional fee of $150 is payable for the subsequent filing of a new declaration (s. 3(4)).

The following information is required to complete Form 3:

1. The type of declaration — that is, new, renewal, change, dissolution, or withdrawal.

2. The firm name under which the limited partnership will be conducted.

3. The mailing address, including street number, name, municipality, and postal code. The copy of the registration will be mailed to this address.

4. The address of the limited partnership's principal place of business in Ontario, including the municipality, the street and number, if any, and the postal code, and the mailing address of the limited partnership.

5. The general nature of the business of the limited partnership.

6. The jurisdiction of formation.

7. Information regarding general partners: For each general partner who is an individual, the partner's surname, the given name by which the partner is commonly known, another given name, if any, and the partner's residential address or address for service, including municipality, the street and number, if any, and the postal code.

    For each general partner that is not an individual, the partner's name and address or address for service, including the municipality, the street and number, if any, and the postal code, and the partner's Ontario corporation number, if any.

    Where a person is signing for a general partner under power of attorney, that person must sign in the "Signature" space and check the "Power of Attorney" box.

8. In the case of an extra-provincial limited partnership, an indication that a power of attorney exists. This does not apply to an extra-provincial limited partnership formed in another Canadian jurisdiction.

For the attorney of an extraprovincial limited partnership who is an individual, the attorney's surname, the given name by which the attorney is commonly known, another given name, if any, and the attorney's residential address or address for service, including the municipality, the street and number, if any, and the postal code.

For the attorney of an extra-provincial limited partnership that is not an individual, the attorney's name and address or address for service including the municipality, the street and number, if any, and the postal code, and the attorney's Ontario corporation number, if any.

Declarations filed on or after April 1, 1994 have a business identification number (BIN) assigned by the registrar. The BIN must be set out on a declaration of change, dissolution, or withdrawal or a new declaration. Declarations filed before April 1, 1994 do not have BINs. A number will be assigned when the first new declaration is filed on or after that date.

Beginning in May 2001, the Ministry of Consumer and Business Services issues a master business licence (MBL) upon registration of a sole proprietor, partnership, limited partnership, or business name that can be used as proof of registration at financial institutions and to facilitate any other business-related registration with the Ontario government.

EXTRA-PROVINCIAL REGISTRATION OF A GENERAL OR LIMITED PARTNER IN AN EXTRA-PROVINCIAL PARTNERSHIP BEING REGISTERED IN ONTARIO

You may be instructed to register an extra-provincial partnership in Ontario and undoubtedly you will ask yourself whether you need to register the general partner and/or the limited partner if they are corporations. If the limited partner(s) are not carrying on business in Ontario other than by way of their interest as a limited partner, you will not need to extra-provincially register.

The general partner, however, probably will be carrying on business in Ontario, since the partnership is registered extra-provincially, and will have to obtain either an extra-provincial licence and/or file Form 2 under the *Corporations Information Act*. However, consider the specific situation to determine whether both the general and limited partner(s) are carrying on business.

CHANGES
Ontario limited partnerships (s. 19)

When the firm name of a limited partnership is changed, a new declaration must be filed with the registrar.

A declaration of change, signed by at least one of the general partners, must be filed with the registrar for every change in information, other than a change in the firm name, required to be stated in the original declaration. If there is a change of address set out in a declaration, the declaration of change must be filed within 15 days after the change takes place. There is no filing fee.

For the purposes of the LPA, a change does not take place until a declaration of change is filed with the registrar. The declaration of change does not alter the expiry date of the original registration.

Extra-provincial limited partnerships (s. 25)

When there is a change in the firm name of an extra-provincial limited partnership, a new declaration must be filed with the registrar.

A declaration of change must be filed for every change in the information, other than a change in the firm name, filed in the original declaration. The declaration of change is signed by at least one of the general partners.

FILING DECLARATION OF DISSOLUTION

Ontario limited partnership (s. 23)

A declaration of dissolution, signed by at least one of the general partners, must be filed with the registrar when the limited partnership is dissolved, or when all the limited partners cease to be limited partners. The partnership is dissolved when the declaration of dissolution is filed. There is no filing fee.

Extra-provincial limited partnership (s. 25(8))

The declaration and the power of attorney may be cancelled by filing a declaration of withdrawal signed by at least one of the general partners with the registrar.

LIMITED PARTNERSHIP AGREEMENTS

It is advisable to have a written limited partnership agreement to deal with matters not addressed in either the PA, LPA, or with matters provided for in these statutes that the partners desire to alter by agreement.

When structuring a limited partnership with a corporation as the general partner, it is advisable to ensure that the directors, officers, and employees of the general partner are not also limited partners. Case law has held that if an individual who is a limited partner is also a director, officer, or employee of the corporate general partner and takes part in the control of the business of the limited partnership, that limited partner loses his or her limited liability.

KEY TERMS

common law

designated partner

extra-provincial limited partnership

REFERENCES

Business Names Act (BNA), RSO 1990, c. B.17, as amended.

Day, Midge, *Ontario Corporate Procedures*, 3d ed. (Toronto: Thomson Professional Publishing, 1995).

Gilmore, Daryl E., *Drafting the Commercial Agreement* (Toronto: Law Society of Upper Canada, 1987).

Knowles, H.J., *Partnership: A Statutory Annotation* (Toronto: Butterworths, 1979).

Law Society of Upper Canada, *Business Law*, Bar Admission Course Materials (Toronto: LSUC, 2001).

Limited Partnerships Act (LPA), RSO 1990, c. P.16, as amended.

Manzer, Alison R., *A Practical Guide to Canadian Partnership Law* (Aurora, ON: Canada Law Book, 1995).

Partnerships Act (PA), RSO 1990, c. P.5, as amended.

Smyth, J.E., D.A. Soberman, and A.J. Easson, *The Law and Business Administration in Canada*, 9th ed. (Toronto: Prentice-Hall, 2001).

FORMS AND PRECEDENTS

Figure 2.1: Form 3, *Limited Partnerships Act*

Figure 2.2: Form 5, *Business Names Act*

Figure 2.3: Master business licence (MBL)

REVIEW QUESTIONS

1. What constitutes carrying on business in partnership?

2. What are the consequences of not registering the partnership?

3. What is the main value of the partnership agreement?

4. Give two examples of where a partner's duty of good faith would arise.

5. You have been asked to attend to the registration of a new partnership under the name "The Summer Gardner." There will be two partners: David Green and Garden Centres Inc. David Green has already been operating a sole proprietorship under the same name. Draft the required documents and prepare a letter to the client forwarding the documents for signature. Identify any questions or information required.

6. What features distinguish a limited partnership from a general partnership?

7. Black and White have formed a limited partnership. Black is a limited partner. Describe White's position. Include any restrictions on his acts. What types of conduct should Black avoid if he is to continue to enjoy limited liability?

8. Describe the registration requirements for a limited partnership.

9. How would you go about obtaining a copy of the record of limited partners?

10. Is a limited partner's right in the limited partnership assignable? If so, describe how this would be accomplished.

11. When is a limited partnership dissolved? How is the partnership property distributed?

12. What is the penalty for not registering a declaration?

13. What records must be maintained by a limited partnership, and where?

CASE STUDY

Case study 2.1: Registration of an extra-provincial limited partnership and business name

On May 1 Jessie Bruton had a telephone conference call with Richard Thorn and Allan Hill to discuss procedures with respect to obtaining an extra-provincial licence for a corporation and registering an extra-provincial partnership by the end of the month. Richard explained the situation as follows.

313131 Canada Limited is a subsidiary of a Swiss corporation and operates a chemical plant in Port Hopeful. The initial startup costs were over $200,000 and, because it is a new operation, there have been the typical startup losses in the first year. To ensure that the Swiss parent can receive some tax benefits from these losses, they have decided to transfer the plant assets into a German limited partnership. To receive these tax benefits, the transfer needs to be completed by the end of May. The closing has been established for May 31. The Hungry for Money Bank is financing the purchase. Thorn & Hill represent the German partnership and have to provide an opinion to the lender that the limited partnership is properly registered in Ontario.

Jessie is asked to draft the documents to register the extra-provincial limited partnership and a business name for use by the limited partnership.

See figures 2.1 and 2.2 for the documents drafted.

FIGURE 2.1 FORM 3, LIMITED PARTNERSHIPS ACT

PRINTED IN CANADA
Imprime au Canada

DATA BUSINESS FORMS S49627 P65

 Ontario

Ministry of
Consumer and
Business Services

Ministère des Services
aux consommateurs
et aux entreprises

INSTRUCTIONS

It is important to read these notes before completing the attached form

Print all information clearly in CAPITAL LETTERS using black ink.

Complete all sections of the form. Incomplete forms will be returned.

Fees: • there is a fee payable for new declarations and renewals
• fees may be paid in cash, money order or cheque
• payable to the **Ontario Minister of Finance**
• do not send cash in the mail
• a handling fee will be charged for a non-negotiable cheque.

Please forward both copies of the enclosed form to the Ministry of
Consumer and Business Services. The Client copy will no longer
be certified consistent with Ontario Regulation 175 / 94 Section 4.
The Client copy will be **returned**, with a validation in the bottom right-hand corner.

Return completed forms to: Ministry of Consumer and Business Services
Companies and Personal Property Security Branch
393 University Ave., Suite 200
Toronto ON M5G 2M2

Please do not separate the form

Refer to these notes while completing form

1.   Registration Type - Check the appropriate box:
New   (Fee payable)
•   a new declaration is the first filing of the firm name
•   a change of firm name is considered a new declaration
(For name change check box marked **New** as well as box
marked **Name Change**)
Renewal (Fee payable)
•   a declaration expires in five years and must be renewed
•   (For name change check box marked **Renewal** as well as
box marked **Name Change**)
Change (No fee payable)
•   a change should be filed when there is a change in
address, activity or information regarding general partners
Dissolution (No fee payable)
•   Limited Partnerships formed in Ontario may cancel the
Declaration by filing a declaration of dissolution
Withdrawal (No fee payable)
•   Extra-provincial Limited Partnerships in Ontario may
cancel the Declaration by filing a declaration of withdrawal
BIN
For a new declaration or renewal with name change or a renewal,
change, dissolution or withdrawal, enter **Business Identification
No. (BIN)**, if previously issued.

2.   Firm Name - Please print the business name of the Limited
Partnership. The firm name must be set out in Block Capital
Letters in the squares provided and must commence on the first
line of the grid in the first square. Each square of the grid
represents a letter of the alphabet, a punctuation mark, or a
space. If there is not sufficient space on the grid for the name,
please use additional form(s). Please complete all items on
additional form(s) and note the number of each additional page in
the top right-hand corner of each form.

3.   Mailing Address - Include street number, name, municipality
and postal code. Your copy of the registration will be mailed
to this address.

4.   Address of Principal Place of Business in Ontario - Include street,
number, name, municipality and postal code. A post office box is
not acceptable in a business address. If there is more than one
place of business, select one as the principal place.

5.   General Nature of Business - include a brief description of the
activity being carried on by the firm.

6.   Jurisdiction of Formation - the name of the jurisdiction in which
the Limited Partnership was formed. Please do not use abbreviations.

7.   Information regarding General Partners:

Item 7 must be completed by all general partners. If there is
more than one general partner, set out the information in
Item 7 on additional Form 3's as required.

The general partners of every limited partnership must keep a
record of limited partners at the principal place of business in
Ontario. This information must be made available to the public
upon request. It must include the full name and residence
address or address for service of each limited partner and the
contribution made to the Limited Partnership.

If the general partner is not an individual or a corporation, then set
out the general partner's name in the "Additional Information"
space.

Where a person is signing for the general partner under power of
attorney, that person must sign in the "Signature" space and
check the "Power of Attorney" box.

If a **New Declaration or Renewal** is being filed, each general
partner must sign the form. If the general partner is a corporation,
set out the corporation name in the Additional Information box and
include the Ontario Corporation Number. An authorized signing
officer must sign. Print the name of the officer under the signature.

If a **Change, Withdrawal or Dissolution** is being filed, at least
one general partner must sign the form. If the general partner is a
corporation, an authorized signing officer must sign. Print the
name of the officer under the signature.

8.   Information Regarding Attorney/Representative for an Extra-
Provincial Limited Partnership:

Item 8 does not apply to an Extra-Provincial Limited Partnership
formed in another Canadian jurisdiction that has an office or other
place of business in Ontario.

An Extra-Provincial Limited Partnership shall execute a power of
attorney in the Declaration under the Limited Partnerships Act
(Form 3) to appoint a person resident in Ontario or a corporation
having its head or registered office in Ontario to be the attorney
and representative in Ontario of that Extra - Provincial Limited
Partnership.

The representative's name, Ontario address and signature must
be set out in item 8. If a corporation is appointed, an authorized
signing officer must sign. Print the name of the officer under the
signature and set out the Ontario Corporation Name & Number.

If the representative is not an individual or a corporation, then set
out the representative's name in the "Additional information" space.

Upon request, the representative must make available to the public,
at its Ontario address, both the executed power of attorney and a
record of the limited partners.

07191 (08/2002)   (français au verso)

FIGURE 2.1 CONCLUDED

Ontario

Ministry of
Consumer and
Business Services

Ministère des Services
aux consommateurs
et aux entreprises

Page_____ of / de_____

Print clearly in CAPITAL LETTERS / Écrivez clairement en LETTRES MAJUSCULES

1. Declaration Type
   Type de déclaration

   A [X] New / Nouvelle   B [ ] Renewal / Renouvellement   C [ ] Change / Changement   D [ ] Dissolution / Dissolution   E [ ] Withdrawal / Retrait

   For Name Change, check also box A or B and enter BIN
   Si modification de la raison sociale,
   cochez aussi A ou B et indiquez le NIE

   [ ] Name Change
   Modification de la
   raison sociale

   Enter Business Identification Number if A or B with Name Change or B, C, D or E.
   Indiquer le numéro d'identification d'entreprise si A ou B avec modification
   de la raison sociale ou B, C, D ou E.

   BIN
   NIE

2. Firm Name
   Raison sociale de la
   société en commandite

   GERMAN LIMITED PARTNERSHIP

3. Mailing Address
   Adresse postale

Street Number / N° de rue	Street Name / Nom de la rue	Suite No./ Bureau n°
P.O. BOX 250		

City / Town / Ville	Province / Province	Country / Pays	Postal Code/ Code postal
PORT HOPEFUL	ON	CANADA	P1H 2P2

4. Principal Place of Business in Ontario / Établissement principal en Ontario   [ ] Same as above / comme ci-dessus

Street Number N° ce rue	Street Name Nom de la rue	Suite No. Bureau n°
1	CHEERFUL DRIVE	100

City / Town Ville	Province Province	Postal Code Code postal
PORT HOPEFUL	Ontario	P1H 2P2

5. General Nature of Business / Nature générale de l'activité exercée

   OWNER AND OPERATOR OF CHEMICAL PLANT

6. Jurisdiction of Formation / Territoire de la création

   GERMANY

7. Information Regarding General Partner(s) / Renseignements sur le ou les commandités

Last Name Nom de famille	First Name Prénom	Middle Initial Initiale (2e prénom)

Street Number N° ce rue	Street Name Nom de la rue	Suite No. Bureau n°
1	CHEERFUL DRIVE	100

City / Town Ville	Province Province	Country Pays	Postal Code Code postal
PORT HOPEFUL	ON	CANADA	P1H 2P2

   Additional Information
   Renseignements supplémentaires: SWISS PARENT

   Ontario Corporation No.
   N° de la personne morale en Ontario: 1234890

   [ ] Power of Attorney / Procuration

   Signature: X

   Print Name of Signatory
   Nom du signataire en lettres moulées: John Donut, President

8. Information Regarding Attorney/Representative / Renseignements sur le procureur/représentant d'une société en commandite extraprovinciale

Last Name Nom de famille	First Name Prénom	Middle Initial Initiale (2e prénom)
MUFFIN	JOAN	

Street Number N° de rue	Street Name Nom de la rue	Suite No. Bureau n°
1	CHEERFUL DRIVE	100

City / Town Ville	Province Province	Country Pays	Postal Code Code postal
PORT HOPEFUL	ON	CANADA	P1H 2P2

   Additional Information
   Renseignements supplémentaires:

   Signature: X

   Print Name of Signatory
   Nom du signataire en lettres moulées: John Donut, President

   Corporation Name
   Raison sociale de la personne morale:

   MINISTRY USE ONLY - RESERVÉ À L'USAGE DU MINISTÈRE

   Ontario Corporation No.
   N° de la personne morale en Ontario:

07191 (08/2002)

#

MINISTRY COPY / COPIE DU MINISTÈRE
Do not Separate Copies / Ne pas détacher les copies

FIGURE 2.2 FORM 5, BUSINESS NAMES ACT

Ontario

Ministry of
Consumer and
Business Services

Ministère des Services
aux consommateurs
et aux entreprises

Registration   Form 5
under the *Business Names Act* - Partnership/Limited Partnership
Enregistrement   Formule 5
en vertu de la Loi sur les noms commerciaux
(Société en nom collectif / société en commandite)

INSTRUCTIONS

It is important to read these notes before completing the attached form.

Print all information clearly in CAPITAL LETTERS using black ink.

Complete all sections of the form. Incomplete forms will be returned.

Fees: • there is a fee payable for new registrations and renewals;
• fees may be paid in cash, money order or cheque;
• payable to the **Ontario Minister of Finance;**
• do not send cash in the mail;
• a handling fee will be charged for a non-negotiable cheque.

Please forward both copies of the form to the Ministry of
Consumer and Business Services. The Client copy will no longer
be certified consistent with Ontario Regulation 175 / 94 Section 4.
The Client copy will be **returned**, with a validation in the bottom right-hand corner.

Return completed forms to: Ministry of Consumer and Business Services
Companies and Personal Property Security Branch
393 University Ave., Suite 200
Toronto ON M5G 2M2

Please do not separate the form.

Refer to these notes while completing form.

1. **Registration Type** - Check the appropriate box:

    New *(Fee payable)*
    • a new registration is the first filing of the
    partnership business name
    • a change of partnership business name is
    considered a new registration
    Renewal *(Fee payable)*
    • a registration expires in five years and must be
    renewed
    Amendment *(No fee payable)*
    • an amendment should be filed whenever there is
    a change in address or change of activity
    Cancellation *(No fee payable)*
    • a cancellation should be submitted if you stop
    using the partnership business name

    BIN
    For renewal, amendment or cancellation, enter "Business
    Identification No.".

2. **Partnership Business Name** - Please print the partnership
business name. This is the name you are registering. The
partnership business name must be set out in Block Capital
Letters in the squares provided and must commence on the
first line of the 'grid' in the first square. Each square of the
grid represents a letter of the alphabet, a punctuation mark,
or a space. If there is not sufficient space on the grid for the
name, please use additional form(s). Please complete all
items on additional form(s) and note the number of each
additional page in the top right-hand corner of each form.

3. **Mailing Address** - Include street number, name,
municipality and postal code. Your copy of the
registration will be mailed to this address.

4. **Address of Principal Place of Business in Ontario** -
Include street, number, name, municipality and postal
code. A post office box is not acceptable in a business
address. If there is more than one place of business,
select one as the principal place. Where the business
address is outside Ontario, set out the words "Not
Applicable" in item 4. If this is the case, please ensure
that Item 3, the mailing address, includes the street
address of the principal place of business outside of
Ontario, as a post office box is not acceptable.

5. **Activity** - Include a brief description of the activity being
performed.

6. **Type of Registrant** - Check the appropriate box for
either a General Partnership or a Limited Partnership.

7. **Firm Name** - set out the exact name previously
registered by the partnership.

8. **Firm's BIN** - set out the corresponding Business
Identification Number for the firm.

9. **Print the name of the person authorizing the
registration** *(either a general partner or a person
acting under a power of attorney).*

    Additional Information: If the person authorizing the
    registration is not an individual, *(e.g. corporation, trust,
    syndicate),* **set out the name, together with the name of
    the individual authorized to sign on that person's
    behalf**, in "Additional Information", and do not complete the
    space above. Eg:

    **xxxx Limited
    Authorized to Sign: Last and First Name**

07215 (03/2004)

en français au verso

FIGURE 2.2 CONCLUDED

| Ministry of Consumer and Business Services | Ministère des Services aux consommateurs et aux entreprises | **Registration Form 5** under the *Business Names Act* - Partnership/Limited Partnership
Enregistrement Formule 5
en vertu de la Loi sur les noms commerciaux
(Société en nom collectif / société en commandite) |

Print clearly in CAPITAL LETTERS
Écrivez clairement en LETTRES MAJUSCULES

1. Registration Type
Type d'enregistrement

If B, C, or D enter "Business Identification Number"
En cas de B, C ou D, inscrivez le n° d'identification de l'entreprise.

Page 1 ___ of / de 1 ___

A ☑ New *Nouveau*   B ☐ Renewal *Renouvellement*   C ☐ Amendment *Modification*   D ☐ Cancellation *Révocation*

BIN Business Identification No.
NIE *N° d'identification de l'entreprise*

2. Partnership Business Name
Nom commercial

GERMAN CHEMICAL

3. Mailing Address
Adresse postale

Street No./ *N° de rue*   Street Name / *Nom de la rue*   Suite No. / *Bureau n°*
1 CHEERFUL DRIVE

City / Town / *Ville*   Province / *Province*   Postal Code / *Code postal*
PORT HOPEFUL ON   P1H 2P2

Country / *Pays*
CANADA

4. Address of principal place of business in Ontario *(P.O. Box not acceptable)*
Adresse de l'établissement principal en Ontario (Case postale non acceptée)   Same as above ☑ *comme ci-dessus*

Street No. / *N° de rue*   Street Name / *Nom de la rue*   Suite No. / *Bureau n°*   City / Town / *Ville*
1   CHEERFUL DRIVE   PORT HOPEFUL

Province / *Province*   Postal Code / *Code postal*   Country / *Pays*
ONTARIO   P1H 2P2   CANADA

5. Give a brief description of the ACTIVITY being carried out under the business name.
Résumez brièvement le genre d'ACTIVITÉ exercée sous le nom commercial.

OWNER AND OPERATOR OF CHEMICAL PLANT

6. Type of Registrant
Type d'entité enregistrée   A ☐ General Partnership *Société en nom collectif*   B ☑ Limited Partnership *Société en commandite*

7. Firm Name
Raison sociale de la société

SWISS PARENT

8. BIN Business Identification No. for Firm Name *(refer to #7)*
NIE de la société désignée en 7

9. Print name of person authorizing this registration *(either a general partner or a person acting under a power of attorney).*
Indiquez en lettres majuscules le nom de la personne autorisant l'enregistrement (associé, commandité ou personne habilitée en vertu d'une procuration).

Last Name / *Nom de famille*   First Name / *Prénom*   Middle Initial / *Initiale 2e prénom*
MUFFIN   JOAN

Additional Information:
If the person authorizing the registration is not an individual, *(e.g. corporation, trust, syndicate,* **set out the name, together with the name of the individual authorized to sign on that person's behalf,** in "Additional Information", and do not complete the space above. Eg:
xxxx Limited
Authorized to Sign: Last and First Name

Renseignements supplémentaires :
Si l'enregistrement est autorisé par une entreprise (personne morale, société de fiducie, consortium, etc.), **indiquez ci-dessous la raison sociale de l'entité et le nom de la personne habilitée à signer** *(voir Instructions, art. 9).*

MINISTRY USE ONLY - *RÉSERVÉ AU MINISTÈRE*

Additional Information *(name)* / *Renseignements supplémentaires (raison sociale)*

Authorized to Sign / *Signataire autorisé*
Last Name / *Nom de famille*   First Name / *Prénom*

07215 (03/2004)

FIGURE 2.3   MASTER BUSINESS LICENCE (MBL)

 Ontario

Master Business Licence

Date Issued:
(yyyy-mm-dd)

Business Number:

Business Name and Mailing Address:

**Business
Address:**

Telephone: Ext: Fax:

Email:

**Legal
Name(s):**

**Type of
Legal Entity:**

**Business
Activity:**

VOID

Business Information	Number	Effective Date (yyyy-mm-dd)	Expiry Date (yyyy-mm-dd)

Page 1 of 1

To the Client: Clients should do a corporation search to ensure that the information pertaining to corporations contained on this Master Business Licence is correct and up to date.

To the Client: When the Master Business Licence is presented to any Ontario business program, you are not required to repeat information contained on this licence. Each Ontario business program is required to accept this licence when presented as part of its registration process. Call the Ontario Business Connects Helpline at 1-900-565-1921 or (416) 314-9151 or TDD (416) 326-9566 if you have any problems.

To the Ontario business program: A client is not required to repeat any information contained in this licence in any other form used in your registration process.

CS 2002-11-12

CHAPTER 3

Corporations

CHAPTER OVERVIEW

This chapter briefly discusses the history of corporations; the different methods of incorporation in Canada, including by royal charter, letters patent, and articles of incorporation; the characteristics and nature of corporations; and the advantages and disadvantages of incorporation as a means of carrying on business. It also examines the organization of Corporations Canada and the Ontario Companies and Personal Property Security Branch of the Ministry of Consumer and Business Services.

CHAPTER OBJECTIVES

After completing this chapter, you should be able to:

1. Describe briefly the history of corporations in Canada.

2. List the different methods by which corporations come into existence.

3. Identify the major characteristics of corporations.

4. Analyze the advantages and disadvantages of using a corporation to carry on business.

5. Seek required information from Corporations Canada or the Ontario Companies and Personal Property Security Branch of the Ministry of Consumer and Business Services.

A BRIEF HISTORY OF THE CANADIAN CORPORATION

A discussion of the historical development of Canadian corporations can be the subject of an entire book; however, some knowledge of the history of Canadian corporations will help you understand some of the provisions that appear on documents of corporations in jurisdictions outside Canada and Ontario.

Canadian corporate history started in Europe and then spread to England. In the early 15th century, Italian artists and craftsmen would often meet over a meal to discuss such matters of mutual concern as their division of labour and hours of work. The group would then petition the king to correct these common problems. These groups were known as *cum panis* organizations, which means "with bread."[1]

The legal concept that grew out of these organizations was that the group can be considered a separate and distinct legal personality apart from its members. In those times, however, such organizations had no "legal status."

The concept of *cum panis* spread across Europe and eventually arrived in England. The economy in pre-16th-century England was not a "free market economy." Instead, the royal power to control trade was exercised by a comprehensive "guild" system. Anyone carrying on a particular business had to do so in conjunction with the rules of the appropriate guild. Guilds were approved by the king in return for periodic payments and the concept that they were separate entities grew. The guild system protected the individual trader from competition outside the trader's guild.

As the merchants carried out their trades, they had to deal with any problems that arose on their own. To facilitate their business activities, they developed a set of rules and acceptable trade practices resulting in a body of business customs later known as the "law merchant."[2]

With exploration of America, oversees trade in England grew and the guild concept broke down as persons who were not members of guilds began to engage in commerce.

letters patent
a document issued by the Crown through its representative to create a commercial entity

Oversees trading companies, often referred to as "regulated companies," were initially set up on a guild-like basis — the Crown issued "**letters patent**," also sometimes called a "royal charter" to create a commercial entity. A well-known example of this type of company is the Hudson's Bay Company formed in 1670. These entities were granted a monopoly over trade in a given geographic area. Each member initially traded on his own capital and inventory according to the rules of the entity.

joint stock company
a company created by statute whose members traded on the capital of all other members

Gradually, a commercial system developed whereby each member could trade on the "joint stock" of all other members. Members would subscribe to a **joint stock company** for capital to finance business ventures. The members jointly shared the benefits of the venture as well as the losses. If new capital was needed, "calls" were made on the existing members of the company for further funds. These companies continued to develop until the "South Sea Bubble" scandal of 1720 prompted the enactment of *The Bubble Act*, which severely restricted the formation of incorporated business associations.[3]

With the advent of the Industrial Revolution and the need for capital to fund new business ventures, *The Bubble Act* was repealed in 1825 and in 1844 *The Joint Stock Companies Act* came into force. This Act did not provide limited liability and the legal treatment of members was akin to that of partners.

The first English statute to give limited liability to members was enacted in 1855 — *The Limited Liability Act*. This Act required the word "Limited" or "Ltd." to be part of the company's name so as to notify the public that the company's investors had limited liability. This statute did not survive long and was soon replaced by *The Joint Stock Companies Act* of 1856, which became the precedent for all modern corporate statutes in the United Kingdom and its colonies. This statute provided as a matter of right incorporation that was based on a "memorandum of association," negotiated among company investors and filed with the government.

In Canada, the first joint stock companies were incorporated in 1849 when Upper and Lower Canada passed an act for the incorporation of companies for building roads and bridges. These companies had a single purpose and did not have limited liability. There was no royal grant required and they were formed by registration upon presentation of the appropriate documents.

In 1850, the united provinces of Canada passed an *Act To Provide for the Formation of Incorporated Joint Stock Companies, for Manufacturing, Mining, Mechanical or Chemical Purposes*. This Act also provided that companies were formed by registration. These companies did have separate legal identity and limited liability but their "lives" were limited to 50 years. You will find that some extra-provincial registration forms, such as those in Quebec and Newfoundland, still ask if the life of the corporation applying for extra-provincial registration is "limited."

During the period 1850 to 1864, general corporation statutes were enacted in Canada. These statutes followed the American view that incorporation was a "privilege" granted by the government in the issuance of letters patent.

DIFFERENT METHODS OF INCORPORATION IN CANADA

The historical development of the Canadian corporation has resulted in a number of different methods of incorporation.

Royal charters

Royal charter is the oldest method of incorporation. In the 17th century, the king of England had the prerogative to issue letters patent or a royal charter. This was how the Hudson's Bay Company became incorporated.

Special acts

At the end of the 19th century, the Canadian Parliament began to pass special statutes to incorporate companies — **special act corporations** — for large projects that were virtually impossible to finance in any other way. These projects were often of a quasi-public nature — railroads, canals, waterworks, and other public utilities, for example.

> **special act corporation or company**
> a corporation formed by a special statute passed by Parliament to undertake special projects

Special acts were used to incorporate such companies as Bell Telephone and the Canadian Pacific Railway. They were also used to create special government (or Crown) corporations like the Central Mortgage and Housing Corporation, the Canadian Broadcasting Corporation, and Air Canada.

General acts

Today, almost all companies are incorporated under the provisions of a general, governing corporate statute — the Ontario *Business Corporations Act* (OBCA) and the *Canada Business Corporations Act* (CBCA), for example. Jurisdictions across Canada have enacted several different methods of incorporation under their respective governing statutes. See table 3.1 on page 64.

MEMORANDUM OF ASSOCIATION

Incorporation by **memorandum of association** requires that applicants register a document that sets out such fundamental terms of their agreement as the powers of the corporation, rules governing how the corporation is to be managed, etc. This document is the "birth certificate" of the company and is comparable to the charter of a royal charter company. As soon as the applicants register the memorandum with the appropriate government office, the company comes into existence.

LETTERS PATENT

In some jurisdictions, the "birth certificate" of a company was known as its letters patent. This method was a direct offspring of the royal charter except that it was issued under the authority of the Crown's representative in each jurisdiction rather than by the Crown directly. The general governing statute regulates the conditions under which the Crown representative — a government agency — may issue letters patent. A letters patent company's rules that govern the corporation are set out in the corporate bylaws or in the governing statute. The bylaws, however, are not filed and therefore are not "public."

The actual steps taken by the applicants using this method do not differ materially from those steps taken where a memorandum of association is registered.

In early 1980, Quebec introduced part 1A of the *Companies Act*. Companies in existence did not have to continue under part 1A unless they amended their articles or amalgamated. All new incorporations, however, were brought under part 1A. Incorporation was no longer possible under part 1, which remained in existence for those corporations that were originally incorporated under it. Part 1 companies were incorporated by letters patent that were issued subject to approval by the Crown's representative. Part 1A companies are incorporated by certificate and articles of incorporation, which are filed as of right, provided that the documents have been completed correctly.

The only province today that issues letters patent for share capital corporations is Prince Edward Island. Letters patent are, however, issued to not-for-profit corporations incorporated under the *Canada Corporations Act* and the *Corporations Act* (Ontario).

ARTICLES OF INCORPORATION

Ontario modernized its corporate statute by enacting the OBCA on January 1, 1970. Ontario undertook a further major review of this statute and introduced amendments to make it more comparable to the federal statute in July 1983. Other significant amendments took place in March 1995 and April 1995.

In 1975, the CBCA came into force, superseding the *Canada Corporations Act*. Other provinces that adopted the "articles" approach are:

- Saskatchewan — 1978

- Quebec under part 1A of the *Companies Act* — 1980s

- Alberta — 1981

- New Brunswick — 1981

- Manitoba — 1987

- Newfoundland — 1990

The significance of these statutes is that, unlike the issuance of letters patent at the discretion of the Crown's representative, they provide for incorporation as of right, provided that the required steps are followed. In these provinces the "birth certificate" of a corporation is known as the **articles of incorporation**.

articles of incorporation
a document filed with the appropriate government authority that provides for incorporation as of right, provided that the required steps are followed

THE NATURE AND CHARACTERISTICS OF CORPORATIONS

Corporations are one of the most important forms of doing business in Canada. Their composition varies widely from the small sole shareholder/director corporation to the large public company. The following discussion reviews the major characteristics of corporations — characteristics that have made this form of business popular.

Separate legal entity

Unlike other forms of business, a corporation is a legal entity that is separate in law from its owners — the shareholders. The corporation may own property, carry on business, and incur liabilities but it does so in its own name. The shareholders own shares in the corporation but they do not own the business, assets, or liabilities of the corporation.

Once the corporation is incorporated under the CBCA, OBCA, or other governing statute, it has the capacity and the rights, powers, and privileges of a natural person.

A sole shareholder, for example, is not liable for the debts and liabilities of the corporation, nor is the corporation liable for the debts and liabilities of its shareholders. A judgment against a corporation is not a judgment against its shareholders, and neither is a judgment against a shareholder a judgment against the corporation.

Shareholders' limited liability

Flowing from the fact that a corporation is a separate legal entity is the fact that a shareholder's liability is limited to his or her investment in the corporation. If, for example, a shareholder purchased 100 common shares for $10, his or her total liability would be $10. This is somewhat simplified, because there are circumstances under which this would not be true, but these circumstances will be discussed later.

Section 45(1) of the CBCA provides that

> [t]he shareholders of a corporation are not, as shareholders, liable for any liability, act or default of the corporation except under subsection 38(4), 118(4) or (5), 146(5) or 226(4) or (5).

This clearly illustrates, that with the exception of certain actions such as a reduction of capital that was not completed in compliance with the CBCA, a shareholder has a limited liability. The provisions in OBCA s. 92(1) are substantially the same.

Creation by law

A corporation must be "created" before it comes into existence. Under the CBCA and the OBCA, this means a corporation must file articles of incorporation with the appropriate government body and be issued a certificate of incorporation.

Perpetual existence

Because a corporation is a separate legal entity from its shareholders, it has perpetual existence. This means that the corporation continues to exist even if one of the shareholders dies or withdraws from the corporation. Even if all of the shareholders were to die, the corporation would still continue to exist. A corporation can cease to exist only when a majority of the shareholders resolve to dissolve it, upon a court order, or by order of the Director appointed under the governing statute.

Separate management

A corporation may have many owners and in some instances it would be impracticable for all of the shareholders of the corporation to try to manage its business and affairs. The corporate statutes provide for a centralized management structure. The directors are charged, subject to any unanimous shareholder agreement restricting their rights, with the responsibility for managing or supervising the management of the business and affairs of the corporation. The only functions the shareholders generally perform are the election of the directors and the appointment of auditors. The shareholders of a closely held corporation — that is, one with a limited number of shareholders — may adopt a unanimous shareholder agreement that limits the responsibilities of the directors either in whole or in part to manage the corporation. The corporate statutes also provide that the directors may delegate certain responsibilities for the management of the corporation to "officers."

ADVANTAGES AND DISADVANTAGES OF INCORPORATION

These characteristics of corporations mean that there are certain advantages and disadvantages to carrying on business in this fashion. The following is a brief summary of some of the major advantages and disadvantages. These are discussed more fully in chapter 7.

Advantages	*Disadvantages*
• limited liability of shareholders	• cost of formation and maintenance
• perpetual existence	• cumbersome structure
• tax advantages	
• estate planning	

REGULATION OF CORPORATIONS

The Canadian constitution

Each provincial government and the government of Canada has the right to bring corporations into existence and to govern their activities, wherever incorporated.

The power to create corporations under provincial legislation is explicitly defined in s. 92 of the *Constitution Act, 1867*:

> In each Province the Legislature may exclusively make Laws in relation to Matters coming within the Classes of Subjects next hereinafter enumerated; that is to say, ...
>
> 11. The Incorporation of Companies with Provincial Objects.

Although there is no equivalent power in s. 91 of this Act — the section that sets out federal "powers" — the following preamble to s. 91 has been relied on as the source of the federal power to incorporate business corporations:

> It shall be lawful for the Queen, by and with the Advice and Consent of the Senate and House of Commons, to make Laws for the Peace, Order, and good Government of Canada, in relation to all Matters not coming within the Classes of Subjects by this Act assigned exclusively to the Legislatures of the Provinces.

The only case where specific power of incorporation is given to the federal jurisdiction is with respect to the incorporation of banks.

Note that the *Constitution Act, 1867* does not provide specific "powers" for the regulation of provincial or federal corporations. Rather, the power to regulate evolves from the assignment of matters in this statute.

The governing statutes and regulations

The governing statutes provide a framework for the regulation of corporations. They provide rules for incorporating and maintaining corporations, including: incorporation; issue, transfer, and other share transactions; the rights of shareholders; protection of minority shareholders; directors and officers; director and shareholder meetings; proxies; record keeping; auditors and financial statements; fundamental changes; takeover or issuer bids; liquidation and dissolution; and remedies, offences, and penalties for non-compliance.

In addition to the statutes, regulations are also passed that expand on some of the requirements in the statutes, deal with "prescribed" material, provide for the regulation of forms under the statutes, and set fees.

Table 3.1 is a list of the general statutes governing corporations in each Canadian jurisdiction and each jurisdiction's method of incorporation.

Government department and ministries

Understanding the way in which the various government departments and ministries work is essential to getting your work processed in an efficient and timely manner. In addition, getting to know the government personnel who process the work can also be advantageous, particularly in emergency situations. For example, you may be asked to continue a corporation into the federal jurisdiction and amalgamate it right away with another federal corporation. Unless you understand the

TABLE 3.1 GOVERNING STATUTES AND VEHICLES OF INCORPORATION BY JURISDICTION

Province	Statute	Vehicle of incorporation
Canada	*Canada Business Corporations Act*, RSC 1985, c. C-44, as am.	articles
Alberta	*Business Corporations Act*, RSA 2000, c. B-9, as am.	articles
British Columbia[a]	*Business Corporations Act*, SBC 2002, c. 57	notice of articles
Manitoba	*The Corporations Act*, RSM 1987, c. C225, as am.	articles
New Brunswick	*Business Corporations Act*, SNB 1981, c. B-9.1, as am.	articles
Newfoundland and Labrador	*Corporations Act*, RSN 1990, c. C-36, as am.	articles
Northwest Territories	*Business Corporations Act*, SNWT 1996, c. C.19	articles
Nova Scotia	*Companies Act*, RSNS 1989, c. 81, as am.	memorandum of association
Nunavut	*Business Corporations Act Nunavut*, SNWT 1998, c. 19, as am.	articles
Ontario	*Business Corporations Act*, RSO 1990, c. B.16, as am.	articles
Prince Edward Island	*Companies Act*, RSPEI 1988, c. C-14, as am.	letters patent
Quebec[b]	*Companies Act*, RSQ c. C-38, as am.	articles
Saskatchewan	*The Business Corporations Act*, RSS 1978, c. B-10, as am.	articles
Yukon	*Business Corporations Act*, RSY 1986, c. 15, as am.	articles

[a] The *Business Corporations Act*, SBC 2002, c. 57, came into force on March 29, 2004 and replaces the *Company Act*, RSBC 1996, c. 62, as amended. The old act provided for incorporation by way of memorandum of association and articles; the new act provides for incorporation by way of notice of articles and articles.

[b] Companies in existence before the passage of part 1A continue to be created by letters patent.

processing time required and the different methods of filing the documents, you will not be able to properly advise the lawyers, and thus the clients, you work for.

Think of the relevant government department as a "resource" that will provide the information you need to make your filings in a timely manner.

The following is a brief explanation of how Corporations Canada and the Companies and Personal Property Security Branch of the Ministry of Consumer and Business Services in Ontario work. Also included as an appendix to this chapter is a list of the addresses for the equivalent government departments in other jurisdictions in Canada along with their Web addresses.

Corporations Canada

Corporations Canada[4] is situated at:

Jean Edmonds Tower South
9th Floor
365 Laurier Avenue West
Ottawa, ON K1A 0C8
telephone: 1-866-333-5556
fax: 613-941-0601
Web site: http://strategis.gc.ca/corporations

Corporations Canada is responsible for incorporating new businesses and not-for-profit corporations. This division of Industry Canada also obtains and disseminates corporate information to the public, ensures compliance with the law, investigates complaints against corporate management, and commences or defends legal proceedings against or by corporations.

It has an extensive and user-friendly Web site called **Strategis**, which you are encouraged to visit and investigate. Corporations Canada publishes information kits and policies, procedures, and guidelines for all of the various procedures and filings under the CBCA.

There are a number of ways to file documents with Corporations Canada:

- in person, by visiting either the office in Ottawa or any regional office;

- by mail, to the Ottawa office;

- by fax, to the Ottawa office; or

- online, either through the Corporations Canada Web site or by e-mail.

Corporations Canada has four sections — the Office of the Director General; the Strategic Technologies, Marketing and Communications Directorate; the Incorporation and Disclosure Services Directorate; and the Compliance and Policy Directorate.

Strategis
an information site and online database of resources for businesses, operated by Corporations Canada

OFFICE OF THE DIRECTOR GENERAL

This office is primarily responsible for ensuring the achievement of the overall objectives of Corporations Canada. It also has personnel and financial responsibilities.

The Registration Section includes the Office of the Registrar General, which guards the Great Seal of Canada. Documents are issued under the formal documents regulations, the *Public Officers Act*, and the *Seals Act* (Commission, Land Grants, Proclamations, etc.). This section accepts and keeps on file railway deposits under ss. 104 and 105 of the *Canada Transportation Act*.

STRATEGIC TECHNOLOGIES, MARKETING AND COMMUNICATION DIRECTORATE

The Informatics Services Section is responsible for implementing the technology components of the business initiative. The Transformation, Marketing and Communications Section is charged with increasing the value of federal incorporation to small and medium-sized businesses throughout the entire life cycle of a corporation. In other words, it develops new products and services and attempts to reduce costs.

INCORPORATION AND DISCLOSURE SERVICES DIRECTORATE

This directorate of Corporations Canada is headed by a "Director" and is divided into the following sections: the Public and Corporate Services Section and the Document Production and Information Processing Section.

The Public and Corporate Services Section

This section provides fundamental services to Corporations Canada's clientele through the operation of several working sections.

The Corporate Examination Unit is responsible for the examination of all CBCA applications, as well as those for not-for-profit corporations, co-operatives, etc. This unit also processes requests for corrected CBCA certificates and all requests for a change of corporate name. The unit has three levels of examiners who review documents before filing them.

The Information Unit is responsibile for responding to all inquiries relating to federal corporations — for example, information with respect to incorporation dates, directors' names, registered addresses, and status — and for providing information through the distribution of various administrative forms, kits, and information statements relating to policies and procedures of Corporations Canada.

The Certification and Customer Relations Units issue certificates of compliance to federal corporations and deal with requests for copies and certified copies of publicly available corporate documents.

Corporations Canada operates a number of field offices throughout Canada, including one located in the Yonge-Richmond Centre, 151 Yonge Street, 4th Floor, Toronto, ON M5C 2W7; telephone: 416-973-5000. These offices provide information and assistance as well as accept documents sent to Corporations Canada. Generally, documents delivered to a field office before 2:40 p.m. will be forwarded to Ottawa for next-day delivery. The date on any certificate delivered to a regional office before 5:00 p.m. will be that day, provided that everything is satisfactory with regard to the documentation.

Document Production and Information Processing Section

This section provides a range of electronic publication and data processing services for Corporations Canada. For example, it looks after the directorate's site on Strategis (the Web site) and conducts tasks related to the maintenance of the directorate's corporations database.

COMPLIANCE AND POLICY DIRECTORATE

The Compliance and Policy Directorate is also headed by a Director who is responsible for the Policy Section, the Compliance and Preliminary Inquiries Section, and the Arrangements and Exemptions Section.

Policy Section

This section is responsible for business planning and for coordinating Corporations Canada input into statutory amendments, developing compliance and operational policy, and developing regulatory proposals.

Compliance and Preliminary Inquiries Section

This section reviews complaints on non-compliance with the corporate statutes and audits Corporations Canada's records for non-compliance.

Arrangements and Exemptions Section

This section reviews applications for arrangements and for exemptions from certain CBCA requirements.

Full information about Corporations Canada can be found on the Strategis Web site under "Staff Roles and Responsibilities," which lists the names of Corporations Canada personnel and outlines how to contact them.

Ontario Companies Branch

The Ministry of Consumer and Business Services is divided into various branches, each of which is responsible for the administration of specific statutes. One of these branches is the Companies and Personal Property Security Branch ("the Ontario Companies Branch").

The Ontario Companies Branch is located at:

375 University Avenue
2nd Floor
Toronto, ON M5G 2M2
telephone: 416-314-8880 or 1-800-361-3223
fax: 416-314-4852
Web site: http://www.cbs.gov.on.ca

The Ontario Companies Branch is responsible for providing all manner of business registrations and incorporation services, which in turn are maintained in an accessible public record. The following statutes are administered by the Ontario Companies Branch:

- *Business Corporations Act*,

- *Business Names Act*,

- *Corporations Act*,

- *Corporations Information Act*,

- *Extra-Provincial Corporations Act*,

- *Limited Partnerships Act*,

- *Partnerships Act*,

- *Personal Property Security Act*, and

- *Repair and Storage Liens Act*.

More specifically, the Ontario Companies Branch is responsible for incorporating businesses and not-for-profit corporations; business registrations such as business names, partnerships, and sole proprietorships; and for all property security registrations in the province of Ontario. These corporate, business, and security registrations are stored in databases that are maintained by the Ontario Companies

Branch. The **Ontario Business Information System (ONBIS)** is the electronic database of information on companies, sole proprietorships, partnerships, limited partnerships, and business names registered in Ontario.

The Ontario Companies Branch publishes information sheets setting out policies, procedures, and guidelines for all of the various procedures and filings under the various statutes regulated by it. These are available online and are also contained in some of the consolidated statute publications.

Unlike Corporations Canada, which has maintained control over the registrations, filings, and searches that it provides, the Ontario Companies Branch has contracted out many of its services to private agencies — Cyberbahn Inc. and Oncorp Direct Inc. To access and use the Ontario Companies Branch electronic filing and searching facilities, you must use one of these service providers.

Contact information for the two service providers is as follows:

Cyberbahn Inc.
300 — 268 Adelaide Street West
Toronto, ON M5H 1X6
telephone: 416-595-9522
   or 1-800-806-0003
fax: 416-599-8163:
Web site: http://www.cyberbahn.ca

OnCorp Direct Inc.
1033 — 316 Bay Street
Toronto, ON M5S 3A5
telephone: 416-964-CORP (2677)
   or 1-800-461-7772
fax: 416-964-3975
Web site: http://www.oncorp.com

Documents can be filed directly with the Ontario Companies Branch in a number of ways:

- in person, by visiting either the office in Toronto or any regional office;

- by mail, to Toronto; or

- online, through a service provider (Cyberbahn Inc. or OnCorp Direct Inc.).

The Ontario Companies Branch is administered by a Director. Although it is not divided into branches in the same way as Corporations Canada, the branch is divided into sections or departments with a team manager in charge of each section. Descriptions of the sections that you will be most concerned with follow.

PUBLIC OFFICE

The Public Office section is responsible for reviewing business names, corporate services — incorporations (including not-for-profit corporations), extra-provincial licensing, etc. — and for searching the public record.

PUBLIC RECORDS

The Public Records section is responsible for reviewing annual returns and notices of change. It is also responsible for attending to filing deficiencies.

COMPLIANCE

The Compliance section is responsible for the filing of annual returns, notices of change, and the sending of notices of default for non-compliance with the provisions of the statutes administered by the Ontario Companies Branch.

PERSONAL PROPERTY SECURITY REGISTRATION

This section is responsible for the registration of liens on property under the *Personal Property Security Act* (PPSA) and the *Repair and Storage Liens Act*. This is accomplished through a system called the personal property security registration (PPSR) system. Under this system, the lender files a document called a financing statement with the Ontario Companies Branch, which then provides notice that the lender and borrower have entered into a security arrangement. This notice contains such specific details of the lien as the debtor's name and the date on which the agreement was entered. These notices are compiled electronically by the PPSR and are available for searching by any lender or buyer electronically.

KEY TERMS

articles of incorporation

joint stock company

letters patent

memorandum of association

Ontario Business Information Systems (ONBIS)

special act corporation or company

Strategis

REFERENCES

Business Corporations Act (Ontario) (OBCA), RSO 1990, c. B.16, as amended.

Canada Business Corporations Act (CBCA), RSC 1985, c. C-44, as amended.

Canada Corporations Act, RSC 1970, c. C-32.

Constitution Act, 1867, 30 & 31 Vict., c. 3 (UK).

Corporations Act (Ontario), RSO 1990, c. C.38, as amended.

Day, Midge, *Ontario Corporate Procedures*, 3d ed. (Toronto: Thomson Professional Publishing, 1995).

Industry Canada, Corporations Canada, *Staff Roles and Responsibilities*, Strategis Web site: http://strategis.gc.ca.

Law Society of Upper Canada, *Business Law*, Bar Admission Notes (Toronto: LSUC, 2000).

McGuiness, Kevin P., *The Law and Practice of Canadian Business Corporations* (Markham, ON: Butterworths, 1999).

Personal Property Security Act (PPSA), RSO 1990, c. P.10, as amended.

Repair and Storage Liens Act (Ontario), RSO 1990, c. R.25, as amended.

Smyth, J.E., D.A. Soberman, and A.J. Easson, *The Law and Business Administration in Canada*, 9th ed. (Toronto: Prentice-Hall, 2001).

Van Duzer, J. Anthony, *The Law of Partnerships and Corporations* (Toronto: Irwin Law, 1997).

Welling, Bruce L., *Corporate Law in Canada: The Governing Principles*, 2d ed. (Markham, ON: Butterworths, 1991).

APPENDIX   CONTACT INFORMATION

British Columbia
Ministry of Finance & Corporate Relations
Corporate and Personal Property Registries
2nd floor, The Waddington Building
940 Blanshard Street
Victoria, BC V8W 3E6
telephone: 250-387-7848
fax; 250-356-9422
Web site: http://www.fin.gov.bc.ca/registries/corppg/default.htm

Alberta
Alberta Registries
Corporate Registries
18th Floor, Commerce Place
10155 — 102 Street
Edmonton, AB T5J 4L4
telephone: 780-422-7330
fax: 780-422-1091
e-mail: Alberta.Registries@gov.ab.ca
Web site: http://www.gov.ab.ca/gs

Saskatchewan
Department of Justice
Corporations Branch
1871 Smith Street
Regina, SK S4P 3V7
telephone: 306-787-2962
fax: 306-787-8999
e-mail: corporations@justice.gov.sk.ca
Web site: http://www.saskjustice.gov.sk.ca

Manitoba
Manitoba Consumer and Corporate Affairs
Companies Office
1010 Woodsworth Building, 10th Floor
405 Broadway Avenue
Winnipeg, MB R3C 3L6
telephone: 204-945-2500
fax: 204-945-1459
e-mail: companies@gov.mb.ca
Web site: http://www.gov.mb.ca/cca/comp_off/index.html

Ontario
Ministry of Consumer and Business Services
Companies and Personal Property Security Branch
375 University Avenue, 2nd Floor
Toronto, ON M5G 2M2
telephone: 416-314-8880 or
    1-800-361-3223 (Compliance Certificates)
    416-314-0102 (Searches)
fax: 416-314-4852
e-mail: cbsinfor@cbs.gov.on.ca
Web site: http://www.ccr.gov.on.ca

Quebec
Direction des entreprises
L'Inspecteur général des institutions financières
800, Place d'Youville, 9e étage
Québec (QC) G1R 4Y5
telephone: 418-643-3625
fax: 418-646-9660
e-mail: edi@igif.gouv.qc.ca
Web site: http://www.igif.gouv.qc.ca

Direction des entreprises
L'Inspecteur général des institutions financières
800, Place Victoria Niveau Promenade, CP 355
Montréal (QC) H4Z 1H9
telephone: 1-888-291-4443 (appels provenant du Québec)
418-643-3625 (appels provenant hors du Québec)
fax: 514-873-6431
Web site: http://www.igif.gouv.qc.ca

New Brunswick
Corporate Affairs Branch
Service New Brunswick
432 Queen Street
Fredericton, NB E3B 1B6
telephone: 506-453-2703
fax: 506-453-2613
Web site: http://www.snb.ca

Mailing address:
Corporate Affairs Branch
Service New Brunswick
PO Box 1998
Fredericton, NB E3B 5G4

Nova Scotia
Service Nova Scotia and Municipal Relations Registry of Joint Stock Companies
Maritime Centre, 9th Floor
1505 Barrington Street Box 1529
Halifax, NS B3J 2K4
telephone: 902-424-7770
fax: 902-424-4633
e-mail: joint-stocks@gov.ns.ca
Web site: http://www.gov.ns.ca/snsmr/rjsc

Prince Edward Island
Consumer, Corporate and Insurance Services Department of
    Community Affairs and Attorney General
105 Rochford Street, 5th Floor
PO Box 2000
Charlottetown, PE C1A 7N8
telephone: 902-368-4551
fax: 902-368-5283
e-mail: skfurlotte@gov.pe.ca
Web site: http://www.gov.pe.ca

Newfoundland and Labrador
Department of Government Services and Lands, Consumer and Commercial Affairs
    Registrar of Companies
PO Box 8700, Confederation Building
Confederation Building Ground Floor, East Block
St. John's, NL A1B 4J6
telephone: 709-729-3317
fax: 709-729-0232
Web site: http://www.gov.nf.ca/gsl/cca/cr
    Corporate searches are done by private agents in Newfoundland and Labrador
        (for a list of these agents, write to this address)

Yukon
Department of Corporate Affairs
(J-9) Registrar of Companies
PO Box 2703 2134
Second Avenue
Whitehorse, YT Y1A 2C6
telephone: 867-667-5442
fax: 867-393-6251
e-mail: corporateaffairs@gov.yk.ca
Web site: http://www.gov.yk.ca/depts/community/corp

Northwest Territories
Department of Justice, GNWT
Registrar
Legal Registries
1st Floor, Stuart Hodgson Bldg.
5009 — 49th Street
Yellowknife, NT X1A 2L9
telephone: 867-873-7492
fax: 867-873-0243
Web site: http://www.gov.nt.ca

Nunavut
Department of Justice
Nunavut Legal Registries Division
PO Box 1000, Station 570
1st Floor, Brown Building
Iqaluit, NU X0A 0H0
telephone: 867-975-6190
fax: 867-975-6194
e-mail: tkusch@gov.nu.ca

NOTES

1. Midge Day, *Ontario Corporate Procedures*, 3d ed. (Toronto: Thomson Professional Publishing, 1995), at 23.

2. J.E. Smyth, D.A. Soberman, and A.J. Easson, *The Law and Business Administration in Canada*, 9th ed. (Toronto: Prentice-Hall, 2001), at 26.

3. The South Sea Company was established by an act of the English Parliament and had a monopoly to conduct England's trade with Spain's colonies in the West Indies and South America. The monopoly was based on the expectation that Spain would grant trading concessions in the peace treaty between England and Spain that was under negotiation at the time. The South Sea Company had the further purpose of relieving the government of its unsecured public debt. Investors were given stock in the company in exchange for their government bonds. Speculation ran high and the stock became overinflated. Inevitably, the stock crashed, bankrupting investors and bringing down the government. Following the scandal, the Bank of England assumed responsibility for the public debt and *The Bubble Act* was passed to control the formation of business associations.

4. The information for this section was obtained from material contained on the Corporations Canada Web site: http://strategis.gc.ca/corporations.

REVIEW QUESTIONS

1. List three different methods of incorporation in Canada.

2. Explain the difference between memorandum of association, letters patent, and articles of incorporation. Indicate which is applicable to each jurisdiction in Canada.

3. List and discuss the main characteristics of corporations.

4. What do we mean when we refer to a "special act" corporation? Give an example.

5. John Green, Mary Green, and Robert Black have decided to open a business selling widgets. They are unsure as to what business structure to use — a corporation or a partnership. They intend to borrow money to get started and are concerned that their homes will not be seized by creditors. They intend to carry on business only in southern Ontario because they want to keep the business a small, personable, hands-on operation. Discuss the pros and the cons of the different business structures.

6. Describe the different methods of filing documents with Corporations Canada and the Ontario Companies Branch.

PART II

Setting up a corporation to do business

CHAPTER 4

Corporate management

CHAPTER OVERVIEW

This chapter discusses the statutory provisions that affect directors and officers in CBCA and OBCA corporations, including provisions that relate to first directors; the number of directors; qualifications of directors; the residency of directors; the election and appointment of directors; and how a director ceases to be a director. It also covers the statutory and fiduciary duties and liabilities of directors, including giving notice of conflicts of interest; the standard of care required; statutory liabilities; and quasi-criminal liabilities. The reader will briefly consider directors' liabilities under unanimous shareholder agreements, and when directors can delegate their responsibilities. The chapter outlines how officers are designated and appointed and how persons dealing with corporations are able to rely on the "indoor management rule." The chapter concludes by examining the indemnification provisions contained in the governing statutes and describes how directors may purchase liability insurance to protect themselves against third-party liability.

CHAPTER OBJECTIVES

After completing this chapter, you should be able to:

1. Identify the different players involved in managing a corporation and the roles that they play.

2. Explain why a corporation must have directors and the statutory consequences of not having any directors.

3. Explain the different ways an individual can become a director.

4. Describe those individuals who are disqualified from being directors.

5. List the different ways in which directors cease to be directors.

6. Explain the procedure for removing a director.

7. Analyze when directors must give notice of conflicts of interest and recite the procedures for doing this.

8. Describe directors' duties and liabilities under the CBCA, the OBCA, and other relevant statutes.

9. Recognize which duties directors may delegate to a managing director, committee of directors, or officers.

10. Define the "indoor management rule."

11. Discuss the methods to protect directors in carrying out their duties.

INTRODUCTION

In chapter 3, we briefly discussed the concept of "centralized management" and identified the important players in controlling the performance of a corporation — namely, the directors, shareholders, and officers. Each player has different responsibilities, some of which are set out in the CBCA and the OBCA, and others that are based on common law principles. Consider the following:

directors
individuals responsible for managing the business and affairs of a corporation for the benefit of the shareholders

- Subject to any unanimous shareholder agreement, **directors** are responsible for managing, or supervising the management of, the business and affairs of the corporation for the benefit of the shareholders (CBCA s. 102(1); OBCA s. 115(1));

shareholders
the "owners" of a corporation who elect the directors

- **shareholders** are the "owners" who elect the directors; and

officers
individuals who manage a corporation's day-to-day activities under the supervision of the directors

- **officers** are individuals who manage the corporation's day-to-day activities under the supervision of the directors.

The CBCA (s. 2(1)) and OBCA (s. 1(1)) define "director" as "a person occupying the position of director by whatever name called." So, although in most corporations directors are, in fact, called "directors," this is not necessary. That is the reason why such designations as "board of governors" or "board of trustees" are sometimes used in not-for-profit corporations.

FIRST DIRECTORS OF A CORPORATION

Both the CBCA and the OBCA require the naming of directors at the time of incorporation. Under the CBCA (s. 106(2)), the first directors are named in the notice of directors (Form 6), which accompanies the articles of incorporation. Each director named in the notice holds office from the issue of the certificate of incorporation until the first meeting of shareholders.

The procedure is slightly different under the OBCA (s. 119(1)) in that the first directors are named in the articles. They also hold office from the date of endorsement of the certificate of incorporation until the first shareholder meeting. However, until the first meeting of shareholders, the resignation of a director named in the articles is not effective unless, at the time that the resignation is to become effective, a successor has been elected or appointed (s. 119(2)).

NUMBER OF DIRECTORS

Both the CBCA (s. 102(2)) and the OBCA (s. 115(2)) require that a **non-offering corporation** have at least one or more directors. An **offering corporation** must have at least three directors:

- in a CBCA corporation, at least two of whom are not officers or employees of the corporation or its affiliates (CBCA s. 102(2)); and

- in an OBCA corporation, at least one-third of whom are not officers or employees of the corporation or any of its affiliates (OBCA s. 115(3)).

A corporation may also have a "**floating board**" — that is, a board of directors of a corporation that has a minimum and maximum number of directors specified in the articles (for example, a minimum of 1 director and a maximum of 10 directors); or a "**fixed board**" — that is, a board of directors of a corporation that has a set number of directors specified in the articles. Where the articles of the corporation provide for "cumulative" voting (discussed below), the articles must also provide for a fixed board, not a floating board.

Under the CBCA, where a corporation has a floating board, there is no provision for determining the number of directors at any given time. The shareholders, by ordinary resolution at their first meeting and at each successive annual meeting, elect the directors, thereby determining the number of directors. However, it is not unusual to find a provision in the articles setting out how to determine the number of directors to be elected at annual meetings.

Section 125(3) of the OBCA provides a mechanism for determining the number of directors on a floating board where a minimum and maximum number is set out in the articles. This number must be fixed by special resolution of the shareholders, or alternatively the shareholders can empower the directors to determine this number. Where no resolution has been passed fixing the number, the number of directors of the corporation is the number of directors named in its articles (OBCA s. 125(4)). For example, if an Ontario corporation names three directors in its articles of incorporation and the shareholders do not pass a special resolution determining the number of directors, the number of directors will be deemed to be three because that is the number of directors named in the articles.

DIRECTORS' QUALIFICATIONS

There are no legal requirements to becoming a director. However, the CBCA (s. 105(1)) and the OBCA (s. 118(1)) do provide that the following persons are "disqualified" from being a director of a corporation:

1. anyone who is less than 18 years of age;

2. anyone who is of unsound mind and has been so found by a court in Canada or elsewhere;

3. a person who is not an individual; or

4. a person who has the status of bankrupt.

non-offering corporation
a corporation that does not offer its shares for sale to the public

offering corporation
a corporation that offers its shares for sale to the public

floating board
a board of directors of a corporation that has a minimum and maximum number of directors determined in the articles

fixed board
a board of directors of a corporation that has a set number of directors determined in the articles

For many years, directors were required to hold shares of the corporation in which they were a director. Now, unless the articles so provide, directors are not required to hold shares of the corporation.

A director of a CBCA or OBCA corporation must be an "individual." This is defined in the statutes as "a natural person, but does not include a partnership, unincorporated association, unincorporated syndicate, unincorporated organization, trust, or a natural person in his or her capacity as trustee, executor, administrator or other legal representative."

In England, for example, a corporation is still allowed to serve as a director.[1] The advantage of this provision appears to be that a notice of change is not required if the officer appointed to perform the role of the director corporation is changed, and this could be useful where a director corporation owns a number of subsidiaries. The closest concept to this in Canada is the "unanimous shareholder agreement," which strips the directors of their powers and provides for shareholders to manage the corporation. Unanimous shareholder agreements are discussed in chapter 9.

DIRECTOR RESIDENCY

Shopping around for jurisdictions that do not have director residency requirements has now become commonplace. We will discuss the attributes of the various provinces in Canada in this regard in chapter 7. For now, both the CBCA and the OBCA provide for a certain percentage of the board of directors to be **resident Canadian**.

resident Canadian
defined under the CBCA and the OBCA variously but essentially as an individual who is a Canadian citizen ordinarily resident in Canada, a Canadian citizen not ordinarily resident in Canada who is a member of a prescribed class of persons, or a permanent resident of Canada within the meaning of the federal *Immigration Act* and ordinarily resident in Canada

CBCA corporations

Since November 24, 2001, the CBCA (s. 105(3)) provides that at least 25 percent of the directors of a corporation must be resident Canadians. However, if a corporation has fewer than four directors, at least one director must be a resident Canadian.

There are two exceptions. One exception is for the boards of corporations whose ownerships are restricted — for example, airlines or book publishers. In these corporations, a majority of the directors of the corporation must be resident Canadians and if there is only one or two directors, that director or one of the two directors, as the case may be, must be a resident Canadian (CBCA ss. 105(3.1) and (3.3)).

The second exception is for "holding" companies. Not more than one-third of the directors of a holding corporation need be resident Canadians if certain revenue thresholds are met. This applies if the holding corporation earns in Canada, directly or through its subsidiaries, less than 5 percent of the gross revenues of the holding corporation and all of its subsidiary bodies corporate together, as shown in the most recent consolidated financial statements of the holding corporation, or in the financial statements of the holding corporation and its subsidiary bodies corporate at the end of the last completed financial year of the holding corporation (CBCA s. 105(4)).

The CBCA (s. 2(1)) defines "resident Canadian" as follows:

"resident Canadian" means an individual who is
(a) a Canadian citizen ordinarily resident in Canada,
(b) a Canadian citizen not ordinarily resident in Canada who is a member of a prescribed class of persons, or

(c) a permanent resident within the meaning of subsection 2(1) of the *Immigration and Refugee Protection Act* and ordinarily resident in Canada, except a permanent resident who has been ordinarily resident in Canada for more than one year after the time at which he or she first became eligible to apply for Canadian citizenship.

Paragraph (c) of this definition can be problematic for those who want to be a director and who have lived in Canada for a number of years but, although eligible, have never taken Canadian citizenship.

For purposes of paragraph (b), s. 13 of the regulations prescribes the classes of persons who are exempt. These include persons working overseas with the government of Canada, employees of a Canadian-controlled corporation, students at recognized educational institutions, and seniors over the age of 60 who had their 60th birthday while living in Canada and have lived outside Canada for less than 10 consecutive years.

OBCA corporations

Under the OBCA (s. 118(3)), a majority of the directors of every corporation other than a non-resident corporation must be resident Canadians. Where a corporation has only one or two directors, that director or one of the two directors, as the case may be, must be a resident Canadian. A "non-resident corporation" is a corporation incorporated before April 27, 1965 that has never carried on business in Canada and never was a resident of Canada.

The OBCA definition of "resident Canadian" varies from the CBCA definition in that paragraph (c) does not restrict a permanent resident who has been ordinarily resident in Canada for more than one year after the time at which such person first became eligible to apply for Canadian citizenship from becoming a director.

The classes of prescribed persons are substantially the same as those in the CBCA, but there are some subtle differences, and you should refer to s. 26 of the OBCA regulations for the complete text. For example, a person who has reached his or her 60th birthday can have been living outside Canada since that time; and an educational institution must be recognized only by the province of Ontario.

BECOMING A DIRECTOR

There are four ways in which individuals become directors of corporations:

1. pursuant to the issuance of a certificate of incorporation;

2. by an election by shareholders;

3. by an appointment by directors to fill a vacancy; and

4. as *ex officio* directors by reason of their office.

Becoming a director pursuant to the issuance of a certificate of incorporation

See the discussion above with respect to the procedure for becoming a first director pursuant to the issuance of the certificate of incorporation.

Becoming a director by election by shareholders

Unless the articles provide for "cumulative" voting for directors, the shareholders, at their first meeting and at each succeeding annual meeting at which an election of directors is required, are required by an ordinary resolution to elect directors to hold office for a term expiring not later than the close of the third annual meeting of shareholders following the election (CBCA s. 106(3); OBCA s. 119(4)).

Directors are not required to hold office for the same "**term**" — that is, the period of time for which the director is elected to act as a director. They can hold office for **staggered terms**; in other words, directors are elected for different periods (CBCA s. 106(4); OBCA s. 119(5)). If a director is not elected for a defined term, the director ceases to hold office at the close of the first annual meeting of shareholders following the director's election (CBCA s. 106(5); OBCA 119(6)). Directors can also be elected for "rotating terms," which means that directors are elected for the same length of term but at alternate annual meetings.

If directors are not elected at a meeting of shareholders when required, the incumbent directors continue in office until their successors are elected (CBCA s. 106(6); OBCA s. 119(7)). This ensures that a board of directors remains in place.

If, by reason of the lack of consent, disqualification, incapacity, or death of any candidates, shareholders fail to elect the required number of directors, the directors elected at that meeting can exercise all the powers of the directors if the number of directors so elected constitutes a quorum (CBCA s. 106(7); OBCA s. 119(8)).

Under certain circumstances, the directors in office must, without delay, call a special meeting of shareholders to fill a vacancy. If they fail to call a meeting, or if there are no directors in office, any shareholder can call the meeting. These circumstances are (CBCA s. 111(2); OBCA s. 124(3)):

1. if there is not a quorum of directors; or

2. where there is a floating board in a CBCA corporation, and there has been a failure to elect the number or minimum number of directors provided for in the articles; or

3. where there is a floating board in an OBCA corporation, and there has been a failure to elect the number of directors required by the articles or by s. 125.

term
when applied to the election of directors, the period of time for which the director is elected to act as a director

staggered term
a varied period of time for which directors are elected

Becoming a director by appointment to fill a vacancy

There are two circumstances that give rise to a "vacancy" on the board of directors: (1) on the disqualification, removal, resignation, or death of the director; and (2) when the directors, between meetings, increase the number of directors.

VACANCY DUE TO DISQUALIFICATION, REMOVAL, RESIGNATION, OR DEATH OF A DIRECTOR

A quorum of directors of a corporation may fill a vacancy among directors that arises due to any reason other than

- an increase in the number or minimum or maximum number of directors; or

- a failure to elect the number or minimum number of directors provided for in the articles or otherwise required to be elected at any annual meeting of shareholders (CBCA s. 111(1); OBCA s. 124(1)).

INCREASE IN NUMBER OF DIRECTORS BY DIRECTORS

In a CBCA corporation, if authorized in the articles of the corporation, the directors may appoint one or more additional directors to hold office for a term expiring not later than the close of the next annual meeting of shareholders, where the total number of directors so appointed does not exceed one-third of the number of directors elected at the previous annual meeting of shareholders (CBCA s. 106(8)).

A similar provision appears in the OBCA where the directors are empowered by the shareholders to appoint additional directors (OBCA s. 124(2)).

For example, (1) if the corporation's articles provide for a minimum of 1 director and a maximum of 10 directors, (2) if the articles provide that the directors may appoint one or more additional directors (CBCA corporation) or if the shareholders have passed a special resolution empowering the directors to determine the number of directors (OBCA corporation), and (3) if the number of directors within the minimum number and maximum number has been fixed at 6 directors, the directors can only increase this number to 8 and appoint 2 more directors. They cannot increase it to 9 and appoint 3 more directors because this would result in the total number being more than one and one-third times the original number of 6.

If the holders of any class of shares of a corporation have an exclusive right to elect one or more directors and a vacancy occurs among those directors, the remaining directors elected by the holders of that class can fill the vacancy, or if there are no such remaining directors, any holder of shares of that class can call a meeting of the holders of shares of that class for the purpose of filling the vacancy (CBCA s. 111(3); OBCA s. 124(4)).

The right of the directors to fill vacancies can be restricted. The articles may provide that a vacancy among the directors can be filled only by a vote of the shareholders, or by a vote of the holders of any class or series of shares having an exclusive right to elect one or more directors if the vacancy occurs among the directors elected by that class or series (CBCA s. 111(4); OBCA s. 124(5)).

A director appointed or elected to fill a vacancy holds office for the unexpired term of his or her predecessor (CBCA s. 111(5); OBCA s. 124(6)).

Becoming a director by virtue of holding another office

"***Ex officio***" directors are not expressly authorized in either the CBCA or the OBCA. However, they are common in not-for-profit corporations and are expressly provided for in the *Corporations Act* (Ontario). An *ex officio* director is a director who becomes a director because he or she holds some other office and the corporate articles or bylaws provide that he or she becomes a director of a corporation because of holding such a position.

ex officio
by virtue of office — a person holding an office who becomes a director because he or she holds that office

CUMULATIVE VOTING FOR ELECTION OF DIRECTORS

Sometimes you will find that the holders of a class or series of shares of a corporation have the exclusive right to elect one or more directors.

cumulative voting
a right sometimes given to shareholders whereby every shareholder entitled to elect directors can cast a number of votes equal to the number of votes attached to that shareholder's shares multiplied by the number of directors to be elected; in some cases, the shareholder may cast all his or her votes in favour of one candidate or distribute the votes among the candidates in any manner he or she sees fit

Cumulative voting is a right that is sometimes given to shareholders. It means that every shareholder entitled to vote at an election of directors has the right to cast at the meeting a number of votes equal to the number of votes attached to the shares held by the shareholder, multiplied by the number of directors to be elected. The shareholder may cast all his or her votes in favour of one candidate, or distribute them among the candidates in such a manner as the shareholder sees fit. A separate vote of shareholders will be taken with respect to each candidate nominated for director unless a unanimous resolution is passed permitting two or more persons to be elected by a single resolution. If there are more candidates than positions available, the candidate who receives the least number of votes is eliminated until the number of candidates who remain equals the number of positions to be filled (CBCA s. 107; OBCA s. 120).

A reasonably significant minority may accumulate all their votes in favour of one or two candidates and thus ensure their election to the board, giving the minority an effective voice in the management of the corporation.

Cumulative voting is more helpful to minority groups when a large number of directors is to be elected. If the number of directors is small, or if only a small proportion of them is elected each year, cumulative voting is less effective in assisting the minority to elect a member to the board. Here is an example of cumulative voting:

> A shareholder has 100 common shares, each of which carries one vote at meetings of shareholders. At the annual meeting of shareholders, the shareholders are electing 5 directors. The shareholder has the choice of casting her 500 votes (100 common shares × the number of directors being elected (5) = 500 votes) for one candidate or among as many of the candidates as she sees fit. By casting all her votes against one candidate, the minority shareholder may be lucky enough to elect the candidate of her choice.

To achieve cumulative voting, a special provision to this effect must be included in the articles. If cumulative voting provisions are desired, there must be a fixed number of directors.

DIRECTOR CONSENTS
Federal corporations (CBCA s. 106(9))

A director who is elected or appointed to hold office as a director is not a director and is deemed not to have been elected or appointed to hold office as a director unless

1. the director was present at the meeting when the election or appointment took place and did not refuse to hold office as a director; or

2. the director was not present at the meeting when the election or appointment took place and

a. the director consented to hold office in writing before the election or appointment or within 10 days after it, or

b. the director has acted as a director pursuant to the election or appointment.

Ontario corporations (OBCA ss. 119(9) and (10))

The election or appointment of a director is not effective unless the person elected or appointed consents in writing before or within 10 days after the date of the election or appointment. Despite this requirement, the OBCA also provides that if the person elected or appointed consents in writing after this time period, the election or appointment will be valid.

CEASING TO BE A DIRECTOR

Directors can resign, be removed, or cease to hold office for a number of reasons including the following:

1. the director dies;

2. the director resigns — the resignation becomes effective at the time a written resignation is sent to the corporation, or at the time specified in the resignation, whichever is later;

3. the director becomes disqualified; or

4. the director is removed — the shareholders of a corporation may by ordinary resolution at an annual or special meeting remove any director or directors from office (CBCA s. 109(1); OBCA s. 122(1)).

Removal of directors

If the shareholders propose to remove a director, the notice calling the meeting must set out this fact and a copy of the resolution must be attached.

A director who

- receives a notice or otherwise learns of a meeting of shareholders called for the purpose of removing him or her from office; or

- receives a notice or otherwise learns of a meeting of directors or shareholders at which another person is to be appointed or elected to fill the office of director, whether because of the resignation or removal of the director or because his or her term of office has expired or is about to expire — for example, at an annual meeting —

can submit to the corporation a written statement giving the reasons for the director's resignation or the reasons the director opposes any proposed action or resolution, as the case may be (CBCA s. 110(2); OBCA s. 123(2)).

When a corporation receives such a statement, it must forthwith send a copy of the statement to every shareholder entitled to receive a notice of meetings of shareholders and to the director appointed under the governing statute, unless the statement is included in or attached to a management proxy or information circular (CBCA s. 110(3); OBCA s. 123(3)).

These provisions of the CBCA and the OBCA make a good argument for effecting the removal of directors by meeting of the shareholders or a sole shareholder. However, except where there is conflict over the removal, it is quite common to use a shareholders' resolution to remove directors.

Where the holders of a special class or series have the exclusive right to elect a director, this director can be removed only by an ordinary resolution at a meeting of the shareholders of that class or series (CBCA s. 109(2); OBCA s. 122(2)).

A vacancy created by the removal of a director may be filled at the meeting at which the director is removed (CBCA s. 109(3); OBCA s. 122(3)).

Where there is cumulative voting, a director may be removed from office only if the number of votes cast in favour of the director's removal is greater than the product of the number of directors required by the articles and the number of votes cast against the motion (CBCA s. 107(f); OBCA s. 120(f)).

If all directors resign

Section 109(4) of the CBCA provides that if all the directors resign or have been removed without replacement, a person who manages or supervises the management of the business and affairs of the corporation is deemed to be a director for the purposes of the CBCA. The exceptions set out in s. 109(5) include:

1. an officer who manages the business or affairs of the corporation under the direction or control of a shareholder or other person;

2. a lawyer, notary, accountant, or other professional who participates in the management of the corporation solely for the purpose of providing professional services; or

3. a trustee in bankruptcy, receiver, receiver-manager, or secured creditor who participates in the management of the corporation or exercises control over its property solely for the purpose of the realization of security or the administration of a bankrupt's estate, in the case of a trustee in bankruptcy.

The OBCA has similar provisions in ss. 115(4) and (5).

HOW DIRECTORS ACT

Generally speaking, decisions of the board of directors are made at meetings of the directors or by way of signed resolutions. Minutes of these meetings and the resolutions must be maintained by the corporation in accordance with the record-keeping requirements of the corporate statutes. When a solicitor gives a legal opinion that the corporation has been duly incorporated and properly organized, these minutes and resolutions will be reviewed, possibly by law clerks, to ensure that all appropriate steps have been taken.

You will find an in-depth discussion of the requirements for directors' meetings in chapter 11.

DIRECTOR DUTIES AND LIABILITIES

Under the general corporate statutes, directors are required to fulfill a number of legal duties, and additional duties may be set out in the bylaws or in a unanimous shareholder agreement. The director's primary duty is to the corporation and not to any particular shareholder or class of shareholder. Liabilities also arise under other statutes such as the *Income Tax Act* and the *Securities Act*, which impose further burdens on directors.

Under the CBCA s. 122(1) and the OBCA s. 134(1), every director and officer of a corporation in exercising their powers and discharging their duties must

- act honestly and in good faith with a view to the best interests of the corporation; and

- exercise the care, diligence, and skill that a reasonably prudent person would exercise in comparable circumstances.

Fiduciary duty

The law imposes upon directors a "fiduciary" obligation to act honestly, in good faith, and in the best interests of the corporation, and to observe a minimum standard of care. Every director and officer, in carrying out his or her responsibilities, is required to act with:

- *Honesty* — Directors and officers must be entirely truthful in their dealings with the board and the corporation.

- *Legality* — They must comply with the statute governing the corporation, the regulations, articles, bylaws, and any unanimous shareholder agreement.

- *Good faith* — They must act in an impartial and disinterested manner and without regard to their own personal interests.

- *Best interests of the corporation* — They must act at all times in the best interests of the corporation. The best interests of the corporation include the best interests of the shareholders. They must consider the shareholders' interests as a group, not the special interests of a particular shareholder or group of shareholders. They must be attentive to the interests of minority shareholders and creditors to ensure that any actions taken to benefit the majority of the shareholders are not oppressive or unfairly prejudicial or do not unfairly disregard the interests of minority shareholders and creditors.

Conflicts of interest

The disclosure of interest rules under CBCA s. 120 were amended on November 24, 2001. They provide that a director or an officer of a corporation must disclose to the corporation the nature and extent of any interest that the director or officer has in a material contract or material transaction, whether made or proposed, with the corporation. This disclosure may be done in writing or by requesting to have their interest noted in the minutes of meetings of directors or of meetings of committees of directors. The director or officer need only disclose an interest if the director or officer:

1. is a party to the contract or transaction;

2. is a director, an officer, or an individual acting in a similar capacity of a party to the contract or transaction; or

3. has a material interest in a party to the contract or transaction.

See figure 4.1 at the end of the chapter for a general notice of interest to be given by a director who has a material interest in a party to the contract or transaction.

If disclosure of the interest is made, if the directors approve the contract or transaction, and if the contract or transaction was reasonable and fair to the corporation when it was approved, the director or officer is not accountable to the corporation or its shareholders for any profit realized from the contract or transaction.

Furthermore, even if the above conditions are not met, a director or officer acting honestly and in good faith is not accountable to the corporation or to its shareholders for any profit realized from a contract or transaction for which disclosure is required if:

1. the contract or transaction is approved or confirmed by special resolution at a meeting of shareholders;

2. disclosure of the interest was made to the shareholders in a manner sufficient to indicate its nature before the contract or transaction was approved or confirmed; and

3. the contract or transaction was reasonable and fair to the corporation when it was approved or confirmed.

A conflict of interest may arise through direct ownership of an asset being sold to the corporation, or it may arise in more indirect ways. For example, a director may be a shareholder in another corporation that is selling to or buying from the corporation in which he or she is a director, or the person making a contract with the corporation may be acting as agent or trustee for the director. This problem arises frequently with related corporations. They may not necessarily be in the relationship of parent and subsidiary. It may be merely that one or more directors of one corporation are shareholders and perhaps directors of a second corporation. The question of what constitutes a "material" contract is one that has to be determined on the basis of the specific circumstances. What is considered "material" in one situation, may not be "material" in another.

A director or officer is required to disclose his or her interest within the time frames set out in the statutes. For a director, this is:

1. at a meeting at which a proposed contract or transaction is first considered;

2. if the director was not, at the time of the meeting referred to in (1), interested in a proposed contract or transaction, at the first meeting after the director becomes so interested;

3. if the director becomes interested after a contract is made or transaction is entered into, at the first meeting after the director becomes so interested; or

4. if an individual who is interested in a contract or transaction later becomes a director, at the first meeting after such individual becomes a director.

If the contract or transaction is one that does not normally require approval by the directors or shareholders, a director or officer must disclose the nature and extent of their interest immediately after becoming aware of the contract or transaction. This disclosure can be done in writing to the corporation or by request to have the interest noted in the minutes of meetings of directors or of meetings of committees of directors.

A director who is required to make a disclosure is not allowed to vote on any resolution to approve the contract or transaction, unless the contract or transaction:

1. relates primarily to his or her remuneration as a director, officer, employee, or agent of the corporation or an affiliate;

2. is for indemnity or insurance; or

3. is with an affiliate.

For any of the following reasons, a director or officer is permitted to make a general notice to the board of directors declaring that he or she is to be regarded as interested in a contract or transaction made with a party:

1. the director or officer is a director or officer or is acting in a similar capacity of a party referred to in the contract or transaction;

2. the director or officer has a material interest in the party; or

3. there has been a material change in the nature of the director's or the officer's interest in the party.

If these rules are not followed, a court may, on application of the corporation or any of its shareholders, set aside the contract or transaction on any terms that it sees fit, or require the director or officer to account to the corporation for any profit or gain realized on it, or do both those things.

The disclosure of interest rules under OBCA s. 132 vary from the amended CBCA rules and more closely follow the CBCA rules before their amendment. The following are some of the differences:

1. An OBCA director is also able to vote under ss. 132(5)(a) and (d) on a contract or transaction if it is an arrangement by way of security for money loaned to or obligations undertaken by the director for the benefit of the corporation or an affiliate; or one with an affiliate.

2. Under s. 132(6), the general notice of interest is not required to reflect the director's or officer's interest in a material change in the interest.

3. Unlike CBCA s. 120(6.1), the OBCA does not specifically give shareholders the right to examine the portions of any minutes of meetings of directors or of committees of directors that contain disclosures under this section, as well as any other documents that contain those disclosures, during the usual business hours of the corporation.

Standard of care

The minimum standard of care imposed by the CBCA (s. 122) and the OBCA (s. 134) requires that a director "exercise the care, diligence and skill that a reasonably prudent person would exercise in comparable circumstances."

Failure to meet this requirement exposes a director or officer to liability to the corporation for damages arising out of his or her negligence or bad faith.

Generally, the standard of care directors must meet is to behave as carefully as the directors would have acted under the same circumstances if they were acting on their own behalf. Although there are no specific rules as to what a director must do to conform to this standard, the following are some examples:

- Directors must be informed as to the policies, business, and affairs of the corporation; they must have an understanding of how business is conducted, revenue is earned, and resources are used.

- They must use common sense and act carefully.

- They must make reasonable and informed decisions with regard to the business affairs of the corporation.

- They must ensure understanding of the issues they are being asked to vote on; insist on receiving accurate and timely information from senior officers and management to help them make decisions; and ask questions and be sure to receive all necessary information on which to make a decision.

- Finally, they must use outside experts wisely — that is, ensure that the qualifications of the experts are adequate and appropriate.

The level of skill expected of a director depends to some extent on his or her qualifications. Generally, a higher degree of skill will be expected of an experienced business person than a lay person. Consider also such things as the director's qualifications and experiences, the information available to the director, the time available for the decision-making process, and the alternatives available.

As part of acting "diligently," a director should attempt to attend all directors' meetings. A director should also prepare himself or herself adequately to take an active role in the meeting. Directors are deemed to have agreed with all resolutions passed at a meeting at which they were not present, unless the director dissents from the resolution within seven days of becoming aware of the resolution. Inaction at a meeting is deemed to be consent to the decisions made at the meeting. If the director disagrees with a decision made at a meeting, he or she should ask to have the disagreement noted in the minutes. If absent, the director should take positive steps to register a dissent. Furthermore, a director should read and understand fully the financial statements of the corporation and question any entries in the statements that are either not understood or need further clarification. These actions may not be sufficient to absolve a director of responsibility for a business decision, but they will demonstrate the director's desire to exercise diligence.

Liabilities under the CBCA and OBCA

In addition to imposing a fiduciary duty and a standard of care on directors, the governing statutes also impose a number of specific liabilities on directors. These include statutory and wage liabilities.

STATUTORY LIABILITIES

Directors of a corporation who vote for or consent to a resolution authorizing the issue of a share for a consideration other than money are jointly and severally (and under the CBCA "or solidarily") liable to the corporation to make good any amount by which the consideration received is less than the fair equivalent of the money that the corporation would have received if the share had been issued for money on the date of the resolution (CBCA s. 118(1); OBCA s. 130(1)).

Directors of a corporation who vote for or consent to a resolution authorizing any of the following are jointly and severally (and under the CBCA "or solidarily") liable to restore to the corporation any amounts so distributed or paid and not otherwise recovered by the corporation (CBCA s. 118(2); OBCA s. 130(2)):

- declaration and payment of dividends;

- purchase, redemption, or acquisition of the corporation's own shares;

- authorization of payment of an unreasonable commission to a person in connection with purchases of the corporation's shares;

- payment of an indemnity contrary to the provisions of the Act; and

- authorization of payments to shareholders that interfere with or jeopardize other shareholders' rights to dissent and receive fair value for their shares, or if such payments cause the rights of other shareholders or the corporation's creditors to be oppressed.

LIABILITY FOR EMPLOYEE WAGES

Under CBCA s. 119(1):

> Directors of a corporation are jointly and severally, or solidarily, liable to employees of the corporation for all debts not exceeding six months wages payable to each such employee for services performed for the corporation while they are such directors respectively.

Under OBCA s. 131(1):

> The directors of a corporation are jointly and severally liable to the employees of the corporation for all debts not exceeding six months' wages that become payable while they are directors for services performed for the corporation and for the vacation pay accrued while they are directors for not more than twelve months under the *Employment Standards Act*, and the regulations thereunder, or under any collective agreement made by the corporation.

Other statutory liabilities

There are many other statutes that impose liabilities on a director. These include:

- the *Income Tax Act* (Canada) for failure to deduct, remit, or withhold taxes under the Act; and

- environmental statutes, securities legislation, the *Consumer Protection Act*, the *Co-operative Corporations Act*, the *Corporations Tax Act*, the *Day Nurseries Act*, the *Employment Standards Act, 2000*, and the *Occupational Health and Safety Act*.

Quasi-criminal liability

The governing statutes (CBCA ss. 250(1) and 251(1); OBCA s. 256(2)) also impose quasi-criminal liability on directors of a corporation by making it an offence for a director:

- to make or assist in making a report or statements in any material, information, evidence, or documents required to be provided or filed under such statutes that contain untrue or misleading statements of material facts;

- to fail to file any documents required to be filed;

- to refuse to provide information to government agencies, etc., when required to do so; or

- to fail to observe or comply with any directions, orders, decisions, rulings, or other requirements under any provisions of the governing statutes or regulations.

Directors' liabilities under a unanimous shareholder agreement

Both the CBCA (s. 146) and the OBCA (s. 108) provide that a unanimous shareholder agreement (USA) or declaration may restrict the rights and powers of the directors. In addition, under a USA, the rights, powers, and duties of the directors may be shifted to the shareholders of the corporation.

Under a USA, the accompanying liabilities of the directors are also expressly shifted to the shareholders and, accordingly, the directors are relieved of their rights, powers, duties, and liabilities.

USAs may address any particular powers of the directors, and need not cover all of those powers. Thus, a USA must be read carefully to determine exactly which of the rights, powers, and duties (and, therefore, liabilities) of the directors have been transferred to the shareholders. If the rights, powers, and duties still belong to the directors, so too do the resulting liabilities.

Delegation of directors' duties

Directors have some flexibility in the delegation of their powers (CBCA s. 115; OBCA s. 127). Directors may appoint a managing director (who must also be a director and resident Canadian) or a committee of directors and delegate to them any of the powers of the directors except the authority:

- to submit to the shareholders any question or matter requiring the approval of the shareholders;

- to fill a vacancy among the directors or in the office of auditor or appoint additional directors;

- to issue securities except as authorized by the directors;

- to issue shares of a series except as authorized by the directors;

- to declare dividends;

- to purchase, redeem, or otherwise acquire shares issued by the corporation;

- to pay a commission for the purchase of shares except as authorized by the directors;

- to approve a management proxy circular;

- to approve a takeover bid circular or directors' circular;

- to approve any financial statements; or

- to adopt, amend, or repeal bylaws.

In large corporations, the board may consist of 15, 20, or more directors and it is not uncommon for the board to appoint a "management committee," usually consisting of about 5 or 6 directors. This committee then directs the day-to-day affairs of the corporation and refers only the more important matters to the less-frequent meetings of the full board.

OFFICERS

Generally speaking, it is the officers of a corporation who look after the day-to-day activities of a corporation (CBCA s. 121; OBCA s. 133).

Subject to the articles, the bylaws, or any unanimous shareholder agreement, the directors may designate the offices of the corporation, appoint as officers persons of full capacity, specify their duties, and delegate to them powers to manage the business and affairs of the corporation, with the exception of the same list of powers that directors may not delegate to committees or a managing director.

Under predecessor statutes, and today under not-for-profit legislation, the statutes and the bylaws designate certain officers that a corporation is required to appoint — a president and a secretary, for example. It is important, therefore, when you are dealing with an older corporation that is incorporated under a predecessor statute, to review the bylaws for the provisions with regard to the appointment of officers.

A director may be appointed to any office of the corporation and may hold two or more offices.

As a rule, the duties of the officers are set out in the bylaws or administrative or standing resolutions. The bylaws will usually provide for several corporate officers. The most popular are a chair of the board, chief executive officer, chief financial officer, chief operating officer, president, one or more vice-presidents with varying levels of seniority, secretary, and treasurer. Under the governing statutes, none of the positions are mandatory and corporations are free to designate and appoint such officers as their board of directors sees fit.

INDOOR MANAGEMENT RULE

Pursuant to CBCA s. 18 and OBCA s. 19, persons dealing with a corporation are entitled to rely on the fact that directors and officers are properly elected and appointed; have the appropriate authorities to exercise the powers and perform the duties that are customary in the business of the corporation or usual for a director, officer, or agent; and have authority to issue and execute documents on behalf of the corporation. This is commonly referred to as the "indoor management rule."

INDEMNIFICATION

Under CBCA s. 124 and OBCA s. 136, a corporation may indemnify a director or officer of a corporation, a former director or officer, or a person who acts at the corporation's request for another entity from costs and expenses incurred in respect of any civil, criminal, or administrative proceeding to which the individual is made a party where such director or officer:

1. acted honestly and in good faith with a view to the best interests of the corporation or other entity; and

2. in the case of a criminal or administrative proceeding that is enforced by a monetary penalty, the individual has reasonable grounds for believing that his or her conduct was lawful.

Under the CBCA, the individual is entitled to be indemnified for the costs of the defence of any proceeding where it fulfills the above two conditions, provided that it was not judged to have committed any fault, or omitted to do anything that the individual ought to have done. The standard is less stringent under the OBCA, and provides that such an individual is entitled to indemnity if the two conditions are fulfilled and the individual was "substantially successful" on the merits of his or her defence of the action or proceeding.

When an action is brought by or on behalf of the corporation and the director or officer is made a party by reason of his or her acting as such, the corporation may, with the approval of the court, indemnify such person against all costs, charges, and expenses reasonably incurred by them in connection with the action, provided that they acted honestly and in good faith and their conduct was lawful as required above.

The CBCA also provides that a corporation may advance monies to such individuals for the costs, charges, and expenses of a proceeding. If the individual does not fulfill the conditions of acting honestly and in good faith and, in the case of a criminal action, the individual had reasonable grounds for believing that the individual's conduct was lawful, the individual must repay the money to the corporation.

INSURANCE

In addition to the indemnity provisions of the governing statutes, corporations may also purchase and maintain insurance for the benefit of a director or officer against any liability incurred by that person in the performance of his or her duties as a director and officer, except where the liability relates to the failure to act honestly and in good faith with a view to the best interests of the corporation. This insurance covers third-party liabilities of the kinds discussed above (CBCA s. 124(6); OBCA s. 136(4)).

Alternatively, a director may personally obtain insurance to cover potential liability to third parties.

REMUNERATION

Finally, given the great number of duties and liabilities placed on directors and officers, subject to the articles, bylaws, or any unanimous shareholder agreement, the directors are authorized to fix the remuneration of the directors, officers, and employees of the corporation (CBCA s. 125; OBCA s. 137). It is not unusual for directors to be paid "directors' fees." These fees might include an annual lump sum or an amount paid for attendance at meetings of the board and will almost always include expenses incurred in connection with board meetings.

KEY TERMS

cumulative voting

directors

ex officio

fixed board

floating board

non-offering corporation

offering corporation

officers

resident Canadian

shareholders

staggered terms

term

REFERENCES

Business Corporations Act (Ontario) (OBCA), RRO 1990, c. B.16, as amended.

Business Corporations Act (Ontario) General Regulations, RRO 1990, reg. 62.

Canada Business Corporations Act (CBCA), RSC 1985, c. C-44, as amended.

Canada Business Corporations Regulations, 2001, SOR/2001-512.

Consumer Protection Act, RSO 1990, c. C.31, as amended.

Co-operative Corporations Act, RSO 1990, c. C.35, as amended.

Corporations Tax Act, RSO 1990, c. C.40, as amended.

Day, Midge, *Ontario Corporate Procedures*, 3d ed. (Toronto: Thomson Professional Publishing, 1995).

Day Nurseries Act, RSO 1990, c. D.2, as amended.

Employment Standards Act, 2000, SO 2000, c. 41.

Income Tax Act, RSC 1985, c. 1 (5th Supp.), as amended.

Law Society of Upper Canada, *Business Law,* Bar Admission Course Materials (Toronto: LSUC, 2001).

McGuiness, Kevin P., *The Law and Practice of Canadian Business Corporations* (Markham, ON: Butterworths, 1999).

Occupational Health and Safety Act, RSO 1990, c. O.1, as amended.

Securities Act, RSO 1990, c. S.5, as amended.

Smyth, J.E., D.A. Soberman and A.J. Easson, *The Law and Business Administration in Canada*, 9th ed. (Toronto: Prentice-Hall, 2001).

Van Duzer, J. Anthony, *The Law of Partnerships and Corporations* (Toronto: Irwin Law, 1997).

Welling, Bruce L., *Corporate Law in Canada: The Governing Principles*, 2d ed. (Markham, ON: Butterworths, 1991).

FORMS AND PRECEDENTS

Figure 4.1: General notice of interest

NOTES

1. Kevin P. McGuiness, *The Law and Practice of Canadian Business Corporations* (Markham, ON: Butterworths, 1999).

REVIEW QUESTIONS

1. List the three principal offices involved in the operation of a corporation.

2. Describe how a first director takes office.

3. How many directors does a "non-offering" federal or Ontario corporation require?

4. Can someone of 16 years of age be a director?

5. Explain the difference in residency requirements between CBCA and OBCA corporations.

6. Your client is 65 years of age and living in Switzerland. Can she be a director of (a) a CBCA corporation; and (b) an OBCA corporation? Explain your answer.

7. List four ways a director can take office.

8. If a director of a CBCA or OBCA corporation has not consented to act as a director, is he or she a validly elected director?

9. Does the failure to sign a consent to act as a director affect the validity of resolutions voted on by the director?

10. Explain the circumstances in which a director can fill a vacancy of directors.

11. How does a director cease to hold office?

12. Give a brief description of the duties and liabilities of directors.

13. What must a director do if he or she realizes that he or she has a conflict of interest in a matter brought before a board meeting?

14. In what matters may directors be personally interested yet still vote on?

15. List three situations where a director may be liable under the governing corporate statutes.

16. If a shareholder has signed a unanimous shareholder declaration restricting all of the powers of the director, who is liable for those acts?

17. To whom may directors delegate? What must they not delegate?

18. What is the indoor management rule?

19. When can a director and officer be indemnified?

20. Can a corporation purchase insurance to protect its directors from liability?

21. When would directors' remuneration be appropriate?

FIGURE 4.1   GENERAL NOTICE OF INTEREST

GENERAL NOTICE OF INTEREST

TO: **OBA Canada Inc. (the "Corporation")**

AND TO: **The Directors Thereof**

DISCLOSURE

Pursuant to subsection 120(1) of the *Canada Business Corporations Act*, I hereby disclose that I:

1. am a director or officer of _____ and _____ (collectively, the "Parties");

2. have a material interest in each of the Parties; and

3. am to be regarded as interested, for the foregoing reasons, in a contract or transaction made with any of the Parties.

DATED the __ day of _____, ____.

_____

Name of Director

CHAPTER 5

Shares

CHAPTER OVERVIEW

This chapter introduces the concept of shares and examines the rights and remedies of shareholders. It discusses authorized capital; the various classes of shares; the most common rights, privileges, restrictions, and conditions attaching to shares; and outlines how to choose an appropriate capital structure for a corporation. The chapter illustrates various share transactions, then discusses the ability of a corporation to hold shares in itself, and concludes by outlining the procedure to follow if a shareholder loses a share certificate.

CHAPTER OBJECTIVES

After completing this chapter, you should be able to:

1. Describe the meaning of "shares."

2. Explain the concept of "piercing the corporate veil."

3. Identify the rights and remedies of shareholders.

4. Discuss how to determine the share capital structure in the articles of incorporation.

5. List the common rights, privileges, restrictions, and conditions affecting shares.

6. Describe the procedures for issue, transfer, redemption, purchase, and other transactions affecting shares.

INTRODUCTION

The issuance of "**shares**" to "shareholders" is one of the most important procedures in the operation of a corporation. Shareholders are the owners of a corporation. It is

shares
a percentage of the ownership of a corporation that entitles its holder to certain rights in the corporation

through shareholder investment that a corporation obtains the capital necessary to carry on its business. Shareholding may be referred to as "equity financing." The portion of this equity ownership represents the influence that shareholders have over the election of the directors of the corporation, their share of the profits of the corporation, and the amount they receive on the dissolution or windup of the corporation. Corporations can have as few as one shareholder and, if an offering corporation — that is, a corporation offering its shares to the public — an unlimited number of shareholders.

For example, BirdBaths Limited might have a total of five shareholders and a total issued capital of 1,000 common shares. Shareholder A holds 20 percent, shareholder B holds 25 percent, shareholder C holds 15 percent, shareholder D holds 30 percent, and shareholder E holds 10 percent. The important factor is not necessarily "how many" shares each shareholder holds but the percentage of the total number of shares issued. See graph 5.1.

Owning shares does not provide the holder with ownership in the assets of the corporation because it is the corporation itself that is the legal owner of its property and assets. Instead, owning shares provides the shareholder with certain rights, including the right to elect directors, the right to receive dividends, and the right to receive property of the corporation upon windup or dissolution after the interests of the creditors of the corporation have been satisfied. Shares are an interest in the capital of the corporation.[1]

PAR VALUE

par value
an arbitrary sum prescribed in the corporation's articles, which was the minimum amount for which a share could be issued

All shares authorized under both the CBCA and the OBCA are without nominal or par value (CBCA s. 24(1); OBCA s. 22(1)). Before December 15, 1975 under the CBCA and July 29, 1983 under the OBCA, shares in a corporation were said to have "nominal or par value." **Par value** was an arbitrary sum prescribed in the articles, which was the minimum amount for which a share could be issued. It allowed each shareholder to purchase shares at a cost not less than the cost paid by previous shareholders.

Par value does not relate to the market value of the share, which may be anywhere from 1 cent to $1,000 for a share with a par value of $1. In fact, use of a par value could create hardship to a corporation. For example, a share with a par value of $100 might currently be trading at $75. If the corporation required more capital, it would be difficult to find purchasers willing to pay the par value. In order to make the shares attractive, the corporation would have to reduce its par value to a more realistic figure. The concept of par value, although still relevant in some jurisdictions, is mainly of historical interest in federal and Ontario corporations.

SEPARATE PERSONALITY

Despite the concept of "separate personality" for corporations, the law does not allow abuse of the limited liability concept. For example, in cases of fraud, the law may ignore the separate corporate existence and "pierce the corporate veil" to hold the individuals controlling the corporation responsible for their acts. The courts,

GRAPH 5.1   OWNERSHIP OF A CORPORATION

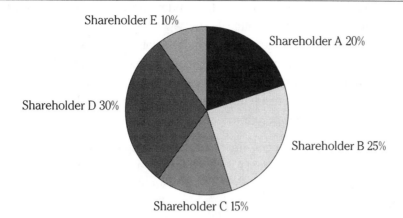

however, are cautious to preserve the principle of separate legal existence and tend to treat each case on its own merits.

One of the leading cases on the principle of the separate legal existence of corporations came before the British House of Lords in 1897 in *Salomon v. Salomon & Co. Ltd.* The circumstances of this case are represented in the following excerpt from the decision of the House of Lords:

> Salomon had carried on the successful business of shoe manufacturer for many years. In 1892 he formed a corporation in which he held almost all the shares (the few remaining shares being held by members of his family) and sold his business to the corporation. As part of the purchase price he took back bonds as a secured creditor of the corporation. Unfortunately a series of strikes in the shoe industry eventually drove the corporation into insolvency, and a trustee was appointed to wind it up. Salomon tried to enforce his rights as a secured creditor, but was resisted by the trustee for the general creditors. The trustee claimed that the corporation was merely a sham for Salomon, that he was the true owner of the business and the true debtor — as such, he should not be permitted to act as a creditor and take priority over his own creditors but should surrender the bonds to them and pay off all debts owned by the corporation. The lower courts supported the trustee's position, but the House of Lords decided in favour of Salomon. The Lords said that either the corporation was a true legal entity or it was not. Since there was neither fraud nor any intention to deceive, since all transactions had been fully disclosed to all parties and the statutory regulations complied with, the corporation was duly created and had validly granted the bonds to Salomon. Accordingly he ranked as a secured creditor of the corporation.

The separate personality of corporations may be ignored under certain circumstances including the following:

1. *Taxation.* In order to prevent tax evasion, the corporate veil may be ignored, for example, in a sale of assets between a controlling shareholder and a corporation or between two related corporations.

2. *Residence.* It may be important to decide where a corporation resides in determining which statutes apply to it. Residency may vary according to the

test imposed by the relevant statute and, accordingly, a corporation may be considered to reside in one jurisdiction under one statute and in another jurisdiction under another statute.

The place of residence is important for taxation matters. For example, a non-resident corporation pays tax on income earned within the jurisdiction, whereas a resident corporation pays tax on all of its income.

In some cases, the residency of the controlling shareholders determines the residency of the corporation.

3. *Agency.* In certain instances, the courts have accepted the claim that a corporation acted as an agent for the shareholders, and therefore, the acts of the corporation should be attributed to the shareholders as its principals (for example, the *Salomon* case).

4. *Fraud.* Once the court believes that fraud exists, it will not allow the objection that a corporation as a separate entity rather than its shareholders has committed the fraud.

SHAREHOLDER RIGHTS

A fundamental principle of corporate law in the area of shareholder rights, is that the "majority rules." In other words, the holders of a majority of the voting shares, indirectly through the directors, govern the actions of the corporation. Although shareholders do not have direct managerial powers, they have the right to:

- elect directors to manage the affairs of the corporation;

- receive financial information at regular intervals; and

- review the performance of directors, including approval of bylaws and certain corporate acts requiring special resolutions.

Despite these powers, one of the problems of the corporate system is the inability of the shareholders to control an independent management.

The corporate statutes attempt to provide mechanisms for the protection of minority groups of shareholders. These mechanisms include cumulative voting and class elections. Both of these mechanisms were discussed in chapter 4. In addition, minority shareholders may use the oppression remedy, appraisal rights, and derivative actions as a means of protection.

Oppression remedy (CBCA s. 241; OBCA s. 248)

oppression remedy
a shareholder remedy where a complainant may apply to the court for an order to rectify the matters complained of; the complainant must satisfy the court that the specified concerns are oppressive or unfairly prejudicial to, or that they unfairly disregard the interests of, a security holder, creditor, director, or officer of the corporation

A complainant who is a shareholder, director, or officer of the corporation or any of its affiliates, the Director appointed under the CBCA, in the case of a federally incorporated company, or, in the case of an offering corporation, the relevant securities commission, may apply to the court for an order — an **oppression remedy** — to rectify the matters complained of. The complainant must satisfy the court that the specified concerns are oppressive or unfairly prejudicial to, or that they unfairly disregard the interests of, a security holder, creditor, director, or officer of the corporation.

Appraisal rights of dissenting shareholders (CBCA s. 190; OBCA s. 185)

A shareholder who has voted against certain resolutions may exercise its **appraisal rights** and require a corporation to purchase its shares upon the shareholder's complying with the requirements set out in the statutes.

Derivative actions (CBCA s. 239; OBCA s. 246)

A complainant may apply to the court for permission to bring an action on behalf of the corporation or to intervene in an action to which the corporation is a party — **derivative actions** — for the purpose of prosecuting, defending, or discontinuing the action on behalf of the corporation.

appraisal rights
a shareholder remedy where a dissenting shareholder may require a corporation to purchase its shares upon the shareholder's complying with the requirements set out in the statutes

derivative action
a shareholder remedy where a complainant may apply to the court for permission to bring an action on behalf of the corporation or to intervene in an action to which the corporation is a party, for the purpose of prosecuting, defending, or discontinuing the action on behalf of the corporation

AUTHORIZED CAPITAL

When a corporation is formed, the articles of incorporation will set out the number and class of shares that the corporation is authorized to issue. There can be a fixed number or an unlimited number of shares authorized. The number of shares is fixed when it is important to control the number of shares of the class to be issued (for example, when shares of one class are issued in exchange for property on an estate freeze) or if there are concerns about dilution of the value of the shares. If there is a fixed number, the corporation cannot issue more than that number. If the corporation does issue more, the number of shares in excess of the authorized number will not be considered to be validly issued shares. However, both the CBCA and the OBCA provide a remedy for this. When a corporation realizes there has been an "overissue" of shares, it can amend its articles to increase the authorized number, and when the articles of amendment become effective, the over-issued shares become validly issued as of the original date of their issue. Alternatively, if there is another share available that is similar in all respects to the class of shares that has been overissued, the shareholder may "compel" the corporation to issue that class of share in surrender of the overissued class (CBCA s. 52; OBCA s. 58).

CLASSES OF SHARES

A corporation may have one or more classes of shares.

The CBCA (s. 24(3)) provides that where a corporation has only one class of shares, the rights of the holders are equal and include the rights to:

- vote at any meeting of shareholders of the corporation;

- receive any dividend declared by the corporation; and

- receive the remaining property of the corporation on dissolution.

The OBCA (s. 22(3)) has a similar provision, but it does not include the right to receive dividends.

If there is more than one class of shares, the rights attaching to each class must be set out in the articles and the rights mentioned above must attach to at least one of the classes but not necessarily to the same class (CBCA ss. 24(3) and (4); OBCA ss. 22(3) and (4)).

Although the CBCA and the OBCA do not define the classes of shares that a corporation may issue, there are usually three main types of shares for non-offering corporations: common shares, special shares, and preferred shares.

With respect to offering corporations, a policy under the *Securities Act* (Ontario) provides for the designation and description of publicly traded shares.

Common shares

common shares
shares that entitle their owners to participate fully in the corporation and to receive dividends and any remaining property of the corporation available for distribution on its dissolution or windup

Common shares (sometimes called "participating shares") typically entitle their owners to participate fully in the corporation and to receive dividends and any remaining property of the corporation available for distribution on its dissolution or windup. Thus, the common shares are generally thought of as being the "equity" shares because the capital value of the corporation accrues to these shares and they receive everything that is left for distribution to shareholders after payment to the holders of classes with prior rights.

Special shares

special shares
shares that have rights, privileges, restrictions, and conditions that do not apply to common shares

Special shares are shares that are not common shares. They typically have specific rights, privileges, restrictions, and conditions — often based on tax considerations — that do not apply to common shares.

Preferred shares

preferred shares (or preference shares)
shares that have priority over other classes of shares

Preferred shares or **preference shares** are shares that have priority over other classes of shares in respect of the payment of dividends or the distribution of assets on windup or dissolution. For example, a preferred share may provide that its holder receive a dividend before any dividends are paid to holders of other classes. Preferred shares may be voting or non-voting, and may have rights of redemption and retraction (see below).

NAMING SHARE CLASSES

Neither the CBCA nor the OBCA restricts the naming of share classes. The name choice is, therefore, left to the incorporator. Generally, where there is only one class of shares, they will be called "common shares." Where there is more than one class, the name will often bear a resemblance to the characteristics of the shares. For example, shares that have preference or priority over the common shares will generally be called "preferred shares." Shares that are neither common shares nor preferred shares might be called "special shares."

Examples of how the capital clause in the articles might read are:

For one class of shares:

The corporation is authorized to issue an unlimited number of common shares.

For two classes of shares:

The corporation is authorized to issue:

- an unlimited number of preferred shares; and
- an unlimited number of common shares.

For three classes of shares:

The corporation is authorized to issue:

- an unlimited number of class A special shares;
- 200,000 class B special shares; and
- an unlimited number of common shares.

DECIDING ON THE NUMBER AND CLASSES OF SHARES

It is common for the articles of a corporation to authorize the issuance of more than one class of shares with different rights attaching to each class. Some reasons to have more than one class of shares are:

- to provide different conditions for different classes of investors;
- to provide different "paid-up capital" considerations under the *Income Tax Act* (Canada); and
- to provide a shareholder with a "freeze" on increasing equity while at the same time providing an opportunity for the shareholder to earn income from the corporation by way of dividends.

It may be important for tax reasons to ensure that each class is distinguished from each of the other classes. In *Champ v. The Queen*, the directors of a corporation decided to declare a dividend on one class of shares and not on the other. The Minister of National Revenue ruled that the dividend was declared on both classes because the articles did not distinguish between the classes and that the decision to have two classes was made to avoid the payment of tax.

In addition to the number of classes of shares, a corporation's articles will set out the number of shares authorized in each class. This can be an unlimited or a fixed number. Most often, the articles authorize an unlimited number of shares. However, a fixed number of shares might be authorized when a property is rolled over into the corporation and a fixed number of shares is issued in exchange for the property. No further shares of that class will be authorized.

The decision on what classes and numbers of shares to use is often made by the corporation's lawyer in conjunction with its accountant.

SHARES ISSUABLE IN SERIES

Another "type" of share is a "**series**" share. A "series" is a subdivision of shares within a class of shares; it is not a separate class of shares. The CBCA (s. 27(1)) provides that a corporation may authorize the issuance of any class of shares in series and may do either or both of the following: (1) authorize the directors to fix

series
a subdivision of shares within a class of shares

the number of shares in and the rights and conditions attaching to the series; or (2) fix the number of shares in and the rights and conditions attaching to the shares of each series.

The provisions in the OBCA (s. 25(1)) do not explicitly provide that a corporation may do either or both of the foregoing, but corporate law practitioners generally interpret the OBCA provisions as providing this. Directors may create a new series of shares by filing articles of amendment. The newly created shares may not be issued, however, until the certificate of amendment is issued.

Series shares are useful for offering corporations or corporations with a large number of potential investors. The creation of a new class of shares requires special resolution authorization of the shareholders; but the creation of an additional series of a class does not. This allows the directors flexibility to negotiate different conditions attaching to the shares of a new series — for example, different dividend rates to reflect the market conditions at the time the shares are issued. Series shares of the same class cannot provide for priority with respect to the payment of dividends or the return of capital on dissolution with respect to other shares in the same series because all shares in a series are equal.

COMMON RIGHTS, PRIVILEGES, RESTRICTIONS, AND CONDITIONS ATTACHING TO SHARES

The conditions attaching to shares can be as complex as the specific situation demands, but there are certain standard share provisions, discussed below. See the sample share conditions in figure 5.1 at the end of this chapter, as well as the share conditions in Schedule A of figure 7.1.

The right to receive dividends and take in specie

Dividends are distributions to shareholders made out of the profits, or retained earnings, of a corporation. They can be paid in cash or in property, shares (stock), or *in specie* (for example, the shares of another corporation). Unless restricted by a unanimous shareholder agreement (USA), the bylaws, or the articles, the power to declare dividends is given to the directors. Dividends are not paid until they are declared and they do not become a debt of a corporation until they are declared. Directors may not delegate their authority to declare dividends. Directors cannot declare or cause the corporation to pay dividends without meeting the financial solvency tests set out in the corporate statutes (CBCA s. 42; OBCA s. 38(3)). This means that directors may not declare and cause the corporation to pay dividends if, after the payment of the dividend, there are reasonable grounds to believe that the corporation cannot pay its liabilities as they become due, or the realizable value of its assets is less than all of its liabilities and stated capital of all classes. If they authorize and the corporation pays a dividend contrary to the solvency provisions (CBCA s. 118(2)(c); OBCA s. 130(2)(d)), directors are jointly and severally liable for any amounts not recovered.

The amount of the dividend is determined as follows:

- The dividend amount may be a fixed rate or amount such as a dollar value, a percentage of paid-up capital, or the redemption amount.

- The dividend amount may be a variable rate that is tied to the prime lending rate or to some formula based on profits.

- Directors may be given the discretion to set the rate at the time of issue, and the dividend rate is said to be discretionary.

The payment of dividends can be

- *Cumulative* — Regardless of whether or not the directors "declare" the dividends, the shareholders' right to receive the dividend remains, although the right to sue for unpaid dividends does not arise until the directors "declare" the dividends. Cumulative dividends "accumulate" every year at a specified rate and must be fully paid before any dividends are paid on other classes of shares. Cumulative dividends are often used in cases where a shareholder considers the investment to be a "loan" to the corporation; the cumulative dividends ensure an annual income on the investment.

- *Non-cumulative* — The right to receive a non-cumulative dividend expires at the end of each financial year of the corporation unless it is declared. If declared, the dividend must be paid to the shareholders; if it is not paid, it becomes a debt of the corporation to the shareholders.

- *Partially cumulative* — When a share contains a right to cumulative dividends and then to a further share in the profits of the corporation through non-cumulative dividends, it is said to be "partially cumulative."

- *Discretionary* — When corporate directors have the ability to make the decision about when dividends are to be paid, the dividends are said to be "discretionary." This discretion can be a useful tax-planning vehicle.

Other considerations when drafting dividend provisions are:

- In what priority do the different share classes receive dividends?

- Once a fixed dividend is paid, do the shareholders have any right to participate further in dividends?

- How often will dividends be paid — for example, monthly, quarterly, or annually?

Return of capital on windup

The priority in which shareholders will share in a return of capital of the corporation on its dissolution, liquidation, or windup should also be set out in the conditions attaching to each share class. The amount that the shareholders of the class will receive should also be considered. Once again, this amount may be a fixed amount — for example, $10 — or the initial issue price of the share, the redemption price, or an amount based on some formula. A corporation will also have to pay any dividends declared and not paid.

Participating or non-participating shares

Participating shares entitle shareholders to share fully in the rights to receive dividends and the return of capital on windup. Shares are non-participating if they entitle shareholders to receive a fixed dividend or a fixed amount on windup and no more.

Redemption by the corporation

Subject to the solvency restrictions imposed in the corporate statutes (discussed later in this chapter), a corporation may redeem any redeemable shares issued by it at prices not exceeding the redemption price stated in the articles or calculated according to a formula stated in the articles. The timing of the redemption must also be stated in the articles (CBCA s. 36.1; OBCA s. 32(1)). Shares cannot be redeemed unless the right to redeem is set out in the share conditions.

The right to redeem may be useful in cases where the corporation wishes to rid itself of an investor so as to eliminate the need to pay dividends or otherwise restructure its capital.

Redemption by the shareholder (retraction)

Another common share condition is the shareholders' retraction privilege. That privilege enables a shareholder to demand that a corporation buy back its shares based on the conditions set out in the articles. Care should be taken when including this provision in articles because it may not always be in the best interests of a corporation to have a shareholder make such a demand. Upon receiving a notice of retraction from a shareholder, a corporation has limited time in which to come up with the funds to pay out the shareholder. Once again, a corporation is able to redeem the shares subject to meeting the financial solvency tests that are set out in the corporate statutes.

Purchase

Both the CBCA and the OBCA provide that, subject to its articles, a corporation may purchase any of its issued shares provided that the financial solvency tests set out in the statutes are met. Although this right to purchase is given by the corporate statute, it is often in the best interests of the corporation to provide a method for such purchase in the share conditions.

Priority of classes

The share conditions attaching to each class of shares should clearly set out the priority of the classes with respect to the payment of dividends and return of capital on windup, dissolution, etc.

Conversion

Shares may be converted into other classes of shares in accordance with the provisions set out in the articles. These provisions should include the timing of the conversion, the number of shares of the other class that the shareholder will receive, the method for initiating the conversion, and when the conversion is deemed to have taken place.

Pre-emptive rights

pre-emptive rights
any further issue of shares must first be offered to the existing shareholders of the same or another class or series of shares on such terms as are provided in the articles or USA before being offered to others

The articles and, in the case of an OBCA corporation, a USA may provide for **pre-emptive rights**. This means that any further issue of shares must first be offered to the existing shareholders of the same or another class or series of shares on such terms as are provided in the articles or USA before being offered to others (CBCA s. 28(1); OBCA s. 26).

Under the CBCA (s. 28(2)), the pre-emptive right does not apply where shares are issued

- for consideration other than money;

- as a stock dividend; or

- pursuant to the exercise of conversion privileges, options, or rights previously granted by the corporation.

This right protects the existing shareholders' proportionate holdings by offering to existing shareholders the opportunity to purchase new shares in proportion to their existing holdings before new shares are offered to new shareholders. This can prevent dilution of a shareholder's ownership. A pre-emptive right would therefore be more advantageous to a small or medium-sized corporation than to a large corporation. Large corporations do, however, sometimes offer existing shareholders the right to purchase one new share at a fixed price for a specified number of shares already held. For example, a corporation may offer existing shareholders the right to purchase 1 new share for every 10 shares currently held, on payment of a set price.

Voting rights and restrictions

Both the CBCA (s. 140(1)) and the OBCA (s. 102(1)) provide that unless the articles state otherwise, each share of a corporation entitles the holder to one vote at a meeting of shareholders. If the corporation does not wish a class of shares to have voting rights, a restriction on voting must be included in the articles. Alternatively, in order to provide more control, it is sometimes desirable to give a class more than one vote per share. This, too, must be set out in the share conditions.

A share may therefore be voting or non-voting, have limited voting rights, or be given voting rights when dividends are in arrears for a specified period of time, or in the event of a takeover by a majority of the voting shareholders.

When drafting the voting rights to be set out in the articles, remember that the CBCA and the OBCA provide that shares that are otherwise non-voting are voting shares under certain circumstances. The following are some of the circumstances set out in the statutes:

1. On certain amendments to the articles (CBCA s. 176; OBCA s. 170).

2. On amalgamation (CBCA s. 183(3)). Note the difference in s. 176(3) in the OBCA, which provides that the holders of a class or series of shares are entitled to vote separately as a class or series on the amalgamation if the amalgamation agreement contains a provision that, if contained in a proposed amendment to the articles, would entitle such holders to vote separately as a class or series under s. 170.

3. On continuance (CBCA s. 188(4)).

4. On a sale, lease, or exchange of all or substantially all of the property of a corporation other than in the ordinary course of business of the corporation

(CBCA s. 189(6)). Under the OBCA (s. 184(6)), shareholders holding non-voting shares are entitled to vote only if the sale would affect the rights of the holders differently from the holders of shares of a voting class.

5. On voluntary liquidation (CBCA s. 211(3)).

6. On voluntary dissolution (CBCA s. 210(2)).

7. On consent in writing by shareholders of a non-offering corporation if an auditor is not appointed (CBCA s. 163(3); OBCA s. 148).

8. On arrangement (OBCA s. 182(4)).

Exclusion of right to separate vote

Under certain circumstances, shareholders that are entitled to vote may be entitled to vote separately as a class. For example, all the shareholders entitled to vote on a resolution vote together in the meeting, and the shareholders whose shares are entitled to a separate vote vote a second time with all of the other shareholders of that class. They may be asked to vote in a separate room, without the shareholders of any other class being present, or they may simply vote as a class in the same room. The separate vote concept allows shareholders of one class to vote without being influenced or harassed by the vote of the shareholders of another class who may be differently affected. To be considered "passed," the resolution must be passed by the votes of each class, voting separately, and all the shareholders voting together.

The CBCA (s. 176) and OBCA (s. 170) provide that, unless the articles state otherwise, shareholders of each class are entitled to vote separately as a class on the following matters:

- increasing or decreasing the maximum number of shares authorized of such class or increasing the maximum number of shares authorized of a class having equal or superior rights;

- effecting an exchange, reclassification, or cancellation of the shares of such class or series; and

- creating a new class or series of shares equal or superior to the shares of such class.

Sometimes, a corporation will wish to restrict the right to a separate vote (CBCA s. 176(1); OBCA s. 170(1)). If this is the case, the restriction must be included in the articles.

ISSUANCE OF SHARES

Shareholders can receive shares in a number of different ways including:

- issuance from the treasury,

- transfer from another shareholder,

- transmission upon the death of a shareholder,

- gift,

- stock dividend,

- share split,

- rollover, and

- amalgamation.

Issuance from the treasury

Subject to provisions to the contrary in the articles, bylaws, or a USA, shares may be issued at the discretion of the directors. The principles of contract law govern the issuance and there will be:

- an offer — the share subscription,

- an acceptance — the directors issue the shares,

- a communication of the acceptance — the delivery of the share certificate, and

- consideration paid — the purchase price.

Upon issuing shares, you must also carefully consider the provisions of the relevant securities legislation.

The number of shares issued and outstanding in the capital of the corporation is said to be the "**issued capital**" of the corporation.

issued capital
number of shares issued and outstanding in the capital of the corporation

THE SHARE SUBSCRIPTION

The share subscription indicates the shareholder's commitment to purchase shares of the corporation. In most circumstances, a short subscription will be prepared containing the number and class of shares to be purchased, the price per share, and the name in which the shares are to be issued. Very often, the purchase price will be tendered with the subscription. In other circumstances, a longer form of subscription agreement will be required.

DIRECTORS' RESOLUTION ISSUING SHARES

Once a subscription is received or a potential investor otherwise indicates a desire to purchase the shares, the directors (subject to any provisions in a USA or the by-laws restricting the powers of the directors) pass a resolution acknowledging acceptance of the subscription, fixing the consideration for the shares, and issuing the shares as fully paid and non-assessable upon receipt of payment.

PAYMENT FOR SHARES

A shareholder can submit payment for shares by cash or cheque (when the amount is large, it is not uncommon to ask for a certified cheque).

Shares can also be paid for in property or past service that is no less in value than the fair equivalent of the money that the corporation would have received if the shares had been issued for money (CBCA s. 25(3); OBCA s. 23(3)).

Where shares of an OBCA corporation are issued for non-cash consideration, the directors must specifically determine in the resolution issuing the shares

1. the amount of money the corporation would have received if the shares had been issued for money, and either

2. the fair value of the property or past service in consideration of which the share is issued, or

3. that such property or past service has a fair value that is not less than the amount of money that would have been received if the shares were issued for money (OBCA s. 23(4)).

Shares are not considered "issued" until they have been fully paid for in money, property, or past service. A promissory note is not considered property.

STATED CAPITAL

Both the CBCA (s. 26(1)) and the OBCA (s. 24(1)) require a corporation to maintain a "stated capital account" for each class of shares. This is a notional account, which does not show up on the financial statements. When shares are issued, the full amount of the consideration received is added to the stated capital for that class, subject to an exemption for non-arm's-length transactions. Where shares are issued for property or past service, the amount added to the stated capital account is the amount of consideration that would have been received if the shares had been issued for money (that is, the amount determined by the directors, as discussed above). When shares of a corporation are issued in payment of a dividend, the amount to be added to the stated capital account is the declared amount of the dividend stated as an amount of money (CBCA 43(2); OBCA s. 38(2)).

Because additions and reductions can be made to stated capital, the corporate "stated capital" is not always the same as the "paid-up capital."

In summary, stated capital can be altered by

- an issuance of shares for cash,

- an issuance of shares as consideration for the purchase of property,

- an issuance of shares on a stock dividend,

- a redemption and repurchase of shares,

- an addition to stated capital by special resolution of the shareholders,

- a reduction of stated capital by special resolution of the shareholders, and

- a conversion of shares into another class.

ISSUANCE OF SHARE CERTIFICATE

When the above steps are complete and the shares have been fully paid for, a corporation will generally issue a share certificate to evidence the title of the shareholders to their shares. Every shareholder is entitled to receive a share certificate at no cost. If shares are held jointly, only one certificate need be issued. Shares of a corporation are deemed to be personal property.

There is no set "format" for a share certificate but it must contain the information set out in CBCA (ss. 49(7), (8), and (13)) and OBCA (ss. 56(1), (2), and (3)) as follows:

- the name of the corporation;

- the words "incorporated under the *Canada Business Corporations Act*" or "subject to the *Canada Business Corporations Act*" or "incorporated under the law of the Province of Ontario" or words to that effect;

- the name of the person to whom the certificate is issued;

- the number, class, and series (if any) that the certificate represents;

- if the corporation has more than one class of shares, the rights and conditions attaching to each class (althernatively, reference may be made that a copy can be obtained from the corporation); and

- the authority of the directors to fix the rights, privileges, restrictions, and conditions of subsequent series, if applicable.

There are certain circumstances where notice must be given "conspicuously" on a share certificate in order to make the circumstances binding on a transferee of the shares. This is often referred to as a **legend**. Conspicuous notice must be given when there is:

- a restriction on the issue or transfer;

- a lien in favour of the corporation;

- a unanimous shareholder agreement in existence; and

- the transferor shareholder is a dissenting shareholder.

The Ontario *Securities Act* multilateral instrument no. 45-502 also places a requirement on closely held corporations that trade securities in Ontario to place an inscription (a legend), which gives notice of the holdback provisions, on certificates issued to accredited investors.

Share certificates must be signed by at least one director or officer of a corporation. The CBCA allows this signature to be printed or otherwise mechanically reproduced on the certificate, but the OBCA requires at least one manual signature. Any other signature required on a security certificate may be printed or otherwise mechanically reproduced. Bylaws or administrative resolutions are often drafted to require two signatures.

A share certificate can be issued in "registered" or in "bearer" form. "Registered" form means that the certificate specifies the name of the person who is entitled to the rights it evidences and that its transfer can be recorded in a securities register. "Bearer" form means that it is payable to the bearer according to its terms and not by reason of any endorsement.

TABLE 5.1   CHECKLIST OF POINTS TO CONSIDER WHEN ISSUING SHARES

1. Are there enough unissued shares remaining in the corporation's unissued capital to allow for the issuance?

2. Are all (a) redemptions of shares, (b) purchases for cancellation of shares, and (c) previously allotted but unissued shares (for example, shares set aside for stock options) taken into account for computing the available number of shares?

3. Is there a limit on the aggregate consideration for which shares may be issued in the articles, and will the aggregate consideration be below this limit after the issuance?

4. Are there pre-emptive rights contained in the articles of the corporation or in a unanimous shareholder agreement? Are they being complied with?

5. Are there any restrictions or preconditions in the articles or bylaws as to issuance of shares? Have they been complied with?

6. Are the conditions of a shareholder agreement being complied with?

7. Is this a "trade" of securities under the *Securities Act*?

8. Is the corporation a closely held issuer as defined under the *Securities Act*?

9. What is the residency of the shareholder?

10. Which of the following exemptions under the *Securities Act* is being relied on for the issuance of shares?

    a. closely held issuer?

    b. accredited investor?

    c. incorporator?

    d. other exemptions under rule 45-501 made under the *Securities Act*?

    e. other exemptions under rule 45-503 made under the *Securities Act*?

11. Are there any forms to file or fees to pay under section 7 of rule 45-501 under the *Securities Act*?

12. Have the directors fixed the consideration for the issuance of the shares and, subject to any unanimous shareholder agreement, passed the appropriate resolution issuing the shares?

13. Have the directors of the corporation received a subscription for the shares?

14. Has payment been made for the shares?

15. Has the shareholders' register and ledger been updated?

16. Has a share certificate been issued? If so, does it contain the appropriate share legends?

TABLE 5.2 CHECKLIST OF POINTS TO CONSIDER WHEN TRANSFERRING SHARES

1. Is the transfer a "trade" of securities?

2. Is the corporation a closely held issuer under the *Securities Act*?

3. Which exemption under the *Securities Act* is being relied on for transfer? Has the appropriate document been prepared?

4. Have the appropriate forms been filed and fees paid under the *Securities Act*?

5. Have the transfer restrictions set out in the articles, bylaws, or shareholder agreement been complied with?

6. Has the appropriate resolution authorizing the transfer been prepared?

7. Was an old certificate endorsed by the shareholder for transfer, or was a share transfer form obtained separately? If share certificates are lost, has a certificate of loss been prepared?

8. Were new share certificates issued with their appropriate legends?

9. Were the shareholders' register, the share transfer register, and the shareholders' ledgers updated?

OWNERSHIP OF SHARES

Shares may be owned or registered

- individually;
- jointly, with right of survivorship;
- jointly, as tenants in common; or
- in trust for another person.

If shares are held in trust, such as for a minor or on behalf of a person who wishes to remain anonymous, it is customary to have a trust declaration prepared that will set out the rights of the trust relationship and provide that all dividends paid on the shares held in trust are the property of the "beneficial" owner of the shares and not the "registered" owner.

Transfer of shares (CBCA ss. 76 to 81; OBCA ss. 86 to 91)

Another way to become a shareholder is by receiving shares upon a transfer from an existing shareholder. The corporation is not a party to this transaction, but in a closely held corporation, the articles, bylaws, or a shareholder agreement will contain restrictions on the transfer of shares. In addition, a shareholder agreement will probably provide certain conditions to be met before a shareholder can go ahead and freely transfer the shares. The terms, including the price, are arrived at independently of the corporation, by the shareholder (transferor) and the purchaser (transferee) of the shares. The corporation is obliged to register the transfer if the requirements of the statutes are met.

The certificate should be endorsed on its back, delivered to the transferee, and presented to the corporation for transfer. Alternatively, a form of share transfer may be signed by the holder and delivered to the transferee, who should present the transfer document to the corporation for recording in its share records.

The transferee is entitled to receive a new certificate for the shares. The corporation is also entitled to charge a small fee for preparing and issuing the certificate.

Gifting shares

Another method of conveying shares from the shareholder to another person is by way of "gift." To accomplish this, all the conditions for transferring the shares must be met, but generally there will also be a "deed of gift" entered into between the transferor and transferee that confirms the terms of the gift. When shares are gifted, there is a restriction under the *Income Tax Act* that the shares cannot be disposed of within 10 years; otherwise, the transferee is subject to any taxes payable at the time of transfer.

Transmission of shares (CBCA s. 51; OBCA s. 67)

If a shareholder dies, becomes incompetent, or goes bankrupt and there are transfer restrictions on the right to transfer shares, the corporation may treat the heir of the deceased, executor, administrator, trustee in bankruptcy, etc. as a registered shareholder. However, the person so treated must deposit with the issuer

1. the original grant of probate, letters of administration, or a court-certified copy or a notarized copy of such documents;

2. an affidavit or declaration of transmission; and

3. the security certificate.

The transfer of the shares from the trustee or executor to the beneficiary must then be approved in accordance with the transfer restrictions in the articles, bylaws or a USA.

Redemption, cancellation, and purchase of shares (CBCA ss. 34, 35, and 36; OBCA ss. 30, 31, and 32)

Subject to the CBCA and OBCA and the articles of a corporation, a corporation may purchase any of its issued shares provided that it is not insolvent — that is, if there are no reasonable grounds for believing that

1. the corporation is or will be unable, after payment, to pay its liabilities as they become due; or

2. the realizable value of the corporation's assets will be, after payment, less than the aggregate of

a. its liabilities, and

b. its stated capital of all classes.

A less onerous solvency test applies if the corporation purchases or redeems its shares:

1. to settle or compromise a debt or claim asserted by or against the corporation;

2. to eliminate fractional shares; or

3. to fulfill the terms of a non-assignable agreement under which the corporation has an option or is obliged to purchase shares owned by a current or former director, officer, or employee of the corporation.

In this case, the test substitutes for the stated capital of all classes the amount required to pay the holders of shares who have a right to be paid, on a redemption or a liquidation, before the holders of the shares to be purchased or acquired (CBCA s. 35(3); OBCA s. 31(3)).

A corporation may purchase or redeem its redeemable shares at prices not exceeding the price in the articles if it meets another form of solvency test. This test substitutes for its stated capital of all classes of shares the amount that would be required to pay the holders of shares who have a right to be paid, on a redemption or in a liquidation, rateably with or prior to the holders of the shares to be purchased or redeemed (in other words, equal or senior to the shares being purchased or redeemed) (CBCA s. 36(1); OBCA 32(1)).

If the purchase is to comply with a court order to purchase securities of a shareholder under CBCA s. 241 and OBCA s. 248, the corporation must meet the solvency test set out in CBCA s. 241(6) and OBCA s. 248(6).

Similarly, with respect to satisfying the claim of a dissenting shareholder, the corporation must meet the solvency test set out in CBCA s. 190(26) and OBCA s. 185(30).

Subject to a USA that restricts the powers of the directors, it is common for the directors to pass a resolution authorizing the purchase or redemption of shares.

Conversion

Shares issued by a corporation, subject to the articles, may be converted into shares of another class. Most often, the share provisions in the articles will provide that a notice of conversion be delivered by the shareholder to the corporation together with the share certificate(s), showing the shares to be converted. The directors will then pass a resolution approving the conversion, and a certificate representing the new class of shares issued will be prepared and delivered to the shareholder.

Options and warrants (CBCA s. 29; OBCA s. 27)

A corporation may issue certificates, warrants, or options or rights to acquire securities of the corporation.

A "**warrant**" is a certificate or other document issued by a corporation as evidence of conversion privileges or options or rights to acquire securities of the corporation.

warrant
a certificate or other document issued by a corporation as evidence of conversion privileges or options or rights to acquire securities of the corporation

option
a right to acquire securities of a corporation on specified conditions and prices at specified times

An "**option**" is a right to acquire securities of a corporation on specified conditions and prices at specified times.

If the articles limit the number of authorized shares, where a corporation has

1. granted privileges to convert any warrants or options issued by the corporation into shares, or into shares of another class or series, or

2. has issued or granted options or rights to acquire shares,

the corporation must "reserve" and continue to reserve sufficient authorized shares to meet the exercise of such conversion privileges, options, and rights.

Corporation holding its own shares (CBCA s. 30(1); OBCA s. 28(1)) and subsidiary acquiring shares of parent (CBCA s. 30(2); OBCA s. 29(8))

Generally, a corporation cannot hold shares in itself or in its parent company except as trustee, or as security for a transaction entered into by it in the ordinary course of a business that includes the lending of money.

The CBCA (ss. 31(4) to (6)) allows a subsidiary to acquire shares of the parent corporation in certain circumstances. This may be necessary for tax reasons where a Canadian corporation holds foreign subsidiaries that want to merge with or take over foreign companies, in order to provide the appropriate tax advantages to shareholders of the target corporation. The regulations of the CBCA set out the conditions that must exist before and after the acquisition.[2] These conditions include the following:

1. the subsidiary must not be resident in Canada;

2. the value paid for the shares must be equal to their fair market value;

3. the shares must be widely held and actively traded on a Canadian stock exchange; and

4. the acquisition must be for the sole purpose of transferring the shares to shareholders of a non-Canadian corporation that deals at arm's length, as determined by the *Income Tax Act*, with the corporation and its subsidiary.

After the acquisition, the subsidiary must immediately transfer the shares to the shareholders of the non-Canadian corporation and cannot retain a beneficial interest in the shares. After the transfer, the non-Canadian corporation must become a subsidiary of the parent but cannot become a resident in Canada. The subsidiary transferring the shares cannot become a Canadian corporation.

If the conditions after the acquisition are not met within 30 days, the parent corporation must cancel the shares, return the amount paid for the shares, and deduct that amount from the corporation's stated capital account.[3]

There is another situation in which a corporation is allowed to hold shares in itself. A corporation may hold shares in itself for the purpose of assisting the corporation or any of its affiliates or associates to qualify under any prescribed law of Canada or a province to receive licences, permits, grants, payments, or other benefits by reason of attaining or maintaining a specified level of Canadian ownership or control.

Replacing a lost certificate (CBCA s. 80(2); OBCA s. 90(2))

If a share certificate is lost, the corporation may issue a replacement certificate if the owner

1. requests a replacement certificate before the issuer has notice that a purchaser has acquired the security;

2. files an indemnity bond to protect the issuer from any loss that it may suffer by issuing a new certificate; and

3. satisfies any other reasonable requirements imposed by the issuer.

In closely held corporations, these requirements are usually satisfied by obtaining a Certificate of Loss and Indemnity from the shareholder and having the board pass a resolution to authorize the issue of a replacement share certificate.

KEY TERMS

appraisal rights	par value
common shares	pre-emptive rights
derivative action	preferred shares (or preference shares)
issued capital	series
legend	shares
oppression remedy	special shares
option	warrant

REFERENCES

Business Corporations Act (Ontario) (OBCA), RSO 1990, c. B.16, as amended, parts III, VI, and XIV.

Canada Business Corporations Act (CBCA), RSC 1985, c. C-44, as amended, parts V, VII, and XV.

Champ v. The Queen, [1983] CTC 1 (FCTD).

Chapin, Beverly C., *Share Provisions: Clauses with Clout: Advanced Corporate and Basic Securities Law for Law Clerks* (Toronto: Law Society of Upper Canada, Department of Continuing Legal Education, 1994).

Day, Midge, *Ontario Corporate Procedures*, 3d ed. (Toronto: Thomson Professional Publishing, 1995).

Income Tax Act, RSC 1985, c. 1 (5th Supp.), as amended.

Law Society of Upper Canada, *Business Law*, Bar Admission Course Materials (Toronto: LSUC, 2003).

Levitt, Brian M., "An Overview in the Context of Its Predecessor Statute and the Canada Business Corporations Act," in Canadian Bar Association, Seminar Material, *The New Ontario Business Corporations Act* (Toronto: CBA, June 7, 1982).

Salomon v. Salomon & Co. Ltd., [1897] AC 22 (HL).

Securities Act, RSO 1990, c. S.5, as amended.

Smyth, J.E., D.A. Soberman, and A.J. Easson, *The Law and Business Administration in Canada*, 9th ed. (Toronto: Prentice-Hall, 2001).

Van Duzer, J. Anthony, *The Law of Partnerships and Corporations* (Toronto: Irwin Law, 1997).

Welling, Bruce L., *Corporate Law in Canada: The Governing Principles*, 2d ed. (Markham, ON: Butterworths, 1991).

Westlake, Brian C., "Share Capital and Related Matters," in Law Society of Upper Canada, Seminar Material, *Working with the Ontario Business Corporations Act* (Toronto: LSUC, April 8, 1992).

FORMS AND PRECEDENTS

Figure 5.1: CBCA sample share conditions for two classes of shares (common and non-cumulative preferred)

NOTES

1 Kevin P. McGuiness, *The Law and Practice of Canadian Business Corporations* (Markham, ON: Butterworths, 1999), at 285.

2 *Canada Business Corporations Regulations, 2001*, SOR/2001-512, s. 36.

3 Industry Canada, Regulatory Impact Analysis Statement (for changes to the *Canada Business Corporations Act* and Regulations, effective November 24, 2001).

REVIEW QUESTIONS

1. What features distinguish a "non-offering" corporation from an "offering" corporation?

2. Define the following:

   a. par value

   b. share

   c. shareholder

d. oppression remedy

e. appraisal rights

f. derivative action

g. authorized capital

h. common share

i. special share

j. preferred share

k. series

l. pre-emptive rights

m. warrant

n. option

3. Outline three possible rights a shareholder may have if a corporation has only one class of shares.

4. Explain what is meant by "piercing the corporate veil."

5. If a corporation had two classes of shares, discuss how you would name the shares.

6. List and explain four standard share conditions you may wish to attach to a class of preferred shares.

7. How is a series share created?

8. Can a shareholder pay for shares with property or past services? Discuss.

9. What is stated capital? How can it be altered?

10. What advice would you give a shareholder that is dissatisfied with a transaction?

11. Discuss the procedure for the following:

a. issuance of shares

b. transfer of shares

c. transmission of shares

d. redemption of shares

12. If a shareholder loses a share certificate, what steps would a closely held corporation take?

13. Are the following statements true or false?

a. Officers elect directors to manage the affairs of the corporation.

b. Cumulative voting is always included in articles.

c. The statutes set out the number and class of shares that a corporation must issue.

d. Common shareholders always have the right to vote.

e. Preferred shares have a preference over other classes.

f. Series shares can be created by the directors.

g. Dividends can be paid by the issuance of shares in the corporation.

h. The redemption right need not be set out in the share conditions.

i. The bylaws can restrict the directors' right to issue shares.

j. If cumulative dividends are not declared and not paid, the shareholders lose the right to receive them.

k. Non-voting shares become voting in certain circumstances.

l. Shares can be paid for in property.

m. Share certificates must be signed by the president and secretary.

FIGURE 5.1 CBCA SAMPLE SHARE CONDITIONS

CBCA
TWO CLASSES:
COMMON AND NON-CUMULATIVE PREFERRED

AUTHORIZED CAPITAL

The Corporation is authorized to issue:

(a) an unlimited number of preferred shares (herein referred to as the "Preferred Shares"); and

(b) an unlimited number of common shares (herein referred to as the "Common Shares").

SHARE PROVISIONS

The rights, privileges, restrictions and conditions attaching to the Preferred Shares and the Common Shares (herein collectively referred to as the "Share Provisions") are as follows:

I INTERPRETATION

1. **Definitions.** Where used in these Share Provisions, the following capitalized words and phrases shall, unless there is something in the context otherwise inconsistent therewith, have the following meanings, respectively:

(a) **"Act"** means the Canada Business Corporations Act, R.S.C. 1985, c. C-44, as now enacted or as the same may from time to time be amended, re-enacted or replaced (and, in the case of such amendment, re-enactment or replacement, any references herein shall be read as referring to such amended, re-enacted or replaced provisions);

(b) **"Business Day"** means a day other than a Saturday, Sunday or any other day treated as a holiday in the municipality in Canada in which the Corporation's registered office is then situated;

(c) **"Close of Business"** means 5:00 o'clock in the afternoon on a Business Day;

(d) **"Common Shareholder"** means a person recorded in the securities register of the Corporation for the Common Shares as being the registered holder of one or more Common Shares;

(e) **"Directors"** or **"Board of Directors"** means the board of directors of the Corporation;

(f) **"Dividend Payment Date"** means the date upon which any fixed preferential non-cumulative cash dividends become due and payable in accordance with any resolution of the Board of Directors declaring such dividend;

FIGURE 5.1 CONTINUED

(g) **"Liquidation Distribution"** means a distribution of assets of the Corporation among its shareholders arising on the liquidation, dissolution or winding up of the Corporation, whether voluntary or involuntary, or any other distribution of assets of the Corporation among its shareholders for the purpose of winding up its affairs;

(h) **"Preferred Shareholder"** means a person recorded in the securities register of the Corporation for the Preferred Shares as being the registered holder of one or more Preferred Shares;

(i) **"Redemption Date"** means, with respect to the Preferred Shares, the date specified for redemption in the notice in writing of the intention of the Corporation to redeem such Preferred Shares; and

(j) **"Redemption Price"** means the sum of $1.00 together with all declared and unpaid preferential, non-cumulative cash dividends on the Preferred Shares.

2. **Gender, etc.** Words importing only the singular number include the plural and vice versa, and words importing any gender include all genders.

3. **Currency.** Unless otherwise explicitly set forth herein, all references herein to "**dollars**" or "**$**" shall refer to the lawful currency of Canada, and all amounts payable hereunder shall be payable in the lawful currency of Canada.

4. **Business Day.** If any date upon which any dividends are payable by the Corporation, or upon which any other action is required to be taken by the Corporation or any shareholder hereunder, is not a Business Day, then such dividend shall be payable or such other action shall be required to be taken on or by the next succeeding day which is a Business Day.

5. **Headings.** The division of these Share Provisions into sections, paragraphs, subparagraphs or other subdivisions and the insertion of headings are for convenience of reference only and shall not affect the construction or interpretation hereof.

6. **Governing Statute.** These Share Provisions shall be governed by and are subject to the applicable provisions of the Act and all other laws binding upon the Corporation and, except as otherwise expressly provided herein, all terms used herein which are defined in the Act shall have the meanings respectively ascribed thereto in the Act.

II PREFERRED SHARES

1. Dividends

1. **Fixed Dividend Rate.** The Preferred Shareholders shall be entitled to receive and the Corporation shall pay thereon, as and when declared by the Board of Directors out of monies of the Corporation properly applicable to the payment of dividends, fixed preferential non-cumulative cash dividends at a rate equal to $0.08 per share per annum. The Board of Directors shall be entitled from time to

FIGURE 5.1 CONTINUED

time to declare part of the fixed preferential non-cumulative cash dividend for any financial period notwithstanding that such dividend for such financial period shall not be declared in full.

2. **Non-Cumulative.** If, within six months after the expiration of any financial period of the Corporation, the Board of Directors, in its discretion, shall not declare the said dividend or any part thereof on the Preferred Shares for such financial period, then the rights of the holders of the Preferred Shares to such dividend or to any undeclared part thereof for such financial period shall be forever extinguished.

3. **No Participation in Further Dividends.** The Preferred Shareholders shall not be entitled to any dividends other than or in excess of the fixed preferential non-cumulative cash dividends hereinbefore provided for.

4. **Dividend Payment.** Dividends (less any tax or other amounts required to be deducted or withheld by the Corporation) on the Preferred Shares shall be paid to the holder of record thereof determined at the Close of Business on the Business Day immediately preceding the applicable Dividend Payment Date by cheque payable on the Dividend Payment Date in lawful money of Canada at par at any branch in Canada of the Corporation's bankers for the time being or, in respect of any particular holder, by any other means agreed upon between the Corporation and such holder provided that such other means provides for payment on the Dividend Payment Date. The mailing of such cheque on or before the applicable Dividend Payment Date by ordinary unregistered first class pre-paid mail addressed to a Preferred Shareholder at his address as it appears in the securities register of the Corporation for the Preferred Shares or, in the event of the address of any such holder not so appearing, then at the last address of such holder known to the Corporation or, in the case of joint holders, to the address of that one of the joint holders whose name stands first in such register, or the payment by such other means shall be deemed to be payment of the dividends represented thereby and payable on such date to the extent of the amount of such payment unless the cheque is not paid upon presentation or payment by such other means is not received.

5. **Stale Cheques.** Dividends which are represented by a cheque which has not been presented to the Corporation's bankers for payment or that otherwise remain unclaimed for a period of six years from the date on which they were declared to be payable shall be forfeited to the Corporation.

6. **Restrictions on Subordinate Shares.** Except with the consent in writing of all outstanding Preferred Shareholders, the Corporation shall not call for redemption nor purchase or otherwise acquire for value less than all the then outstanding Preferred Shares nor purchase or otherwise acquire for value any Common Shares or any shares of any other class of the Corporation ranking junior to the Preferred Shares so long as any Preferred Shares are outstanding, unless and until the fixed preferential non-cumulative cash dividend has been declared and

FIGURE 5.1 CONTINUED

paid or set apart for payment for the then current financial period of the Corporation on all the Preferred Shares outstanding.

2. Liquidation

1. **Liquidation Preference.** In the event of any Liquidation Distribution, the Preferred Shareholders shall be entitled to receive from the assets and property of the Corporation for each Preferred Share held by them respectively the Redemption Price before any amount shall be paid or any property or assets of the Corporation distributed to the Common Shareholders or shares of any other class ranking junior to the Preferred Shares with respect to priority in a Liquidation Distribution.

2. **No Participation in Surplus Assets.** After payment to the Preferred Shareholders of the amount so payable to them as above provided, they shall not be entitled to share in any further distribution of the property or assets of the Corporation.

3. Purchase by the Corporation

1. Subject to the Articles and the provisions of the Act, the Corporation may at any time or from time to time purchase (if obtainable) all or any part of the outstanding Preferred Shares at the lowest price at which, in the opinion of the Board of Directors, such shares are obtainable but not exceeding the Redemption Price. Except where outstanding Preferred Shareholders all consent to the purchase, the Corporation may purchase such shares only pursuant to tenders received by the Corporation upon request for tenders addressed to the holders of all the Preferred Shares, and the Corporation shall accept only the lowest tenders. Where, in response to the invitation for tenders, two or more Preferred Shareholders submit tenders at the same price and the tenders are accepted by the Corporation as to only part of the Preferred Shares offered, the Corporation shall accept part of the Preferred Shares offered in such tender in proportion as nearly as may be to the total number of Preferred Shares offered in each such tender (disregarding fractions).

4. Redemption

1. **Option to Redeem.** Subject to the Articles and the provisions of the Act, the Corporation may, upon giving notice as hereinafter provided, redeem at any time the whole or from time to time any part of the then outstanding Preferred Shares on payment for each share to be redeemed of the Redemption Price.

2. **Notice of Redemption.** In the case of the redemption of Preferred Shares pursuant to the provisions of section 4.1 hereof, the Corporation shall at least seven days before the Redemption Date deliver, send by facsimile transmission (or other electronic communication) or mail to each person who at the date of such mailing or other communication is a registered holder of Preferred Shares to be redeemed a notice in writing of the intention of the Corporation to redeem such Preferred Shares. Such notice shall be delivered, sent by facsimile transmission (or other electronic communication) or mailed by letter, postage prepaid, ad-

FIGURE 5.1   CONTINUED

dressed to each such Preferred Shareholder at his address as it appears on the records of the Corporation or, in the event of the address of any such Preferred Shareholder not so appearing, then to the last known address of such Preferred Shareholder except, however, that accidental failure to give any such notice to one or more of such shareholders shall not affect the validity of such redemption. Such notice shall set out:

(a)   the Redemption Price;

(b)   the Redemption Date;

(c)   if only part of the Preferred Shares held by the person to whom it is addressed is to be redeemed, the number thereof so to be redeemed;

(d)   if certificates representing the Preferred Shares called for redemption are to be presented and surrendered at a place other than the registered office of the Corporation, the place or places designated therefor; and

(e)   the specified bank or specified trust company where the respective holders of Preferred Shares called for redemption may present and surrender certificates representing such shares.

3. **Payment.** On or after the Redemption Date, the Corporation shall pay or cause to be paid to or to the order of the registered holders of the Preferred Shares to be redeemed the Redemption Price thereof on presentation and surrender of the certificates representing the Preferred Shares called for redemption at the registered office of the Corporation or any other place or places designated in the notice of redemption.

4. **Partial Redemption.** If only part of the shares represented by any certificate be redeemed, a new certificate for the balance shall be issued at the expense of the Corporation.

5. **Effect of Redemption.** Subject to the provisions of section 4.6 hereof, on and after the Redemption Date, the Preferred Shares called for redemption shall cease to be entitled to dividends, and the holders thereof shall not be entitled to exercise any of the rights of shareholders in respect thereof unless payment of the Redemption Price shall not be made upon presentation of certificates in accordance with the foregoing provisions, in which case, the rights of the Preferred Shareholders shall remain unaffected.

6. **Deposit of Redemption Price.** The Corporation shall have the right at any time after the mailing or other communication notice of its intention to redeem any Preferred Shares as aforesaid to deposit the Redemption Price for the shares so called for redemption or of such of the said shares represented by certificates as have not at the date of such deposit been surrendered by the holders thereof in connection with such redemption to a special account in a specified chartered bank or specified trust company in Canada, named in such notice of redemption, to be paid without interest to or to the order of the respective holders of such Preferred Shares called for redemption upon presentation and surrender

FIGURE 5.1   CONTINUED

to such bank or trust company of the certificates representing the same. Upon such deposit being made or upon the Redemption Date, whichever is the later, the Preferred Shares in respect whereof such deposit shall have been made shall be deemed to be redeemed and the rights of the Preferred Shareholders thereof after such deposit or such Redemption Date, as the case may be, shall be limited to receiving without interest their proportionate part of the total Redemption Price so deposited against presentation and surrender of the said certificates held by them respectively. Any interest allowed on any such deposit shall belong to the Corporation. Redemption monies that are represented by a cheque which has not been presented to the Corporation's bankers for payment or that otherwise remain unclaimed (including, without limitation, monies held on deposit to a special account as provided for above) for a period of six years from the Redemption Date shall be forfeited to the Corporation.

7. **Selecting Shares for Partial Redemption.** If only part of the Preferred Shares is at any time to be redeemed, the shares so to be redeemed shall be selected *pro rata* (disregarding fractions) from among the Preferred Shareholders of record thereof as at the date of the notice of redemption or in such other manner as the Board of Directors in its sole discretion may deem equitable.

5. Retraction

1. **Option to Retract.** Subject to the Articles and the provisions of the Act, every Preferred Shareholder may, at his option and in the manner hereinafter provided, require the Corporation to redeem at any time all or part of the Preferred Shares held by such holder upon payment for each share to be redeemed of the Redemption Price.

2. **Retraction Procedure.** In the case of the redemption of Preferred Shares under the provisions of section 5.1 hereof, the holder thereof shall surrender the certificate or certificates representing such Preferred Shares at the registered office of the Corporation accompanied by a notice in writing (herein referred to as a "**Retraction Notice**") signed by such holder requiring the Corporation to redeem all or a specified number of the Preferred Shares represented thereby. As soon as practicable but, in any event, not later than 30 days following receipt of a Retraction Notice, the Corporation shall pay or cause to be paid to or to the order of the registered holder of the Preferred Shares to be redeemed the Redemption Price thereof. If only a part of the shares represented by any certificate be redeemed, a new certificate for the balance shall be issued at the expense of the Corporation.

6. Restrictions

1. So long as any of the Preferred Shares are issued and outstanding, the Corporation shall not without, but may from time to time, with the approval of all outstanding Preferred Shareholders:

FIGURE 5.1 CONTINUED

(a) declare or pay or set apart for payment any dividends on the Common Shares or any other shares of any other class ranking junior to the Preferred Shares with respect to priority in the payment of dividends if:

    (i) the realizable value of the Corporation's assets is less than the aggregate of its liabilities and the Redemption Price of all Preferred Shares then issued and outstanding; or

    (ii) after the payment, the realizable value of the Corporation's assets would be less than the aggregate of its liabilities and the Redemption Price of all Preferred Shares then issued and outstanding; or

(b) redeem, purchase or otherwise pay off or purchase out of the surplus or capital any Common Shares or any shares of any other class ranking junior to the Preferred Shares with respect to priority in a Liquidation Distribution.

7. Voting

1. **Voting Restrictions.** The Preferred Shareholders shall not be entitled as such (except as hereinafter specifically provided and except as otherwise provided by the Act) to receive notice of or to attend any meeting of the shareholders of the Corporation and shall not be entitled to vote at any such meeting.

2. **Limited Notice Rights.** The Preferred Shareholders shall, however, have the right to receive notice of and to attend and vote at all meetings of shareholders called for the purpose of authorizing the dissolution of the Corporation pursuant to the Act or a sale, lease or exchange of all or substantially all of the property of the Corporation other than in the ordinary course of business pursuant to the Act.

8. Creation of Additional Shares and Amendments

1. **Restrictions on Authorized Capital.** No class of shares may be created ranking as to a Liquidation Distribution or dividends in priority to or on a parity with the Preferred Shares, without the approval of the Preferred Shareholders given by special resolution.

2. **Variation of Rights.** The provisions hereof contained in Part II attaching to the Preferred Shares or any sections hereof may be deleted, varied, modified, amended or amplified by articles of amendment but only with the approval of the Preferred Shareholders given by special resolution.

9. Priority

1. The Common Shares shall rank junior to the Preferred Shares and shall be subject in all respects to the rights, privileges, restrictions and conditions attaching to the Preferred Shares.

III COMMON SHARES

1. **Dividends.** Subject to the prior rights of the Preferred Shareholders and to any other class of shares ranking senior to the Common Shares with respect to priority in the payment of dividends, the Common Shareholders shall be entitled to

FIGURE 5.1 CONCLUDED

receive dividends and the Corporation shall pay dividends thereon, as and when declared by the Board of Directors out of monies properly applicable to the payment of dividends, in such amount and in such form as the Board of Directors may from time to time determine and all dividends which the Board of Directors may declare on the Common Shares shall be declared and paid in equal amounts per share on all Common Shares at the time outstanding.

2. **Liquidation.** In the event of any Liquidation Distribution, the Common Shareholders shall, subject to the prior rights of the Preferred Shareholders and to any other shares ranking senior to the Common Shares with respect to priority in a Liquidation Distribution, be entitled to receive the remaining property and assets of the Corporation.

3. **Purchase by the Corporation.** Subject to the Articles and the provisions of the Act, the Corporation may at any time or from time to time purchase (if obtainable) all or any part of the outstanding Common Shares at the lowest price at which, in the opinion of the Board of Directors, such shares are obtainable. Except where all of the outstanding Common Shareholders consent to the purchase, the Corporation may purchase such shares only pursuant to tenders received by the Corporation upon request for tenders addressed to all of the Common Shareholders, and the Corporation shall accept only the lowest tenders. Where, in response to the invitation for tenders, two or more shareholders submit tenders at the same price and the tenders are accepted by the Corporation as to only part of the Common Shares offered, the Corporation shall accept part of the Common Shares offered in such tender in proportion as nearly as may be to the total number of Common Shares offered in each such tender (disregarding fractions).

4. **Voting.** The Common Shareholders shall be entitled to receive notice of and to attend (in person or by proxy) and be heard at all meetings of the shareholders of the Corporation (except for meetings at which only holders of another specified class or series of shares of the Corporation are entitled to vote separately as a class or series) and shall have one vote for each Common Share held at all such meetings.

CHAPTER 6

Names

CHAPTER OVERVIEW

This chapter outlines the criteria for determining whether a proposed corporate name is one that complies with federal and Ontario corporate statutes and regulations. It discusses the three elements that make up a corporate name and the six criteria that are used in determining whether the name complies with the legislation. Also covered are use of a French name, use of a number name, and special approval and consents that may be required before using a name, as well as the sources and procedures for name searches and an overview of the NUANS system. Finally, this chapter briefly discusses business names, trademarks, and domain names.

CHAPTER OBJECTIVES

After completing this chapter, you should be able to:

1. State whether a corporate name meets the statutory requirements of the jurisdiction of the proposed incorporation.

2. Analyze whether a name will be considered "confusing" with another name.

3. Determine the sources for conducting a name search for a corporate name before incorporation or change of name.

4. Recognize when and how to have a name "pre-approved" for use by a federal corporation.

INTRODUCTION

Choosing a corporate name is an important step in identifying a business to the public. A corporate name must not be confusing with another corporate name such that members of the public will be confused about the entity with which they are dealing. In order to protect the public and avoid such confusion, there are a number of legal considerations:

1. The corporate statutes provide extensive rules and regulations with regard to the use of the corporate name.

2. Both Corporations Canada and the Ontario Companies Branch provide extensive name guidelines to assist applicants in choosing a good name.

3. The common law provides protection for previously registered names.

4. The corporate statutes, the *Trade-marks Act*, and the business names statutes all provide some protection for registered names.

The ultimate responsibility for choosing a name rests with the client, who must assume full responsibility for any risk of confusion with existing business names and trademarks. However, it is the lawyer's role, among others, to advise the client about whether the proposed name complies with the relevant legislation, whether there are any other confusing names, and the consequences of using the name if it does not meet the previous two criteria.

CORPORATE NAMES

Finding a good corporate name can often be very difficult and clients sometimes do not understand the process or the ramifications of using a name that may be similar to that used by another business. A brief explanation to the client at the start of the process can often alleviate their confusions. The following overview of the basic concepts to be used in assessing a name will provide you with the information to do this.

Elements of a corporate name

A corporate name should generally consist of the following elements:

- a distinctive element that is the unique identifier of the name;

- a descriptive element that describes the line of business; and

- a legal element that indicates the legal status of the corporation as an incorporated body.

DISTINCTIVE ELEMENT

coined word
a word that has been created and is unrelated to any other word

Finding a unique word to identify a business requires creativity. Often, a unique word is a "**coined word**." That is, a word that has been created by the client, or the client's advisers, and is unrelated to any other word. Some examples of "coined" words are *Exxon* and *Telus*.

The distinctive element can also be a combination of dictionary words used in a creative manner — for example, *Shell Oil* — or initials or characters or the name of a person or thing.

DESCRIPTIVE ELEMENT

The descriptive element of the name describes the activities that the corporation will carry on. For example, the use of the words "sales," "manufacturing," and "exporting" will identify the business of the corporation. Other descriptive words could be more specific descriptions of a product — for example, "hardware," "embroidery," or "drapery."

LEGAL ELEMENT

Corporations incorporated under the CBCA and the OBCA must use as part of their name one of the following words (CBCA s. 10(1); OBCA (s. 10(1)):

- "Limited," "Limitée," "Incorporated," "Incorporée," "Corporation," or the corresponding abbreviation ("Ltd.," "Ltée," "Inc.," or "Corp.").

A federal corporation may also use "Société par actions de régime fédéral" or the corresponding abbreviation "SARF."

Both the CBCA (s. 10(1)) and the OBCA (s. 10(1)) provide that a corporation can use and be legally designated by either the full or the corresponding abbreviated form.

Guidelines for choosing an acceptable name

Both the CBCA and the OBCA and their regulations set out extensive requirements for corporate names. In addition, Corporations Canada has prepared a *Name Granting Compendium* that provides detailed information to assist in choosing a name. The compendium can be viewed online on the Strategis Web site.

The Ontario Companies and Personal Property Security Branch ("Ontario Companies Branch") has detailed information on the requirements for the name of a business corporation in the *Business Incorporator's Handbook*, which is available in hard copy from the Ontario Government Bookstore in Toronto (telephone: 1-800-668-9938 or in Toronto at 416-326-5320). Information is also available online at the government of Ontario Web site.

The *Name Granting Compendium* suggests that to decide whether a name is acceptable, you must consider whether the name is

- absolutely prohibited,

- qualifiedly prohibited,

- obscene,

- lacking in distinctiveness,

- confusing, or

- deceptively misdescriptive.

The following is a brief summary of the rules affecting the use of corporate names. You are encouraged to carefully review the statutes, the regulations, the federal *Name Granting Compendium*, and the Ontario *Business Incorporator's Handbook* for a more detailed description of what constitutes an acceptable corporate name.

ABSOLUTELY PROHIBITED

The CBCA and the OBCA provide that a corporation may not use a name that contains certain prohibited words.

Section 21 of the CBCA regulations prohibits the use of the words

- "Air Canada,"

- "Canada Standard" or "CS,"

- "cooperative," "co-op," or "pool" when it connotes a cooperative venture,

- "Parliament Hill,"

- "Royal Canadian Mounted Police,"

- "United Nations," or

- French translations of the above.

The OBCA (s. 9(1)) provides that, in addition to words and expressions prohibited by the regulations, and subject to complying with the conditions set out in the regulations, a corporation must not have a name that is the same as or similar to the name of a known

- body corporate,

- trust,

- association,

- partnership,

- sole proprietorship, or

- individual,

whether in existence or not, or a name that is the same as or similar to the known name under which any of the above entities identifies himself, herself, or itself to the public if the use of the name would be likely to deceive.

In addition, OBCA reg. 62/90, s. 15 prohibits the use of the words:

- "amalgamated," unless the corporation is an amalgamated corporation;

- "architect" or "architectural," where such words suggest the practice of the profession except with the written consent of the Council of the Ontario Association of Architects;

- "association";

- "college," "institute," or "university," where the inference is that it is a university, college of applied arts and technology, or other postsecondary education institution;

- "condominium";

- "cooperative";

- "council";

- "digits" or words that lead to the inference that the name is a number name;

- "engineer" or "engineering," where such words suggest the practice of the profession, except with the written consent of the Association of Professional Engineers of Ontario;

- "housing," unless the corporation is sponsored by or connected with a government;

- "veteran," unless there is continuous use of the name for a period of at least 20 years before the acquisition of the name; and

- "numerals" indicating the year of incorporation unless it is the successor to the business or it is a year of amalgamation of the corporation.

QUALIFIEDLY PROHIBITED

In addition to words that are absolutely prohibited, some words may be "qualifiedly prohibited" if, for example, they connote a relationship with a government body, a profession, or a financial institution.

Under the CBCA, the following words are considered to be qualifiedly prohibited where the name connotes that the corporation

- carries on business under royal, vice-regal, or governmental patronage, approval, or authority, unless the appropriate government department or agency requests the name in writing; or

- is sponsored or controlled by or is affiliated with the government of Canada, the government of a province, the government of a country other than Canada, or a political subdivision or agency of any such government, unless the appropriate government, political subdivision, or agency consents in writing to the use of the name.

Examples quoted in the *Name Granting Compendium* include:

- Sports Canada,

- Canadian Association of Postmasters, and

- Health & Welfare Programmers Association.

Under the OBCA, the following names are qualifiedly prohibited without the consent of the appropriate authority:

- if the name suggests an association with the Crown or the government of Canada, a municipality, any province or territory of Canada, or any department, ministry, branch, bureau, service, board, agency, commission, or activity of any such government or municipality unless consent of the appropriate government department or agency is obtained;

- if the name suggests that the corporation is sponsored or controlled by or is associated or affiliated with a university or an association of accountants, architects, engineers, lawyers, physicians, surgeons, or any other professional association recognized by the laws of Canada or a province or territory of Canada;

- if the name suggests that the corporation carries on the business of a bank, loan company, insurance company, trust company, other financial intermediary, or stock exchange that is regulated by a law of Canada or a province or territory of Canada; and

- any word or expression that suggests that a corporation is connected with a political party or leader of a political party if the corporation has a political purpose.

There are rules restricting the use of the name of a province in the name of a corporation unless the corporation is incorporated in that province. For example, in order to use "Alberta," "British Columbia," "Manitoba," "New Brunswick," "Newfoundland," "Nova Scotia," or "Saskatchewan" in the corporate name, it may be necessary to obtain consent from the relevant government.

There is, however, no restriction on the use of the word "Canada" for use by a provincial corporation.

Generally speaking, it is acceptable to use the name of a foreign country in the name of a corporation; however, ensure that this use does not make the name "deceptively misdescriptive" by misdescribing the place or origin of the goods or services.

OBSCENE WORDS

Both the CBCA and the OBCA contain a provision against the use of any language in a name that is obscene or connotes a business that is scandalous, obscene, or immoral.

TOO GENERAL OR LACKING IN DISTINCTIVENESS

A name may be considered not distinctive in cases where it is too general — for example, it describes only the line of business, it is primarily or only a surname used alone, or it is primarily or only a geographic name used alone — as in "Book Sales," "Brown Ltd.," or "Uxbridge Ltd."

secondary meaning
when applied to a corporate name, a meaning that has acquired distinctiveness through use over a period of time

Consider that sometimes "distinctiveness" is inherent or acquired through use over a period of time, in which case the name may be said to have "**secondary meaning**" — for example, Dominion Glass, Maple Leaf Gardens, Coca-Cola, and McDonalds.

CONFUSING

The essence of choosing a good corporate name is to set a corporation apart from its competitors so that there is no chance for confusion. There are three reasons a name may be considered confusing:

1. if it is a name that leads to the inference that the business carried on by the corporation under the proposed name and the business carried on by any other person are one business;

2. if it is a name that leads to the inference that a corporation is associated with a person and that person is not associated with the corporation; and

3. if it is a name used by one corporation that is so similar to the name of another person that someone will think that they are dealing with the same person.

Notwithstanding the above, both the CBCA and the OBCA do have provisions for corporations to acquire similar or even identical names. The provisions are complicated and a careful reading of the regulations is necessary. The following is a summary.

Under the CBCA (reg. 2001-512, ss. 28, 30, and 31):

1. A name that is confusing with the name of a corporation that has not carried on business in the two years immediately before the date of a request to use the corporate name is prohibited unless the existing corporation consents in writing and undertakes in writing to dissolve immediately or change its name before the corporation that proposes to use the name begins to use it.

2. A name that is confusing with the name of an existing corporation is prohibited unless:

    a. it is the name of a corporation that is the successor to the business of the existing corporation and the existing corporation has ceased or will, in the immediate future, cease to carry on business under that corporate name and undertakes in writing to dissolve or change its name before the successor corporation begins carrying on business under that name; or

    b. the name of the existing or proposed corporation sets out the year of incorporation, or the year of the most recent amendment to the articles of the corporation, in parentheses, immediately before the legal ending.

3. If an existing corporation acquires, or will acquire, all or substantially all of the property of an affiliated corporation, it may use the name of the affiliated corporation only if the affiliated corporation undertakes in writing to dissolve, or to change its name, before the existing corporation begins to use the name.

4. If a proposed corporation is to acquire all or substantially all of the property of a corporation that is to be an affiliate of the proposed corporation, the proposed corporation can only use the name of the affiliated corporation if the affiliated corporation undertakes in writing to dissolve, or to change its name, before the proposed corporation begins using the corporate name.

The following are the provisions under the OBCA (reg. 62, ss. 4 and 6) regarding similar names:

1. Corporation A may have a name similar to corporation B where corporation A is not or will not be affiliated with corporation B, if corporation A is the successor to the business of corporation B, and corporation B has ceased or will cease to carry on business; or corporation B undertakes in writing to dissolve or to change its name before corporation A commences to use it and the name sets out the year of acquisition of the name in brackets; words, numerals, or initials are added, deleted, or substituted; or a different legal ending is used.

2. A corporation cannot acquire a name identical to the name or former name of another corporation, whether in existence or not, unless

    a. the other corporation was incorporated outside Ontario and has never carried on business in Ontario, or

b. at least 10 years have elapsed since the other corporation was dissolved or changed its name.

3. A corporation may acquire a name identical to that of another corporation if the following criteria are met:

   a. neither corporation is an offering corporation;

   b. the corporations are affiliated or associated with one another or are controlled by related persons;

   c. the corporation that acquires the name is a successor to the business of the other corporation; and

   d. the other corporation has been dissolved or has changed its name.

DECEPTIVELY MISDESCRIPTIVE

A name that misleads the public with regard to the type of business or services it provides, the condition under which the goods or services are produced or supplied, or the place of origin of the goods or services is also prohibited.

Use of a French name

If a corporation is going to carry on business in Quebec, the *Charter of the French Language Act* of Quebec provides that it must use a French name. The corporation should, therefore, provide for the use of a French name in its articles. This can be accomplished either by having an English name and a French name or by having a special provision in the articles authorizing the use of its name in the French language. The French Language Office in Montreal will provide a French translation of an English name; alternatively, a Quebec law firm can also provide a translation.

The disadvantage of using the special provision for a French name is that the name will not appear on the Ontario corporation profile report or on a federal Strategis report. It will be discovered only upon a review of a copy of the articles of the corporation. Thus, theoretically, a corporation may use a French name in which to take security. If the name is buried in the special provisions, a search by a subsequent creditor may not discover the provision in the articles but only if a corporation profile is obtained. The result will be that searches under the French name will not be conducted and a prior personal property security registration against the corporation may not be discovered.

Both the CBCA (s. 10(3)) and the OBCA (s. 10(2)) provide that a corporation may set out its name in its articles in an English form, a French form, an English form and a French form (for example, Henry Birks & Sons Inc. and Henry Birks et Fils Inc.), or a combined English and French form (for example, Henry Birks & Sons et Fils Ltd./Ltée). A corporation may use and may be legally designated by any such form. The Ontario regulations provide that the name of a corporation must always be displayed with a "/" between the English and French versions of the name on any correspondence with the Ministry of Consumer and Business Services.

Use of a number name

It is not mandatory to have a "word" name for a corporation. All jurisdictions in Canada provide for a number name such as "6666666 Ontario Inc." The number name assigned federally and in Ontario will be the corporate number issued to each corporation upon incorporation.

Often a number name is used when a quick incorporation is needed and there is no time to complete a thorough search of a word name. The number name can later be changed to a word name by filing articles of amendment. Sometimes a number name will be used where no importance is attached to the name of the corporation — for example, when the corporation is a holding corporation.

It is possible to reserve a bank of number names. This could be useful if a corporation name is needed on short notice — for example, for the purposes of entering into a conract.

Special approvals and consents to use of a name

There are certain circumstances under which it may be necessary to obtain approval to the use of the name from a professional association or university — for example, "University of Montreal Debating Society" or "Greater Toronto Engineers Association."

Also, a corporate name may be available provided that consent to the use of the name is obtained from some individual, corporation, or trademark owner.

NAME SEARCHES

Before filing articles of incorporation, an applicant must determine that there are no similar names. Both the CBCA (Form 1 instructions and Incorporation Kit instructions) and the OBCA (reg. 62, s. 18(1)1) require that a NUANS search report that is dated not more than 90 days before the date of submission accompany the articles.

There is always the possibility that an existing name does not appear on the NUANS report. Therefore, in order to complete a thorough search for the availability of the name that will have considerable public exposure, it is recommended that the following additional sources be searched:

- trademarks — the NUANS report provides two pages of similar trademarks; further searches should be made;

- trade directories;

- local telephone books; and

- domain names.

Fortunately, there are some search houses that have developed extensive computerized searches that include databases of the above. For example, Marque d'Or's "Natscope" offers extended federal and Ontario-biased name search reports including all of the above. It is highly recommended that these extended searches be used for any names that will have public exposure.

GOVERNMENT APPROVAL OF A CORPORATE NAME

Corporations Canada provides a process for "pre-approving" corporate names by submitting a completed form by e-mail, fax, or mail for its consideration. A response will be received within a couple of days stating that the name is available, is not available because of specified similar names, or may be available with certain specified consent. It is a good idea to obtain pre-approval of a corporate name where time permits because this can save time and expense for your client when the articles are submitted.

If similar names appear on the NUANS search report, and the client's instructions are to proceed to "pre-clear" the name, the request should include arguments why the name should be approved. Some common arguments include the following:

- the amount of public exposure the name will have and the likelihood of confusion;

- the distinctiveness of any part of the name and the extent to which it has become known;

- the length of time the name has been in use;

- the industry in which the name will be used;

- the proposed corporation's clientele;

- the geographic region in which the name will be used; and

- the degree of any similarity between the name and the similar name or trademark from the point of view of sound, visual image, or suggested ideas.

The Ontario Companies Branch does not provide a similar procedure. The onus is on the incorporator or the applicant to ensure that the name conforms to law and is not similar to any known name.

AN OVERVIEW OF THE NUANS SYSTEM

The newly upgraded automated name search (NUANS) system was established by what is now Industry Canada on January 1, 1981. Hewlett Packard Company (HP) has a licence from Industry Canada to administer the system.

The **NUANS system** is a computerized search system that compares a proposed corporate name or trademark with databases of existing names or trademarks. The system employs a number of automated search strategies to evaluate corporate names based on their phonetics, letter content, coined words, synonyms, distinctive versus descriptive terms, line of business, geographic proximity, etc. It then produces a list of names and trademarks that are found to be most similar.

A name submitted for a NUANS search report is added immediately to the name base as a proposed name during the search process. It will be retained on the database for an assigned reservation period sufficient to accommodate the formal incorporation process. There is usually a three- to six-month delay between incorporation and registration on the database. To compensate for this, any names that have been proposed through the NUANS system stay on record for up to six months.

NUANS system
a computerized search system that compares a proposed corporate name or trademark with databases of existing names or trademarks

NUANS search reports can be ordered from a search house — that is, from an independent private sector business that is approved by HP to conduct searches in the NUANS system. Some of these search houses provide an "online" service if the customer has either an account set up with the search house or a major credit card.

In addition to the NUANS search report, these search houses offer preliminary searches on names, usually at no cost. The results of the preliminary search often offer more names than the actual NUANS itself.

Although generally accurate, there are some shortcomings in the NUANS system. It is possible that the same search conducted on different days will produce different results. The database contains the names of all corporations incorporated in all jurisdictions in Canada, but it does not contain Quebec corporations incorporated on or after January 1, 1994. Table 6.1 illustrates the data that are uploaded from the provinces into the NUANS system. Although the data are uploaded weekly by HP, the provinces accumulate the information for different periods of time before forwarding it on to HP. These time frames are also set out in the table. In addition, due to a province's update cycle, the data forwarded by the provinces may not be up to date at the time it is forwarded.

The NUANS Web site has a lot of information about the NUANS report including the report layout, different types of reports available, a list of recognized name search houses, mnemonics, and various other information.

SEARCH SYSTEMS IN OTHER JURISDICTIONS IN CANADA

For extra-provincial registrations, it is often useful to know the methods used to search names in other jurisdictions. Table 6.2 provides a list of the name search systems in place in jurisdictions across Canada.

DIRECTOR'S RIGHT TO CHANGE NAME

The CBCA (ss. 12(2) and (5)) and the OBCA (ss. 12(1) and (2)) provide that if a corporation, through inadvertence or otherwise, has acquired a name contrary to the provision in the respective statutes, the Director under the Act may direct the corporation to change its name. If the corporation does not do so, the Director may revoke the name and assign a new name to the corporation.

BUSINESS NAMES

If a corporation identifies itself to the public in Ontario using a name other than its full corporate name, it has to register that name under the *Business Names Act* (BNA). Registration under the BNA does not provide much protection for the name. There are extensive name requirements set out in the regulations to the BNA that are similar to those found in the CBCA and the OBCA. Registration of business names under the BNA is discussed in greater detail in chapter 9.

Although registration under the BNA does not require a name search, it is prudent practice to search the business name before registration and alert your

TABLE 6.1 INFORMATION AVAILABLE IN NUANS REPORT

Jurisdiction	Information available in NUANS report	Update cycle
Alberta	Names of corporations, societies, extra-provincial corporations, professional corporations, reserved names, and business names	Weekly
British Columbia	Names of corporations, societies, extra-provincial corporations, and reserved names Note: (a) BC business names are not included; (b) does not keep inactive names.	Weekly
Federal	Names of corporations and reserved names Note: Limited trademark registrations and applications are also listed.	Weekly
Manitoba	Names of corporations, societies, extra-provincial corporations, reserved names, and business names Note: Inactive names are kept for no more than two years.	Monthly
New Brunswick	Names of corporations, societies, extra-provincial corporations, reserved names, and business names	Monthly
Newfoundland and Labrador	Names of corporations	Every two months
Northwest Territories	Names of corporations Note: NWT business names are not included.	Every two months
Nova Scotia	Names of corporations, societies, extra-provincial corporations, reserved names, and business names Note: Does not keep inactive names for more than 1 day.	Every two months
Nunavut	Names of corporations Note: NU business names are not included.	Every two months
Ontario	Names of corporations, societies, extra-provincial corporations, reserved names, and business names	Weekly
Prince Edward Island	Names of corporations, societies, extra-provincial corporations, reserved names, and business names	Monthly

TABLE 6.1   CONTINUED

Jurisdiction	Information available in NUANS report	Update cycle
Quebec	As of December 31, 1993 no information on corporate names or business names is available	
Saskatchewan	Names of corporations, societies, extra-provincial corporations, reserved names, and business names	Monthly
Yukon	Names of corporations Note: YT business names are not included.	Every two months

client to any similar names. This will avoid the chance of a "passing off" action being brought against your client by the prior user of a similar name. **Passing off** is a common law tort whereby one person carries on a business under a name that tends to mislead the public into thinking that the business is being carried on by another person. Passing off does not have to be intentional — deceit can be unintended.

passing off
a common law tort whereby one person carries on a business under a name that tends to mislead the public into thinking that the business is being carried on by another person

TRADEMARKS

Ultimate business name protection in Canada is obtained by registering the name as a trademark under the *Trade-marks Act* (Canada) (TMA). A **trademark** is a word, symbol, or design, or a combination of these, used to identify wares, goods, or services of one business and differentiate them from those of others. To register a trademark, you must file an application with the Trade-marks Office in Hull, Quebec. Before registration, the Trade-marks Office undertakes examinations to determine compliance with the provisions of the TMA. The usual process for registration involves the following:

trademark
a word, symbol, or design, or a combination of these, used to identify wares, goods, or services of one business and differentiate them from those of others

1. a preliminary search of existing trademarks;

2. an application;

3. an examination of the application by the Trade-marks Office;

4. publication of the application in the official trademarks journal;

5. the receipt of opposition (challenges) to the application; and

6. the allowance and registration (if there is no opposition).

DOMAIN NAMES

Technological advancements have caused the development of another important type of name — namely, "domain" names. A **domain name** is an address for individuals and businesses on the World Wide Web. For example, www.ilco.on.ca is a domain name.

domain name
an address for individuals and businesses on the World Wide Web

TABLE 6.2   NAME SEARCH SYSTEMS IN USE IN JURISDICTIONS ACROSS CANADA

Jurisdiction	Name search system
Alberta	NUANS reports obtained from accredited search houses. Reports are required for both incorporation and business name registration.
British Columbia	Name searches and reservations are conducted by the government and are required for both incorporation and business name registration.
Federal	NUANS report conducted by search houses. Report required for incorporation.
Manitoba	NUANS reports conducted by government for both incorporation and business name registration.
New Brunswick	Maritime-biased NUANS report conducted by government for both incorporation and business name registration.
Newfoundland and Labrador	Government conducts name search for incorporation.
Northwest Territories	Government conducts name search and reserves names for both incorporation and business name registration.
Nova Scotia	Government conducts name search and reserves names for both incorporation and business name registration.
Nunavut	Government conducts name search and reserves names for incorporation and business name registration.
Ontario	NUANS reports conducted by search houses. Reports are required for incorporation.
Prince Edward Island	Government conducts name search and reserves names for incorporation and business name registration.
Quebec	Government conducts name search and reserves names for incorporation. Names must be in French.
Saskatchewan	Government conducts name search and reserves names for incorporation and business name reservation.
Yukon	Government conducts name search and reserves names for both incorporation and business name registration.

There are two types of top-level domains: country codes, which were created for use by countries — for example, ".ca," ".us," and ".uk" — and generic codes, which were created for use by anyone using the Internet — for example, ".com," ".biz," and ".org."

Canadian businesses wishing to register a domain name using the .ca country code do so through the Canadian Internet Registration Authority (CIRA). Instructions, restrictions, and policies regarding .ca registrations are contained on the CIRA Web site.

Businesses wishing to register .com, .biz, .org, etc., domain names do so through the Internet Corporation for Assigned Names and Numbers (ICANN).

To register domain names, contact any one of numerous registrars who are accredited by ICANN and CIRA and who are accessible through the Internet.

KEY TERMS

coined word	passing off
domain name	secondary meaning
NUANS system	trademark

REFERENCES

Business Corporations Act (Ontario) (OBCA), RSO 1990, c. B.16, as amended.

Business Names Act (Ontario) (BA), RSO 1990, c. B.17, as amended.

Canada Business Corporations Act (CBCA), RSC 1985, c. C-44, as amended.

Canadian Internet Registration Authority (CIRA) at http://www.cira.org.

Industry Canada, Corporations Canada, *Name Granting Compendium*, April 22, 1999.

Industry Canada, Corporations Canada, *Small Business Guide to Federal Incorporation*, 1998.

Internet Corporation for Assigned Names and Numbers (ICANN) at http://www.icann.org.

MacMillan, Anna I., *Basic Corporate Law for Legal Secretaries and Law Clerks, Corporate Names — the Basics*, Law Society of Upper Canada, Department of Continuing Legal Education, June 16, 1993.

McGuiness, Kevin P., *The Law and Practice of Canadian Business Corporations* (Markham, ON: Butterworths, 1999).

Trade-marks Act, RSC 1985, c. T-13, as amended.

FORMS AND PRECEDENTS

Figure 6.1: Form requesting name decision

Figure 6.2: Federal-biased NUANS search report

Figure 6.3: Industry Canada name decision letter

REVIEW QUESTIONS

1. List the three elements generally found in a corporate name.

2. Describe the circumstances in which a CBCA corporation can use a name that is confusing with an existing corporation.

3. Describe the circumstances in which an Ontario corporation can have an identical name to another corporation.

4. Identify when a corporation would want to use a number name.

5. Give two circumstances in which consent to the use of the name might be required.

6. Consider and discuss the quality of the following names:

   a. Unilock Ltd.

   b. The Health Hut

   c. Arrest-A-Fire Protection Systems Ltd.

7. Download from the Industry Canada Web site (Strategis) the *Name Granting Compendium*. Consider the quality of the following names, all of which are taken from the compendium, then look them up in the compendium and compare thoughts about the quality of the names with what you find in the compendium:

   • Health and Welfare Programmers Association

   • Birdbaths Alberta Ltd.

   • University of Montreal Debating Society

   • Suncraft Shoes Ltd.

   • Legault Inc.

   • Star & Associates Ltd.

8. The names on the left listed below are proposed. The name opposite the proposed name is an existing name. On the basis of Industry Canada's *Name Granting Compendium*, comment on whether the proposed names are acceptable:

Proposed name	*Existing name*
Uniso Professional Shoemakers' Society	North American Professional Shoemakers' Association
Maple Leaf Bicycles Inc.	Maple Leaf Inc.
ABC (Canada) Inc.	ABC Inc.
Newton Tool Quebec Ltd.	Newton Tool (Canada) Ltd.

9. Explain your reasons for recommending the use of an extended name search report when selecting a corporate name.

10. Describe the process for obtaining government approval of a name for a CBCA corporation.

11. Define the following terms:

    a. coined word

    b. Secondary meaning

    c. NUANS system

    d. trademark

    e. domain name

    f. passing off

12. Indicate whether the following statements are true or false:

    a. The legal element must be the last word in the name.

    b. A word that is absolutely prohibited under the CBCA or the OBCA is acceptable for use in a name.

    c. A name containing the word "engineer" for an engineering practice to be incorporated under the OBCA can be used only with the consent of the Association of Professional Engineers of Ontario.

    d. A proposed CBCA corporation may use a name similar to a corporation that dissolved three years before the proposed business intends to incorporate.

    e. A proposed OBCA corporation may use a name identical to a corporation that ceased to carry on business 11 years before the proposed business intends to incorporate.

    f. A corporation may use a French name.

    g. A NUANS search reserves the proposed name for 90 days.

    h. The highest level of protection for the use of a name in Canada is achieved by registration under the *Trade-marks Act* (Canada).

FIGURE 6.1   FORM REQUESTING NAME DECISION

 Industry Canada   Industrie Canada

Corporate Name Information Form

for faster approval of your corporate name

Use of this form is voluntary. Information that you provide will be used by the Corporations Canada for the sole purpose of making a decision regarding your proposed corporate name. Any personal information submitted is protected under the provisions of the *Privacy Act* and will be stored in Personal Information Bank number IC-PPU-049.

Often, the Corporations Canada must reject a proposed corporate name simply because we do not have enough information. To avoid this, you should complete this form so we can make a decision about your corporate name quickly.

1
What is the proposed name of your corporation?

The name must not just describe the activities of the proposed corporation, like Shoe Manufacturing Inc. There must be something distinctive in the name, like Turner Shoe Manufacturing Inc.

> BSJ GARDEN ORNAMENT SALES INC.

2
What will be the activities of your proposed corporation?
(Please see *Name Granting Guidelines*, Chapter 1.6)

In as much detail as possible and using non-technical language, please describe in the space provided:

A | The likely nature of the proposed corporation's business

> SALES OF GARDEN ORNAMENTS

B | The likely nature of its clientele

> PEOPLE INTERESTED IN GARDENING

C | The territory in which it is likely to operate

> ACROSS CANADA

3
From where did you get your proposed corporate name?
(Please see *Name Granting Guidelines*, Chapter 1.6)

Please explain where the distinctive term (e.g. "Turner" in Turner Consulting Ltd.) in your proposed corporate name came from (a person? an idea? another corporation?).

> INCORPORATORS' INITIALS

IC 2691 (2004/03)

Canada

FIGURE 6.1 CONTINUED

4 Does your proposed corporate name contain a personal name?

If yes, please confirm either statement A or B.

(Please see *Name Granting Guidelines*, Chapter 4.1)

☐ **A** The personal name belongs to an individual who will be an incorporator or a director of the proposed corporation.

☐ **B** One of the following documents is attached:

☐ A signed statement of consent and material interest by the individual whose name appears in your corporate name.

☐ An affidavit stating that the personal name used in your proposed corporate name is fictitious and is not the name of an individual who is well-known or known personally to you.

5 Are Corporations staff likely to think that your proposed corporate name is confusing with an existing trademark, an existing or recently dissolved corporation, or unincorporated business name which appears on the NUANS?

If yes, please list those potential problems (existing trade-marks or incorporated or unincorporated business names) in the space below. (Remember, there are two types of confusion: where the names are so similar that someone may think they are the *same* business, and where the names are so similar that someone may think they are *related*.)

Then, please select option A or one or more of B, C, D.

☐ **A** If your proposed name is not likely to cause confusion despite its similarity to the corporate or unincorporated names and/or trademark you have identified, please explain why confusion is not likely in the space below (e.g. differences of goods/services, type and level of sophistication of clientele, likely territory of operation, etc.).

IC 2691 (2004/03) p.2

FIGURE 6.1 CONCLUDED

☐ **B**   If your proposed name is likely to appear **related** to any of the corporate or unincorporated names or trademarks you have identified above, please attach the **written consent of the corporation or owner of the trademark or unincorporated business name**.

☐ **C**   If your proposed name is so similar to the name of an unincorporated business you have identified that the public is likely to think that they are the **same** business, please attach the **written consent and undertaking of the owner to stop doing business under that trade name or transfer its rights to your proposed corporation.**

☐ **D**   If your proposed name is so similar to an existing or recently dissolved corporate name you have identified that the public is likely to think that they are the **same** corporation, please **indicate which of the following consents is attached:**

     ☐   The consent and **undertaking of the existing corporation to dissolve or change its name, including** (please indicate which):

         ☐   confirmation that your proposed corporation will include in its name **the year of incorporation or amendment, in parentheses**; or

         ☐   confirmation that your proposed corporation will be **affiliated with the existing corporation and will receive substantially all its property in the immediate future.**

     ☐   The **consent and undertaking of the existing corporation, which has been inactive for two years, to dissolve or to change its name.**

---

6   **Does your proposed corporate name use the word "Group"?**
(Please see *Name Granting Guidelines*, Chapter 4.6)

If yes,
1) please list in the space below the incorporated and unincorporated business names, if any, appearing on your attached NUANS search report that will be members of the group.

2) please explain why other very similar names or trademarks, if any, appearing on the NUANS report would not appear to be part of the proposed group.

IC 2691 (2004/03) p.3

FIGURE 6.2   FEDERAL-BIASED NUANS SEARCH REPORT

```
1"THE PROVISION OF THE INFORMATION CONTAINED IN THIS REPORT IS SUBJECT TO THE
             TERMS AND CONDITIONS CONTAINED ON THE BACK HERE OF."
   Industry Canada, NUANS 5PAGE                      MILTOM  ATR V=14,26

   ? BSJ GARDEN ORNAMENT SALES INC.           78413116           PAGE 1/5
                                              CANADA             2003Oc21
   ===================================================================

   BSJ GARDEN ORNAMENT SALES INC             CD 78413116          2003Oc21
                                                PROP.MILTOM

   BSJ GARDEN ORNAMENT SALES INC             ON 78413090          2003Oc21
                                                PROP.MILTOM

   LES CONSULTANTS B.B.S.J. INC              QC 27474360          1990Ja16
     LONGUEUIL (C

   BEST BUSINESS SERVICES LTD                NT C166652           1998Au27

   JANES HONEY BEES LTD                      BC 0658872           2002No20

   BSJ CONSTRUCTION CONSULTANTS              NS 3023960           1998No02
     WELLINGTON                                 PBN

   DR. DAVID B. SKINNER, PROFESSIONAL CORPORATION  YK 70888441    1981J122

   B. S. GARMENT INC                         ON 799533            1988Oc18
     SCAR. ONTARI

   B.S.J.D. INVESTMENTS LIMITED              ON 529395            1982No26
     WILLOWDALE O                              Inactive  Cancelled 1988No07

   BLUE STORM MEDIA INC                      CD 3974367           2001No26
     QC

   BRAEMA DEVELOPMENT INC                    MB 78413637          2003Oc21
                                                PROP.MANTOBA

   E B SYSTEMS LIMITED                       MB 0348155           1974De30
              "Misc.Services,n.e.s."           MbShrNDist

   BASEMENT STUDIOS                          Sk 101032925         Rg2002Ma07
     REGINA                    Partnrshp "SOUND EDITING STUDIO, SOUND RECORDING,

   BSJ CONSTRUCTION                          OB 101061315         2000Se26
     PICKERING                                                    Sole_Prop

   BRAINSTORMIN BUSINESS SOLUTIONS           OB 130305816         2003Mr17
     TORONTO                                                      Sole_Prop

   HBS SYSTEMS, INC                          PE 025703      VN    1998A123
                                                ExtraProv

   HBS SYSTEMS, INC                          MB 3839134  Delaware 1997J122
          "Services Incident..Agriculture"     EPShrNDist         1998Ma20

   BEREAVEMENT ASSOCIATION (ST. JOHNS REGION) INC  NF C125104     1997J103
```

FIGURE 6.2 CONTINUED

```
1"LES RENSEIGNEMENTS CONTENUS DANS CE RAPPORT SONT SUJETS AUX CLAUSES ET
             CONDITIONS ENONCEES A L'ENDOS DE CE DOCUMENT."
     Industry Canada, NUANS 5PAGE                    MILTOM  ATR V=14,26

     ? BSJ GARDEN ORNAMENT SALES INC.          78413116        PAGE 2/5
                                               CANADA          2003Oc21

     ==========================================================================

     DAVDEL BOATS                              SK 78412781        2003Oc21
                                                  PROP.SASK

     ST. JOHNS BUILDING CORPORATION OF AMHERSTBURG  ON 098109     1959Fe26
        AMHERSTBURG

     BROKEN ARROW DESIGN LTD                   AB 78413135        2003Oc21
                                                  PROP.AB ACC

     BSJ INVESTMENTS INC              .        NB 60039686        1987Jn10
        MONCTON       E1C5T9                      Bus.Corp        1997Jl16

     THE BASEMENT CLOTHING STORE               OB 120776273       2002Au13
        NEWMARKET                                                 Genl.Part

     BRISTOL BAILIFF & DOCUMENT SERVICES       NS 78410595        2003Oc21
                                                  PROP.N.S.

     GESTION BE-SOJOMA INC                     CD 729116          1978Jl18
        RIMOUSKI                                        Dissolved 1983Se23

     CANADIAN BROWN SWISS ASSOCIATION          CD 99791998 FinInstn 1985Ja02

     BESSEYS MOVING SERVICES INC               NF C186031         1999Se09

     REIGN STORM E-BUSINESS SOLUTIONS          OB 100221910       2000Fe25
        MISSISSAUGA                                              Sole_Prop

     EXPLORATION BREX INC                      CD 2199378         1987Jn02
        ABITIBI-TEMI                                              2003Oc06

     GESTION JOANNE BISSONNETTE INC            CD 2640562         1990Se04
        QC

     B.S.J. HOLDINGS LTD                       Ab 0203940341      1988De06
                                                                  2002De05

     BZJ FLYING INC                            Sk    557790       1981Ma25
        SASKATOON                                         *Struck 1989Oc31

     SORRENTO BUSINESS IMPROVEMENT ASSOCIATION BC 0042773 BCsociety 2001Fe27

     BOISES ST-GERMAIN INC.                    CD 3670767         1999Oc19
        MESSINES

     JEANS BEEZEE LTEE                         CD 276359          1978Fe15
        MONTREAL                                        Dissolved 1982Ja22

     BEEZEE JEANS LTD                          CD 276359          1978Fe15
        MONTREAL                                        Dissolved 1982Ja22
```

FIGURE 6.2   CONTINUED

```
 1"THE PROVISION OF THE INFORMATION CONTAINED IN THIS REPORT IS SUBJECT TO THE
           TERMS AND CONDITIONS CONTAINED ON THE BACK HERE OF."
Industry Canada, NUANS 5PAGE                         MILTOM  ATR V=14,26

? BSJ GARDEN ORNAMENT SALES INC.            78413116            PAGE 3/5
                                            CANADA              2003Oc21

============================================================================

B. S. SYSTEMS CANADA                        MB 3857256              1998Jl07
             "Misc.Services,n.e.s."         Proprietor   Expired 2001Jl07

OWEN SOUND SENIOR MENS FASTBALL TEAM        ON 1157665             1996Fe19
  OWEN SOUND O

BSJ PRODUCTIONS                             OB 111190310           2001No16
  TORONTO                                                        Sole_Prop

BRAINSTORM PRODUCT DEVELOPMENT INC          ON 1140365            1995Jl24
  THORNHILL ON

BSJ EQUIPMENT INC                           ON 2002741            2001Al27
  OAKVILLE ONT

BSJ AUTO SERVICES INC                       ON 1357203            1999Ma26
  BRAMPTON ONT

ORGANISME DE GESTION DU MATERIEL DE CONSTRUCTION  QC 28692523     1991De09
DES BATIMENTS A L'HOME..                    Non-Prof
  NICOLET

ORGANISME DE GESTION DU MATERIEL DE CONSTRUCTION  QC 30896682     1993Ma04
DES BATIMENTS A L'HOME..                    Non-Prof
  SHAWINIGAN (

BSJ.EVANS                                   OB 130165582          2003Fe11
  TORONTO                                                       Sole_Prop

B.S.J. SERVICES LTD                         Ab 0202505723         1981Mr25
                                               *Struck           1984Se01

B.S.J. PARTRIDGE PROFESSIONAL CORPORATION   Ab 0205631187         1993Ma10
                                             *Struck Legal       1995No01

SARNIA-LAMBTON BUSINESS DEVELOPMENT CORPORATION   ON 758315       1988Ma04
  SARNIA ONTAR

B S J ENTERPRISES INC                       Ab 0206102774         1994Ma09
                              *Struck New_Name Nu1995De12 1997No01

BORTS-GERTSMAN MANAGEMENT CONSULTANTS LTD    CD 1007602           1980Se24
  OTTAWA-CARLE                                                    1999Jn08

B S J TOOL & DIE                            OB 990303232          1999Mr18
  ETOBICOKE                                                     Sole_Prop

BSJ NETWORKING SOLUTIONS                    OB 111178091          2001No14
  MISSISSAUGA                                                   Sole_Prop
```

FIGURE 6.2 CONTINUED

```
CONTENTS OF THIS REPORT ARE DEPENDENT ON THE INPUT PARAMETERS
SELECTED BY THE USER. PENDING APPLICATIONS ARE UPDATED WHERE NECESSARY
AT ADVERTISEMENT AND REGISTRATION.  TYPICALLY THERE IS A 6 WEEK LAPSE
BETWEEN FILING & AVAILABILITY FOR SEARCH.  ERRORS/OMISSIONS SHOULD BE
REPORTED TO THE TRADE MARKS OFFICE BY TELEPHONING (819) 994-9614.

Industry Canada NUANS - TRADEMARK REPORT          MILTOM  ATT V=14,26
                  78413116            CLASS=14,26       PAGE 4/5
                                                        2003Oc21.

           ? BSJ
                                        *
UNBSJ SEAWOLVES       906342
    9(1)niii:Pub.Auth 1993Oc18  Advertised       UNIVERSITY OF NEW BRUN
                                        *
BSJ                   399408-TMA 223708           14.Jewellery products.
           Expunged   1976Jn28 1977Oc14          JACOB WEISS, TRADING A
                                        *
BSD                   887505 TMA 509881                    14.Jewellery.
           Use-1990   1998Au20 1999Mr24          BOB SIEMON DESIGNS, IN
                                        *
ABS                   1172261      14,26.Real and imitation jewellery; earrings,
           Use-1994Jn 2003Mr28  Formalized       rings, clasps, pendants, b>
                                                    BLUMER GMBH (A COMPANY
                                        *
JBS MANAGEMENT SYSTEM1128108    35,19,42,9.Management software for use in truss
           Prop.use   2002Ja15  Allowed          fabrication business to enabl>
                                                    JAGER BUILDING SYSTEMS
                                        *
JS ;                  421918 TMA 338632           14,26.Rings, bracelets, pendants,
                      1978Mr07 1988Mr31  cufflinks, earrings, charms and other >
                                                    J.B. SIMPSON MFG. INC.
                                        *
BS-                   586238 TMA 361488                      14.Jewelry.
                      1987Jn25 1989Oc27          SUPAPRORN ASAVAKUL TRA
                                        *
SSJ                   764061 TMA 446774           14.All fine gold jewellery; namely
                      1994Se22 1995Au25          rings, bracelets, and necklaces.
                                                    SERKIZ GOKDAG,
                                        *
SBJ;                  538926-TMA 316083           14,26.Rings, bracelets, pendants,
           Expunged   1985Mr27 1986Jl04  earrings, necklaces, bangles and brooc>
                                                    SARKIS BERBERIAN JEWEL
                                        *
BST                   377036 TMA 206968           42,9,Scientific and commercial data
           Use-1967Oc 1974Jl12 1975Ma09  processing and computerized type-se>
                                                    CONSEILLERS EN GESTION
                                        *
SB ;                  644664 TMA 386993           14,26.Chains, rings, earrings,
                      1989No14 1991Jl26  bracelets, pendants, tie bars, tie
                                             pins, > HACIK SELELENK, CARRYI
                                        *
BJS                   713069 TMA 415860   37,42,35,19,Engineering and consulting
           Use-1990Jn 1992Se17 1993Au20  services in the field of constructing
                                             b> LINEAR DYNAMICS, INC.
                                        *
SJ ;                  826386 TMA 514394           35,14,42,26.Manufacture of gold
                      1996Oc30 1999Au12  jewellery ornaments, namely, necklaces,
                                             earrin> SHIVANI JEWELLERS
                                        *
SJF                   853619 TMA 528778           14.Precious metal jewellry.
                      1997Au18 2000Jn05          529779 B.C. LTD. DBA S
```

FIGURE 6.2 CONTINUED

LE CONTENU DE CE RAPPORT DE MARQUE DE COMMERCE EST DEPENDANT DES
PARAMETRES DES DONNEES CHOISIS PAR L'UTILISATEUR. LES DEMANDES EN
SUSPENS SONT MISES-A-JOUR LORSQUE NECESSAIRE, LORS DE L'ANNONCE ET DE
L'ENREGISTREMENT. TYPIQUEMENT, IL Y A UN DELAI DE 6 SEMAINES ENTRE LE
DEPOT ET LA DISPONIBILITE POUR FIN DE RECHERCHE. TOUTES ERREURS
/OMISSIONS DOIVENT-ETRE RAPPORTEES AU BUREAU DES MARQUES DE COMMERCE
EN TELEPHONANT A (819) 994-9614.

```
Industrie Canada NUANS - TRADEMARK REPORT        MILTOM  ATT V=14,26
                    78413116            CLASS=14,26        PAGE 5/5
                                                          2003Oc21.

        ? BSJ

                                *
V.S.J. ;           1065042 TMA 563031    14,25,9,10.Bijoux en or et en argent
                   2000Jn27 2002Jn04   (bagues, breloques, boucles d'oreilles,
                                                > DIAMANT ELINOR INC.
                                *
BSD                483458-             14,26.Jewellery, namely, rings, pendants,
             Prop.use  1982Mr10   Abandoned            earings, bracelets.
                                                   VARTAN DEMERDJIAN TRAD
                                *
FSJ ;              1116117        16,28,41,35.Marketing of our club for entity
             Use-2000Mr 2001Se21   Searched    identification purposes (although>
                                                   FORT ST.JOHN SOCCER CL
                                *
JS ;               581780 TMA 356479   14,41.Jewellery and metal art produced
                   1987Al10 1989Jn02      from both precious and non-precio>
                                                   JOHN ADAM SCHNEIDER,
                                *
SB ;               635641 TMA 393789        14,6,42,20.Bijoux pour femmes,
                   1989Jl10 1992Fe07     comportant notamment; des bagues,
                                         bracelets, b> SPOSABELLA CANADA INC.
                                *
XBS;               788284 TMA 473105        9,41,14.Audio apparatus and audio
             Use-1987Se01 1995Jl24 1997Mr19  instruments for receiving, recording,
                                                   am> MATSUSHITA ELECTRIC IN
                                *
J'S ;              825101 TMA 484239   35,25,14,42.Jewellery, including rings,
             Use-1995Se01 1996Oc03 1997Oc17   pendants, bracelets, earrings and
                                              watc>  J'S CONCEPT LIMITED
                                *
J * S;             1073970 TMA 564375                    14.Jewellery.
             Use-2000Fe02 2000Se11 2002Jl05           JEWELSTAR CORPORATION,
                                *
DBS                1082798 TMA 571214                  6,9.Metal wire.
                   2000No15 2002No25              FORT WAYNE METALS RESE
                                *
SAJ                1184673                              14.Jewellery.
             Prop.use  2003Jl14   Formalized        SIGNATURE ACCESSORIES
                                *
JST                1165392                              14.Jewelry.
             Use-1999Se10 2003Ja21   Formalized      SUMIT DIAMOND CORPORAT
                                *
SJL                1141416        14.22 Kt gold jewellery (bangals, rings,
             Prop.use  2002Ma21  Allowed neckless, chains).  ARVINDER SINGH
                                *
SBT;               323504 TMA 168371                14.Jewellery of all kinds.
                   1969Jn20 1970Mr20                 SHAYEN SAHEN TUNTOGLU
                                *

TM Update 2003Oc21 ApplNo 1192300 Filed 2003Se30
```

FIGURE 6.2 CONCLUDED

TERMS AND CONDITIONS

Definitions:
'Customer' refers to a person, firm or other entity who receives a NUANS Report directly or indirectly from HP pursuant to a written agreement with HP, or who relies on such Report without the benefit of any written agreement with HP.

"HP" shall at all times refer to Hewlett-Packard (Canada) Co.

(a)   There are no representations or warranties, expressed or implied, oral or written, in fact or by operation of law or otherwise, except as herein expressly stated. In no event shall HP be liable for any indirect, special or consequential damages for any reason whatsoever including any damages arising out of Customer's access to or use of services, data or reports provided under the Agreement between the Customer and HP, including responsibility or liability resulting from the inaccuracy and/or omissions of NUANS Reports or NUANS Database Pre-Searches.

(b)   HP'S liability for direct damages resulting from HP'S negligence or breach of contract in the execution of services (including delivery of data and reports) under its Agreement with the Customer shall be limited to the total charge for the services giving rise to the loss or damage.

(c)   Where a Customer is required to re-order a NUANS Report because the Customer did not receive the first report or because of a demonstrable omission or inaccuracy therein, HP'S sole liability in the case of non-receipt by Customer shall be to waive all charges with respect thereto, provided that in all such cases HP shall not be liable for any failure in the case of an Act of God, riots, insurrection, or any other event beyond HP'S direct control, and provided in all cases that the Customer provide HP with satisfactory evidence of one of the above-mentioned failures within fifteen (15) days of the alleged date of such failure.

(d)   The Customer agrees to indemnify HP and to hold it harmless from any loss or liability to the Customer, or to any third parties for any injuries or damages not caused by HP'S negligence which result from the Customer's access to or use of any such report or data and operation of any machines in the control of HP, from the Customer's use of HP'S premises or premises which HP is authorized to use, or from any error or inaccuracy in the preparation and formulation of a request for a NUANS Report.

(e)   The Customer acknowledges that HP is subject to certain time and other restrictions in compiling its data base for purposes of delivering a NUANS Report or a NUANS Database Pre-Search and the Customer shall so advise any third party to whom it disseminates such Report or Pre-Search. HP shall not be held liable by the Customer or by any third party for the failure of a NUANS Report or a NUANS Database Pre-Search to disclose any name with prior rights. HP expressly excludes all liability and damages resulting from the inaccuracy or incompleteness of, or omissions from, any NUANS Report.

CONDITIONS GÉNÉRALES

Définitions:
On entend par 'client' une personne, une entreprise ou toute autre entité qui reçoit directement ou indirectement de HP un rapport NUANS en conformité avec une entente écrite avec HP, ou qui compte sur un tel rapport sans avoir conclu d'entente écrite avec HP.

Le terme "HP" fait toujours référence à Hewlett-Packard (Canada) Cie

(a)   Sauf mention contraire dans le présent contrat, HP ne reconnaît aucune représentation ni garantie expresse ou implicite, verbale ou écrite, dans les faits ou par l'effet de la loi ou de toute autre disposition. HP ne peut en aucun cas être tenue responsable de dommages spéciaux, indirects ou accessoires, dont les dommages résultants de l'obtention ou de l'utilisation par le client des données, rapports ou services fournis en vertu des présentes, y compris toute responsabilité découlant d'inexactitudes ou d'omissions dans les rapports NUANS ou dans les rapports de recherche préliminaire NUANS.

(b)   La responsabilité de HP pour tout dommage direct résultant de la négligence de HP ou de la violation du contrat dans l'exécution des services (y compris la fourniture de données et de rapports) en vertu des présentes sera limitée au montant total des frais exigés pour les services qui ont donné lieu à la perte ou au dommage.

(c)   Si le client est obligé de redemander un rapport NUANS parce que HP a omis de produire le premier rapport selon ses obligations, la seule responsabilité de HP consistera à renoncer à tous les frais associés à cette demande, à condition que HP soit exemptée de toute responsabilité si le manquement est dû à un cas de force majeure, à des émeutes, à des insurrections ou à toute autre cause indépendante de la volonté de HP; par ailleurs, le client sera aussi tenu de fournir à HP des pièces justificatives satisfaisantes d'un tel manquement dans un délai de quinze (15) jours suivant la date prétendue de chaque manquement.

(d)   Le Client convient d'indemniser HP et de le dégager de toute responsabilité découlant d'une perte ou d'une obligation pour le client ou une tierce partie en raison de blessures ou de dommages qui ne résultent pas de la négligence de HP, mais plutôt du fait que le client a obtenu et utilisé le rapport ou les données et a fait fonctionné de l'équipement sous le contrôle de HP, qu'il a utilisé les locaux de HP ou des locaux que HP est autorisée à utiliser, ou qu'une erreur ou une inexactitude s'est glissée dans la préparation ou la formulation d'une demande de rapport NUANS.

(e)   Le client reconnaît que HP est soumise à certaines restrictions liées au temps et à d'autres facteurs lorsqu'elle compile sa base de données en vue de produire un rapport NUANS ou un rapport de recherche préliminaire NUANS et il devra donc en prévenir toute tierce partie à qui il transmet le rapport NUANS ou le rapport de recherche préliminaire NUANS. HP ne peut être tenue responsable par le client ou toute tierce partie en cas d'omission de divulgation dans le rapport NUANS ou le rapport de recherche préliminaire NUANS de toute dénomination et remarque de commerce avec droit prioritaire. HP décline expressément toute responsabilité découlant d'inexactitudes ou d'omissions dans le rapport NUANS.

FIGURE 6.3   INDUSTRY CANADA NAME DECISION LETTER

 Industry Canada
Corporations Canada
9th floor
Jean Edmonds Towers South
365 Laurier Avenue West
Ottawa, Ontario K1A 0C8

Industrie Canada
Corporations Canada
9e étage
Tour Jean Edmonds sud
365, avenue Laurier ouest
Ottawa (Ontario) K1A 0C8

03-10-31

Client Number / Numéro de Client
1199

Request Number / Numéro de Demande
1394922

MILLER THOMSON

NAME DECISION   DÉCISION DE LA DÉNOMINATION

With reference to your name request for:
Concernant votre demande de la dénomination:

BSJ GARDEN ORNAMENT SALES INC.

THE PROPOSED NAME IS AVAILABLE
FOR USE AS A CORPORATE NAME

HOWEVER

Such availability is subject to the applicants
assuming full responsibility for any risk of
confusion with existing business names and
trade marks (including those set out in the
relevant NUANS search report(s)).
Acceptance of such responsibility will
comprise an obligation to change the name to a
dissimilar one in the event that representations
are made and established that confusion is
likely to occur. (The use of any name granted
is subject to the laws of the jurisdiction where
the company carries on business.)

Such availability is based on the current
NUANS search report and any other facts
known to Corporations Canada at this time.
New information coming to our attention prior
to or on filing articles could effect this
availability. If any printing or other use of the
name is made before the certificate is issued, it
will be done at the risk of the applicant.

LA DÉNOMINATION PROPOSÉE EST
DISPONIBLE:

CEPENDANT

Telle disponibilité est sujette à ce que les
requérants assument toute responsabilité de
risque de confusion avec toutes dénominations
commerciales, et toutes marques de commerce
existantes (y compris celles qui sont citées dans
le(s) rapport(s) de recherche NUANS
pertinent(s)). Cette acceptation de
responsabilité comprend l'obligation de
changer la dénomination de la société en une
dénomination différente advenant le cas où des
représentations sont faites établissant qu'il
existe une probabilité de confusion.
(L'utilisation de tout nom octroyé est sujette à
toute loi de la juridiction où la société exploite
son entreprise)

Telle disponibilité est basée sur le rapport de
recherche NUANS actuel et des autres faits
connus par Corporations Canada en ce
moment. Il est possible que de nouvelles
informations recueillies, avant ou depuis
l'émission de cette lettre affectent la
disponibilité de la dénomination. Si des
imprimés ou autre usage de la dénomination
sont faits avant l'émission du certificat les
requérants assumeront entièrement ce risque.

FIGURE 6.3 CONTINUED

NOTE:

1) Your NUANS report expires: 2004-01-19

2) The NUANS search report upon which this decision in based has a life of 90 days. The reservation of your name will expire at the end of that period unless, prior to that date, you have been incorporated, or you have requested and received a new name decision on the basis of a new NUANS search report.

3) There is no personalized telephone service on corporate names. Please note that requests for reconsideration of a deficient corporate name must be made in one of the following manners:

a) **Electronic Applications:** Reconsideration of deficient corporate names originally **submitted online with Articles of Incorporation**, as non-pre approved names, **can only be resubmitted online** by selecting the "Articles of Incorporation Resubmission" option from our "Corporations Canada On-line Filing Centre" at: https://strategis.ic.gc.ca/secure/cgi-bin/sc_mrksv/corpdir/corpFiling/main.cgi?lang=e

To access the "Articles of Incorporation Resubmission" login screen, enter the Resubmission Number and the Request Number printed on the first page of the attached **deficiency notice.**

b) **Electronic Applications:** Reconsideration of deficient corporate names originally **submitted online without Articles of Incorporation**, as name pre-approvals, **must be made in writing** and can be sent by fax to area code (613) 941-5782 or toll free at 1-877-568-9922.

c) **Applications submitted by other means:** Any requests for reconsideration of deficient

NOTA:

1) Votre rapport de recherche NUANS échoira le: 2004-01-19

2) La recherche de nom NUANS sur laquelle cette décision est basée n'est valide que pour 90 jours. La réservation de nom expire à la fin de cette période à moins que, dans l'intervalle, vous ne soyez constitué en société ou que vous n'ayez renouvellé votre rapport de recherche et obtenu une nouvelle décision de nom favorable.

3) Nous n'offrons pas de service personnalisé de consultation orale pour les noms corporatifs. Toutes demandes de reconsidération d'une dénomination sociale doivent être soumises de l'une des façons suivantes:

a) **Demandes électroniques:** Les reconsidérations de dénominations sociales **soumises en ligne avec Statuts constitutifs,** avec l'option dénomination non pré-approuvée, **peuvent seulement être resoumises en ligne** en choisissant l'option "Resoumission de Statuts constitutifs" disponible du "Centre de dépôt des formulaires en ligne de Corporations Canada à: https://strategis.ic.gc.ca/secure/cgi-bin/sc_mrksv/corpdir/corpFiling/main.cgi?lang=f

Pour accéder à l'écran "Inscription d'une resoumission", entrer le Numéro de resoumission et le Numéro de demande imprimés sur la première page de l'**avis de défaut** ci-attaché.

b) **Demandes électroniques:** Les reconsidérations de dénominations sociales **soumises en ligne sans Statuts constitutifs,** comme demande de pré-approbation, **doivent être soumises par écrit** et peuvent être envoyées par télécopieur en composant le (613) 941-5782 ou sans frais le 1-877-568-9922.

c) **Autres demandes:** Les reconsidérations de dénominations sociales **non soumises en**

FIGURE 6.3 CONTINUED

corporate names **not submitted online,** with or without Articles of Incorporation, **must be made in writing** and can be sent by fax to area code (613) 941-5782 or toll free at 1-877-568-9922.

ligne, avec ou sans Statuts constitutifs, **doivent être soumises par écrit** et peuvent être envoyées par télécopieur en composant le (613) 941-5782 ou sans frais le 1-877-568-9922.

Alain Gratton
_____
Signature

WE ASK FOR YOU COOPERATION IN QUOTING OUR REQUEST NUMBER, YOUR CLIENT ID AND THE DATE OF THE MOST RECENT DECISION (A COPY OF 1ST PAGE OF THE NAME DECISION (NOT THE FAX SHEET) WOULD BE SUITABLE FOR THIS PURPOSE) IN ANY FUTURE SUBMISSIONS WITH RESPECT TO THE NAME.

NOUS DEMANDONS VOTRE COOPÉRATION EN CITANT NOTRE NUMÉRO DE DEMANDE, VOTRE NUMÉRO DE CLIENT, ET LA DATE D LA DÉCISION LA PLUS RÉCENTE (UNE COPIE DE LA PREMIÈRE PAGE DE LA DÉCISION DE LA DEMANDE (PAS LA PAGE COUVERTURE) SERAIT ACCEPTABLE) DANS DES SOUMISSIONS FUTURES RELATIVEMENT À CETTE DÉNOMINATION SOCIALE.

FIGURE 6.3 CONCLUDED

 Industry Canada
Corporations Directorate
9th floor
Jean Edmonds Towers South
365 Laurier Avenue West
Ottawa, Ontario K1A 0C8

Protecting Your Corporate Name

The granting of a corporate name by the Director under the *Canada Business Corporations Act* (CBCA) generally confers a degree of protection for that corporate name. However, the granting of names under the CBCA does not in itself confer any rights to those names vis-à-vis corporate names or trade names which may have existed at the time of granting but which did not appear on the NUANS search report or which the Director did not, at the time of granting, consider likely to cause confusion. Similarly, the granting of a corporate name may not protect you from earlier or subsequent trade marks of other parties.

The following gives a succinct overview of the relationship between trade name, corporate name and trade mark rights and some general guidance as to how you can best protect your corporate name and the goodwill associated with it.

1.   Before an applicant applies for a corporate name, it is important for him or her to ensure that there are no similar existing corporate names, trade names or trade marks. A NUANS search report, including trade marks which are registered or proposed for registration, is required to be filed with articles of incorporation, amendment, etc. and is usually very reliable. Since, however, the NUANS system is not foolproof, the applicant remains responsible for any likelihood of confusion.

While a name granted by the Director will appear on future NUANS searches required for incorporation in the federal and most provincial jurisdictions, you may wish to conduct your own NUANS searches on a periodic basis after your name has been approved. This would be done in order to ensure, to your own satisfaction, that no confusing corporate or business name has subsequently been approved in the jurisdiction(s) in which you are carrying on business, and to give you up-to-date information about trade marks that have been applied for or registered subsequent to the granting of your corporate name.

2.   Using a corporate name which is similar to a registered trade mark may result in liability for infringement of the registered trade mark, even if the trade mark was registered after the corporate name was granted. This is so because, under trade marks law, the holder of a corporate name bears the responsibility for ensuring that no new trade marks are registered which are confusing with that name. Information on registered and advertised trade marks can be obtained from the *Trade Marks Journal*, distributed weekly by Public Works and Government Services Canada* or by conducting a search of one of the various electronic trade mark databases.** The holder of a corporate name has the right, in certain circumstances, to oppose the registration of a trade mark or to have a trade mark registration expunged.

3.   Registration of a trade mark is the best way to obtain the exclusive right to use the mark in all of Canada in association with the wares and services for which the registration is obtained. While the Trade Marks Office** can provide basic guidance, it is recommended that a specialist (a trade mark agent or trade mark lawyer) be consulted. It should be noted that trade mark registration is not available for corporate names in all circumstances.

*   Canada Communications Group - Publishing
Supply and Services Canada
45 Sacré-Coeur Blvd.
Hull QC K1A 0S9
Tel.: 1-800-567-4422

**   Trade Marks Office
Industry Canada
Phase I, Place du Portage
Hull QC K1A 0C9
Tel.: (819) 953-8098 (re: on-line databases)
Tel.: (819) 997-1420 (re: general inquiries)

CHAPTER 7

The formation of corporations

CHAPTER OVERVIEW

This chapter describes the various issues a lawyer will consider when advising a client whether and in which jurisdiction to incorporate. It explains how to complete the documents for making an application for incorporation and outlines the various methods of filing the articles of incorporation to receive the certificate of incorporation.

CHAPTER OBJECTIVES

After completing this chapter, you should be able to:

1. Recognize the issues concerning incorporation.

2. Compare the criteria of carrying on business in partnership and carrying on business through a corporation.

3. Identify the major characteristics of the various jurisdictions in Canada that may be relevant to determine where to incorporate.

4. Complete documents to incorporate a corporation under the CBCA and OBCA.

5. Explain the procedures for filing the articles of incorporation under the CBCA and the OBCA.

INTRODUCTION

Chapter 3 described the fundamental concepts of corporations and examined some of the advantages of carrying on business using a corporation. This information will be put into practice when a client comes to a lawyer for advice on starting up a business. Typically, the client will have an initial meeting with a lawyer who will discuss a number of issues, including those contained in this chapter. If the client decides to incorporate, the lawyer will often instruct a law clerk in the preparation of the documents to complete the incorporation. It is important, however, for the law clerk to have a solid understanding of the issues to ensure that the resulting articles contain the appropriate information and to provide backup to the client if the lawyer is inaccessible.

THE ISSUES SURROUNDING INCORPORATION

The following are some of the issues a lawyer may discuss with a client in the process of deciding whether to incorporate.

Is incorporation legally possible?

If the business to be carried on is the practice of a profession that is governed by a statute, a corporation may practise the profession only if the governing statute expressly permits such practice — for example, the Law Society of Upper Canada has granted permission for a solicitor to use a limited liability corporation.

Taxation

Probably the next most important incorporation issue is that of taxation. It is not unusual for a lawyer to refer the client to the client's accountant, or at least communicate with the client's accountant, who may have more in-depth knowledge of the client's financial affairs. Here are some points to consider when deciding whether incorporation is the best decision from a tax perspective:

1. Income or loss in a partnership is determined at the partnership level but taxed at the individual level. In a corporation, income or loss is determined and taxed at the corporate level. Because a corporation is a "separate legal entity," it files a federal and provincial tax return in its own name.

2. A corporation pays the maximum rate of tax on every dollar of taxable income. An individual pays tax based on a progressive scale.

3. A corporation can provide tax flexibility because the individual is not required to pay tax until the money is taken out of the corporation in the form of salary, dividend, or bonus. Other methods are also available for taking income out of the corporation, such as redemption and retraction of shares.

4. The $500,000 lifetime capital gains exemption under the *Income Tax Act* is applicable to individuals selling shares in a Canadian-controlled private corporation (CCPC) but not to corporations holding such shares. If, therefore, a shareholder sells his or her shares in a CCPC, he or she will be exempt from capital gains realized on the sale for up to $500,000.

5. If a CCPC carries on business in Canada throughout the taxation year, and earns active business income qualifying for the small business deduction, the combined tax rate on the first $225,000 of active business income is reduced. This limit increases to $250,000 in 2004, $275,000 in 2005, and $300,000 thereafter.

6. Other tax breaks may be available to a corporation through the *Corporations Tax Act* (Ontario).

7. If the corporation incurs a non-capital loss in its early years of existence, that loss may be deducted against profits made in the past three years, in the current year, or in the next seven years. A capital loss, on the other hand, can be deducted from capital gains realized in the past three years and in all future years.

Limits on an investor's liability

As mentioned in chapter 3, a corporation is a legal entity separate and apart from its shareholders. It is the corporation that owns and operates the business, incurs the liabilities, and makes a profit or incurs a loss. The shareholder may be considered an "investor" in the corporation and, as such, only risks the value of his or her investment. In a partnership or sole proprietorship, each partner is a co-owner of the partnership assets and is, therefore, liable to the full extent of the assets for the liabilities of the business. If the proposed business involves a lot of risk, it may be better to incorporate.

Principals involved in the business

NUMBER

Each partner in a partnership is responsible for the acts of the other partners. If a large number of individuals are to be involved in the ownership of a business, it may be better to incorporate rather than carry on business in partnership.

EASE OF INTEREST TRANSFER

It is generally easier to transfer a share in a corporation than to execute a new partnership agreement, or amend an existing agreement, every time a partner is replaced.

RELATIONSHIP OF PROPOSED PRINCIPALS

The degree to which the principals are actively involved in running the business also makes a difference. Principals who are to be actively involved in the business may wish to hold common shares and have the right to vote on certain important matters, while other shareholders may not wish to be involved in the running of the business and may choose to hold special shares. So, if there are differences in the levels of risk that shareholders are to be exposed to, a limited partnership or corporation may be the best business vehicle to use. One partner can bind the partnership but one shareholder cannot bind a corporation without authority from the board of directors.

Raising capital

Corporations often raise capital by selling shares. This form of investment may be perceived as more prestigious to potential investors than issuing "units" in a partnership or a limited partnership.

Perpetual existence

Unless there are provisions to the contrary in a partnership agreement, death or a dispute resulting in the dissolution of a partnership and the formation of a new partnership will result in renegotiation of contracts, filing notices, entering into new agreements, and providing new bank signing authorities. A corporation continues notwithstanding the death of a shareholder or director. However, if the venture is for a single purpose, a partnership may be more easily formed and dissolved than a corporation.

Flexibility of structure

Although corporations are governed by the corporate statute in the jurisdiction in which they are formed, provisions may be inserted in the articles or in a unanimous shareholder agreement to provide considerable flexibility for relationships between shareholders.

Estate planning

Consideration should also be given to the other assets owned by the principals of a business and the long-range planning for the disposition of these assets. For example, a common objective of incorporation is to set up a business that will provide financial benefit to members of the principal's family while retaining the business under the control and direction of the principal. It is possible to structure the corporation so that the equity growth will be owned by successive generations.

Business name protection

Both the CBCA and the OBCA provide that a corporation may not be incorporated using a name that will be confusing with that of an existing corporation.

Value of goodwill

A corporation, being a separate entity from an individual, can build up an asset in the form of "goodwill."

Statutory framework

The corporate statute that governs the corporation will provide standardized guidelines for the manner in which the corporation conducts its affairs.

Costs to establish and operate corporations and partnerships

Table 7.1 illustrates the relative government filing fees for corporations, partnerships, and sole proprietorships.

Other costs to consider include legal fees for incorporation and organization, and maintaining the corporation; legal fees for preparing partnership agreements; and accounting fees for performing a corporate audit.

TABLE 7.1   FILING FEES

Entity	Initial registration		Annual filing fees	
	Paper filing	Electronic filing	Paper filing	Electronic filing
	dollars			
Corporation — federal	250	200	40	20
Corporation — Ontario	360	300*	nil	nil*
General partnership — Ontario	80	60	nil**	nil
Limited partnership — Ontario	210	n/a	nil**	nil
Sole proprietorship — Ontario	80	60	nil**	nil

   * Service provider charges administrative fee for electronic filing.

** Renewal required every five years.

CONSIDERING THE LEGAL JURISDICTION OF A CORPORATION

After the decision to incorporate is made, the next decision is in which jurisdiction to incorporate. It used to be that in Ontario, one simply chose between becoming a federal or an Ontario corporation. This choice has been complicated by the developing competition between the various jurisdictions in Canada. Technology has also assisted this development, because it is now possible to make records available at a registered or head office electronically. Most often lawyers will choose to incorporate in the province in which the principals of the corporation are resident, presuming that is the province in which the law firm will be able to give legal opinions. If your client incorporates in another jurisdiction, you may be required to retain counsel in that jurisdiction, which may increase your client's costs. Nonetheless, to offer the best corporate advice to their client, lawyers (and law clerks) must be aware of the provisions for incorporating in different provinces.

There may be compelling startup and spinoff reasons why corporations will shop for jurisdictions. Considerations will include tax treatment, securities, or corporate governance issues. Corporations go jurisdiction shopping not only in Canada but offshore as well.

The following are some highlights of provisions in the corporate statutes in jurisdictions in Canada that may be attractive in different circumstances.

Federal incorporation

NAME

Unlike the case in Ontario, a business incorporating federally must receive approval of its name from Corporations Canada before incorporating. This requirement provides greater name protection than that offered by most provinces.

CARRYING ON BUSINESS

A federal corporation has the right to carry on business across Canada with the assurance of being able to operate under its own name. Despite this right, federal corporations are subject to the same extra-provincial registration requirements as Ontario corporations.

PRESTIGE

If your client is going to carry on business outside Canada, it may be more "prestigious" to do this using a federal corporation.

DIRECTORS' RESIDENCY

The residency requirements of the CBCA are less onerous than those of the OBCA. At least 25 percent of the directors of a CBCA corporation must be resident Canadians; if it has fewer than four directors, at least one director must be a resident Canadian. An Ontario corporation must have a majority of resident Canadian directors; if it has two directors, one director must be a resident Canadian.

FINANCIAL ASSISTANCE RULES

Unlike the OBCA, the CBCA has no restrictions on or requirements to notify shareholders regarding the lending of money or giving a guarantee or other forms of financial assistance.

FINANCIAL DISCLOSURE

A corporation that does not offer securities to the public may resolve not to appoint an auditor.

ELECTRONIC MEETINGS

If it chooses to do so, a federal corporation may now hold meetings entirely by electronic means. Shareholders and directors can participate in meetings and vote electronically. Only directors, not shareholders, may hold electronic meetings in Ontario corporations.

Nova Scotia unlimited liability companies (NSULC)[1]

The provision for "unlimited liability companies" has been available in Nova Scotia since 1900 but it has been widely used only since 1992. The so called check-the-box rules implemented by the Internal Revenue Service in the United States on January 1, 1997 clarified the availability of these entities as flowthrough vehicles of US investors in Canada and greatly increased their popularity. These rules provide that "any Canadian corporation or company formed under any federal or provincial law which provides that the liability of all of the members of such corporation or company will be unlimited" can qualify for partnership (branch) status. These companies are therefore often attractive to Canadian subsidiaries of US-based corporations, particularly when the Canadian company is in a loss situation, because that loss flows to the US-based corporation.

Shareholders (or members) of an NSULC have unlimited joint and several liability for the obligations of the company upon its dissolution. Before becoming a shareholder or member of an NSULC, a person or company should consider the degree to which it is exposed to liability and whether this exposure can somehow be reduced by using an intervening limited liability entity. The shareholders of an unlimited liability company have no direct liability to creditors or other obligors of the company. The responsibility of these shareholders arises only when the entity is liquidated with insufficient assets to satisfy its obligations.

An added attraction of NSULCs — and indeed all companies incorporated in Nova Scotia — is that there are no Canadian residency requirements for directors.

New Brunswick corporations

New Brunswick has often been considered by the legal profession as the "Delaware of Canada." The state of Delaware in the United States is known to have one of the most flexible corporate statutes in the United States. New Brunswick has this reputation in part because of its liberal residency laws. Both federal and Ontario corporations are required to have a certain percentage of resident Canadian directors. This requirement can be especially onerous for foreign subsidiaries. Consider, for example, a US corporation that is coming into Canada to distribute its products on a multilevel marketing basis. For tax purposes, it decides to set up an Ontario corporation, which must have a Canadian-resident director. Often, a client just starting up a business in Canada will not know anyone suitable to be a director or someone who is willing to be subject to the liabilities of being a director.

There is no requirement under the New Brunswick *Business Corporations Act* (NBBCA) to have any resident Canadian directors. Some well-known US companies such as Wal-Mart Canada Inc. have chosen to incorporate a Canadian subsidiary under the NBBCA.

Other attractive provisions under the NBBCA include the ability to opt out of the related-party financial assistance provisions by inserting appropriate language in the articles as well as the fact that there is no statutory liability imposed on directors for unpaid employee wages or vacation pay that becomes payable while they are directors. Note, however, that provincial employee standards legislation may provide for such a liability in other provinces including Ontario.

Other jurisdictions that do not require resident Canadian directors are British Columbia (as of March 29, 2004), Nova Scotia, Quebec, Yukon, and Prince Edward Island.

Alberta corporations

The Alberta *Business Corporations Act* has an interesting provision, which may make it an appealing jurisdiction in which to incorporate. A corporation governed by this statute is able to amalgamate with an extra-provincial corporation if one of the amalgamating corporations is the wholly owned subsidiary of the other, provided that the extra-provincial statute also permits the amalgamation. The amalgamated corporation becomes subject to the laws of Alberta. This same provision is also available in the Northwest Territories.

Table 7.2 compares some of the important issues to consider when deciding on the jurisdiction in which to incorporate.

Despite the varying provisions across Canada, the statute of choice in Ontario still remains the CBCA or the OBCA. According to Wayne Gray, a partner with the law firm of McMillan Binch LLP, an Ontario lawyer is likely to consider a provincial statute outside Ontario only in three situations:

- if residency is an issue, lawyers might consider British Columbia, New Brunswick, Nova Scotia, or any of the territories, none of which impose any resident Canadian requirements on the board;

- if flowthrough tax treatment for US investors is attractive, an NSULC is the only option; and

- where, for tax reasons, it is necessary to have a subsidiary acquire and hold shares in the parent corporation, the provisions of the statutes in British Columbia and Nova Scotia are more permissive than the CBCA or the OBCA.

PREPARATION OF DOCUMENTS FOR FILING ARTICLES OF INCORPORATION

Incorporation under the CBCA and the OBCA is a matter of right provided that the incorporator delivers the prescribed documents completed with the information required. Neither Corporations Canada nor Ontario Companies Branch personnel review the contents of the articles; they will be interested only in ensuring that the forms are complete and correctly signed. The onus is on the incorporator to ensure that the contents are correct.

Form of documents

To incorporate a corporation under the CBCA or the OBCA, one or more incorporators must complete and file articles of incorporation with the Director of the respective statute. An incorporator must be at least 18 years of age, not of unsound mind as found by a court in Canada or elsewhere, and not a bankrupt. An incorporator may also be a corporation.

For a CBCA corporation, the federal Director fixes the form and contents of the articles as set out in s. 6. The Strategis Web site provides information on how to complete the form.

The articles for an OBCA corporation must be in the form prescribed by the regulations to the OBCA. O. reg. 289/00 has strict document requirements including paper size, numbering of pages, and quality of paper.

Contents of articles

The contents of the articles are similar under both statutes with some exceptions:

1. The names and addresses of the directors and the address for the registered office are set out in the OBCA articles. The CBCA requires this information to be set out in separate forms — namely, Form 3, Notice of Registered Office and Form 6, Notice of Directors.

2. The address for the directors of a CBCA corporation is the residence address, but the address for Ontario directors is an address for service.

TABLE 7.2   A COMPARISON OF INCORPORATION PROVISIONS ACROSS CANADA

Juris-diction	Residency requirements	Restriction on intercorporate shareholdings	Financial assistance restrictions	Proxy solicitation	Directors' liability for unpaid wages and vacation pay
Canada	Yes for directors but none for board committees	Limited circumstances in which corporation may hold shares in itself or a holding company	None	Yes, if number of shareholders is 50 or more unless exemption	Yes — up to 6 months of unpaid wages and order obtained vacation pay
BC	No	None	Limited disclosure requirements in the company's records	Limited rules for pre-existing reporting companies	None — except note that where employees report for work in BC, there is a liability under the employment standards legislation
Alta.	Yes — requires 50% resident directors (except where corporation earns less than 5% of its revenue within Canada)	Limited circumstances in which corporation may hold shares in itself or a holding company	Disclosure to shareholders required	Yes	No liability for vacation pay but liability for 6 months' wages
Sask.	Yes (except where corporation earns less than 5% of its revenue within Canada)	Limited circumstances in which corporation or subsidiary may hold shares in itself or a holding company	Disclosure to shareholders required	Yes, if number of shareholders is more than 15 (two or more joint holders being counted as one) unless exemption order is obtained	Yes — liability to employees for all wages while they were directors
Man.	Yes	Yes — limited circumstances in which corporation may hold shares in itself or a holding company	Yes	Yes, if number of shareholders is 15 or more unless exemption order obtained	Up to 6 months of unpaid wages for each employee
Ont.	Majority of Canadian residents; only 1 required when there are 2 directors	Yes — limited circumstances in which company may hold shares in itself or a holding company	Post-transaction disclosure to shareholders	Reporting issuers only	Up to 6 months of unpaid wages and up to 12 months of unpaid vacation pay
Que.	No	Yes — however, only if holding as a mandatory, hypothecary, creditor, or administrator of property of another person	Limited circumstances in which financial assistance may be given	None	Up to 6 months of unpaid wages

TABLE 7.2 CONCLUDED

Juris-diction	Residency requirements	Restriction on intercorporate shareholdings	Financial assistance restrictions	Proxy solicitation	Directors' liability for unpaid wages and vacation pay
NB	None	Yes — limited circumstances in which corporation may hold its own shares	Can opt out of related-party provisions but not for share purchase	None	None
NS	None	None	None	None	None
PEI	None	None	Specific circumstances under which a loan or guarantee is permitted	None	None
NL	Yes — except where corporation earns less than 5% of its revenue within Canada	Yes — limited circumstances in which corporation may hold its own shares	Specific circumstances under which a loan or guarantee is permitted	Yes	None
YT	None	Yes — limited circumstances in which corporation may hold its own shares	Yes	Mandatory solicitation of proxies if there are more than 15 shareholders unless waived by all shareholders entitled to vote at a meeting of shareholders	Yes — under the *Labour Standards Act* including wages, holiday pay, and pay in lieu of notice
NWT	None	Limited circumstances in which corporation or subsidiary may hold shares in itself or a holding company	Specific circumstances under which a loan or guarantee is permitted, and information regarding financial assistance must be included in financial statement	Mandatory solicitation of proxies if there are more than 15 shareholders unless waived by all shareholders entitled to vote at a meeting of shareholders	Yes — up to 6 months of unpaid wages
NU	None	Limited circumstances in which corporation may hold shares in itself or a holding company	Specific circumstances under which a loan or guarantee is permitted, and information regarding financial assistance must be included in financial statement	Mandatory solicitation of proxies if there are more than 15 shareholders unless waived by all shareholders entitled to vote at a meeting of shareholders	Yes — up to 6 months of unpaid wages

3. A CBCA corporation must have a registered office in a "place" within Canada. An Ontario corporation must have a registered office address in Ontario. The Ontario ministry will not accept a post office box as the address but will accept a street and number or an RR number, municipality, and postal code.

The following is a description of the information that must appear in the articles of incorporation. It is presented in the order in which the information appears in s. 6 of the CBCA, but the same information is required for articles to be filed under the OBCA:

1. The name of the corporation. This must comply with the name requirements set out in the relevant statute. A French version of the name must be added if the corporation intends to carry on business in Quebec. For a review of the name provisions, see chapter 6.

2. For a CBCA corporation, the articles should indicate the province in Canada where the registered office is to be situated. For an Ontario corporation, the articles must provide the address of the registered office address in Ontario, which should state the street and number or RR number. If the address is a multi-office building, the articles must also provide the suite number, the name of the municipality or post office, and the postal code.

3. The classes and any maximum number of shares that the corporation is authorized to issue and the conditions attaching to each class of shares. For a review on selecting the appropriate share structure for the corporation, see chapter 5.

4. Restrictions, if any, on share transfers. You must provide the restrictions, if any, on the issue, transfer, or ownership of shares (CBCA s. 6(1)(d); OBCA s. 42(1)). It is quite common for corporations with a small number of shareholders to provide for a restriction on the transfer of shares to ensure that control of the corporation is restricted. A common share transfer provision will require the approval of a majority of the voting shareholders or the directors. There may be further provisions with regard to the transfer of shares in a unanimous shareholder agreement (see chapter 8).

5. The number of directors, or the minimum and maximum number of directors of the corporation. The provisions that relate to directors are discussed in chapter 4.

6. Any restrictions on the business that the corporation may carry on. Both the CBCA and the OBCA provide that a corporation has all the powers and privileges of a natural person and, generally, there will be no restrictions on the proposed corporation's business or powers. However, there are certain circumstances when it may be necessary or desirable to include a restriction on the business, either for tax purposes or because some other body governing the business of the corporation so requires. For example, a professional corporation incorporated by a lawyer to practise law is governed by the Law Society of Upper Canada and the business must be restricted to providing legal services.

7. Any additional provisions permitted by the relevant statute or bylaw to be set out in the bylaws of the corporation. Both the CBCA and the OBCA allow for

any provision permitted by the statute or permitted by law to be included in the articles. The more common provisions included are:

a. A statement regarding the corporation being a closely held issuer.

b. A provision for the corporation to have a lien on the shares of a shareholder who is indebted to the corporation.

c. In the articles of a CBCA corporation, you may wish to provide a mechanism for fixing the number of directors within the minimum and maximum number. As well, it may be useful to authorize the directors of the corporation between annual meetings of shareholders to appoint one or more additional directors to serve until the next annual meeting. If this provision is included, it should also provide that the number of additional directors may not at any time exceed one-third of the number of directors who held office at the expiration of the last annual meeting. The total number of directors of the corporation after any such appointment may not exceed the maximum number of directors permitted by the articles. Section 106(8) of the CBCA permits this only if the articles so provide.

d. Pre-emptive rights of shareholders (discussed in chapter 5).

e. Cumulative voting (discussed in chapter 5).

f. Election of directors for staggered terms.

g. Election and retirement of directors in rotation.

h. The use of a foreign version of a corporate name outside Canada (CBCA).

i. Use of the corporate name in any language (OBCA).

Special approvals required for incorporation

Certain applications for incorporation may require pre-approval by a regulating body before filing to ensure that a licence will be issued by that body. For example, real estate brokers must be pre-approved by the registrar of real estate brokers and business brokers and insurance agents must be pre-approved by the superintendent of insurance.

There may also be other statutory requirements that corporations must meet. Some examples include:

- an engineering company must obtain written consent to the use of the word "engineer," "engineering," and the French equivalents or any variation of it from the Association of Professional Engineers of Ontario; and

- a firm practising architecture must obtain the written consent of the Council of the Ontario Association of Architects to the use of the word "architect," "architectural," and the French equivalents or any variation of it.

Procedures for filing articles of incorporation

The filing procedures for federal and Ontario corporations vary slightly and are outlined below.

FEDERAL CORPORATIONS

The documents required to be filed to incorporate a corporation under the CBCA are:

- articles of incorporation (Form 1), in duplicate bearing an original signature of the incorporator;

- notice of registered office (Form 3), in duplicate, bearing the original signature of the incorporator;

- notice of directors (Form 6), in duplicate, bearing the original signature of the incorporator;

- except where you are requesting a number name, a federal-biased NUANS report dated not more than 90 days before the date on which the articles are submitted;

- name decision letter, if obtained (if you have not requested this, the name will be reviewed when the application is submitted, which may delay the issuance of the certificate of incorporation, especially if there is any concern about the name);

- any consents to the use of the name; and

- a cheque payable to the receiver general for Canada.

The forms used for incorporating are available from the administrative forms section of the Strategis Web site. It is not mandatory to use the forms provided, but if you choose not to, you must ensure that all the required information is provided and on 8½ × 11-inch paper.

The above documents may be filed with Corporations Canada by any of four different methods:

1. *Electronically* — if you have a major credit card, you may complete and file articles by going to the Electronic Filing Centre on the Strategis Web site. This service is available 7 days a week, 24 hours a day. You will receive immediate acknowledgment of filing and the certificate of incorporation will be e-mailed to you either the same day or the following day depending on the time of filing and the complexity of the application. Generally, documents submitted before 1 p.m. (EST) on any business day should be processed on the same day by 5 p.m. (EST). If documents are filed electronically, no signature is required, but a copy of the articles as filed should be signed by the incorporator and maintained with the records of the corporation.

   The Ontario Companies Branch service providers Cyberbahn Inc. and Oncorp Direct Inc. also offer electronic filing of federal articles of incorporation at an additional cost.

2. *By fax* — you can fax the above documents to 613-941-0999. These will be processed and the certificate of incorporation with be faxed back to you within three days. An originally signed copy of the articles should be maintained with the records of the corporation.

3. By mail or delivery to one of Corporations Canada's regional offices. The addresses of these offices are on the Strategis Web site. The certificate of incorporation will be mailed back to you within two to three weeks.

4. In person, by delivering the documents to the counter at 9th floor, Jean Edmonds Tower South, 365 Laurier Avenue West, Ottawa, Ontario K1A 0C8. The certificate of incorporation will be available within one hour (subject to longer procedural time at Christmas and New Year), if delivered between 8:30 a.m. and 2:30 p.m.

A federal corporation may also pre-reserve a block of number names.

ONTARIO CORPORATIONS

The documents required to incorporate an Ontario corporation are:

- articles of incorporation, in duplicate, bearing the original signature(s) of the incorporator(s) on both copies;

- unless a number name is requested, an original Ontario-biased computer-printed search report from the NUANS system maintained by Industry Canada dated not more than 90 days before the submission of the articles;

- any consents to the use of the name;

- consent to act as a first director for any director who is not an incorporator (instead of delivering this document to the Ontario Director, it must be kept at the registered office address; upon request and without charge, a director, shareholder, or creditor is permitted by the corporation to inspect such consent during the normal business hours of the corporation and to make a copy);

- cheque payable to the Minister of Finance, Ontario, if filed by hard copy; and

- cover letter to ministry, if filed by hard copy.

There are two methods of filing articles of incorporation for Ontario incorporations:

1. *Electronically* — The Ontario Companies Branch has two service providers, Cyberbahn Inc. and Oncorp Direct Inc. To file electronically, you must have opened an account with one of these intermediaries. Upon filing electronically, you will immediately be able to print the certificate of incorporation together with a copy of the electronic terms and conditions, to which the incorporator or a person authorized by the incorporator must agree. It is good practice to receive a signed copy of the electronic terms and conditions to be kept in your file to evidence approval by the client or lawyer acting on behalf of a client. When filing electronically, you are required to provide the NUANS report reference number, the date of the report, and the proposed name searched, and not the report itself. You must keep a paper or electronic copy of the NUANS report and of any consent or consent and undertaking required under the OBCA.

2. *Paper copy* — By delivering hard copies of the documents directly to the Ontario ministry's office in Toronto or to one of the regional offices listed on the ministry's Web site either in person or by mail. If you deliver articles of incorporation to

the ministry in person, you will receive the certificate of incorporation immediately. If the articles of incorporation are mailed to the ministry, the certificate of incorporation will be mailed to you within two to four weeks.

Cost of filing

The ministry's fees for filing articles are subject to change at any time, but at the time of printing they were as follows:

	Electronic filing	Paper filing
Canada	$200	$250
Ontario	$300 plus the service provider's fee	$360

Electronic filings

Because no signatures are required on documents filed electronically, it is good practice to adopt the habit of having your client sign off on the articles and other documents for filing and to keep this signed copy in the minute book.

Endorsing articles

The certificate of incorporation issued by the Director under the CBCA or the OBCA is conclusive proof that the corporation has been incorporated under the respective statutes on the date set out in the certificate with the exception of any proceedings to cancel the certificate for cause.

If a particular date is required for incorporation, this can be requested but cannot be more than 30 days subsequent to the date of delivery of the articles. You must emphasize the date requested either by using bold or highlighted letters in your cover letter if the documents are being submitted to Ontario Companies Branch or verbally if the documents are being filed in person.

Issuance of corporation number

The federal Director or the Ontario Director assigns every corporation a number, referred to as the "corporation number." If the Director endorses a certificate and sets out this number incorrectly, the Director can substitute a corrected certificate that bears the date of the certificate it replaces. This number should be used in all correspondence with the relevant government departments.

REFERENCES

Business Corporations Act (Alberta), RSA 2000, c. B-9, as amended.

Business Corporations Act (New Brunswick) (NBBCA), SNB 1981, c. B-9.1.

Business Corporations Act (Ontario) (OBCA), RSO 1990, c. B.16, as amended, part II — Incorporation.

Canada Business Corporations Act (CBCA), RSC 1985, c. C-44, as amended, part II — Incorporation.

Flaherty, Eamonn J., *Key Legal Issues in the Creation and Development of a Small Enterprise* (Toronto: Miller Thomson LLP, July 10, 2001).

Gray, Wayne D., *Shopping for That Perfect Corporate Statute* (Toronto: McMillan Binch, May 2000).

Industry Canada, Corporations Canada, *Canada Business Corporations Act Incorporation Kit* (Ottawa: Industry Canada, April 1, 2001).

Latreille, Marie-Andrée, Goodman Phillips & Vineberg, *The Annual Congress Collection of the Bar of Quebec*, 1998 Permanent Training Service of the Bar of Quebec, at 155ff.

Law Society of Upper Canada, *Methods of Carrying On Business*, Bar Admission Course Materials, phase 3 (Toronto: LSUC, September 2000).

Ontario Ministry of Consumer and Business Services, Companies Branch, Information Sheet [BC-8] — Incorporation (Business Corporations), April 3, 2000.

Reagh, Charles, *Introduction to the Nova Scotia Companies Act*, Corporate Brief number 49 (Toronto: CCH Canadian Limited, September 1998).

FORMS AND PRECEDENTS

Figure 7.1: Certificate and articles of incorporation (CBCA Form 1)

Figure 7.2: Notice of registered office (CBCA Form 3)

Figure 7.3: Notice of directors (CBCA Form 6)

Figure 7.4: Articles of incorporation (OBCA Form 1)

Figure 7.5: Consent to act as a first director (OBCA Form 2)

NOTE

1. The author thanks Charles Reagh of Stewart, McKelvey, Stirling & Scales, Halifax, Nova Scotia for the information contained in this section.

REVIEW QUESTIONS

1. List three reasons to incorporate as opposed to doing business in partnership.

2. List three reasons to incorporate under the CBCA.

3. What is an NSULC? When would you likely use one?

4. List the incorporation documents required to be filed:

    a. in Canada

    b. in Ontario

5. Which of the following jurisdictions do not have any residency requirements for directors?

    a. Canada

    b. Ontario

    c. New Brunswick

    d. Quebec

    e. Nova Scotia

    f. British Columbia

6. Does the Director under either the CBCA or the OBCA have the right to refuse incorporation? If so, describe the circumstances when this might occur.

7. Your client has signed the articles of incorporation and returned them to you for filing. It's December 1 and you have a NUANS report dated August 7. Will the NUANS report be accepted by the ministry? Explain.

8. Prepare a questionnaire for incorporation to send to the client for completion and return to you. This should include a request for all the information you will need to file the articles of incorporation and indicate any special information the client may need to know in order to answer your questions.

9. You have been instructed to prepare articles of incorporation for a new federal corporation — "Ariel Sunshine Publications Inc." The client, Ariel Sunshine, will be the first director and incorporator. Her address is 79 Lakeside Drive, Craigleith, Ontario. The registered office will be the client's residence address. There will be one class of shares. Prepare the necessary documents and all covering letters to incorporate this venture as a federal corporation. State any assumptions you have made.

CASE STUDIES

Case study 7.1: Federal incorporation

Peter Black and his two friends Shirley Smith and Roger Jones contacted the law firm of Thorn & Hill to incorporate a federal company for their new business venture of selling garden ornaments to the public across Canada. Mr. Thorn, the senior partner, instructed his corporate law clerk, Jessie, to prepare the necessary documents.

Mr. Thorn and Jessie met with Mr. Black to obtain the necessary information and to explain the process of incorporation to him. During the meeting, Jessie completed her firm's incorporation questionnaire.

Mr. Black suggested the name "Black, Smith and Jones Inc." Jessie told him that this name did not comply with the regulations under the CBCA because the name consisted only of surnames. She suggested that he use a name that described the business but also had a unique identifier to distinguish the name from any other name. After consultation with his partners, Mr. Black decided to use the name "BSJ Garden Ornament Sales Inc." Jessie obtained and reviewed the federal-biased NUANS report and confirmed that the name did not appear to be similar to any other names on the report. She told Mr. Black that the NUANS reports can contain errors, and that if anyone complained to the Director under the CBCA that the name was similar to their name, the Director could require Mr. Black to change the name. Jessie then submitted the NUANS report and the form to request a name decision to Corporations Canada by facsimile. Within 24 hours, she received a response indicating that the name was available. For a copy of the form requesting the name decision, the federal-biased NUANS report, and the name decision letter, see figures 6.1, 6.2, and 6.3 at the end of chapter 6.

Since Ms Smith's father intended to lend money to the new corporation, it was decided to incorporate with two classes of shares: preferred shares and common shares. The three owners (Black, Smith, and Jones) will each receive an equal number of common shares, while Ms Smith's father will receive non-voting preferred shares with the right to receive dividends.

Mr. Black indicated that Ms Smith, Mr. Jones, and he will be the directors, but that he alone would be the incorporator. The registered office address will be the new office address for the corporation.

See figures 7.1, 7.2, and 7.3 at the end of this chapter. The documents are prepared on the basis of the amended and restated Rule 45-501, effective January 12, 2004.

Case study 7.2: Ontario incorporation

Jessie received instructions from Mr. Hill to incorporate an Ontario corporation for a long-time client of the firm who wanted to establish a holding corporation to buy another piece of property. The client was David Green. Mr. Green would be the incorporator and Mr. and Mrs. Green would be the directors and officers. Only one class of shares was required and Mr. Green would own all the shares. Mr. Green was happy to use a number name corporation. The year-end would be April 1. The corporation would not appoint an auditor but the accountants would be ABC Accounting LLP and the bank would be the Royal Bank. Either one of Mr. and Mrs. Green would have signing authority for cheques and contracts.

See figures 7.4 and 7.5 at the end of this chapter.

FIGURE 7.1   CERTIFICATE AND ARTICLES OF INCORPORATION (CBCA FORM 1)

 Industry Canada   Industrie Canada

Certificate   **Certificat**
of Incorporation   **de constitution**

Canada Business   **Loi canadienne sur**
Corporations Act   **les sociétés par actions**

Name of corporation-Dénomination de la société   Corporation number-Numéro de la société

I hereby certify that the above-named   Je certifie que la société susmentionnée, dont
corporation, the articles of incorporation of   les statuts constitutifs sont joints, a été
which are attached, was incorporated under   constituée en société en vertu de la
the *Canada Business Corporations Act*.   *Loi canadienne sur les sociétés par actions*.

Director - Directeur   Date of Incorporation - Date de constitution

Canada

FIGURE 7.1 CONTINUED

I◆I Industry Canada	Industrie Canada	**FORM I** **ARTICLES OF INCORPORATION** **(SECTION 6)**	**FORMULAIRE I** **STATUTS CONSTITUTIFS** **(ARTICLE 6)**
Canada Business Corporations Act	Loi canadienne sur les sociétés par actions		

1 -- Name of the Corporation   Dénomination sociale de la société

BSJ Garden Ornament Sales Inc.

2 -- The province or territory in Canada where the registered office is situated   La province ou le territoire au Canada où est situé le siège social

Province of Ontario

3 -- The classes and any maximum number of shares that the corporation is authorized to issue   Catégories et le nombre maximal d'actions que la société est autorisée à émettre

The annexed Schedule A is incorporated in this form.

4 -- Restrictions, if any, on share transfers   Restrictions sur le transfert des actions, s'il y a lieu

The annexed Schedule B is incorporated in this form.

5 -- Number (or minimum and maximum number) of directors   Nombre (ou nombre minimal et maximal) d'administrateurs

A minimum of one and a maximum of 10 directors.

6 -- Restrictions, if any, on the business the corporation may carry on   Limites imposées à l'activité commerciale de la société, s'il y a lieu

There are no restrictions.

7 -- Other provisions, if any   Autres dispositions, s'il y a lieu

The annexed Schedule C is incorporated in this form.

8 -- Incorporators - Fondateurs

Name(s) - Nom(s)	Address (including postal code) Adresse (inclure le code postal)	Signature	Tel. No. - N° de tél.
Peter Black	123 Sesame Street, Port Ellen, ON L3R 0C9		541-321-3333

FOR DEPARTMENTAL USE ONLY - À L'USAGE DU MINISTÈRE SEULEMENT

IC 3419 (2003/06)

Canada I◆I

FIGURE 7.1 CONTINUED

SCHEDULE A TO THE ARTICLES OF INCORPORATION
OF
BSJ GARDEN ORNAMENT SALES INC.
(the "Corporation")

The Corporation is authorized to issue:

(a)   an unlimited number of preferred shares (herein referred to as the "Preferred Shares"); and

(b)   an unlimited number of common shares (herein referred to as the "Common Shares").

The rights, privileges, restrictions and conditions attaching to the Preferred Shares and the Common Shares (herein collectively referred to as the "Share Provisions") are as follows:

PART I - INTERPRETATION

1.   **Definitions.** Where used in these Share Provisions, the following capitalized words and phrases shall, unless there is something in the context otherwise inconsistent therewith, have the following meanings, respectively:

(a)   **"Act"** means the Canada Business Corporations Act, R.S.C. 1985, c. C-44, as now enacted or as the same may from time to time be amended, re-enacted or replaced (and, in the case of such amendment, re-enactment or replacement, any references herein shall be read as referring to such amended, re-enacted or replaced provisions);

(b)   **"Business Day"** means a day other than a Saturday, Sunday or any other day treated as a holiday in the municipality in Canada in which the Corporation's registered office is then situated;

(c)   **"Close of Business"** means 5:00 o'clock in the afternoon on a Business Day;

(d)   **"Common Shareholders"** means a person recorded in the securities register of the Corporation for the Common Shares as being the registered holder of one or more Common Shares;

(e)   **"Directors"** or **"Board of Directors"** means the board of directors of the Corporation;

(f)   **"Dividend Payment Date"** means the date upon which any fixed preferential non-cumulative cash dividends become due and payable in accordance with any resolution of the Board of Directors declaring such dividend;

(g)   **"Liquidation Distribution"** means a distribution of assets of the Corporation among its shareholders arising on the liquidation, dissolution or winding up of the Corporation, whether voluntary or involuntary, or any other distribution of assets

FIGURE 7.1 CONTINUED

of the Corporation among its shareholders for the purpose of winding up its affairs;

(h) **"Preferred Shareholders"** means a person recorded in the securities register of the Corporation for the Preferred Shares as being the registered holder of one or more Preferred Shares;

(i) **"Redemption Date"** means, with respect to the Preferred Shares, the date specified for redemption in the notice in writing of the intention of the Corporation to redeem such Preferred Shares; and

(j) **"Redemption Price"** means the sum of $1.00 together with all declared and unpaid preferential, non-cumulative cash dividends on the Preferred Shares.

2. **Gender, Etc.** Words importing only the singular number include the plural and vice versa, and words importing any gender include all genders.

3. **Currency.** Unless otherwise explicitly set forth herein, all references herein to **"dollars"** or **"$"** shall refer to the lawful currency of Canada, and all amounts payable hereunder shall be payable in lawful currency of Canada.

4. **Business Day.** If any date upon which any dividends are payable by the Corporation, or upon which any other action is required to be taken by the Corporation or any shareholder hereunder, is not a Business Day, then such dividend shall be payable or such other action shall be required to be taken on or by the next succeeding day which is a Business Day.

5. **Headings.** The division of these Share Provisions into sections, paragraphs, subparagraphs or other subdivisions and the insertion of headings are for convenience of reference only and shall not affect the construction or interpretation hereof.

6. **Governing Statute.** These Share Provisions shall be governed by and are subject to the applicable provisions of the Act and all other laws binding upon the Corporation and, except as otherwise expressly provided herein, all terms used herein which are defined in the Act shall have the meanings respectively ascribed thereto in the Act.

PART II - PREFERRED SHARES

1. **Dividends**

1.1 **Fixed Dividend Rate.** The Preferred Shareholders shall be entitled to receive and the Corporation shall pay thereon, as and when declared by the Board of Directors out of monies of the Corporation properly applicable to the payment of dividends, fixed preferential non-cumulative cash dividends at a rate equal to $0.08 per share per annum before any dividends shall be paid to the Common Shareholders or the holders of shares of any other class ranking junior to the Preferred Shares with respect to priority in the payment of dividends. The Board of Directors shall be entitled from time to time to declare part of the fixed preferential non-cumulative cash dividend for any financial

FIGURE 7.1 CONTINUED

A-3

period notwithstanding that such dividend for such financial period shall not be declared in full.

1.2   **Non-Cumulative.** If, within six months after the expiration of any financial period of the Corporation, the Board of Directors, in its discretion, shall not declare the said dividend or any part thereof on the Preferred Shares for such financial period, then the rights of the holders of the Preferred Shares to such dividend or to any undeclared part thereof for such financial period shall be forever extinguished.

1.3   **No Participation in Further Dividends.** The Preferred Shareholders shall not be entitled to any dividends other than or in excess of the fixed preferential non-cumulative cash dividends hereinbefore provided for.

1.4   **Dividend Payment.** Dividends (less any tax or other amounts required to be deducted or withheld by the Corporation) on the Preferred Shares shall be paid to the holder of record thereof determined at the Close of Business on the Business Day immediately preceding the applicable Dividend Payment Date by cheque payable on the Dividend Payment Date in lawful money of Canada at par at any branch in Canada of the Corporation's bankers for the time being or, in respect of any particular holder, by any other means agreed upon between the Corporation and such holder provided that such other means provides for payment on the Dividend Payment Date. The mailing of such cheque on or before the applicable Dividend Payment Date by ordinary unregistered first class pre-paid mail addressed to a Preferred Shareholder at his address as it appears in the securities register of the Corporation for the Preferred Shares or, in the event of the address of any such holder not so appearing, then at the last address of such holder known to the Corporation or, in the case of joint holders, to the address of that one of the joint holders whose name stands first in such register, or the payment by such other means shall be deemed to be payment of the dividends represented thereby and payable on such date to the extent of the amount of such payment unless the cheque is not paid upon presentation or payment by such other means is not received.

1.5   **Stale Cheques.** Dividends which are represented by a cheque which has not been presented to the Corporation's bankers for payment or that otherwise remain unclaimed for a period of six years from the date on which they were declared to be payable shall be forfeited to the Corporation.

1.6   **Restrictions on Subordinate Shares.** Except with the consent in writing of all outstanding Preferred Shareholders, the Corporation shall not call for redemption nor purchase or otherwise acquire for value less than all the then outstanding Preferred Shares nor purchase or otherwise acquire for value any Common Shares or any shares of any other class of the Corporation ranking junior to the Preferred Shares so long as any Preferred Shares are outstanding, unless and until the fixed preferential non-cumulative cash dividend has been declared and paid or set apart for payment for the then current financial period of the Corporation on all the Preferred Shares outstanding.

FIGURE 7.1   CONTINUED

A-4

2.   **Liquidation**

2.1   **Liquidation Preference.** In the event of any Liquidation Distribution, the Preferred Shareholders shall be entitled to receive from the assets and property of the Corporation for each Preferred Share held by them respectively the Redemption Price before any amount shall be paid or any property or assets of the Corporation distributed to the Common Shareholders or the holders of shares of any other class ranking junior to the Preferred Shares with respect to priority in a Liquidation Distribution.

2.2   **No Participation in Surplus Assets.** After payment to the Preferred Shareholders of the amount so payable to them as above provided, they shall not be entitled to share in any further distribution of the property or assets of the Corporation.

3.   **Purchase by the Corporation.**

3.1   Subject to the Articles and the provisions of the Act, the Corporation may at any time or from time to time purchase (if obtainable) all or any part of the outstanding Preferred Shares at the lowest price at which, in the opinion of the Board of Directors, such shares are obtainable but not exceeding the Redemption Price. Except where outstanding Preferred Shareholders all consent to the purchase, the Corporation may purchase such shares only pursuant to tenders received by the Corporation upon request for tenders addressed to the holders of all the Preferred Shares, and the Corporation shall accept only the lowest tenders. Where, in response to the invitation for tenders, two or more Preferred Shareholders submit tenders at the same price and the tenders are accepted by the Corporation as to only part of the Preferred Shares offered, the Corporation shall accept part of the Preferred Shares offered in such tender in proportion as nearly as may be to the total number of Preferred Shares offered in each such tender (disregarding fractions).

4.   **Redemption**

4.1   **Option to Redeem.** Subject to the Articles and the provisions of the Act, the Corporation may, upon giving notice as hereinafter provided, redeem at any time the whole or from time to time any part of the then outstanding Preferred Shares on payment for each share to be redeemed of the Redemption Price.

4.2   **Notice of Redemption.** In the case of the redemption of Preferred Shares pursuant to the provisions of section 4.1 hereof, the Corporation shall at least seven days before the Redemption Date deliver, send by facsimile transmission (or other electronic communication) or mail to each person who at the date of such mailing or other communication is a registered holder of Preferred Shares to be redeemed a notice in writing of the intention of the Corporation to redeem such Preferred Shares. Such notice shall be delivered, sent by facsimile transmission (or other electronic communication) or mailed by letter, postage prepaid, addressed to each such Preferred Shareholder at his address as it appears on the records of the Corporation or, in the event of the address of any such Preferred Shareholder not so appearing, then to the last known address of such Preferred Shareholder except, however, that accidental failure to give any such notice to

FIGURE 7.1 CONTINUED

A-5

one or more of such shareholders shall not affect the validity of such redemption. Such notice shall set out:

(a)   the Redemption Price;

(b)   the Redemption Date;

(c)   if only part of the Preferred Shares held by the person to whom it is addressed is to be redeemed, the number thereof so to be redeemed;

(d)   if certificates representing the Preferred Shares called for redemption are to be presented and surrendered at a place other than the registered office of the Corporation, the place or places designated therefor; and

(e)   the specified bank or specified trust company where the respective holders of Preferred Shares called for redemption may present and surrender certificates representing such shares.

4.3   **Payment.** On or after the Redemption Date, the Corporation shall pay or cause to be paid to or to the order of the registered holders of the Preferred Shares to be redeemed the Redemption Price thereof on presentation and surrender of the certificates representing the Preferred Shares called for redemption at the registered office of the Corporation or any other place or places designated in the notice of redemption.

4.4   **Partial Redemption.** If only part of the shares represented by any certificate be redeemed, a new certificate for the balance shall be issued at the expense of the Corporation.

4.5   **Effect of Redemption.** Subject to the provisions of section 4.6 hereof, on and after the Redemption Date, the Preferred Shares called for redemption shall cease to be entitled to dividends, and the holders thereof shall not be entitled to exercise any of the rights of shareholders in respect thereof unless payment of the Redemption Price shall not be made upon presentation of certificates in accordance with the foregoing provisions, in which case, the rights of the Preferred Shareholders shall remain unaffected.

4.6   **Deposit of Redemption Price.** The Corporation shall have the right at any time after the mailing or other communication notice of its intention to redeem any Preferred Shares as aforesaid to deposit the Redemption Price for the shares so called for redemption or of such of the said shares represented by certificates as have not at the date of such deposit been surrendered by the holders thereof in connection with such redemption to a special account in a specified chartered bank or specified trust company in Canada, named in such notice of redemption, to be paid without interest to or to the order of the respective holders of such Preferred Shares called for redemption upon presentation and surrender to such bank or trust company of the certificates representing the same. Upon such deposit being made or upon the Redemption Date, whichever is the later, the Preferred Shares in respect whereof such deposit shall have been made shall be deemed to be redeemed and the rights of the Preferred Shareholders thereof after such deposit or such Redemption Date, as the case may be, shall be limited to receiving without interest their proportionate

FIGURE 7.1   CONTINUED

A-6

part of the total Redemption Price so deposited against presentation and surrender of the said certificates held by them respectively. Any interest allowed on any such deposit shall belong to the Corporation. Redemption monies that are represented by a cheque which has not been presented to the Corporation's bankers for payment or that otherwise remain unclaimed (including, without limitation, monies held on deposit to a special account as provided for above) for a period of six years from the Redemption Date shall be forfeited to the Corporation.

4.7   **Selecting Shares for Partial Redemption.** If only part of the Preferred Shares is at any time to be redeemed, the shares so to be redeemed shall be selected *pro rata* (disregarding fractions) from among the Preferred Shareholders of record thereof as at the date of the notice of redemption or in such other manner as the Board of Directors in its sole discretion may deem equitable.

5.   **Retraction**

5.1   **Option to Retract.** Subject to the Articles and the provisions of the Act, every Preferred Shareholder may, at his option and in the manner hereinafter provided, require the Corporation to redeem at any time all or part of the Preferred Shares held by such holder upon payment for each share to be redeemed of the Redemption Price.

5.2   **Retraction Procedure.** In the case of the redemption of Preferred Shares under the provisions of section 5.1 hereof, the holder thereof shall surrender the certificate or certificates representing such Preferred Shares at the registered office of the Corporation accompanied by a notice in writing (herein referred to as a "**Retraction Notice**") signed by such holder requiring the Corporation to redeem all or a specified number of the Preferred Shares represented thereby. As soon as practicable but, in any event, not later than 30 days following receipt of a Retraction Notice, the Corporation shall pay or cause to be paid to or to the order of the registered holder of the Preferred Shares to be redeemed the Redemption Price thereof. If only a part of the shares represented by any certificate be redeemed, a new certificate for the balance shall be issued at the expense of the Corporation.

6.   **Restrictions.**

6.1   So long as any of the Preferred Shares are issued and outstanding, the Corporation shall not without, but may from time to time with, the approval of all outstanding Preferred Shareholders:

(a)   declare or pay or set apart for payment any dividends on the Common Shares or any other shares of any other class ranking junior to the Preferred Shares with respect to priority in the payment of dividends if:

(i)   the realizable value of the Corporation's assets is less than the aggregate of its liabilities and the Redemption Price of all Preferred Shares then issued and outstanding; or

FIGURE 7.1 CONTINUED

A-7

> (ii) after the payment, the realizable value of the Corporation's assets would be less than the aggregate of its liabilities and the Redemption Price of all Preferred Shares then issued and outstanding; or

(b) redeem, purchase or otherwise pay off or purchase out of the surplus or capital any Common Shares or any shares of any other class ranking junior to the Preferred Shares with respect to priority in a Liquidation Distribution.

7. Voting

7.1 **Voting Restrictions.** The Preferred Shareholders shall not be entitled as such (except as hereinafter specifically provided and except as otherwise provided by the Act) to receive notice of or to attend any meeting of the shareholders of the Corporation and shall not be entitled to vote at any such meeting.

7.2 **Limited Notice Rights.** The Preferred Shareholders shall, however, have the right to receive notice of and to attend and vote at all meetings of shareholders called for the purpose of authorizing the dissolution of the Corporation pursuant to the Act or a sale, lease or exchange of all or substantially all of the property of the Corporation other than in the ordinary course of business pursuant to the Act.

8. Creation of Additional Shares and Amendments

8.1 **Restrictions on Authorized Capital.** No class of shares may be created ranking as to a Liquidation Distribution or dividends in priority to or on a parity with the Preferred Shares, without the approval of the Preferred Shareholders given by special resolution.

8.2 **Variation of Rights.** The provisions hereof contained in Part II attaching to the Preferred Shares or any sections hereof may be deleted, varied, modified, amended or amplified by articles of amendment but only with the approval of the Preferred Shareholders given by special resolution.

9. Priority.

9.1 The Common Shares shall rank junior to the Preferred Shares and shall be subject in all respects to the rights, privileges, restrictions and conditions attaching to the Preferred Shares.

PART III - COMMON SHARES

1. Dividends.

1.1 Subject to the prior rights of the Preferred Shareholders and to the holders of any other class of shares ranking senior to the Common Shares with respect to priority in the payment of dividends, the Common Shareholders shall be entitled to receive dividends and the Corporation shall pay dividends thereon, as and when declared by the Board of Directors out of monies properly applicable to the payment of dividends, in such amount and in such form as the Board of Directors may from time to time determine and all

FIGURE 7.1   CONTINUED

A-8

dividends which the Board of Directors may declare on the Common Shares shall be declared and paid in equal amounts per share on all Common Shares at the time outstanding.

2.   **Liquidation.**

2.1   In the event of any Liquidation Distribution, the Common Shareholders shall, subject to the prior rights of the Preferred Shareholders and to the holders of any other shares ranking senior to the Common Shares with respect to priority in a Liquidation Distribution, be entitled to receive the remaining property and assets of the Corporation.

3.   **Purchase by the Corporation.**

3.1   Subject to the Articles and the provisions of the Act, the Corporation may at any time or from time to time purchase (if obtainable) all or any part of the outstanding Common Shares at the lowest price at which, in the opinion of the Board of Directors, such shares are obtainable. Except where all of the outstanding Common Shareholders consent to the purchase, the Corporation may purchase such shares only pursuant to tenders received by the Corporation upon request for tenders addressed to all of the Common Shareholders, and the Corporation shall accept only the lowest tenders. Where, in response to the invitation for tenders, two or more shareholders submit tenders at the same price and the tenders are accepted by the Corporation as to only part of the Common Shares offered, the Corporation shall accept part of the Common Shares offered in such tender in proportion as nearly as may be to the total number of Common Shares offered in each such tender (disregarding fractions).

4.   Voting.

4.1   The Common Shareholders shall be entitled to receive notice of and to attend (in person or by proxy) and be heard at all meetings of the shareholders of the Corporation (except for meetings at which only holders of another specified class or series of shares of the Corporation are entitled to vote separately as a class or series) and shall have one vote for each Common Share held at all such meetings.

FIGURE 7.1 CONTINUED

B-1

SCHEDULE B TO THE ARTICLES OF INCORPORATION
OF
BSJ GARDEN ORNAMENT SALES INC.

No shares shall be transferred without either:

(a)   the approval of the directors of the Corporation expressed by a resolution passed by the board of directors of the Corporation at a meeting of the directors or by an instrument or instruments in writing signed by a majority of the directors; or

(b)   the approval of the holders of a majority of the voting shares of the Corporation for the time being outstanding expressed by a resolution passed at a meeting of shareholders or by an instrument or instruments in writing signed by the holders of a majority of such shares.

FIGURE 7.1   CONTINUED

SCHEDULE C TO THE ARTICLES OF INCORPORATION
OF
BSJ GARDEN ORNAMENT SALES INC.

Other Provisions (if any, are):

1.   The outstanding securities of the Corporation may be beneficially owned, directly or indirectly, by not more than 35 persons or companies, exclusive of:

(i)   persons or companies that are, or at the time they last acquired securities of the Corporation were, accredited investors as such term is defined in the Ontario Securities Commission ("OSC") Rule 45-501 Exempt Distributions as amended from time to time;

(ii)   current or former directors or officers of the Corporation or of an affiliated entity of the Corporation; and

(iii)   employees of the Corporation or an affiliated entity of the Corporation, or current or former consultants as defined in MI 45-105, who in each case beneficially own only securities of the Corporation that were issued as compensation by, or under an incentive plan of, the Corporation or an affiliated entity of the Corporation;

provided that:

A.   two or more persons who are the joint registered holders of one or more securities of the Corporation are counted as one beneficial owner of those securities; and

B.   a corporation, partnership, trust or other entity is counted as one beneficial owner of securities of the Corporation unless the entity has been created or is being used primarily for the purpose of acquiring or holding securities of the Corporation, in which event each beneficial owner of an equity interest in the entity or each beneficiary of the entity, as the case may be, is counted as a separate beneficial owner of those securities of the Corporation.

2.   The Corporation has a lien on a share registered in the name of a shareholder or his legal representative for a debt of that shareholder to the Corporation.

3.   The number of directors of the Corporation shall be determined from time to time as follows:

(a)   where directors are to be elected at a meeting of shareholders, the number shall be determined by resolution of the board of directors and set out in the notice calling the meeting of shareholders; and

FIGURE 7.1 CONCLUDED

C-2

(b)   where directors are to be elected by way of a written resolution of shareholders, the number shall be set out in the resolution;

provided that the number of directors may not be less than the minimum number nor more than the maximum number of directors set out in the articles.

4.   The directors of the Corporation, may, between annual meetings of shareholders of the Corporation, appoint one or more additional directors to serve until the next annual meeting, provided that the number of additional directors shall not at any time exceed one-third of the number of directors who held office at the expiration of the last annual meeting and provided further that the total number of directors of the Corporation after any such appointment shall not exceed the maximum number of directors permitted by the articles.

FIGURE 7.2 NOTICE OF REGISTERED OFFICE (CBCA FORM 3)

Industry Canada   Industrie Canada

Canada Business   Loi canadienne sur les
Corporations Act   sociétés par actions

FORM 3
NOTICE OF REGISTERED OFFICE OR
NOTICE OF C ANGE OF ADDRESS OF REGISTERED OFFICE
(SECTION I)

FORMULAIRE 3
A IS DE D SIGNATION OU
DE C ANGEMENT D'ADRESSE DU SIÈGE SOCIAL
(ARTICLE I)

1 -- Name of the Corporation - Dénomination sociale de la société	2 -- Corporation No. - Nº de la société
BSJ Garden Ornament Sales Inc.	

3 -- Street address of Registered Office - Adresse civique du siège social

123 Sesame Street
Port Ellen, ON L3R 0C9

(and mailing address, if different from that of registered office) - (si l'adresse postale diffère de celle du siège social)

CAUTION: Address of registered office must be within the province or territory that is described in the Articles at Item 2; otherwise an amendment to the Articles is required, using Form 4, in addition to this form (see paragraph 173(1) b) of the Act).
A IS : L'adresse du siège social doit se situer dans les limites de la province ou du territoire indiqué dans les statuts à la rubrique 2. Sinon, il faut modifier les statuts en déposant le formulaire 4, en plus du présent formulaire (voir l'alinéa 173(1) b) de la Loi).

4 -- Effective Date of Change - Date de prise d'effet

Not Applicable

5 -- Previous Address of Registered Office - Adresse précédente du siège social

Not Applicable

Signature	Printed Name - Nom en lettres moulées	6 -- Capacity of - En qualité de	7 -- Tel. No. - Nº de tél.
	Peter Black	Incorporator	541-321-3333

FOR DEPARTMENTAL USE ONLY - À L'USAGE DU MINISTÈRE SEULEMENT

IC 3420 (2003/06)

Canada

FIGURE 7.3   NOTICE OF DIRECTORS (CBCA FORM 6)

Industry Canada	Industrie Canada	**FORM 6** **NOTICE OF DIRECTORS** **NOTICE OF C ANGE** **OF DIRECTORS OR NOTICE OF** **C ANGE OF ADDRESS OF A** **PRES ENT DIRECTOR** **SECTIONS I 6 AND I I3(I)**	**FORM ULAIRE 6** **LISTE DES ADM INISTRATEURS** **A IS DE C ANGEMENT** **DES ADM INISTRATEURS OU A IS DE** **C ANGEM ENT D'ADRESSE D'UN** **ADM INISTRATEUR ACTUEL** **ARTICLES I 6 ET I I3(I)**
Canada Business Corporations A ct	Loi canadienne sur les sociétés par actions		

1 -- Name of the Corporation - Dénomination sociale de la société

BSL Garden Ornament Sales Inc.

2 -- Corporation No. - N° de la société

3 -- The follow ing persons became directors of this corporation - Les personnes suivantes sont devenues administrateurs de la présente société

Name - Nom	Effective Date Date d'entrée en vigueur	Residential A ddress - A dresse domiciliaire	Resident Canadian - Y /N Résident canadien - O/N
Not Applicable			

4 -- The follow ing persons ceased to be directors of this corporation - Les personnes suivantes ont cessé d'être administrateurs de la présente société

Name - Nom	Effective Date Date d'entrée en vigueur	Residential A ddress - A dresse domiciliaire
Not Applicable		

5 -- The directors of this corporation now are - Les administrateurs de la présente société sont maintenant

Name - Nom	Residential A ddress - A dresse dom iciliaire	Resident Canadian - Y /N Résident canadien - O/N
See attached Schedule A		

6 -- Change of address of a present director - Changement d'adresse d'un administrateur actuel

Name - Nom	Effective Date Date d'entrée en vigueur	Former Residential A ddress A dresse domiciliaire précédente	New Residential A ddress Nouvelle adresse résidentielle
Not Applicable			

Signature	Printed Name - Nom en lettres moulées Peter Black	7 -- Capacity of - En qualité de Incorporator	8 -- Tel. No. - N° de tél. 541-321-3333

FOR DEPARTMENTAL USE ONLY - À L'US AGE DU M INISTÈRE SEULEM ENT

IC 3103 (2003/06)

Canadä

FIGURE 7.3 CONCLUDED

Schedule A to Form 6
Notice of Directors

Name	Residential Address	Resident Canadian
Peter Black	1 First Street, Port Ellen, ON L3R 0A9	Yes
Shirley Smith	2 Second Street, Port Ellen, ON L3R 0B9	Yes
Roger Jones	3 Third Street, Port Ellen, ON L3R 0D9	Yes

FIGURE 7.4 ARTICLES OF INCORPORATION (OBCA FORM 1)

For Ministry Use Only
À l'usage exclusif du ministère

Ontario Corporation Number
Numéro de la société en Ontario

ARTICLES OF INCORPORATION
STATUTS CONSTITUTIFS

Form 1
Business
Corporations
Act

*Formule 1
Loi sur les
sociétés par
actions*

1. The name of the corporation is: (Set out in BLOCK CAPITAL LETTERS)
   Dénomination sociale de la société : (Écrire en LETTRES MAJUSCULES SEULEMENT)

0	1	1	1	1	1	1	1		O	N	T	A	R	I	O		I	N	C	.						

2. The address of the registered office is:
   Adresse du siège social :

   111 Red Street

   (Street & Number or R.R. Number & if Multi-Office Building give Room No.)
   (Rue et numéro ou numéro de la R.R. et, s'il s'agit d'un édifice à bureaux, numéro du bureau)

   White Port   ONTARIO | P | 3 | P | 0 | P | 9 |

   (Name of Municipality or Post Office)   (Postal Code)
   (Nom de la municipalité ou du bureau de poste)   *(Code postal)*

3. Number (or minimum and maximum number) of directors is/are: minimum/*minimal*   maximum/*maximal*
   Nombre (ou nombres minimal et maximal) d'administrateurs :   1   10

4. The first director(s) is/are:
   Premier(s) administrateur(s) :

   First name, middle names and surname
   Prénom, autres Prénoms et nom de famille

The first director(s)	Address for service, giving Street & No. or R.R. No., Municipality, Province, Country and Postal Code *Domicile élu, y compris la rue et le numéro, le numéro de la R.R. ou le nom de la municipalite, la province, le pays et le code postal*	Resident Canadian? Yes or No *Résident canadien? Oui/Non*
David Green	111 Red Street White Port, ON P3P 0P9	Yes
Carol Green	111 Red Street White Port, ON P3P 0P9	Yes

07116 (01/2002)

FIGURE 7.4 CONTINUED

2

5. Restrictions, if any, on business the corporation may carry on or on powers the corporation may exercise.
   Limites, s'il y a lieu, imposées aux activités commerciales ou aux pouvoirs de la société.

There are no restrictions.

6. The classes and any maximum number of shares that the corporation is authorized to issue:
   Catégories et nombre maximal, s'il y a lieu, d'actions que la société est autorisée à émettre :

An unlimited number of common shares.

07116 (01/2002)

FIGURE 7.4 CONTINUED

3

7. Rights, privileges, restrictions and conditions (if any) attaching to each class of shares and directors authority
    with respect to any class of shares which may be issued in series:
    *Droits, privilèges, restrictions et conditions, s'il y a lieu, rattachés à chaque catégorie d'actions et pouvoirs des
    administrateurs relatifs à chaque catégorie d'actions qui peut être émise en série :*

None

07116 (01/2002)

FIGURE 7.4   CONTINUED

4

8. The issue, transfer or ownership of shares is/is not restricted and the restrictions (if any) are as follows:
   L'émission, le transfert ou la propriété d'actions est/n'est pas restreint. Les restrictions, s'il y a lieu, sont les suivantes :

No shares may be transferred without either:

(a) the approval of the directors of the Corporation expressed by a resolution passed by the board of directors of the Corporation at a meeting of the directors or by an instrument or instruments in writing signed by a majority of the directors; or

(b) the approval of the holders of a majority of the voting shares of the Corporation for the time being outstanding expressed by a resolution passed at a meeting of shareholders or by an instrument or instruments in writing signed by the holders of a majority of such shares.

07116 (01/2002)

FIGURE 7.4 CONTINUED

5

9. Other provisions if any:
   Autres dispositions, s'il y a lieu :

1. The outstanding securities of the Corporation may be beneficially owned, directly or indirectly, by not more than 35 persons or companies, exclusive of:

(i) persons or companies that are, or at the time they last acquired securities of the Corporation were, accredited investors as such term is defined in the Ontario Securities Commission ("OSC") Rule 45-501 Exempt Distributions as amended from time to time;

(ii) current or former directors or officers of the Corporation or of an affiliated entity of the Corporation; and

(iii) employees of the Corporation or an affiliated entity of the Corporation, or current or former consultants as defined in MI 45-105, who in each case beneficially own only securities of the Corporation that were issued as compensation by, or under an incentive plan of, the Corporation or an affiliated entity of the Corporation;

provided that:

A. two or more persons who are the joint registered holders of one or more securities of the Corporation are counted as one beneficial owner of those securities; and

B. a corporation, partnership, trust or other entity is counted as one beneficial owner of securities of the Corporation unless the entity has been created or is being used primarily for the purpose of acquiring or holding securities of the Corporation, in which event each beneficial owner of an equity interest in the entity or each beneficiary of the entity, as the case may be, is counted as a separate beneficial owner of those securities of the Corporation.

2. The Corporation has a lien on a share registered in the name of a shareholder or his legal representative for a debt of that shareholder to the Corporation.

07116 (01/2002)

FIGURE 7.4   CONCLUDED

10. The names and addresses of the incorporators are:
     Noms et adresses des fondateurs :

First name, middle names and surname or corporate name *Prénom, autres prénoms et nom de famille ou dénomination sociale*	Full address for service or address of registered office or of principal place of business giving street & No. or R.R. No., municipality and postal code *Domicile élu au complet, adresse du siège social ou adresse de l'établissement principal, y compris la rue et le numéro ou le numéro de la R.R., le nom de la municipalité et le code postal*
David Green	111 Red Street White Port, ON P3P 0P9

These articles are signed in duplicate.
Les présents statuts sont signés en double exemplaire.

Signatures of incorporator(s) /
Signatures des fondateurs

David Green

FIGURE 7.5   CONSENT TO ACT AS A FIRST DIRECTOR (OBCA FORM 2)

Form 2
*Business
Corporations
Act*

*Formule 2
Loi sur les
sociétés par
actions*

CONSENT TO ACT AS A FIRST DIRECTOR
CONSENTEMENT DU PREMIER ADMINISTRATEUR

I,/Je soussigné(e), _____ Carol Green _____
(First name, middle names and surname)
(Prénom, autres Prénoms et nom de famille)

address for service
domicile élu

_____ 111 Red Street, White Port, ON P3P 0P9 _____
(Street & No. or R.R. No., Municipality, Province, Country & Postal Code)
(Rue et numéro, ou numéro de la R.R., nom de la municipalité, province, pays et code postal)

hereby consent to act as a first director of
accepte par la présente de devenir premier administrateur de

_____ 01111111 ONTARIO INC. _____
(Name of Corporation)
(Dénomination sociale de la société)

_____ Carol Green _____
(Signature of the Consenting Person)
(Signature de l'acceptant)

07117 (06/01)

CHAPTER 8

Post-incorporation organization

CHAPTER OVERVIEW

This chapter describes the steps required to organize a corporation after it has been incorporated to put it into a legal position to carry on business. It covers items to be conducted by the directors, including the issuance of shares, enactment of bylaws, and appointment of officers, as well as items to be conducted by the shareholders, including the confirmation of bylaws, fixing the number of directors, appointing an auditor or consenting to audit exemption, and the election of permanent directors. The chapter explains how to set up a minute book for a newly incorporated corporation, including preparation of the statutory registers and shareholder ledgers. Finally, it discusses the contents of the solicitor's report to the client.

CHAPTER OBJECTIVES

After completing this chapter, you should be able to:

1. List the various steps required to organize a newly incorporated CBCA or OBCA corporation.

2. Identify whether these steps should be taken by signed resolution or conducted at meetings.

3. Describe the procedures for issuing shares, making bylaws, and issuing share certificates.

4. Organize a minute book and complete the appropriate ledgers and registers.

5. Explain the provisions in the CBCA and the OBCA affecting auditors.

6. Write a letter to the client reporting on the incorporation and organization.

ORGANIZATION

post-incorporation organization

the passage of certain resolutions and the preparation of certain documents to set the corporation up to be in a legal position to do business

The incorporation of a business is just the beginning of its life; there are many events that follow. These events include organization, amendments, continuance, amalgamation, and then eventually, perhaps, dissolution. The first step is the **post-incorporation organization**. Once the corporation is brought into existence by the issuance of a certificate of incorporation, the directors and shareholders are required to pass certain resolutions and prepare certain documents to set the corporation up to be in a legal position to do business. These steps must be conducted accurately. If, for example, the shares are not properly issued, there may be an argument by a proposed purchaser of the shares, for example, that there are no shareholders. If anything should happen to the initial director, there will be no one available to issue the shares and, therefore, no shareholder to elect a new director. This may pose a problem if the owner decides to sell the corporation or if a bank requires a pledge of the shares as collateral for a loan. If you follow the steps described below, you will leave an accurate record of the initial steps in the corporation's management. This will eliminate the possibility of any deficiencies in the initial organization process when a proposed purchaser completes the minute book due diligence.

Here are the steps required to properly organize a corporation after incorporation:

1. Pass directors' resolutions (CBCA s. 104(1); OBCA s. 117(1)) to accomplish such things as:

   a. making bylaws;

   b. adopting forms of share certificates and corporate records;

   c. authorizing the issuance of shares;

   d. appointing officers;

   e. appointing an auditor to hold office until the first annual meeting of shareholders;

   f. making banking arrangements; and

   g. transacting any other business, which may include:

      i. considering authorizing a member of your law firm or any individual who has the relevant knowledge of the corporation to sign notices of change in registered office and directors and the annual return pursuant to CBCA ss. 262.1(1) and (2);

      ii. considering whether the corporation will communicate with its shareholders by electronic means; and

      iii. adopting any pre-incorporation contracts entered into on behalf of the corporation.

2. Pass shareholders' resolutions to accomplish such things as:

   a. confirming the bylaws passed by the directors;

b. fixing the number of directors within the minimum and maximum number provided in the articles or empowering the directors to do so; and

c. electing permanent directors.

3. Obtain consents to act as directors.

4. Issue share certificates.

5. Prepare banking documents.

6. Set up a minute book for the corporation that includes all registers and shareholder ledgers.

7. Obtain a corporate seal for the corporation, if required. Both the CBCA and the OBCA provide that a corporation may, but need not, have a corporate seal.

8. File an initial return under the *Corporations Information Act* (Ontario)(CIA). A CBCA corporation carrying on business in Ontario files Form 2 under the CIA and an OBCA corporation files Form 1 under the CIA.

9. Satisfy all requirements of the *Securities Act* (Ontario) with regard to the issuance of shares.

10. Prepare a letter to the client reporting on all of the above.

The procedures for organizing a corporation will vary depending on whether the first directors are nominees of the client or members of the law firm incorporating the corporation. In addition, in some cases minutes will be prepared, while in other cases resolutions will be signed. Some of the matters that are attended to will be done pursuant to requirements in the statute. Other matters will be completed as a matter of practice.

The following guidelines will help you decide whether to pass resolutions by way of consent in writing or at meetings.

- *Meeting.* If all of the first directors or shareholders are not available to sign resolutions, it may be more convenient to hold a meeting to pass the necessary resolutions because only a **quorum** is required for the transaction of business at meetings. Sometimes, people prefer to "meet" to conduct business rather than sign resolutions. If there are a number of directors, it may be easier to hold a meeting as opposed to circulating resolutions to each director for his or her signature.

quorum
the minimum number of directors or shareholders that must be present at a meeting to constitute a valid meeting

- *Written resolution.* If all of the directors or shareholders entitled to vote on the resolution at a meeting are available to sign resolutions in writing, a written resolution is as valid as if it had been passed at a meeting (CBCA ss. 117(1) and 142(1); OBCA ss. 129 and 104(1)). Written resolutions are generally used when there is only one or a small number of directors or shareholders. A resolution becomes effective on the day it is signed by the last person required to sign.

Director organization meetings or resolutions (CBCA s. 104(1); OBCA s. 117(1))

Both the CBCA and the OBCA provide that after incorporation, a meeting of the directors of a corporation will be held at which the directors may pass resolutions organizing the corporation.

A meeting of directors can be called by an incorporator or first director by giving not less than five days' notice to each director named in the articles, stating the time and place of the meeting (CBCA s. 104(3); OBCA s. 117(4)).

The following items may be dealt with at the first meeting of directors:

MAKING BYLAWS

Unless the articles, the bylaws, or a unanimous shareholder agreement provide otherwise, the directors may pass resolutions to make, amend, or repeal bylaws that regulate the business or affairs of a corporation (CBCA s. 103; OBCA s. 116). **Bylaws** are regulations made by a corporation to govern its internal affairs. They are different from resolutions that are passed as routine acts by the directors and shareholders.

Neither the CBCA nor the OBCA "require" a corporation to pass bylaws, but it is general practice to do so. There are several places in the statutes that refer to exceptions in the bylaws. For example, CBCA s. 25(1) provides that, "Subject to the articles, the by-laws and any unanimous shareholder agreement and to section 28, shares may be issued at such times and to such persons and for such consideration as the directors may determine." The bylaws may vary this provision.

There are two approaches to what is included in general bylaws. Some practitioners prefer the bylaws to contain only the most basic matters that are relevant to the organization of the corporation, thus leaving management to refer to the statute for matters not contained in the bylaws. As well, should the corporate statute requirements be amended, no bylaw amendment is necessary. This is commonly referred to as a "short form" of bylaw. The alternative approach is to include all information that a corporate secretary requires when organizing meetings, issuing shares, etc. This type of bylaw is generally referred to as a "long form" of bylaw.

Some of the typical provisions found in bylaws include:

* Matters affecting the business of the corporation such as the form of the corporate seal (if any), the financial year-end date, and designating who may sign contracts on behalf of the corporation.

* The manner of election of directors, the place where director meetings may be held, the quorum for directors' meetings, how to call a directors' meeting, notice requirements, who will act as chair and secretary of the meeting, and whether or not the chair will have a **casting vote**.

* A brief description outlining the duties of the officers of the corporation and their appointment.

* A section relating to the protection of directors and officers, including indemnification.

* The directors' ability to issue shares, the form of the share certificates, who may sign share certificates, and the maintenance of the transfer register.

bylaws
regulations made by a corporation to govern its internal affairs

casting vote
a vote that decides between two equal parties, especially when used by the chair of a meeting

- The rules for calling and conducting shareholder meetings, including quorum, persons entitled to be present, governing votes, and who will act as chair and secretary of the meetings.

- Borrowing provisions — the right to borrow is given automatically under the statutes unless restricted by the articles, bylaws, or a unanimous shareholder agreement (CBCA s. 189(1); OBCA s. 184(1)).

Precedent bylaws for federal and Ontario corporations are available from legal stationers such as Dye & Durham. Other precedents are contained in the corporation manuals published by legal publishers such as those cited in the reference section at the end of this chapter. Your law firm will also likely have its own form of bylaw. Using a precedent is the first step in drafting a bylaw. You must become thoroughly familiar with what is in the precedent. Sometimes changes, additions, and deletions will be required.

Once the directors have made a bylaw, they submit it to the shareholders at the next meeting of shareholders for confirmation. The shareholders can approve, amend, or reject the bylaw (CBCA s. 103(2); OBCA s. 116(2)).

A bylaw is effective from the time it is made by the directors until it is confirmed, confirmed as amended, or rejected by the shareholders. Where the bylaw is confirmed, or confirmed as amended, it continues in effect in the form in which it is confirmed (CBCA s. 103(3); OBCA s. 116(3)).

If the bylaw is rejected by the shareholders, or if the directors fail to present it to the shareholders for confirmation, the bylaw ceases to have any effect on the date of such rejection, or on the date of the shareholders' meeting at which it should have been presented for confirmation. In this case, any further resolution of the directors to make a bylaw similar to the rejected bylaw is not effective until confirmed by the shareholders (CBCA s. 103(4); OBCA s. 116(4)).

There are two common methods to prepare and sign bylaws:

1. *By resolution of the directors and shareholders passed at a meeting.* In this case, the bylaw is signed at the end by the president and secretary to indicate that it has been passed by the directors and confirmed by the shareholders.

2. *By written resolution.* In this case, the bylaw is passed and signed by all the directors and all the shareholders at the end of the bylaw.

Unless otherwise provided in the bylaws, the procedure to amend or repeal a bylaw is the same as the procedure for passing it in the first place.

ADOPTING FORMS OF SHARE CERTIFICATES

As discussed in chapter 5, shareholders are entitled, at their option or upon request, to receive a share certificate evidencing their ownership of shares of the corporation.

CORPORATE RECORDS

The authority to maintain records for a corporation arises from the requirement in the statutes to maintain various specified accounting and corporate records. The information in table 8.1 identifies the type of records to be maintained, the location of the records, who has access to the records, and what happens if a corporation does not maintain records.

TABLE 8.1   PROVISIONS FOR RECORD KEEPING UNDER THE CBCA AND THE OBCA

Provision	Canada	Ontario
Corporate records to be maintained	• Articles and all amendments • Bylaws and all amendments • Unanimous shareholder agreements • Minutes of meetings and shareholder resolutions • Copies of all notices of registered office and directors • Securities register containing the information set out in CBCA s. 50	• Articles and all amendments • Bylaws and all amendments • Copy of any unanimous shareholder agreement known to the directors • Minutes of meetings and shareholder resolutions • A register of directors in which are set out the names and residence addresses while directors, including the street and number, if any, of all persons who are or have been directors of the corporation with the dates on which each became or ceased to be a director • A securities register that complies with OBCA s. 141(1)
	Records to be maintained at registered office or any other place in Canada designated by the directors (CBCA s. 20(1))	Records to be maintained at registered office or at such other place in Ontario designated by the directors (OBCA s. 140(1))
		Register of transfers in which all transfers of securities issued by the corporation in registered form and the date and other particulars of each transfer (OBCA s. 141(2))
		To be maintained at the registered office of a corporation or at such other places in Ontario designated by the directors, and the branch register or registers of transfers may be kept at such offices of the corporation or other places, either within or outside Ontario, designated by the directors
	Minutes of meetings and resolutions of the directors (CBCA s. 20(2))	Minutes of meetings and resolutions of the directors (OBCA s. 140(2))
	To be kept at registered office or such other place as the directors think fit and shall be open to inspection by directors at all reasonable times (CBCA s. 20(4))	
	Minutes of meetings and resolutions of any committees of the board (CBCA s. 20(2))	Minutes of meetings and resolutions of any committees of the board (OBCA s. 140 (2)
	To be kept at registered office or such other place as the directors see fit and shall be open to inspection by directors at all reasonable times (CBCA s. 20(4))	
Period for retention of corporate records	6 years after date of dissolution (CBCA s. 225) (subject to any other requirements)	Where a corporation has been voluntarily wound up under OBCA ss. 192 to 235, there is no responsibility on the liquidator if its documents and records are not forthcoming to anyone claiming to be interested in them (OBCA s. 236); however, note requirements of other statutes

TABLE 8.1 CONTINUED

Provision	Canada	Ontario
Accounting records to be maintained	Adequate accounting records (CBCA s. 20(2))	Adequate accounting records (OBCA s. 140(2))
	To be kept at registered office or such other place as the directors think fit and shall be open to inspection by directors at all reasonable times (CBCA s. 20(4))	
Period for retention of accounting records	6 years after the end of the financial year to which the records relate (subject to requirements to maintain records longer pursuant to any other statute) (CBCA s. 20(2.1))	6 years from the end of the last fiscal period to which they relate (subject to requirements of any taxing authority of Ontario, the government of Canada, or any other jurisdiction to which the corporation is subject) (OBCA s. 140(2))
When accounting records are kept outside Canada	Accounting records adequate to enable the directors to ascertain the financial position of the corporation with reasonable accuracy on a quarterly basis shall be kept at the registered office or any other place in Canada designated by the directors (CBCA s. 20(5))	Adequate accounting records may be kept at a place other than the registered office of the corporation if the records are available for inspection during regular office hours at the registered office by means of a computer terminal or other electronic technology (OBCA s. 144(2))
When records or registers kept outside Canada	Despite CBCA ss. 20(1) and 20(5) but subject to the *Income Tax Act*, the *Excise Tax Act*, the *Customs Act*, and any other act administered by the Minister of National Revenue, a corporation may keep all or any of its corporate records and accounting records referred to in subsection (1) or (2) at a place outside Canada, if: (a) the records are available for inspection, by means of a computer terminal or other technology, during regular office hours at the registered office or any other place in Canada designated by the directors; and (b) the corporation provides the technical assistance to facilitate an inspection referred to in paragraph (a) (CBCA s. 20(5.1))	Records listed in OBCA ss. 140 and 141 may be kept at a place other than the registered office of the corporation if the records are available for inspection during regular office hours at the registered office by means of a computer terminal or other electronic technology (OBCA s. 144(2))
Form of records	All registers and other records required to be prepared and maintained may be in a bound or looseleaf form or in a photographic film form, or may be entered or recorded by any system of mechanical or electronic data processing or any other information storage device that is capable of reproducing any required information in intelligible written form within a reasonable time (CBCA s. 22(1))	Records may be kept in a bound or looseleaf book or may be entered or recorded by any system of mechanical or electronic data processing or any other information storage device (OBCA s. 139(1))

TABLE 8.1 CONCLUDED

Provision	Canada	Ontario
Access to corporate records	Shareholders and creditors, their personal representatives, and the federal Director may examine the records described in CBCA s. 20(1) during the usual business hours of the corporation, and may take extracts from the records free of charge (CBCA s. 21(1)) Shareholders are entitled on request and without charge to one copy of the articles and bylaws and any unanimous shareholder agreement (CBCA s. 21(2))	The records mentioned in OBCA s. 140, the securities register, and the register of transfers must, during normal business hours of a corporation, be open to examination by any director (OBCA s. 144(1)) Shareholders and creditors of a corporation, their agents, and legal representatives may examine the records referred to in OBCA s. 140(1) during the usual business hours of the corporation and may take extracts from them, free of charge (OBCA s. 145(1)) Shareholders are entitled on request and without charge to one copy of the articles and bylaws and any unanimous shareholder agreement (OBCA s. 145(2))
Penalties for not keeping records in accordance with the Act	If a corporation fails to comply with CBCA s. 20 without reasonable cause, it is guilty of an offence and on summary conviction is liable to a fine not exceeding $5,000 (CBCA s. 20(6))	Every person who commits an act contrary to or fails or neglects to comply with any provision of the OBCA or the regulations is guilty of an offence and on conviction is liable to a fine of not more than $2,000 or to imprisonment for a term of not more than one year, or to both, or if such person is a corporation, to a fine of not more than $25,000 Where a corporation is guilty of an offence, every director or officer of it who, without reasonable cause, authorized, permitted, or acquiesced in such offence is also guilty of an offence and on conviction is liable to a fine of not more than $2,000 or to imprisonment for a term of not more than one year, or to both (OBCA ss. 258(1)(j) and 258(2))
Notices and annual returns	No provision in CBCA to keep copies of filed Forms 3, 6, or 22	The CIA provides that a corporation must maintain an up-to-date paper or electronic record of the prescribed information set out in returns and notices that it has filed under that Act and make the record available for examination by any shareholder, member, director, officer, or creditor of the corporation during its normal business hours at its registered office or principal place of business in Ontario (CIA s. 5(2))

In addition to the period for retention of records under the corporate statutes, consideration must also be given to any other statute to which the corporation is subject that may have retention provisions. For example, under the *Income Tax Act* (ITA), the Canada Revenue Agency (CRA) may periodically audit a corporation to "encourage compliance with the self-assessment tax system."[1] Part of the audit will include a review of the corporation's records. A CRA auditor may review the minutes of directors' and shareholders' meetings, for example, to discover reasons for a corporation's entering into a particular transaction or to provide some other facts that relate to some subjective element of a taxing provision. Section 230(1) of the ITA requires taxpayers to keep records and books of account that will ensure that taxes payable under the ITA or the taxes or other amounts that should have been deducted, withheld, or collected be determined. ITA s. 230(4) and regulation 5800 provide time limits for the retention of documents, including time limits for retaining minutes of directors' and shareholders' meetings. ITA s. 230(4) also has provisions that relate to keeping electronic records.

CRA *Information Circular* 78-10R3, dated October 5, 1998, relating to the retention and destruction of books and records can be downloaded from the CRA Web site.

Other statutes with provisions relating to record retention include the *Excise Tax Act*, the *Retail Sales Tax Act* (Ontario), the *Customs Act*, the *Employment Standards Act 2000* (Ontario), the *Employment Insurance Act*, and s. 24 of the Canada Pension Plan. Other references may be found in the *Business Records Protection Act*, the *Workplace Safety and Insurance Act, 1997* (Ontario), the *Limitations Act* (Ontario), the *Copyright Act*, and the *Trade-marks Act*.

CBCA s. 23(1) and OBCA s. 13 provide that a corporation may, but need not, adopt a corporate seal. The CBCA also provides that a document is not invalid merely because the seal is not attached. If a corporate seal is desired, the impression of the seal should be adopted by resolution of the directors or by way of the general operating bylaws.

It is customary to keep the "corporate" records in a **minute book**. The minute book comes complete with divider tabs for the following sections:

minute book
a book in which the corporate records of a corporation are maintained

- articles and all amendments;

- bylaws and all amendments;

- shareholder agreement, if any;

- minutes of meetings and resolutions of directors and shareholders;

- copies of all notices filed;

- register of directors;

- register of officers;

- securities register;

- register of transfers;

- share ledgers; and

- register of debt obligations.

In many minute books you will find the directors' minutes and resolutions separated from the shareholders' minutes and resolutions. Practically, this separation can be very confusing, especially when you are asked to conduct a review of the minute book, because you will find yourself flipping back and forth between the two sections. The separation of the resolutions arises because shareholders' minutes and resolutions are subject to inspection by shareholders and creditors, their personal representatives, and the Director under the statutes. Directors' minutes and resolutions, on the other hand, need only be made available to the directors. The minutes and resolutions of directors and shareholders of an offering corporation should be separated, but those of a non-offering corporation need not be.

Once the corporation is organized and the resolutions are signed, they are filed in the minute book together with the articles and bylaws. The registers and ledgers should be prepared and the appropriate notices filed under the CIA (see below).

PREPARATION OF REGISTERS AND SHARE LEDGERS

When you order the minute book and tabs for the corporation, you will receive forms for completing the following, which will contain information similar to that shown below.

1. Directors' register

Name and residence address	Resident Canadian (Y/N)	Date became a director	Date ceased to be a director
Oreole Sunshine 77 Sunset Strip Blue Vale, ON L0G 1M0	Y	January 26, 1981	

2. Officers' register

Name and residence address	Position	Date became a director	Date ceased to be a director
Oreole Sunshine 77 Sunset Strip Blue Vale, ON L0G 1M0	President	January 26, 1981	

3. Shareholders' common share register

Date	Name	Shares held	
		No. of shares	Cert. no.
January 26, 1981	Oreole Sunshine	1,000	C-001

4. Shareholders' ledger

Name: Oreole Sunshine
Address: 77 Sunset Strip
                Blue Vale ON L0G 1M0
Class of shares: Common shares

Date	Cert. no.	Trans. no.	To or from whom transferred	Shares Sold	Shares Bought	Shares Balance
Jan. 26, 1981	C-001	—	From treasury	0	1,000	1,000
Aug. 28, 1992	—	1	To Cleo Nightingale	500	0	500
Aug. 28, 1992	C-003	—	Cert. issued for balance of shares outstanding	—	—	500

5. Register of transfers

Transfer number	Date	Class of shares	Certificates surrendered No.	Certificates surrendered Shares	Transferred from name	Transferred to name	Certificates issued No.	Certificates issued Shares	Certificates issued Initials
1	Aug. 28, 1992	Com	C-001	1,000	Oreole Sunshine	Cleo Nightingale	C-002	500	EG

6. Register of debt obligations

Date	Nature of debt obligation incl. class or series	Name and address of holder of debt obligation	Principal amount of debt obligation	Date discharged
Feb. 10, 1983	Series A Debenture no. SA-001	West Pacific Loan Company, 66 Golden Archway, Heavenly, ON L4I 6X2	$100,000	

There are many "corporate record databases" available for sale that have the capability of preparing these forms automatically once correct information is entered into the database.

ISSUE OF SHARES

As discussed in chapter 5, the issuance of shares is an important step. If not handled properly, deficiencies in this step can cause problems for the corporation when it needs to borrow money, or when its shares are to be sold publicly. Deficiencies may mean that the solicitor acting for the corporation may be unable to give an unconditional opinion as to the ownership of the shares.

The number of shares to be issued will depend on the particular circumstances and the amount and means by which capital is to be injected into the corporation. Sometimes a corporation will issue one common share for $1, and further capital will be injected by means of a shareholder loan to the corporation. Alternatively, an initial share may be issued and the assets of a sole proprietorship rolled over into the corporation in return for the issue of a larger number of shares representing the value of the capital transferred. The decision of how to capitalize the corporation will generally be made by an accountant or tax lawyer. It is important that the consideration for the shares be received before the shares are issued because shares are not legally considered issued until the consideration for the shares is fully paid in money or in property or past service (CBCA s. 25(3); OBCA s. 23(3)).

Sometimes you will find $1 taped onto the subscription for the shares filed in the minute book. This is not a good practice to follow because it may encourage an omission of this amount in the financial statements of the corporation. It is much better to deposit the dollar into the corporation's bank account.

When determining the value of property or past services for CBCA or OBCA purposes, the directors may take into account reasonable charges and expenses of organization and reorganization and payment for property and past service reasonably expected to benefit the corporation.

Shares are issued as "fully paid" and "non-assessable," and the holders are not liable to the corporation or to its creditors for the value of the shares. This means that unless an agreement has been entered into to the contrary, shareholders will not be subject to "assessments" by the corporation for additional capital investment.

The procedure for the issue of shares is discussed more fully in chapter 5, but the following is a summary for the initial issuance of shares after incorporation:

1. The proposed shareholder delivers a subscription to the corporation together with payment of the subscription price. The subscription sets out

   a. the number of shares the subscriber wishes to purchase,

   b. the price per share,

   c. the name in which the shares are to be issued, and

   d. the fact that payment is attached.

2. The directors (subject to any restrictions in the articles, the bylaws, or a unanimous shareholder agreement and any pre-emptive rights attaching to the shares) pass a resolution providing for the issuance of the shares. The resolution

   a. accepts the subscription,

   b. fixes the consideration for the shares and determines that the shares will be issued upon receipt of the specified price,

   c. issues the shares as fully paid and non-assessable, and

   d. authorizes the delivery of a share certificate to the shareholder.

3. Once payment is received, the corporation issues a share certificate reflecting the number of shares subscribed for and issued. The share certificate may be given to the shareholder, in which case you should obtain a receipt; in a closely held corporation, the certificate may be retained with the corporate records.

4. All documents required for compliance with *Securities Act* (Ontario) rule 45-501 are signed.

APPOINTING OFFICERS (CBCA s. 124; OBCA s. 136)

Unless otherwise specified in the articles, bylaws, or a unanimous shareholder agreement, the directors have the responsibility to designate the offices of the corporation, appoint individuals to these positions, decide on their duties, and delegate to them powers to manage the business and affairs of the corporation. For a discussion of officers, see chapter 4.

APPOINTING AN AUDITOR AND INFORMATION ABOUT AUDITORS (CBCA ss. 162 TO 172; OBCA ss. 148 TO 160)

If it is not proposed to hold a meeting or obtain a written resolution of shareholders immediately, the directors may appoint an auditor to hold office until the first annual meeting of shareholders.

The following are some of the important provisions of the statutes with regard to auditors.

Appointment of auditor (CBCA s. 162(1); OBCA s. 149(2))

The directors may appoint the initial auditor of a corporation. After that, it is the responsibility of the shareholders to appoint an auditor at each annual meeting to hold office until the close of the next annual meeting. If an auditor is not appointed by the shareholders, the auditor in office continues in office until a successor is appointed.

Exemption from audit requirements (CBCA s. 163; OBCA s. 148)

Under the CBCA, the shareholders of a non-offering corporation may "resolve" not to appoint an auditor. Any resolution passed to do this is valid only until the next succeeding annual meeting of shareholders. The resolution must be consented to by all the shareholders, including shareholders not otherwise entitled to vote.

The OBCA provision is similar. With respect to a financial year of an OBCA corporation, a non-offering corporation is exempt from the requirement to appoint an auditor if all of the shareholders consent in writing to the exemption for that year.

Notice of appointment of auditor (OBCA s. 149(9))

An OBCA corporation must give notice in writing to an auditor of the auditor's appointment as soon as the appointment is made. There is no equivalent requirement in the CBCA.

Filling a vacancy (CBCA s. 166; OBCA s. 149(3))

The directors may fill any vacancy in the office of auditor. You should, however, always check the articles and any unanimous shareholder agreement carefully to make sure there are no auditor provisions.

Auditor's right to attend shareholders' meetings (CBCA s. 168(1); OBCA s. 151(1))

The auditor is entitled to receive notice of every meeting of shareholders and, at the expense of the corporation, to attend and be heard on matters relating to the auditor's duties.

Examination and right of access of records by auditor (CBCA ss. 169(1) and 170(1); OBCA ss. 153(1) and (5))

An auditor of a corporation is entitled to make whatever examination of the records of the corporation that is, in the opinion of the auditor, necessary to enable the auditor to report in the prescribed manner on the financial statements to be placed before the shareholders.

Resignation of auditor (CBCA s. 164(2); OBCA s. 150)

A resignation of an auditor becomes effective at the time a written resignation is sent to the corporation or at the time specified in the resignation, whichever is later.

Disqualification as auditor (CBCA 161(3); OBCA ss. 152(1) and (3))

An auditor must be independent of a corporation and its affiliates, directors, and officers. As soon as an auditor becomes disqualified to be such, the auditor must resign.

Removal of auditor (CBCA s. 165; OBCA s. 149(4))

The shareholders of a corporation can, except where the auditor has been appointed by order of the court, remove an auditor before the expiration of the auditor's term. This is done by passing an ordinary resolution at a special meeting duly called for the purpose.

MAKING BANKING ARRANGEMENTS

To conduct business, a corporation will require a bank account. Financial institutions have their own standard documents to open an account. These forms can be obtained from the financial institution and prepared for the corporation, but many banks prefer to have the customer visit the bank in person. However the documents are completed, they — or at least a banking resolution — should be approved by the directors and inserted into the minute book because it is a "certified" copy of this resolution that is delivered to the financial institution.

The following forms are generally required. Some banks have each form as a separate document while others combine all the documents into one standard form.

1. *Operation and verification of account agreement.* This agreement establishes the terms and conditions of the corporation's account with the bank. It includes provisions for cheques being debited to the customer's account; procedures for overdrawing on the account; bank charges; and procedures regarding the verification of statements.

2. *Banking resolution.* The banking resolution names the persons who are able to sign cheques on behalf of the corporation. It is preferable to name the positions of the persons having the authority to sign because if the person named is an officer of the corporation and that person resigns and someone else is appointed to the position, there is no need to pass another resolution. It will then only be necessary to let the bank know that the officer has changed by filing a new list of directors and officers and a signature card with the bank. Sometimes, of course, this is not possible, and you will be required to name specific individuals — for example, when someone who can sign cheques is not an "officer" of the corporation.

Some corporations appoint "authorized cheque signers" and the resolution states this and appoints a senior officer to advise the bank from time to time of the names of the persons authorized to sign cheques. A new bank resolution is not required to be filed when an authorized cheque signer changes. The person appointed by the corporation to designate the authorized cheque signers will write a letter to the bank advising of a new authorized cheque signer.

Examples of cheque-signing authorities are:

a. the president alone;

b. any one of the directors and officers; or

c. any officer for amounts up to and including $2,000 and any two officers for amounts over $2,000.

3. *Certificate of incumbency.* This is a list of directors and officers certified by the secretary of the corporation or another authorized officer.

4. *Certificate of non-restriction.* A corporation is authorized by statute to borrow and this certificate provides that there are no restrictions in the articles, bylaws, or a unanimous shareholder agreement regarding the corporation's ability to borrow. Although not necessary because of the statutory authority, some banks still request "borrowing bylaws" to be passed. The borrowing bylaw reproduces the borrowing language from the statute.

5. *Specimen signature card.* Each person who is authorized to sign cheques must provide the bank with a specimen signature.

6. *Verification of authorized signatories.* The Proceeds of Crime (Money Laundering) Act (PCMLA) came into force on October 10, 1991 and regulations under this Act came into force on March 24, 1993. The object of the PCMLA at that time was to establish record-keeping requirements in the financial field in order to facilitate certain investigations and prosecutions of drug offences. Since then, the PCMLA has undergone significant changes, most recently in December 2001, when it became known as the *Proceeds of Crime (Money Laundering) and Terrorist Financing Act* (PCMLTFA). The objects of the PCMLTFA, in part, are to "implement specific measures to detect and deter money laundering and the financing of terrorist activities to facilitate the investigation and prosecution of money laundering and terrorist financing offences" (PCMLTFA s. 3). The regulations under the PCMLTFA require financial institutions to ascertain the identity of every individual who signs a signature card for an account with that financial institution. With respect to a corporate account where the signature card is signed by more than three individuals, the identity of at least three individuals who signed the card must be verified. The regulations provide that verifying the identity of an individual may be made by reference to the individual's birth certificate, driver's licence, provincial health insurance card, passport, or to any similar document. Most banks require individuals to present this identification in person at the bank, although account managers may use some discretion in these procedures.

TRANSACT ANY OTHER BUSINESS

Miscellaneous directors' resolutions may be required in the following instances:

1. If the corporation is subject to the CBCA, you may wish to consider passing a directors' resolution to authorize a member of your law firm or any individual who has the relevant knowledge of the corporation to sign notices of change in registered office and directors and the annual return pursuant to CBCA ss. 262.1(1) and (2).

2. Again, if the corporation is subject to the CBCA, consider whether the corporation will communicate with its shareholders by electronic means. If so, you may wish to pass a separate bylaw authorizing this, or you may wish to include this in your general bylaw.

3. If a contract has been entered into before the corporation came into existence, the corporation can "by any action or conduct" signify its intention to be bound by the contract (CBCA s. 14(2); OBCA s. 21(2)). This is generally done by way of a directors' resolution. Unless specifically provided otherwise in the contract, until a corporation "adopts" such a contract, the person who originally entered into the contract on behalf of the corporation is bound by the terms of the contract. Once the corporation adopts the contract, it is entitled to the benefits of the contract as if the corporation had been in existence at the date the contract was signed and had been a party to the contract.

Business conducted by shareholders at their first meeting

In addition to the directors passing "organizational" resolutions, it is customary for the shareholders to meet and pass organizational resolutions. Shareholders typically pass resolutions

1. approving the bylaws passed by the directors either with or without variation;

2. fixing the number of directors (If the corporation is an OBCA corporation, the shareholders are required pursuant to s. 125(3) to fix the number of directors and may empower the directors to fix the number of directors. If the shareholders do not pass such a resolution, the number of directors remains the number named in the articles (OBCA s. 125(4)). If the corporation is subject to the CBCA, this provision does not exist, but you may have included a procedure for fixing the number of directors in your articles. Once the number of directors has been determined, the shareholders will pass a resolution electing the permanent directors to hold office until the first annual meeting.); and

3. either appointing auditors, if the directors have not done so, or exempting the corporation from appointing auditors and complying with the audit requirements of the statute.

Directors' consents

Chapter 4 discussed the need for directors to consent to their election. It is common practice to have a "consent" signed by the directors and inserted into the minute book.

Procedure for conducting organization business

As mentioned at the beginning of this chapter, the order in which the organization is conducted will vary depending on who the first director is. The above order of business would be appropriate to follow when the client is the first director. The following order of business should be followed if you are using a first director who is a member of your law firm:

1. The first director passes resolutions

   a. to adopt forms of security certificates and corporate records, including the corporate seal, if any; and

   b. to authorize the issue of securities.

2. The first director resigns.

3. Shareholders pass resolutions to fix the number of directors and elect permanent directors.

4. Permanent directors pass resolutions

   a. to make bylaws;

   b. to appoint officers;

   c. to appoint an auditor to hold office until the first annual meeting of shareholders;

   d. to make banking arrangements; and

   e. to transact any other business.

5. Shareholders pass resolutions

   a. to approve the bylaws passed by the directors; and

   b. either to appoint auditors, if the directors have not done so, or to exempt the corporation from appointing auditors and complying with the audit requirements of the statute. (Bear in mind that if there are non-voting shareholders, they must also consent to the exemption from audit.)

All other organization matters are the same. In addition, you should prepare an "indemnity" by the shareholder for the law firm director (for further discussion of indemnification, see chapter 4).

Satisfy all requirements under the Securities Act (Ontario)

You should ensure that all appropriate documents necessary to comply with the provisions of the *Securities Act* (Ontario) are completed, and any required filings are made or fees paid with the Ontario Securities Commission.

File an initial return

If the corporation you are organizing is an Ontario corporation or a federal corporation carrying on business in Ontario, the provisions of the *Corporations Information Act* (Ontario) (CIA) apply. Section 2 of the CIA provides:

> (1) Every corporation other than an extra-provincial corporation or a corporation of a class exempted by the regulations shall file with the Minister [of Consumer and Business Services] an initial return setting out the prescribed information as of the date of filing.
>
> (2) The initial return shall be filed within sixty days after the date of incorporation, amalgamation or continuation of the corporation.

The information to be included in the return filed under this section is:

1. The name of the corporation.

2. The Ontario corporation number of the corporation.

3. The date of its incorporation or amalgamation, whichever is the most recent.

4. The names and addresses for service of the corporation's directors, including municipality, street and number, if any, and postal code.

5. The date on which each director became a director and, where applicable, the date on which a director ceased to be a director.

6. If the corporation is a corporation with share capital, a statement as to whether each director is or is not a resident Canadian.

7. The names and addresses for service, including municipality, street and number, if any, and postal code, of the corporation's five most senior officers. Note that filings will not be accepted with more officers listed. The corporate client should determine this information.

8. The date on which each person referred to in (7) became a senior officer and, where applicable, the date on which a person ceased to be a senior officer.

9. The addresses of the corporation's head or registered office, including municipality, street and number, if any, and postal code.

10. The mailing address, if different from the registered office address.

11. Whether the preferred language of communication with the corporation is English or French.

The initial return (Form 1) can be filed online through one of the ministry's service providers (Cyberbahn Inc. or Oncorp Direct Inc.) or by mailing or personally delivering a paper copy of Form 1 to the ministry at its Toronto address. There is no government fee to file Form 1, but if you choose to file electronically, the service providers have a small filing fee. No original signature is required on the form but it must be verified by the certificate of an officer or director of the corporation or other individual having knowledge of the affairs of the corporation.

Section 3(1) of the CIA provides that

> Every extra-provincial corporation [including CBCA corporations], other than a corporation of a class exempted by the regulations [including corporations subject

to the *Bank Act* (Canada), corporations that operate railways or telegraph lines or carry on the business of a railway express company or the business of leasing or hiring railway sleeping, parlour, or dining cars in Ontario, corporations subject to the *Telephone Act*, International Bank for Reconstruction and Development approved by the *Bretton Woods and Related Agreements Act* (Canada), and municipalities within the meaning of the *Municipal Affairs Act*], that begins to carry on business in Ontario shall file with the Minister an initial return setting out the prescribed information as of the date of filing.

Once again, this return, which is on Form 2, must be filed within 60 days after the date the corporation begins to carry on business in Ontario.

Form 2 must contain:

1. the name of the corporation;

2. the Ontario corporation number of the corporation;

3. the date of its incorporation or amalgamation, whichever is the most recent;

4. the name of the jurisdiction in which the corporation was incorporated, continued, or amalgamated;

5. the address of the corporation's head or registered office, including municipality, street and number, if any, and postal code;

6. the date on which the corporation commenced activities in Ontario, and, where applicable, the date on which it ceased activities in Ontario;

7. the name and office address of the corporation's chief officer or manager in Ontario, if any, including municipality, street and number, if any, and postal code, the date on which the person assumed this position, and, where applicable, the date on which the person ceased to hold this position;

8. the address of the corporation's principal office in Ontario, if any, including municipality, street and number, if any, and postal code;

9. if the corporation is required by law to have an agent for service in Ontario, the name and address of its agent, including municipality, street and number, if any, and postal code, and the Ontario corporation number of the agent, if the agent is a corporation (this section is not applicable to CBCA corporations);

10. whether the preferred language of communication with the corporation is English or French; and

11. the immediate former name of the corporation.

To date, the initial return for extra-provincial corporations (Form 2) can be filed only by mailing or delivering a paper copy to the ministry at its Toronto address. No original signature is required on the form but it must be verified by the certificate of an officer or director of the corporation or other individual having knowledge of the affairs of the corporation. Once again, there is no government filing fee. Ontario Companies Branch policy requires that a photocopy of the page of the most recent articles or other constating documents, containing the correct name and incorporation/amalgamation date, accompany the initial return.

The CIA (s. 5(2)) provides that a corporation must maintain an up-to-date paper or electronic record of the prescribed information set out in returns and notices that it has filed under the Act and make the record available for examination by any shareholder, member, director, officer, or creditor of the corporation during its normal business hours at its registered office or principal place of business in Ontario.

Reporting to your client

When you have completed the post-incorporation organization and had all documents signed and filed in the minute book, it is time to communicate with your client so that the client knows what has been done and what must be done to maintain the corporation in good standing going forward. This is generally accomplished by way of a report letter. The report letter is usually quite a lengthy document. For this reason, if there is any action required from the client, it is advisable to prepare a short cover letter referring to the "formal" report letter and outlining the actions requested of the client.

The report letter customarily addresses:

- particulars of incorporation, including jurisdiction and date, and special provisions in the articles;

- particulars of the authorized and issued share capital and any restrictions on the transfer of shares, including share conditions;

- particulars of any restrictions on the business of the corporation;

- particulars about the registered office;

- particulars about banking, authorized signing officers, and the financial year-end;

- names of persons who may sign contracts on behalf of the corporation;

- particulars about the number and names of the directors and officers of the corporation and their liabilities and standards of care required;

- requirements for director meetings, such as notice, quorum, and dates, if any;

- particulars about the names of the shareholders and number of shares held by each;

- requirements for shareholder meetings, including notice, quorum, proxies, place, etc.;

- particulars about the auditor or accountant and a reiteration of the exemption for non-offering corporations;

- particulars about taxes to be paid;

- requirements of corporate records to be maintained;

- particulars of registration of any business names, domain names, or trademarks;

- particulars about initial filings under the CIA; and

- particulars of bylaws.

Practices vary as to when the account will be sent to the client for the incorporation. Some firms include the account with their final report letter. Other firms send the account separately. The account will give a detailed explanation of the services performed together with a breakdown of disbursements incurred, which may include the following:

- name search fee;
- incorporation fee;
- fee for registration of business name;
- minute book;
- corporate seal;
- share certificates;
- photocopying;
- telephone calls; or
- facsimile transmissions.

The report letter is often addressed to the corporation and marked to the attention of the senior officer. By directing the report to the corporation, certain incorporation and organization expenses may be written off by the corporation against its income.

KEY TERMS

bylaws

casting vote

minute book

post-incorporation organization

quorum

REFERENCES

Business Corporations Act (Ontario) (OBCA), RSO 1990, c. B.16, as amended.

Business Records Protection Act, RSO 1990, c. B.19, as amended.

Canada Business Corporations Act (CBCA), RSC 1985, c. C-44, as amended.

Canada Pension Plan, RSC 1985, c. C-8, as amended.

Copyright Act, RSC 1985, c. C-42, as amended.

Corporations Information Act (Ontario) (CIA), RSO 1990, c. C.39, as amended.

Customs Act, RSC 1985, c. 1 (2d Supp.), as amended.

Debbo, Brennan, *Record Retention* (Toronto: Miller Thomson LLP, July 2002).

Employment Insurance Act, SC 1996, c. 23.

Employment Standards Act, 2000, SO 2000, c. 41.

Excise Tax Act, RSC 1985, c. E-15, as amended.

Income Tax Act, RSC 1985, c. 1 (5th Supp.), as amended.

Limitations Act, RSO 1990, c. L.15, as amended.

Proceeds of Crime (Money Laundering) and Terrorist Financing Act, SC 2000, c. 17.

Retail Sales Tax Act, RSO 1990, c. R.31, as amended.

Securities Act, RSO 1990, c. S.2, as amended.

Trade-marks Act, RSC 1985, c. T-13, as amended.

Workplace Safety and Insurance Act, 1997, SO 1997, c. 16, sched. A.

FORMS AND PRECEDENTS

Figure 8.1: Sample organization proceedings for a federal corporation, including share certificates, bylaws, and report letter

Figure 8.2: Sample organizaion proceedings for an Ontario corporation, including share certificates, bank documents, bylaws, initial return Form 1, and report letter

NOTES

1. The author thanks Brennan Debbo, a former associate tax lawyer with Miller Thomson LLP, for providing this information.

REVIEW QUESTIONS

1. Describe what is meant by "post -incorporation organization" of a corporation.

2. List the steps required to organize a federal corporation.

3. List two methods of accomplishing the organization and explain briefly what is meant by each.

4. List four matters that will be approved by the directors.

5. List two matters that will be dealt with by the shareholders.

6. Describe the procedure for issuing shares.

7. List three items of business that you would consider conducting for a CBCA corporation that are not part of the standard organization.

8. Kitten Toys Inc. is a federal corporation operating in Ontario. What filings must be made after it starts up its business?

9. Are the following statements true or false?

   a. Once a corporation is incorporated, there are no further legal steps required.

   b. The directors may not be able to pass the initial organizational resolutions because there may be a unanimous shareholder agreement in place restricting their powers.

   c. A resolution fixing the number of directors between the minimum and maximum number of directors is an ordinary resolution of the shareholders.

   d. All corporations must have a corporation seal.

   e. The *Securities Act* (Ontario) does not apply to a non-offering corporation.

   f. A written resolution of the directors can be signed by a quorum of directors.

   g. When the directors pass a bylaw, it must be approved by the shareholders before it becomes effective.

   h. A corporation can destroy its records whenever it feels like it.

   i. Shares must be fully paid for before they can be issued.

   j. A corporation that is not offering its shares to the public may, if all of the voting and non-voting shareholders consent, waive the requirement to appoint an auditor.

   k. An initial return under the *Corporations Information Act* must be filed for Ontario corporations within 10 days of incorporation.

CASE STUDIES

Case study 8.1: Federal post-incorporation organization

BSJ Garden Ornament Sales Inc. was incorporated under the CBCA on December 24, 2003. Jessie filed the original copies of the signed articles of incorporation, Form 3, Form 6, and the name decision letter by facsimile with Corporations Canada. The cover letter requested that the fees for the incorporation be taken out of the deposit account that Thorn & Hill maintained with Corporations Canada.

As soon as she received the certificate of incorporation, Jessie prepared the post-incorporation organization documents. She used the information she obtained from Mr. Black at their first meeting, which included the following:

#	Type of information required	Information		
1.	Full name, residence address, and citizenship of directors and officers	Peter Black President	1 First St. Port Ellen ON L3R 0A9	Canadian
		Shirley Smith Vice-president	2 Second St. Port Ellen ON L3R 0B9	Canadian
		Roger Jones Secretary	3 Third St. Port Ellen ON L3R 0D9	Canadian
2.	Name of shareholders, number of shares issued, and consideration	Peter Black	1 common	$1.00
		Shirley Smith	1 common	$1.00
		Roger Jones	1 common	$1.00
		Clarence Smith	1,000 preferred	$1,000
3.	Name of bank and bank signing authorities	Royal Bank of Canada Any two of the directors		
4.	Financial year-end	December 31		
5.	Name of auditor	ABC Accounting LLP		
6.	Contract signing authority	Any 2 directors and officers		
7.	Provinces where corporation will carry on business	Ontario		

See figure 8.1 at the end of this chapter. The documents are prepared on the basis of the amended and restated rule 45-501, effective January 12, 2004.

Case study 8.2: Ontario post-incorporation organization

01111111 Ontario Inc. was incorporated under the *Business Corporations Act* (Ontario) on October 31, 2003. Two originally signed copies of the articles of incorporation and the consent to act as director, together with a cheque in the amount of $360 made payable to the Minister of Finance (Ontario) and a cover letter, were filed by Jessie in person at the Companies and Personal Property Security Branch on University Avenue in Toronto. The certificate of incorporation was issued immediately. The number name of the corporation was 01111111 Ontario Inc.

As soon as Jessie received the certificate of incorporation, she prepared the post-incorporation organization documents. She used the information that Mr. Hill had given her with his original instructions.

See figure 8.2 at the end of this chapter. The documents are prepared on the basis of the amended and restated rule 45-501, effective January 12, 2004.

FIGURE 8.1   SAMPLE ORGANIZATION PROCEEDINGS FOR A FEDERAL CORPORATION

SUBSCRIPTION

TO: **BSJ GARDEN ORNAMENT SALES INC.**
                 (the "Corporation")

AND TO: **THE DIRECTORS THEREOF**

The undersigned subscribes for the number and class of shares in the capital of the Corporation set out below and tenders herewith the total subscription price as follows:

SUBSCRIBER	NUMBER AND CLASS OF SHARES	TOTAL SUBSCRIPTION PRICE
Peter Black	1 - common	$1.00

The undersigned requests that the said shares be issued as fully paid and non-assessable to the undersigned and that a certificate or certificates representing such shares be issued in the name of and delivered to the undersigned.

The undersigned undertakes to advise the Corporation of any change in beneficial ownership of the said shares.

DATED as of the 24th day of December, 2003.

_____
                                         Peter Black

FIGURE 8.1   CONTINUED

SUBSCRIPTION

TO: **BSJ GARDEN ORNAMENT SALES INC.**
                (the "Corporation")

AND TO: **THE DIRECTORS THEREOF**

The undersigned subscribes for the number and class of shares in the capital of the Corporation set out below and tenders herewith the total subscription price as follows:

SUBSCRIBER	NUMBER AND CLASS OF SHARES	TOTAL SUBSCRIPTION PRICE
Shirley Smith	1 - common	$1.00

The undersigned requests that the said shares be issued as fully paid and non-assessable to the undersigned and that a certificate or certificates representing such shares be issued in the name of and delivered to the undersigned.

The undersigned undertakes to advise the Corporation of any change in beneficial ownership of the said shares.

DATED as of the 24th day of December, 2003.

_____
Shirley Smith

FIGURE 8.1   CONTINUED

SUBSCRIPTION

TO: **BSJ GARDEN ORNAMENT SALES INC.**
             (the "Corporation")

AND TO: **THE DIRECTORS THEREOF**

The undersigned subscribes for the number and class of shares in the capital of the Corporation set out below and tenders herewith the total subscription price as follows:

SUBSCRIBER	NUMBER AND CLASS OF SHARES	TOTAL SUBSCRIPTION PRICE
Roger Jones	1 - common	$1.00

The undersigned requests that the said shares be issued as fully paid and non-assessable to the undersigned and that a certificate or certificates representing such shares be issued in the name of and delivered to the undersigned.

The undersigned undertakes to advise the Corporation of any change in beneficial ownership of the said shares.

DATED as of the 24th day of December, 2003.

_____
                                          Roger Jones

FIGURE 8.1 CONTINUED

SUBSCRIPTION

TO: **BSJ GARDEN ORNAMENT SALES INC.**
         (the "Corporation")

AND TO: **THE DIRECTORS THEREOF**

The undersigned subscribes for the number and class of shares in the capital of the Corporation set out below and tenders herewith the total subscription price as follows:

SUBSCRIBER	NUMBER AND CLASS OF SHARES	TOTAL SUBSCRIPTION PRICE
Clarence Smith	1,000 - preferred	$1,000

The undersigned requests that the said shares be issued as fully paid and non-assessable to the undersigned and that a certificate or certificates representing such shares be issued in the name of and delivered to the undersigned.

The undersigned undertakes to advise the Corporation of any change in beneficial ownership of the said shares.

DATED as of the 24th day of December, 2003.

_____
Clarence Smith

FIGURE 8.1 CONTINUED

RESOLUTIONS OF THE BOARD OF DIRECTORS

OF

BSJ GARDEN ORNAMENT SALES INC.
(the "Corporation")

BY-LAW NUMBER 1

RESOLVED that a by-law relating generally to the conduct of the business and affairs of the Corporation is made as By-law Number 1, and the President and Secretary of the Corporation are directed to sign the by-law and insert a copy in the minute book.

APPOINTMENT OF OFFICERS

RESOLVED that the following persons are appointed as the officers of the Corporation, to hold such office or offices until they resign or are removed by the directors:

Name	Position Held
Peter Black	President
Shirley Smith	Vice President
Roger Jones	Secretary

FORM OF SHARE CERTIFICATES

RESOLVED that:

1. The form of share certificate for the common shares in the capital of the Corporation, a specimen of which is annexed hereto, is approved and adopted.

2. The form of share certificate for the preferred shares in the capital of the Corporation, a specimen of which is annexed hereto, is approved and adopted.

3. Until changed by resolution the President and Secretary of the Corporation are authorized to sign all share certificates on behalf of the Corporation.

ISSUANCE OF COMMON SHARES

RESOLVED that:

1. The subscriptions of Peter Black, Shirley Smith, and Roger Jones (the "Subscribers") for an aggregate of three common shares (the "Shares") in the capital of the Corporation, which subscriptions are annexed hereto, be and the same are hereby accepted.

FIGURE 8.1 CONTINUED

Page 2

2. The directors of the Corporation hereby determine the sum of $3.00, namely $1.00 per share, as the aggregate consideration for the issuance of the Shares subscribed for by the Subscribers.

3. The Corporation having received the sum of $3.00 in full payment of the aggregate consideration for the Shares, three common shares in the capital of the Corporation be and the same are hereby issued to the Subscribers as follows:

Name of Subscriber	Number
Peter Black	1
Shirley Smith	1
Roger Jones	1

4. It is hereby directed that certificates representing the Shares be issued to the Subscribers in the number of shares set out opposite their respective names above.

ISSUANCE OF PREFERRED SHARES

RESOLVED that:

1. The subscription of Clarence Smith (the "Subscriber") for 1,000 preferred shares (the "Shares") in the capital of the Corporation, which subscription is annexed hereto, be and the same is hereby accepted.

2. The directors of the Corporation hereby determine the sum of $1,000.00, as the aggregate consideration for the issuance of the Shares subscribed for by the Subscriber.

3. The Corporation having received the sum of $1,000.00 in full payment of the consideration for the Shares, 1,000 preferred shares in the capital of the Corporation be and the same are hereby issued to the Subscriber.

4. It is hereby directed that a certificate representing the Shares be issued to the Subscriber.

FIGURE 8.1 CONTINUED

CORPORATE SEAL

RESOLVED that the corporate seal of the Corporation shall be in the form impressed hereon.

BANKING DOCUMENTS

RESOLVED that:

1. A bank account be established with Royal Bank of Canada and that the resolution regarding banking and security annexed hereto is approved and adopted.

2. The directors and officers of the Corporation are authorized and directed to execute and deliver to the Corporation's bankers such banking documents as are requisite or necessary to open an account with such bank.

FINANCIAL YEAR

RESOLVED that until changed by resolution of the directors, the financial year of the Corporation shall end on December 31 in each year.

AUTHORITY TO SIGN NOTICES

RESOLVED that the firm of Thorn & Hill LLP (the "Corporation's Solicitors") be appointed solicitors for the Corporation and any partner, associate or corporate law clerk employed by the Corporation's Solicitors who has the relevant knowledge of the Corporation is authorized to sign and file (electronically or otherwise):

(a)   any notice of registered office or change in the address of the registered office;
(b)   any notice of directors, notice of change of directors or notice of change in director's address; and
(c)   any annual return.

EXTRA PROVINCIAL / TERRITORIAL REGISTRATION

RESOLVED that any officer or director of the Corporation may execute such document or documents as may be required to apply for extra provincial or extra-territorial licenses in those provinces and territories where the Corporation will carry on business and to appoint attorneys or attorneys for service in respect of such extra-provincial or extra-territorial licenses.

FIGURE 8.1   CONTINUED

LOCATION OF BOOKS AND RECORDS

RESOLVED that the Corporation maintains, at its registered office or at the offices of Miller Thomson LLP, the records and registers specified in Sections 20 and 50 (3) of the *Canada Business Corporations Act*.

THE UNDERSIGNED, being all the directors of the Corporation, pass the foregoing resolutions pursuant to the provisions of the *Canada Business Corporations Act*.

DATED as of the 24th day of December, 2003.

_____   _____
Peter Black   Roger Jones

_____
Shirley Smith

FIGURE 8.1   CONTINUED

Certificate No.

For _____ Common Shares

Issued to

Dated

From whom transferred

Dated
No. Original Certificate
No. Original Shares
No. of Shares Transferred

Received Certificate No. _____

for _____ Shares

this _____ day of _____ ,

INCORPORATED UNDER THE CANADA BUSINESS CORPORATIONS ACT

No.   Common Shares

BSJ GARDEN ORNAMENT SALES INC.

SPECIMEN

This is to Certify that

is the registered holder of _____ Common Shares of

BSJ GARDEN ORNAMENT SALES INC.

The class or series of shares represented by this Certificate has rights, privileges, restrictions or conditions attached thereto and the Corporation will furnish to the holder, on demand and without charge, a full copy of the text of,

(i) the rights, privileges, restrictions and conditions attached to the said shares and to each class authorized to be issued and to each series insofar as the same have been fixed by the directors, and

(ii) the authority of the directors to fix the rights, privileges, restrictions and conditions of subsequent series, if applicable.

LIEN ON SHARES.   The Corporation has a lien on the shares represented by this Certificate for any debt of the shareholder to the Corporation.

RESTRICTIONS ON TRANSFER.   There are restrictions on the right to transfer the shares represented by this Certificate.

IN WITNESS WHEREOF the Corporation has caused this Certificate to be signed by its duly authorized officers

this _____ day of _____ .

FIGURE 8.1   CONTINUED

CERTIFICATE
FOR

COMMON
SHARES OF

BSJ GARDEN ORNAMENT SALES INC.

ISSUED TO

DATE

For Value Received, _____ hereby assign and transfer unto _____ Common Shares represented by the within Certificate.

Dated _____ , _____.

In the presence of

_____

_____

FIGURE 8.1 CONTINUED

Certificate No. _____

For _____ Preferred Shares

Issued to

Dated

From whom transferred

Dated

No. Original Certificate

No. Original Shares

No. of Shares Transferred

Received Certificate No. _____

for _____ Shares

this _____ day of _____, _____

INCORPORATED UNDER THE CANADA BUSINESS CORPORATIONS ACT

BSJ GARDEN ORNAMENT SALES INC.

Preferred Shares

No.

SPECIMEN

This is to Certify that

is the registered holder of _____ Preferred Shares of

BSJ GARDEN ORNAMENT SALES INC.

The class or series of shares represented by this Certificate has rights, privileges, restrictions or conditions attached thereto and the Corporation will furnish to the holder, on demand and without charge, a full copy of the text of,

(i) the rights, privileges, restrictions and conditions attached to the said shares and to each class authorized to be issued and to each series insofar as the same have been fixed by the directors, and

(ii) the authority of the directors to fix the rights, privileges, restrictions and conditions of subsequent series, if applicable.

LIEN ON SHARES. The Corporation has a lien on the shares represented by this Certificate for any debt of the shareholder to the Corporation.

RESTRICTIONS ON TRANSFER. There are restrictions on the right to transfer the shares represented by this Certificate.

IN WITNESS WHEREOF the Corporation has caused this Certificate to be signed by its duly authorized officers this _____ day of _____, _____.

FIGURE 8.1 CONTINUED

For Value Received, _____ hereby assign and
transfer unto _____
Preferred Shares represented by the within
Certificate.

Dated _____ , _____.

In the presence of

_____

_____

FIGURE 8.1 CONTINUED

RESOLUTIONS OF THE SHAREHOLDERS

OF

BSJ GARDEN ORNAMENT SALES INC.
(the "Corporation")

CONFIRMATION OF BY-LAW NO. 1

WHEREAS the directors have made By-law No. 1 and submitted it to the shareholders for approval;

RESOLVED, as an ordinary resolution, that By-law No. 1 is confirmed.

ELECTION OF DIRECTORS

RESOLVED, as an ordinary resolution, that:

1.   The number of directors to be elected within the minimum and maximum number of directors set out in the articles of incorporation is one.

2.   The following individuals are elected as the directors the Corporation until the first annual meeting of the shareholders of the Corporation or until they otherwise cease to hold office as a director of the Corporation:

> Peter Black
> Roger Jones
> Shirley Smith

APPOINTMENT OF AUDITOR

RESOLVED, as an ordinary resolution, that ABC Accounting LLP is appointed the auditor of the Corporation to hold office until a successor is elected or appointed, at such remuneration as may be fixed by the directors, the directors being authorized to fix such remuneration.

THE UNDERSIGNED, being all the shareholders of the Corporation entitled to vote thereon, pass the foregoing resolutions pursuant to the provisions of the *Canada Business Corporations Act*.

DATED as of the 24th day of December, 2003.

_____   _____
Peter Black   Roger Jones

_____
Shirley Smith

FIGURE 8.1   CONTINUED

DIRECTOR'S CONSENT AND ACKNOWLEDGEMENT

TO: **BSJ GARDEN ORNAMENT SALES INC.**
(the "Corporation")

I, the undersigned, in accordance with the provisions of the *Canada Business Corporations Act* Canada (the "Act"):

(1)   Consent to act as a director of the Corporation, such consent to continue in effect unless revoked by instrument in writing delivered to the Corporation.

(2)   Acknowledge and declare that I am:

☐   a Canadian citizen ordinarily resident in Canada; **OR**

☐   a Canadian citizen <u>not</u> ordinarily resident in Canada who is a member of a prescribed class of persons (refer to Schedule A); **OR**

☐   a permanent resident within the meaning of the *Immigration Act* and ordinarily resident in Canada, except a permanent resident who has been ordinarily resident in Canada for more than one year after the time at which I first became eligible to apply for Canadian citizenship; **OR**

☐   none of the above

(3)   Undertake to advise the Corporation, in writing, forthwith after any change in citizenship, residence or status of lawful admission for permanent residence.

(4)   Acknowledge that:

a)   I am not under 18 years of age;

b)   I am not a person who has been found by a court in Canada or elsewhere to be of unsound mind; and

c)   I am not an undischarged bankrupt.

(5)   Consent to any director participating in a meeting of the directors or of a committee of directors by means of a telephonic, electronic or other communication facility that permits all participants to communicate adequately with each other during the meeting.

FIGURE 8.1 CONTINUED

(6)   Acknowledge that the Corporation will rely upon the foregoing consents and undertakings for the purpose of ensuring compliance by the Corporation with the provisions of the Act.

DATED as of the 24th day of December, 2003.

_____

Peter Black
1 First Street
Port Ellen, Ontario L3R 0A9

FIGURE 8.1   CONTINUED

SCHEDULE A

"Resident Canadian" Class of Persons Prescribed
SOR/2001-3-12, section 13 made under the *Canada Business Corporations Act* (the "Act")

For the purposes of the definition of "resident Canadian" in subsection 2 (1) of the Act, the following classes of persons are prescribed:

1.   persons who are full-time employees of the Government of Canada, or a province, of an agency of any of those governments or of a federal or provincial Crown corporation, if the principal reason for their residence outside Canada is to act as employees;

2.   persons who are full-time employees, if the principal reason for their residence outside Canada is to act as employees, of a body corporate,

    (i)   of which more than 50 per cent of the voting shares are beneficially owned or over which control or direction is exercised by resident Canadians,

    (ii)   a majority of directors of which are resident Canadians, or

    (iii)   that is a subsidiary of a body corporate described in subparagraph (i) or (ii);

3.   persons who are full-time students at a university or other educational institution recognized by the educational authorities of a majority of the provinces of Canada and have been resident outside Canada for fewer than 10 consecutive years;

4.   persons who are full-time employees of an international association or organization of which Canada is a member; and

5.   persons who were, at the time of reaching their 60th birthday, ordinarily resident in Canada and have been resident outside of Canada for fewer than 10 consecutive years.

FIGURE 8.1 CONTINUED

DIRECTOR'S CONSENT AND ACKNOWLEDGEMENT

TO: BSJ GARDEN ORNAMENT SALES INC.
(the "Corporation")

I, the undersigned, in accordance with the provisions of the *Canada Business Corporations Act* Canada (the "Act"):

(1)   Consent to act as a director of the Corporation, such consent to continue in effect unless revoked by instrument in writing delivered to the Corporation.

(2)   Acknowledge and declare that I am:

☐   a Canadian citizen ordinarily resident in Canada; **OR**

☐   a Canadian citizen <u>not</u> ordinarily resident in Canada who is a member of a prescribed class of persons (refer to Schedule A); **OR**

☐   a permanent resident within the meaning of the *Immigration Act* and ordinarily resident in Canada, except a permanent resident who has been ordinarily resident in Canada for more than one year after the time at which I first became eligible to apply for Canadian citizenship; **OR**

☐   none of the above

(3)   Undertake to advise the Corporation, in writing, forthwith after any change in citizenship, residence or status of lawful admission for permanent residence.

(4)   Acknowledge that:

a)   I am not under 18 years of age;

b)   I am not a person who has been found by a court in Canada or elsewhere to be of unsound mind; and

c)   I am not an undischarged bankrupt.

(5)   Consent to any director participating in a meeting of the directors or of a committee of directors by means of a telephonic, electronic or other communication facility that permits all participants to communicate adequately with each other during the meeting.

FIGURE 8.1   CONTINUED

(6)   Acknowledge that the Corporation will rely upon the foregoing consents and undertakings for the purpose of ensuring compliance by the Corporation with the provisions of the Act.

DATED as of the 24th day of December, 2003.

_____

Roger Jones
3 Third Street
Port Ellen, Ontario L3R 0D9

FIGURE 8.1 CONTINUED

SCHEDULE A

"Resident Canadian" Class of Persons Prescribed
SOR/2001-3-12, section 13 made under the *Canada Business Corporations Act* (the "Act")

For the purposes of the definition of "resident Canadian" in subsection 2 (1) of the Act, the following classes of persons are prescribed:

1. persons who are full-time employees of the Government of Canada, or a province, of an agency of any of those governments or of a federal or provincial Crown corporation, if the principal reason for their residence outside Canada is to act as employees;

2. persons who are full-time employees, if the principal reason for their residence outside Canada is to act as employees, of a body corporate,

    (i)   of which more than 50 per cent of the voting shares are beneficially owned or over which control or direction is exercised by resident Canadians,

    (ii) a majority of directors of which are resident Canadians, or

    (iii) that is a subsidiary of a body corporate described in subparagraph (i) or (ii);

3. persons who are full-time students at a university or other educational institution recognized by the educational authorities of a majority of the provinces of Canada and have been resident outside Canada for fewer than 10 consecutive years;

4. persons who are full-time employees of an international association or organization of which Canada is a member; and

5. persons who were, at the time of reaching their 60th birthday, ordinarily resident in Canada and have been resident outside of Canada for fewer than 10 consecutive years.

FIGURE 8.1 CONTINUED

DIRECTOR'S CONSENT AND ACKNOWLEDGEMENT

TO: **BSJ GARDEN ORNAMENT SALES INC.**
(the "Corporation")

I, the undersigned, in accordance with the provisions of the *Canada Business Corporations Act* Canada (the "Act"):

(1)   Consent to act as a director of the Corporation, such consent to continue in effect unless revoked by instrument in writing delivered to the Corporation.

(2)   Acknowledge and declare that I am:

☐   a Canadian citizen ordinarily resident in Canada; **OR**

☐   a Canadian citizen <u>not</u> ordinarily resident in Canada who is a member of a prescribed class of persons (refer to Schedule A); **OR**

☐   a permanent resident within the meaning of the *Immigration Act* and ordinarily resident in Canada, except a permanent resident who has been ordinarily resident in Canada for more than one year after the time at which I first became eligible to apply for Canadian citizenship; **OR**

☐   none of the above

(3)   Undertake to advise the Corporation, in writing, forthwith after any change in citizenship, residence or status of lawful admission for permanent residence.

(4)   Acknowledge that:

a)   I am not under 18 years of age;

b)   I am not a person who has been found by a court in Canada or elsewhere to be of unsound mind; and

c)   I am not an undischarged bankrupt.

(5)   Consent to any director participating in a meeting of the directors or of a committee of directors by means of a telephonic, electronic or other communication facility that permits all participants to communicate adequately with each other during the meeting.

FIGURE 8.1 CONTINUED

(6)   Acknowledge that the Corporation will rely upon the foregoing consents and undertakings for the purpose of ensuring compliance by the Corporation with the provisions of the Act.

DATED as of the 24th day of December, 2003.

———————————————————————
Shirley Smith
2 Second Street
Port Ellen, Ontario L3R 0B9

FIGURE 8.1   CONTINUED

SCHEDULE A

"Resident Canadian" Class of Persons Prescribed
SOR/2001-3-12, section 13 made under the *Canada Business Corporations Act* (the "Act")

For the purposes of the definition of "resident Canadian" in subsection 2 (1) of the Act, the following classes of persons are prescribed:

1.   persons who are full-time employees of the Government of Canada, or a province, of an agency of any of those governments or of a federal or provincial Crown corporation, if the principal reason for their residence outside Canada is to act as employees;

2.   persons who are full-time employees, if the principal reason for their residence outside Canada is to act as employees, of a body corporate,

   (i)   of which more than 50 per cent of the voting shares are beneficially owned or over which control or direction is exercised by resident Canadians,

   (ii)   a majority of directors of which are resident Canadians, or

   (iii)   that is a subsidiary of a body corporate described in subparagraph (i) or (ii);

3.   persons who are full-time students at a university or other educational institution recognized by the educational authorities of a majority of the provinces of Canada and have been resident outside Canada for fewer than 10 consecutive years;

4.   persons who are full-time employees of an international association or organization of which Canada is a member; and

5.   persons who were, at the time of reaching their 60th birthday, ordinarily resident in Canada and have been resident outside of Canada for fewer than 10 consecutive years.

FIGURE 8.1   CONTINUED

BY-LAW NO. 1
A by-law relating generally to
the transaction of the business and affairs
of
BSJ GARDEN ORNAMENT SALES INC.
(the "Corporation")

TABLE OF CONTENTS

FIGURE 8.1   CONTINUED

Page   ii

FIGURE 8.1 CONTINUED

BY-LAW NO. 1
a by-law relating generally to
the conduct of
the business and affairs of
BSJ GARDEN ORNAMENT SALES INC.
(the "Corporation")

BE IT MADE as a by-law of the Corporation as follows:

1.   **INTERPRETATION**

1.1   **Definitions.** In this by-law and all other by-laws and resolutions of the Corporation, unless the context otherwise requires:

(a)   the following terms shall have the meanings specified:

    (i)   "Act" means the *Canada Business Corporations Act*, or any statute that may be substituted therefor, including the regulations made thereunder, as amended from time to time;

    (ii)   "Articles" means the Articles of Incorporation of the Corporation as amended or restated from time to time;

    (iii)   "Board" means the board of directors of the Corporation;

    (iv)   "Chairperson of the Board" means the Director appointed by the Board from time to time to hold that office;

    (v)   "Corporation" means BSJ Garden Ornament Sales Inc.

    (vi)   "Defaulting Shareholder" means a shareholder of the Corporation who defaults in the payment of any Shareholder Debt when the same becomes due and payable;

    (vii)   "Director" means a member of the Board;

    (viii)   "Liened Shares" means the whole or any part of the shares registered in the name of a Defaulting Shareholder;

    (ix)   "meeting of shareholders" means an annual meeting of shareholders or a special meeting of shareholders, or both, and includes a meeting of any class or series of any class of shareholders;

    (x)   "Officer" means an officer of the Corporation;

    (xi)   "Shareholder Debt" means any principal or interest due in respect of any indebtedness owing by the holder of shares of any class or series in the

FIGURE 8.1 CONTINUED

Corporation, including, without limitation, an amount unpaid in respect of a share issued by a body corporate on the date it was continued under this Act;

(b)   terms that are defined in the Act are used in this by-law with the same meaning; and

(c)   words importing the singular number shall include the plural number and vice versa, and words importing the masculine gender shall include the feminine and neuter genders.

2.   DIRECTORS

2.1   Number of Directors. The minimum and maximum number of Directors of the Corporation shall be such as are from time to time set forth in the Articles. The number of Directors within such range shall be determined from time to time as set forth in the Articles.

2.2   Election and Term. The Directors shall be elected by the shareholders after the effective date of this By-law and at each succeeding annual meeting at which an election of Directors is required, and shall hold office until the next annual meeting of shareholders or, if elected for an expressly stated term, for a term expiring not later than the close of the third annual meeting of shareholders following the election.

2.3   Remuneration and Expenses. Each Director shall be remunerated for his services as a Director at such rate as the Board may from time to time determine. In addition, each Director shall be paid such sums in respect of the out-of-pocket expenses incurred by him in attending meetings of the Board, meetings of any committee of the Board of which he is a member, or meetings of shareholders, or otherwise incurred by him in connection with the performance of his duties as a Director, as the Board may from time to time determine. Nothing herein contained shall preclude any Director from receiving remuneration for serving the Corporation as an Officer or employee or in any other capacity.

3.   MEETINGS OF DIRECTORS

3.1   Quorum. A majority of the number of Directors which then constitutes the Board shall constitute a quorum for the transaction of business at any meeting of the Board. If it is necessary to determine the number of Directors constituting a quorum at a time when one or more vacancies exist on the Board, such a determination shall be made as if such vacancies did not exist.

3.2   Calling of Meetings. A meeting of the Board may be held at any time upon call by the Board, the Chairperson of the Board, the President or any other Officer so empowered by the Board.

3.3   Place of Meetings. Each meeting of the Board shall be held at such place within or outside Ontario as may be determined by the person calling the meeting.

FIGURE 8.1 CONTINUED

Page 3

3.4 Notice. Subject as hereinafter provided, notice of every meeting of the Board shall be given to each Director at least 48 hours prior to the meeting. Notwithstanding the foregoing:

(a) no notice need be given of the first meeting of the Board subsequent to a meeting of shareholders at which Directors are elected if such Board meeting is held immediately following the meeting of shareholders; and

(b) the Board may appoint a day or days in any month or months for regular meetings at a place and hour to be named.

A copy of any resolution by the Board fixing the time and place of regular meetings of the Board shall be sent to each Director forthwith after being passed, but no other notice shall be required for any such regular meeting. The accidental failure to give notice of a meeting of the Board to a Director or any error in such notice not affecting the substance thereof shall not invalidate any action taken at the meeting.

3.5 Votes to Govern. Every question at a meeting of the Board shall be decided by a majority of the votes cast on the question. In the event of an equality of votes on any question at a meeting of the Board, the Chairperson of the Board shall not be entitled to a second or casting vote.

4. OFFICERS

4.1 Appointment. Subject to any Unanimous Shareholder Agreement, the Board may from time to time designate the officers of the Corporation and from time to time appoint a Chairperson of the Board, managing director, president, one or more vice-presidents (to which title may be added words indicating seniority of function), a secretary, a treasurer and such other officers as the Board may determine, including, without limitation, one or more assistants to any of the officers so appointed. One person may hold more than one office. The Board may specify the duties of and, in accordance with these By-laws and subject to the Act, delegate to such officers powers to manage the business and affairs of the Corporation. Except for the Chairperson of the Board and the managing director, an officer may but need not be a Director.

4.2 Chairperson of the Board. The Board may from time to time appoint a Chairperson of the Board who shall be a Director. If appointed, the Board may assign to the Chairperson of the Board any of the powers and duties that are by any provisions of these By-laws assigned to the managing director or to the president. The Chairperson shall have such other powers and duties as the Board may specify.

4.3 President. If appointed, the president shall be the chief executive officer and subject to the authority of the Board shall have general supervision of the business and affairs of the Corporation. The president shall have such other powers and duties as the Board may specify.

4.4 Secretary. Unless otherwise determined by the Board, the secretary shall attend and be the secretary of all meetings of the Board, shareholders and committees of the Board that he or she attends. The secretary shall enter or cause to be entered in records kept for that purpose minutes of all proceedings at meetings of the Board, shareholders and committees of the Board,

FIGURE 8.1 CONTINUED

whether or not he or she attends such meetings. The secretary shall give or cause to be given, as and when instructed, all notices to shareholders, Directors, officers, auditors and members of committees of the Board. The secretary shall be the custodian of the stamp or mechanical device generally used for affixing the corporate seal of the Corporation and of all books, records and instruments belonging to the Corporation, except when some other officer or agent has been appointed for that purpose. The secretary shall have such other powers and duties as otherwise may be specified.

4.5   Treasurer. The treasurer shall keep proper accounting records in compliance with the Act and shall be responsible for the deposit of money, the safekeeping of securities and the disbursement of the funds of the Corporation. The treasurer shall render to the Board whenever required an account of all his or her transactions as treasurer and of the financial position of the Corporation. The treasurer shall have such other powers and duties as otherwise may be specified. A person appointed to the positions of Secretary and Treasurer, may, but need not be, known as the Secretary-Treasurer.

4.6   Powers and Duties. The powers and duties of all officers shall be such as the terms of their engagement call for or as the Board or (except for those whose powers and duties are to be specified only by the Board) the chief executive officer may specify. The Board and (except as aforesaid) the chief executive officer may, from time to time and subject to the provisions of the Act and any Unanimous Shareholder Agreement, vary, add to or limit the powers and duties of any officer. Any of the powers and duties of an officer to whom an assistant has been appointed may be exercised and performed by such assistant, unless the Board or he chief executive officer otherwise directs.

5.   PROTECTION OF DIRECTORS, OFFICERS AND OTHERS

5.1   Limitation of Liability. Every Director and officer of the Corporation in exercising his or her powers and discharging his or her duties shall act honestly and in good faith with a view to the best interests of the Corporation and exercise the care, diligence and skill that a reasonably prudent person would exercise in comparable circumstances. Subject to the foregoing, no Director or officer shall be liable for the acts, omissions, failures, neglects or defaults of any other Director, officer or employee, or for joining in any act for conformity, or for any loss, damage or expense suffered or incurred by the Corporation through the insufficiency or deficiency of title to any property acquired by the Corporation or for or on behalf of the Corporation, or for the insufficiency or deficiency of any security in or upon which any of the moneys of the Corporation shall be invested, or for any loss or damage arising from the bankruptcy, insolvency or tortious act of any person with whom any of the moneys, securities or effects of the Corporation shall be deposited, or for any loss occasioned by any error of judgment or oversight on his or her part, or for any other loss, damage or misfortune which shall happen in the execution of the duties of his or her office or in relation thereto. Nothing herein shall relieve any Director or officer from the duty to act in accordance with the Act and the regulations thereunder or from liability for any breach thereof.

FIGURE 8.1 CONTINUED

Page 5

5.2 Indemnity

(a) The Corporation shall indemnify a Director or officer of the Corporation, a former director or officer of the Corporation or another individual who acts or acted at the Corporation's request as a director or officer (or an individual acting in a similar capacity) of another entity, against all costs, charges and expenses, including, without limitation, an amount paid to settle an action or satisfy a judgment, reasonably incurred by the individual in respect of any civil, criminal, administrative, investigative or other proceeding in which the individual is involved because of that association with the Corporation or other entity.

(b) The Corporation shall advance monies to a Director, officer or other individual for the costs, charges and expenses of a proceeding referred to in Section 5.2(a). The individual shall repay the monies if he or she does fulfil the conditions of Section 5.2(c).

(c) The Corporation shall not indemnify an individual under Section 5.2(a) unless he or she:

(i) acted honestly and in good faith with a view to the best interests of the Corporation or, as the case may be, to the best interests of the other entity for which he or she acted as a director or officer or in a similar capacity at the Corporation's request; and

(ii) in the case of a criminal or administrative action or proceeding that is enforced by a monetary penalty, he or she had reasonable grounds for believing that his or her conduct was lawful.

(d) The Corporation shall also indemnify the individual referred to in Section 5.2(a) in such other circumstances as the Act or law permits or requires. Nothing in these By-laws shall limit the right of any person entitled to indemnity to claim indemnity apart from the provisions of these By-laws.

5.3 Insurance. Subject to the Act, the Corporation may purchase and maintain such insurance for the benefit of any individual referred to in Section 5.2(a) as the Board may from time to time determine.

6. SECURITIES

6.1 Security Certificates. Every holder of one or more securities of the Corporation shall be entitled, at his or her option, to a security certificate, or to a non-transferable written certificate of acknowledgement of his or her right to obtain a security certificate, stating the number and class or series of shares held by him or her as shown on the securities register. The certificates shall be in such form as the Board may from time to time approve and need not be under the corporate seal. Unless otherwise ordered by the Board, any such certificate shall be signed by one or more of the Directors or officers of the Corporation, or the signature shall be printed or otherwise mechanically reproduced on the certificate.

FIGURE 8.1 CONTINUED

Page 6

6.2 Enforcement of Lien. If any Defaulting Shareholder defaults in the payment due in respect of any Shareholder Debt when the same becomes due and payable and continues in default for a period of 15 days after the Corporation has given notice in writing of such default to the Defaulting Shareholder:

(a) the Corporation may sell all or any part of the Liened Shares at a *bonafide* public or private sale or auction;

(b) the terms and manner of the auction or sale shall be in the sole discretion of the Corporation;

(c) the Corporation may accept any offer which it in its absolute discretion considers advisable upon such terms, whether for cash or credit or partly cash and partly credit, as it in its discretion considers advisable;

(d) notice of any public or private sale or auction shall be given to the Defaulting Shareholder at least 15 days prior to the date on which such sale is held;

(e) the proceeds of such sale shall be used and applied in descending order as follows:

   (i) first, to the cost and expense of such sale incurred by the Corporation, including, without limitation, legal fees, disbursements and charges;

   (ii) second, to reimburse the Corporation for out-of-pocket expenses incurred in connection with the sale;

   (iii) third, for the payment in full of the Shareholder Debt and all other sums due to the, Corporation by the Defaulting Shareholder; and

   (iv) the balance, if any, to the Defaulting Shareholder;

(f) if the proceeds of the sale are insufficient to pay the Shareholder Debt, the Defaulting Shareholder shall remain liable for any such deficiency;

(g) the Corporation may apply any dividends or other distributions paid or payable on or in respect of the Liened Shares in repayment of the Shareholder Debt;

(h) where the Liened Shares are redeemable pursuant to the Articles or may be repurchased at a price determined pursuant to the terms of any Unanimous Shareholder Agreement, the Corporation may redeem or repurchase all or any part of the Liened Shares and apply the redemption or repurchase price to the Shareholder Debt; and

(i) the Corporation may refuse to register a transfer of all or part of the Liened Shares until the Shareholder Debt is paid

In exercising one or more of the rights granted in this Section 6.2, the Corporation shall not prejudice or surrender any other rights of enforcement of its lien which may by law be available

FIGURE 8.1 CONTINUED

Page 7

to it, or any other remedy available to the Corporation for collection of the Shareholder Debt, and the Defaulting Shareholder shall remain liable for any deficiency remaining.

7.   MEETINGS OF SHAREHOLDERS

7.1   Meeting Held by Electronic Means

(a)   Any person entitled to attend a meeting of shareholders may vote and otherwise participate in the meeting by means of a telephonic, electronic or other communication facility made available by the Corporation that permits all participants to communicate adequately with each other during the meeting. A person participating in a meeting of shareholders by such means is deemed to be present at the meeting.

(b)   Directors who call (but not shareholders who requisition) a meeting of shareholders may determine that:

    (i)   the meeting shall be held, in accordance with the regulations, entirely by means of a telephonic, electronic or other communication facility that permits all participants to communicate adequately with each other during the meeting; and

    (ii)   any vote shall be held, in accordance with the regulations, entirely by means of a telephone, electronic or other communication facility that the Corporation has made available for that purpose.

(c)   Any vote at a meeting of shareholders may be carried out by means of a telephonic, electronic or other communication facility, if the facility:

    (i)   enables the votes to be gathered in a manner that permits their subsequent verification; and

    (ii)   permits the tallied votes to be presented to the Corporation without it being possible for the Corporation to identify how each shareholder or group of shareholders voted.

7.2   Calling Meetings. The Board shall call an annual meeting of shareholders not later than 15 months after the holding of the last preceding annual meeting but no later than six months after the end of the Corporation's preceding financial year and may at any time call a special meeting of shareholders.

7.3   Notice of Meetings. Notice of each meeting of shareholders shall be sent not less than 10 days before the meeting to each shareholder entitled to vote at the meeting, to each Director, to the auditor of the Corporation and to any other persons who, although not entitled to vote at the meeting, are entitled or required under any provision of the Act, the Articles or any by-law of the Corporation to attend the meeting. The accidental failure to give notice of a meeting of shareholders to any person entitled to notice thereof or any error in such notice not affecting the substance thereof shall not invalidate any action taken at the meeting.

FIGURE 8.1 CONTINUED

7.4   Persons Entitled to be Present. The only persons entitled to attend a meeting of shareholders shall be those persons entitled to vote thereat, the Directors, Officers and auditor of the Corporation and any other persons who, although not entitled to vote at the meeting, are entitled or required under any provision of the Act, the Articles or any by-law of the Corporation to attend the meeting. Any other person may be admitted to the meeting only on the invitation of the Chairperson of the meeting or with the consent of the meeting.

7.5   Quorum. At any meeting of shareholders, the holders of [a majority] of the shares entitled to vote at a meeting of shareholders whether present in person or represented by proxy, shall constitute a quorum for the transaction of business.

7.6   Voting.

(a)   Subject to the Act, Voting at any meeting of shareholders shall be by a show of hands except where, either before or after a vote by show of hands, a ballot is required by the Chairperson of the meeting or is demanded by any person present and entitled to vote at the meeting. On a show of hands, each person present at the meeting and entitled to vote thereat shall, subject to the Act, have one vote. On a ballot, each person present at the meeting and entitled to vote thereat shall, subject to the Act and the Articles, have one vote for each share in respect of which such person is entitled to vote. A ballot so required or demanded shall be taken in such manner as the Chairperson of the meeting directs.

(b)   Unless otherwise required by the Act or the Articles, every question at a meeting of shareholders shall be decided by a majority of the votes cast on the question. In the event of an equality of votes on any question at a meeting of shareholders either upon a show of hands or upon a ballot, the Chairperson of the meeting shall not be entitled to a second or casting vote.

7.7   Proxyholders and Representatives.   Every shareholder entitled to vote at a meeting of shareholders may appoint a proxyholder, or one or more alternative proxyholders, as his or her nominee to attend and act at the meeting in the manner and to the extent authorized and with the authority conferred by the proxy. A Proxy shall be in writing or electronic signature executed by the shareholder or his or her attorney and shall conform with the requirements of the Act. Alternatively, every shareholder which is a body corporate or other legal entity may authorize by resolution of its directors or governing body an individual to represent it at a meeting of shareholders and that individual may exercise on the shareholder's behalf all the powers it could exercise if it were an individual shareholder. The authority of such an individual shall be established by depositing with the Corporation a certified copy of the resolution, or in such other manner as may be satisfactory to the secretary of the Corporation or the chairperson of the meting. Any such proxyholder or representative need not be a shareholder. The proxy is valid only at the meeting in respect of which it is given or any adjournment thereof.

FIGURE 8.1 CONTINUED

7.8 **Joint Shareholders.** If two or more persons hold shares jointly, any one of them present in person or duly represented at a meeting of shareholders may, in the absence of the other or others, vote the shares, but if two or more of those persons are present in person or represented and vote, they shall vote as one the shares jointly held by them.

7.9 **Presiding Officer.** The Chairperson of the Board or, a Director designated by him, or failing such designation, a Director designated by the Board, shall preside at a meeting of shareholders. If neither the Chairperson of the Board nor any Director is present within 30 minutes after the time appointed for the holding of a meeting of shareholders, the shareholders present shall choose a shareholder then present to be chairperson of the meeting.

8. EXECUTION OF INSTRUMENTS

8.1 Deeds, transfers, assignments, contracts and any other documents of the Corporation shall be signed on behalf of the Corporation by any two persons:

(a) one of whom holds the office of Chairperson of the Board, managing director, president, vice-president or is a Director; and

(b) the other of whom is a Director or holds one of the aforesaid offices or the office of secretary, treasurer, assistant secretary or assistant treasurer or any other office created by by-law or by the Board.

8.2 In addition, the Board may from time to time authorize any other person or persons to sign any particular instruments.

8.3 The secretary or, any other officer or any Director, may sign certificates and similar instruments (other than share certificates) on the Corporation's behalf with respect to any factual matters relating to the Corporation's business and affairs, including, without limitation, certificates verifying copies of the Articles, By-laws, resolutions and minutes of meetings of the Corporation. Any signing officer may affix the corporate seal to any instrument requiring the same.

8.4 The signature of any person authorized to sign on behalf of the Corporation may, if specifically authorized by resolution of the Board, be written, printed, stamped, engraved, lithographed or otherwise mechanically reproduced or may be an electronic signature. Anything so signed shall be as valid as if it had been signed manually, even if that person has ceased to hold office when anything so signed is issued or delivered, until revoked by resolution of the Board.

9. SHAREHOLDERS' AGREEMENT

9.1 **Conflicting Provisions.** Notwithstanding anything contained in the by-laws, the provisions of the by-laws shall be amended to the extent necessary to give effect to the provisions of any shareholders' agreement in force between the Corporation and its shareholders, and to the extent that there is any conflict between the provisions of the by-laws and any such shareholders' agreement, the provisions of such shareholders' agreement shall prevail.

FIGURE 8.1 CONTINUED

10.   EFFECTIVE DATE

10.1   These By-laws shall come into force when made by the Board in accordance with the Act.

MADE by the Board as of the 24th day of December, 2003.

_____

Peter Black, President

_____

Roger Jones, Secretary

Confirmed by the Shareholders as of the 24th day of December, 2003.

_____

Peter Black, President

_____

Roger Jones, Secretary

FIGURE 8.1 CONTINUED

ACKNOWLEDGEMENT

The undersigned hereby acknowledges that as at the date hereof it is a "closely-held issuer" as such term is defined in Ontario Securities Commission ("OSC") Rule 45-501 Exempt Distributions (refer to Schedule A for a complete copy of the definition).

In connection with trades made on this date of three common shares and 1,000 preferred shares of the undersigned:

(a)   No Offering Memorandum has been issued by the undersigned;

(b)   Following such trades; the undersigned will continue to be a closely-held issuer and the aggregate proceeds received by the undersigned and any other issuer engaged in common enterprise with the undersigned, in connection with trades made in reliance upon the "closely-held issuer" exemption contained in section 2.1 of the Ontario Securities Commission Rule 45-501 (the "Exemption") will not exceed $3,000,000;

(c)   No selling or promotional expenses have been or will be paid or incurred in connection with trades made in reliance on the Exemption except for services performed by a dealer registered under the *Securities Act* (Ontario).

DATED as of the 24th day of December, 2003.

BSJ GARDEN ORNAMENT SALES INC.

By: _____
        Peter Black
        President

        _____
        Roger Jones
        Secretary

We/I have the authority to bind the Corporation

FIGURE 8.1 CONTINUED

SCHEDULE A

"Closely-held issuer" means an issuer, other than a mutual fund or non-redeemable investment fund, whose

(a)   shares are subject to restrictions on transfer requiring the approval of either the board of directors or the shareholders of the issuer (or the equivalent in a non-corporate issuer) contained in constating documents of the issuer or one or more agreements among the issuer and holders of its shares; and

(b)   outstanding securities are beneficially owned, directly or indirectly, by not more than 35 persons or companies, exclusive of:

(i)   persons or companies that are, or at the time they last acquired securities of the Corporation were, accredited investors (as such term is defined in the Ontario Securities Commission ("OSC") Rule 45-501 Exempt Distributions as amended from time to time);

(ii)   current or former directors or officers of the Corporation or of an affiliated entity of the Corporation; and

(iii)   current or former employees of the Corporation or an affiliated entity of the Corporation, or current or former consultants as defined in MI 45-105, who in each case beneficially own only securities of the Corporation that were issued as compensation by, or under an incentive plan of, the Corporation or an affiliated entity of the Corporation;

provided that:

(A)   two or more persons who are the joint registered holders of one or more securities of the Corporation are counted as one beneficial owner of those securities; and

(B)   a corporation, partnership, trust or other entity shall be counted as one beneficial owner of securities of the Corporation unless the entity has been created or is being used primarily for the purpose of acquiring or holding securities of the Corporation, in which event each beneficial owner of an equity interest in the entity or each beneficiary of the entity, as the case may be, is counted as a separate beneficial owner of those securities of the Corporation."

FIGURE 8.1 CONTINUED

BSJ GARDEN ORNAMENT SALES INC.

REGISTER OF DIRECTORS

NAME AND ADDRESS	RES. CDN (YES/NO)	DATE APPOINTED	DATE RESIGNED
Peter Black 1 First Street, Port Ellen, Ontario, Canada, L3R 0A9	Yes	Dec. 24, 2003	
Shirley Smith 2 Second Street, Port Ellen, Ontario, Canada, L3R 0B9	Yes	Dec. 24, 2003	
Roger Jones 3 Third Street, Port Ellen, Ontario, Canada, L3R 0D9	Yes	Dec. 24, 2003	

FIGURE 8.1   CONTINUED

BSJ GARDEN ORNAMENT SALES INC.
REGISTER OF OFFICERS

NAME AND ADDRESS	OFFICE HELD	DATE APPOINTED	DATE RESIGNED
Peter Black 1 First Street, Port Ellen, Ontario, Canada, L3R 0A9	President	Dec. 24, 2003	
Shirley Smith 2 Second Street, Port Ellen, Ontario, Canada, L3R 0B9	Vice President	Dec. 24, 2003	
Roger Jones 3 Third Street, Port Ellen, Ontario, Canada, L3R 0D9	Secretary	Dec. 24, 2003	

Page 1 of 1

FIGURE 8.1   CONTINUED

BSJ GARDEN ORNAMENT SALES INC.
SHAREHOLDERS' REGISTER

common

DATE ISSUED	NAME	NUMBER OF SHARES	CERTIFICATE NUMBER	DATE CANCELLED
Dec 24/2003	Peter Black	1	C-001	
Dec 24/2003	Shirley Smith	1	C-002	
Dec 24/2003	Roger Jones	1	C-003	
	Total Outstanding	3		

Page 1 of 1

FIGURE 8.1 CONTINUED

BSJ GARDEN ORNAMENT SALES INC.
SHAREHOLDERS' REGISTER

preferred

DATE ISSUED	NAME	NUMBER OF SHARES	CERTIFICATE NUMBER	DATE CANCELLED
Dec 24/2003	Clarence Smith	1,000	P-001	
	Total Outstanding	1,000		

Page 1 of 1

FIGURE 8.1 CONTINUED

Certificate No. C-001
For One Common Share
Issued to
Peter Black

Dated December 24, 2003.

From whom transferred
Issued from Treasury
Dated _____
No. Original Certificate _____
No. Original Shares _____
No. of Shares Transferred _____

Received Certificate No. _____
for _____ Shares
this _____ day of _____, _____,

INCORPORATED UNDER THE CANADA BUSINESS CORPORATIONS ACT

No. C-001   One Common Share

BSJ GARDEN ORNAMENT SALES INC.

This is to Certify that

is the registered holder of

Peter Black

One   Common Share of

BSJ GARDEN ORNAMENT SALES INC.

The class or series of shares represented by this Certificate has rights, privileges, restrictions or conditions attached thereto and the Corporation will furnish to the holder, on demand and without charge, a full copy of the text of,
(i) the rights, privileges, restrictions and conditions attached to the said shares and to each class authorized to be issued and to each series insofar as the same have been fixed by the directors, and
(ii) the authority of the directors to fix the rights, privileges, restrictions and conditions of subsequent series, if applicable.

LIEN ON SHARES. The Corporation has a lien on the shares represented by this Certificate for any debt of the shareholder to the Corporation.
RESTRICTIONS ON TRANSFER. There are restrictions on the right to transfer the shares represented by this Certificate.

IN WITNESS WHEREOF the Corporation has caused this Certificate to be signed by its duly authorized officers
this 24th day of December, 2003.

_____
President

_____
Secretary

FIGURE 8.1 CONTINUED

CERTIFICATE
FOR

One

COMMON
SHARE OF

BSJ GARDEN ORNAMENT SALES INC.

ISSUED TO
Peter Black

DATE
December 24, 2003

For Value Received, _____ hereby assign and transfer unto _____ Common Shares represented by the within Certificate.

Dated _____ , _____.

In the presence of

_____

_____

FIGURE 8.1 CONTINUED

Certificate No. C-002
For One Common Share
Issued to
Shirley Smith

Dated December 24, 2003.

From whom transferred
Issued from Treasury
Dated
No. Original Certificate
No. Original Shares
No. of Shares Transferred

Received Certificate No.
for _____ Shares
this _____ day of _____, _____

No. C-002

One Common Share

INCORPORATED UNDER THE CANADA BUSINESS CORPORATIONS ACT

BSJ GARDEN ORNAMENT SALES INC.

This is to Certify that
is the registered holder of

Shirley Smith
One
Common Share of

BSJ GARDEN ORNAMENT SALES INC.

The class or series of shares represented by this Certificate has rights, privileges, restrictions or conditions attached thereto and the Corporation will furnish to the holder, on demand and without charge, a full copy of the text of,
(i) the rights, privileges, restrictions and conditions attached to the said shares and to each class authorized to be issued and to each series insofar as the same have been fixed by the directors, and
(ii) the authority of the directors to fix the rights, privileges, restrictions and conditions of subsequent series, if applicable.

LIEN ON SHARES. The Corporation has a lien on the shares represented by this Certificate for any debt of the shareholder to the Corporation.
RESTRICTIONS ON TRANSFER. There are restrictions on the right to transfer the shares represented by this Certificate.

IN WITNESS WHEREOF the Corporation has caused this Certificate to be signed by its duly authorized officers this 24th day of December, 2003.

_____
President

_____
Secretary

FIGURE 8.1 CONTINUED

CERTIFICATE
FOR

One

COMMON
SHARE OF

BSJ GARDEN ORNAMENT SALES INC.

ISSUED TO
Shirley Smith

DATE
December 24, 2003

For Value Received, _____ hereby assign and transfer unto _____ Common Shares represented by the within Certificate.

Dated _____ , _____ .

In the presence of

_____

_____

FIGURE 8.1   CONTINUED

Certificate No. C-003
For One Common Share
Issued to
Roger Jones

Dated December 24, 2003.

From whom transferred
Issued from Treasury
Dated
No. Original Certificate
No. Original Shares
No. of Shares Transferred

Received Certificate No. _____
for _____ _____ Shares
this _____ day of _____ , _____

INCORPORATED UNDER THE CANADA BUSINESS CORPORATIONS ACT

No. C-003   One Common Share

BSJ GARDEN ORNAMENT SALES INC.

This is to Certify that   Roger Jones
is the registered holder of   One   Common Share of

BSJ GARDEN ORNAMENT SALES INC.

The class or series of shares represented by this Certificate has rights, privileges, restrictions or conditions attached thereto and the Corporation will furnish to the holder, on demand and without charge, a full copy of the text of,
(i) the rights, privileges, restrictions and conditions attached to the said shares and to each class authorized to be issued and to each series insofar as the same have been fixed by the directors, and
(ii) the authority of the directors to fix the rights, privileges, restrictions and conditions of subsequent series, if applicable.

LIEN ON SHARES.   The Corporation has a lien on the shares represented by this Certificate for any debt of the shareholder to the Corporation.
RESTRICTIONS ON TRANSFER.   There are restrictions on the right to transfer the shares represented by this Certificate.

IN WITNESS WHEREOF the Corporation has caused this Certificate to be signed by its duly authorized officers this 24th day of December, 2003.

_____   _____
President   Secretary

FIGURE 8.1   CONTINUED

CERTIFICATE
FOR

One

COMMON
SHARE OF

BSJ GARDEN ORNAMENT SALES INC.

ISSUED TO
Roger Jones

DATE
December 24, 2003

For Value Received, _____ hereby assign and

transfer unto _____

Common Shares represented by the within

Certificate.

Dated _____ , _____ .

In the presence of

_____

_____

FIGURE 8.1 CONTINUED

Certificate No. P-001
For 1,000 Preferred Shares
Issued to
Clarence Smith

Dated December 24, 2003.

From whom transferred
Issued from Treasury
Dated
No. Original Certificate
No. Original Shares
No. of Shares Transferred

Received Certificate No.
for _____ Shares
this _____ day of _____ ,

INCORPORATED UNDER THE CANADA BUSINESS CORPORATIONS ACT

No. P-001   1,000 Preferred Shares

BSJ GARDEN ORNAMENT SALES INC.

This is to Certify that
is the registered holder of

Clarence Smith
1,000   Preferred Shares of

BSJ GARDEN ORNAMENT SALES INC.

The class or series of shares represented by this Certificate has rights, privileges, restrictions or conditions attached thereto and the Corporation will furnish to the holder, on demand and without charge, a full copy of the text of,
(i) the rights, privileges, restrictions and conditions attached to the said shares and to each class authorized to be issued and to each series insofar as the same have been fixed by the directors, and
(ii) the authority of the directors to fix the rights, privileges, restrictions and conditions of subsequent series, if applicable.

LIEN ON SHARES. The Corporation has a lien on the shares represented by this Certificate for any debt of the shareholder to the Corporation.
RESTRICTIONS ON TRANSFER. There are restrictions on the right to transfer the shares represented by this Certificate.

IN WITNESS WHEREOF the Corporation has caused this Certificate to be signed by its duly authorized officers this 24th day of December, 2003.

_____   _____
President   Secretary

FIGURE 8.1   CONTINUED

CERTIFICATE
FOR

1,000

PREFERRED
SHARES OF

BSJ GARDEN ORNAMENT SALES INC.

ISSUED TO
Clarence Smith

DATE
December 24, 2003

For Value Received, _____ hereby assign and transfer unto _____
Preferred Shares represented by the within Certificate.

Dated _____ , _____.

In the presence of

_____

_____

FIGURE 8.1 CONTINUED

BSJ GARDEN ORNAMENT SALES INC.

SHAREHOLDERS' LEDGER

NAME: Peter Black

ADDRESS: 1 First Street, Port Ellen, Ontario, Canada, L3R 0A9

CLASS: common

Date	Cert. No.	Trans. No.	To Whom or From Whom	Transferred	Acquired	Balance Held
Dec. 24, 2003	C-001	0	Issue From Treasury	0	1	1

FIGURE 8.1   CONTINUED

BSJ GARDEN ORNAMENT SALES INC.

SHAREHOLDERS' LEDGER

NAME: Shirley Smith

ADDRESS: 2 Second Street, Port Ellen, Ontario, Canada, L3R 0B9

CLASS: common

Date	Cert. No.	Trans. No.	To Whom or From Whom	Transferred	Acquired	Balance Held
Dec. 24, 2003	C-002	0	Issue From Treasury	0	1	1

FIGURE 8.1   CONTINUED

BSJ GARDEN ORNAMENT SALES INC.
SHAREHOLDERS' LEDGER

NAME: Roger Jones

ADDRESS: 3 Third Street, Port Ellen, Ontario, Canada, L3R 0D9

CLASS: common

Date	Cert. No.	Trans. No.	To Whom or From Whom	Transferred	Acquired	Balance Held
Dec. 24, 2003	C-003	0	Issue From Treasury	0	1	1

FIGURE 8.1 CONTINUED

BSJ GARDEN ORNAMENT SALES INC.

SHAREHOLDERS' LEDGER

NAME: Clarence Smith

ADDRESS: 4 Fourth Street, Port Ellen, Ontario, Canada, L3R 0C8

CLASS: preferred

Date	Cert. No.	Trans. No.	To Whom or From Whom	Transferred	Acquired	Balance Held
Dec 24, 2003	P-001	0	Issue From Treasury	0	1	1,000

FIGURE 8.1   CONTINUED

December 31, 2003

PERSONAL AND CONFIDENTIAL

BSJ Garden Ornament Sales Inc.
123 Sesame Street
Port Ellen ON L3R 0C9

Attention: Mr. Peter Black, President

Dear Sirs/Madams:

Re: **BSJ Garden Ornament Sales Inc.** (the "Corporation")
        Incorporation and Organization
        Our File No.: 1111111

We have now completed the incorporation and organization of the Corporation and are pleased
to submit our report in connection therewith.

A.   **<u>INCORPORATION</u>**

1. **Articles of Incorporation**

Pursuant to the *Canada Business Corporations Act* (the "Act"), the Corporation was incorporated
by the filing of Articles of Incorporation by facsimile with the Director, Corporations Canada
(the "Director") and the issue of a Certificate of Incorporation incorporating the Corporation
effective as of December 24, 2003. The Certificate and Articles of Incorporation (the "Articles")
have been placed in the minute book of the Corporation. A photocopy is enclosed for your
records.

2. **Corporate Name**

In clearing the corporate name, we relied on a computer search of corporate names and
trademarks to determine if there were names similar to the Corporation's name. The results of the

FIGURE 8.1   CONTINUED

search which disclosed several similar, although not identical pre-existing corporate names were confirmed to you by our letter of October 30, 2003 prior to the filing of the Articles and you instructed us to proceed to incorporate using the name set out in the Articles. Nevertheless, the possibility always exists that a "passing off" action may be brought by a person who considers that the Corporation's name is confusing with his or her corporation's name. In addition, the Director has the right to change the name of any corporation if he considers the name is likely to deceive, or is the same as or similar to any other name.

Subsection 10(5) of the Act states that a corporation shall set out its name in legible characters in all contracts, invoices, negotiable instruments and orders for goods or services issued or made by or on behalf of the corporation and in all documents sent to the Director. The Act does not require the full corporate name to appear on letterhead. If, however, a contract is set out in letter form, it will be necessary to have the full corporate name appear in the body of the letter or on the signing page in order to meet the requirements of the Act.

Nevertheless, a recent case found that the failure to use the full correct corporate name on a supply order led to personal liability against the principal of a corporation. Accordingly, we strongly recommend that the full correct corporate name (as it appears in the Corporation's Articles) be used at all times, especially on all contracts entered into by or on behalf of the Corporation. Please feel free to contact us if you have any questions in this regard.

3. Registered Office

The Act provides that a corporation shall at all times have a registered office in the province specified in its Articles. The Articles provide that the province in Canada where the registered office is located is Ontario. The street address of the registered office as indicated on the Form 3 Notice of Registered Office filed with the Articles is:

> 123 Sesame Street
> Port Ellen ON L3R 0C9

4. Business and Powers

The Act provides that a corporation has the capacity, rights, powers and privileges of a natural person. Restrictions on the business or powers that a corporation may exercise can, however, be included in the Articles. No such restrictions have been included in the Articles of the Corporation.

The Corporation should also consider whether any local, municipal or other licensing and registration requirements must be met before commencement of business.

5. Authorized Capital

The Corporation is authorized to issue an unlimited number of common shares and an unlimited number of preferred shares.

FIGURE 8.1 CONTINUED

The rights, privileges, restrictions and conditions attaching to the Preferred Shares and the Common Shares are set out in the Articles.

6. **Exemption from Prospectus and Registration Requirements of the** *Securities Act* **(Ontario)**

To qualify the Corporation as a "closely-held issuer" for the purposes of the *Securities Act* (Ontario), shares must be subject to restrictions on transfer. The Act prohibits a corporation from imposing restrictions on the issue, transfer or ownership of shares except such restrictions as are authorized by its articles. We have therefore included the following restriction in the Corporation's Articles:

"No shares shall be transferred without either:

(a) the approval of the directors of the Corporation expressed by a resolution passed by the board of directors of the Corporation at a meeting of the directors or by an instrument or instruments in writing signed by a majority of the directors; or

(b) the approval of the holders of a majority of the voting shares of the Corporation for the time being outstanding expressed by a resolution passed at a meeting of shareholders or by an instrument or instruments in writing signed by the holders of a majority of such shares".

In addition to the above, a "closely-held" issuer is limited as to the number and type of security holders. We have included the following provisions in the Articles of the Corporation to address this limitation:

1. "The outstanding securities of the Corporation may be beneficially owned, directly or indirectly, by not more than 35 persons or companies, exclusive of:

(i) persons or companies that are, or at the time they last acquired securities of the Corporation were, accredited investors as such term is defined in the Ontario Securities Commission ("OSC") Rule 45-501 Exempt Distributions as amended from time to time;

(ii) current or former directors or officers of the Corporation or an affiliated entity of the Corporation; and

(iii) current or former employees of the Corporation or an affiliated entity of the Corporation, or current or former consultants as defined in MI 45-105, who in each case beneficially own only securities of the Corporation that were issued as compensation by, or under an incentive plan of, the Corporation or an affiliated entity of the Corporation;

provided that:

FIGURE 8.1   CONTINUED

Page 4

A.   two or more persons who are the joint registered holders of one or more securities of the Corporation are counted as one beneficial owner of those securities; and

B.   a corporation, partnership, trust or other entity is counted as one beneficial owner of securities of the Corporation unless the entity has been created or is being used primarily for the purpose of acquiring or holding securities of the Corporation, in which event each beneficial owner of an equity interest in the entity or each beneficiary of the entity, as the case may be, is counted as a separate beneficial owner of those securities of the Corporation."

B.   **ORGANIZATION**

7. **By-law No. 1**

By-law No. 1, a general by-law relating to the business and affairs of the Corporation, was passed by the directors and confirmed by the shareholders effective as of December 24, 2003. This by-law expands upon various provisions of the Act and should be read in conjunction with the Act. Among other matters, it addresses the quorum and procedure for directors' and shareholders' meetings, the duties of officers and certain other matters relating to the operation of the Corporation.

8. **Directors**

The Articles of the Corporation provide that it may have a minimum of one director and a maximum of 10 directors.

The Articles also provide that the number of directors shall be determined from time to time as follows:

(a)   where the directors are to be elected at a meeting of shareholders, the number shall be determined by resolution of the board of directors and set out in the notice calling the meeting of shareholders; and

(b)   where the directors are to be elected by way of a written resolution of shareholders, the number shall be set out in the resolution;

provided that the number of directors may not be less than the minimum number nor more than the maximum number of directors set out in the articles.

The current directors of the Corporation are Peter Black, Shirley Smith and Roger Jones, who were elected by the shareholders effective as of December 24, 2003.

The Act requires at least 25% of the directors to be resident Canadian, as such term is defined in the Act. However, if the Corporation has less than four directors, at least one director must be a resident Canadian.

FIGURE 8.1 CONTINUED

9. Officers

The officers of the Corporation were appointed by the directors effective as of December 24, 2003 and are:

Name	Position Held
Peter Black	President
Shirley Smith	Vice President
Roger Jones	Secretary

10. Delegation

The directors may appoint a managing director or committee of directors and, subject to statutory limitations, delegate powers to such managing director or committee. The managing director must be a resident Canadian as defined by the Act.

11. Banking

The directors have authorized the Corporation to establish a bank account with Royal Bank of Canada and determined that any two directors may sign cheques on behalf of the Corporation. A copy of the banking agreement delivered to the bank is attached to the resolution filed in the minute book.

12. Execution of Documents

By-law No. 1 provides that deeds, transfers, assignments, contracts and any other documents of the Corporation shall be signed on behalf of the Corporation by any two persons:

(a)   one of whom holds the office of Chairperson of the Board, managing director, president, vice-president or is a Director; and

(b)   the other of whom is a Director or holds one of the aforesaid offices or the office of secretary, treasurer, assistant secretary or assistant treasurer or any other office created by by-law or by the Board.

13. Corporate Seal

A corporate seal, adopted by resolution of the directors effective as of December 24, 2003, was obtained for the Corporation.

14. Shareholders

The following shares were issued:

FIGURE 8.1 CONTINUED

Page 6

Name of Shareholder	Number and Class of Shares	Total Subscription Price	After 11/29/01 Issued to Accredited Investor (Y/N)	Certificate No.
Peter Black	1 - common	$ 1.00	No	C-001
Shirley Smith	1 - common	$ 1.00	No	C-002
Roger Jones	1 - common	$ 1.00	No	C-003
Clarence Smith	1,000 - preferred	$ 1,000	No	P-001

These shares were issued as fully paid and non-assessable. We confirm our understanding that payment for the shares has been made, as the validity of their issue is dependent upon payment therefor.

15. Appointment Of Auditor

A resolution was passed by the shareholders dated December 24, 2003 appointing ABC Accounting LLP as the auditor of the Corporation, to hold office until their successor is appointed.

16. Financial Year End

By resolution of the directors effective as of December 24, 2003, the financial year end of the Corporation was determined as December 31 in each year.

C. MANDATORY FILINGS

17. Change of Registered Office

The Corporation is required to file with the Director a notice of any change of municipal address of its registered office on Form 3 within 15 days of such change.

If the Corporation wishes to change the province in which the registered office is situated, a special resolution must first be passed followed by the filing of Articles of Amendment.

18. Change of Director

A director shall, within 15 days after changing his or her address, send the Corporation a notice of that change.

The Corporation shall, within 15 days after:

    (a)   a change is made among its directors, or

    (b)   it receives a notice of change of address of a director,

send to the Director a notice of change setting out the change on Form 6.

FIGURE 8.1 CONTINUED

Page 7

19. Annual Returns

Pursuant to the Act, the Corporation must submit an annual return to the Director together with the prescribed fee within six months after the date of the end of the taxation year of the corporation.

The annual return may either be filed together with the Corporate Income Tax Return or separately.

The Act provides that where a corporation is in default for a period of one year in sending to the Director any fee, notice or document required by the Act, the Director may dissolve the corporation by issuing a certificate of dissolution under section 212 of the Act or he/she may apply to a court for an order dissolving the corporation. The Director is required to give 120 days notice of his/her decision to dissolve the corporation to the corporation and to each director of the corporation, and to publish notice of his/her decision to dissolve the corporation in a publication generally available to the public.

20. Federal and Ontario Corporate Tax Returns

The Corporation must file an annual income tax return with each of Canada Customs and Revenue Agency, the Ministry of Finance, Corporations Tax Branch (Ontario) and each province or jurisdiction in which it carries on business. Canada Customs and Revenue Agency and the Ministry of Finance, Corporations Tax Branch (Ontario) will each assign to the Corporation an account number, which account number must be quoted in all correspondence with that particular tax department. The Corporation's initial income tax return must be filed no later than six (6) months after its first tax year-end. In addition, if the Corporation supplies goods or services, it may have to become registered for goods and service tax under the *Excise Tax Act* (Canada) and for Ontario retail sales tax under the *Retail Sales Tax Act* (Ontario). It will have to also file the necessary returns thereunder. We confirm that we will not be responsible for the filing of any of these tax returns or for reminding the Corporation of its obligation to do so.

Corporations are also required to ensure that all taxing authorities are kept informed of any address change.

21. Business Names

The *Business Names Act* (Ontario) (the "BNA") provides in part that no corporation shall carry on business or identify itself to the public under a name other than its corporate name unless the name is registered by that corporation.

Failure to register, renew or amend a business name registration causes the corporation to be unable to maintain a proceeding in a court in Ontario in connection with that business except with leave of the court. However, no contract is void or voidable by reason only that it was entered into by a corporation which was in contravention of BNA or the regulations at the time the contract was made.

FIGURE 8.1   CONTINUED

There are significant monetary penalties under the BNA for failure to comply with the requirement for registration of a business name. If a corporation is guilty of failure to file as required by the BNA, it is on conviction liable to a fine of not more than $25,000. If a corporation is guilty of an offence, every director or officer of the corporation and every person acting as its representative in Ontario who authorized, permitted or acquiesced in such an offence is also guilty of an offence and on conviction is liable to a fine of not more than $2,000.

If at any time the Corporation carries on business under its corporate name without the legal ending or under any business name, please advise us accordingly so that appropriate registration under this legislation may be made.

22. Extra-Provincial Registrations

(a)   **Ontario.** Any corporation incorporated federally or in any other province or territory in Canada (a "Domestic Extra-Provincial Corporation") need not obtain a licence under the *Extra-Provincial Corporations Act* (Ontario) in order to carry on business in Ontario.

It is necessary for a Domestic Extra-Provincial Corporation carrying on business in Ontario to file a Form 2 Initial Return pursuant to the *Corporations Information Act* (Ontario).

This Return was prepared, signed and filed with the Examination and Notice Section, Companies and Personal Property Security Branch, Ministry of Consumer and Business Services. A duplicate copy has been inserted in the minute book.

(b)   **Other Canadian Jurisdictions.** The Corporation has the capacity to carry on its business, conduct its affairs and exercise its powers throughout Canada to the extent that the laws of such jurisdiction permit. Extra-Provincial registration is required by most Canadian provinces/territories before the Corporation may commence its business within such province or territory.

D.   <u>ONGOING MAINTENANCE</u>

23. Transaction of Business

Any by-law or resolution passed at any time during the Corporation's existence by the signatures of all of the directors or all of the shareholders entitled to vote on that resolution is as valid as if it had been passed at a properly constituted meeting of the directors or shareholders.

24. Annual Proceedings

Pursuant to the Act, the directors of a corporation shall call an annual meeting of shareholders;

(a)   not later than eighteen months after the corporation comes into existence; and

FIGURE 8.1 CONTINUED

(b)   subsequently not later than 15 months after holding the last preceding annual meeting but no later than six months after the end of the Corporation's preceding financial year-end.

The purpose of an annual meeting of shareholders is to consider minutes of any earlier meetings, the financial statements and auditor's report for the latest financial year of the corporation, the re-election of the incumbent directors and the reappointment of the incumbent auditor. Any business other than those specified is deemed to be special business.

As mentioned above, a resolution in writing signed by all the shareholders entitled to vote on that resolution at a meeting of shareholders is as valid as if it had been passed at a meeting of the shareholders.

The Director, or any interested person, may apply to a court for an order dissolving a Corporation if the Corporation has failed for two or more consecutive years to comply with the Act with respect to holding annual meetings of the shareholders.

Each year, four to five months after the financial year end of the Corporation, we will automatically prepare the required annual proceedings, including directors' resolution approving, among other things, the financial statements, and forward them to you for dating and signature once the financial statements for that year are completed.

25. Authority to Sign Notices

To facilitate the timely filing of certain notices under the Act, the Directors have authorized any partner, associate or corporate law clerk employed by Thorn & Hill LLP who has the relevant knowledge of the Corporation to sign and file (electronically or otherwise):

(a)   any notice of registered office or change in the address of the registered office;

(b)   any notice of directors, notice of change of directors or notice of change in director's address; and

(c)   any annual return.

E.   <u>CORPORATE RECORDS</u>

26. Minute Book and Corporate Seal

Unless the directors otherwise designate, the corporate books and records of a corporation must be maintained at the registered office of such corporation. By resolution of the directors passed effective as of December 24, 2003, the Corporation was authorized to maintain its books and records either at its registered office or at the offices of Thorn & Hill LLP.

FIGURE 8.1 CONTINUED

For your convenience we have included a checklist of matters for your review to determine whether or not there are other matters which require attention. If we can be of assistance to you in any of these matters, please contact the undersigned for the appropriate referral.

We trust that this has been completed to your satisfaction and should you have any questions or comments respecting this matter, please feel free to contact us.

Yours truly,

Richard Thorn

RT/msu
Enclosures

cc: Jessie Bruton

FIGURE 8.1   CONCLUDED

CHECK LIST OF
POST INCORPORATION CONSIDERATIONS
FOR
BSJ GARDEN ORNAMENT SALES INC.

If you would like our assistance with any of the following matters, please check the appropriate box and fax this form to Richard Thorn at 415.123.1111. Richard Thorn will have a solicitor specialized in the particular area contact you.

☐   advice on creditor-proofing assets

☐   lease or other occupancy arrangements

☐   trade-mark and domain name registrations

☐   securing accounts receivable

☐   insurance

☐   employment contracts or manuals

☐   notification under the *Investment Canada Act*

☐   securing shareholder loans

☐   shareholder agreement

☐   contribution or indemnity for guarantees of corporate obligations

☐   sales contracts and commercial credit guarantees

☐   form of purchase order

☐   health, safety and environmental matters

☐   incentive plans

☐   exempt financing

FIGURE 8.2   SAMPLE ORGANIZATION PROCEEDINGS FOR AN ONTARIO CORPORATION

SUBSCRIPTION

TO: **01111111 ONTARIO INC.**
   (the "Corporation")

AND TO: **THE DIRECTORS THEREOF**

The undersigned subscribes for the number and class of shares in the capital of the Corporation set out below and tenders herewith the total subscription price as follows:

SUBSCRIBER	NUMBER AND CLASS OF SHARES	TOTAL SUBSCRIPTION PRICE
David Green	1 - common	$1.00

The undersigned requests that the said shares be issued as fully paid and non-assessable to the undersigned and that a certificate or certificates representing such shares be issued in the name of and delivered to the undersigned.

The undersigned undertakes to advise the Corporation of any change in beneficial ownership of the said shares.

DATED as of the 31st day of October, 2003.

_____
David Green

FIGURE 8.2 CONTINUED

RESOLUTIONS OF THE BOARD OF DIRECTORS

OF

01111111 ONTARIO INC.
(the "Corporation")

APPOINTMENT OF OFFICERS

RESOLVED that the directors hereby appoint the following as the officers of the Corporation, to hold the office shown opposite each respective name at the pleasure of the board:

Name	Position Held
David Green	President
Carol Green	Secretary

FORM OF SHARE CERTIFICATES

RESOLVED that:

1. The form of share certificate for the common shares in the capital of the Corporation, a specimen of which is annexed hereto, is approved and adopted.

2. Until changed by resolution the President and Secretary of the Corporation are authorized to sign all share certificates on behalf of the Corporation.

ISSUANCE OF COMMON SHARES

RESOLVED that:

1. The subscription of David Green (the "Subscriber") for one common share (the "Share") in the capital of the Corporation, which subscription is annexed hereto, be and the same is hereby accepted.

2. The directors of the Corporation hereby determine the sum of $1.00, as the consideration for the issuance of the Share subscribed for by the Subscriber.

3. The Corporation having received the sum of $1.00 in full payment of the consideration for the Share, one common share in the capital of the Corporation be and the same is hereby issued to the Subscriber.

4. It is hereby directed that a certificate representing the Share be issued to the Subscriber.

FIGURE 8.2 CONTINUED

CORPORATE SEAL

RESOLVED that the corporate seal of the Corporation shall be in the form impressed hereon.

BANKING DOCUMENTS

RESOLVED that:

1. A bank account be established with Royal Bank of Canada and that the resolution regarding banking and security annexed hereto is approved and adopted.

2. The directors and officers of the Corporation are authorized and directed to execute and deliver to the Corporation's bankers such banking documents as are requisite or necessary to open an account with such bank.

FINANCIAL YEAR

RESOLVED that the financial year of the Corporation shall end on April 30 in each year.

AUTHORITY TO SIGN NOTICES

RESOLVED that the firm of Miller Thomson LLP (the "Corporation's Solicitors") be appointed solicitors for the Corporation and any partner, associate or corporate law clerk employed by the Corporation's Solicitors who has the relevant knowledge of the affairs of the Corporation is authorized to sign and file (electronically or otherwise):

    (i)   any initial return;
    (ii)   any notice of change; and
    (iii) any annual return;

as required by the *Corporations Information Act* (Ontario).

EXTRA PROVINCIAL / TERRITORIAL REGISTRATION

RESOLVED that any officer or director of the Corporation may execute such document or documents as may be required to apply for extra-provincial or extra-territorial licenses in those provinces and territories where the Corporation will carry on business and to appoint attorneys or attorneys for service in respect of such extra-provincial or extra-territorial licenses.

EXECUTION OF INSTRUMENTS

RESOLVED that any director or officer of the Corporation is authorized on behalf of the Corporation to sign, whether under corporate seal or otherwise, contracts, documents, deeds,

FIGURE 8.2 CONTINUED

transfers, assignments, agreements, releases, obligations or instruments in writing requiring the signature of the Corporation and affix the corporate seal as may be required.

LOCATION OF BOOKS AND RECORDS

RESOLVED that the Corporation maintains, at its registered office or at the offices of Thorn & Hill LLP, the records and registers specified in the *Business Corporations Act* (Ontario).

THE UNDERSIGNED, being all the directors of the Corporation, pass the foregoing resolutions pursuant to the provisions of the *Business Corporations Act* (Ontario).

DATED as of the 31st day of October, 2003.

David Green	Carol Green

FIGURE 8.2 CONTINUED

Certificate No. _____

For _____ Common Shares

Issued to _____

Dated _____

From whom transferred

Dated _____
No. Original Certificate _____
No. Original Shares _____
No. of Shares Transferred _____

Received Certificate No. _____

for _____ Shares

this _____ day of _____, _____

INCORPORATED UNDER THE LAWS OF THE PROVINCE OF ONTARIO

01111111 ONTARIO INC.

Common Shares

No. _____

This is to Certify that
is the registered holder of _____ Common Shares of

01111111 ONTARIO INC.

The class or series of shares represented by this Certificate has rights, privileges, restrictions or conditions attached thereto and the Corporation will furnish to the holder, on demand and without charge, a full copy of the text of,
(i) the rights, privileges, restrictions and conditions attached to the said shares and to each class authorized to be issued and to each series insofar as the same have been fixed by the directors, and
(ii) the authority of the directors to fix the rights, privileges, restrictions and conditions of subsequent series, if applicable.

LIEN ON SHARES. The Corporation has a lien on the shares represented by this Certificate for any debt of the shareholder to the Corporation.
RESTRICTIONS ON TRANSFER. There are restrictions on the right to transfer the shares represented by this Certificate.

IN WITNESS WHEREOF the Corporation has caused this Certificate to be signed by its duly authorized officers
this _____ day of _____, _____ .

FIGURE 8.2 CONTINUED

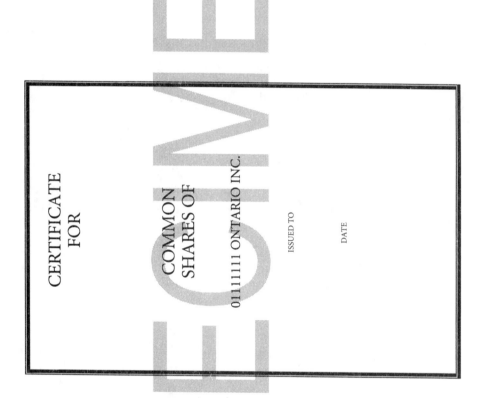

For Value Received, _____ hereby assign and
transfer unto _____
Common Shares represented by the within
Certificate.
Dated _____, _____.
In the presence of

_____

_____

FIGURE 8.2   CONTINUED

RESOLUTIONS OF THE SOLE SHAREHOLDER

OF

01111111 ONTARIO INC.
(the "Corporation")

NUMBER OF DIRECTORS

RESOLVED, as a special resolution, that:

1.   Until changed by special resolution, the number of directors of the Corporation shall be two.

2.   Until changed by special resolution, the number of directors to be elected at the annual meeting of the shareholders shall be two.

ELECTION OF DIRECTORS

RESOLVED, as an ordinary resolution, that the following be and are elected as the directors of the Corporation to hold office until the first annual meeting of the Corporation or until their successors have been duly elected or appointed:

David Green
Carol Green

EXEMPTION FROM AUDIT REQUIREMENTS

WHEREAS the Corporation is not an offering corporation within the meaning of the *Business Corporations Act* (Ontario) (the "Act");

RESOLVED, as a unanimous resolution, that the Corporation be exempt from the requirements of the Act regarding the appointment and duties of an auditor for the first financial period ending April 30, 2004.

APPOINTMENT OF ACCOUNTANT

RESOLVED, as an ordinary resolution, that ABC Accounting LLP is appointed the accountant of the Corporation to hold office until a successor is elected or appointed, at such remuneration as may be fixed by the directors, the directors being authorized to fix such remuneration.

FIGURE 8.2   CONTINUED

THE UNDERSIGNED, being the sole shareholder of the Corporation, passes the foregoing resolutions pursuant to the provisions of the *Business Corporations Act* (Ontario).

DATED as of the 31st day of October, 2003.

_____

David Green

FIGURE 8.2   CONTINUED

DIRECTOR'S CONSENT AND ACKNOWLEDGEMENT

TO: 01111111 ONTARIO INC.
(the "Corporation")

I, the undersigned, in accordance with the provisions of the *Business Corporations Act* (Ontario) (the "Act"):

(1)   Consent to act as a director of the Corporation, such consent to continue in effect unless revoked by instrument in writing delivered to the Corporation.

(2)   Acknowledge and declare that I am:

☐   a Canadian citizen ordinarily resident in Canada; **OR**

☐   a Canadian citizen <u>not</u> ordinarily resident in Canada who is a member of a prescribed class of persons (refer to Schedule A); **OR**

☐   a permanent resident within the meaning of the *Immigration Act* and ordinarily resident in Canada; **OR**

☐   none of the above

(3)   Undertake to advise the Corporation, in writing, forthwith after any change in citizenship, residence or status of lawful admission for permanent residence.

(4)   Acknowledge that:

a)   I am not under 18 years of age;

b)   I am not a person who has been found by a court in Canada or elsewhere to be of unsound mind; and

c)   I am not an undischarged bankrupt.

(5)   Consent to any director participating in a meeting of the directors or of a committee of directors by means of such telephonic, electronic or other communication facilities as permit all persons participating in the meeting to communicate with each other simultaneously and instantaneously.

FIGURE 8.2   CONTINUED

Page 2

(6)   Acknowledge that the Corporation will rely upon the foregoing consents and undertakings for the purpose of ensuring compliance by the Corporation with the provisions of the Act.

DATED as of the 31st day of October, 2003.

David Green
111 Red Street
White Port, ON P3P 0P9

FIGURE 8.2   CONTINUED

SCHEDULE A

"Resident Canadian" Class of Persons Prescribed
Ont. Reg. 62, s. 26 made under the *Business Corporations Act* (Ontario) (the "Act")

For the purposes of clause (b) of the definition of "resident Canadian" in subsection 1(1) of the Act, the following classes of persons are prescribed:

1.   Full-time employees of the Government of Canada, a province or a territory of Canada or of an agency of any such government or of a federal or provincial crown corporation.

2.   Full-time employees of a body corporate,

        (i)   of which more than 50 per cent of the voting securities are beneficially owned or over which control or direction is exercised by resident Canadians, or

        (ii)   a majority of directors of which are resident Canadians,

        where the principal reason for the residence outside Canada is to act as such employees;

3.   Full-time students at a university outside of Canada or at another educational institution outside of Canada recognized by the province.

4.   Full-time employees of an international association or organization of which Canada is a member.

5.   Persons who were, at the time of reaching their 60th birthday, ordinarily resident in Canada and have been resident outside of Canada since that time.

FIGURE 8.2 CONTINUED

DIRECTOR'S CONSENT AND ACKNOWLEDGEMENT

TO: **01111111 ONTARIO INC.**
(the "Corporation")

I, the undersigned, in accordance with the provisions of the *Business Corporations Act* (Ontario) (the "Act"):

(1)   Consent to act as a director of the Corporation, such consent to continue in effect unless revoked by instrument in writing delivered to the Corporation.

(2)   Acknowledge and declare that I am:

☐   a Canadian citizen ordinarily resident in Canada; **OR**

☐   a Canadian citizen <u>not</u> ordinarily resident in Canada who is a member of a prescribed class of persons (refer to Schedule A); **OR**

☐   a permanent resident within the meaning of the *Immigration Act* and ordinarily resident in Canada; **OR**

☐   none of the above

(3)   Undertake to advise the Corporation, in writing, forthwith after any change in citizenship, residence or status of lawful admission for permanent residence.

(4)   Acknowledge that:

a)   I am not under 18 years of age;

b)   I am not a person who has been found by a court in Canada or elsewhere to be of unsound mind; and

c)   I am not an undischarged bankrupt.

(5)   Consent to any director participating in a meeting of the directors or of a committee of directors by means of such telephonic, electronic or other communication facilities as permit all persons participating in the meeting to communicate with each other simultaneously and instantaneously.

FIGURE 8.2   CONTINUED

Page 2

(6)   Acknowledge that the Corporation will rely upon the foregoing consents and undertakings for the purpose of ensuring compliance by the Corporation with the provisions of the Act.

DATED as of the 31st day of October, 2003.

_____

Carol Green
111 Red Street
White Port, ON P3P 0P9

FIGURE 8.2   CONTINUED

SCHEDULE A

"Resident Canadian" Class of Persons Prescribed
Ont. Reg. 62, s. 26 made under the *Business Corporations Act* (Ontario) (the "Act")

For the purposes of clause (b) of the definition of "resident Canadian" in subsection 1(1) of the Act, the following classes of persons are prescribed:

1.   Full-time employees of the Government of Canada, a province or a territory of Canada or of an agency of any such government or of a federal or provincial crown corporation.

2.   Full-time employees of a body corporate,

    (i)   of which more than 50 per cent of the voting securities are beneficially owned or over which control or direction is exercised by resident Canadians, or

    (ii)   a majority of directors of which are resident Canadians,

    where the principal reason for the residence outside Canada is to act as such employees;

3.   Full-time students at a university outside of Canada or at another educational institution outside of Canada recognized by the province.

4.   Full-time employees of an international association or organization of which Canada is a member.

5.   Persons who were, at the time of reaching their 60th birthday, ordinarily resident in Canada and have been resident outside of Canada since that time.

FIGURE 8.2 CONTINUED

BY-LAW NO. 1
A by-law relating generally to
the transaction of the business and affairs
of
01111111 ONTARIO INC.
(the "Corporation")

TABLE OF CONTENTS

FIGURE 8.2 CONTINUED

BY-LAW NO. 1
A by-law relating generally to
the transaction of
the business and affairs of
01111111 ONTARIO INC.
(the "Corporation")

RESOLVED as a by-law of the Corporation that:

1.   INTERPRETATION

1.1   Definitions. In this By-law and all other by-laws and resolutions of the Corporation, unless the context otherwise requires:

(a)   the following terms shall have the meanings specified:

(i)   **"Act"** means the *Business Corporations Act* (Ontario), or any statute that may be substituted therefor, including the regulations made thereunder, as amended from time to time;

(ii)   **"Articles"** means the Articles of Incorporation of the Corporation as amended or restated from time to time;

(iii)   **"Board"** means the board of directors of the Corporation;

(iv)   **"Chair of the Board"** means the Director appointed by the Board from time to time to hold that office;

(v)   **"Corporation"** means 01111111 Ontario Inc.;

(vi)   **"Director"** means a member of the Board;

(vii)   **"meeting of shareholders"** means an annual meeting of shareholders or a special meeting of shareholders, or both, and includes a meeting of any class or series of any class of shareholders;

(viii)   **"Officer"** means an officer of the Corporation;

(b)   terms that are defined in the Act are used in this By-law with the same meaning; and

(c)   words importing the singular number shall include the plural number and vice versa, and words importing the masculine gender shall include the feminine and neuter genders.

FIGURE 8.2   CONTINUED

Page 2

2.   DIRECTORS AND OFFICERS

2.1   **Number of Directors.**   The minimum and maximum number of Directors of the Corporation shall be such as are from time to time set forth in the Articles.   The number of Directors within such range shall be determined from time to time by special resolution or, subject to the provisions of the Act, by the Board if so empowered by special resolution.

2.2   **Election and Term.**   The Directors shall be elected at each annual meeting of shareholders to hold office until the next annual meeting or until their respective successors are elected or appointed.   At any annual meeting every retiring Director shall, if qualified, be eligible for re-election.

2.3   **Quorum.**   A majority of the number of Directors from time to time shall constitute a quorum for the transaction of business at any meeting of the Board.   If it is necessary to determine the number of Directors constituting a quorum at a time when one or more vacancies exist on the Board, such a determination shall be made as if such vacancies did not exist.

2.4   **Calling of Meetings.**   A meeting of the Board may be held at any time upon call by the Board, the Chair of the Board, the President or any other Officer so empowered by the Board.

2.5   **Place of Meetings.**   Each meeting of the Board shall be held at such place within or outside Ontario as may be determined by the person calling the meeting.

2.6   **Notice.**   Subject as hereinafter provided, notice of every meeting of the Board shall be given to each Director at least 48 hours prior to the meeting.   Notwithstanding the foregoing:

(a)   no notice need be given of the first meeting of the Board subsequent to a meeting of shareholders at which Directors are elected if such Board meeting is held immediately following the meeting of shareholders; and

(b)   the Board may appoint a day or days in any month or months for regular meetings at a place and hour to be named.

A copy of any resolution by the Board fixing the time and place of regular meetings of the Board shall be sent to each Director forthwith after being passed, but no other notice shall be required for any such regular meeting.   The accidental failure to give notice of a meeting of the Board to a Director or any error in such notice not affecting the substance thereof shall not invalidate any action taken at the meeting.

2.7   **Votes to Govern.**   Every question at a meeting of the Board shall be decided by a majority of the votes cast on the question.   In the event of an equality of votes on any

FIGURE 8.2 CONTINUED

Page 3

question at a meeting of the Board, the Chair of the Board shall not be entitled to a second or casting vote.

2.8   **Audit, Executive and Other Committees.** Subject to the provisions of the Act, the Board may appoint annually from among its members an Audit Committee and one or more other committees of Directors, including a committee designated as an Executive Committee, and delegate to such committee or committees any of the powers of the Board except those powers which, under the Act, a committee of Directors has no authority to exercise.

Unless otherwise determined by the Board, each committee appointed by the Board shall have the power to fix the quorum for its meetings at not less than a majority of its members, to elect its presiding officer and to fix its rules of procedure.

2.9   **Appointment of Officers.** The Board may from time to time appoint Officers, specify their duties and delegate to them such powers as the Board deems advisable and which are permitted by the Act to be so delegated. The Board may also from time to time appoint persons to serve the Corporation in such positions other than as Officers, with such titles and such powers and duties and for such terms of service, as the Board deems advisable. One person may hold or discharge the functions of more than one officer or other position.

2.10   **Remuneration and Expenses.** Each Director shall be remunerated for his/her services as a Director at such rate as the Board may from time to time determine. In addition, each Director shall be paid such sums in respect of the out-of-pocket expenses incurred by him/her in attending meetings of the Board, meetings of any committee of the Board of which he/she is a member, or meetings of shareholders, or otherwise incurred by him/her in connection with the performance of his/her duties as a Director, as the Board may from time to time determine. Nothing herein contained shall preclude any Director from receiving remuneration for serving the Corporation as an Officer or employee or in any other capacity.

2.11   **Indemnity.** Without limit to the right of the Corporation to indemnify any person to the full extent permitted by law, the Corporation shall indemnify a Director or Officer, a former Director or Officer, or a person who acts or acted at the Corporation's request as a director or officer of a body corporate of which the Corporation is or was a shareholder or creditor, and his/her heirs and legal representatives, against all costs, charges and expenses, including an amount paid to settle an action or satisfy a judgment, reasonably incurred by him/her in respect of any civil, criminal or administrative action or proceeding to which he/she is made a party by reason of being or having been a Director or Officer, or director or officer of such body corporate, if

(a)   he/she acted honestly and in good faith with a view to the best interests of the Corporation; and

FIGURE 8.2 CONTINUED

Page 4

(b)   in the case of a criminal or administrative action or proceeding that is enforced by a monetary penalty, he/she had reasonable grounds for believing that his/her conduct was lawful.

3.   <u>SHAREHOLDERS</u>

3.1   Annual and Special Meetings. The Board shall call an annual meeting of shareholders not later than 15 months after the holding of the last preceding annual meeting and may at any time call a special meeting of shareholders.

3.2   Place of Meetings. Each meeting of shareholders shall be held at such place within or outside Ontario as the Board determines.

3.3   Notice of Meetings. Notice of each meeting of shareholders shall be sent not less than 10 days nor more than 50 days before the meeting to each shareholder entitled to vote at the meeting, to each Director, to the auditor of the Corporation and to any other persons who, although not entitled to vote at the meeting, are entitled or required under any provision of the Act, the Articles or any by-law of the Corporation to attend the meeting. The accidental failure to give notice of a meeting of shareholders to any person entitled to notice thereof or any error in such notice not affecting the substance thereof shall not invalidate any action taken at the meeting.

3.4   Persons Entitled to be Present. The only persons entitled to attend a meeting of shareholders shall be those persons entitled to vote thereat, the Directors, Officers and auditor of the Corporation and any other persons who, although not entitled to vote at the meeting, are entitled or required under any provision of the Act, the Articles or any by-law of the Corporation to attend the meeting. Any other person may be admitted to the meeting only on the invitation of the chair of the meeting or with the consent of the meeting.

3.5   Quorum. At any meeting of shareholders, the holders of a majority of the shares entitled to vote at a meeting of shareholders whether present in person or represented by proxy, shall constitute a quorum for the transaction of business.

3.6   Voting.

(a)   Voting at any meeting of shareholders shall be by a show of hands except where, either before or after a vote by show of hands, a ballot is required by the chair of the meeting or is demanded by any person present and entitled to vote at the meeting. On a show of hands, each person present at the meeting and entitled to vote thereat shall, subject to the Act, have one vote. On a ballot, each person present at the meeting and entitled to vote thereat shall, subject to the Act and the Articles, have one vote for each share in respect of which such person is entitled to vote. A ballot so required or demanded shall be taken in such manner as the chair of the meeting directs.

FIGURE 8.2 CONTINUED

(b)   Unless otherwise required by the Act or the Articles, every question at a meeting of shareholders shall be decided by a majority of the votes cast on the question. In the event of an equality of votes on any question at a meeting of shareholders either upon a show of hands or upon a ballot, the chair of the meeting shall not be entitled to a second or casting vote.

(c)   Subject to the Act and the Articles, where, after the date on which a list of shareholders entitled to receive notice of a meeting is prepared in accordance with the Act, a shareholder named in such list transfers any of his/her shares, the transferee of such shares shall be entitled to vote such shares at the meeting if, at any time before the meeting, the transferee

   (i)   produces properly endorsed share certificates, or

   (ii)   otherwise establishes that he/she owns such shares.

3.7   Representatives. Upon filing proof of his/her appointment reasonably sufficient to the chair of a meeting of shareholders,

(a)   a person who holds shares as a personal representative,

(b)   an individual who has been duly authorized to represent at the meeting a shareholder which is a body corporate or an association, or

(c)   a proxyholder or alternate proxyholder of a personal representative, body corporate or association,

shall be entitled to vote at the meeting in respect of the shares in respect of which such person has been appointed.

3.8   Joint Shareholders. Where two or more persons are registered jointly as the holders of shares of the Corporation,

(a)   any notice, cheque or other document directed to such persons shall be sent to them at their address as recorded in the Corporation's share register or, if there be more than one address recorded for them in that register, at the first such address;

(b)   any one of such persons may give a receipt on behalf of them for a share certificate that is issued in respect of their shares, or for any dividend that is paid in respect of their shares, or for any warrant or other evidence of a right to subscribe for securities of the Corporation that is issued in respect of their shares, or for any evidence of the rights in respect of any conversion, exchange or other change in the share capital of the Corporation that is issued in respect of their shares; and

FIGURE 8.2   CONTINUED

Page 6

(c)   any one of such persons present in person or represented by proxy at a meeting of shareholders and entitled to vote thereat may, in the absence of the other or others, vote their shares as if he/she were solely entitled thereto, but, if more than one of such persons is so present or represented, they shall vote as one the shares jointly held by them.

For the purposes of this section, several personal representatives of a shareholder in whose names shares of the Corporation are registered shall be deemed to hold such shares jointly.

3.9   Presiding Officer. The Chair of the Board or, a Director designated by him/her, or failing such designation, a Director designated by the Board, shall preside at a meeting of shareholders. If neither the Chair of the Board nor any Director is present within thirty minutes after the time appointed for the holding of a meeting of shareholders, the shareholders present shall choose a shareholder then present to be chair of the meeting.

3.10   Scrutineers. At any meeting of shareholders, the chair of the meeting may appoint one or more persons, who may but need not be shareholders, to serve as scrutineers at the meeting.

3.11   Dividends. A dividend payable to any shareholder

(a)   in cash may be paid by cheque payable to the order of the shareholder, or

(b)   in shares may be paid by a share certificate in the name of the shareholder,

and shall be mailed to such shareholder by prepaid ordinary or air mail in a sealed envelope addressed (unless he/she has directed otherwise) to him/her at his/her address as shown in the Corporation's share register. The mailing of such cheque or share certificate, as the case may be, unless in the case of a cheque it is not paid on due presentation, shall discharge the Corporation's liability for the dividend to the extent of the sum or number of shares represented thereby plus the amount of any tax which the Corporation has properly withheld. In the event of the non-receipt of any such dividend cheque or share certificate, the Corporation shall issue to the shareholder a replacement cheque or share certificate, as the case may be, for the same amount or number of shares on such reasonable terms as to indemnity and evidence of non-receipt as the Board, or any Officer or agent designated by the Board, may require.

4.   <u>EXECUTION OF DOCUMENTS</u>

4.1   The Board may from time to time determine the Officers or other persons by whom certificates, contracts or other documents of the Corporation shall be executed and the manner of execution thereof, including the use of printed or facsimile reproductions of any or all signatures and the use of a corporate seal or a printed or facsimile reproduction thereof.

FIGURE 8.2 CONTINUED

Page 7

5. **BORROWING**

5.1 The Board may from time to time, in such amounts and on such terms as it deems expedient, without authorization of the shareholders:

(a) borrow money upon the credit of the Corporation;

(b) issue, reissue, sell or pledge debt obligations of the Corporation;

(c) except as limited by law, give a guarantee on behalf of the Corporation to secure performance of an obligation of any person; and,

(d) mortgage, hypothecate, pledge or otherwise create a security interest in all or any property of the Corporation, owned or subsequently acquired, to secure any obligation of the Corporation.

The foregoing resolution making By-law No. 1 of the Corporation is passed by all of the directors of the Corporation pursuant to the *Business Corporations Act* (Ontario).

DATED as of the 31st day of October, 2003.

_____   _____
David Green   Carol Green

The foregoing resolution making By-law No. 1 of the Corporation is confirmed without variation by the sole shareholder of the Corporation pursuant to the *Business Corporations Act* (Ontario).

DATED as of the 31st day of October, 2003.

_____
David Green

FIGURE 8.2 CONTINUED

<table>
<tr><td>Ministry of Consumer and Business Services</td><td>Ministère des Services aux consommateurs et aux enterprises</td><td>Companies and Personal Property Security Branch
393 University Ave Suite
200 Toronto ON M5G 2M2</td><td>Direction des compagnies et des sûretés mobilières
393 av., University bureau 200
Toronto ON M5G 2M2</td></tr>
</table>

For Ministry Use Only
À l'usage du ministère seulement
Page/Page 1 **of/de** 2

Form 1 - Ontario Corporation/
Formule 1 - Personnes morales en Ontario

Initial Return/Notice of Change/
Rapport Initial/Avis de modification
Corporations Information Act/*Loi sur les renseignements exigés des personnes morales*

Notice of Change

1.

	Initial Return Rapport Initial	Avis de modification
Business Corporations/ Société par actions	☒	☐
Not-For-Profit Corporation/ Personne morale sans but lucratif	☐	☐

Please type or print all information in block capital letters using black ink.
Prière de dactylographier les renseignements ou de les écrire en caractères d'imprimerie à l'encre noire.

2.
Ontario Corporation Number
Numéro matricule de la personne morale en Ontario

01111111

3. Date of Incorporation or Amalgamation/
Date de constitution ou fusion

Year/Année	Month/Mois	Day/Jour
2003	10	31

For Ministry Use Only
À l'usage du ministère seulement

4. Corporation Name Including Punctuation/Raison sociale de la personne morale, y compris la ponctuation

01111111 ONTARIO INC.

5. Address of Registered or Head Office/Adresse du siège social
c/o a/s

Street No./N° civique: **111**
Street Name/Nom de la rue: **RED STREET**
Suite/Bureau:

Street Name (cont'd)/Nom de la rue (suite)

City/Town/Ville: **WHITE PORT**   **ONTARIO, CANADA**

Postal Code/Code postal: **P3P 0P9**

For Ministry Use Only
À l'usage du ministère seulement

6. Mailing Address/Adresse postale

☒ Same as Registered or Head Office/
Même que siège social

☐ Not Applicable/
Ne s'applique pas

Street No./N° civique

Street Name/Nom de la rue   Suite/Bureau

Street Name (cont'd)/Nom de la rue (suite)

City/Town/Ville

Province, State/Province, État   Country/Pays   Postal Code/Code postal

7. Language of Preference/Langue préférée   English - Anglais ☒   French - Français ☐

8. **Information on Directors/Officers must be completed on Schedule A as requested.** If additional space is required, photocopy Schedule A./**Les renseignements sur les administrateurs ou les dirigeants doivent être fournis dans l'Annexe A, tel que demandé.** Si vous avez besoin de plus d'espace, vous pouvez photocopier l'Annexe A.

Number of Schedule A(s) submitted/Nombre d'Annexes A présentées **1** (At least one Schedule A must be submitted/Au moins une Annexe A doit être présentée)

9.
(Print or type name in full of the person authorizing filing / Dactylographier ou inscrire le prénom et le nom en caractères d'imprimerie de la personne qui autorise l'enregistrement)

I/Je   **DAVID GREEN**

certify that the information set out herein, is true and correct.
atteste que les renseignements précités sont véridiques et exacts.

Check appropriate box
Cocher la case pertinente

D) ☒ Director/Administrateur

O) ☒ Officers/Dirigeant

P) ☐ Other individual having knowledge of the affairs of the Corporation/Autre personne ayant connaissance des activités de la personne morale

NOTE/REMARQUE: Sections 13 and 14 of the **Corporations Information Act** provide penalties for making false or misleading statements or omissions. Les articles 13 et 14 de la **Loi sur les renseignements exigés des personnes morales** prévoient des peines en cas de déclaration fausse ou trompeuse, ou d'omission.

FIGURE 8.2 CONTINUED

Form 1 - Ontario Corporation/Formule 1 - Personnes morales de l'Ontario
Schedule A/Annexe A

For Ministry Use Only
A l'usage du ministère seulement
Page/Page 2 of/de 2

Please type or print all information in block capital letters using black ink. Prière de dactylographier les renseignements ou de les écrire en caractères d'imprimerie à l'encre noire.	Ontario Corporation Number Numéro matricule de la personne morale en Ontario 01111111	Date of Incorporation or Amalgamation Date de constitution ou fusion Year/Année Month/Mois Day/Jour 2003 · 10 · 31

DIRECTOR / OFFICER INFORMATION - RENSEIGNEMENTS RELATIFS AUX ADMINISTRATEURS/DIRIGEANTS
Full Name and Address for Service/Nom et domicile élu

Last Name/Nom de famille	First Name/ Prénom	Middle Names/Autres prénoms
GREEN	DAVID	

Street Number/Numéro civique: 111 Suite/Bureau:

*OTHER TITLES (Please Specify)
*AUTRES TITRES (Veuillez préciser)

Chair / Président du conseil
Chair Person / Président du conseil
Chairman / Président du conseil
Chairwoman / Président du conseil
Vice-Chair / Vice-président du conseil
Vice-President / Vice-président
Assistant Secretary / Secrétaire adjoint
Assistant Treasurer / Trésorier adjoint
Chief Manager / Directeur exécutif
Executive Director / Directeur administratif
Managing Director / Administrateur délégué
Chief Executive Officer / Directeur général
Chief Financial Officer / Agent en chef des finaces
Chief Information Officer / Directeur général de l'information
Chief Operating Officer / Administrateur en chef des opérations
Chief Administrative Officer / Directeur général de l'administration
Comptroller / Contrôleur
Authorized Signing Officer / Signataire autorisé
Other (Untitled) / Autre (sans titre)

Street Name/Nom de la rue: RED STREET

Street Name (cont'd)/Nom de la rue (suite):

City/Town/Ville: WHITE PORT

Province, State/Province, État	Country/Pays	Postal Code/Code postal
ONTARIO	CANADA	P3P 0P9

Director Information/Renseignements relatifs aux administrateurs

Resident Canadian/Résident canadien: ☒ YES/OUI ☐ NO/NON

(Resident Canadian applies to directors of business corporations only.)/
(Résident canadien ne s'applique qu'aux administrateurs de sociétés par actions)

Date Elected/Date d'élection	Year/Année 2003	Month/Mois 10	Day/Jour 31	Date Ceased/Date de cessation	Year/Année	Month/Mois	Day/Jour

Officer Information/Renseignements relatifs aux dirigeants

	PRESIDENT/PRÉSIDENT	SECRETARY/SECRÉTAIRE	TREASURER/TRÉSORIER	GENERAL MANAGER/DIRECTEUR GÉNÉRAL	*OTHER/AUTRE
	Year/Année Month/Mois Day/Jour	Year/Année Month/Mois Day/Jour	Year/Année Month/Mois Day/Jour	Year/Année Month/Mois Day/Jour	Year/Année Month/Mois Day/Jour
Date Appointed/Date de nomination	2003 · 10 · 31				
Date Ceased/Date de cessation					

DIRECTOR / OFFICER INFORMATION - RENSEIGNEMENTS RELATIFS AUX ADMINISTRATEURS/DIRIGEANTS
Full Name and Address for Service/Nom et domicile élu

Last Name/Nom de famille	First Name/ Prénom	Middle Names/Autres prénoms
GREEN	CAROL	

Street Number/Numéro civique: 111 Suite/Bureau:

*OTHER TITLES (Please Specify)
*AUTRES TITRES (Veuillez préciser)

Chair / Président du conseil
Chair Person / Président du conseil
Chairman / Président du conseil
Chairwoman / Président du conseil
Vice-Chair / Vice-président du conseil
Vice-President / Vice-président
Assistant Secretary / Secrétaire adjoint
Assistant Treasurer / Trésorier adjoint
Chief Manager / Directeur exécutif
Executive Director / Directeur administratif
Managing Director / Administrateur délégué
Chief Executive Officer / Directeur général
Chief Financial Officer / Agent en chef des finaces
Chief Information Officer / Directeur général de l'information
Chief Operating Officer / Administrateur en chef des opérations
Chief Administrative Officer / Directeur général de l'administration
Comptroller / Contrôleur
Authorized Signing Officer / Signataire autorisé
Other (Untitled) / Autre (sans titre)

Street Name/Nom de la rue: RED STREET

Street Name (cont'd)/Nom de la rue (suite):

City/Town/Ville: WHITE PORT

Province, State/Province, État	Country/Pays	Postal Code/Code postal
ONTARIO	CANADA	P3P 0P9

Director Information/Renseignements relatifs aux administrateurs

Resident Canadian/Résident canadien: ☒ YES/OUI ☐ NO/NON

(Resident Canadian applies to directors of business corporations only.)/
(Résident canadien ne s'applique qu'aux administrateurs de sociétés par actions)

Date Elected/Date d'élection	Year/Année 2003	Month/Mois 10	Day/Jour 31	Date Ceased/Date de cessation	Year/Année	Month/Mois	Day/Jour

Officer Information/Renseignements relatifs aux dirigeants

	PRESIDENT/PRÉSIDENT	SECRETARY/SECRÉTAIRE	TREASURER/TRÉSORIER	GENERAL MANAGER/DIRECTEUR GÉNÉRAL	*OTHER/AUTRE
	Year/Année Month/Mois Day/Jour	Year/Année Month/Mois Day/Jour	Year/Année Month/Mois Day/Jour	Year/Année Month/Moi Day/Jour	Year/Année Month/Mois Day/Jour
Date Appointed/Date de nomination		2003 · 10 · 31			
Date Ceased/Date de cessation					

07200 (03/2002)
DSG 10/2002

FIGURE 8.2   CONTINUED

Certificate No. C-001
For One Common Share
Issued to
David Green

Dated October 31, 2003.

From whom transferred
Issued from Treasury
Dated
No. Original Certificate
No. Original Shares
No. of Shares Transferred

Received Certificate No. _____
for _____ Shares
this _____ day of _____, _____

INCORPORATED UNDER THE LAW OF THE PROVINCE OF ONTARIO

01111111 ONTARIO INC.

One Common Share

No. C-001

This is to Certify that

is the registered holder of

David Green

One

Common Share of

01111111 ONTARIO INC.

The class or series of shares represented by this Certificate has rights, privileges, restrictions or conditions attached thereto and the Corporation will furnish to the holder, on demand and without charge, a full copy of the text of,
(i) the rights, privileges, restrictions and conditions attached to the said shares and to each class authorized to be issued and to each series insofar as the same have been fixed by the directors, and
(ii) the authority of the directors to fix the rights, privileges, restrictions and conditions of subsequent series, if applicable.

LIEN ON SHARES.   The Corporation has a lien on the shares represented by this Certificate for any debt of the shareholder to the Corporation.
RESTRICTIONS ON TRANSFER.   There are restrictions on the right to transfer the shares represented by this Certificate.

IN WITNESS WHEREOF the Corporation has caused this Certificate to be signed by its duly authorized officers this 31st day of October, 2003.

_____
President

_____
Secretary

FIGURE 8.2 CONTINUED

CERTIFICATE
FOR

One

COMMON
SHARE OF

01111111 ONTARIO INC.

ISSUED TO
David Green

DATE
October 31, 2003

For Value Received, _____ hereby assign and transfer unto _____ Common Shares represented by the within Certificate.

Dated _____ , _____.

In the presence of

_____

_____

FIGURE 8.2   CONTINUED

ACKNOWLEDGEMENT

The undersigned hereby acknowledges that as at the date hereof it is a "closely-held issuer" as such term is defined in Ontario Securities Commission ("OSC") Rule 45-501 Exempt Distributions (refer to Schedule A for a complete copy of the definition).

In connection with trades made on this date of one common share of the undersigned:

(a)   No Offering Memorandum has been issued by the undersigned;

(b)   Following such trades; the undersigned will continue to be a closely-held issuer and the aggregate proceeds received by the undersigned and any other issuer engaged in common enterprise with the undersigned, in connection with trades made in reliance upon the "closely-held issuer" exemption contained in section 2.1 of the Ontario Securities Commission Rule 45-501 (the "Exemption") will not exceed $3,000,000; and

(c)   No selling or promotional expenses have been or will be paid or incurred in connection with trades made in reliance on the Exemption except for services performed by a dealer registered under the *Securities Act* (Ontario).

DATED as of the 31st day of October, 2003.

01111111 ONTARIO INC.

By: _____
David Green
President

FIGURE 8.2 CONTINUED

SCHEDULE A

"Closely-held issuer" means an issuer, other than a mutual fund or non-redeemable investment fund, whose

(a)   shares are subject to restrictions on transfer requiring the approval of either the board of directors or the shareholders of the issuer (or the equivalent in a non-corporate issuer) contained in constating documents of the issuer or one or more agreements among the issuer and holders of its shares; and

(b)   outstanding securities are beneficially owned, directly or indirectly, by not more than 35 persons or companies, exclusive of:

(i)   persons or companies that are, or at the time they last acquired securities of the Corporation were, accredited investors (as such term is defined in the Ontario Securities Commission ("OSC") Rule 45-501 Exempt Distributions as amended from time to time);

(ii)   current or former directors or officers of the Corporation or an affiliated entity of the Corporation; and

(iii)   current or former employees of the Corporation or an affiliated entity of the Corporation, or current or former consultants as defined in MI Rule 45-105, who in each case beneficially own only securities of the Corporation that were issued as compensation by, or under an incentive plan of, the Corporation or an affiliated entity of the Corporation;

provided that:

(A)   two or more persons who are the joint registered holders of one or more securities of the Corporation are counted as one beneficial owner of those securities; and

(B)   a corporation, partnership, trust or other entity shall be counted as one beneficial owner of securities of the Corporation unless the entity has been created or is being used primarily for the purpose of acquiring or holding securities of the Corporation, in which event each beneficial owner of an equity interest in the entity or each beneficiary of the entity, as the case may be, is counted as a separate beneficial owner of those securities of the Corporation."

FIGURE 8.2 CONTINUED

01111111 ONTARIO INC.

01111111

REGISTER OF DIRECTORS

NAME AND ADDRESS	RES. CDN (YES/NO)	DATE APPOINTED	DATE RESIGNED
David Green 111 Red Street White Port, ON P3P 0P9	Yes	Oct 31, 2003	
Carol Green 111 Red Street White Port, ON P3P 0P9	Yes	Oct 31, 2003	

FIGURE 8.2 CONTINUED

01111111 ONTARIO INC.

01111111

REGISTER OF OFFICERS

NAME AND ADDRESS	OFFICE HELD	DATE APPOINTED	DATE RESIGNED
David Green 111 Red Street White Port, ON P3P 0P9	President	Oct 31, 2003	
Carol Green 111 Red Street White Port, ON P3P 0P9	Secretary	Oct 31, 2003	

FIGURE 8.2   CONTINUED

01111111 ONTARIO INC.

SHAREHOLDERS' REGISTER

common

Date Issued	Name	Number of Shares	Certificate Number	Date Cancelled
Oct. 31, 2003	David Green	1	C-001	

FIGURE 8.2   CONTINUED

01111111 ONTARIO INC.

01111111

SHAREHOLDERS' LEDGER

NAME: David Green

ADDRESS: 111 Red Street, White Port, ON P3P 0P9

CLASS: common

Date	Cert. No.	Trans. No.	To Whom or From Whom	Transferred	Acquired	Balance Held
Oct. 31, 2003	C-001	0	Issue From Treasury	0	1	1

FIGURE 8.2   CONTINUED

Direct Line: 905.666.1212
E-mail: ghill@thornhill.ca

November 5, 2003

PERSONAL AND CONFIDENTIAL

01111111 Ontario Inc.
111 Red Street
White Port ON P3P 0P9

Attention: Mr. David Green, President

Dear Sirs/Madams:

Re: 01111111 Ontario Inc. (the "Corporation")
Incorporation and Organization
Our File No.: 1111111

We have now completed the incorporation and organization of the Corporation and are pleased to submit our report in connection therewith.

A.   INCORPORATION

1. **Articles of Incorporation**

Pursuant to the *Business Corporations Act* (Ontario) (the "Act"), the Corporation was incorporated by the filing of Articles of Incorporation with the Director appointed under the Act (the "Director") and the issue of a Certificate of Incorporation incorporating the Corporation effective as of October 31, 2003. The Certificate and Articles of Incorporation (the "Articles") have been placed in the minute book of the Corporation. A photocopy is enclosed for your records.

2. **Corporate Name**

Subsection 10(5) of the Act states that a corporation shall set out its name in legible characters in all contracts, invoices, negotiable instruments and orders for goods or services issued or made by

FIGURE 8.2 CONTINUED

Page 2

or on behalf of the corporation and in all documents sent to the Director. The Act does not require the full corporate name to appear on letterhead. If, however, a contract is set out in letter form, it will be necessary to have the full corporate name appear in the body of the letter or on the signing page in order to meet the requirements of the Act.

Nevertheless, a recent case found that the failure to use the full correct corporate name on a supply order led to personal liability against the principal of a corporation. Accordingly, we strongly recommend that the full correct corporate name (as it appears in the Corporation's Articles) be used at all times, especially on all contracts entered into by or on behalf of the Corporation. Please feel free to contact us if you have any questions in this regard.

3. Registered Office

The Act provides that a corporation shall at all times have a registered office in a municipality or geographic township within Ontario.

The Articles provide that the registered office of the Corporation is located in the City of White Port is:

> 111 Red Street
> White Port, Ontario, P3P 0P9

Any change in the address of the registered office within the present municipality may be effected by resolution of the directors. Any change in location from one municipality to another within Ontario may be effected only by special resolution of the shareholders.

4. Business and Powers

The Act provides that a corporation has the capacity, rights, powers and privileges of a natural person. Restrictions on the business or powers that a corporation may exercise can, however, be included in the Articles. No such restrictions have been included in the Articles of the Corporation.

5. Authorized Capital

The Corporation is authorized to issue an unlimited number of common shares.

6. Exemption from Prospectus and Registration Requirements of the *Securities Act* (Ontario)

To qualify the Corporation as a "closely-held issuer" for the purposes of the *Securities Act* (Ontario), shares must be subject to restrictions on transfer. The Act prohibits a corporation from imposing restrictions on the issue, transfer or ownership of shares except such restrictions as are authorized by its articles. We have therefore included the following restriction in the Corporation's Articles:

FIGURE 8.2   CONTINUED

Page 3

"No shares shall be transferred without either:

(a) the approval of the directors of the Corporation expressed by a resolution passed by the board of directors of the Corporation at a meeting of the directors or by an instrument or instruments in writing signed by a majority of the directors; or

(b) the approval of the holders of a majority of the voting shares of the Corporation for the time being outstanding expressed by a resolution passed at a meeting of shareholders or by an instrument or instruments in writing signed by the holders of a majority of such shares".

In addition to the above, a "closely-held" issuer is limited as to the number and type of security holders. We have included the following provisions in the Articles of the Corporation to address this limitation:

1. "The outstanding securities of the Corporation may be beneficially owned, directly or indirectly, by not more than 35 persons or companies, exclusive of:

(i) persons or companies that are, or at the time they last acquired securities of the Corporation were, accredited investors as such term is defined in the Ontario Securities Commission ("OSC") Rule 45-501 Exempt Distributions as amended from time to time;

(ii) current or former directors or officers of the Corporation or an affiliated entity of the Corporation; and

(iii) current or former employees of the Corporation or an affiliated entity of the Corporation, or current or former consultants as defined in MI Rule 45-105, who in each case beneficially own only securities of the Corporation that were issued as compensation by, or under an incentive plan of, the Corporation or an affiliated entity of the Corporation;

provided that:

A. two or more persons who are the joint registered holders of one or more securities of the Corporation are counted as one beneficial owner of those securities; and

B. a corporation, partnership, trust or other entity is counted as one beneficial owner of securities of the Corporation unless the entity has been created or is being used primarily for the purpose of acquiring or holding securities of the Corporation, in which event each beneficial owner of an equity interest in the entity or each beneficiary of the entity, as the case may be, is counted as a separate beneficial owner of those securities of the Corporation."

FIGURE 8.2 CONTINUED

B.   <u>ORGANIZATION</u>

7. By-law No. 1

By-law No. 1, a general by-law relating to the business and affairs of the Corporation, was passed by the directors and confirmed by the sole shareholder effective as of October 31, 2003. This by-law expands upon various provisions of the Act and should be read in conjunction with the Act.   Among other matters, it addresses the quorum and procedure for directors' and shareholders' meetings, the duties of officers and certain other matters relating to the operation of the Corporation.

8. Directors

The Articles of the Corporation provide that it may have a minimum of one director and a maximum of 10 directors. By special resolution of the sole shareholder passed effective as of October 31, 2003, the number of directors within such minimum and maximum was fixed at two.

The current directors of the Corporation are David Green and Carol Green, who were elected by the sole shareholder effective as of October 31, 2003.

The Act requires that if a corporation has two or fewer directors, the sole director or one of the two directors, as the case may be, must be a "resident Canadian" as that term is defined in the Act. If a corporation has three or more directors, a majority of the directors must be resident Canadians.

9. Officers

The officers of the Corporation were appointed by the directors effective as of October 31, 2003 and are:

Name	Position Held
David Green	President
Carol Green	Secretary

10. Delegation

The directors may appoint a managing director or committee of directors and, subject to statutory limitations, delegate powers to such managing director or committee. The managing director and a majority of the members of any committee must be resident Canadians as defined by the Act.

11. Banking

The directors have authorized the Corporation to establish a bank account with Royal Bank of Canada and determined that any officer may sign cheques on behalf of the Corporation. A copy

FIGURE 8.2   CONTINUED

of the banking agreement delivered to the bank is attached to the resolution filed in the minute book.

12. Execution of Documents

By-law No. 1 provides that contracts, documents or instruments in writing required to be executed by the Corporation may be signed on behalf of the Corporation by such person or persons as the directors may from time to time by resolution designate. By resolution of the directors effective as of October 31, 2003, any director or officer of the Corporation may sign contracts, documents or instruments in writing requiring execution by the Corporation.

13. Corporate Seal

A corporate seal, adopted by resolution of the directors dated October 31, 2003, was obtained for the Corporation.

14. Shareholders

The following shares were issued:

Name of Shareholder	Number and Class of Shares	Total Subscription Price	After 11/29/01 Issued to Accredited Investor (Y/N)	Certificate No.
David Green	1- common	$ 1.00	No	C-001

This share was issued as fully paid and non-assessable. We confirm our understanding that payment for the share has been made, as the validity of its issue is dependent upon payment therefor.

15. Exemption from Audit Requirements

A corporation that is not offering its securities to the public may, with the written consent of all shareholders, be exempted from the requirement of appointing an auditor and having an annual audit. This consent must be given in each and every year to which it relates.

A waiver of the requirement for appointment of an auditor and having an annual audit was signed by the sole shareholder of the Corporation effective as of October 31, 2003.

16. Appointment Of Accountant

A resolution was passed by the sole shareholder effective as of October 31, 2003 appointing ABC Accounting LLP as the accountant of the Corporation, to hold office until their successor is appointed. The making is not mandatory.

FIGURE 8.2 CONTINUED

17. Financial Year End

By resolution of the directors effective as of October 31, 2003, the financial year end of the Corporation was determined as April 30 in each year.

C.   MANDATORY FILINGS

15. Initial Return

Under the *Corporations Information Act* (Ontario), the Corporation is required to file with the Minister of Consumer and Business Services an Initial Return within 60 days of incorporation, setting out certain basic corporate information including the registered office address, principal place of business address, if any, the names, address for service and dates of election or appointment of the directors and officers of the corporation. The Corporation must maintain an up–to–date paper or electronic record of the prescribed information set out in any return filed and make it available to any shareholder, director, officer or creditor of the corporation during normal business hours at its registered office or principal place of business in Ontario. The Initial Return for the Corporation was filed on November 1, 2003 and a copy is attached hereto.

16. Change of Information in Initial Return

The Corporation must file with the Minister of Consumer and Business Services a notice of any change in the information filed in the Initial Return, within 15 days of such change.

17. Annual Returns

The Corporation is required to file a return each year with the Minister of Consumer and Business Services either by delivering the return to the Minister of Finance or by delivering it to the Minister of Consumer and Business Services. The return must be filed, in the case where a tax return is required under the *Corporations Tax Act*, within the time period for delivery of the tax return, or where no tax return is required , within six months of its financial year end.

18. Federal and Ontario Corporate Tax Returns

The Corporation must file an annual income tax return with each of Canada Customs and Revenue Agency, the Ministry of Finance, Corporations Tax Branch (Ontario) and each province or jurisdiction in which it carries on business. Canada Customs and Revenue Agency and the Ministry of Finance, Corporations Tax Branch (Ontario) will each assign to the Corporation an account number, which account number must be quoted in all correspondence with that particular tax department. The Corporation's initial income tax return must be filed no later than six (6) months after its first tax year-end. In addition, if the Corporation supplies goods or services, it may have to become registered for goods and service tax under the *Excise Tax Act* (Canada) and for Ontario retail sales tax under the *Retail Sales Tax Act* (Ontario). It will have to also file the necessary returns thereunder. We confirm that we will not be responsible for the filing of any of these tax returns or for reminding the Corporation of its obligation to do so.

FIGURE 8.2 CONTINUED

Corporations are also required to ensure that all taxing authorities are kept informed of any address change.

If the Director is notified by the Minister of Finance that a corporation is in default in complying with the provisions of the *Corporations Tax Act*, the Director may give notice by registered mail to the corporation or by publication once in *The Ontario Gazette* that an order dissolving the corporation will be issued unless the corporation remedies its default within ninety days after the giving of the notice. The implications of this are:

- Forfeiture of corporate assets to the Crown;

- Loss of limited liability and insurance coverage; and

- Inability to claim tax losses.

The government requires corporations with tax due to pay a late filing penalty of up to 17 per cent on the outstanding balance, escalating up to 50 per cent for repeat late non-filers. In addition, directors of corporations may be prosecuted for failure to file and fined $200 per day.

19. Business Names

The *Business Names Act* (Ontario) (the "BNA") provides in part that no corporation shall carry on business or identify itself to the public under a name other than its corporate name unless the name is registered by that corporation.

Failure to register, renew or amend a business name registration causes the corporation to be unable to maintain a proceeding in a court in Ontario in connection with that business except with leave of the court. However, no contract is void or voidable by reason only that it was entered into by a corporation which was in contravention of BNA or the regulations at the time the contract was made.

There are significant monetary penalties under the BNA for failure to comply with the requirement for registration of a business name. If a corporation is guilty of failure to file as required by the BNA, it is on conviction liable to a fine of not more than $25,000. If a corporation is guilty of an offence, every director or officer of the corporation and every person acting as its representative in Ontario who authorized, permitted or acquiesced in such an offence is also guilty of an offence and on conviction is liable to a fine of not more than $2,000.

If at any time the Corporation carries on business under its corporate name without the legal ending or under any business name, please advise us accordingly so that appropriate registration under this legislation may be made.

20. Extra-Provincial Registrations

The Corporation has the capacity to carry on its business, conduct its affairs and exercise its powers outside of Ontario to the extent that the laws of such extra-provincial jurisdiction permit.

FIGURE 8.2 CONTINUED

The issuance of an extra-provincial licence or the filing of an appropriate notice is required by most Canadian provinces before the Corporation may commence its business within such province.

The Corporation should also consider whether any local, municipal or other licensing and registration requirements must be met before commencement of business.

D.   **ONGOING MAINTENANCE**

21. **Transaction of Business**

Any by-law or resolution passed at any time during the Corporation's existence by the signatures of all of the directors or all of the shareholders entitled to vote on that resolution is as valid as if it had been passed at a properly constituted meeting of the directors or shareholders.

22. **Annual Proceedings**

Pursuant to the Act, the directors of a corporation,

    (a)   shall call an annual meeting of shareholders not later than 18 months after the corporation comes into existence and subsequently not later than 15 months after holding the last preceding annual meeting; and

    (b)   may at any time call a special meeting of shareholders.

The purpose of an annual meeting of shareholders is to consider minutes of any earlier meetings, the financial statements and auditor's report for the latest financial year of the corporation, the re-election of the incumbent directors and the reappointment of the incumbent auditor. Any business other than those specified is deemed to be special business.

As mentioned above, a resolution in writing signed by all the shareholders entitled to vote on that resolution at a meeting of shareholders is as valid as if it had been passed at a meeting of the shareholders.

Each year, four to five months after the financial year end of the Corporation, we will automatically prepare the required annual proceedings, including directors' resolution approving, among other things, the financial statements, and forward them to you for dating and signature once the financial statements for that year are completed.

E.   **CORPORATE RECORDS**

23. **Minute Book and Corporate Seal**

Unless the directors otherwise designate, the corporate books and records of a corporation must be maintained at the registered office of such corporation. By resolution of the directors passed

FIGURE 8.2 CONCLUDED

effective as of October 31, 2003, the Corporation was authorized to maintain its books and records either at its registered office or at the offices of Thorn & Hill LLP.

We trust that this has been completed to your satisfaction and should you have any questions or comments respecting this matter, please feel free to contact us.

Yours truly,

Gregory Hill

GH/msu
Enclosures

cc: Jessie Bruton

CHAPTER 9

Post-organization considerations

CHAPTER OVERVIEW

This chapter outlines the other matters that a corporation must consider after the initial post-incorporation organization. They include: adopting pre-incorporation contracts; setting up tax accounts; registering business names; considering extra-provincial registration; considering any required licences; providing indemnities for the directors and officers; and drawing up shareholder agreements.

CHAPTER OBJECTIVES

After completing this chapter, you should be able to:

1. Identify the steps required to register a corporation for tax purposes in Ontario.

2. Discuss the provisions of the *Corporations Tax Act*.

3. Apply the provisions of the *Business Names Act* to business name registrations in Ontario.

4. Describe the difference between a shareholder agreement and a unamimous shareholder agreement.

5. Relate some of the contents of a shareholder agreement.

ADOPTING A PRE-INCORPORATION CONTRACT (CBCA s. 14; OBCA s. 21)

A person may enter into any written or oral contract on behalf of a corporation to be incorporated. This type of contract is referred to as a "**pre-incorporation contract**." Examples of pre-incorporation contracts are an agreement of purchase

pre-incorporation contract
a written or oral contract entered into by a person on behalf of a corporation to be incorporated

and sale of property and a lease of a premises that has to be signed before the corporation has been incorporated. This person, which may be an individual, partnership, association, body corporate, or personal representative, is personally bound by the contract and is entitled to receive its benefits. When a corporation is incorporated, it has a reasonable length of time to adopt the contract. Once the contract is adopted by the corporation, the corporation is bound by the contract and is subject to its provisions, and the person signing the contract is no longer bound by it.

A corporation can confirm and adopt a pre-incorporation contract by any action that signifies its intention to be bound by the contract — for example, passing a directors' resolution.

PURCHASE OF EXISTING BUSINESS

If the principals involved in the corporation were previously in business — for example, in a partnership — there may be certain assets and liabilities to be assumed by the new corporation. This may be accomplished by purchasing the existing business. An agreement is drawn up outlining the business to be purchased and providing for an evaluation of its property. This agreement is then approved by the directors of the corporation, either by passing a resolution at a meeting or having it signed by all of the directors (see chapter 8).

A new corporation may not have much cash, and shares of the corporation may be issued to the sole proprietor or partner to pay for the assets that were transferred into the corporation.

SETTING UP GOVERNMENT ACCOUNTS

Before commencing business or shortly thereafter, a corporation should consider which business accounts to establish with various government bodies. Corporations may be required to pay federal income tax as well as Ontario corporations tax. In addition, if the corporation offers goods and services for sale, it will be required to pay goods and services tax (GST) or harmonized sales tax (HST) pursuant to the *Excise Tax Act*. New Brunswick, Newfoundland and Labrador, and Nova Scotia have harmonized their sales taxes with the federal GST, and one registration is all that is required for GST and provincial sales tax in these provinces.

The most common government accounts that a corporation will establish are:

Federal

- corporate tax;

- GST;

- payroll deduction; and

- import/export.

Ontario

- corporate tax;

- retail sales tax;

- employer health tax; and

- workplace safety and insurance premiums.

Canada Revenue Agency

When a federal or Ontario corporation is incorporated, the information is transmitted from Corporations Canada or the Ontario Companies and Personal Property Security Branch ("Ontario Companies Branch") to the Canada Revenue Agency (CRA). In most cases, new corporations will automatically receive a business number (BN) from the CRA within 45 days of incorporation. The BN is a numbering system to streamline the way businesses deal with government. The CRA will mail a notice of issuance of the BN to the corporation and request specific information with respect to the setup of accounts. If the accounts are required before receiving notification of the BN, you will have to initiate the registrations for your client, as described below. The four major accounts are:

1. *Corporate tax account.* This account receives payment of corporate income tax under the *Income Tax Act* (ITA).

2. *GST/HST account.* Whether a corporation is required to register for GST depends on the nature of the goods or services it sells or provides and the amount of its sales. If the corporation's annual, worldwide GST/HST taxable sales, including those of any associates, are more than $30,000 ($50,000 for a public service body) in the immediate preceding four consecutive calendar quarters or in a single calendar quarter, the corporation is required to register. It may, however, register voluntarily — for example, to provide the ability to claim the GST/HST paid on business startup expenses from the time of registration.

3. *Payroll deduction account.* This account is required if your client has employees because the corporation is required to make regular payroll deductions (income tax, CPP premiums, and EI premiums) for its employees and remit these amounts periodically.

4. *Import/export account.* If your client intends to import commercial shipments from, or export commercial goods to, other countries, an import/export account is required for the payment of applicable duties under the *Excise Tax Act*.

The BN consists of 15 characters and is divisible into two parts. The first part consists of 9 digits, which identify the business. The second part consists of 2 letters, which identify the type of account, and 4 digits, which identify the account number. The letters and accounts they identify are:

- RC — corporate income tax;

- RM — import/export;

- RP — payroll deductions; and

- RT — GST/HST.

There are a number of different ways to register for the BN and open the CRA accounts:

1. *By phone.* You can call toll-free 1-888-959-5525 to register. Be ready to answer all questions contained in part A of Form RC1, "Request for a Business Number." You will first have to fax or mail a copy of the certificate of incorporation or amalgamation. You can download a copy of the form from the CRA Web site.

2. *By mail, fax, or personal delivery to any tax service office listed on the CRA Web site.* If you deliver the form personally on behalf of your client, you have to provide the tax office with a completed Form RC59, "Business Consent Form," or prepare a letter of authorization from your client authorizing the CRA to deal with you as a representative of your client. As your client's representative, you will be able to register the business, access all BN accounts, make account inquiries, and provide information to update accounts. Authorized representatives remain authorized until their authority is revoked.

3. *By Ontario Business Connects workstation.* You will need the name of the business and the mailing and physical addresses (including the postal code). If you are registering an unincorporated business, you will need the name and social insurance number (SIN) of the sole proprietor or one of the partners. If you are registering an incorporated business, you will need

   a. the name and SIN of an officer or a director;

   b. the certificate of incorporation number;

   c. the date of incorporation; and

   d. the jurisdiction.

4. *Online.* Register online by using the Business Registration Online (BRO) service provided by the CRA and its provincial partners, Nova Scotia and Ontario, at www.businessregistration.gc.ca.

Shortly after registration, the CRA will send a letter to the corporation confirming the BN accounts and summarizing the information provided on registration.

If the business has been incorporated for more than two months, or has a GST/HST number, there may already be a BN. In this case, if you are opening any of the above accounts, you will need to provide the BN and the name and address of the business.

If the business is in Quebec, the CRA BN does not include GST/HST accounts because the Ministère du Revenu du Québec (MRQ) administers the GST/HST system on behalf of the CRA. If you need to register for the GST/HST in Quebec, contact the MRQ at:

Ministère du Revenu du Québec
3800 Marly Street
Ste-Foy, QC G1X 4A5
Telephone: 1-800-567-4692

Ontario corporations tax

Corporations tax is collected by the province of Ontario under the authority of the *Corporations Tax Act* (CTA). Each corporation that is liable to pay tax must file an Ontario corporations tax return (CT23) within six months of its taxation year-end.

APPLICATION OF CTA

The CTA applies to every corporation that is incorporated under the laws of Canada or a province of Canada (that is, all corporations with or without share capital) that have a permanent establishment in Ontario. It also applies to foreign corporations (that is, those incorporated outside Canada) that have a permanent establishment in Ontario, own real property, timber resource property, or a timber limit in Ontario, and derive the income from those properties.

The definition of permanent establishment is complex. Refer to s. 4 of the CTA to determine what constitutes a permanent establishment.

TAXES ADMINISTERED

The CTA levies three types of taxes:

1. *Income tax.* This tax is payable on a corporation's taxable income for each taxation year.

2. *Capital tax.* This tax is payable on a corporation's taxable paid-up capital (which includes paid-up capital stock, earned capital, and surplus, reserves, shareholders' loans, and indebtedness). Non-Canadian corporations are taxed on taxable paid-up capital employed in Canada.

   Certain small corporations with year-ends after April 20, 1988 are exempt from capital tax if both their total assets and their gross revenue as reported on their financial statements meet a certain requirement (CTA s. 68).

   Other corporations may be subject to capital tax at a rate of $3/10$ of 1 percent of the amount taxable or at some other flat rate.

3. *Premium tax.* This tax is payable by insurance companies that carry on business in Ontario and is based on the total taxable premiums written in the province.

EXEMPTION FROM FILING RETURNS

Depending on which criteria the corporation satisfies, it must complete one of the following:

- CT23 Corporations Tax and Annual Return,

- CT23 Short-Form Corporations Tax and Annual Return, or

- Exempt from Filing (EFF) declaration.

It is useful for corporate law clerks to know when a corporation is exempt from filing Form CT23, for example, when dealing with the dissolution of an inactive corporation. A corporation is exempt from filing when it

1. has filed a federal income tax return (T2) with the CRA for the taxation year;

2. had no Ontario taxable income for the taxation year;

3. had no Ontario corporations tax payable for the taxation year;

4. was a Canadian-controlled private corporation throughout the taxation year (that is, generally a private corporation with 50 percent or more of its shares owned by Canadian residents as defined by the ITA);

5. had provided its CRA business number to the Ministry of Finance, Corporations Tax Branch (which may be required so that item 1 can be substantiated); and

6. is *not* subject to the corporate minimum tax (that is, alone or as part of an associated group whose total assets exceed $5 million or whose total revenues exceed $10 million for the taxation year).

TAXATION YEAR

A corporation cannot have a financial year that ends more than 53 weeks from the date of incorporation. For example, a business incorporated on January 27, 1992 would not be required to file a return until its January 31, 1993 year-end. If, however, a corporation is incorporated on November 1, 1992 and has a year-end of December 31, it will be required to file a return as of December 31, 1992.

If no return is filed, the Corporations Tax Branch will assume that the corporation has a year-end one year from the date of incorporation.

ACCOUNT NUMBER

When a corporation is incorporated in Ontario, the Ontario Companies Branch downloads information into the system maintained by the Corporations Tax Branch. Every new corporation is assigned an account number, but this account remains dormant until a CT23 return is filed. The Corporations Tax Branch has a link with the CRA's system from which it can pick up all corporations that no longer qualify as exempt corporations and have not filed the required CT23. Starting in 2000, corporations must file an EFF declaration with their annual return in order to be exempt.

DISSOLUTION PROCESS

Section 241(1) of the OBCA provides that where the Ontario Director is notified by the Minister of Finance that a corporation is in default in complying with the provisions of the CTA, the Director may give notice by registered mail to the corporation or by publication once in the *Ontario Gazette* that an order dissolving the corporation will be issued unless the default is remedied within 90 days after the notice is given.

If a corporation is dissolved as outlined above, any interested person may apply to the Ontario Director to have the corporation revived. The Director may in his or her discretion by order, upon such terms and conditions as he or she sees fit to impose, revive the corporation. On revival, the corporation is restored to its legal position, including all its property, rights, etc., and is subject to all its liabilities as of the date of the dissolution to the same extent as if it has not been dissolved.

The Corporations Tax Branch notifies the corporation by letter of the impending cancellation of its charter for failure to comply with the provisions of the CTA. If this letter is returned undelivered, the charter may be cancelled without the directors or officers of the corporation being aware that this has happened. Dissolution of the corporation in this manner may result in any property owned by the corporation being forfeited to the Crown (OBCA s. 244(1)).

BOOKS AND RECORDS

Section 87 of the CTA requires a corporation that pays taxes to keep records and books of account in the same manner as those kept under the ITA (see chapter 8) at its permanent establishment in Ontario or at such other place as is designated by the Minister of Finance.

The corporation is required to keep these records until written permission for their disposal is obtained from the minister.

A tax information bulletin issued in February 1981 by the Minister of Finance indicated that the minister had signed a general consent for the destruction of books and records held for Ontario tax purposes provided that the books and records to be destroyed relate to a fiscal year that ended more than five years before the beginning of the fiscal year in which the books and records are destroyed and the following conditions are satisfied:

- the books and records to be destroyed must relate to a period for which all returns have been filed and all taxes assessed have been paid;

- there must not be any outstanding dispute with regard to any tax payable;

- the time limit for filing a notice of objection to any assessment or statement of disallowance must have expired without the filing of such notice of objection;

- there must not be an outstanding demand from the Ministry of Finance for the production of books and records or a written notice requiring the retention of books and records; and

- the corporation must not have filed a waiver with the Minister of Finance or the CRA.

Note that a number of other statutes regulate the keeping of records. This is discussed in chapter 8.

PENALTIES

There are monetary penalties imposed under the CTA upon conviction of the corporation, its directors and officers, or agents of the corporation for

- failure to file a return;

- failure to keep adequate records or to permit access to these records by a person authorized by the minister; and

- making a false statement.

In addition, if a corporation fails to file a return, a total of three demand notices will be sent to the corporation, after which steps may be taken to dissolve the corporation pursuant to s. 241 of the OBCA discussed above.

Retail sales tax (Ontario)

Retail sales tax (RST) is a consumption tax imposed under the *Retail Sales Tax Act* on consumers who purchase taxable goods or services. It is administered by the RST branch of the Ontario Ministry of Finance.

A corporation will require an RST vendor permit to charge, collect, and remit RST on taxable sales if it

- regularly sells taxable goods;

- regularly provides taxable services;

- regularly sells insurance;

- charges more than $4 admission to a place of amusement;

- is a manufacturing contractor — that is, the manufactured cost of goods used in real property contracts is more than $50,000 in any fiscal year;

- is a non-resident contractor doing business in Ontario;

- sells taxable goods or services at flea markets, fairs, or exhibitions;

- regularly imports taxable goods or taxable services into Ontario for its own use; or

- purchases goods exempt from RST that it plans to resell, but later takes these goods from inventory for its own use.

There are tax-exempt goods and services (see *Retail Sales Tax Act*, ss. 1.1 and 7 to 9). You can register for a vendor permit

1. by telephone,

2. by mail or fax,

3. in person, at an Ontario Ministry of Finance Tax Office, or

4. at an Ontario Business Connects workstation.

An RST number will be assigned immediately. If you are registering on behalf of your client, you will need to provide a letter of authorization. You will also need to provide a photocopy of the first page of the articles of incorporation.

For more information, contact the RST branch at

- the Ministry of Finance's Web site,

- the TAX FAX service at 1-877-4-TAX-FAX (1-877-482-9329), or

- any Ontario Ministry of Finance tax office.

Employer health tax (Ontario)

Employer health tax (EHT) is paid by employers who have a permanent establishment in Ontario and who:

- have employees who report for work at the Ontario permanent establishment, or have employees who do not report for work at a permanent establishment of the employer but are paid from an Ontario permanent establishment of the employer; and

- have a total Ontario remuneration for the year (paid to employees or former employees) that exceeds the exemption amount allowed. As of January 1, 1999, the exemption amount is $400,000 of annual payroll. Eligible employers who are associated are required to share the exemption among members of the associated group.

Employers who meet the above criteria are required to register by

- calling one of the EHT Regional Offices.

- completing an information questionnaire, which can be obtained from EHT regional offices (listed in the *EHT Guide for Employers*), and returning it to the nearest regional office; or

- registering through an Ontario Business Connects workstation.

Upon registration, the employer will receive an EHT account number.

Workplace safety and insurance

Most businesses in Ontario that employ workers must register with the Workplace Safety and Insurance Board (WSIB) within 10 days of hiring their first full- or part-time worker. A few industries are not required to register, such as banks, trust companies, insurance companies, trade unions, private day cares, travel agencies, clubs, photographers, barbers, hair salons, shoeshine stands, taxidermists, and funeral directors and embalmers. WSIB benefits replace lost earnings to workers and cover health-care costs resulting from work-related injuries and illnesses.

To register with the WSIB, download the form from www.wsib.on.ca or call 1-800-387-8638, then either mail the completed form to the address below or fax it to 416-344-4684. The form takes 4-6 weeks to process. Upon registration, an information package will be sent out to your client's business.

Contact the WSIB for further information at:

Workplace Safety and Insurance Board
200 Front Street West
Toronto, ON M5V 3J1
Telephone: 416-344-1000 or 1-800-387-0750 (Ontario only)
Fax: 416-344-3410
E-mail: wsibcomm@wsib.on.ca
Web: http://wsib.on.ca

WSIB offices are also in cities across Ontario.

MUNICIPAL BUSINESS LICENCES

Many cities or municipalities require a corporation to obtain a business licence before commencing business in their area. You should advise your client to check with the local municipality before commencing business. In most cases, the licence fee is minimal.

SPECIAL REGULATORY LICENCES

There are a number of special regulatory licences that may be required by a business to protect the interests and safety of consumers. The following are some of the statutes that impose licensing requirements:

- *Liquor Licence Act*
- *Day Nurseries Act*
- *Mortgage Brokers Act*
- *Real Estate and Business Brokers Act*
- *Travel Industry Act*
- *Automobile Dealers Act*

Contact the Ministry of Consumer and Business Services for information about these licensing requirements at 1-800-268-1142 or 416-326-8555.

EXTRA-PROVINCIAL REGISTRATION

If your client intends to conduct business in a jurisdiction other than Ontario, you should consult an agent in that jurisdiction about whether the corporation is required to register before carrying on business. The registration of corporations doing business in another jurisdiction in Canada is discussed in greater detail in chapter 10.

REGISTERING A BUSINESS NAME

When discussing the setup of your client's business, you should ask whether the client intends to carry on business under the name of the corporation or under another name. For example, your client may have incorporated a number company, but be doing business under another name. In this case, you must ensure that your client's "business name" is registered. There is no requirement for registering a trade or a business name of a corporation federally, but most provinces have requirements affecting business names. Only Newfoundland and Labrador do not have specific registration requirements for business names.

In Ontario, the *Business Names Act* (BNA) provides that no body corporate is permitted to carry on business in Ontario or identify itself to the public in Ontario by a name or style other than its corporate name, unless the name or style is first registered with the Ontario Companies Branch (BNA s. 2(1)).

Registrations under the BNA can be renewed on an ongoing basis for periods of five years (BNA s. 4(1.1)). Regulation 122/91 under the BNA contains restrictions on names including words and expressions that are specifically prohibited and those that suggest an activity that is not carried on by the registrant. Although it is not mandatory in Ontario to conduct any form of name search before registering a business name, most practitioners will carry out searches, which may include a NUANS search. For more discussion of names and name searches, see chapter 6.

Failure to register under the BNA can result in fines upon conviction. Furthermore, if a corporation has failed to register its name or style, it cannot maintain a court action or proceeding in Ontario with respect to any contract it has made (BNA ss. 7(1) and 10). A saving provision, however, allows for the name or style to be registered after an action or proceeding is commenced with leave of the court, provided that the failure to register the name was inadvertent and the public has not been deceived (BNA s. 7(2)).

Registration of a name or style under the BNA does not confer on the corporation any right to the name or style registered that the corporation does not otherwise have. However, common law rights may accrue over time, through, among other things, use of the name.

Notwithstanding the registration and/or use of a business name or style, the corporation must set out its name in legible characters in all contracts, invoices, negotiable instruments, and orders for goods or services issued or made by or on behalf of it (BNA s. 2(6); CBCA s. 10(5); OBCA s. 10(5)).

Registration of a business name under the BNA is achieved by completing Form 2 and filing it with the Ontario Companies Branch. Chapter 1 sets out the different methods of filing under the BNA. The form can be submitted by an officer or director of the corporation, or an attorney acting under a power of attorney that authorizes the attorney to submit the form on behalf of the corporation.

Any change to the information appearing on Form 2 requires the filing of an amended registration within 15 days of the change. When a business name is no longer being used, a "cancellation" of the name may be filed. There are no government fees for these filings but the service providers' fees will still apply.

PROVIDING INDEMNIFICATION TO DIRECTORS AND OFFICERS

Chapter 4 discussed the ability of a corporation to indemnify its directors, officers, and certain others against costs, charges, and expenses incurred in connection with defending an action. If a corporation permits such indemnification, it may enter into an "indemnification" agreement with the person being indemnified, or it may simply include such provision in the bylaws or a resolution. In accordance with the CBCA (s. 120(5)) and the OBCA (s. 132(5)), a director is permitted to vote on a resolution to approve a contract or transaction with respect to his or her indemnity.

UNANIMOUS SHAREHOLDER AGREEMENT

unanimous shareholder agreement (USA)
a written agreement among all of the shareholders of a corporation or among all of the shareholders and a person who is not a shareholder (for example, a director), or a declaration made by the sole beneficial shareholder, that restricts in whole or in part the powers of the directors to manage the business and affairs of the corporation

A **unanimous shareholder agreement** (USA) is a written agreement that restricts in whole or in part the powers of the directors to manage the business and affairs of a corporation. Such an agreement may be among all of the shareholders of the corporation or among all of the shareholders and a person who is not a shareholder (for example, a director), or it may be a declaration made by the sole beneficial shareholder of the corporation (CBCA ss. 146(1) and (2); OBCA s. 108(2)).

Under a USA, the shareholders assume the rights, powers, duties, and legal obligations that have been removed from the directors.

There are two main reasons for having a USA. First, a USA offers more control and protection of shareholder interests than a simple shareholder agreement. At common law, even if all of the shareholders are parties to a shareholder agreement, they are not permitted to agree as to how they will act in their capacities as directors. Thus, it is possible there could be no agreement about how the corporation would be managed.

Second, a USA can serve as a form of protection to directors if the corporation has only one or a few shareholders. For example, because the CBCA and the OBCA require a majority of directors to be resident Canadians, employees of a subsidiary of a foreign corporation or the subsidiary's lawyers may be appointed directors. The subsidiary will likely be operated as a "division" of the foreign corporation, with instructions coming from the officers and senior executives of the parent directly to employees of the subsidiary. Under these circumstances, it makes sense to have a USA, which shifts the power of the directors onto the shareholders, so that the legal situation reflects the commercial reality.

Where shares that are subject to a USA are transferred, the transferee of the shares is deemed to be a party to the agreement (CBCA s. 146(3); OBCA s. 108(4)). The transferee must, however, be aware of the existence of the USA — that is, the existence of a USA must be noted conspicuously on the share certificate. If a share purchaser is not aware of the existence of a USA, and subsequently becomes aware of it, he or she may rescind the transaction within 30 days after becoming aware of the USA (CBCA s. 146(4)).

SHAREHOLDER AGREEMENTS

If there is more than one shareholder in a corporation, the shareholders should be advised to enter into a shareholder agreement. It is always better to anticipate disputes when people are on good terms than to resolve disputes when relations have soured. Shareholder agreements are used to set out the processes by which shareholders will deal with certain issues. The issues can be broad, such as an agreement that regulates the operation of a corporation, or narrow, such as how a shareholder may dispose of his or her shares. For example, a shareholder agreement may

- include an agreement on how shareholders (all together or in a group) will vote their shares;
- place restrictions on the transfer of shares; or
- provide for methods of dispute resolution.

The question whether the corporation itself should be a party to the agreement must also be settled. In general, if any of the terms and conditions are binding on or enforceable by the corporation, the corporation should be a party to the agreement. If, however, the agreement relates only to shareholder relationships, it is not necessary to include the corporation in the agreement. The corporation will become a party to the agreement, and thus bound by its terms, when it has signed the agreement.

Content of shareholder agreements

The basic purpose of a shareholder agreement is to contractually alter the arrangements that the statutes and common law would otherwise permit.

The following is a brief outline of the contents of a shareholder agreement.

RECITALS

The recitals are intended to specify the purpose of the shareholder agreement and to provide background information needed to understand the terms of the agreement.

INTERPRETATION

The interpretation provisions of a shareholder agreement are relatively standard and appear in many other kinds of agreements. Such provisions:

- define the various expressions found in the agreement;
- state that words importing their singular form include their plural, etc.;
- explain that headings in the agreement are for convenience;
- stipulate the laws that are applicable to the agreement;
- explain severability (that is, if one term is illegal, the rest remain in force);
- outline the entire agreement between the parties;
- stipulate the currency to be used (for example, Canadian dollars); and
- contain a number of appendices.

TERM OF AGREEMENT

A clause regarding the term of the agreement indicates when the agreement takes effect and how it may be terminated. If no termination date is determined, there will be uncertainty as to when the shareholder agreement will end.

THE CORPORATION

If the parties to a shareholder agreement are all of the shareholders of the corporation, it is usual to stipulate in the agreement what the initial articles and bylaws of the corporation will provide.

In addition, a shareholder agreement may stipulate how the articles and bylaws are to be amended, if the amendments are not to be carried out in accordance with the terms of the governing statute.

OTHER PARTIES

If the parties to the agreement include all of the shareholders of the corporation, the agreement is a USA. If a party is an individual, state the full name and residence address. If a party is a corporation, state its name and the jurisdiction under which it was incorporated. Also, list all parties in control of a corporate shareholder.

Make sure that you identify the "beneficial" owners of the shares, and not the "registered" owners of the shares.

SHARE OWNERSHIP

This clause describes the outstanding shareholders of the corporation at the date of the agreement.

If it is known that the corporation is undercapitalized and more capital will be required for a particular project (such as an acquisition), the agreement may contain a clause that imposes an obligation on the shareholders to purchase more shares. In addition, the agreement may specify a remedy if a shareholder is unable or unwilling to meet this obligation.

LEGEND

A USA is ineffective against a transferee who does not have actual notice of its existence, unless the agreement or a reference to it is noted conspicuously on the share certificate. A clause to this effect is included in the agreement.

A shareholder agreement that is not unanimous is not binding unless the new shareholder signs the shareholder agreement. Usually, therefore, the shareholder agreement also provides that any subscription or transfer of shares is conditional upon the subscriber's or transferee's first becoming a party to the shareholder agreement.

PRE-EMPTIVE RIGHTS

Sometimes shareholders will want to have the right to purchase shares of the corporation if the corporation seeks additional capital by way of a share offering. The most common "pre-emptive" right is one that entitles existing shareholders to purchase additional shares in proportion to their existing shareholdings.

This clause could be included in the articles of incorporation. However, since the articles are a public document and a shareholder agreement is not, it may be desirable to include pre-emptive rights in the shareholder agreement.

DISPOSAL OF INTERESTS

A clause regarding the disposal of interests is usually included because the shareholders wish to control who may own shares in the corporation. Furthermore, the shareholders will want to establish rules to deal with the situation when an existing shareholder wants out of the business, or they may wish to require mandatory share transfers under certain circumstances, such as when a shareholder is no longer willing or able to contribute to the business or when there is a dispute. There are a number of ways to deal with the disposal of interests:

1. Corporate law permits shareholders to sell their shares to whomever they wish, subject only to the approval, if any, required by the articles of incorporation — for example, approval by the board of directors. A shareholder agreement often limits the transfer of shares to the arrangements permitted under the agreement.

2. The occasions when transfers are permitted are then set out in the agreement. These may include transfers as security for loans (pledge); transfers to family members; transfers to heirs on the death of a shareholder; transfers to other shareholders; limits on a pledge of shares upon consent of other holders; and transfers to a wholly owned subsidiary for business reasons where the shareholder is a corporation.

3. Sometimes it may be desirable to provide for a mandatory transfer of shares — that is, a compulsory buy–sell arrangement. A mandatory transfer provision might be used if a shareholder is no longer able (due to retirement, disability, or death) or willing to work in the business of the corporation; on a breach of agreement; or as a way to resolve a dispute. However, before using such a clause, make sure your client has the financial resources to buy the shares of the other shareholder(s). These provisions are sometimes referred to as "shotgun" provisions.

4. A right of first refusal allows transfers on a restrictive basis. Shares are first offered to existing shareholders, and if they refuse or cannot buy them, the shares are offered to third parties.

DIRECTORS

Provisions regarding the election and replacement of directors are included to ensure that the shareholders signing the agreement have the right to elect a certain number of directors. This provision can also establish a quorum of directors to be present at meetings. The agreement may also set out the right of different shareholders to elect a nominee director.

OFFICERS

Officers are appointed by the directors, subject to the articles, the bylaws, and any unanimous shareholder agreement. The initial officers may be specified in a shareholder agreement together with a mechanism to change the holder of any office. In some cases, employment contracts may be entered into with senior officers, and a copy may be appended to the agreement.

MEETINGS

Provisions regarding quorum requirements for meetings of directors and shareholders may be included.

FINANCIAL MATTERS

Shareholder agreements may include provisions regarding the auditor of the corporation, the financial year of the corporation, the manner in which the corporation may borrow money, auditor waiver, and banking arrangements

MANAGEMENT RESTRICTIONS

Sometimes it is sufficient to stipulate the number of directors and the manner in which they will be elected. Additional control can be attained by requiring special majorities of the directors to make certain decisions. A shareholder agreement may also stipulate that certain matters will be determined only by the shareholders and not by the directors. In addition, some decisions may not be made without the approval of some or all of the parties to the agreement.

DISPUTES

Corporate law allows disputes between shareholders to be determined by the relative voting power of different shareholders. A shareholder agreement may provide other methods of resolving disputes which are binding on the shareholders who are parties to the agreement. A mandatory transfer of shares between parties is one method of resolving a dispute.

If the dispute is a question of fact, the agreement may stipulate that an arbitrator be appointed. However, this provision will not work if the disagreement concerns interpretation of a clause in the agreement. Such a dispute would require a court decision.

ENFORCEMENT

It is usual to require the parties to the agreement to agree with one another that they will use their powers as shareholders of the corporation and as persons entitled to nominate directors to ensure that the terms of the agreement are carried out.

AMENDMENT

A shareholder agreement may be amended and the original agreement states how this will happen. Because the original agreement is unanimous, it is usual to require unanimous approval for amendments.

NOTICES

An agreement may provide in various circumstances for notice to be given to the parties. Usually, therefore, there will be a clause setting out the required provisions with respect to the giving of notice, such as the number of days and the address of the parties to whom notice must be given.

TIME OF THE ESSENCE

Where time is expressly or impliedly of the essence of a contract, this provision requires all parties to strictly observe their obligations with respect to time.

VOTING

Corporate law allows shareholders to vote their shares as they see fit in their own interest.

A shareholder agreement may also include an agreement as to how the parties will vote their shares. Such a provision is included to enhance the influence of, or to protect the interests of, shareholders who sign the agreement by determining ahead of time how they will collectively vote their shares.

A final word of caution about USAs. In *Sportscope Television Network Ltd. v. Shaw Communications Inc.*, Justice Blair held that a USA comprises one of the constating documents of a corporation and, as such, the USA intended to govern an amalgamated corporation (Amalco) should be stipulated in the amalgamation agreement. According to Wayne Gray:

> Given *Sportscope*, counsel acting on behalf of the amalgamating corporations or the amalgamated corporation resulting therefrom should take steps to ensure either that: (i) the amalgamation agreement expressly contemplates that the USA for one of the amalgamating corporations will carry forward and be binding on Amalco and the shareholders thereof; or (ii) the continuing shareholders of Amalco enter into a restated USA or another ratifying agreement.

KEY TERMS

pre-incorporation contract

unanimous shareholder agreement (USA)

REFERENCES

Business Corporations Act (OBCA), RSO 1990, c. B.16, as amended.

Business Names Act (BNA), RSO 1990, c. B.17, as amended.

Canada Customs and Revenue Agency, *The Business Number and Your Canada Customs and Revenue Agency Accounts* (Ottawa: CCRA, 2001).

Canadian Bar Association, *Basic Corporation Practice* (Ottawa: CBA, 1989).

Corporations Information Act (CIA), RSO 1990, c. C.39, as amended.

Corporations Tax Act (CTA), RSO 1990, c. C.40, as amended.

Day, Midge, *Ontario Corporate Procedures*, 3d ed. (Toronto: Thomson Professional Publishing, 1995).

Gray, Wayne D. "Creation and Termination of Unanimous Shareholder Agreements: *Sportscope Television Network Ltd. v. Shaw Communications Inc.*" (2000), vol. 34 *Canadian Business Law Journal* 146.

Law Society of Upper Canada, *Business Law Reference Materials*, 36th Bar Admission Course, phase 3 (Toronto: LSUC, November 1994).

Ontario Ministry of Finance, Retail Sales Tax Branch, *Small Business Pointers: The Basics of Retail Sales Tax*, publication no. SBP 901 (Toronto: Queen's Printer for Ontario, 2001).

Ontario Ministry of Finance, Tax Revenue Division, *EHT Guide for Employers*, publication no. 2436 (Toronto: Queen's Printer for Ontario, 1997, rev. ed. 2003).

Retail Sales Tax Act, RSO 1990, c. R. 31, as amended.

Sportscope Television Network Ltd. v. Shaw Communications Inc. (1999), 46 BLR (2d) 87; 92 OTC 33 (Gen. Div.).

FORMS AND PRECEDENTS

Figure 9.1: Form RC1, Request for a business number

Figure 9.2: Application for a vendor permit (Ontario)

Figure 9.3: Information questionnaire — Employer health tax (Ontario)

Figure 9.4: Application form for WSIB

Figure 9.5: Business name registration by a corporation

REVIEW QUESTIONS

1. Describe briefly the provisions of the *Business Names Act*, and name two business entities to which it applies.

2. What does a unanimous shareholder agreement permit that would otherwise be prohibited?

3. What are two reasons for drafting a unanimous shareholder agreement?

4 What would be the purpose of a shareholder agreement? Discuss five topics for inclusion in the agreement.

5. John and Mary are going to incorporate. They find premises they want to lease and they are asked to sign a simple agreement to lease. Can they sign this on behalf of the proposed corporation? What would the corporation have to do to become bound by the contract?

6. What advice would you give to a client who is about to become a director of a corporation?

7. What is an executive committee?

8. Your corporate client wishes to use a trade name in Ontario. What advice would you give your client?

9. What are the requirements for a financial year-end of a corporation? What happens if a corporation does not set a year-end?

10. What are the penalties for not complying with the *Corporations Tax Act*?

CASE STUDY

Case study 9.1: Ontario business name registration

Mr. Green, the principal of 01111111 Ontario Inc., sends Jessie Bruton, the corporate law clerk working at Thorn & Hill, an e-mail asking her to register the business name "Sunny Shores Realty" for use by 01111111 Ontario Inc. He explains that he is going to use this name for the rental of his new property. Jessie obtains an Ontario NUANS report to find out if there are any other similar business names that are likely to be confusing with Mr. Green's business name. She discovers that there are not. She then proceeds to prepare Form 2 under the *Business Names Act* (Ontario). She can register electronically or by delivering a copy to the Ontario Companies Branch. Since time is short, she elects to file the form electronically through one of the ministry's service providers. She faxes the prepared form to Mr. Green and asks him to approve it and to signify his approval by initialing the form and faxing it back to her. Once she receives the approved copy of the Form 2, she proceeds with the electronic filing.

See figure 9.5 at the end of this chapter.

FIGURE 9.1   FORM RC1, REQUEST FOR A BUSINESS NUMBER

	Canada Customs and Revenue Agency	Agence des douanes et du revenu du Canada		BN	

REQUEST FOR A BUSINESS NUMBER (BN)

FOR OFFICE USE ONLY

Complete this form to apply for a Business Number (BN). If you are a sole proprietor with more than one business, your BN will apply to all your businesses. **All businesses have to complete parts A and F.** For more information, see our pamphlet called *The Business Number and Your Canada Customs and Revenue Agency Accounts.* If you have questions, including where to send this form, call us at 1-800-959-5525.

Note: If your business is in the province of Quebec and you wish to register for GST/HST, do not use this form. Contact the ministère du Revenu du Québec. However, if you wish to register for any of the other three accounts mentioned below, complete the appropriate parts indicated in the following instructions.

- To open a GST/HST account, complete parts A, B, and F
- To open a payroll deductions account, complete parts A, C, and F.
- To open an import/export account, complete parts A, D and F.
- To open a corporate income tax account, complete parts A, E and F.

Part A – General information

A1 | Identification of business (For a corporation, enter the name and address of the head office.)

Name

Operating, trading, or partnership name (if different from the name on the left). If you have more than one business or if your business operates under more than one name, enter the name(s) here. If you need more space, include the information on a separate piece of paper.

Business address (This must be a physical address, not a post office box.) | Postal or zip code

Mailing address (if different from business address) | Postal or zip code

Contact person – Complete this area to identify an employee of your business as your contact person in all matters pertaining to your BN accounts. To identify a person for specific accounts, complete the "Contact Person" lines in Area B1, C1, D1, or E1. To authorize a representative who is not an employee of your business, complete form RC59, *Business Consent Form.* See our pamphlet for more information.

First name | Last name | Title | Telephone number | Fax number

A2 | Client ownership type | Language of correspondence ☐ English ☐ French

☐ Individual   If so, are you a sole proprietor?   Yes ☐   No ☐   Are you an employer of a domestic?   Yes ☐   No ☐

☐ Partnership

☐ Other   Are you incorporated?   Yes ☐   No ☐   (All corporations have to provide a copy of the certificate of incorporation or amalgamation.)

Complete this part to provide information for the individual, partner(s), corporate director(s), or officer(s) of your business. **If you need more space, include the information on a separate piece of paper.**

First name | Last name | Work telephone number | Work fax number

Title
President and Director | Social insurance number | Home telephone number | Home fax number

First name | Last name | Work telephone number | Work fax number

Title | Social insurance number | Home telephone number | Home fax number

A3 | Type of operation   Check the box below that best describes your type of operation.

☐ Charity   ☐ Union   ☐ Association   ☐ Financial institution   ☐ University/school   ☐ Municipal government

☐ Society   ☐ Hospital   ☐ Non-profit   ☐ Religious body   ☐ Trust   ☐ None of the above

A4 | Major commercial activity

Clearly describe your major business activity. Give as much detail as possible in the space provided.

Specify up to three main products that you mine, manufacture, or sell, or services you provide or contract. Also, estimate the percentage of revenue that each product or service represents.   ____ %   ____ %   ____ %

RC1 E (01)

Canada

FIGURE 9.1 CONTINUED

A5   **GST/HST information** – For more information, see our pamphlet called *The Business Number and Your Canada Customs and Revenue Agency Accounts.*

Do you provide or plan to provide goods or services in Canada or to export outside Canada?	Yes ☐ No ☐
If *no*, you generally cannot register for GST/HST. However, certain businesses may be able to register. See our pamphlet for details.	
Are your annual **worldwide** GST/HST taxable sales, including those of any associates, more than $30,000 ($50,000 if you are a public service body)? If *yes*, you have to register for GST/HST. **Note**: Special rules apply to charities and public institutions. See our pamphlet for details.	Yes ☐ No ☐
Do you solicit orders in Canada for prescribed goods to be sent by mail or courier to an address in Canada? Prescribed goods include printed materials such as books, newspapers, periodicals, magazines, and an audio recording that relates to those publications and that accompanies them when they are sent to Canada.	Yes ☐ No ☐
Do you operate a taxi or limousine service?	Yes ☐ No ☐
Are you a non-resident who charges admissions directly to audiences at activities or events in Canada?	Yes ☐ No ☐
If you answer *yes* to either of these questions, you **have to** register for GST/HST, regardless of your revenue.	
Do you wish to register voluntarily? By registering voluntarily, you must begin to charge GST/HST and file returns even if your worldwide GST/HST taxable sales are $30,000 or less ($50,000 or less if you are a public service body). See our pamphlet for more information.	Yes ☐ No ☐

Part B – GST/HST account information – Complete B1 to B4 if you need a BN GST/HST account (except for businesses in the province of Quebec). See our pamphlet for details.

Do you want us to send you GST/HST information?   Yes ☐   No ☐

B1   **GST/HST account identification** – Check the box if the information is the same as in Part A1. ☐

Mailing address for GST/HST purposes	c/o	Account name (enter the name under which you carry on business.)
	Address	
		Postal or zip code

Contact person – Complete this area to identify an employee of your business as your contact person in all matters pertaining to your GST/HST account. To authorize a representative who is not an employee of your business, complete form RC59, *Business Consent Form*. See our pamphlet for more information.

First name	Last name		Language of correspondence ☐ English ☐ French
Title		Telephone number ( )	Fax number ( )

B2   **Filing information**

Enter your fiscal year-end. ☐☐ ☐☐ Month Day	If you do not provide us with a date, we will enter December 31. If you want to select a fiscal year-end that is not December 31, see our pamphlet for more information.	Enter the effective date of registration for GST/HST purposes. ☐☐ ☐☐ ☐☐ Year Month Day	See our pamphlet for information about when you need to register for GST/HST.

B3   **Reporting period**

Unless you are a charity or a financial institution, we will assign you a reporting period based on your total estimated annual GST/HST taxable sales in Canada (including those of your associates). In the column on the left below, check the box that corresponds to your estimated sales. In certain cases, you may be able to change this assigned reporting period. To do so, check the box in the column on the right below that corresponds to your choice. For more information, see our pamphlet.

Total estimated annual GST/HST taxable sales in Canada (including those of your associates)	Reporting period assigned to you, unless you choose to change it (see next column)	Options
More than $6,000,000 ☐	Monthly	No options available
More than $500,000 up to $6,000,000 ☐	Quarterly	☐ Monthly
$500,000 or less ☐	Annual	☐ Monthly or ☐ Quarterly
Charities	Annual	☐ Monthly or ☐ Quarterly
Financial institutions	Annual	☐ Monthly or ☐ Quarterly

B4   **Type of Operation**

04 ☐ Listed financial institution   08 ☐ Non-resident   09 ☐ Taxi or limousine operator   99 ☐ None of these types

FIGURE 9.1 CONTINUED

Part C

Payroll deductions account information — Complete C1 and C2 if you need a BN payroll deductions account.

C1 Payroll deductions account

Check the box if the information is the same as in Part A1. ☐

Account name

Address

| | Postal or zip code |

Mailing address for payroll deductions	c/o
	Address
		Postal or zip code

Contact person – Complete this area to identify an employee of your business as your contact person in all matters pertaining to your payroll deductions accounts. To authorize a representative who is not an employee of your business, complete Form RC59, *Business Consent Form*. See our pamphlet for more information.

| First name | Last name | Language of correspondence ☐ English ☐ French |

| Title | Telephone number ( ) | Fax number ( ) |

Do you want us to send you the New Employers Kit, which includes *Payroll Deductions Tables* and information?   Yes ☐   No ☐

C2 General information

a)   What type of payment are you making?

☐ Payroll   ☐ Registered retirement savings plan

☐ Registered retirement income fund   ☐ Other (specify) _____

b)   How often will you pay your employees or payees? Please check the pay period(s) that apply.

☐ Daily   ☐ Weekly   ☐ B-weekly   ☐ Semi-monthly

☐ Monthly   ☐ Annually   ☐ Other (specify) _____

c)   Will you design your own computer program for payroll purposes?   Yes ☐   No ☐   If *yes*, do you need our payroll formulas?   Yes ☐   No ☐

d)   Do you want to receive the *Payroll Deductions Tables*?   Yes ☐   No ☐

If *yes*, select one of the following.   Paper ☐   Diskette ☐

e)   Do you use a payroll service?   Yes ☐   No ☐   *f yes*, which one? (enter name) _____

f)   What is the maximum number of employees you expect to have working for you at any time n the next 12 months? _____

g)   When will you make the first payment to your employees or payees?

| | | | | | |
Year   Month   Day

h)   Duration of business operation   Year round ☐   Seasonal ☐

If seasonal, please check month(s) of operation. | J | F | M | A | M | J | J | A | S | O | N | D |

i)   If the business is a corporation, is the corporation a subsidiary or an affiliate of a foreign corporation?   Yes ☐   No ☐   If *yes*, enter country: _____

j)   Are you a franchisee?   Yes ☐   No ☐   If *yes*, enter the name and country of the franchisor: _____

FIGURE 9.1 CONCLUDED

Part D – Import/export account information

Complete D1 and D2 if you need a BN import/export account for commercial purposes. (You do not need to register for an import/export account for personal importations). Complete a separate form for each branch or division of your corporation that requires an import/export account for commercial purposes.

D1 | Import/export account identification – Check the box if the information is the same as in Part A1. ☐

Import/export account name

Address

Postal or zip code

Mailing address (if different from above)
c/o
Address

Postal or zip code

Contact person – Complete this area to identify an employee of your business as your contact person in all matters pertaining to your import/export accounts. To authorize a representative who is not an employee of your business, complete form RC59, *Business Consent Form*. See our pamphlet for more information.

First name | Last name | Language of correspondence ☐ English ☐ French

Title | Telephone number ( ) | Fax number ( )

Do you want us to send you import/export account information? Yes ☐ No ☐

D2 | Import/export information

Type of account: ☐ Importer ☐ Exporter ☐ Both ☐ Meeting, convention, and incentive travel (MCIT)

If you are applying for an exporter account, you **must** provide all of the following information.

Enter the type of goods you are or will be exporting.

Enter the estimated annual value of goods you are or will be exporting. $ _____

Part E – Corporate income tax account information – Complete E1 if you need a BN corporate income tax account.

E1 | Corporate income tax account identification – Check the box if the information is the same as in Part A1. ☐

Mailing address for corporate tax purposes
c/o
Address

Postal or zip code

Contact person – Complete this area to identify an employee of your business as your contact person in all matters pertaining to your corporate tax accounts. To authorize a representative who is not an employee of your business, complete form RC59, *Business Consent Form*. See our pamphlet for more information.

First name | Last name | Language of correspondence ☐ English ☐ French

Title | Telephone number ( ) | Fax number ( )

Part F – Certification – All businesses have to complete and sign this part. You can sign this form if you are a sole proprietor, a partner, a corporate director, or an officer or authorized employee of the company. You can also sign it if the Canada Customs and Revenue Agency has on file Form RC59, *Business Consent Form* authorizing you as the company's representative.

I certify that the information given on this form is, to the best of my knowledge, true and complete.

Print your name _____ Signature _____

Title _____ Date [Year] [Month] [Day]

Printed in Canada

FIGURE 9.2 APPLICATION FOR A VENDOR PERMIT (ONTARIO)

 Ontario Ministry of Finance
Retail Sales Tax

Application for Vendor Permit
Pursuant to Section 5 of the *Retail Sales Tax Act*

Note: Please type or print when completing this form.
For assistance in completing this form refer to the telephone directory blue pages for the Ontario Tax Office telephone number.

1. Legal Name
Check the box that applies to your business and enter the appropriate name in the space below.

☐ **Proprietorship** (One Owner) - full name of owner (e.g. "John F. Smith")
☐ **Partnership** (More than one Owner) - full name of two principal partners (e.g. "John G. Jones and Jane S. Doe")
☐ **Corporation** (An Incorporated Business) - full corporate name, no abbreviations (e.g. "Future Ontario Limited" rather than "Future Ont. Limited")
☐ **Association** - full names of any two members/officers

If a corporation enter number shown on Certificate of
Incorporation issued by the Companies Branch, Ontario
Ministry of Consumer and Commercial Relations. ▶

2. Business or Trade Name
If the same name as Legal Name check (✓) this box ☐ OR complete ▼

3. Business Address and Telephone
Street No./Street Name/Suite No./Apt. No. or Lot No./Concession and Township

Post Office/City/Town or Village/R.R. No. | Fax No. (include Area Code)

Province | Postal Code | Telephone No. (include Area Code)

Do you have more than one Ontario business location?
☐ Yes   ☐ No   If yes, attach a list of all locations.

4. Mailing Address (where tax returns and tax information can be sent.)
If identical to Business Address please check (✓) this box ☐ OR complete ▼

Street No./Street Name/Suite No./Apt. No. or Lot No./Concession and Township

Post Office/City/Town or Village/R.R. No.

Province | Postal Code | Telephone No. (include Area Code)

5. Home Address and Telephone
Enter the Name, Title, Home Address of the Owner; or two Partners, or two Officers of the Corporation; or two Members/Officers of the Association.

Name | Title

Street No./Street Name/Suite No./Apt. No. or Lot No./Concession and Township

Post Office/City/Town or Village/R.R. No. | Province | Postal Code | Telephone No. (include Area Code)

Name | Title

Street No./Street Name/Suite No./Apt. No. or Lot No./Concession and Township

Post Office/City/Town or Village/R.R. No. | Province | Postal Code | Telephone No. (include Area Code)

1953G (02-01)

FIGURE 9.2 CONCLUDED

6. Do you already have a Retail Sales Tax Vendor Permit?

☐ Yes ☐ No   If yes, enter permit number.

7. Are you purchasing an existing business?

☐ Yes ☐ No   If yes, give trade name and retail sales tax vendor permit number of previous business.

Closing Date of Previous Business (if applicable)

Trade Name

Permit Number

8. Enter date business commences under your ownership.

Year   Month   Day

9. Describe the type of business you will be operating: if it will be ☐ full-time ☐ part-time and type of items sold, etc.

Full-Time	Part-Time

10. Do you prefer communication in French?

☐ Yes ☐ No

11. Please complete this section if your business does not operate for a full 12 months.

A. Operating for 1 day only

Year   Month   Day

B. If operating less than 30 days

From: To:

Year   Month   Day   Year   Month   Day

C. If operating less than 12 months, enter "X" in each box for the months you are open.

Jan	Feb	Mar	Apr	May	Jun	Jul	Aug	Sep	Oct	Nov	Dec

12. Bank Name and Address (where you have your business account)

Name

Address

City	Province	Postal Code	Telephone No. (include Area Code)

13. This application must be signed by:

(a) the Owner, if a proprietorship
(b) two Partners, if a partnership
(c) two Officers, if a corporation
(d) two Members/Officers, if an association

The above statements are hereby certified to be true and correct to the best of my knowledge.

Signature	Title	Date
Signature	Title	Date

Personal information on this form is collected under the authority of Section 5 of the *Retail Sales Tax Act*, R.S.O. 1990 R31 and will be used for the purposes of registering the applicant and issuing a retail sales tax vendor permit. Questions about this collection may be directed to the Ministry Information Centre at 1-800-263-7965.

Formulaire de demande également disponible en français

(R) 1953G (02-01)

FIGURE 9.3 INFORMATION QUESTIONNAIRE — EMPLOYER HEALTH TAX (ONTARIO)

☺ Ontario Ministry of Finance
Ministère des Finances

PO Box 640. 33 King Street West / CP 640. 33 rue King ouest
Oshawa ON L1H 8P5

Information Questionnaire
Questionnaire de renseignements

Your Reference No.
Votre n° de référence

Please refer to the enclosed Instruction Sheet for explanations of terms used in this form. / *Veuillez vous référer à la Feuille d'instructions ci-jointe, laquelle définit les termes utilisés dans le présent formulaire.*

For general enquiries call us toll-free: / *Pour renseignements généraux appelez-nous sans frais :*

English Language Enquiries / *Services en anglais*	**1-800-263-7965**
French Language Enquiries / *Services en français*	**1-800-668-5821**
TTY / ATS	**1-800-263-7776**

Language of choice:
Langue de préférence :

☐ English / *anglais* ☐ French / *français*

[A] Provide the following information: / *Fournissez l'information suivante :*

Business or Trade Name / *Nom commercial ou de l'entreprise*

Business Address in Ontario (Street No. & Name/Con.) / *Adresse commerciale en Ontario (N° et nom de la rue/de la con.)* Suite / *Bureau*

City / *Ville*   Province   Postal Code / *Code postal*

Telephone No. (Area Code) / *N. de téléphone (ind. régional)*   Ext. / *Poste*   Facsimile No. (Area Code) / *N° de télécopieur (ind. régional)*

[B] Corporations Tax Information / *Renseignements aux fins de l'imposition des corporations*

1. a. If you have a fixed Fiscal Year End, please enter the Month and Day
   Si la fin de votre exercice financier est fixe, inscrivez-en le mois et le jour . . . .

   month/*mois*   day/*jour*

   b. If you have a Floating Fiscal Year End, please enter the Day, Week # and Month
   (eg TU.3.12 for Tues. 3rd week in Dec) (See Instructions)
   Si la fin de votre exercice financier est flottante, inscrivez-en le jour, le numéro de la semaine et le numéro du mois (par ex. Ma.03.12 pour mardi, troisième semaine de décembre) (Voir instructions)

   day/*jour*   week/*semaine*   month/*mois*

2. Method of filing: (See Instructions)   E-File / *Électronique*   CT-23 or/ou CT-8   Plain Paper Form / *Papier ordinaire*   Exempt / *Exempté*
   Méthode de production : (Voir renseignements)

3. For companies incorporated outside Ontario: Date business started in Ontario.
   Dans le cas des corporations constituées en dehors de l'Ontario, date marquant le début de l'exploitation de l'entreprise en Ontario.

   year / *année*   mon./*mois*   day/*jour*

4. Your Revenue Canada account number
   Votre numéro de compte assigné par Revenu Canada . . . . . . ☐☐☐☐☐ - ☐☐☐☐ **R C** - ☐☐☐☐

5. Contact Person for Corporations Tax Returns / *Personne-ressource pour les déclarations d'impôts des corporations*

Name / *Nom*	Title / *Titre*	Telephone / *Téléphone*	Ext. / *Poste*	Fax / *N° télec.*
Street No. & Name / *N° et nom de la rue*		City / *Ville*	Province/State / *État*	PC/Zip / *Code postal/Zip*

[C] Employer Health Tax Registration - If you have not registered for Employer Health Tax purposes and wish to do so, please complete the following information. / *Inscription à l'impôt-santé des employeurs - Si vous n'êtes pas encore inscrit à l'impôt-santé des employeurs et désirez le faire, répondez aux questions qui suivent.*

1. Your Revenue Canada account number
   Votre numéro de compte assigné par Revenu Canada . . . . . ☐☐☐☐☐ - ☐☐☐☐ **R P** - ☐☐☐☐

2. Are you an Associated Employer? (See Instructions)
   Êtes-vous un employeur associé? (Voir renseignements) . . . . Yes / *Oui* ☐   No / *Non* ☐

3. What will be your payroll starting date?
   Indiquez le commencement de votre service de la paie. . . . .

   year / *année*   mon./*mois*   day/*jour*

4. What is the estimated annual gross payroll for permanent establishments in Ontario?
   Donnez une estimation des salaires bruts annuels payés pour tous les établissements permanents en Ontario. $ ☐☐☐ . 00

5. If your business operates on a seasonal basis, indicate the payroll month(s).
   Si votre entreprise est saisonnière, indiquez les mois de paie. . . . .

   Jan Feb Mar Apr May Jun Jul Aug Sep Oct Nov Dec
   Jan Févr Mar Avr Mai Juin Juill Août Sept Oct Nov Déc

6. Check the appropriate box below IF this application is a result of:
   Cochez la case appropriée ci-dessous SI la présente demande est effectuée à la suite d'une :

   ☐ Amalgamation / *Fusion*
   ☐ Incorporation of an existing business / *Constitution en personne morale s'une entreprise existante*
   ☐ Division of a corporation / *Division d'une corporation*
   ☐ Acquisition of an existing ongoing business / *Acquisition d'une entreprise permanente existante*

7. Contact Person for Employer Health Tax Returns / *Personne-ressource pour les déclarations d'impôt-santé des employeurs*

Name / *Nom*	Title / *Titre*	Telephone / *Téléphone*	Ext. / *Poste*	Fax / *N° télec.*
Street No. & Name / *N° et nom de la rue*		City / *Ville*	Province/State / *État*	PC/Zip / *Code postal/Zip*

FIGURE 9.3 CONCLUDED

B Corporations Tax Information / *Renseignements aux fins de l'imposition des corporations*

1. a. If you have a fixed Fiscal Year End, please enter the Month and Day
   Si la fin de votre exercice financier est fixe, inscrivez-en le mois et le jour ....

month/mois	day/jour

   b. If you have a Floating Fiscal Year End, please enter the Day, Week # and Month
   (eg. TU 3.12 for Tues. 3rd week in Dec) (See Instructions)
   Si la fin de votre exercice financier est flottante, inscrivez-en le jour, le numéro de la semaine et le numéro du mois (par ex. Ma 03.12 pour mardi, troisième semaine de décembre) (Voir instructions) ....

day/jour	week/semaine	month/mois

2. Method of filing: (See Instructions)
   Méthode de production : (Voir renseignements) .... E-File / *Électronique* — CT-23 or/ou CT-8 ——   Plain Paper Form / *Papier ordinaire* ——   Exempt / *Exempté* ——

3. For companies incorporated outside Ontario: Date business started in Ontario.
   Dans le cas des corporations constituées en dehors de l'Ontario, date marquant le début de l'exploitation de l'entreprise en Ontario. ....

year / année	mon /mois	day/jour

4. Your Revenue Canada account number
   Votre numéro de compte assigné par Revenu Canada .... ☐☐☐☐☐☐☐☐ - ☐☐☐☐ - **R C** - ☐☐☐☐

5. Contact Person for Corporations Tax Returns / *Personne-ressource pour les déclarations d'impôts des corporations*

Name / *Nom*	Title / *Titre*	Telephone / *Téléphone*	Ext. / *Poste*	Fax / *N° télec.*
Street No. & Name / *N° et nom de la rue*	City / *Ville*		Province/State / *État*	PC/Zip / *Code postal/Zip*

C Employer Health Tax Registration - If you have not registered for Employer Health Tax purposes and wish to do so, please complete the following information. / ***Inscription à l'impôt-santé des employeurs*** - *Si vous n'êtes pas encore inscrit à l'impôt-santé des employeurs et désirez le faire, répondez aux questions qui suivent.*

1. Your Revenue Canada account number
   Votre numéro de compte assigné par Revenu Canada .... ☐☐☐☐☐☐☐☐ - ☐☐☐☐ - **R P** - ☐☐☐☐

2. Are you an Associated Employer? (See Instructions)
   Êtes-vous un employeur associé? (Voir renseignements) .... Yes / *Oui* ☐   No / *Non* ☐

3. What will be your payroll starting date?
   Indiquez le commencement de votre service de la paie. ....

year / année	mon / mois	day/jour

4. What is the estimated annual gross payroll for permanent establishments in Ontario?
   Donnez une estimation des salaires bruts annuels payés pour tous les établissements permanents en Ontario. .... $ ☐☐☐,☐☐☐,☐☐☐ **.00**

5. If your business operates on a seasonal basis, indicate the payroll month(s).
   Si votre entreprise est saisonnière, indiquez les mois de paie. ....

Jan	Feb	Mar	Apr	May	Jun	Jul	Aug	Sep	Oct	Nov	Dec
Jan	*Févr*	*Mar*	*Avr*	*Mai*	*Juin*	*Juill*	*Août*	*Sept*	*Oct*	*Nov*	*Déc*

6. Check the appropriate box below IF this application is a result of:
   Cochez la case appropriée ci-dessous Si la présente demande est effectuée à la suite d'une :

   ☐ Amalgamation / *Fusion*   ☐ Incorporation of an existing business / *Constitution en personne morale s'une entreprise existante*   ☐ Division of a corporation / *Division d'une corporation*   ☐ Acquisition of an existing ongoing business / *Acquisition d'une entreprise permanente existante*

7. Contact Person for Employer Health Tax Returns / *Personne-ressource pour les déclarations d'impôt-santé des employeurs*

Name / *Nom*	Title / *Titre*	Telephone / *Téléphone*	Ext. / *Poste*	Fax / *N° télec.*
Street No. & Name / *N° et nom de la rue*	City / *Ville*		Province/State / *État*	PC/Zip / *Code postal/Zip*

D Other Ministry of Finance Account Numbers / *Autres numéros de compte du ministère des Finances*

Employer Health Tax No. / *N° d'impôt-santé des employeurs* ☐☐☐ - ☐☐☐ - ☐☐   Retail Sales Tax No. / *N° de taxe de vente au détail* ☐☐☐☐ - ☐☐☐

E Certification - To the best of my knowledge, the above information is correct. / ***Attestation*** - *Autant que je sache, les renseignements ci-dessus sont exacts.*

Name (please print) / *Nom (en lettres moulées)*	Signature	Date

Personal information contained on this form is collected under the authority of the Employer Health Tax Act, RSO 1990, c.E 11, s.40 and will be used for tax purposes. Questions about this information collection should be directed to: Freedom of Information Liaison Officer, Employer Health Tax Branch, PO Box 640, 33 King St West, Oshawa ON L1H 8P5, (905) 436-4489. / *Les renseignements personnels contenus dans ce formulaire sont recueillis en vertu de la Loi sur l'impôt prélevé sur les employeurs relatif aux services de santé, L.R.O. de 1990, chap. E.11, article 40 et seront utilisés aux fins d'impôt. Prière d'adresser toute question relative à cette demande à l'officier de liaison, Accès l'information, Direction de l'impôt-santé des employeurs, CP 640, 33 rue King ouest, Oshawa ON L1H 8P5, (905) 436-4489.*

PX2046   001

FIGURE 9.4   APPLICATION FORM FOR WSIB

WSIB Workplace Safety & Insurance Board
CSPAAT Commission de la sécurité professionnelle et de l'assurance contre les accidents du travail

200 Front Street West, 3rd Floor
Toronto ON
M5V 3J1

Telephone: (416) 344-1007
Fax: (416) 344-2707
Toll Free: 1-800-387-0080

Employer Registration

Account Number	Firm Number

All information is strictly confidential.

Issue Date (dd-mmm-yyyy)

Mailing Address	
Town/City	
Province	Postal Code
Telephone Number ( )	Fax Number ( )
Website Address	
Email Address	

Section A : Should You Register?

Do you currently hire workers, or (sub)contractors considered by the WSIB to be workers, or plan to hire them in the future?   ☐ yes   ☐ no

If you have answered "yes", how many workers do you generally have? _____
Please complete this form.

If you have answered "no" to the above question, an account may still be established for optional insurance. If you do not wish to request optional insurance, do not fill in this form.

Domestic Employers: If you employ a domestic for more than 24 hours a week, complete this form

Section B: Previous Registration

Do the owner(s), partners or executive officer(s) have, or have they previously had, an account with the WSIB?   ☐ yes   ☐ no

If you have answered "no", go to Section C.

If you have answered "yes", please provide the following information for the previous account. If there is information about more than one account, please use page 3.

Legal Name		Address		
City	Province	Postal Code	Telephone Number ( )	WSIB Account Number

Section C: Employer Name(s) & Identification

Please complete this section in full. A copy of the documents filed with the Ministry of Consumer and Business Services or any other supporting documents must be attached to this form.

Legal Name

Place an "X" in the box that describes the ownership of your operation.   ☐ Sole Proprietorship   ☐ Partnership   ☐ Corporation   ☐ Other   Language Preference ☐ English ☐ French

Trade Name(s)

CCRA No. (Revenue Canada)	Employer Health Tax No.	Bank Name	Branch

Section D: Address(es)

Work Location

Please provide the physical location where the employer is carrying on business activities (i.e. not a box number or general delivery).
If there is more than one work location, please use page 3.

Address

Postal Code	Area Code Telephone Number ( )	Area Code FAX Number ( )	Email Address (if different)

Payroll Address

Only fill out this section if the physical location of your payroll records differs from your work location address.

Address

Postal Code	Area Code Telephone Number ( )	Area Code FAX Number ( )	Email Address (if different)

0775A (08/02)

www.wsib.on.ca

FIGURE 9.4   CONTINUED

Section E: Business Activity

Describe your business activity, including equipment or machinery used and materials contained in your product, in the area below.

Business Activity Description	Dates (e.g. 01JAN1996) (Include all workers' and contractors' labour)	Estimated Insurable Earnings for the Current Calendar Year	For WSIB Use Only
	Date Help First Employed (ddmmmyyyy)		
	Date Help First Employed (ddmmmyyyy)		
	Date Help First Employed (ddmmmyyyy)		

If there are more than three business activities, please use page 3.

If there is more than one business activity, do you maintain segregated payrolls for each business activity?   ☐ yes   ☐ no

Please provide the trade names and business activities of three competitors.

Name	Business Activity

Section F: Owner/Executive Details

Please provide the following details about the owner, managing partner, or chief executive officer.

First Name	Middle Name	Last Name

Date of Birth (e.g. 01JAN1995)	Social Insurance Number	Title

Home Address   (This address must be a physical address and not a box number or a general delivery).

City	Province	Postal Code	Area Code Telephone No.
			( )

If the employer has more partner(s) or executive officer(s) than the one individual shown above, please use page 3.

Personal information on this form is collected under the authority of the Workplace Safety and Insurance Act, 1997, and may be used to register/determine your status for coverage and to administer and enforce the Act. If you have any questions, please contact your Customer Service Representative/Account Manager or call 1-800-387-8638.

Section G: Associated Employer(s)

Does the employer have an associated relationship with one or more other employers?   ☐ yes   ☐ no

If yes, does the employer have any business dealings with the associated employer(s)?   ☐ yes   ☐ no

If you have answered "yes" to both these questions, please provide the name and address of the associated employer. If there is more than one employer, please use page 3.	Legal Name			
Address	City	Province	Postal Code	Account Number

Section H: Certification

I hereby certify that I am the employer (or authorized officer) responsible for paying all WSIB premiums on this account (and any linked accounts) for which the individual or entity identified under "Legal Name" in Section C is legally liable. To the best of my knowledge, the information on this form and on any documents attached is true and correct.

Name (please print)	Title

Signature	Area Code Telephone Number	Date Completed (e.g. 01JAN1996) d d m m m y y y y
	( )	

For WSIB Use Only	Letters/Forms Issued	WSIB Representative	Signature

0775A2   www.wsib.on.ca

FIGURE 9.4 CONCLUDED

WSIB Workplace Safety & Insurance Board
ONTARIO
CSPAAT Commission de la sécurité professionnelle et de l'assurance contre les accidents du travail

Employer Registration
Page 3

All information is strictly confidential.

Legal Name

'5A3

www.wsib.on.ca

FIGURE 9.5   BUSINESS NAME REGISTRATION BY A CORPORATION

 Ontario

Ministry of
Consumer and
Business Services

Ministère des Services
aux consommateurs
et aux entreprises

Registration
under the Business Names Act - Corporations

Enregistrement
en vertu de la *Loi sur les noms commerciaux (Personnes morales)*

Form 2
Formule 2

INSTRUCTIONS   **It is important to read these notes before completing the attached form.**

Print all information clearly in CAPITAL LETTERS using black ink.

Complete all sections of the form. Incomplete forms will be returned.

Fees: • there is a fee payable for new registrations and renewals;
• fees may be paid in cash, money order or cheque;
• payable to the **Ontario Minister of Finance;**
• do not send cash in the mail;
• a handling fee will be charged for a non-negotiable cheque.

Please forward both copies of the enclosed form to the Ministry of
Consumer and Business Services. The Client copy will no longer
be certified consistent with Ontario Regulation 175 / 94 Section 4.
The Client copy will be **returned**, with a validation in the bottom right-hand corner.

Return completed forms to: Ministry of Consumer and Business Services
Companies and Personal Property Security Branch
393 University Ave., Suite 200
Toronto ON M5G 2M2

Please do not separate the form.

Refer to these notes while completing form

1. Registration Type - Check the appropriate box:
New (Fee payable)
• a new registration is the first filing of the business name
• a change of business name/identification name is considered a new registration

Renewal (Fee payable)
• a registration expires in five years and must be renewed

Amendment (No fee payable)
• an amendment should be filed whenever there is a change in address, activity or corporation name

Cancellation (No fee payable)
• a cancellation should be submitted if you stop using the business name

BIN
For renewal, amendment or cancellation, enter "Business Identification No" (BIN).

2. Business Name - Please print the business name. This is the name you are registering. The business name must be set out in Block Capital Letters in the squares provided and must commence on the first line of the 'grid' in the first square. Each square of the grid represents a letter of the alphabet, a punctuation mark, or a space. If there is not sufficient space on the grid for the name, please use additional form(s). Please complete all items on additional form(s) and note the number of each additional page in the top right-hand corner of each form.

3. Mailing Address - Include street number, name, municipality and postal code. Your copy of the registration will be mailed to this address.

4. Business Address in Ontario - Include street number, name, municipality and postal code. A post office box is not acceptable in a business address. If there is more than one place of business, select one as the principal place. Where the business address is outside Ontario, set out the words "Not Applicable" in item 4. If this is the case, please ensure that Item 3, the mailing address, includes the street address of the principal place of business outside of Ontario, as a post office box is not acceptable.

5. Activity - Include a brief description of the activity being performed.

6. Corporation Name - the name of the corporation that is registering the business name.

7. Ontario Corporation Number - the number assigned to the corporation named in item 6.

8. Jurisdiction - the name of the jurisdiction in which the corporation was incorporated. Please do not use abbreviations.

9. Address of the Head or Registered Office of the corporation - include the number, street, municipality and postal code of the head or registered office address. **A post office box is not acceptable.**

10. Print the name of the person authorizing the registration, (either an officer, or a director, or a person acting under a power of attorney.)

Additional Information: If the person authorizing the registration is not an individual, set out the name in "Additional Information" and do not complete the boxes for the last, first and middle names.

07197 (05/2002)   en français au verso

FIGURE 9.5 CONCLUDED

Ministry of
Consumer and
Business Services

Ministère des Services
aux consommateurs
et aux entreprises

Registration Form 2
under the Business Names Act - Corporations
Enregistrement Formule 2
en vertu de la *Loi sur les noms commerciaux (Personnes morales)*

Print clearly in CAPITAL LETTERS /
Écrivez clairement en LETTRES MAJUSCULES

1. Registration Type
Type d'enregistrement

Page_____ of / de _____

If B, C, or D enter "Business Identification Number" /
En cas de B, C ou D, inscrivez le n° d'identification de l'entreprise.

A ☑ New
Nouvel

B ☐ Renewal
Renouvellement

C ☐ Amendment
Modification

D ☐ Cancellation
Révocation

BIN Business Identification No./
NIE le n° d'identification de l'entreprise

2.
Business or
Identification
Name / Nom
commercial
ou
d'identification

SUNNY SHORES REALTY

3.
Mailing
Address
Adresse
postale

Street No./ N° de rue   Street Name / Nom de la rue   Suite No. / Bureau n°
111 RED STREET

City / Town / Ville   Province / Province   Postal Code / Code postal
WHITE PORT ONTARIO P3P 0P9

Country / Pays
CANADA

4. Address of principal place of business in Ontario
Adresse de l'établissement principal en Ontario
(P.O. Box not acceptable
Case postale non acceptée)

☑ Same as above /
comme ci-dessus

Street No./ N° de rue   Street Name / Nom de la rue   Suite No./ Bureau n°
111   RED STREET

City / Town / Ville   Province / Province   Postal Code/ Code postal
WHITE PORT   ONTARIO   P3P 0P9

Country / Pays
CANADA

5. Give a brief description of the **ACTIVITY** being carried out under the business/identification name.
Résumez brièvement le genre d'**ACTIVITÉ** exercée sous le nom commercial ou d'identification

REAL ESTATE RENTAL

6. Corporation Name
Personne morale

01111111 ONTARIO INC.

7. Ontario corporation number
Numéro matricule de la personne morale en Ontario

01111111

8. Jurisdiction in which the corporation was incorporated
Le territoire de compétence où la personne morale a été constituée

ONTARIO

9. Address of Head or Registered Office of the corporation (P.O. Box not acceptable)
Adresse du siège social ou du bureau enregistré de la personne morale. *(Case postale non acceptée)*

Street No./ N° de rue   Street Name / Nom de la rue   Suite No./ Bureau n°
111   RED STREET

City / Town / Ville   Province / Province   Postal Code/ Code postal
WHITE PORT   ONTARIO   P3P 0P9

Country / Pays
CANADA

10. Print name of person authorizing this registration *(either an officer, or a director, or a person acting under a power of attorney)*
Indiquez en lettres majuscules le nom de la personne autorisant l'enregistrement *(dirigeant, administrateur, ou personne habilitée en vertu d'une procuration).*

Last Name / Nom de famille   First Name / Prénom   Middle Initial / initiale 2° prénom
GREEN   DAVID

If person authorizing the registration is not an individual (eg. corporation, trust, syndicate),
print name below and do not complete last, first and middle names above.
Si la personne qui autorise l'enregistrement n'est pas un individu (c'est-à-dire une
personne morale, un trust ou syndicat) ne pas remlir le nom de famille, prénom et 2°

MINISTRY USE ONLY - RÉSERVÉ AU MINISTÈRE

Additional Information / Renseignements supplémentaires

07197 (02/2003)

PART III

Maintaining a corporation

CHAPTER 10

Extra-provincial/ territorial registration

CHAPTER OVERVIEW

This chapter outlines the issues concerning the registration of Canadian corporations to carry on business in jurisdictions other than the one in which they are incorporated. It discusses the need to determine whether or not the corporation is considered to be "carrying on business" in another jurisdiction, as well as the various issues that confront extra-provincially licensed corporations such as registration, tax filings, municipal licences, filing notices of changes, and annual filings. It also reviews the provisions of the Ontario *Extra-Provincial Corporations Act* and the procedures that corporations formed outside Canada must follow before carrying on business in Ontario. Finally, it outlines the requirements that other Canadian incorporated or amalgamated corporations must meet in order to do business in Ontario.

CHAPTER OBJECTIVES

After completing this chapter, you should be able to:

1. Determine whether a corporation formed in one jurisdiction is carrying on business in another jurisdiction and is required to register or be licensed to do so.

2. Determine when to consult with local counsel about whether extra-provincial registration is required.

3. List the provinces that have reciprocal legislation that exempts certain corporations from the need to register, and explain those provisions.

4. Explain the basic issues affecting extra-provincial corporations in Canada, including the registration process, the effects of failing to register, the use of name, the appointment of an agent, the filing of notices of changes, and annual returns.

5. Apply the provisions of the *Extra-Provincial Corporations Act* to foreign corporations carrying on business in Ontario.

INTRODUCTION

On incorporation, a federal corporation is given the capacity to carry on its business throughout Canada and to conduct its affairs in any jurisdiction outside Canada to the extent that the laws of that jurisdiction permit (CBCA ss. 15(2) and (3)). Analogously, an Ontario corporation "has the capacity to carry on its business, conduct its affairs and exercise its powers in any jurisdiction outside Ontario to the extent that the laws of such jurisdiction permit" (OBCA s. 16). However, most jurisdictions have licensing or registration provisions that must be complied with before a corporation formed in one jurisdiction can carry on its business in another jurisdiction. These provisions enable people doing business with the corporation to search the public registry in the jurisdiction in which the corporation is doing business and find out an address for service of documents on the corporation in that jurisdiction.

EXTRA-PROVINCIAL/TERRITORIAL REGISTRATION

All provinces and territories in Canada, and many foreign jurisdictions, require corporations formed in another jurisdiction to follow a registration process before carrying on business.

The following discussion considers some of the issues confronting a corporation that intends to carry on its business in other jurisdictions.

Carrying on business

The first question you are likely to hear from a solicitor or client is, "Does the corporation need to register?" To determine this, you need to know the business that the corporation carries on. Then, you have to review the relevant statute in that jurisdiction to determine

1. whether it is considered an "extra-provincial/territorial" corporation in that jurisdiction; and

2. if it is, what the definition of "carrying on business" is in terms of the client's business.

Sometimes, the answer will be obvious. For example, your client may be a corporation that has a branch or division operating in another jurisdiction. Other times, the answer will not be so obvious. For example, your client may be a corporation that holds a mortgage in land or has entered into a general security agreement with a debtor in another jurisdiction. Where it is not abundantly clear that the corporation is carrying on business, you should consult with local counsel about whether you need to register the corporation.

Different industries may also be governed by different legislation. Common examples are banking and trust companies, insurance companies, and railways. As well, not-for-profit corporations are often governed by different legislation. For example, in British Columbia the extra-provincial registration of not-for-profit companies is governed by the *Society Act* (see chapter 15 for further discussion on the extra-provincial/territorial registration of not-for-profit corporations).

Other questions arise when you are dealing with corporations that are general or limited partners of a partnership registered in the jurisdiction. In general, limited partners that do not carry on business, except by virtue of being a limited partner in a partnership registered in the jurisdiction, will not have to register, whereas the general partner will. However, you should always check the relevant statute in the jurisdiction in which you are registering. If you are unsure, seek the assistance of local counsel or recommend to your responsible lawyer that he or she do so.

Although the definitions of "carrying on business" vary in each jurisdiction, there are some common themes. If a corporation has a "presence" (for example, a representative, warehouse, office, place of business, or resident agent) in another jurisdiction, it will be required to register. If a corporation advertises in a telephone book, it will likely have to register. If a corporation intends to hold land, it will have to register. However, a corporation that holds a security interest may not have to register. Table 10.1 at the end of the chapter lists the definitions of carrying on business in the Canadian provinces and territories.

Determining whether a corporation "carries on business" in another jurisdiction may be difficult, so it is important to understand that the final opinion should always come from a solicitor qualified to opine in the jurisdiction concerned. There have been many legal cases on the subject of what constitutes "carrying on business," and you do not want your client to end up being the subject of one of these cases.

Failure to register

The main consequence of failing to register a provincial corporation in another province or territory is that it will be incapable of maintaining an action, suit, or other court proceeding in the province and may be unable to hold land. Monetary penalties may also be levied on the corporation and its directors, officers, and registered agents for contravening the extra-provincial registration requirements and upon being found guilty of an offence. In contrast, while a federal corporation is "required" to register in a province in order to carry on business there, failure to do so will not impair its rights in the province. You should check the relevant statute carefully to determine which corporations they apply to and the consequences of failing to register.

Corporate name

Federal corporations have the right to use their corporate name in any Canadian jurisdiction. Other corporations must complete a search to satisfy the registering body that their name does not conflict with an existing name in the jurisdiction in which they are attempting to register. The name restrictions on carrying on business are generally similar to those on incorporation. If a similar corporate name already exists in the jurisdiction in Canada in which a corporation is attempting to register, the corporation may be required to use an "assumed name." Alternatively, the corporation may be able to provide a consent from a corporation with a similar name if the corporations are in different market segments, geographic areas, etc.

Appointing an agent for service

A corporation registering to carry on business in another jurisdiction must appoint an **agent for service**. In most cases, this person can be an individual or a corporation. The agent's responsibilities are simply to be available to receive service of documents and to pass them on as quickly as possible to the principal. For this reason, it is imperative to appoint someone reliable. The agent can be someone from the client's local office, if there is one, or a solicitor. Unless you are dealing with a sophisticated client or a client that has reliable office staff to deal with documents that are served on it, it is strongly recommended that a reputable law firm be used as registered agent.

Registration process

To qualify to do business in the various jurisdictions in Canada, a corporation has to file prescribed documents with the jurisdiction. The jurisdiction will then issue a "certificate of registration" and a registration number, which will authorize the corporation to carry on its business. This process requires the filing of certain forms with the jurisdiction. The forms can be found on government Web sites, as well as in most corporate record databases on the market today.

A corporation is generally required to register before commencing business in the jurisdiction. In some provinces, however, such as Alberta, Manitoba (federal corporations only), New Brunswick, Prince Edward Island, Yukon, the Northwest Territories, and Nunavut, a corporation must register within 30 days after commencing business, and in British Columbia a corporation must register within two months after commencing business.

The Nova Scotia *Corporations Registration Act* (ss. 3(2) and (3)) provides an exemption from registration for corporations formed in a jurisdiction that provides a similar exemption from registration for corporations formed in Nova Scotia. These provinces must be designated by the governor in council. Only New Brunswick has been designated for the purpose of exemption.

The reciprocal provision in New Brunswick is found in s. 195.1 of the New Brunswick *Business Corporations Act* (NBBCA), which provides for exemption to be made by regulation. Only corporations formed in Nova Scotia have been exempted from the registration requirements of the NBBCA.

The governments of Canada, Newfoundland and Labrador, Nova Scotia, and Ontario are working together to simplify the registration process for federal corporations that do their filing online. They have initiated a Joint On-line Registration Pilot, which was up and running as of August 8, 2002. Under this system, federal corporations in these provinces can access online forms through one portal at Industry Canada's Electronic Filing Centre to incorporate federally and register extra-provincially in any one or all of the collaborating provinces. Federal corporations can also access online forms necessary to complete federal and provincial annual returns. On the basis of information collected from the corporation during the process of filing articles of incorporation, the online service automatically selects the appropriate provincial forms and inserts relevant information. If any information is missing, the online service guides the user through any additional requirements. When the forms are complete, the online filing centre makes the corporation's information available to the province. If payments cannot be collected, or if provincial forms require a signature, the Electronic Filing Centre sends the necessary forms and complete instructions to the filer by e-mail.

Documents generally required for registration

The documents generally required to complete an extra-provincial/territorial registration are:

1. a registration statement,

2. an appointment of agent for service,

3. a notarial or government-certified copy of the articles of incorporation,

4. a certified copy of the corporation's bylaws (Newfoundland and Labrador only)

5. a certificate of status, and

6. a fee payable to the provincial treasury.

Business identifiers

In an effort to develop a convenient way for businesses to identify themselves when communicating with federal and provincial authorities, the provinces of British Columbia, Manitoba, Nova Scotia, and New Brunswick have entered into partnership with the Canada Revenue Agency (CRA) to use the federal business number (BN).

Each of the four provinces requests federal BNs as part of the extra-provincial registration process. If a BN has not been assigned, the province can obtain the number. The federal BNs for existing registrations are being requested when annual filings are completed.

Annual reporting

All jurisdictions in Canada have an annual reporting requirement. A corporation doing business in the jurisdiction must file an annual return or annual summary, either as of the anniversary of registration or upon a specified date, and pay a fee. Annual return requirements are discussed in greater detail in chapter 12.

Fees payable

Fees for registration vary across Canada. They range from no fees at all in Ontario for filing Form 2 under the *Corporations Information Act* for a domestic extra-provincial/territorial corporation, to a fee of $500 in Newfoundland and Labrador. Newfoundland and Labrador is the only jurisdiction whose fees are based on authorized capital. In Nova Scotia, registration fees are prorated to the month of registration.

Taxation

When a corporation is registered and carries out its business in another jurisdiction, it may become subject to local jurisdiction taxes. There is a registration process for tax purposes, including corporate tax and sales tax. New Brunswick, Newfoundland and Labrador, and Nova Scotia have harmonized their sales taxes with the federal goods and services tax (GST). As a result, only one registration for GST and harmonized sales tax (HST) is needed in these provinces. There is no provincial sales tax in Alberta, so registration for sales tax is not necessary. Registration for corporate taxes is separate from registration for sales taxes. For an in-depth discussion of corporate tax and retail sales tax registrations in Ontario, see chapter 9.

Licensing

Besides registering under the business statute in another jurisdiction, a corporation may be required to obtain an industry-specific licence in order to carry on business in the jurisdiction. For example, multilevel marketers, insurance brokers, real estate brokers, investment brokers, and motor vehicle dealers must be licensed to carry on business at the provincial level.

In addition, municipalities have bylaws that require certain businesses to be licensed.

CHANGES AFTER INITIAL REGISTRATION/LICENSING

Corporations that are registered to carry on business in another jurisdiction are generally obligated to report changes in their structure that take place in the governing jurisdiction. For example, many provinces require notice of articles of amendment, articles of continuance, articles of amalgamation, change of directors, and changes in registered office.

Deregistration process

Just as there is a process for registering a corporation to do business in another jurisdiction, there is also a process for "de-registering." The procedure is generally a simple one such as filing a letter from the corporation or a statement signed by a director or officer that the corporation no longer intends to carry on business in that jurisdiction.

Revocation of authority by province

If a corporation does not comply with the reporting requirements of the jurisdiction in which it carries on business, its registration may be revoked. Generally, revocation occurs after failure to file annual returns for a couple of years, failure to make payment of the annual fees, or failure to maintain a registered agent.

Notice will usually be given by the jurisdiction, allowing a period of time in which the offence can be rectified. If the offence is not rectified, the corporation will be deregistered.

To continue carrying on business, the corporation may be "reinstated" by complying with the outstanding filing requirements and, in some cases, by paying the fees due since the date of non-compliance. In some cases, a new application for registration is required.

EXTRA-PROVINCIAL LICENSING FOR A FOREIGN CORPORATION IN ONTARIO

The following discussion presents a detailed look at the requirements regarding foreign corporations carrying on business in Ontario. The statute that governs foreign corporations doing business in Ontario is the *Extra-Provincial Corporations Act* (EPCA).

Carrying on business in Ontario (EPCA ss. 1(2)–(3))

For the purposes of the EPCA (s. 1(2)), a corporation is said to be "carrying on business in Ontario" if

1. it has a resident agent, representative, warehouse, office or place where it carries on its business in Ontario;

2. it holds an interest, otherwise than by way of security, in real property situate in Ontario; or

3. it otherwise carries on its business in Ontario.

A corporation does not carry on business by reason only that it takes orders for or buys or sells goods, wares, and merchandise; or offers or sells services of any type by use of travellers or through advertising or correspondence (EPCA s. 1(3)).

Classes of extra-provincial corporations (EPCA s. 2(1))

The EPCA (s. 1(1)) defines an "extra-provincial corporation" as "a corporation, with or without share capital, incorporated or continued otherwise than by or under the authority of an Act of the Legislative Assembly" of Ontario. The EPCA (s. 2(1)) divides extra-provincial corporations into three classes:

- *Class 1.* Corporations incorporated or continued by or under the authority of an Act of a legislature of a province of Canada.

- *Class 2.* Corporations incorporated or continued by or under the authority of an Act of the Parliament of Canada or of the legislature of a territory of Canada.
    (Class 1 and 2 corporations are referred to in this chapter as domestic EP corporations.)

- *Class 3.* Corporations incorporated or continued under the laws of a jurisdiction outside Canada.
    (Class 3 corporations are referred to in this chapter as foreign EP corporations.)

Foreign EP corporations must be licensed under the EPCA before they can carry on business in Ontario.

Subject to the EPCA, the *Corporations Information Act* (Ontario) (CIA), and any other act, domestic EP corporations are exempt from obtaining a licence under the EPCA (EPCA s. 4(1)). These corporations are merely required to complete and file Form 2 under the CIA. This procedure will be discussed later in the chapter.

Use of name of extra-provincial corporation (EPCA s. 10)

Domestic and foreign EP corporations are not allowed to use or identify themselves in Ontario by a name that contains a word or expression prohibited by the regulations. That is:

1. the name cannot be the same as or, except where a number name is used, similar to

    a. the name of a known corporation, trust, association, partnership, sole proprietorship, or individual, whether in existence or not, or

    b. the known name under which any body corporate, trust, association, partnership, sole proprietorship or individual carries on its business or identifies itself;

2. the name cannot be used if the use of that name would be likely to deceive; or

3. the name cannot be used if it does not meet the requirements prescribed by the regulations.

Domestic and foreign EP corporations may, subject to their incorporating instruments, the CIA, and any other act, use and identify themselves in Ontario by a name other than their corporate name.

If, through inadvertence, a class 1 or class 3 extra-provincial corporation (that is, not a federal corporation) uses or identifies itself by a name contrary to s. 10 of the EPCA, the Ontario Director may, after giving the corporation an opportunity to be heard, order it to cease using the name in Ontario. Where the name is contained in a licence, the Director may order that the corporation apply for an amended licence under a different name within the time specified in the order. If a class 1 corporation does not comply, the Director may apply to the court for an order. If a foreign EP corporation fails to apply for an amended licence pursuant to the order, the Ontario Director may cancel the licence (EPCA s. 11).

Procedure for applying for extra-provincial licence (O. reg. 365, s. 6)

An application for an extra-provincial licence is made by submitting the following documents to the Ontario Director in paper format:

1. An Application for Extra-Provincial Licence (Form 1 under the EPCA), in duplicate, each copy of which must bear the original signature of a director or officer of the corporation. If the corporation has a corporate seal, the seal must be affixed to the application. If the corporation does not have a corporate seal, this fact must be indicated in the cover letter to the Ontario Director that accompanies the application.

a. Note that item 6 of Form 1 contemplates that the corporation has been authorized to make the application by a resolution passed by the directors of the corporation.

b. Item 7 of Form 1 should be completed with the address of a "principal office" or "chief place of business" in Ontario. If there is none, state so.

c. Item 8 of Form 1 should be completed only if the corporation has a chief officer or manager in Ontario. If there is none, state so.

d. Item 9 of Form 1 should be completed with a short description of the business that the corporation intends to carry on in Ontario.

2. An original Ontario-biased NUANS report, dated not more than 90 days prior to the submission of the application.

   If an identical name appears on the NUANS as "proposed," the name will not be accepted unless the extra-provincial corporation provides a written consent from the person who first proposed the name.

3. A certificate of status, signed by an official of the governing jurisdiction who is authorized to so certify, stating

   a. the name of the extra-provincial corporation,

   b. the date of its incorporation or amalgamation,

   c. the jurisdiction to which the corporation is subject, and

   d. that the corporation is a valid and subsisting corporation.

4. An appointment of an agent for service in Form 2 under the EPCA duly executed by the corporation under corporate seal, if any.

   A foreign EP corporation must ensure the continuing appointment of an Ontario-resident individual, aged 18 years or older, or a corporation with its head office or registered office in Ontario as its agent for service in Ontario on whom service of process, notices, or other proceedings may be made. Service on the agent is deemed to be service on the corporation (EPCA s. 19(1)).

5. A cheque payable to the Minister of Finance (Ontario) for the filing fee.

If the Ontario Director is not satisfied on the basis of the documents filed that the extra-provincial corporation is validly subsisting in the jurisdiction in which it purports to be incorporated, the corporation may be required to provide the director with a legal opinion in writing from a lawyer authorized to practise in that jurisdiction that the extra-provincial corporation is a valid and subsisting corporation in that jurisdiction.

If the certificate of status or any legal opinion is not in English or French, a notarized translation will be required.

Once the Ontario Director is satisfied with the application, he or she will endorse the application with the date (generally the date on which the Director receives the application) and an Ontario corporation number. If the corporation is not going to start its business activities immediately, the applicant may request a later date. The licence becomes effective on the date shown in the endorsement. It can take six to eight weeks for an application to be processed (EPCA ss. 5(2), (3), and (4)).

The Ontario Director may make a licence (or an amended licence) subject to restrictions on the business of a corporation, and to such other limitations or conditions as are specified in the licence or amended licence (EPCA s. 5(5)).

Endorsement refused (EPCA ss. 6 and 8)

If the Ontario Director refuses to endorse an application for an extra-provincial licence, the corporation may appeal his or her decision to the Divisional Court.

Contraventions of the EPCA

Section 4(2) of the EPCA provides that no foreign EP corporation shall carry on any of its business in Ontario without a licence under the EPCA. Furthermore, no person acting as representative or agent for a foreign EP corporation shall carry on any of its business in Ontario unless the corporation has a licence under the EPCA.

A foreign EP corporation that contravenes the EPCA, faces three consequences.

MONETARY PENALTIES

There are monetary penalties for every person who, without reasonable cause, contravenes the EPCA, the regulations, or the conditions of a licence issued under the EPCA. If guilty of such an offence, upon conviction, individuals such as a director, officer, or registered agent are liable to a fine of up to $2,000 and corporations are liable to fines up to $25,000 (EPCA ss. 20 (1) and (2)).

ABILITY TO MAINTAIN AN ACTION

A foreign EP corporation that does not have a current appointment of an agent for service, or that has not obtained a required licence under the EPCA, cannot maintain an action or other proceeding in any court or tribunal in Ontario in respect of any contract made by it (EPCA s. 21(1)).

Fortunately, such a contravention can be easily remedied. The foreign EP corporation can take immediate steps to obtain a licence under the EPCA, at which time an action or other proceeding may be maintained as if the default had been corrected before the action or proceeding was instituted (EPCA s. 21(2)).

POWER TO HOLD LAND

Once a foreign EP corporation has obtained a licence under the EPCA, it has power to acquire, hold, and convey any land or interest therein in Ontario necessary for its actual use and occupation or for carrying on its undertaking (EPCA s. 22). A corporation cannot register a document under the land registry or land titles systems in Ontario unless it has been issued an Ontario corporation number.

Steps to take after the licence is issued

Within 60 days of commencing to carry on business in Ontario, an extra-provincial corporation is required to file an initial return (Form 2) under the CIA. There is no government filing fee.

Consider also whether the licensed extra-provincial corporation needs to file a business name under the BNA or apply for any other provincial licence such as a motor vehicle dealer's licence. In addition, municipal licensing may also be required.

Filing annual returns

Foreign EP corporations that hold an extra-provincial licence to carry on business in Ontario are required to file annual returns under the CIA. The return must be delivered to the Minister of Finance. Alternatively, a return that is filed electronically may be delivered to the Minister of Consumer and Business Services. As of the date of writing, there is no government filing fee.

Provincial taxes

Extra-provincial corporations that carry on business in Ontario are subject to the same tax considerations as Ontario corporations. You should therefore ask your client whether you will be responsible for making tax registrations such as the following:

- CRA business number and various tax accounts such as GST, import/ export, payroll deductions, and corporate income tax under the *Income Tax Act* (Canada);

- provincial corporations tax under the *Corporations Tax Act* (Ontario);

- provincial retail sales tax under the *Retail Sales Tax Act* (Ontario);

- Workplace Safety and Insurance Board premiums; and

- employer health tax under the *Employer Health Tax Act* (Ontario).

The procedures for registration with respect to these accounts are discussed more fully in chapter 9.

Procedures regarding changes

When an extra-provincial corporation makes changes either to its name or to the status of its activities, the EPCA and the CIA require notice to be given.

CHANGE OF NAME OR JURISDICTION (EPCA S. 12(1))

When a foreign EP corporation changes its name (or has been ordered to change its name) or has been continued under the laws of another jurisdiction, it must apply for an amended licence on the prescribed form. The application, accompanied by a certificate of status and other relevant documents, such as a NUANS report in the case of a change of name, must be delivered to the Ontario Director.

CEASING TO CARRY ON BUSINESS (EPCA S. 12(2))

Where a foreign EP corporation has not carried on any of its business in Ontario for two consecutive years, it is required to apply for termination of its licence. If it does not do so, the Ontario Director, upon giving the corporation an opportunity to be heard, may make an order to cancel the licence.

CORRECTED CERTIFICATE (EPCA S. 13(1))

Where an extra-provincial corporation's licence contains an error, the Ontario Director can request return of the licence. Alternatively, the corporation can apply to the Director for a corrected licence, in which case it must return the original licence. The Director will endorse a corrected licence if he or she is of the opinion that it is appropriate to do so and is satisfied that the corporation has met all the licence requirements. The corrected licence generally bears the date of the licence it replaces.

REQUIREMENTS FOR DOMESTIC EP CORPORATIONS CARRYING ON BUSINESS IN ONTARIO

Every domestic EP corporation that begins to carry on business in Ontario is required to file with the Ministry of Consumer and Business Services (MBCS) an initial return under the CIA, setting out the prescribed information as of the date of the date of filing. The initial return is to be filed within 60 days after the corporation begins to carry on business in Ontario. Once the initial return is filed, the MCBS issues an Ontario corporation number to the corporation.

Documents required to be filed

To obtain an Ontario corporation number, a domestic EP corporation must file the following documents:

1. a cover letter to the MCBS;

2. Form 2 — Extra-Provincial Corporations, Initial Return; and

3. a photocopy of the first page of the most recent articles or other constating documents containing the correct name and incorporation/amalgamation date, filed with the jurisdiction to which the corporation is subject.

Form 2s are filed manually at the counter of the MCBS or by mail. Electronic filing is not yet available. The forms do not require a signature. There is no fee for filing an initial return or a notice of change (see below). Allow 48 hours for processing an initial return to obtain the Ontario corporation number.

Amalgamation outside Ontario

On the amalgamation of a domestic EP corporation with another corporation in its home jurisdiction, a new initial return must be filed, together with a copy of the certificate and first page of the articles of amalgamation. A new Ontario corporation number will be assigned.

Continuance outside Ontario

If a domestic EP corporation that is registered in Ontario continues into another jurisdiction outside Ontario, it is required to file Form 2 — Notice of Change under the CIA, together with a copy of the certificate and articles of continuance.

Continuance out of Ontario and EP domestic registration back into Ontario

If an Ontario corporation continues federally or into another province and continues to do business in Ontario, after continuance a notice of change should be filed, together with a copy of the certificate and articles of continuance. The Ontario corporation number issued will be the same as the Ontario corporation number of the corporation prior to continuance. The notice of change should indicate the date of incorporation in Ontario as the date on which it commences business activities in Ontario.

Information required to complete Form 2 for a domestic EP corporation

The following information is required to complete Form 2:

1. the corporation name, including punctuation;

2. the date of incorporation/amalgamation;

3. the address of the registered or head office;

4. the address of the principal office in Ontario, if applicable;

5. the former corporation name, if applicable;

6. the date the corporation commenced business activity in Ontario;

7. the jurisdiction of incorporation;

8. the name and office address of the corporation's chief officer/manager in Ontario, if applicable; and

9. the name of director, officer, or other individual having knowledge of the affairs of the corporation who will certify that the information set out in the form is true and correct.

Changes

Every corporation that has filed an initial return with the MCBS must file a notice of change for every change in the information contained in the initial return. This filing must be made within 15 days after the change takes place. If a corporation ceases to do business in Ontario, it must also file a notice of change and set out the date on which it ceased to carry on business in Ontario.

Documents required to be filed regarding a change

The following information must be filed in order to amend the Public Record:

1. a cover letter to the MCBS;

2. Form 2 — Extra-Provincial Corporations, Notice of Change; and

3. a photocopy of the first page of the articles of amendment (in the event of a name change), articles of amalgamation, or other constating documents

containing the correct name and incorporation/amalgamation date, filed with the jurisdiction to which the corporation is subject.

KEY TERM

agent for service

REFERENCES

Business Corporations Act (British Columbia), SBC 2002, c. 57.

Business Corporations Act (New Brunswick) (NBBCA), SNB 1981, c. B-9.1, as amended.

Canada, Industry Canada, "Allan Rock and Walter Noel Announce Improved Services for Newfoundland and Labrador Businesses," *Release*, August 8, 2002, available online at http://www.ic.gc.ca (announcement of a Joint On-Line Registration Pilot).

Canada Business Corporations Act (CBCA), RSC 1985, c. C-44, as amended.

Corporations Information Act (Ontario) (CIA), RSO 1990, c. C.39, as amended.

Corporations Registration Act (Nova Scotia) (NSCRA), RSNS 1989, c. 101, as amended.

Corporations Tax Act (Ontario), RSO 1990, c. C.40, as amended.

Employer Health Tax Act (Ontario), RSO 1990, c. E.11, as amended.

Extra-Provincial Corporations Act (Ontario) (EPCA), RSO 1990, c. E.27, as amended.

Income Tax Act (Canada), RSC 1985, c. 1 (5th Supp.), as amended.

Kingston, R.A., *Canada Corporation Manual* (Toronto: Carswell, 2003).

Retail Sales Tax Act (Ontario), RSO 1990, c. R.31, as amended.

Securities Act (British Columbia), RSBC 1996, c. 418, as amended.

FORMS AND PRECEDENTS

Figure 10.1: Form 1, *Extra-Provincial Corporations Act*, application for extra-provincial licence

Figure 10.2: Form 2, *Extra-Provincial Corporations Act*, appointment of agent for service

Figure 10.3: Form 2, *Corporations Information Act*, initial return

Figure 10.4: Sample resolution authorizing application for extra-provincial registration in Ontario

Figure 10.5: Report letter to client for obtaining extra-provincial licence in Ontario

Figure 10.6: Initial return (Form 2) under the *Corporations Information Act* for domestic extra-provincial registration in Ontario

REVIEW QUESTIONS

1. List three common characteristics of carrying on business in another jurisdiction.

2. What are two possible consequences for a corporation that carries on business in a jurisdiction other than the jurisdiction in which it is formed and that does not comply with the registration requirements?

3. Are the following statements true or false?

   a. A Nova Scotia corporation does not have to register to carry on business in New Brunswick.

   b. A New Brunswick corporation does not have to register to carry on business in Nova Scotia.

   c. An extra-provincial corporation has to maintain its minute book in a jurisdiction in which it registers to carry on business.

   d. Corporations are not required to file annual returns in jurisdictions in Canada in which they carry on business other than their home jurisdiction.

   e. Directors and officers of an Ontario extra-provincially registered corporation may be liable for monetary penalties if a domestic EP corporation fails to comply with the EPCA.

4. Why does a corporation have to appoint a registered agent?

5. Can a corporation use its name in another province? Explain.

6. List four documents that you might have to prepare in order to register a corporation in another province.

7. Give three examples of tax registrations that a corporation may be required to make after registering extra-provincially.

8. List two occasions when an extra-provincial corporation may be required to file a notice of change under the CIA.

9. Explain the definition of carrying on business in Ontario under the EPCA.

10. Explain the difference in the registration requirements under the EPCA for foreign EP corporations and domestic EP corporations.

11. List the documents required for an application for an extra-provincial licence in Ontario. Who would be required to apply?

12. Can a foreign EP corporation hold land in Ontario without an extra-provincial licence?

EXERCISE

ABC Luxury Motor Vehicle Dealer, an Ontario general partnership in which ABC Limited is the general partner and Luxury Motor Vehicle Dealer is the limited partner, wants to carry on its business across Canada. Make a document list and list of questions you would want to ask in connection with preparing the documents for registration.

CASE STUDIES

Case study 10:1: Registration in Ontario of a foreign EP corporation

One day Jessie Bruton received a memorandum from Richard Thorn, a partner at Thorn & Hill LLP, advising her that his client Big Bad Batteries Corp., a Delaware corporation, wishes to start doing business in Ontario on November 5, 2003. He instructed Jessie to contact Katherine Smith-Power, the president of Big Bad Batteries Corp., for any information she needed. Since it was the beginning of September, Jessie knew she had to process the documentation quickly in order to have it filed with the Ontario Companies Branch in time to have the extra-provincial licence issued by November 5. She prepared an e-mail to Ms Smith-Power's executive assistant requesting the information, which the assistant returned by annotating Jessie's original e-mail. This information is as in the table on the facing page.

After receiving the necessary information, Jessie obtained an Ontario-biased NUANS report to verify that there were no other similar names. Then she prepared the necessary documents and sent them to Big Bad Batteries Corp. for signature with the request to return them to her so that she could file the documents no later than September 22. While the documents were out for signature, Jessie requested a certificate of good standing from Delaware. When the signed documents were returned, Jessie filed the application for extra-provincial licence, the appointment of agent for service, the NUANS report, the certificate of status, and a cheque for the filing fees, together with a covering letter, with the Ontario Companies Branch. When the licence was issued, Jessie immediately filed the initial return (Form 2) under the *Corporations Information Act* and prepared a report letter to Ms Smith-Power outlining the particulars of registration.

See figures 10.1 to 10.5 at the end of this chapter.

Information requested	Response
1. Proper name of the corporation to be licensed	Big Bad Batteries Corp.
2. Governing jurisdiction	Delaware
3. Date of incorporation in Delaware	August 18, 2000
4. Full address of head or registered office	1234 Power Street Jolt, Delaware USA 23435
5. Date of the resolution of the directors of Big Bad Batteries Corp. authorizing the corporation to apply for the extra-provincial licence in Ontario	September 10, 2003
6. Full address of principal office in Ontario, if determined	None
7. Chief officer or manager in Ontario if determined, and residential address	None
8. Any other name under which the corporation may carry on its business	None
9. Date the corporation proposes to commence business in Ontario	November 5, 2003
10. Description of the business activities	Distribution of batteries
11. Name and position of the individual who will sign the application	Katherine Smith-Power, President
12. Name and business address of the agent for service	Richard Thorn of Thorn & Hill LLP

Case study 10:2: Registration in Ontario of a domestic EP corporation

Consider the case studies in chapters 7 and 8 regarding the incorporation and organization of BSJ Garden Ornament Sales Inc. as a federal corporation. Recall that Mr. Black advised Jessie that this corporation would carry on business in Ontario. As part of the organization proceedings, Jessie prepared an initial return (Form 2) for filing under the *Corporations Information Act*. This was filed within 60 days of BSJ commencing business in Ontario.

See figure 10.6 at the end of this chapter.

TABLE 10.1   CANADIAN PROVINCIAL AND TERRITORIAL DEFINITIONS OF "CARRYING ON BUSINESS"

Province	Definition of carrying on business	Consequences of not registering
British Columbia[a] *Business Corporations Act*, SBC 2002, c. 57 Part 11 — Extraprovincial Companies Register within 2 months of commencing business (s. 375.1)	s. 1(1) "foreign corporation" means a corporation that (a) is not a company, (b) has issued shares, (c) is not required under the Cooperative Association Act to be registered under that Act, and (d) was 　(i) incorporated otherwise than by or under an Act, 　(ii) continued under section 308 or otherwise transferred by a similar process into a jurisdiction other than British Columbia, or 　(iii) the result of an amalgamation under Division 4 of Part 9 or a similar process, or of an amalgamation or similar process in a jurisdiction other than British Columbia; "foreign entity" means (a) a foreign corporation, or (b) a limited liability company; *Name display* s. 27(1) A company or extraprovincial company must display its name or, in the case of an extraprovincial company that has adopted an assumed name under this Act, its assumed name, in legible English or French characters, (a) in a conspicuous position at each place in British Columbia at which it carries on business, (b) in all its notices and other official publications used in British Columbia, (c) on all its contracts, business letters and orders for goods, and on all its invoices, statements of account, receipts and letters of credit used in British Columbia, and (d) on all bills of exchange, promissory notes, endorsements, cheques and orders for money used in British Columbia and signed by it or on its behalf.	s. 426(1)(b) A person commits an offence who ... contravenes section 375(1). s. 428(3) A foreign entity that commits an offence under section 426(1)(b) is liable to a fine in a prescribed amount for each day that the offence continues.

---

a Under the *Business Corporations Act*, SBC 2002, c. 57, a corporation that is extra-provincially registered in British Columbia when the Act enters into force will not be required to register under the Act.

TABLE 10.1 CONTINUED

Province	Definition of carrying on business	Consequences of not registering

British Columbia (cont'd.)	*Carrying on business*
	
	s. 375(2) [A] foreign entity is deemed to carry on business in British Columbia if
	
	  (a) its name, or any name under which it carries on business, is listed in a telephone directory
	
	    (i) for any part of British Columbia, and
	
	    (ii) in which an address or telephone number in British Columbia is given for the foreign entity,
	
	  (b) its name, or any name under which it carries on business, appears or is announced in any advertisement in which an address or telephone number in British Columbia is given for the foreign entity,
	
	  (c) it has, in British Columbia,
	
	    (i) a resident agent, or
	
	    (ii) a warehouse, office or place of business, or
	
	  (d) it otherwise carries on business in British Columbia.
	
	(3) A foreign entity does not carry on business in British Columbia
	
	  (a) if it is a bank,
	
	  (b) if its only business in British Columbia is constructing and operating a railway, or
	
	  (c) merely because it has an interest as a limited partner in a limited partnership carrying on business in British Columbia.
	
	(4) A foreign entity need not be registered under this Act or comply with this Part other than subsection (5) of this section, and may carry on business in British Columbia as if it were registered under this Act, if
	
	  (a) the principal business of the foreign entity consists of the operation of one or more ships, and
	
	  (b) the foreign entity does not maintain in British Columbia a warehouse, office or place of business under its own control or under the control of a person on behalf of the foreign entity.
	
	(5) Every person who is a resident agent or representative of a foreign entity referred to in subsection (4) must file with the registrar
	
	  (a) a notice of agency in the form established by the registrar stating
	
	    (i) the name of the foreign entity,
	
	    (ii) the chief place of business of the foreign entity outside British Columbia, and
	
	    (iii) particulars of the person's agency, and
	
	  (b) a notice of change of agency in the form established by the registrar identifying any change in that name, chief place of business or agency.
	
	(6) Sections 27(1), 384 and 385 apply to a foreign entity referred to in subsection (4) as if it were an extraprovincial company.	

TABLE 10.1 CONTINUED

Province	Definition of carrying on business	Consequences of not registering
Alberta *Business Corporations Act*, RSA 2000, c. B-9, as amended Part 21 Register within 30 days of commencing business	s. 277(1) For the purposes of this Part, an extra-provincial corporation carries on business in Alberta if (a) its name, or any name under which it carries on business, is listed in a telephone directory for any part of Alberta, (b) its name, or any name under which it carries on business, appears or is announced in any advertisement in which an address in Alberta is given for the extra-provincial corporation, (c) it has a resident agent or representative or a warehouse, office or place of business in Alberta, (d) it solicits business in Alberta, (e) it is the owner of any estate or interest in land in Alberta, (f) it is licensed or registered or required to be licensed or registered under any Act of Alberta entitling it to do business, (g) it is, in respect of a public vehicle as defined in the Motor Transport Act, the holder of a certificate of registration under the Motor Vehicle Administration Act, unless it neither picks up nor delivers goods or passengers in Alberta, (h) it is the holder of a certificate issued by the Alberta Motor Transport Board, unless it neither picks up nor delivers goods or passengers in Alberta, or (i) it otherwise carries on business in Alberta. (2) The Registrar may exempt an extra-provincial corporation from the payment of fees under this Part if the Registrar is satisfied that it does not carry on business for the purpose of gain. Alberta Corporate Registry tel. no.: 780-427-2311	s. 294 No act of an extra-provincial corporation, including any transfer of property to or by an extra-provincial corporation, is invalid by reason only (a) that the act or transfer is contrary to or not authorized by its charter or internal regulations or any law of the jurisdiction in which it is incorporated, or (b) that the extra-provincial corporation was not then registered. s. 295(1) An extra-provincial corporation while unregistered is not capable of commencing or maintaining any action or other proceeding in any court in Alberta in respect of any contract made in the course of carrying on business in Alberta while it was unregistered. s. 295(2) If an extra-provincial corporation was not registered at the time it commenced an action or proceeding referred to in subsection (1) but becomes registered afterward, the action or proceeding may be maintained as if it had been registered before the commencement of the action or proceeding. *Penalty* s. 296 A person who contravenes this Part is guilty of an offence and liable to a fine of not more than $5000.

TABLE 10.1 CONTINUED

Province	Definition of carrying on business	Consequences of not registering

Saskatchewan
 	
The Business Corporations Act, RSS 1978, c. B-10, as amended
 	
Register prior to commencing business
	s. 262(1) Every corporation carrying on business in Saskatchewan shall be registered under this part and no corporation shall carry on business in Saskatchewan unless it is so registered.
	
	s. 262(2) For the purposes of this act, a corporation is deemed to be carrying on business if it:
	
	   (a) holds any title, estate or interest in land registered in the name of the corporation under The Land Titles Act;
	
	   (b) has a resident agent or representative or maintains an office, warehouse or place of business in Saskatchewan;
	
	   (c) is licensed or registered or required to be licensed or registered under any statute of Saskatchewan entitling it to do business or to sell securities of its own issue;
	
	   [(d) and (e) repealed]
	
	   (f) otherwise carries on business in Saskatchewan.
	
	A listing in the telephone directory in Saskatchewan under the name of the corporation is deemed to be carrying on business (s. 262(3)).
	
	Corporations Branch tel. no.: 306-787-2962
		s. 275(1) A corporation that is not registered under this Act is not capable of commencing or maintaining any action or other proceeding in a court in respect of a contract made in whole or in part in Saskatchewan in the course of, or in connection with, its business.
		
		This does not apply to a Canada corporation (s. 275(2))
		
		s. 276 Where a corporation was not registered but becomes registered under this Act, any action or proceeding mentioned in subsection 275(1) may be maintained as if the corporation had been registered before the institution of the action or proceeding.
		
		Penalty
		
		s. 302 Every person who, without reasonable cause contravenes a provision of this Act or the regulations for which no punishment is provided is guilty of an offence and liable on summary conviction to a fine not exceeding $500.00.

Manitoba
 	
The Corporations Act, RSM 1987, c. C225, as amended
 	
Register prior to commencing business
 	
Federal corporations must register within 30 days of commencing business (s. 187(3))
	s. 187(1) This part, except where it is expressly provided, applies to every body corporate carrying on its business or undertaking in Manitoba, other than a body corporate licensed under the Insurance Act as an insurer or a body corporate created solely for religious purposes.
	
	s. 187(2) A body corporate is deemed to be carrying on business in Manitoba if:
	
	   it has a resident agent or representative, or a warehouse, office or place of business in Manitoba;
	
	   its name or any name under which it carries on business, together with an address for the body corporate in Manitoba, is listed in a Manitoba telephone directory;
	
	   its name or any name under which it carries on business, together with an address for the body corporate in Manitoba, is included in any advertisement advertising the business or any product of the body corporate;
	
	   it is the registered owner of real property situate in Manitoba; or
	
	   it otherwise carries on its business or undertaking in Manitoba.
	
	Corporations Branch tel. no.: 204-945-2500
		s. 197(1) An extra-provincial body corporate is not capable of commencing or maintaining any action or other proceeding in a court in respect of a contract made in whole or in part in the province, in the course of, or in connection with, the business or undertaking carried on by it, without being registered under the provisions of this Part.
		
		s. 197(3) Registration of a body corporate is deemed to authorize all previous acts of the body corporate and is construed as if the certificate of registration or supplementary certificate of registration had been granted before the body corporate commenced to carry on its business or undertaking in the Province, except for the purpose of a prosecution for an offence under this Part.
		
		Penalty
		
		s. 187(5) Every body corporate that carries on its business or undertaking in the province without being registered, and every director and officer of the body corporate, and every representative or agent acting in any capacity for the body corporate so carrying on its business or undertaking is respectively guilty of an offence and is liable to a penalty of $50 for every day the business or undertaking is so carried on.

TABLE 10.1 CONTINUED

Province	Definition of carrying on business	Consequences of not registering
Ontario *Extra-Provincial Corporations Act*, RSO 1990, c. E.27, as amended Register prior to commencing business pursuant to s. 4(2)	s. 2(1) Extra-provincial corporations shall be classified into the following classes: • Class 1. Corporations incorporated or continued by or under the authority of an Act of a legislature of a province of Canada. • Class 2. Corporations incorporated or continued by or under the authority of an Act of the Parliament of Canada or of the legislature of a territory of Canada. • Class 3. Corporations incorporated or continued under the laws of a jurisdiction outside of Canada. s. 4(2) No extra-provincial corporation within class 3 shall carry on any of its business in Ontario without a licence under this Act to do so, and no person acting as representative for or agent for any such extra-provincial corporation shall carry on any of its business in Ontario unless the corporation has a licence under this Act. s. 1(2) For the purposes of this Act, an extra-provincial corporation carries on its business in Ontario if, (a) it has a resident agent, representative, warehouse, office or place where it carries on its business in Ontario; (b) it holds an interest, otherwise than by way of security, in real property situate in Ontario; or (c) it otherwise carries on its business in Ontario. s. 1(3) An extra-provincial corporation does not carry on its business in Ontario by reason only that, (a) it takes orders for or buys or sells goods, wares and merchandise; or (b) offers or sells services of any type, by use of travellers or through advertising or correspondence. Note: Although class 1 and class 2 corporations are exempt from the licensing requirement, a Form 2 initial notice must be filed with the Ministry of Consumer and Business Services under the *Corporations Information Act*, RSO 1990, c. C.39, as amended, within 60 days after the date the corporation begins to carry on business in Ontario (s. 3). An Ontario corporation number will be assigned. s. 22 Every Corporation, (a) within class 1 or 2; (b) within class 3 that has a licence under this Act; or (c) that is exempt from the licensing requirement under this Act, has power to acquire, hold and convey any land or interest therein in Ontario necessary for its actual use and occupation or for carrying on its undertaking. Companies Branch tel. no.: 416-314-8880	s. 21(1) An extra-provincial corporation within class 3 that is not in compliance … is not capable of maintaining any action or any other proceeding in any court or tribunal in Ontario in respect of any contract made by it. s. 21(2) Where a default referred to in subsection (1) has been corrected, an action or other proceeding may be maintained as if the default had been corrected before the institution of the action or other proceeding. *Penalty* s. 20(1) Every person who, without reasonable cause, (a) contravenes this Act or the regulations; (b) contravenes a condition of a licence; or (c) fails to observe or comply with an order, direction or other requirement made under this Act or the regulations, is guilty of an offence and on conviction is liable to a fine of not more than $2,000 or if such person is a corporation to a fine of not more than $2,000. s. 20(2) Where an extra-provincial corporation is guilty of an offence under subsection (1), every director or officer of the corporation and every person acting as its representative in Ontario who authorized, permitted or acquiesced in such offence is also guilty of an offence and on conviction is liable to a fine of not more than $2,000.

TABLE 10.1 CONTINUED

Province	Definition of carrying on business	Consequences of not registering
Quebec *An Act Respecting the Legal Publicity of Sole Proprietorships, Partnerships and Legal Persons*, RSQ, c. P-45, as amended Register no later than sixty days after the date on which it commenced business (s. 9)	s. 2(3) Every natural person operating a sole proprietorship in Quebec, whether or not it is a commercial enterprise under a name which does not include the person's surname; s. 2(5) Every legal person established for a private interest not constituted in Quebec, but domiciled in Quebec, which carries on an activity in Quebec, including the operation of an enterprise, or possesses an immovable real right, other than a prior claim or hypothec, in Quebec Quebec Registry tel. no.: 418-643-3625	s. 100 Where a person or partnership subject to the requirement of registration has not registered, the examination of an application presented by that person or partnership before a court or a body exercising judicial or quasi judicial functions may be suspended until registration is effected, where so requested by an interested person before the hearing. Sections 101, 102, 103, 104, 105 and 106 provide that an offence is any of failing to register within prescribed time, failure to file annual declaration or an amending declaration. *Penalty* s. 107 Every person guilty of an offence is liable to a fine of not less than \$200 and not more than \$2,000. For a second or subsequent offence, the fines are doubled.

TABLE 10.1 CONTINUED

Province	Definition of carrying on business	Consequences of not registering

New Brunswick
 	
Business Corporations Act, SNB 1981, c. B-9.1 as amended
 	
Part XVII
 	
Register within 30 days of commencing business (s. 196)
	s. 194(1) For the purposes of this Part, an extra-provincial corporation carries on business in New Brunswick if
	
	  (a) its name, or any name under which it carries on business, appears or is announced in any advertisement in which an address in New Brunswick is given for the extra-provincial corporation;
	
	  (b) it has a resident agent or representative or a warehouse, office or place of business in New Brunswick;
	
	  (c) it solicits business in New Brunswick;
	
	  (d) it is the owner of any estate or interest in land in New Brunswick;
	
	  (e) it is licensed or registered or required to be licensed or registered under any Act of New Brunswick entitling it to do business;
	
	  (f) it is the holder of a certificate of registration under the *Motor Vehicle Act;*
	
	  (g) it is the holder of a licence issued under the *Motor Carrier Act;* or
	
	  (h) it otherwise carries on business in New Brunswick.
	
	s. 194(2) Where an extra-provincial corporation has its name or any name under which it carries on business listed in a telephone directory for any part of New Brunswick, that corporation shall be deemed, in the absence of evidence to the contrary, to be carrying on business in New Brunswick.
	
	s. 194(2.1) An extra-provincial corporation is not carrying on business in New Brunswick by reason only that it is a general or limited partner in a limited partnership or an extra-provincial limited partnership that has filed a declaration under the *Limited Partnership Act.*
	
	s. 194(3) The Director may exempt an extra-provincial corporation from the operation of this Part except subsection (4) if he is satisfied that it does not carry on business for the purpose of gain.
	
	s. 194(4) An extra-provincial corporation exempted under subsection (3) shall
	
	  (a) send to the Director the appointment of its attorney for service in the prescribed form, and
	
	  (b) in each year on or before the last day of the month that is the same as the month in which it was incorporated, send to the Director an annual return in the prescribed form or in the form required by the laws of the jurisdiction in which it was incorporated.
	
	(Section 194(4) provides that an exempted extra-provincial corporation under s. 194(3) has to file an appointment of its attorney for service and an annual return each year in the prescribed form.)
	
	Pursuant to s. 195(1), s. 11.1 of the General Regulation under the *Business Corporations Act,* NB reg. 81-147, as amended, provides that an extra-provincial corporation incorporated under the laws of the province of Nova Scotia is exempted from part XVII of the Act.
	
	New Brunswick Corporate Affairs tel. no.: 506-453-2703
		s. 211 No act of an extra-provincial corporation, including any transfer of property to or by an extra-provincial corporation, is invalid by reason only
		
		  (a) that the act or transfer is contrary to or not authorized by its charter or internal regulations or any law of the jurisdiction in which it is incorporated, or
		
		    (b) that the extra-provincial corporation was not then registered.
		
		s. 213(1) An extra-provincial corporation, while unregistered, is not capable of commencing or maintaining any action or other proceeding in any court in New Brunswick in respect of any contract made in the course of carrying on business in New Brunswick while it was unregistered or otherwise in violation of this Part.
		
		s. 213(2) If an extra-provincial corporation is not registered at the time it commences an action or proceeding referred to in subsection (1) but becomes registered afterward, the action or proceeding may be maintained as if it was registered before the commencement of the action or proceeding.
		
		s. 213(3) This section does not apply to an extra-provincial corporation incorporated under the laws of Canada.
		
		Penalty
		
		s. 214(1) An extra-provincial corporation who fails to comply with this Part commits an offence and is liable on a summary conviction to a fine of not more than five thousand dollars and in default of payment is liable to levy by distress and sale in accordance with section 35 of the *Summary Convictions Act.*
		
		s. 214(2) Whether or not the extra-provincial corporation has been prosecuted or convicted, any director or officer of the extra-provincial corporation who knowingly authorizes, permits or acquiesces in such failure commits an offence and is liable on a summary conviction to a fine not exceeding five thousand dollars or to imprisonment for a term not exceeding six months or to both and in default of payment of a fine is liable to imprisonment in accordance with subsection 31(3) of the *Summary Convictions Act.*

TABLE 10.1 CONTINUED

Province	Definition of carrying on business	Consequences of not registering
Nova Scotia *Corporations Registration Act*, RSNS 1989, c. 101, s. 1, as amended Register prior to commencing business	s. 2(b) "[C]arry on business" means the transaction of any of the ordinary business of a corporation, whether by means of an employee or an agent and whether or not the corporation has a resident agent or representative or a warehouse, office or place of business in the Province. s. 3(2) Notwithstanding subsection (1), this Act does not apply to a corporation that is incorporated and registered pursuant to the laws of another province of Canada designated by the Governor in Council. Made under s. 3 of the *Corporations Registration Act*, RSNS 1989, c. 101, OIC 94-185 (March 8, 1994), NS reg. 40/94: The Governor in Council on the report and recommendation of the Minister of Justice dated the 15th day of February, 1994, pursuant to subsections (2) and (3) of Section 3 of Chapter 101 of the Revised Statutes of Nova Scotia, 1989, as amended, the *Corporations Registration Act*, is pleased to designate the Province of New Brunswick for the purpose of exemption under subsection (2) of Section 3, of the Act, effective on, from and after the 1st day of April, 1994. A New Brunswick corporation is also exempt from filing an annual return in Nova Scotia. Registry of Joint Stock Companies tel. no.: 902-424-7770	s. 17(1) Unless and until a corporation holds a certificate of registration that is in force, it shall not be capable of bringing or maintaining any action, suit or other proceeding in any court in the Province in respect to any contract made in whole or in part in the Province in connection with any part of its business done or carried on in the Province while it did not hold a certificate of registration that was in force, provided, however, that this Section shall not apply to any company incorporated by or under the authority of an Act of the Parliament of Canada or by or under the authority of an Act of the Legislature. *Penalty* s. 13(1) If any corporation, whether incorporated before or on the first day of October, 1912, or at any time thereafter, does or carries on in the Province any part of its business while it does not hold a certificate of registration that is in force, such corporation shall be liable to a penalty of fifty dollars for every day on which it so does or carries on any part of its business, and every director, manager, secretary, agent, traveller or salesman of the corporation, who, with notice that the corporation does not hold a certificate of registration that is in force, transacts in the Province any part of the business of the corporation, shall, for every day on which he so transacts the same, be liable to a penalty of fifty dollars.

TABLE 10.1 CONTINUED

Province	Definition of carrying on business	Consequences of not registering
Prince Edward Island *Licensing Act*, RSPEI 1988, c. L-11, as amended Register within 30 days of commencing business	s. 1(e) "[D]oing business," or the expression "carrying on business," means the transaction of any of the ordinary business of a corporation or person, including franchises, whether or not by means of an employee or an agent and whether or not the corporation or person has a resident agent or representative or a warehouse, office or place of business in the province. s. 3(1) The following corporations and persons are required to be licensed under this Act: (a) all railway express companies doing business within this province; (b) all banks, finance companies, loan companies or trust companies doing business within this province; (c) every telegraph or other corporation working a telegraph, telex or other similar method of communication for the use of the public within this province; (d) every corporation or person operating a chain store and every corporation or person operating a branch chain wholesale store, and each branch of such corporation doing business in this province over and above the number of one; (e) each corporation or person operating a branch chain theatre and each branch of such corporation doing business in this province over and above the number one; (f) every electric light company and electric power company doing business in this province and each branch of such corporation, doing business in this province over and above the number of one; (g) the Island Telephone Company Limited; (h) all oil and gas companies carrying on the business in this province of wholesale gasoline; (i) all corporations or persons not ordinarily resident in the province carrying on any construction trade in the province and employing therein one or more persons but the Lieutenant Governor in Council may reduce the license fee payable by any such corporation or person if it would appear to impose an undue hardship in proportion to the small amount of business transacted by the Company; (j) all other persons not hereinbefore specified who are not ordinarily resident in the province and whose chief place of business is located outside of the province, and who carry on business in the province; (k) all franchisees carrying on business in the province, and each branch of each franchise operated by the franchisee; (l) all other companies and corporations not hereinbefore specified which, not being incorporated under the laws of this province, and having their head office or chief place of business located outside of this province, carry on business in Prince Edward Island. Registry tel. no.: 902-368-4550	s. 6(2) Any corporation or person who is required by this Act to obtain a license and who neglects, omits or fails to do so for a period of one month, or whose license stands revoked for a period of one month, in addition to liability for payment of the l9icense fee, is liable to a penalty not exceeding $100 and costs, recoverable on summary conviction or by suite in a court of competent jurisdiction; a similar penalty is recoverable for each successive month during which the omission or revocation is continued. s. 7 Unless and until a corporation holds a license that is in force, it shall not be capable of bringing or maintaining any action, suit or other proceeding in any court in Prince Edward Island in respect to any contract made in whole or in part in Prince Edward Island in connection with any part of its business done or carried on in Prince Edward Island while it did not hold a license that was in force; but this section does not apply to any company incorporated by or under the authority of an Act of the Parliament of Canada, or by or under the authority of an Act of the Legislature of Prince Edward Island.

TABLE 10.1 CONTINUED

Province	Definition of carrying on business	Consequences of not registering
Newfoundland and Labrador *Corporations Act*, RSN 1990, c. C-36, as amended Register prior to commencing business (s. 433)	s. 431(2) For the purposes of this Part, an extra-provincial company is carrying on an undertaking in the province where (a) it holds title to land in the province or has an interest otherwise than by way of security in land; (b) it maintains an office, warehouse or place of business in the province; (c) it is licensed or registered or required to be licensed or registered under a law of the province that entitles it to do business or to sell securities of its own issue; (d) it is the holder of a certificate of registration issued under the Highway Traffic Act respecting a public service vehicle; or (e) in another manner it carries on an undertaking in the province. s. 431(3) For the purposes of subsection (2), where an extra-provincial company is listed with a number under the name of the extra-provincial company in a telephone directory published by a telephone company for use in this province, that extra-provincial company is presumed, in the absence of proof to the contrary, to be carrying on an undertaking in this province. Registry tel. no.: 709-729-3316	s. 452(1) An extra-provincial company, other than a federal company, that is not registered under this Act may not maintain an action, suit or other proceeding in a court in the province in respect of a contract made in whole or in part within the province in the course of or in connection with the carrying on of an undertaking by the company in the province. (2) Notwithstanding subsection (1), where an extra-provincial company, other than a federal company, described in that subsection becomes registered under this Act or has its registration restored, the company may then maintain an action, suit or other proceeding in respect of the contract described in subsection (1) as though it had never been disabled under that subsection whether or not the contract was made or proceeding instituted by the company before the date the company was registered or had its registration restored.
Yukon *Business Corporations Act*, RSYT 1986, c. 15, as amended Register before or within 30 days after it commences business (s. 277(2))	s. 275(1) … [A]n extra-territorial corporation carries on business in the Yukon if it transacts any of the ordinary business of an extra-territorial corporation whether or not the corporation has a resident agent or representative or a warehouse, office or place of business in the Yukon. s. 275(2) [T]he taking of orders by travellers for goods, wares or merchandise to be subsequently imported into the Yukon to fill such orders, or the buying or selling of such goods, wares or merchandise by correspondence, if the corporation has no resident agent or representative or a warehouse, office or place of business in the Yukon, shall be deemed not to be carrying on business. s. 276(1) This Part does not apply to an extra-territorial corporation required to be licensed as an insurer under the Insurance Act. (2) … to a Canada corporation so as to affect its right to carry on business in the Yukon. (3) … to an extra-territorial corporation required to be registered pursuant to the provisions of the *Societies Act* or the *Cooperative Associations Act*. Justice Services Division Corporate Affairs tel. no.: 867-667-5811	s. 296(1) [A]n extra-territorial corporation while unregistered is not capable of commencing or maintaining an action or other proceeding in any court in the Yukon in respect of any contract made in the course of carrying on business in the Yukon while it was unregistered. s. 296(2) [I]f an extra-territorial corporation was not registered at the time it commenced an action or proceeding referred ton in subsection (1) but becomes registered afterward, the action or proceeding may be maintained as if it had been registered before the commencement of the action or proceeding. *Penalty* s. 297(1) [A] person who contravenes this Part commits an offence and is liable to a fine of not more than $5,000. s. 297(2) [A] corporation, firm, broker or other person who acts as the agent or representative of, or in any other capacity, for an extra-territorial corporation which carries on business contrary to the requirements of this Part, commits an offence.

TABLE 10.1 CONCLUDED

Province	Definition of carrying on business	Consequences of not registering
Northwest Territories *Business Corporations Act,* SNWT 1996, c. 19 Register before or within 30 days after it commences business (s. 281(1))	s. 279 An extra-territorial corporation carries on business in the Northwest Territories if: its name, or any name under which it carries on business or operations, is listed in a telephone directory for any part of the Northwest Territories; its name, or any name under which it carries on business or operations, appears or is announced in any advertisement in which an address in the Northwest Territories is given for the extra-territorial corporation; it has a resident agent or representative or a warehouse, office or place of business or operations in the Northwest Territories; it solicits business in the Northwest Territories; it is the owner of any estate or interest in land in the Northwest Territories; it is licensed or registered or required to be licensed or registered under any Act of the Northwest Territories entitling it to do business or carry on operations; it otherwise carries on business or operations in the Northwest Territories. Companies Registry tel. no.: 867-873-7490	s. 298(1) [W]hile it is unregistered, an extra-territorial corporation is not capable of commencing or maintaining any action or other proceeding in any court in the Northwest Territories in respect of any contract made in the course of carrying on business in the Northwest Territories while it was unregistered. s. 298(2) [I]f an extra-territorial corporation was not registered at the time it commenced an action or proceeding referred to in subsection (1) but subsequently becomes registered, the action or proceeding may be maintained as if the extra-territorial corporation had been registered before the commencement of the action or proceeding. *Penalty* s. 299 A person who contravenes any provision of this Part is guilty of an offence and liable on summary conviction to a fine not exceeding $10,000.
Nunavut *Business Corporations Act,* SNWT 1998, c. 34 Register within 30 days of commencing business (s. 281)	s. 279 An extra-territorial corporation carries on business in Nunavut if: its name, or any name under which it carries on business or operations, is listed in a telephone directory for any part of Nunavut; its name, or any name under which it carries on business or operations, appears or is announced in any advertisement in which an address in Nunavut is given for the extra-territorial corporation; it has a resident agent or representative or a warehouse, office or place of business or operations in Nunavut; it solicits business in Nunavut; it is the owner of any estate or interest in land in Nunavut; it is licensed or registered or required to be licensed or registered under any Act of Nunavut entitling it to do business or carry on operations; it otherwise carries on business or operations in Nunavut Nunavut Regional Office tel. no.: 867-979-1605	s. 298(1) [W]hile it is unregistered, an extra-territorial corporation is not capable of commencing or maintaining any action or other proceeding in any court in Nunavut in respect of any contract made in the course of carrying on business in Nunavut while it was unregistered. s. 298(2) [I]f an extra-territorial corporation was not registered at the time it commenced an action or proceeding referred to in subsection (1) but subsequently becomes registered, the action or proceeding may be maintained as if the extra-territorial corporation had been registered before the commencement of the action or proceeding. *Penalty* s. 299 A person who contravenes any provision of this Part is guilty of an offence and liable on summary conviction to a fine not exceeding $10,000.

Ontario	Ministry of Consumer and Business Services	Companies and Personal Property Security Branch 393 University Ave Suite 200 Toronto ON M5G 2M2

Application for Extra-Provincial Licence
Form 1
Extra-Provincial Corporations Act

Instructions for Completing

FEE

The fee for an extra-provincial licence is $330.00, payable in Canadian funds. Cheques or money orders are to be made payable to the Minister of Finance. **Where a cheque is tendered in payment, the name of the corporation must be entered on the face of the cheque.** Do not send cash through the mail.

FORMAT

The application must be in **duplicate** in Form 1 prescribed in Ontario Regulations made under the Extra-Provincial Corporations Act. Applications which do not conform to Form 1 cannot be accepted and will be returned to the applicant submitting the application.

APPEARANCE OF DOCUMENTS

Applications and any supporting documents which are to be filed with the Ministry must be typewritten, or, if completed by hand, printed in BLOCK CAPITAL letters, and must be legible and compatible with microfilming process. Applications and supporting documents must be upon one side of good quality white bond paper 210 mm. x 297 mm. with a margin of 30 mm. on the left hand side or 8 1/2" x 11" with a margin of 1 1/4" on the left hand side. Documents which do not conform to this standard cannot be accepted and will be returned to the applicant submitting the application.

PAGES

The pages are numbered 1 to 3 and must remain in that order. Pages must not be removed. If any item is inapplicable, state "nil" or "not applicable".

Applications with missing pages will not be accepted and will be returned to the applicant.

SUPPLEMENTARY PAGES

If additional pages are required due to lack of sufficient space they must be the same size as all other pages, must have a margin of 30 mm. or 1 1/4" on the left hand side and must be numbered the same as the original with the addition of letters of the alphabet to indicate sequence. For example, supplementary pages for Item 9 would be numbered 2A, 2B, etc. See instructions for **Appearance of Documents.**

SUPPORTING DOCUMENTS

The application must be accompanied by:

a)   an **Appointment of Agent for Service** (Form 2);

b)   a **Certificate of Status** issued under the seal of office and signed by the proper officer (Director, Corporations Branch, etc) of the jurisdiction to which the corporation is subject, setting out the following:

   (i)   the name of the corporation;

   (ii)   date of incorporation/amalgamation or merger;

   (iii)   jurisdiction to which the corporation is subject;

   (iv)   that the corporation is a valid and subsisting corporation; and

c)   **the original NUANS name search report** (See instructions re: Corporate Name).

CORPORATE NAME

Prior to completing the application the officers of the corporation should satisfy themselves that the corporate name is available for use in Ontario. To do this the applicants must obtain from a private search house an **Ontario biased or weighted** NUANS computer printed search report on the name which is to be **cleared** by the Companies Branch of the Ministry. The names and addresses of private search houses are listed in the yellow pages of telephone directories under the heading "Searchers of Records".

The **original** NUANS report dated not more than 90 days before submission of the application must accompany the application. Failure to obtain the NUANS report, or submission of a stale dated report will delay processing of the application.

FIGURE 10.1   CONTINUED

APPLICATION

ITEM 1   The name of the corporation must be set out in BLOCK CAPITAL letters in the spaces provided and must commence on the first line in the first space.

ITEM 2   Set out in BLOCK CAPITAL letters the name **other than** the corporate name under which the corporation is to be licenced in Ontario. If not applicable, please state "none". If this Item is completed, a Form 2 under the Business Names Act must also be filed for the business name with the prescribed fee.

ITEM 3   State the jurisdiction to which the corporation is subject, for example, State of New York, U.S.A., etc.

ITEM 4   State the full date (year, month, day) on which the corporation came into existence either by incorporation, amalgamation or merger, as the case may be.

ITEM 5   The address (where multi-office building include room or suite number) of the head office of the corporation must be set out in full including the **postal/zip code.** Post office box is not an acceptable address for head office. The name of the State and Country must also be set out.

ITEM 6   The full date (year, month, day) on which the corporation was authorized to make the application must be set out.

ITEM 7   The address (where multi-office building, include room or suite number) of the chief place of business in Ontario (if determined) of the corporation must be set out in full including the **postal code.** Post office box is not an acceptable address for principal office. If none, state so.

ITEM 8   Set out one first name, initials and last name and full residence address or address for service (including suite number, if applicable) of the Chief Officer or Manager in Ontario (if determined).

ITEM 9   Set out the business which the corporation intends to carry on in Ontario.

ITEM 10 to 13 incl. must appear in all applications.

EXECUTION

Both copies of the application must be signed by an officer or a director of the corporation and the signatures must be original signatures and not photocopies. Applications containing photocopied signatures will not be accepted. The name of the corporation must be set out above the signature.

The corporate seal must be affixed to both copies of the application. If the jurisdiction to which the corporation is subject does not require its corporations to have a corporate seal, please so indicate when submitting the application.

The application (in duplicate), Appointment of Agent for Service and Consent to Act as Agent for Service (Form 2), together with the fee, Ontario biased NUANS computer printed search report and Certificate of Status should be mailed or delivered to:

> Ministry of Consumer and Business Services
> Companies and Personal Property Security Branch
> 393 University Ave Suite 200
> Toronto ON M5G 2M2

FIGURE 10.1 CONTINUED

Ontario Corporation Number
Numéro de la compagnie en Ontario

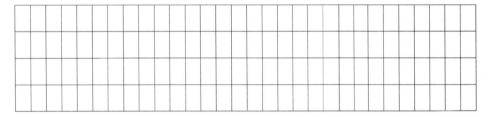

Form 1
Extra-
Provincial
Corporations
Act

Formule 1
*Loi de 1984
sur les
compagnies
extraprovinciales*

1.

APPLICATION FOR EXTRA-PROVINCIAL LICENCE/
DEMANDE EN VUE D'OBTENIR UN PERMIS EXTRAPROVINCIAL

1. The name of the Corporation is (Print in UPPER CASE ONLY) :
Dénomination sociale de la compagnie (Écrire en LETTRES MAJUSCULES SEULEMENT) :

| B | I | G | | B | A | D | | B | A | T | T | E | R | I | E | S | | C | O | R | P | . | | | | | |

2. Business name or style, other than the corporate name, under which the corporation is to be licensed in Ontario, if any (if none, state so): / Nom, autre que la dénomination sociale, sous lequel un permis doit être délivré à la compagnie en Ontario, le cas échéant (si ce n'est pas le cas, veuillez l'indiquer) :

3. Jurisdiction to which subject:/
Compétence législative :

Delaware, United States of America
_____
(Name of Province, State or Country) / (Province, État ou pays)

4. Date of incorporation/amalgamation:/
Date de la constitution ou de la fusion :

2003-08-15
_____
year / année   month / mois   day / jour

5. Full address of the head or registered office: / Adresse du siège social :

1234 Power Street
_____
(Street & Number or R.R. Number & if Multi-Office Building give Room No.) / (Rue et numéro ou numéro de la R.R. et numéro du bureau)

Jolt, Delaware
_____
(Name of Municipality or Post Office) / (Municipalité ou bureau de poste)

23435
Postal/Zip Code / Code postal/zip

United States of America
_____
(Name of State or Country) / (État ou pays)

6. The corporation has been authorized to make this application by a resolution passed by the directors of the corporation at a meeting held on: / La compagnie est autorisée à présenter cette demande au moyen d'une résolution adoptée par ses administrateurs le :

2003-09-10
_____
year / année   month / mois   day / jour

07065(01/2002)

FIGURE 10.1   CONTINUED

7. **Full address** (including postal code) of the principal office or chief place of business in Ontario, if determined (if not, state so): / Adresse de l'établissement principal en Ontario, si elle est établie (si ce n'est pas le cas, l'indiquer) : 2.

N/A
_____

(Street & Number or R.R. Number & if Multi-Office Building give Room No.) / (Rue et numéro ou numéro de la R.R. et numéro du bureau)

_____

(Name of Municipality or Post Office) / (Municipalité ou bureau de poste)   Postal/Zip Code / Code postal/zip

8. Chief officer or manager in Ontario, if determined (if none, state so): /
   Premier dirigeant ou gérant en Ontario, s'il est désigné (si ce n'est pas le cas, l'indiquer) :

Name in full, including all first and middle names / Nom et prénoms	Residence address, giving Street & No. or R.R. No. & Municipality or Post Office and Postal Code: / Adresse personnelle y compris la rue et le numéro ou le numéro de la R.R., et le nom de la municipalité ou du bureau de poste et le code postal
N/A	

9. The business which the corporation intends to carry on in Ontario is: /
   Les activités commerciales que la compagnie entend exercer en Ontario sont les suivantes :

Distribution of batteries.

07065(01/2002)

FIGURE 10.1 CONCLUDED

3.

10. The corporate existence of the corporation is not limited in any way by statute or otherwise and the corporation is a valid and subsisting corporation. / La personnalité morale de la compagnie n'est restreinte d'aucune manière notamment par l'effet de la loi et la compagnie conserve sa validité et son existence juridique.

11. The corporation has the capacity to carry on business in Ontario. / La compagnie est habilitée à exercer ses activités commerciales en Ontario.

12. The corporation has the capacity to hold land without conditions or limitations. / La compagnie est habilitée à posséder des biens-fonds sans condition ni restriction.

13. The corporation hereby acknowledges that upon the licence being issued the corporation shall be subject to the provisions of the Extra-Provincial Corporations Act, the Corporations Information Act, the Corporations Tax Act and to such further and other legislative provisions as the Legislature of Ontario may deem expedient in order to secure the due management of the corporation's affairs and the protection of its creditors within Ontario. / La compagnie reconnaît par la présente que dès la délivrance du permis, elle sera assujettie aux dispositions de la *Loi sur les compagnies extraprovinciales*, de la Loi sur les renseignements exigés des compagnies et associations, de la *Loi sur l'imposition des personnes morales* ainsi qu'aux autres dispositions législatives ultérieures que la Législature de l'Ontario peut juger opportunes afin d'assurer la saine gestion des affaires de la compagnie et la protection de ses créanciers en Ontario.

This application is executed in duplicate. / La présente demande est signée en double exemplaire.

BIG BAD BATTERIES CORP.
_____
(Name of Corporation) / (Dénomination sociale de la compagnie)

By: / Signé : *Katherine Smith-Power*
_____
(Signature) / (Signature)

President
_____
(Description of Office) / (Fonctions)

(Corporate Seal) / (Sceau de la compagnie)

07065(01/2002)

 **Ontario**

Ministry of
Consumer and
Business Services

Companies and Personal
Property Security Branch
393 University Ave Suite 200
Toronto ON M5G 2M2

**Appointment of Agent for Service/
Revised Appointment of Agent for
Service**
Form 2
Extra-Provincial Corporations Act

INSTRUCTIONS FOR COMPLETING

FEES

There is no fee payable for filing an Appointment of Agent for Service/Revised Appointment of Agent for Service.

FORMAT OF DOCUMENTS

The Appointment of Agent for Service or Revised Appointment of Agent for Service must be in Form 2 prescribed by Ontario Regulations made under the *Extra-Provincial Corporations Act.*

GENERAL

An Agent for Service must be a natural person 18 years of age or older, having his/her residence in the Province of Ontario or a corporation (other than the applicant) having its registered office in the Province of Ontario.

Where the Agent is a corporation, the Consent to Act as Agent for Service shall be executed in the name of the corporation under the signature of an officer or a director of the corporation which is to act as the agent.

All information must be typewritten or, if completed by hand, be printed in BLOCK CAPITAL letters. All documents filed with the Branch are microfilmed and must therefore be neat, legible and suitable for microfilming. Documents which do not conform to this standard will be returned to the corporation. We recommend the form be completed using heavy black typewriter ribbon or black pen.

ONTARIO CORPORATION NUMBER

"Ontario Corporation Number" appears in the top right corner of the extra-provincial licence issued to the corporation. Where a Revised Appointment of Agent for Service is prepared, the Ontario corporation number must be set out by the appointing corporation.

EXECUTION STATEMENT

The form must be in duplicate and both copies must have original signatures.

The **Original** Appointment or **Revised** Appointment is to be mailed or delivered to:

Ministry of Consumer and Business Services
Companies and Personal Property Security Branch
393 University Ave Suite 200
Toronto ON M5G 2M2

07064(01/2002)

(en français au verso)

FIGURE 10.2 CONCLUDED

| Form 2
Extra-Provincial
Corporations
Act

Formule 2
Loi sur les
personnes morales
extraprovinciales | Check **(X)** the
appropriate box
Cochez **(X)** la
case appropriée | [X] APPOINTMENT OF AGENT FOR SERVICE
DÉSIGNATION DU MANDATAIRE AUX FINS DE SIGNIFICATION
or / ou
[ ] REVISED APPOINTMENT OF AGENT FOR SERVICE
MODIFICATION DE LA DÉSIGNATION DE MANDATAIRE | Ontario Corporation Number
Numéro de la société en Ontario

2222222 | 1. |

Big Bad Batteries Corp.
_____
(Name of appointing corporation) / (Dénomination sociale de la société désignant le mandataire)
(hereinafter called the "Corporation") hereby nominates, constitutes and appoints / (ci-après appelée la «société») constitue

Richard Thorn
_____
(Name of agent giving first name, initials and surname; or full Corporate Name)
(Mandataire : prénom, initiale et nom de famille; ou dénomination sociale complète)

| Thorn & Hill LLP, 151 All Park Drive, Toronto, ON | M7V 5K8 |

(Business address of the agent, including Street Number, Suite or Room Number and Municipality) — Postal/Zip Code /
(Adresse d'affaires du mandataire : numéro et rue, bureau et municipalité) — *Code postal/zip*

its true and lawful agent for service, to act as such, and as such to sue and be sued, plead and be impleaded in any court in Ontario and generally on behalf of the corporation within Ontario to accept service of process and to receive all lawful notices and, for the purposes of the corporation, to do all acts and to execute all deeds and other instruments relating to the matters within the scope of this appointment. Until due lawful notice of the appointment of another and subsequent agent has been given to and accepted by the Director under the *Extra-Provincial Corporations Act*, service of process or of papers and notices upon the said agent for service shall be accepted by the corporation as sufficient service.

son mandataire aux fins de signification, qui agira en cette qualité, soutiendra à titre de demandeur ou de défendeur les actions en justice intentées en Ontario et, de manière générale, recevra et acceptera en Ontario, au nom de la société, tous actes de procédure et tous avis requis ou autorisés par la loi, accomplira toutes actions et signera tous actes et autres instruments relativement aux affaires entrant dans le cadre du présent mandat. Tant qu'un avis en bonne et due forme visant à désigner un autre mandataire n'aura pas été donné au directeur et accepté par lui, conformément à la Loi sur les personnes morales extraprovinciales, la société accepte comme suffisante la signification au mandataire susmentionné desdits actes de procédure, avis et autres documents.

| Dated / *Date* | 2003 | September | 10 |
| | year / *année* | month / *mois* | day / *jour* |

Big Bad Batteries Corp.
_____
(Name of Corporation / *Dénomination sociale de la société*)

BY:
PAR: *Katherine Smith-Power*   President
_____ _____
(Signature)   (Description of Office / *Titre*)

(Corporate Seal)
(Sceau de la société)
_____ _____
(Signature)   (Description of Office / *Titre*)

CONSENT TO ACT AS AGENT FOR SERVICE
CONSENTEMENT À AGIR EN QUALITÉ DE MANDATAIRE AUX FINS DE SIGNIFICATION

I
Je soussigné(e), _____ Richard Thorn _____
(Name of Agent in full; if Corporation, full Corporate Name)
(Nom complet du mandataire; si personne morale, dénomination sociale complète)

of
dont l'adresse   Thorn & Hill LLP, 151 All Park Drive, Toronto
d'affaires est : _____
(Business address including Street Number, Suite or Room Number and Municipality)
(Adresse d'affaires : numéro et rue, numéro du bureau et municipalité)

Ontario, hereby consent to act as the agent for service in the Province of Ontario of
en Ontario, consens par les présentes à agir, dans la Province de l'Ontario, en qualité de mandataire aux fins de signification de

Big Bad Batteries Corp.
_____
(Name of Corporation / *Dénomination sociale de la société*)

pursuant to the appointment executed by the said corporation on the
en vertu du présent mandat que ladite société a signé le

| 10th | day of / *jour de* | September | , year / *année* | 2003 | ; |

authorizing me to accept service of process and notices on its behalf
ledit mandat m'autorise à recevoir et à accepter au nom de la société tous actes de procédure, avis et autres documents.

| Dated / *Date* | 2003 | September | 10 |
| | year / *année* | month / *mois* | day / *jour* |

Jessie Bruton[X]   *Richard Thorn*[X]
_____   _____
(Signature of witness /   (Signature of the consenting person or Officer/Director of Corporation) /
Signature du témoin)   *(Signature du mandataire; si personne morale, signature du dirigeant/*
           administrateur agissant en son nom)

07064(01/2002)

FIGURE 10.3   FORM 2, CORPORATIONS INFORMATION ACT, INITIAL RETURN

Ⓥ **Ontario**

Ministry of Consumer and Business Services

Ministère des Services aux consommateurs et aux entreprises

Companies and Personal Property Security Branch
393 University Ave, Suite 200
Toronto ON M5G 2M2

Direction des compagnies et des sûretés mobilières
393, av. University, bureau 200
Toronto ON M5G 2M2

Page 1/Page 1

FORM 2- EXTRA PROVINCIAL CORPORATIONS/
FORMULE 2 - PERSONNES MORALES EXTRA-PROVINCIALES
Please type or print all information in block capital letters using black ink.
Prière de dactylographier les renseignements ou de les écrire en caractères d'imprimerie à l'encre noire.

INITIAL RETURN/NOTICE OF CHANGE /
Corporations Information Act
RAPPORT INITIAL/AVIS DE MODIFICATION
Loi sur les renseignements exigés des personnes morales

For Ministry Use Only À l'usage du ministère seulement	2. Ontario Corporation Number Numéro matricule de la personne morale en Ontario	3. Date of Incorporation or Amalgamation Date de constitution, ou fusion			1.	Initial Return Rapport initial	Notice of Change Avis de modification
	2222222	Year/Année	Month/Mois	Day/Jour	Business Corporations/ Société par actions Not-For-Profit Corporation/ Personne morale sans but lucratif	✔	
		2000	08	18			

4. Corporation Name Including Punctuation/Raison sociale de la personne morale, y compris la ponctuation

BIG BAD BATTERIES CORP.

For Ministry Use Only
À l'usage du ministère seulement

5. Address of Registered or Head Office/Adresse du siège social

c/o / a/s

For Ministry Use Only
À l'usage du ministère seulement

Street No./N° civique	Street Name/Nom de la rue	Suite/Bureau
1234	POWER STREET	

Street Name (cont'd)/Nom de la rue (suite)

City/Town/Ville	Province, State/Province, État
JOLT	DELAWARE
Country/Pays	Postal Code/Code postal
UNITED STATES OF AMERICA	23435

6. Address of Principal Office in Ontario/Adresse du bureau principal en Ontario
Street No./N° civique

Same as Above/ Même que celle ci-dessus

✔ Not Applicable/ Ne s'applique pas

Street Name/Nom de la rue   Suite/Bureau

Street Name (cont'd)/Nom de la rue (suite)

City/Town/Ville   ONTARIO, CANADA

Postal Code/Code postal

7. Language of Preference
Langue préférée

English/Anglais ✔   French/Français

8. Former Corporation Name if applicable/Raison sociale antérieure de la personne morale, le cas échéant.

✔ Not Applicable
Ne s'applique pas

9. Date commenced business activity in Ontario/ Date de début des activités en Ontario	10. Date ceased carrying on business activity in Ontario/ Date de cessation des activités en Ontario
Year/Année Month/Mois Day/Jour	Year/Année Month/Mois Day/Jour Not Applicable/ Ne s'applique pas
2003 11 05	

11. Jurisdiction of Incorporation/Amalgamation or Continuation. (Check appropriate box) Do not check more than one box.
Ressort de constitution/de fusion ou prorogation (cocher la case pertinente). Ne cocher qu'une seule case.

1. ALBERTA ALBERTA	2. CANADA CANADA	3. NEW BRUNSWICK NOUVEAU-BRUNSWICK	4. NOVA SCOTIA NOUVELLE-ÉCOSSE	5. QUEBEC QUÉBEC	6. YUKON YUKON	7. BRITISH COLUMBIA COLOMBIE-BRITANNIQUE
8. MANITOBA MANITOBA	9. NEWFOUNDLAND TERRE-NEUVE	10. PRINCE EDWARD ISLAND ÎLE-DU-PRINCE-ÉDOUARD	11. SASKATCHEWAN SASKATCHEWAN	12. NORTHWEST TERRITORIES TERRITOIRES DU NORD-OUEST		13. NUNAVUT NUNAVUT

If other please specify /
Si autre, veuillez préciser

DELAWARE, UNITED STATES OF AMERICA

This information is being collected under the authority of The Corporations Information Act for the purpose of maintaining a public data base of corporate information. /
La Loi sur les renseignements exigés des personnes morales autorise la collecte de ces renseignements pour constituer une banque de données accessible au public.

FOR MINISTRY USE ONLY/À L'USAGE DU MINISTÈRE   See deficiency letter enclosed/Voir l'avis d'insuffisance ci-joint

07201 (02/2002)

FIGURE 10.3 CONCLUDED

FORM 2 - EXTRA PROVINCIAL CORPORATIONS/
FORMULE 2 - PERSONNES MORALES EXTRA-PROVINCIALES

Page 2/Page 2

Please type or print all information in block capital letters using black ink.
Prière de dactylographier les renseignements ou de les écrire en caractères d'imprimerie à l'encre noire.

FOR MINISTRY USE ONLY À L'USAGE DU MINISTÈRE SEULEMENT	Ontario Corporation Number/ Numéro matricule de la personne morale en Ontario	Date of Incorporation or Amalgamation Date de constitution ou fusion Year/Année Month/Mois Day/Jour	For Ministry Use Only À l'usage du ministère seulement
	2222222	2000 08 18	

12. Name and Office Address of the Chief Officer/Manager in Ontario/
Nom et adresse du bureau du directeur général/gérant en Ontario

✔ Not Applicable/Ne s'applique pas

Last Name/Nom de famille   First Name/Prénom   Middle Name/Autres prénoms

Street Number/Numéro civique

Street Name/Nom de la rue

Street Name (cont'd)/Nom de la rue (suite)   Suite/Bureau

City/Town/Ville   Postal Code/Code postal

ONTARIO, CANADA

Date Effective / Date d'entrée en vigueur   Year/Année Month/Mois Day/Jour

Date Ceased / Date de cessation des fonctions   Year/Année Month/Mois Day/Jour

13. Name and Office Address of Agent for Service in Ontario - Check One box
Nom et adresse du bureau du mandataire aux fins de signification en Ontario. Cocher la case pertinente.

☐ Not Applicable/Ne s'applique pas

Only applies to foreign business corporations
S'applique seulement aux personnes morales étrangères

a) ✔ Individual or un particulier ou   b) ☐ Corporation une personne morale

Complete appropriate sections below/Remplir les parties pertinentes ci-dessous.

a) Individual Name/Nom du particulier

Last Name/Nom de famille   First Name/Prénom   Middle Name/Autres prénoms
THORN   RICHARD

b) Ontario Corporation Number/Numéro matricule de la personne morale en Ontario

Corporation Name including punctuation/Raison sociale, y compris la ponctuation

c) Address/Adresse

c/o / a/s
THORN & HILL LLP

Street No./N° civique   Street Name/Nom de la rue   Suite/Bureau
151   ALL PARK DRIVE

Street Name (cont'd)/Nom de la rue (suite)   City/Town/Ville
TORONTO

ONTARIO, CANADA   Postal Code/Code postal
M7V 5K8

14. (Print or type name in full of the person authorizing filing./ Dactylographier ou inscrire le prénom et le nom en caractères d'imprimerie de la personne qui autorise l'enregistrement.

Check appropriate box /
Cocher la case pertinente

D) ☐ Director/Administrateur

I/ Je   RICHARD THORN

O) ☐ Officer/Dirigeant

certify that the information set out herein, is true and correct.
atteste que les renseignements précités sont véridiques et exacts.

P) ✔ Other individual having knowledge of the affairs of the Corporation/Autre personne ayant connaissance des activités de la personne morale

NOTE/REMARQUE: Section 13 and 14 of the **Corporations Information Act** provide penalties for making false or misleading statements, or omissions.
Les articles 13 et 14 de la **Loi sur les renseignements exigés des personnes morales** prévoient des peines en cas de déclaration fausse ou trompeuse, ou d'omission.

This information is being collected under the authority of The Corporations Information Act for the purpose of maintaining a public data base of corporate information. /
La Loi sur les renseignements exigés des personnes morales autorise la collecte de ces renseignements pour constituer une banque de données accessible au public.

FOR MINISTRY USE ONLY/À L'USAGE DU MINISTÈRE   ☐ See deficiency letter enclosed/Voir l'avis d'insuffisance ci-joint

07201 (02/2002)

CERTIFIED COPY OF

RESOLUTIONS OF THE BOARD OF DIRECTORS

OF

BIG BAD BATTERIES CORP.

(the "Corporation")

"EXTRA-PROVINCIAL REGISTRATION

RESOLVED that:

1.   The Corporation be authorized to make such application and to file such documents as may be necessary or desirable to extra-provincially register the Corporation in the Province of Ontario, Canada, pursuant to the *Extra-Provincial Corporations Act*; and

2.   Katherine Smith-Power, President of the Corporation, be authorized and directed to take such action and to sign such documents, whether under the corporate seal or otherwise, as may be necessary or desirable to effect the extra-provincial registration contemplated by this resolution.

EXTRA-PROVINCIAL AGENT FOR SERVICE

RESOLVED that in connection with the extra-provincial registration of the Corporation, Richard Thorn, of Thorn & Hill LLP be appointed as the Agent for Service to act for and on behalf of the Corporation in the province of Ontario."

THE UNDERSIGNED, being the President of the Corporation, certifies the foregoing to be true and correct copy of a resolution of the board directors of the Corporation passed as of the 10th day of September, 2003, and that the forgoing is in full force and effect, unamended, as of the date hereof.

DATED the 10th day of September, 2003.

_____

Katherine Smith-Power

President

Direct line: 416-415-5555
E-mail:: rthorn@thornhill.ca

November 15, 2003

Big Bad Batteries Corp.
1234 Power Street
Jolt, Delaware
U.S.A.   23435

Attention: Katherine Smith-Power, President

Dear Mr. Hill:

Re: Big Bad Batteries Corp. (the "Corporation") – Extra-Provincial Licence in Ontario

We are pleased to report to you on the completion of the extra-provincial licensing of the Corporation in the Province of Ontario.

Issuance of Extra-Provincial Licence

The Director under the *Extra-Provincial Corporations Act* (Ontario) (the "Act") issued an Extra-Provincial Licence to the Corporation pursuant to the provisions of the Act effective on November 5, 2003 (the "Licence").

The Corporation is authorized to carry on in Ontario the business specified in the Licence.

The original copy of the Licence is enclosed for retention with the corporate records of the Corporation. We have maintained a copy for our files

Amendments to Licence

The Corporation is required under the Act to make an application for an amended licence where:

(a)   it has changed its name; or

(b)   it has continued under the laws of another jurisdiction.

FIGURE 10.5   CONTINUED

Termination of Licence

The Act provides that where the Corporation has not carried on any of its business in Ontario for any two consecutive years, it shall make application for termination of its Licence. If it does not do so, the Director appointed under the Act, upon giving the Corporation an opportunity to be heard, may by order cancel the Licence.

Agent for Service

The Corporation is required to ensure the continuing appointment, at all times, of an agent for service in Ontario on whom service of process, notices or other proceedings may be made.

The name and address of the existing agent for service is:

> Richard Thorn
> 151 All Park Drive
> Toronto, Ontario
> M7V 5K8

A duplicate filed copy of the Appointment of Agent for Service is also enclosed.

Our annual fee for acting as agent for service is $250 which fee includes the preparation and filing of the annual return.

Where the name, address or any other particular set out in the Appointment of Agent for Service changes or where an agent is substituted, the Corporation is required to file a revised appointment.

Initial Return

Under the *Corporations Information Act* (Ontario), the Corporation is required to file with the Minister of Consumer and Business Services an Initial Return within 60 days after the date the corporation begins to carry on business in Ontario, setting out certain basic corporate information including the name of the jurisdiction in which the corporation was formed, registered office address, principal place of business address, if any, the name and office address of the corporation's chief officer or manager in Ontario, if any, and name and address of its agent for service in Ontario.

The Initial Return for the Corporation was filed on November 5, 2003. A duplicate filed copy is enclosed for your records.

A Notice of Change (Form 2) of any information filed in the Initial Return must be filed within 15 days after the change takes place.

The Corporation must maintain an up-to-date paper or electronic record of the prescribed information set out in any return filed and make it available to any shareholder, director, officer

FIGURE 10.5 CONCLUDED

Page 3

or creditor of the Corporation during its normal business hours at its registered office or principal place of business in Ontario.

Annual Return

The Corporation is required to file a return each year with the Minister of Consumer and Business Services either by delivering the return to the Minister of Finance or by delivering it to the Minister of Consumer and Business Services. The return must be filed, in the case where a tax return is required, within the time period for delivery of the tax return, or where no tax return is required under the *Corporations Tax Act,* within six months of its financial year end.

Penalties for Non-Compliance

The Act and the CIA have penalties for non-compliance. These penalties include the inability of a corporation to maintain any action or other proceeding in any court in Ontario in respect of any contract made by the corporation and monetary penalties payable on conviction by a corporation and its directors, officers and the representative of the corporation in Ontario.

If you have any questions with respect to the foregoing or if we can be of further assistance, please do not hesitate to contact the writer.

Yours truly,

Richard Thorn

Copy to: Jessie Bruton

Ontario

Ministry of Consumer and Business Services	Ministère des Services aux consommateurs et aux entreprises	Companies and Personal Property Security Branch 393 University Ave, Suite 200 Toronto ON M5G 2M2	Direction des compagnies et des sûretés mobilières 393, av. University, bureau 200 Toronto ON M5G 2M2	Page 1/Page 1

FORM 2- EXTRA PROVINCIAL CORPORATIONS/
FORMULE 2 - PERSONNES MORALES EXTRA-PROVINCIALES
Please type or print all information in block capital letters using black ink.
Prière de dactylographier les renseignements ou de les écrire en caractères
d'imprimerie à l'encre noire.

INITIAL RETURN/NOTICE OF CHANGE /
Corporations Information Act
RAPPORT INITIAL/AVIS DE MODIFICATION
Loi sur les renseignements exigés des personnes morales

For Ministry Use Only À l'usage du ministère seulement	2. Ontario Corporation Number Numéro matricule de la personne morale en Ontario	3. Date of Incorporation or Amalgamation Date de constitution, ou fusion		1. Business Corporations/ Société par actions Not-For-Profit Corporation/ Personne morale sans but lucratif	Initial Return Rapport initial	Notice of Change Avis de modification
		Year/Année Month/Mois Day/Jour	2003 12 24		✔	

4. Corporation Name Including Punctuation/Raison sociale de la personne morale, y compris la ponctuation

BSJ GARDEN ORNAMENT SALES INC.

For Ministry Use Only
À l'usage du ministère seulement

5. Address of Registered or Head Office/Adresse du siège social
c/o / a/s

For Ministry Use Only
À l'usage du ministère seulement

Street No./N° civique	Street Name/Nom de la rue	Suite/Bureau
123	SESAME STREET	

Street Name (cont'd)/Nom de la rue (suite)

City/Town/Ville	Province, State/Province, État
PORT ELLEN	ONTARIO

Country/Pays	Postal Code/Code postal
CANADA	L3R 0C9

6. Address of Principal Office in Ontario/Adresse du bureau principal en Ontario
Street No./N° civique

✔ Same as Above/
Même que celle ci-dessus

☐ Not Applicable/
Ne s'applique pas

Street Name/Nom de la rue   Suite/Bureau

Street Name (cont'd)/Nom de la rue (suite)

City/Town/Ville

ONTARIO, CANADA

Postal Code/Code postal

7. Language of Preference   English/Anglais   French/Français
Langue préférée   ✔

8. Former Corporation Name if applicable/Raison sociale antérieure de la personne morale, le cas échéant.

✔ Not Applicable
Ne s'applique pas

9. Date commenced business activity in Ontario/ Date de début des activités en Ontario	10. Date ceased carrying on business activity in Ontario/ Date de cessation des activités en Ontario
Year/Année Month/Mois Day/Jour 2003 12 24	Year/Année Month/Mois Day/Jour Not Applicable/ Ne s'applique pas

11. Jurisdiction of Incorporation/Amalgamation or Continuation. (Check appropriate box) Do not check more than one box.
Ressort de constitution/de fusion ou prorogation (cocher la case pertinente). Ne cocher qu'une seule case.

1. ☐ ALBERTA ALBERTA	2. ✔ CANADA CANADA	3. ☐ NEW BRUNSWICK NOUVEAU-BRUNSWICK	4. ☐ NOVA SCOTIA NOUVELLE-ÉCOSSE	5. ☐ QUEBEC QUÉBEC	6. ☐ YUKON YUKON	7. ☐ BRITISH COLUMBIA COLOMBIE-BRITANNIQUE
8. ☐ MANITOBA MANITOBA	9. ☐ NEWFOUNDLAND TERRE-NEUVE	10. ☐ PRINCE EDWARD ISLAND ÎLE-DU-PRINCE-ÉDOUARD	11. ☐ SASKATCHEWAN SASKATCHEWAN	12. ☐ NORTHWEST TERRITORIES TERRITOIRES DU NORD-OUEST	13. ☐ NUNAVUT NUNAVUT	

If other please specify /
Si autre, veuillez préciser

This information is being collected under the authority of The Corporations Information Act for the purpose of maintaining a public data base of corporate information. /
La Loi sur les renseignements exigés des personnes morales autorise la collecte de ces renseignements pour constituer une banque de données accessible au public.

FOR MINISTRY USE ONLY/À L'USAGE DU MINISTÈRE   ☐ See deficiency letter enclosed/Voir l'avis d'insuffisance ci-joint

07201 (02/2002)

FIGURE 10.6 CONCLUDED

FORM 2 - EXTRA PROVINCIAL CORPORATIONS/
FORMULE 2 - PERSONNES MORALES EXTRA-PROVINCIALES

Please type or print all information in block capital letters using black ink.
Prière de dactylographier les renseignements ou de les écrire en caractères d'imprimerie à l'encre noire.

FOR MINISTRY USE ONLY À L'USAGE DU MINISTÈRE SEULEMENT	Ontario Corporation Number/ Numéro matricule de la personne morale en Ontario	Date of Incorporation or Amalgamation Date de constitution ou fusion Year/Année Month/Mois Day/Jour	For Ministry Use Only À l'usage du ministère seulement
		2003 12 24	

12. Name and Office Address of the Chief Officer/Manager in Ontario/
Nom et adresse du bureau du directeur général/gérant en Ontario   ✔ Not Applicable/Ne s'applique pas

Last Name/Nom de famille   First Name/Prénom   Middle Name/Autres prénoms

Street Number/Numéro civique

Street Name/Nom de la rue

Street Name (cont'd)/Nom de la rue (suite)   Suite/Bureau

City/Town/Ville   Postal Code/Code postal

ONTARIO, CANADA

Date Effective   Year/Année Month/Mois Day/Jour   Date Ceased   Year/Année Month/Mois Day/Jour
Date d'entrée en vigueur   Date de cessation
                                                               des fonctions

13. Name and Office Address of Agent for Service in Ontario - Check One box
Nom et adresse du bureau du mandataire aux fins de signification en Ontario. Cocher la case pertinente.

✔ Not Applicable/Ne s'applique pas

> Only applies to foreign business corporations
> S'applique seulement aux personnes morales étrangères

a) ☐ Individual or   b) ☐ Corporation
   un particulier ou   une personne morale
Complete appropriate sections below/Remplir les parties pertinentes ci-dessous.

a) Individual Name/Nom du particulier

Last Name/Nom de famille   First Name/Prénom   Middle Name/Autres prénoms

b) Ontario Corporation Number/Numéro matricule de la personne morale en Ontario

Corporation Name including punctuation/Raison sociale, y compris la ponctuation

c) Address/Adresse

c/o / a/s

Street No./N° civique   Street Name/Nom de la rue   Suite/Bureau

Street Name (cont'd)/Nom de la rue (suite)   City/Town/Ville

                          Postal Code/Code postal
ONTARIO, CANADA

14. (Print or type name in full of the person authorizing filing./ Dactylographier ou
inscrire le prénom et le nom en caractères d'imprimerie de la personne qui
autorise l'enregistrement.

Check appropriate box /
Cocher la case pertinente

D) ✔ Director/Administrateur

I /
Je   PETER BLACK   O) ☐ Officer/Dirigeant

certify that the information set out herein, is true and correct.   P) ☐ Other individual having knowledge of the affairs
atteste que les renseignements précités sont véridiques et exacts.   of the Corporation/Autre personne ayant
                                                                             connaissance des activités de la personne morale

NOTE/REMARQUE: Section 13 and 14 of the **Corporations Information Act** provide penalties for making false or misleading statements, or omissions.
Les articles 13 et 14 de la **Loi sur les renseignements exigés des personnes morales** prévoient des peines en cas de déclaration fausse ou trompeuse, ou d'omission.

This information is being collected under the authority of The Corporations Information Act for the purpose of maintaining a public data base of corporate information. /
La Loi sur les renseignements exigés des personnes morales autorise la collecte de ces renseignements pour constituer une banque de données accessible au public.

FOR MINISTRY USE ONLY/À L'USAGE DU MINISTÈRE   ☐ See deficiency letter enclosed/Voir l'avis d'insuffisance ci-joint

07201 (02/2002)

CHAPTER 11

Preparing for directors' and shareholders' meetings

CHAPTER OVERVIEW

This chapter discusses meetings of directors and shareholders. It explains when directors and shareholders may be required to hold meetings, such as after incorporation, annually, and for any special business; outlines the statutory rules for calling and holding meetings; and reviews the alternatives to meetings, including electronic meetings and signed resolutions. It identifies the contents of a notice calling a meeting and the documents required to accompany the notice. Finally, it discusses the organization at the meeting, including who may attend, the residency requirements for directors' meetings, who will act as chair and secretary, and voting.

CHAPTER OBJECTIVES

After completing this chapter, you should be able to:

1. Identify when a directors' or shareholders' meeting is required or when signed resolutions are appropriate.

2. Draft notices of meetings, waivers of meetings, minutes of meetings, and proxies for meetings.

3. Relate the proper procedures for calling and conducting meetings, including electronic voting.

INTRODUCTION

As discussed in chapter 4, directors and shareholders can conduct their business and arrive at decisions by way of meetings. The provisions relating to the calling of and conduct at meetings are generally contained in the corporation's bylaws or in a unanimous shareholder agreement. It is rare, though possible, that such provisions will be contained in the corporation's articles.

Also important for the conduct of meetings are rules of order, which have their origin in British parliamentary procedure. Rules of order are intended to deal with conflict situations arising at meetings and the making, seconding, amending, withdrawing, and voting on of motions made at meetings. The most popular books on rules of order for company meetings are *Wainberg and Nathan's Company Meetings Including Rules of Order*, 5th ed., and *Robert's Rules of Order*. There are also more modern publications relating to rules of order for "productive" meetings, such as *Meyer's Rules of Order*. According to Dean Meyer, "*Robert's Rules of Order* made an immense contribution to the effectiveness of legislative processes. But the book was not designed for modern business meetings." Although *Robert's* and *Wainberg's* are the classic texts on rules of order, some clients may prefer more modern standards, such as *Meyer's*.

In addition to rules of order and provisions in the *Canada Business Corporations Act* (CBCA) and the Ontario *Business Corporations Act* (OBCA), common law and case law also have an impact on procedures and influence statutory provisions regarding meetings.

It is particularly important to be aware of the statutory provisions affecting meetings. They allow you to identify deficiencies during minute book due diligence and to correctly prepare documents for calling meetings and recording the business that takes place at meetings.

Table 11.1 provides a summary of the important statutory provisions regarding meetings. A complete discussion of the various provisions follows.

DIRECTORS' MEETINGS

Clients often pose the question, "From a legal perspective, what items of business do directors need to pass resolutions for?" There are several occasions when the directors will want to meet to conduct the business of the corporation. After the post-incorporation organizational meetings, a board of directors may decide to meet on a regular basis — such as monthly, quarterly, or annually — to discuss and make decisions about the operation of the business. There may be special situations in which directors will meet to conduct business such as to declare dividends, fill a vacancy of a retired director or officer, make or amend bylaws, issue shares, authorize a significant purchase or sale, or authorize a bank loan.

Directors are required to call an annual meeting of shareholders of the corporation and to approve the corporation's financial statements before they are distributed to the shareholders. Immediately after an annual meeting, the newly elected directors meet to appoint officers and committee members.

Directors can also conduct business by way of signed resolutions instead of meeting in person. In addition, directors may participate in an **electronic meeting**

electronic meeting
a meeting conducted by telephonic or other electronic means that allows all participants in the meeting to communicate fully

TABLE 11.1 Statutory provisions affecting meetings

Topic	Directors' meetings		Shareholders' meetings	
	CBCA section	OBCA section	CBCA section	OBCA section
Place of meetings	114(1)	126(1)	132(1)	93(1)
Quorum	114(2)	126(3)	139	101
Transacting business	114(3)	126(6)	None	97
	114(4)	126(7)		
Shareholder requisition of meeting	N/A	N/A	143	105
Shareholder proposal	N/A	N/A	137	99
Calling meeting	114(1)	117(4)	133	94
	104(3)	126(8)		
Notice	114(1)	126(9)	135	96
	114(5)	262	253	262
Electronic notice	252.4	None	252.3	None
Waiver of notice	114(6)	126(10)	136	98
	255	264	255	264
Adjourned meeting	114(7)	126(11)	135(4)	96(3), (4)
One director/ shareholder meeting ...	114(8)	126(12)	139(4)	101(4)
Meeting held by telephone or electronic means	114(9)	126(13)	132(4), (5) Reg. s. 45	94(2)
Consent to participation by telephone or electronic means in Meeting	N/A	N/A	132(4), (5)	None
Place of telephone meeting	None	126(14)	None	93(2)
Consent of director to business at meeting	123(1)	135	N/A	N/A
Record date for receiving notice of shareholder meeting ...	N/A	N/A	134	95(2)
Entitlement to vote at meeting	N/A	N/A	140	102
Chairman's casting vote	N/A	N/A	N/A	97(a)
Voting by proxy	N/A	N/A	148(1)	110(1)
Authority for written resolutions in lieu of meetings	117	129	142	104

that is conducted by telephone or other electronic means, as long as all participants in the meeting can communicate fully.

Calling a meeting of directors

Before preparing the notice of a meeting, you will need to review the corporation's bylaws to determine who has the authority to call the meeting. This will be the person, or persons, who "sign" the notice. It is customary to send out photocopies of the signed notice rather than originally signed copies.

If the bylaws do not specify who has the authority to call a meeting, the OBCA provides that a quorum of directors may call a meeting at any time to transact the business set out in the notice.

The CBCA and the OBCA provide that an incorporator or a director may call the meeting of directors to organize the corporation by giving not less than five days' notice to each director. The notice must state the time and place of the meeting.

Notice of meeting (other than to organize a corporation)

Under the CBCA, notice of a meeting must be given to each director in accordance with the bylaws. If the bylaws do not specify how and when notice is to be given, it appears that common law rules apply. That is, the notice should be given a reasonable time prior to the date of the meeting. Notice may be given electronically, provided that the bylaws do not restrict electronic notification and provided that the addressee has consented to and designated an information system for the receipt of the electronic document.

The OBCA provides that notice must be given 10 days or more before the date of the meeting to each director at the director's latest address as shown on the records of the corporation or in the most recent notice filed under the *Corporations Information Act*, whichever is the more current. The notice may be sent by prepaid mail or delivered personally.

Corporations, particularly larger corporations, may wish to provide for regular directors' meetings. If the date, time, and place of the meetings are specified in the bylaws or in a unanimous shareholder agreement or are determined by previous resolutions, no notice of the meetings is required.

Contents of notice

Unless the bylaws provide otherwise, a notice of a directors' meeting does not need to specify the business to be conducted at the meeting unless,

- for federal corporations, that business is an activity that cannot be delegated by the board as set out in CBCA s. 115(3); or

- for Ontario corporations, a quorum of the directors calls a meeting, in which case the general nature of the business must be specified in the notice calling the meeting (OBCA s. 126(8)).

Other than as required, the business of the meeting may be set out in the notice, as a courtesy to the directors.

Waiver of notice

A director may waive notice of a meeting of directors in any manner and at any time. Attendance of a director at a meeting of directors is considered a waiver of notice of the meeting, except where a director attends a meeting for the express purpose of objecting to the transaction of any business on the grounds that the meeting is not lawfully called (CBCA s. 114(6); OBCA s. 126(10)).

This is a useful provision to know when you discover on a minute book's due diligence review that a director who was not present at the meeting was not given notice and did not sign a waiver of notice. Having a waiver of notice signed after the procedural deficiency is discovered can rectify the problem.

Failure to give notice

If notice of a meeting of directors is not given to or is not waived by a director, the meeting may not be duly constituted and any action taken at the meeting may be invalid. If you encounter this situation, further research into case law will be required to locate any court decisions regarding the failure to give notice.

Place of meeting

The CBCA provides that, unless the articles or bylaws otherwise provide, the directors may meet at any place.

The OBCA provides that a meeting of the board of directors should be held at the registered office of the corporation. The bylaws may provide that a meeting may be held at any place within or outside Ontario. If they provide that meetings may be held outside Ontario, unless the corporation is a "non-resident" corporation as defined in the OBCA, a majority of the meetings of the board of directors must be held at a place within Canada in any financial year of the corporation.

Meetings by telephone

Subject to the bylaws, a director of a CBCA corporation may, in accordance with the regulations, and if all the directors consent, participate in a meeting of directors or of a committee of directors by means of a telephonic, electronic, or other communication facility that permits all participants to communicate adequately with each other during the meeting (CBCA s. 114(9)). Prior to the November 24, 2001 amendments to the CBCA, directors were limited to attending meetings by telephone.

Under the OBCA, unless otherwise provided in the bylaws, if all the directors of a corporation present at or participating in the meeting consent, a meeting of directors or of a committee of directors may be held by means of such telephone, electronic, or other communication facilities as permit all persons participating in the meeting to communicate with each other simultaneously and instantaneously (OBCA s. 126(13)). If a majority of the directors participating in a meeting are in Canada, the meeting is deemed to have been held in Canada (OBCA s. 126(14)).

At the time of writing, there are no regulations in the CBCA or the OBCA affecting the holding of electronic meetings by directors.

Quorum

Quorum requirements vary in the CBCA and the OBCA.

Under the CBCA, subject to the articles or bylaws, a majority of the number of directors or minimum number of directors required by the articles constitutes a quorum at any meeting of directors. Notwithstanding a vacancy among the directors, a quorum of directors may exercise all the powers of the directors (CBCA s. 114(2)).

Section 114(3) of the CBCA sets out the requirements for resident Canadian directors to be present at meetings in order for the directors to transact business:

1. at least 25 percent of the directors present must be resident Canadians, or, if the corporation has fewer than four directors, at least one of the directors present must be resident Canadian; or

2. in corporations where ownership restrictions apply — for example, airlines, telecommunications, uranium mining, book publishing and distribution, and film and video distribution (see CBCA s. 105(3.1)) — a majority of directors present must be resident Canadian, or, if the corporation has only two directors, at least one of the directors present must be resident Canadian; or

3. in a holding corporation, a majority of directors present must be resident Canadians.

Notwithstanding these provisions, directors may transact business at a meeting of directors where the required number of resident Canadian directors is not present if:

- a resident Canadian director who is unable to be present approves in writing, or by telephonic, electronic, or other communication facility, the business transacted at the meeting, and

- the required number of resident Canadian directors would have been present if that director had been present at the meeting (CBCA s. 114(4)).

The OBCA also provides that subject to the articles or bylaws, a majority of the number of directors or minimum number of directors required by the articles constitutes a quorum at any meeting of directors, but in no case is a quorum to be less than two-fifths of the number of directors or minimum number of directors (OBCA s. 126(3)).

Where there are fewer than three directors, all directors must be present to constitute a quorum (OBCA s. 126(4)).

Whether or not there is a vacancy among the directors, a quorum of directors can exercise all the powers of the directors (OBCA s. 126(5)).

Under the OBCA, directors cannot transact business at a meeting of directors unless a majority of directors present are resident Canadians, or, if a corporation has fewer than three directors, one of the directors present is a resident Canadian (OBCA s. 126(6)). The same provisions apply with respect to an absent Canadian director who gives written approval of the business being conducted.

Directors of a non-resident corporation are not subject to this requirement.

Who may attend meetings

It is customary for the bylaws to provide that only directors may attend meetings of directors unless the directors present at the meeting otherwise consent to having another person present. For example, a corporation may wish to have its lawyer or accountant present at a meeting to advise on a certain topic.

Chair and secretary

The procedure for conducting meetings provides for the appointment of a chair and a secretary of the meeting. The bylaws may specify whom the chair and secretary will be. Alternatively, their appointment may be voted on as one of the first items of business at the meeting.

Consent of director who is present to business at meeting

A director who is present at a meeting of directors or committee of directors is deemed to have consented to any resolution passed or action taken at the meeting unless:

1. the director requests a dissent to be entered in the minutes of the meeting;

2. the director sends a written dissent to the secretary of the meeting before the meeting is adjourned; or

3. the director sends a dissent by registered mail or delivers it to the registered office of the corporation immediately after the meeting is adjourned (CBCA s. 123(1); OBCA s. 135(1)).

A director who votes for or consents to a resolution is not entitled to dissent (CBCA s. 123(2); OBCA s. 135(2)).

Consent of director who was not present to business at meeting

A director who was not present at a meeting at which a resolution was passed or action taken is deemed to have consented to such business unless, within seven days after becoming aware of the resolution, the director

1. causes his or her dissent to be placed with the minutes of the meeting, or

2. sends his or her dissent by registered mail or delivers it to the registered office of the corporation (CBCA s. 123(3); OBCA s. 135(3)).

Voting at meetings

Every director has the right to one vote at all meetings of directors, unless the director has declared a conflict of interest in the matter being voted on and has to refrain from voting. For further discussion on conflict of interest, see chapter 4. In order to prevent a tie vote or to maintain control of a corporation, the bylaws will sometimes authorize the chair of the meeting to have a second or "casting" vote.

Directors cannot vote by "proxy" or sign resolutions by power of attorney. They must be present in person in order to cast their vote or they must personally sign all resolutions of directors.

Adjourned meetings

Sometimes, it will be necessary to "adjourn" or interrupt a meeting for a period of time, perhaps to complete some necessary transaction before continuing with the meeting. In this case, notice of an adjourned meeting of directors is not required to be given if the time and place of the adjourned meeting is announced at the original meeting (CBCA s. 114(7); OBCA s. 126(11)).

One-director meeting

Although it is hard to conceptualize having a meeting with only one person present, both the CBCA and the OBCA provide that where a corporation has only one director, that director may constitute a meeting (CBCA s. 114(8); OBCA s. 126(12)).

MEETINGS OF SHAREHOLDERS

Shareholders usually conduct their business at meetings of shareholders. Both offering and non-offering corporations are required by law to hold an **annual meeting** of shareholders to consider the minutes of the previous meeting; receive the director's annual report, the financial statements, and the auditor's report; elect directors; appoint auditors; and conduct any further business properly brought before the meeting.

annual meeting
a meeting of shareholders held to consider the minutes of the previous meeting; receive the directors' annual report, the financial statements, and the auditor's report; elect directors; appoint auditors; and conduct any further business properly brought before the meeting

Calling shareholder meetings

It is the responsibility of the directors to "call" an annual meeting of shareholders

- not later than 18 months after the corporation comes into existence; and

- subsequently, not later than 15 months after holding the last preceding annual meeting (CBCA s. 133(1); OBCA s. 94(1)(a)).

The CBCA also provides that the annual meeting must not be held later than six months after the end of the corporation's preceding financial year.

The directors may also, at any time, call a special meeting of shareholders (CBCA s. 133(2); OBCA s. 94(1)(b))

All business transacted at a special meeting and all business conducted at an annual meeting is deemed to be **special business**, except for:

special business
business conducted at a meeting of shareholders other than consideration of the minutes of an earlier meeting, the financial statements and auditor's report, election of directors, and reappointment of the incumbent auditor

- consideration of the minutes of an earlier meeting;

- the financial statements and auditor's report;

- election of directors; and

- reappointment of the incumbent auditor (CBCA s. 135(5); OBCA s. 96(5)).

Special meetings are therefore held to deal with special items of business.

An annual meeting of shareholders is sometimes referred to as an "annual general meeting." An annual meeting at which special business is to be conducted may be referred to as an "annual and special meeting."

Shareholder resolutions

There are two main types of shareholder resolutions:

- **ordinary resolutions** are resolutions that are passed by at least a majority of the votes cast; and

- **special resolutions** are resolutions that are passed by at least two-thirds of the votes cast in respect of the resolution, or that are signed by all the shareholders who are entitled to vote on the resolution (CBCA s. 2(1); OBCA s. 1(1)).

Note that the OBCA (but not the CBCA) provides that a shareholder's authorized attorney in writing may sign an ordinary or a special resolution for a shareholder.

Special resolutions include resolutions to authorize:

- an amendment to the articles of a corporation;

- a continuance of a corporation into another jurisdiction;

- a long-form amalgamation;

- a sale, lease, or exchange of all or substantially all of the property of a corporation other than in the ordinary course of its business;

- a liquidation and dissolution where the corporation is or has carried on business;

- an addition to or reduction of stated capital; and

- fixing the number of directors of the corporation within the minimum and maximum number allowed in the articles, if the directors have not been empowered to do so (OBCA only).

Where there are only one or two shareholders, they may prefer to sign written resolutions rather than hold a shareholders' meeting. Unlike a meeting, where merely a quorum of shareholders may conduct business, a resolution in writing must be signed by all shareholders who are entitled to vote on the resolution at a meeting. There are two exceptions to the rule allowing written resolutions to be signed by all shareholders in lieu of a meeting:

1. where a director, or

2. where an auditor

submits a written statement giving reasons for his or her resignation or his or her opposition to any proposed action or resolution to remove the person from office (CBCA ss. 110(2), 168(5); OBCA ss. 123(2), 149(6)).

ordinary resolution
a resolution that is passed by at least a majority of the votes cast

special resolution
a resolution that is passed by at least two-thirds of the votes cast in respect of the resolution, or that is consented to in writing by all the shareholders who are entitled to vote on the resolution

Requisitioning a shareholders' meeting

Under certain circumstances, shareholders who are entitled to vote and who collectively hold at least 5 percent of the issued voting shares may "requisition" the directors to call a meeting of shareholders for the purposes stated in the requisition. If the directors do not call a meeting of shareholders to transact the business stated in the requisition within 21 days after receiving it, any shareholder who signed the requisition may call the meeting.

Shareholders may wish to "requisition" a meeting for a variety of reasons:

1. to remove a director or directors;

2. when there is no vote of confidence in the directors and/or the auditors; or

3. to force a buyout of the shares of the corporation.

Notice of meeting

Notice of a shareholders' meeting must be sent to each shareholder who is entitled to vote at the meeting, to each director, and to the corporation's auditor.

For a CBCA corporation, notice must be sent within the prescribed period. At the time of writing, the prescribed period is not less than 21 days and not more than 60 days before the meeting. Corporations that are not distributing corporations can shorten this time by specifying a shorter period in their bylaws. However, the provisions for fixing a record date (discussed below) and sending financial statements to the directors still refer to 21 days before the meeting. Practically speaking, even corporations that are not distributing corporations may still be required to give 21 days' notice in order to comply with these other requirements.

For an OBCA corporation, notice must be sent not less than 21 days for an offering corporation, or not less than 10 days for any other corporation, and not more than 50 days before the meeting.

For both CBCA and OBCA corporations, notice must be sent by prepaid mail addressed to, or delivered personally to, the shareholder at the shareholder's latest address as shown in the records of the corporation.

Under the CBCA, a corporation may deliver notices and proxy materials electronically if the bylaws so provide and if a shareholder consents and designates a system for receiving the electronic communication. There is no provision in the OBCA authorizing electronic delivery of notices.

The CBCA does not define "day." The OBCA (s. 1(1)) defines "day" as

> a clear day and a period of days shall be deemed to commence the day following the event that began the period and shall be deemed to terminate at midnight of the last day of the period except that if the last day of the period falls on a Sunday or holiday the period shall terminate at midnight of the day next following that is not a Sunday or holiday.

Therefore, if the annual meeting of the corporation is to be held on Monday, June 14, 2004 and the bylaws provide for at least 21 days' notice, notice must be given no later than Friday, May 21, 2004. You need to count the number of clear days from and including Saturday, May 22 to and including Saturday, June 12. If the 21st day is Sunday, June 13, the notice period would be considered to end at midnight on Monday June 17. Therefore, the 21 days must end on Saturday, June 12.

It is customary for the officer or employee of the corporation who is responsible for delivering notice of the meeting to make a statutory declaration, setting out the details of the date, time, and method by which notice was given. This declaration is presented to the meeting, and the chair generally directs that it be maintained with the minutes of the meeting.

Record date for notice

For practical purposes, the directors may fix in advance a date, known as the **record date**, for the purpose of deciding which shareholders are entitled to receive notice of a meeting of shareholders. The record date cannot precede the date on which the meeting is to be held by less than 21 days or by more than 50 days.

If a record date is fixed, notice of the date has to be given within a certain time under the CBCA and the OBCA. Under the CBCA (s. 135(1) of the CBCA Regulations), notice must be given within the prescribed period (currently specified in s. 44 of the CBCA Regulations as not less than 21 days and not more than 60 days before the date fixed). Under the OBCA (s. 95(4)), notice must be given not less than 7 days before the meeting.

Notice must be given of the record date

1. by advertisement in a newspaper published or distributed in the place where the corporation has its registered office and in each place in Canada where it has a transfer agent or where a transfer of its shares may be recorded; and

2. by written notice to each stock exchange in Canada on which the shares of the corporation are listed for trading (CBCA s. 134(3); OBCA s. 95(4)).

Note that notice of the record date may be waived in writing by every shareholder of a share of the class or series affected whose name appears in the securities register at the close of business on the day the directors fix the record date (CBCA s. 134(3); OBCA s. 95(4)).

If no record date is fixed, the record date for deciding which shareholders are entitled to receive notice of a meeting of shareholders is at the close of business on the date immediately before the day on which the notice is given, or, if no notice is given, the day on which the meeting is held (CBCA s. 134(2)(a); OBCA s. 95(3)(a)).

It is not necessary to give notice of a meeting to a shareholder whose name is not registered in the records of the corporation. However, a person who does not receive notice of a meeting may still attend and vote at the meeting.

Contents of notice

A notice of a meeting of shareholders at which special business is to be conducted must state:

1. the nature of the business to be conducted, in sufficient detail to permit the shareholder to form a reasoned judgment about it; and

2. the text of any special resolution to be submitted to the meeting (CBCA s. 135(6); OBCA s. 96(6)).

record date (for shareholders entitled to receive notice of meetings) a date fixed in advance by the directors for the purpose of determining which shareholders are

Under the OBCA, a statement of this information can accompany the notice; it does not have to be contained in the notice.

Where a meeting of shareholders will consider a proposal to amend the corporation's articles, the notice must include a statement that dissenting shareholders are entitled to be paid the fair value of their shares in accordance with their rights. Failure to include the statement does not invalidate an amendment (CBCA s. 190; OBCA s. 169(2)).

Waiver of notice

The CBCA and the OBCA permit a shareholder or any other person who is entitled to attend a meeting of shareholders to waive notice of the meeting in any manner and at any time. Attendance at the meeting is considered a waiver of notice, except where the person attends for the express purpose of objecting to the transaction of any business on the grounds that the meeting was not lawfully called (CBCA s. 136; OBCA s. 98).

A waiver of notice is generally used when there are only a few shareholders and giving notice is unnecessary.

Failure to give notice

As with directors' meetings, if notice of a meeting of shareholders is not given, the meeting may not be duly constituted and any action taken at the meeting may be invalid. If you encounter this situation, further research into case law will be required to locate any court decisions regarding the failure to give notice.

Place of meeting

Shareholder meetings of a CBCA corporation are to be held at a place within Canada specified in the bylaws. If no place is specified in the bylaws, meetings must be held at a place within Canada determined by the directors (CBCA s. 132(1)). A meeting may be held outside Canada only if a place is specified in the articles or if all the shareholders who are entitled to vote at the meeting agree that the meeting is to be held at that place (CBCA s. 132(2)). A shareholder who attends a meeting outside Canada is deemed to have agreed to hold the meeting at that place, except where the shareholder attends the meeting for the purpose of objecting to the transaction of any business on the grounds that the meeting is not lawfully held (CBCA ss. 132(3)).

The CBCA does not define "place." It appears to be acceptable to provide, for example, that a meeting be held in Florida. However, it is questionable whether "in the United States of America" would be a sufficient description.

Under the OBCA, a meeting of shareholders, subject to the articles and any unanimous shareholder agreement, must be held at such place in or outside Ontario as the directors determine (OBCA s. 93(1)). If the directors have not determined a place for the meeting, it is to be held at the registered office (OBCA s. 93(1)).

Telephonic or electronic meetings

If a CBCA corporation so provides in its bylaws, shareholders' meetings can be held entirely by telephone or some other electronic means, such as Internet chat rooms, so long as this facility permits all participants to communicate adequately with each other.

Unless the bylaws provide otherwise, any person who is entitled to attend a shareholders' meeting can participate electronically or by telephone or other communication facility so long as the corporation makes available a communication facility, which permits all participants to communicate adequately with each other. For purposes of a quorum, a person who participates electronically in a meeting is deemed to be present at the meeting (CBCA s. 132(4)).

Unless the bylaws provide otherwise, shareholders are entitled to vote telephonically or electronically, provided that the corporation makes available the necessary facility (CBCA s. 141(3)).

The corporation can decide to hold the entire vote telephonically or electronically, provided that it makes available a facility for holding the meeting that will permit verification of the vote (reliability) and permit the votes to be counted without identifying who cast the vote (secret ballot). If a corporation wishes to do this, it must amend its bylaws to so provide (CBCA s. 141(1)).

The provisions of the OBCA are not as detailed as those of the CBCA. They merely provide that shareholder meetings can be held electronically if they are permitted in the articles or bylaws, and that a shareholder who votes at the meeting or establishes a communications link to the meeting is deemed to be present at the meeting (OBCA s. 94(2)).

Quorum

Unless the corporation's bylaws provide otherwise, the holders of a majority of the shares who are entitled to vote at a meeting of shareholders, whether present in person or represented by proxy, constitute a quorum. When a quorum is present at the opening of a meeting of shareholders, the shareholders present may, unless the bylaws provide otherwise, proceed with the business of the meeting, even if a quorum is not present throughout the meeting.

Who may attend

The common law rule is that only those persons who are entitled to vote may be present at a meeting of shareholders. In addition, although the directors are not entitled to vote, the CBCA and the OBCA provide that they have the right to receive notice of, attend, and be heard at every meeting of shareholders (CBCA ss. 135 and 110; OBCA ss. 96(1) and 123(1)). As well, the auditor of a corporation has the right to receive notice of, attend, and be heard at every meeting of shareholders on matters relating to his or her duties as an auditor (CBCA ss. 135(1) and 168(1); OBCA ss. 96(1) and 151(1)).

Strangers may be admitted to a meeting of shareholders only with the consent of the chair or the shareholders at the meeting.

Proxies

entitled to receive notice of a meeting of shareholders

proxy
a document by which a shareholder appoints a "proxyholder" or one or more alternate "proxyholders," who need not be shareholders, as the shareholder's nominee to attend and act at the meeting in the manner, to the extent, and with the authority conferred by the proxy

Every shareholder who is entitled to vote at a meeting of shareholders may, by means of a document called a **proxy**, appoint a "proxyholder" or one or more alternate "proxyholders," who do not have to be shareholders, as the shareholder's nominee to attend and act at the meeting in the manner, to the extent, and with the authority conferred by the proxy (CBCA s. 148(1); OBCA s. 110(1)).

The form of proxy must be signed by the shareholder or the shareholder's attorney authorized in writing. It is valid only at the meeting in respect of which the proxy is given (including an adjourned meeting). A shareholder may revoke a proxy by depositing with the corporation an instrument in writing executed by the shareholder or the shareholder's attorney authorized in writing.

Corporations with 50 or fewer shareholders who are entitled to vote at a meeting are not required to send out management proxies.

Voting

Unless a corporation's articles provide otherwise, each share of a corporation entitles the holder to one vote at a meeting of shareholders (CBCA s. 140(1); OBCA s. 102(1)).

A corporate shareholder can, by resolution of its directors, appoint any individual to represent it at meetings of shareholders, and the corporation must recognize this person (CBCA s. 140(2); OBCA s. 102(2)). This person has all the powers that an individual shareholder has (CBCA s. 140(3); OBCA s. 102(3)).

Unless the bylaws provide otherwise, where shares are held jointly by two or more persons, one of those persons present at a meeting may in the absence of the others, vote the shares. However, if two or more of those persons are present, in person or by proxy, they can vote as one only on the shares jointly held by them (CBCA s. 140(4); OBCA s. 102(4)).

Unless the bylaws provide otherwise, voting at a meeting of shareholders is to be by show of hands, except where a ballot is demanded by a shareholder or proxyholder (CBCA s. 141(1); OBCA s. 103(1)). The usual practice is for the chair to ask all those voting in favour of a motion to raise their right hand. Where a ballot is demanded, the secretary of the meeting will distribute either a form with the motion printed on it or a blank form, and ask each voting shareholder to tick the appropriate box either in favour or against the motion. The scrutineer at the meeting will tally all the votes and present them to the chair, who will advise the shareholders present of the result of the vote.

Subject to any provisions to the contrary in the governing statute, articles or bylaws of a corporation, or a unanimous shareholder agreement, all questions considered at a meeting of shareholders shall be decided by a majority of the votes cast. Unless specifically provided in the bylaws, the chair of the meeting does not have a casting or second vote where there is a tie in the voting.

As discussed above, for practical purposes, the directors may fix in advance the record date for the purpose of deciding which shareholders are entitled to vote at the meeting (CBCA s. 138(2); OBCA s. 100(1)). If, after the record date, a shareholder of an OBCA corporation transfers any shares, and the transferee produces a properly endorsed share certificate or otherwise satisfies the corporation that the transferee owns the shares, not later than 10 days before the meeting, or such shorter period as the bylaws may provide, the transferee's name will be added to the list of shareholders entitled to vote at the meeting (OBCA s. 100(2)).

If a record date for voting is not fixed, the persons entitled to vote are those persons who were entitled to receive notice of the meeting (CBCA s. 138(3); OBCA s. 100(3)). Further, if a shareholder of an OBCA corporation transfers shares after notice of the meeting has been given, the transferee will be entitled to vote the shares if the transferee satisfies the requirements stated above (OBCA s. 100(3)).

One-shareholder meetings

If a corporation has only one shareholder, or only one holder of any class or series of shares, the shareholder present in person or represented by proxy may constitute a meeting (CBCA s. 139(4); OBCA s. 101(4)).

Shareholder proposal

If there is any matter that a shareholder would like to raise at a meeting of shareholders, provided that he or she is entitled to vote at the meeting, the shareholder can give the corporation notice of the proposal and discuss it at the meeting (CBCA s. 137(1); OBCA s. 99(1)). This provision would typically be used in large or public corporations. When the corporation receives notice of a proposal, the proposal is to be included in the management information circular that is sent to shareholders (CBCA s. 137(2); OBCA s. 99(2)). There are, however, restrictions regarding proposals (see CBCA s. 137; OBCA s. 99).

The November 24, 2001 amendments to the CBCA have extended the rights of a shareholder to make a proposal to include "beneficial" shareholders and not just voting shareholders, as is the case in the OBCA.

KEY TERMS

annual meeting	record date
electronic meeting	special business
ordinary resolution	special resolution
proxy	

REFERENCES

Business Corporations Act (Ontario) (OBCA), RSO 1990, c. B.16, as amended, and regulations.

Canada Business Corporations Act (CBCA), RSC 1985, c. C-44, as amended, and regulations.

Corporations Information Act (Ontario) (CIA), RSO 1990, c. C.39, as amended.

Linfield, Derek N. and Stuart Carruthers, "Preparing for an Annual Meeting and a Special Meeting of a Public Company — The Legal Framework," in Canadian Bar Association, Ontario Branch, Continuing Legal Education, *The Nuts and Bolts of Running Company Meetings*, Continuing Legal Education seminar, May 5, 1994 (Toronto: CBAO, 1994).

Meyer, N. Dean, *Meyer's Rules of Order* (Ridgefield, CT: NDMA, 2001).

Nathan, Hartley R., "How To Prepare for Meetings of Directors," in Canadian Bar Association, Ontario Branch, Continuing Legal Education, *The Nuts and Bolts of Running Company Meetings*, Continuing Legal Education seminar, May 5, 1994 (Toronto: CBAO, 1994).

Nathan, Hartley R., ed., *Wainberg and Nathan's Company Meetings Including Rules of Order*, 5th ed. (Toronto: CCH Canadian, 2001).

Robert, Henry M. III, et al., *Robert's Rules of Order Newly Revised*, 10th ed. (Cambridge, MA: Perseus Publishing, 2000).

Stamegna, Carolyn P., "Role of the Secretary with Respect to Company Meetings," in Canadian Bar Association, Ontario Branch, Continuing Legal Education, *The Nuts and Bolts of Running Company Meetings*, Continuing Legal Education seminar, May 5, 1994 (Toronto: CBAO, 1994).

Weist, Robert, "Reform of the Canada Business Corporations Act," in Canadian Bar Association, Ontario Branch, Continuing Legal Education, *Reform of the Canada Business Corporations Act: What Does It Mean for My Practice?* Continuing Legal Education seminar, February 2, 2002 (Toronto: CBAO, 2002).

FORM AND PRECEDENTS

Figure 11.1: Notice of directors' meeting

Figure 11.2: Waiver of directors' meeting

Figure 11.3: Minutes of directors' meeting approving financial statements

Figure 11.4: Notice of annual and special meeting of shareholders

Figure 11.5: Waiver of shareholders' meeting

Figure 11.6: Proxy for shareholders' meeting

Figure 11.7: Minutes for shareholders' meeting

Figure 11.8: Statutory declaration re mailing notice of shareholders' meeting

Figure 11.9: Minutes of directors' meeting appointing officers

REVIEW QUESTIONS

1. List three different types of sources where you would find rules and regulations governing meetings.

2. You are asked to draft a notice of a meeting for an OBCA corporation. Upon reviewing the corporate records, you discover that the resolution passing the bylaws was not properly signed. Explain how you would decide who could sign the notice and how much notice must be given.

3. Under the CBCA and the OBCA, can you give electronic notice of a directors' meeting and a shareholders' meeting? Explain your answer.

4. Draft a notice for a directors' meeting of a CBCA corporation that is being held to declare dividends.

5. Does failure to give notice of a meeting invalidate the proceedings at the meeting?

6. Describe the quorum requirements for directors' and shareholders' meetings.

7. Distinguish between an ordinary resolution and a special resolution.

8. What can a director do if he or she did not attend a meeting of directors and does not agree with the outcome of the meeting?

9. The corporation's annual meeting is set for June 10. The directors set a record date of May 10 for the shareholders entitled to receive notice, and notice of the meeting is given to shareholders on May 15. On May 20, shareholder X transfers his shares to shareholder Y, who, prior to the transfer, did not hold any shares in the corporation. Is shareholder Y entitled to attend and vote at the meeting? Explain your answer.

10. When must an annual meeting be held for a CBCA corporation? For an OBCA corporation?

11. What must be stated in a notice of a shareholders' meeting?

12. Could a shareholder living in Kuwait attend a shareholders' meeting of a CBCA corporation by telephone? Explain what would be required.

13. What is a proxy? Who can sign it?

14. When drafting articles for a CBCA corporation, could you provide that shareholders' meetings be held in Ohio?

FIGURE 11.1   NOTICE OF DIRECTORS' MEETING

NAME OF COMPANY

NOTICE OF MEETING OF DIRECTORS

TAKE NOTICE that a meeting of the board of directors of Company Name will be held at _____ on _____ at _____.

DATED _____.

By order of the president

_____

Secretary

FIGURE 11.2 WAIVER OF DIRECTORS' MEETING

TO: NAME OF CORP (the "Corporation")

AND TO: THE DIRECTORS THEREOF

WAIVER OF NOTICE

The undersigned directors of the Corporation waive notice of the meeting of directors of the Corporation to be held at [PLACE] on [DAY], the [DATE] day of [MONTH], [YEAR] at the hour of [HOUR] o'clock in the [FORE OR AFTER] noon, Eastern Standard Time, and consent to the meeting being held and to the transaction of such business as may properly come before the meeting and any adjournment or adjournments thereof.

DATED the   day of   , *

_____   _____

_____   _____

FIGURE 11.3   MINUTES OF DIRECTORS' MEETING APPROVING FINANCIAL STATEMENTS

MINUTES of a meeting of the board of directors of * (the "Corporation") held at * on *, the * day of * at the hour of * o'clock in the * noon.

PRESENT

There were present:

> *

being {all/a quorum} of the directors of the Corporation.

ALSO PRESENT WITH THE CONSENT OF THE MEETING:

> *

CHAIR AND SECRETARY

The President of the Corporation, *, took the Chair and the Secretary of the Corporation, *, acted as secretary of the meeting.

CONSTITUTION OF MEETING

The Chair stated that notice calling the meeting was mailed to all directors of the Corporation on *. Proof of such mailing has been filed by the secretary of the meeting, and the Chair directed that a copy of the notice with proof of mailing be annexed to the minutes of the meeting.

The Chair declared that [all/a quorum] of the directors being present and notice of the meeting having been given in accordance with the by-laws of the Corporation, the meeting was duly convened and properly constituted for the transaction of business.

ALTERNATIVE

All of the directors being present and all the directors having waived notice of the meeting, the meeting was declared to be duly convened and properly constituted for the transaction of business. The Chair directed the waiver of notice, which was signed by all of the directors, to be annexed to the minutes of the meeting.

APPROVAL OF MINUTES OF PREVIOUS MEETING

After discussion, on motion duly made, seconded and carried the following resolution was passed:

> **RESOLVED** that the minutes of the board of directors' meeting held on * are approved.

APPROVAL OF FINANCIAL STATEMENTS

The Chairman presented to the meeting the financial statements of the Corporation for the financial year ended * together with the auditor's report thereon.

Upon motion duly made, seconded and carried the following resolution was passed:

FIGURE 11.3   CONCLUDED

RESOLVED that the audited financial statements of the Corporation for the financial period ended [month, day and year] are approved and any two [if applicable] of the director[s] of the Corporation are [is] authorized to sign the balance sheet on behalf of the board to evidence such approval.

ANNUAL MEETING OF SHAREHOLDERS

Upon motion duly made, seconded and carried the following resolution was passed:

RESOLVED that the annual meeting of shareholders of the Corporation be held at *on *, the * day of * at the hour of * o'clock in the * noon for the following purposes:

(a)   considering the minutes of the meeting of the shareholders held on   ,   19   ;

(b)   receiving the financial statements of the Corporation for the financial year ended * together with the auditor's report thereon;

(c)   re-electing the incumbent directors of the Corporation for the ensuing year;

(d)   re-appointing the incumbent auditors of the Corporation and authorizing the directors to fix their remuneration; and

(e)   transacting such other business as may properly come before the meeting.

TERMINATION

There being no further business, the meeting on motion terminated.

_____   _____
Chair   Secretary of the meeting

FIGURE 11.4   NOTICE OF ANNUAL AND SPECIAL MEETING OF SHAREHOLDERS

[CORPORATION NAME]
(the "Corporation")

NOTICE OF ANNUAL AND SPECIAL MEETING OF
SHAREHOLDERS

[DATE]

NOTICE IS GIVEN that the annual and special meeting of the shareholders of the Corporation will be held at *[address]* on *[date]* at *[the hour]* (Eastern Standard Time) for the following purposes:

1.   To receive the Annual Report, including the audited financial statements and auditors' report thereon for the financial period ended *[Month, Day, Year]*.

2.   To re-elect the incumbent directors.

3.   To re-appoint the incumbent auditors and authorize the directors to fix their remuneration.

4.   To consider and, if thought fit, pass a special resolution authorizing an amendment to the articles of the Corporation. *[Note: If this is a special meeting, then the notice needs to contain information circular–like disclosure of the special business to be conducted at the meeting.]*

5.   To transact such other business that may properly come before the meeting.

The accompanying letter provides additional information relating to the matters to be dealt with at the meeting and forms part of this Notice. The text of the special resolution to consider at the meeting is set out as Schedule A to this notice. A copy of the annual report, including audited financial statements, also accompanies this Notice.

If you are unable to be present at the meeting, please exercise your right to vote by signing and returning the enclosed form of proxy to the Secretary, *[Corporation Name, Address]*, prior to the meeting.

DATED this   day of   ,   .

BY ORDER OF THE BOARD

[Signed]

Name, Office

FIGURE 11.5   WAIVER OF SHAREHOLDERS' MEETING

TO: NAME OF CORPORATION (the "Corporation")

AND TO: THE SHAREHOLDERS THEREOF

WAIVER OF NOTICE

The undersigned shareholders of the Corporation waive notice of the meeting of shareholders of the Corporation to be held at [PLACE] on [DAY], the [DATE] day of [MONTH], [YEAR] at the hour of [HOUR] o'clock in the [FORE OR AFTER] noon, Eastern Standard Time, and consent to the meeting being held and to the transaction of such business as may properly come before the meeting and any adjournment or adjournments thereof.

DATED the   day of   ,   .

_____   _____
A. Shareholder   B. Shareholder

                                               _____
                                               C. Shareholder

FIGURE 11.6 PROXY FOR SHAREHOLDERS' MEETING

CORPORATION NAME
(the "Corporation")

PROXY SOLICITED ON BEHALF OF MANAGEMENT

FOR ANNUAL AND SPECIAL MEETING OF SHAREHOLDERS TO BE HELD

ON

The undersigned shareholder of the Corporation appoints * , * , or failing him, *, or instead of either of them * , as proxy for the undersigned to attend, act and vote for and on behalf of the undersigned at the annual and special meeting of the shareholders to be held on the * day of *, * and at any adjournments thereof, in the same manner, to the same extent and with the same power as if the undersigned were present at the meeting or any such adjournments.

The undersigned revokes any proxy previously given.

DATED the _____ day of _____, _____.

_____
Name of Shareholder
(please print)

_____
(Signature)

A shareholder has the right to appoint a proxy (who need not be a shareholder) to attend and act for him on his behalf at the meeting other than the persons designated herein. To exercise this right, the shareholder may insert the name of the desired person in the blank space provided herein and strike out the other name or may submit another appropriate proxy.

FIGURE 11.7   MINUTES FOR SHAREHOLDERS' MEETING

MINUTES of the annual meeting of the shareholders of * (**the "Corporation"**) held at *, on * day, the * day of * at the hour of * o'clock in the * noon.

PRESENT

(a)   There were present in person:

*

(b)   There were represented by proxy in favour of *

*

ALSO PRESENT WITH THE CONSENT OF THE MEETING:

*

CHAIR AND SECRETARY

The President of the Corporation,*, took the Chair and the Secretary of the Corporation *, acted as secretary of the meeting.

APPOINTMENT OF SCRUTINEER

The Chair, with the approval of the meeting, appointed * to act as Scrutineer.

CONSTITUTION OF MEETING

The Chair stated that notice calling the meeting was mailed to all directors, shareholders and the auditor of the Corporation on * . Proof of such mailing has been filed by the secretary of the meeting and the Chair directed that a copy of the notice with proof of mailing be annexed to the minutes of the meeting.

The Chair declared that {all/a quorum} of the shareholders being present either in person or by proxy, and notice of the meeting having been given in accordance with the by-laws of the Corporation, the meeting was duly convened and properly constituted for the transaction of business.

APPROVAL OF MINUTES OF PREVIOUS MEETING

After discussion, on motion duly made, seconded and carried the following resolution was passed:

> **RESOLVED, as an ordinary resolution,** that the minutes of the shareholders' meeting held on * are approved.

FIGURE 11.7 CONTINUED

ANNUAL REPORT

The Chair presented to the meeting the annual report of the Corporation containing the financial statements of the Corporation for the financial year ended * as approved by the directors together with the auditor's report thereon.

The Chair then made a few remarks on the annual report.

ELECTION OF DIRECTORS

The Chair advised the meeting that it was in order to proceed with the election of * directors for the ensuing year and confirmed that a majority of the nominees were resident Canadians within the meaning of the *Business Corporations Act* (Ontario).

On motion duly made, seconded and carried the following resolution was passed:

> **RESOLVED, as an ordinary resolution,** that the following individuals are [is] elected as a [the] director[s] of the Corporation until the next annual meeting of the shareholders of the Corporation or until [he, she or they] otherwise cease[s] to hold office as [a] director[s] of the Corporation:

> *
> *
> *

[NOTE: IF ALL SHAREHOLDERS ARE VOTING SHAREHOLDERS INCLUDE THE EXEMPTION FROM AUDIT REQUIREMENTS IF APPROPRIATE.]

EXEMPTION FROM AUDIT REQUIREMENTS

On motion duly made, seconded and carried the following resolution was passed:

> **WHEREAS** the Corporation is not an offering corporation within the meaning of the *Business Corporations Act* (Ontario) (the "Act");

> **RESOLVED, as a unanimous resolution,** that the Corporation be exempt from the requirements of the Act regarding the appointment and duties of an auditor for the financial period ending [month, day and next year end].

APPOINTMENT OF [AUDITORS / ACCOUNTANTS]

On motion duly made, seconded and carried the following resolution was passed:

> **RESOLVED, as an ordinary resolution,** that [accountant/auditor name] is appointed as the [accountant/auditor] of the Corporation until the close of the next annual meeting of the shareholders or it sooner ceases to hold office as such at a remuneration to be fixed by the directors, the directors being authorized to fix such remuneration.

FIGURE 11.7 CONCLUDED

The Chair directed the Secretary to give the Corporation's auditors written notice of their appointment.

CONFIRMATION OF PROCEEDINGS

On motion duly made, seconded and carried the following resolution was passed:

> **RESOLVED, as a special resolution,** that all by-laws, resolutions, contracts, acts and proceedings of the board of directors of the Corporation enacted, passed, made, done or taken since the last annual meeting (or the last resolutions of the shareholders in lieu of the annual meeting) which are:
>
> (a)   referred to or appear in or may be inferred from any resolution, minutes of meeting, financial statements, registers, records or reports concerning the Corporation; and
>
> (b)   now or have been available to the shareholders,
>
> are approved notwithstanding any defect in the procedure for calling or holding any meeting, in the procedure for appointing directors or in the qualification of any director of the Corporation.

TERMINATION

There being no further business, the meeting on motion terminated.

_____   _____
Chair   Secretary of the meeting

PROVINCE OF ONTARIO   )   In the atter of the Annual   eneral   eeting
)   of the Shareholders of
)   *[CORPORATION NAME]*

TO WIT:)

I,   , of the *[City/Town of* _____ *]*, in the rovince of ntario, do solemnly declare that:

1.   I am the *[Title]* of *[Corporation name]* (the Corporation) and as such have nowledge of the matters hereinafter declared.

2.   A copy of the attached notice of the annual general meeting of shareholders of the Corporation together with a form of proxy, accompanied in each case by a copy of the attached *[list documents accompanying notice — for example: annual report containing the financial statements and the report of the auditors to the shareholders, and a copy of the* _____ *]* were sent on the   day of   ,   , by *[registered mail, prepaid post, electronic transmission, courier or hand delivery as appropriate]* to each of the persons who, on the   day of   ,   were shareholders of the Corporation addressed to each such shareholder at *[his/her/its]* last address as shown on the boo s of the Corporation and to the auditor of the Corporation.

And I ma e this solemn declaration conscientiously believing it to be true and nowing that it is of the same force and effect as if made under oath and by virtue of the *Canada Evidence Act.*

DECLARED before me at the   )
[City/Town] of   , in   )
the rovince of ntario, this   )
day of   ,   .   )
)
)   *[Name]*
)   *[Title]*

A Commissioner, etc.

FIGURE 11.9   MINUTES OF DIRECTORS' MEETING APPOINTING OFFICERS

MINUTES of a meeting of the board of directors of * **(the "Corporation")** held at * on *, the * day of * at the hour of * o'clock in the * noon.

PRESENT

There were present:

*

being [all/a quorum] of the directors of the Corporation.

ALSO PRESENT WITH THE CONSENT OF THE MEETING:

*

CHAIR AND SECRETARY

With the unanimous consent of the meeting, * took the Chair and * acted as secretary of the meeting.

CONSTITUTION OF MEETING

The Chair declared that [all/a quorum] of the directors being present and the meeting being held immediately following the meeting of shareholders at which they were elected and no notice being required, the meeting was duly convened and properly constituted for the transaction of business.

APPROVAL OF MINUTES OF PREVIOUS MEETING

After discussion, on motion duly made, seconded and carried the following resolution was passed:

> **RESOLVED** that the minutes of the board of directors' meeting held on * are approved.

APPOINTMENT OF OFFICERS

On motion duly made, seconded and carried the following resolution was passed:

> **RESOLVED** that the following individual[s] are [is] appointed to the office or offices indicated opposite their respective names to hold such office or offices at the pleasure of the board:

Name of Officer	**Office**

TERMINATION

There being no further business, the meeting on motion terminated.

_____   _____
Chair   Secretary of the meeting

CHAPTER 12

Annual matters

CHAPTER OVERVIEW

This chapter discusses the procedures that are required on an annual basis to keep federal and Ontario corporations in good standing, including the need to approve and distribute financial statements and the need to hold an annual meeting of the shareholders. The chapter explains the business conducted at annual meetings and the information required to complete annual minutes or resolutions, as well as examines the declaration and payment of dividends and the allocation of management bonuses. The chapter discusses the need to file annual returns, outlines the information required to complete federal and Ontario annual returns, and gives an overview of the deadlines for filing annual returns in each jurisdiction in Canada.

CHAPTER OBJECTIVES

After completing this chapter, you should be able to:

1. Identify the annual procedures required to keep CBCA and OBCA corporations up to date.

2. List and prepare documents for annual meetings of directors and shareholders.

3. Diarize dates for filing annual returns.

4. Prepare and file annual returns.

INTRODUCTION

Each year after incorporation, a corporation must take certain steps to maintain compliance with the corporate statutes. There are other requirements as well, such as filing corporate tax returns with the Canada Revenue Agency (CRA) and the provincial government, but a discussion of these filings is beyond the scope of this chapter.

The steps required annually include the following:

1. The directors must approve the financial statements (CBCA s. 158(1); OBCA s. 159(1)).

2. A copy of the financial statements must be sent to those shareholders who have not informed the corporation in writing that they do not want a copy of the documents, not less than 21 days before each annual meeting or before the signing of a resolution in lieu of the annual meeting (10 days for an OBCA non-offering corporation) (CBCA s. 159(1); OBCA s. 154(2)).

3. The corporation must hold an annual meeting of its shareholders no more than 18 months after the corporation comes into existence and subsequently no more than 15 months after the previous annual meeting (CBCA s. 133(1); OBCA s. 94(1)). The CBCA also provides that the annual meeting shall be held no later than six months after the end of the corporation's preceding financial year (CBCA s. 133(1)).

4. The directors must put before the shareholders at the annual meeting the financial statements, the report of the auditor (if any), and any further information respecting the financial position of the corporation and the results of its operations required by the articles, the bylaws, or a unanimous shareholder agreement.

5. The corporation must file an annual return (CBCA s. 263; CIA s. 3.1(1)).

APPROVAL OF FINANCIAL STATEMENTS BY DIRECTORS

After the auditors or the accountants prepare the financial statements, they meet with the directors of the corporation to review them. When the board is satisfied that the statements are accurate and complete, they meet or sign a resolution approving the financial statements. Such approval is evidenced in different ways under the CBCA and the OBCA:

1. Under the CBCA, the financial statements must be manually signed by one or more directors or have reproduced on them a facsimile of the signature(s) (CBCA s. 158(1)).

2. Under the OBCA, the financial statements must be signed at the foot of the balance sheet by two of the directors who are duly authorized to sign, or by the director where there is only one (OBCA s. 159(1)).

SENDING FINANCIAL STATEMENTS TO THE SHAREHOLDERS

Typically, in closely held corporations (that is, privately owned, non-offering corporations), the shareholders waive receipt of the financial statements within the required time period. However, in larger corporations, or where the shareholders are different from the directors, it is important to comply on a timely basis with the requirement to send or disclose the financial statements to the shareholders.

When notice of the annual shareholders' meeting is given, the financial statements usually accompany the notice. However, you should be aware that, under the November 24, 2001 CBCA amendments, a corporation need give only 10 days' notice of a meeting of a closely held corporation (CBCA s. 135(1.1)), whereas the financial statements must be sent no later than 21 days before the meeting (CBCA s. 159(1)). If, as allowed under the CBCA, only 10 days' notice is given, the financial statements have to be sent separately, which will likely increase the cost of giving notice (due to the additional postage).

Section 155 of the CBCA provides for "comparative" financial statements for the financial period ended not more than six months prior to the annual meeting and the immediately preceding financial year. The OBCA has a comparable provision (in s. 154), but it applies only to offering corporations, which are required to file financial statements under the *Securities Act*.

ANNUAL MEETINGS

Shareholders' annual meetings

Annual meetings, or annual general meetings as they are sometimes referred to, are called by the directors. The first annual meeting must be held within 18 months of incorporation. After that, a corporation must hold an annual meeting within 15 months of the previous annual meeting and, if it is a CBCA corporation, within 6 months of the immediately preceding financial year-end.

Chapter 11 discussed in detail the procedures for calling and holding meetings. In summary, the annual meeting of a closely held corporation must be held at the registered office of the corporation or at a place provided in the bylaws, or where the directors otherwise determine. Notice of the time and place of the meeting must be given to the directors, the auditors, and the shareholders who are entitled to vote not more than 50 and not less than 10 days prior to the meeting. The notice must set out the business to be conducted at the meeting.

The business transacted at an annual meeting generally includes the following:

1. consideration and approval of the minutes of the previous meeting;

2. the directors' annual report regarding the business and activities of the corporation;

3. a review of the corporation's financial statements, together with the report of the auditor, if any (CBCA s. 155(1); OBCA s. 154(1));

4. the election of directors (CBCA s. 106(3); OBCA s. 119(4));

5. the appointment of auditors, unless the corporation is exempt from the requirement to appoint auditors (CBCA s. 162(1); OBCA s. 149(1));

6. fixing the remuneration to be received by the auditors, or authorizing the directors to fix such remuneration;

7. confirmation of all acts of the directors reflected in the corporation's records since the last annual meeting of the shareholders; such a confirming resolution is usually passed only at an annual meeting of shareholders of a closely held

corporation, and consideration should be given in all cases to ensure that it is prudent to pass the resolution;

8. any special business such as an amendment to the articles or bylaws (note that the meeting then becomes an annual and special meeting of shareholders); and

9. any other business that may properly be brought before the meeting.

A shareholder who is entitled to vote can attend the meeting in person. Alternatively, a shareholder can, by means of a proxy, appoint a proxyholder or one or more alternate proxyholders. A proxyholder, who does not have to be a shareholder, can attend and act at the meeting in the manner, to the extent, and with the authority conferred by the proxy (CBCA s. 148; OBCA s. 110).

In lieu of holding an annual meeting, the business required to be conducted at the meeting can be completed by resolutions in writing signed by all the shareholders who are entitled to vote on the resolutions at a meeting of shareholders. If the corporation is subject to the OBCA, the required business can be completed by resolutions signed by all the shareholders or their attorney authorized in writing (CBCA s. 142; OBCA s. 104).

If a federal corporation fails for two or more consecutive years to hold an annual meeting of shareholders or to pass resolutions in lieu thereof, the federal Director or any interested person may apply to a court for an order dissolving the corporation (CBCA s. 213(1)).

Directors' meetings

As discussed above, the directors must approve the financial statements before forwarding them to the shareholders. The financial statements can be approved at a meeting of directors or by a signed resolution prior to the date of the shareholders' meeting.

In addition, it is customary for newly elected directors to meet immediately after the annual meeting of shareholders to appoint officers and committee members for the following year.

The procedures for holding directors' meetings are discussed fully in chapter 11.

Summary

Whether resolutions are passed at meetings or in writing, the business typically conducted annually to meet the requirements of the CBCA and the OBCA is as follows:

FIRST DIRECTORS' MEETING

- approval of the financial statements and authorization of the directors to sign statements acknowledging that approval

- calling of the annual meeting

SHAREHOLDERS' MEETING

- consideration and approval of the minutes of the previous meeting

- receipt and consideration of the financial statements and the auditor's report, if any

- election of directors

- appointment of auditors, or consent to exemption from audit requirements

- fixing the auditors' remuneration, or authorizing the directors to fix such remuneration

- confirmation of all acts of the directors for the past year

- any other business properly brought before the meeting

SECOND DIRECTORS' MEETING

- appointment of officers

- appointment of committee members (if appropriate)

DECLARATION OF DIVIDENDS

Chapter 5 discussed the right of shareholders to receive dividends. Subject to the corporate statutes, any unanimous shareholder agreement, and the articles, the directors may declare and pay dividends according to the rights attaching to the shares (CBCA s. 43(1); OBCA s. 38(1)). They cannot delegate this power — for example, to a committee or managing director (CBCA s. 115; OBCA s. 127). If the corporation does not meet the financial solvency requirements set out in the corporate statutes, however, the directors cannot declare or pay the dividends (CBCA s. 38(3); OBCA s. 42). Dividends can be paid by issuing shares of the corporation or in the form of money or property.

The directors can fix a record date to determine which shareholders are entitled to receive dividends (CBCA s. 134; OBCA s. 95). If they do not fix a date, the record date is the close of business on the day the resolution approving the dividend is passed.

DECLARATION AND PAYMENT OF BONUSES

It is often the case that bonuses are declared by small and medium-sized businesses before the end of the taxation year but not paid until sometime within 180 days after the corporation's year-end. This is done for tax-planning purposes for both the corporation and the owner-manager as an employee of the corporation. The corporation is entitled to claim a deduction for the bonus in the taxation year in which the bonus is declared, whereas the person who receives the bonus is not liable for tax on the bonus until the bonus is received. The goal of the corporation often is to reduce its taxable income below $200,000 by paying the bonus to the owner-manager, who would have benefited from the corporate profits in any event through dividend payments on shares.

Section 78(4) of the *Income Tax Act* (ITA) provides that where an amount in respect of a taxpayer's expense that is salary, wages, or other remuneration is unpaid on the day that is 180 days after the end of the taxation year in which the expense is incurred, the amount is deemed not to have been incurred as an expense in that year but in the taxation year in which the amount is paid.

There are a number of considerations for a corporation to bear in mind before declaring and paying year-end bonuses to owner-managers in order to maximize the tax benefits to both parties:

1. In order for the corporation to be entitled to deduct the amount of the bonus, the amount must be reasonable (see ITA s. 67) in relation to the nature of the work done for the corporation by the individual receiving the bonus. This requirement is not strictly applied by the CRA to owner-managers who are active in the business. However, the CRA will likely not allow a large bonus payment to a spouse or family member of the business owner to be deducted where they have devoted little time to the business of the corporation.

2. In order for the corporation to receive the tax benefit, the bonus payment must be a liability to the corporation at the end of the taxation year in which it is to be deductible. As a practical matter, a corporation's profits are often not known until the financial statements are prepared, usually within six months after the year-end. Therefore, it may not be possible to determine the actual amount of the bonus to be paid to reduce the corporation's taxable income below $200,000.

   The best evidence of an obligation to pay a bonus is an employment agreement between the owner-manager and the corporation, setting out a formula by which the bonus is to be determined.

   An alternative to an employment agreement is a resolution of the directors (subject to any unanimous shareholder agreement), passed before the end of the year in which the deduction is to be taken, to pay a certain sum to a named individual as additional payment for services rendered. If this is done, the resolution should set out the amount to be paid and the name of the individual to whom it will be paid. The individual should also be notified of the decision. This creates a good legal argument that the obligation to pay the bonus has been created and, accordingly, the bonus will be deductible.

3. In certain cases, the bonus is not determined or declared for some time after the end of the corporation's taxation year. In this case, the CRA may accept a late-declared bonus if it is established that the bonus was declared and paid pursuant to an established policy of the corporation — for example, an incentive program.

CORPORATE ANNUAL RETURNS

The CBCA, the Ontario *Corporations Information Act* (CIA), and the corporate statutes in each jurisdiction in Canada require corporations to file annual returns or renew their corporate registrations. It is no secret that the process for filing returns and renewing registrations under the CBCA and the CIA is inefficient. Effective as of January 1, 1999 for federal corporations, and January 1, 2000 for Ontario corporations, these annual returns form part of the federal T2 corporate tax return and the Ontario CT23 corporations tax return. Consequently, if the annual return is filed at the same time as the tax return, the information provided may differ from the information recorded in the minute book, because the auditor or accountant does not have access to the minute book. This often results in additional cost to the corporation for lawyers' fees to correct the information filed or to prepare corporate documents to reflect the information as it was filed.

Federal annual returns

Section 263(1) of the CBCA provides that, on the prescribed date, every corporation shall send to the federal Director an annual return in prescribed form and the federal Director shall file it.

Section 4 of the CBCA regulations provides that the annual return shall be sent to the federal Director or to the CRA, as the case may be, by a corporation within six months after the end of the corporation's taxation year, setting out the required information as at that time.

The annual return can be prepared on Form 22 or on a document that conforms as closely as possible to it, or on T2 Schedule 80 — Industry Canada — Annual Return – *Canada Business Corporations Act* corporation income tax annual return.

The information required to complete the annual return is:

1. the name of the corporation;

2. the federal corporation number;

3. the CRA business number;

4. the taxation year-end;

5. the registered office address;

6. the mailing address, if it is different from the registered office address;

7. the corporation's main types of business;

8. an indication whether there has been a change in directors — if there has been, Form 6 must also be filed;

9. an indication whether there has been a change in the registered office — if there has been, Form 3 must also be filed;

10. the date of the last annual meeting;

11. an indication whether the corporation has more than 50 shareholders;

12. an indication whether the corporation distributes its securities to the public;

13. an indication whether the corporation has in place a unanimous shareholder agreement referred to in CBCA s. 146(2) that restricts, in whole or in part, the power of the directors to manage the business and affairs of the corporation;

14. the jurisdictions in which the corporation is carrying on business;

15. the date of signing;

16. the capacity and telephone number of the person signing; and

17. the signature of a director, authorized officer, or any solicitor or other person acting on behalf of the corporation.

Form 22 can be filed by paper copy, fax, or electronically with Corporations Canada. If the form is filed with the corporate tax return with the CRA, it takes 6 to 8 weeks for confirmation of the filing to be recorded on the Strategis Web site.

The current filing fee is $40 for a paper copy and $20 for an electronic copy.

If a corporation is in default for a period of one year in sending the annual return to the federal Director, the Director can dissolve the corporation after giving 120 days' notice of his of her decision to the corporation and each director and publishing notice in a publication generally available to the public (CBCA s. 212).

The federal Director also has the authority under CBCA s. 263.1(2) to refuse to issue a certificate of compliance if the annual return is not filed or if the filing fee is not paid. Furthermore, pursuant to a notice to clients dated December 22, 1998, the federal Director can refuse to file any document under the CBCA (for example, articles of amendment) if the annual return is not filed or if the filing fee is not paid.

Ontario annual returns

Every OBCA corporation, not-for-profit corporation under the *Corporations Act*, and foreign extra-provincial corporation must file a return under the CIA each year with the Minister of Consumer and Business Services ("MCBS minister") by delivering it to the Minister of Finance (CIA s. 3.1(1)).

There is an exception for electronically filed forms, which can be filed through the MCBS's service providers directly with the MCBS minister.

Corporations without share capital are exempted from this provision. However, they must file a return each year with the MCBS minister by delivering the return on the anniversary of the date of the corporation's incorporation or amalgamation, whichever is later, or within 60 days after the anniversary (CIA s. 3.1(3)).

The information contained on the annual return is:

1. the name of the corporation;

2. the Ontario corporation number;

3. all changes in the information set out in the notice or return that the corporation more recently filed under the CIA, if applicable; and

4. an indication that there has been no change in the information set out in the notice or return that the corporation most recently filed under the CIA, if applicable.

A corporation that is required to file a corporations tax return under s. 75 of the *Corporations Tax Act* must:

1. deliver the return together with the corporation's tax return for its last completed taxation year, within the time period for the return's delivery, or

2. if the corporation delivers a return to the MCBS electronically, deliver the return within the time period for its delivery.

A corporation that is not required to deliver a corporate tax return must deliver the annual return within six months of its last completed taxation year.

It takes six to eight weeks for confirmation of returns delivered to the Minister of Finance to appear on the public record.

There is no filing fee for filing annual returns in Ontario. However, if the returns are filed electronically, the MCBS's service providers charge a small fee.

Section 5(2) of the CIA provides that a corporation must maintain an up-to-date paper or electronic record of the prescribed information set out in returns and notices that it has filed under the CIA. It must also make the record available for examination by any shareholder, member, director, officer, or creditor of the corporation during its normal business hours at its registered office or principal place of business in Ontario.

The information from the annual return is uploaded into the Ontario Business Information System (ONBIS) and appears on the **corporation profile report**. A corporation profile report is a report produced by the Companies and Personal Property Security Branch of the Ontario MCBS ("Ontario Companies Branch") that displays current information about the corporation on the public record, including all directors, officers, and registered office, as well as some historical information, such as amalgamation and name history.

HISTORY OF ONTARIO ANNUAL RETURNS

The requirement to file annual returns in Ontario has undergone various changes in the past 30 years or so. Understanding these changes is important for those corporations that existed at that time, because you must ensure that the corporation has complied with all the requirements.

Corporations subject to the *Corporations Act* were required to file annual returns as of March 31 in each year. When the *Corporations Information Act* was introduced in 1976, this requirement was eliminated. No annual returns were required in Ontario from 1976 to 1992.

From July 1992 to 1994, the Ministry of Consumer and Commercial Relations (as the MCBS was then known) requested all corporations to file a "special notice" as of their anniversary date and to pay a filing fee. CIA s. 6(1) authorizes the minister at any time to require a corporation to make a special filing for the purpose of updating the public record. The information requested is generally the same as the information required in the initial notice.

As of April 1, 1995, every corporation in Ontario was again required to file an annual return pursuant to s. 3.1(1) of the CIA within 30 days of the anniversary date of incorporation or amalgamation and to pay a filing fee. This requirement was suspended between 1996 and 2000 while the Ministry of Finance, with other Ontario government departments, worked out a method of filing annual returns as part of the corporate tax return as of the end of the corporation's taxation year. The existing requirement became effective for all corporations with a year-end commencing in 2000.

You may still come across corporations that have not yet complied with these requirements. Information about a corporation's status of compliance will appear

corporation profile report
a report produced by the Ontario Companies Branch that displays current information on the public record about a corporation, including all directors, officers, and registered office, as well as some historical information, such as amalgamation and name history

on the corporation profile report or on a certificate of status. If a corporate client has not met its requirements, you will have to file the special notice or annual return and pay the outstanding fees. (No penalties have been added and the fee remains $50 for share capital corporations and $25 for not-for-profit corporations.)

FAILURE TO FILE ANNUAL RETURN

If a corporation fails to comply with a filing requirement under the CIA or fails to pay a fee required under the OBCA, the Ontario Director is authorized to give notice to the corporation or by publication once in the *Ontario Gazette* that an order dissolving the corporation will be issued unless the corporation complies with the requirement or pays the fee within 90 days after the notice is given (OBCA s. 241(3)). If the corporation does not comply, the Director may issue an order to cancel the certificate of incorporation, and the corporation will be dissolved on the date fixed in the order.

The Director's notice to the corporation can be given by prepaid mail to the corporation at its registered office as shown on the public record or delivered personally to the corporation. The notice is deemed to be received by the corporation on the fifth day after mailing.

The notice may also be sent by ordinary mail or by any other method, including registered mail, certified mail, or prepaid courier, to the appropriate address if there is a record by the person who has delivered it that the notice or document has been sent. A notice can also be sent by facsimile, or by any other form of electronic transmission if there is a record that the notice or other document has been sent. A notice sent by electronic means is deemed to be received on the earlier of (1) the day the recipient actually receives it and (2) the first business day after the day the transmission is sent by the Ontario Director.

You should be aware of OBCA s. 274, which has not yet been proclaimed. This section provides that the Ontario Director is not to endorse any certificate under the OBCA if a corporation is in default of a filing requirement under the CIA or has any unpaid fees or penalties outstanding.

Extra-provincial/territorial annual returns

Each province and territory in Canada has a requirement to file an annual return or, in the case of Prince Edward Island, to renew the corporate registration. Table 12.1 sets out the annual return (renewal) filing dates for each jurisdiction in Canada.

TABLE 12.1 ANNUAL RETURN (RENEWAL) FILING DATES

Province	Due date for filing annual returns
Alberta *Business Corporations Act*, RSA 2000, c. B-9; as amended, s. 292	On or before the last day of the month immediately following the month in which the certificate of registration is issued in Alberta.
British Columbia *Business Corporations Act*, SBC 2002, c. 57	Within two months after each anniversary date of the corporation's registration in British Columbia made up to that anniversary date.
Manitoba *The Corporations Act*, RSM 1987, c. C225, as amended, s. 121	Not later than the last day of the month immediately following the month in which the corporation was incorporated or amalgamated.
New Brunswick *Business Corporations Act*, SNB 1981, c. B-9.1, as amended, s. 209	On or before the last day of the month following: (a) the month in which the corporation was first registered in New Brunswick; or (b) the month of its incorporation if it is a federal or Canadian provincial/territorial corporation and it has so elected pursuant to s. 209(3). *Note:* Nova Scotia corporations are required to file an annual return and an appointment of attorney. The annual return can be a copy of the annual return filed in Nova Scotia.
Newfoundland *Corporations Act*, RSN 1990, c. C-36, as amended, s. 408	Not later than the first day of April in each year after the date of registration in Newfoundland containing information as of the preceding December 31. *Note:* Newfoundland is part of the Joint On-line Registration Pilot with the federal government and federal corporations can file their federal annual return and Newfoundland annual return online through Industry Canada's Electronic Filing Centre.
Nova Scotia *Corporations Registration Act*, RSNS, c. 101, as amended, s. 10	In the month during which the anniversary of the incorporation occurs. *Note:* (1) Corporations can file the same document as in the incorporating jurisdiction if it contains all the same information; (2) New Brunswick corporations are exempt from filing annual returns; and (3) Nova Scotia is part of the Joint On-line Registration Pilot with the federal government and federal corporations can file their federal annual return and Nova Scotia annual return online through Industry Canada's Electronic Filing Centre.

TABLE 12.1 CONCLUDED

Province	Due date for filing annual returns
Ontario *Corporations Information Act*, RSO 1990, c. C.39, as amended, s. 3.1(1)	No requirement for "domestic" extra-provincial corporations to file annual return. "Foreign" extra-provincial corporations are required to file annually as of the date of delivery as follows: If a corporation is required to file a tax return: i. deliver the return together with its tax return for its last completed taxation year, within the time period for delivery of the tax return; or ii. deliver the return within the time period for delivery of the tax return if it delivers a return to the Ontario Director electronically. If a corporation is not required to deliver a tax return, deliver the return within six months of its last completed taxation year.
Prince Edward Island *Licensing Act*, RSPEI, 1988, c. L-11, as amended, s. 4(1)	Anniversary of the date of registration.
Quebec *An Act Respecting the Legal Publicity of Sole Proprietorships, Partnerships and Legal Persons*, RSQ, c. P-45, as amended, s. 26	Between September 15 and December 15.
Saskatchewan *The Business Corporations Act*, RSS 1978, c. B-10, as amended, s. 273	The last day of the month following the month in which the corporation was incorporated or amalgamated.
Northwest Territories *Business Corporations Act*, SNWT 1996, c. 19, as amended, s. 292	On or before the last day of the month following the month each year, which is the same as the month in which the company was incorporated or amalgamated. The information is to be current to and including the most recent anniversary date of incorporation or amalgamation.
Nunavut *Business Corporations Act*, SNWT 1996, c. 19, as amended, s. 292	On or before the last day of the month following the month each year, which is the same as the month in which the company was incorporated or amalgamated. The information is to be current to and including the most recent anniversary date of incorporation or amalgamation.
Yukon *Business Corporations Act*, RSYT 1986, c. 15, as amended, s. 293	Before the last day of the month immediately following the corporation's anniversary month of the date of the certificate of registration issued in the Yukon.

KEY TERM

corporation profile report

REFERENCES

Business Corporations Act (Ontario) (OBCA), RSO 1990, c. B.16, as amended.

Campbell, John and Steven Adams, "Selected Tax Aspects of Corporate Reorganizations," Seminar for Corporate Law Clerks, Miller Thomson LLP, March 26, 1996.

Canada Business Corporations Act (CBCA), RSC 1985, c. C-44, as amended, and regulations.

Corporations Information Act (Ontario) (CIA), RSO 1990, c. C.39, as amended.

Corporations Tax Act (Ontario), RSO 1990, c. C.40, as amended.

Extra-Provincial Corporations Act (Ontario) (EPCA), RSO 1990, c. E.27, as amended.

Income Tax Act (Canada) (ITA), RSC 1985, c. 1 (5th Supp.), as amended.

Securities Act (Ontario), RSO 1990, c. S.5, as amended.

FORMS AND PRECEDENTS

Figure 12.1: Federal annual proceedings by resolution

Figure 12.2: Federal annual return — Form 22 and Schedule 80 of T2

Figure 12.3: Ontario annual proceedings by resolution

Figure 12.4: Ontario annual return (extracts from CT23 short-form corporations tax and annual return)

NOTE

1 The discussion in this section is based on John Campbell and Steven Adams, "Selected Tax Aspects of Corporate Reorganizations," Seminar for Corporate Law Clerks, Miller Thomson LLP, March 26, 1996.

REVIEW QUESTIONS

1. List four items that a corporation is required to do annually.

2. How are financial statements approved?

3. When must a corporation hold an annual meeting?

4. List the items of business typically conducted at an annual meeting.

5. If a corporation has six shareholders, can there be signed resolutions in lieu of an annual meeting? Explain.

6. Can a shareholder give a power of attorney to another person to sign resolutions on his or her behalf for

   a. a CBCA corporation?

   b. an OBCA corporation?

7. Can a director give a proxy to another person to attend and vote at a directors' meeting on his or her behalf?

8. List the documents required for an annual shareholders' meeting.

9. When is a CBCA corporation required to file an annual return? List two ways in which the return can be filed.

10. When is an OBCA corporation required to file an annual return? List two ways in which the return can be filed.

11. Is a "domestic" extra-provincial corporation required to file an annual return in Ontario?

12. Is a "foreign" extra-provincial corporation required to file an annual return in Ontario?

13. Are there any penalties for not filing an annual return? Explain, with references to both the CBCA and the OBCA.

EXERCISES

1. Draft directors' and shareholders' annual meeting documents.

2. Complete a federal annual return.

3. Complete an Ontario annual return.

FIGURE 12.1   FEDERAL ANNUAL PROCEEDINGS BY RESOLUTION

Direct Line -
E-mail -

May 5, 2005

PERSONAL AND CONFIDENTIAL

BSJ Garden Ornament Sales Inc.
123 Sesame Street
Port Ellen ON L3R 0C9

Attention: Mr. Peter Black, President

Dear Sirs:

**Re: BSJ Garden Ornament Sales Inc. (the "Corporation")
         Annual Proceedings for the Financial Period Ended December 31, 2004
         Our File No. 1111111/Alpha**

The *Canada Business Corporations Act* (the "CBCA") requires that a corporation hold an annual general meeting of shareholders. Instead of holding an actual meeting, shareholders may sign resolutions to conduct the business of the annual meeting. Our records indicate that it is time to prepare annual resolutions for the Corporation. Accordingly, we enclose for dating and signature the following resolutions and other documents which are required by the CBCA to bring the records of the Corporation up to date for its financial period ended December 31, 2004:

1.   Resolution of the board of directors approving the financial statements of the Corporation for its financial period ended December 31, 2004.

2.   Resolutions of the shareholders in lieu of the annual meeting.

3.   Director's Consent and Acknowledgment for each director.

4.   Resolutions of the board of directors appointing the officers for the ensuing year and authorizing maintenance of the books and records of the Corporation either at its registered office or at our offices.

FIGURE 12.1 CONTINUED

Page 2

If the enclosed documents are acceptable, please arrange to have them signed by the appropriate individuals and return them to us for filing with the Corporation's records.

We have prepared these documents using the information in the Corporation's records in our possession. If this information has changed, please advise us so we can update our records and prepare revised documents.

The CBCA requires that the board approval of the financial statements be evidenced by the signature of one or more directors at the foot of the balance sheet. If you have not yet received the financial statements from your accountants, please wait until you receive them before having the attached documents signed and returned.

In addition, the CBCA requires that corporations file an annual return (the "Return") for the purpose of updating or confirming the basic corporate information of record. The Return must be filed within six months of the corporation's taxation year end.

We understand that the form of Return is being sent out as part of the package with the corporation's annual income tax return from the Canada Revenue Agency. We also maintain an electronic database for the corporations whose records we hold which, to the best of our knowledge, contains information that matches the information currently contained in the Corporation's public file.

Therefore, if you or your accountant have filed the Return, please provide us with a copy that we can place in the Corporation's minute book and use to update our database with any information that is changed or added by the Return. Of course, we would be pleased to assist you in the preparation and filing of the Return, should you instruct us to.

If you have any questions regarding the above please do not hesitate to contact either the undersigned or Jessie Bruton, Corporate Law Clerk, at 905-415-9999.

Yours truly,

Richard Thorn

Encls.

FIGURE 12.1 CONTINUED

RESOLUTION OF THE BOARD OF DIRECTORS
OF
BSJ GARDEN ORNAMENT SALES INC.
(the "Corporation")

FINANCIAL STATEMENTS

RESOLVED that the audited financial statements of the Corporation for the financial period ended December 31, 2004 are approved and any director of the Corporation is authorized to sign the balance sheet on behalf of the board to evidence such approval.

THE UNDERSIGNED, being all of the directors of the Corporation, pass the foregoing resolution pursuant to the provisions of the *Canada Business Corporations Act*.

DATED the   day of   , 2005.

_____   _____
Peter Black   Roger Jones

_____
Shirley Smith

FIGURE 12.1   CONTINUED

RESOLUTIONS OF THE SHAREHOLDERS
OF
BSJ GARDEN ORNAMENT SALES INC.
(the "Corporation")

FINANCIAL STATEMENTS

RESOLVED, as an ordinary resolution, that the audited financial statements of the Corporation for the financial period ended December 31, 2004 are received.

ELECTION OF DIRECTORS

RESOLVED, as an ordinary resolution, that the following individuals are elected as the directors of the Corporation until the next annual meeting of the shareholders of the Corporation or until they otherwise cease to hold office as directors of the Corporation:

Peter Black
Roger Jones
Shirley Smith

APPOINTMENT OF AUDITOR

RESOLVED, as an ordinary resolution, that ABC Accounting LLP is appointed the auditor of the Corporation until the close of the next annual meeting of the shareholders or it sooner ceases to hold office as such at a remuneration to be fixed by the directors, the directors being authorized to fix such remuneration.

CONFIRMATION OF PROCEEDINGS

RESOLVED, as a special resolution, that all by-laws resolutions, contracts, acts and proceedings of the board of directors of the Corporation enacted, passed, made, done or taken since the last annual meeting (or the last resolutions of the shareholders in lieu of the annual meeting) which are:

(a)   referred to or appear in or may be inferred from any resolution, minutes of meeting, financial statements, registers, records or reports concerning the Corporation; and

(b)   now or have been available to the shareholders,

are approved notwithstanding any defect in the procedure for calling or holding any meeting, in the procedure for appointing directors or in the qualification of any director of the Corporation.

FIGURE 12.1 CONTINUED

THE UNDERSIGNED, being all of the shareholders of the Corporation entitled to vote thereon, pass the foregoing resolutions pursuant to the provisions of the *Canada Business Corporations Act*.

DATED the   day of   , 2005.

_____   _____
Peter Black   Roger Jones

_____
Shirley Smith

FIGURE 12.1   CONTINUED

DIRECTOR'S CONSENT AND ACKNOWLEDGEMENT

TO: BSJ GARDEN ORNAMENT SALES INC.
(the "Corporation")

I, the undersigned, in accordance with the provisions of the *Canada Business Corporations Act* (the "Act"):

(1)   Consent to act as a director of the Corporation, such consent to continue in effect unless revoked by instrument in writing delivered to the Corporation.

(2)   Acknowledge and declare that I am:

☐   a Canadian citizen ordinarily resident in Canada; **OR**

☐   a Canadian citizen <u>not</u> ordinarily resident in Canada who is a member of a prescribed class of persons (refer to Schedule A); **OR**

☐   a permanent resident within the meaning of the *Immigration Act* and ordinarily resident in Canada, except a permanent resident who has been ordinarily resident in Canada for more than one year after the time at which I first became eligible to apply for Canadian citizenship; **OR**

☐   none of the above

(3)   Undertake to advise the Corporation, in writing, forthwith after any change in citizenship, residence or status of lawful admission for permanent residence.

(4)   Acknowledge that:

a)   I am not under 18 years of age;

b)   I am not a person who has been found by a court in Canada or elsewhere to be of unsound mind; and

c)   I am not an undischarged bankrupt.

(5)   Consent to any director participating in a meeting of the directors or of a committee of directors by means of a telephonic, electronic or other communication facility that permits all participants to communicate adequately with each other during the meeting.

FIGURE 12.1 CONTINUED

(6)   Acknowledge that the Corporation will rely upon the foregoing consents and undertakings for the purpose of ensuring compliance by the Corporation with the provisions of the Act.

DATED the   day of   , 2005.

_____
Peter Black
1 First Street
Port Ellen, Ontario L3R 0A9

FIGURE 12.1 CONTINUED

SCHEDULE A

"Resident Canadian" Class of Persons Prescribed
SOR/2001-512, section 13 made under the *Canada Business Corporations Act* (the "Act")

For the purposes of the definition of "resident Canadian" in subsection 2 (1) of the Act, the following classes of persons are prescribed:

1. persons who are full-time employees of the Government of Canada, or a province, of an agency of any of those governments or of a federal or provincial Crown corporation, if the principal reason for their residence outside Canada is to act as employees;

2. persons who are full-time employees, if the principal reason for their residence outside Canada is to act as employees, of a body corporate,

    (i) of which more than 50 per cent of the voting shares are beneficially owned or over which control or direction is exercised by resident Canadians,

    (ii) a majority of directors of which are resident Canadians, or

    (iii) that is a subsidiary of a body corporate described in subparagraph (i) or (ii)

3. persons who are full-time students at a university or other educational institution recognized by the educational authorities of a majority of the provinces of Canada and have been resident outside Canada for fewer than 10 consecutive years;

4. persons who are full-time employees of an international association or organization of which Canada is a member; and

5. persons who were, at the time of reaching their 60th birthday, ordinarily resident in Canada and have been resident outside of Canada for fewer than 10 consecutive years.

FIGURE 12.1 CONTINUED 461

DIRECTOR'S CONSENT AND ACKNOWLEDGEMENT

TO: BSJ GARDEN ORNAMENT SALES INC.
(the "Corporation")

I, the undersigned, in accordance with the provisions of the *Canada Business Corporations Act* (the "Act"):

(1)   Consent to act as a director of the Corporation, such consent to continue in effect unless revoked by instrument in writing delivered to the Corporation.

(2)   Acknowledge and declare that I am:

☐   a Canadian citizen ordinarily resident in Canada; **OR**

☐   a Canadian citizen <u>not</u> ordinarily resident in Canada who is a member of a prescribed class of persons (refer to Schedule A); **OR**

☐   a permanent resident within the meaning of the *Immigration Act* and ordinarily resident in Canada, except a permanent resident who has been ordinarily resident in Canada for more than one year after the time at which I first became eligible to apply for Canadian citizenship; **OR**

☐   none of the above

(3)   Undertake to advise the Corporation, in writing, forthwith after any change in citizenship, residence or status of lawful admission for permanent residence.

(4)   Acknowledge that:

a)   I am not under 18 years of age;

b)   I am not a person who has been found by a court in Canada or elsewhere to be of unsound mind; and

c)   I am not an undischarged bankrupt.

(5)   Consent to any director participating in a meeting of the directors or of a committee of directors by means of a telephonic, electronic or other communication facility that permits all participants to communicate adequately with each other during the meeting.

FIGURE 12.1 CONTINUED

(6)   Acknowledge that the Corporation will rely upon the foregoing consents and undertakings for the purpose of ensuring compliance by the Corporation with the provisions of the Act.

DATED the   day of   , 2005.

Roger Jones
3 Third Street
Port Ellen, Ontario L3R 0D9

FIGURE 12.1   CONTINUED

SCHEDULE A

"Resident Canadian" Class of Persons Prescribed
SOR/2001-512, section 13 made under the *Canada Business Corporations Act* (the "Act")

For the purposes of the definition of "resident Canadian" in subsection 2 (1) of the Act, the following classes of persons are prescribed:

1. persons who are full-time employees of the Government of Canada, or a province, of an agency of any of those governments or of a federal or provincial Crown corporation, if the principal reason for their residence outside Canada is to act as employees;

2. persons who are full-time employees, if the principal reason for their residence outside Canada is to act as employees, of a body corporate,

    (i)   of which more than 50 per cent of the voting shares are beneficially owned or over which control or direction is exercised by resident Canadians,

    (ii) a majority of directors of which are resident Canadians, or

    (iii) that is a subsidiary of a body corporate described in subparagraph (i) or (ii)

3. persons who are full-time students at a university or other educational institution recognized by the educational authorities of a majority of the provinces of Canada and have been resident outside Canada for fewer than 10 consecutive years;

4. persons who are full-time employees of an international association or organization of which Canada is a member; and

5. persons who were, at the time of reaching their 60th birthday, ordinarily resident in Canada and have been resident outside of Canada for fewer than 10 consecutive years.

FIGURE 12.1   CONTINUED

DIRECTOR'S CONSENT AND ACKNOWLEDGEMENT

TO: BSJ GARDEN ORNAMENT SALES INC.
(the "Corporation")

I, the undersigned, in accordance with the provisions of the *Canada Business Corporations Act* (the "Act"):

(1)   Consent to act as a director of the Corporation, such consent to continue in effect unless revoked by instrument in writing delivered to the Corporation.

(2)   Acknowledge and declare that I am:

☐   a Canadian citizen ordinarily resident in Canada; **OR**

☐   a Canadian citizen <u>not</u> ordinarily resident in Canada who is a member of a prescribed class of persons (refer to Schedule A); **OR**

☐   a permanent resident within the meaning of the *Immigration Act* and ordinarily resident in Canada, except a permanent resident who has been ordinarily resident in Canada for more than one year after the time at which I first became eligible to apply for Canadian citizenship; **OR**

☐   none of the above

(3)   Undertake to advise the Corporation, in writing, forthwith after any change in citizenship, residence or status of lawful admission for permanent residence.

(4)   Acknowledge that:

a)   I am not under 18 years of age;

b)   I am not a person who has been found by a court in Canada or elsewhere to be of unsound mind; and

c)   I am not an undischarged bankrupt.

(5)   Consent to any director participating in a meeting of the directors or of a committee of directors by means of a telephonic, electronic or other communication facility that permits all participants to communicate adequately with each other during the meeting.

FIGURE 12.1   CONTINUED

(6)   Acknowledge that the Corporation will rely upon the foregoing consents and undertakings for the purpose of ensuring compliance by the Corporation with the provisions of the Act.

DATED the   day of   , 2005.

_____

Shirley Smith
2 Second Street
Port Ellen, Ontario L3R 0B9

FIGURE 12.1   CONTINUED

SCHEDULE A

"Resident Canadian" Class of Persons Prescribed
SOR/2001-512, section 13 made under the *Canada Business Corporations Act* (the "Act")

For the purposes of the definition of "resident Canadian" in subsection 2 (1) of the Act, the following classes of persons are prescribed:

1. persons who are full-time employees of the Government of Canada, or a province, of an agency of any of those governments or of a federal or provincial Crown corporation, if the principal reason for their residence outside Canada is to act as employees;

2. persons who are full-time employees, if the principal reason for their residence outside Canada is to act as employees, of a body corporate,

    (i)   of which more than 50 per cent of the voting shares are beneficially owned or over which control or direction is exercised by resident Canadians,

    (ii)   a majority of directors of which are resident Canadians, or

    (iii) that is a subsidiary of a body corporate described in subparagraph (i) or (ii)

3. persons who are full-time students at a university or other educational institution recognized by the educational authorities of a majority of the provinces of Canada and have been resident outside Canada for fewer than 10 consecutive years;

4. persons who are full-time employees of an international association or organization of which Canada is a member; and

5. persons who were, at the time of reaching their 60th birthday, ordinarily resident in Canada and have been resident outside of Canada for fewer than 10 consecutive years.

FIGURE 12.1 CONCLUDED

RESOLUTIONS OF THE BOARD OF DIRECTORS
OF
BSJ GARDEN ORNAMENT SALES INC.
(the "Corporation")

APPOINTMENT OF OFFICERS

RESOLVED that the following individuals are appointed to the office or offices set opposite their respective names, to hold office at the pleasure of the board:

Peter Black	-	President
Shirley Smith	-	Vice President
Roger Jones	-	Secretary

LOCATION OF BOOKS AND RECORDS

RESOLVED that the Corporation maintains, at its registered office or at the offices of Miller Thomson LLP, the records and registers specified in the *Canada Business Corporations Act*.

THE UNDERSIGNED, being all of the directors of the Corporation, pass the foregoing resolutions pursuant to the provisions of the *Canada Business Corporations Act*.

DATED the   day of   , 2005.

_____   _____
Peter Black   Roger Jones

_____
Shirley Smith

FIGURE 12.2 FEDERAL ANNUAL RETURN — FORM 22 AND SCHEDULE 80 OF T2

Industry Canada Industrie Canada Canada Business Loi canadienne sur les Corporations Act sociétés par actions	**FORM 22 ANNUAL RETURN** (section 263)	**FORMULAIRE 22 RAPPORT ANNUEL** (article 263)

Filing for Year - Dépôt pour l'année
2003

See Instructions on the Reverse Side - Voir les instructions au verso

1 -- Corporation Name and Registered Office Address - Dénomination sociale de la société et adresse du siège social

BSJ Garden Ornament Sales Inc.

123 Sesame Street, Port Ellen, ON, Canada, L3R 0C9

(and mailing address, if different from that of registered office) - (ainsi que l'adresse postale si elle diffère de celle du siège social)

2 -- Corporation No. - N° de la société
454545

3 -- Business No. - N° d'entreprise
123123123

4 -- Taxation Year End
Fin de l'année d'imposition
M: 1 2 D-J: 3 1

5 -- Main Types of Business - Catégories principales d'activité commerciale

Sales

6 -- Has there been a change of director(s)?
Est-ce qu'il y a eu un changement d'administrateur(s) ?

☐ Yes - Oui   ☒ No - Non

If yes, has Form 6 been: - Si oui, le formulaire 6 a-t-il été :

☐ Filed - Déposé   ☐ Attached - Annexé

7 -- Has there been a change of registered office?
Est-ce qu'il y a eu un changement du siège social ?

☐ Yes - Oui   ☒ No - Non

If yes, has Form 3 been: - Si oui, le formulaire 3 a-t-il été :

☐ Filed - Déposé   ☐ Attached - Annexé

8 -- Date of Last Annual Meeting
Date de la dernière assemblée annuelle   ▶   Y-A M D-J

9 -- Is the Corporation a distributing corporation or a reporting issuer?
La société est-elle une société ayant fait appel au public ou un émetteur assujetti ?   ▶ ☐ Yes Oui ☒ No Non

10 -- Does the corporation have more than 50 shareholders?
La société a-t-elle 50 actionnaires ou plus ?   ▶ ☐ Yes - Oui   ☒ No - Non

11 -- Does the Corporation have in place a unanimous shareholder agreement referred to in subsection 146(1) of the Act that restricts the powers of the directors?
La société dispose-t-elle d'une convention unanime des actionnaires visée au paragraphe 146(1) de la Loi qui restreint les pouvoirs des administrateurs ?   ▶ ☐ Yes Oui ☒ No Non

12 -- Jurisdictions in which the corporation is carrying on business - Provinces et territoires où la société exerce ses activités

Prov./Territory-Prov./Territoire	Address of the principal place of business or address for service - Adresse principale de la société ou adresse aux fins de signification
Ontario	123 Sesame Street, Port Ellen, ON, Canada, L3R 0C9

Tel. No. - N° de tél.	Signature	Printed Name - Nom en lettres moulées Peter Black	13 -- Capacity of - En qualité de President

FOR DEPARTMENTAL USE ONLY - A L'USAGE DU MINISTÈRE SEULEMENT

IC 2580 (2003/04)

Canada

FIGURE 12.2 CONTINUED

Canada Customs
and Revenue Agency
and Industry Canada

Agence des douanes
et du revenu du Canada
et Industrie Canada

SCHEDULE 80

INDUSTRY CANADA – ANNUAL RETURN – *CANADA BUSINESS CORPORATIONS ACT*

Name of corporation	Business Number	Taxation year end
BSJ GARDEN ORNAMENT SALES INC.	123123123	Year: 2 0 0 3 Month: 1 2 Day: 3 1

Corporations incorporated under the *Canada Business Corporations Act* (CBCA) may satisfy the CBCA requirements to file an annual return with the Director, CBCA, by completing this schedule and filing it with the *T2 Corporation Income Tax Return* (T2 return) within six months of the taxation year end, (as that term is defined under the *Income Tax Act*).

By completing Schedule 80, you are consenting to Canada Customs and Revenue Agency's disclosure of the information provided on this annual return, and certain information from the T2 return (i.e., corporation name, Business Number, taxation year end, head office address, mailing address, and the major business activity), to Industry Canada, Director, CBCA, as part of the joint initiative to ease the reporting burden for common clients.

Schedule 80 is deemed to be signed by a director or authorized officer if it is attached to a signed *T2 Corporation Income Tax Return*.

If you do not consent to the above, you can file directly with Industry Canada using their prescribed forms.

Part 1 – Corporate Information

Does the corporation distribute its securities to the public? . . . . **110**   1 Yes ☐   2 No ☒

Does the corporation have 15 or more shareholders? . . . . **111**   1 Yes ☐   2 No ☒

Does the corporation have in place a unanimous shareholder agreement referred to in subsection 146(2) of the *Canada Business Corporations Act*? A unanimous shareholder agreement is a written agreement among all the shareholders of a corporation that restricts, in whole or in part, the powers of the directors to manage the business and affairs of the corporation by giving to the shareholders certain powers usually conferred to the Board of Directors . . . . **112**   1 Yes ☐   2 No ☒

What was the date of the last annual meeting? . . . . *None held yet* . . . . **113** | | | | | | | |
  Year   Month   Day

Part 2 – Director Information

Has there been a change of directors of the corporation? . . . . **120**   1 Yes ☐   2 No ☒

If *yes*, has Form 6, *Notice of Change of Directors* been filed pursuant to the provisions of the CBCA? . . . . . **121**   1 Yes ☐   2 No ☐

If the answer is *no* at line 121, please indicate if you have completed and attached
Schedule 81 – *Notice of Change of Directors* – CBCA with this form . . . . **122**   1 Yes ☐   2 No ☐

Part 3 – Filing Fee

An annual return filing fee of $40.00 payable to the Receiver General for Canada is prescribed by the
regulations to the CBCA. Have you included this payment with this T2 return? . . . . **130**   1 Yes ☒   2 No ☐

Please use the attached remittance voucher to make your payment.

T2 SCH 80 E (02)   (Ce formulaire existe en français.)   **Canadä**

FIGURE 12.2 CONTINUED

Part 4 – Registered Office

Is the Registered Office address of the corporation the same as the Head Office address
identified on page 1 of the T2 return? . . . . **200**   1 Yes [X]   2 No [ ]

If the answer is *no* at line 200, please provide the address of the Registered Office in the space below:

201 Street

City	Province / Territory	Postal code

Has there been a change of Registered Office since you last filed your annual return? . . . . **210**   1 Yes [ ]   2 No [X]

If *yes*, has Form 3, *Notice of Change of Registered Office* been filed pursuant to the
provisions of the CBCA? . . . . **211**   1 Yes [ ]   2 No [ ]

If the answer is *no* at line 211, you may complete a *Notice of Change of Registered Office* by providing the information in this part. The notice will be deemed to be received by the Director, CBCA, at the time and date that this return is received by Revenue Canada. Where required by the Act, the changes being reported by the filing of this form must be authorized by the director(s) or shareholder(s). If the address of the Registered Office is changed to a place located outside of the area specified in the Articles, an amendment to the Articles, will be necessary.

Effective date of the change of Registered Office . . . . **220** | | | | | | |
Year   Month   Day

Place in Canada where the Registered Office is currently situated.

221 Place Ontario

Previous address of the Registered Office.

231 Street

City	Province / Territory	Postal code

Part 5 – Jurisdiction In Which The Corporation Is Carrying On Business

For each provincial/territorial jurisdiction in which the corporation is carrying on business, state the address of the principal place of business or address for service, including the city, province, and postal code. A corporation is presumed to be "carrying on business" if it has an address in the province/territory or having there, either directly or through the agency of a representative acting under a general mandate, an establishment, a post office box or the use of a telephone line, or carrying out in the province/territory any act for the purpose of profit.

	240 Address of the principal place of business or address for service	City	Province / Territory	Postal code
1.	123 Sesame Street	Port Ellen	ON	L3R 0C9
2.				
3.				
4.				
5.				
6.				
7.				
8.				
9.				
10.				
11.				
12.				

Certification

Please complete this area if this schedule is filed separately from the signed T2 return.

I, **950** _____ **951** _____ **954** _____ President _____
(Surname in block letters)   (First name in block letters)   Position, office, or rank

am an authorized signing officer of the corporation. I certify that I have examined this schedule, and that the information given on this schedule is, to the best of my knowledge, correct and complete.

955 | 2 | 0 | 0 | 4 | 0 | 5 | 3 | 1 | _____   **956**   555-777-0000
Year   Month Day   Date   Signature of an authorized signing officer of the corporation   Telephone number

Printed in Canada

FIGURE 12.2   CONTINUED

Please use this voucher only to pay your Canada Business Corporations Act (CBCA) annual return filing fee. Complete all boxes and the name area on the voucher to ensure we allocate your payment correctly. See the reverse for further instructions.

▌✹▐ Canada Customs and Revenue Agency and Industry Canada	Agence des douanes et du revenu du Canada et Industrie Canada	**BUSINESS REMITTANCE VOUCHER** **Annual Return Filing Fee**	T2 SCH 80 E (02)

Business Number

123123123

Trans. Type

I

Corporation's Name

BSJ Garden Ornament Sales Inc.

Taxation Year End

Year	Month	Day
2 0 0 3	1 2	3 1

Amount Paid

40.00

FIGURE 12.2   CONCLUDED

Return the voucher to your taxation centre with your *T2 Corporation Income Tax Return* and Schedule 80, *Industry Canada - Annual Return*, and your cheque or money order made payable to the Receiver General for Canada. **Do not** make your payment at your financial institution.

To help us credit your payment, write your business number on the back of your cheque or money order.

We will charge a fee for any dishonoured payment.

DO NOT staple, paper clip, tape or fold voucher or your cheque

DO NOT mail cash

FIGURE 12.3   ONTARIO ANNUAL PROCEEDINGS BY RESOLUTION

August 15, 2004

PERSONAL AND CONFIDENTIAL

01111111 Ontario Inc.
111 Red Street
White Port ON   P3P 0P9

Attention: David Green, President

Dear Sirs:

Re: 01111111 Ontario Inc.. (the "Corporation")
Annual Proceedings for the Financial Period Ended April 30, 2004
Our File No. 3232

The *Business Corporations Act* (Ontario) (the "OBCA") requires that a corporation hold an annual general meeting of shareholders. Instead of holding an actual meeting, shareholders may sign resolutions to conduct the business of the annual meeting. Our records indicate that it is time to prepare annual resolutions for the Corporation. Accordingly, we enclose for dating and signature the following resolutions and other documents which are required by the OBCA to bring the records of the Corporation up to date for its financial period ended April 30, 2004:

1.   Resolution of the board of directors approving the financial statements of the Corporation for its financial period ended April 30, 2004.

2.   Resolutions of the shareholders in lieu of the annual meeting.

3.   Director's Consent and Acknowledgment for each director.

4.   Resolutions of the board of directors appointing the officers for the ensuing year and authorizing maintenance of the books and records of the Corporation either at its registered office or at our offices.

FIGURE 12.3   CONTINUED

Page 2

If the enclosed documents are acceptable, please arrange to have them signed by the appropriate individuals and return them to us for filing with the Corporation's records.

We have prepared these documents using the information in the Corporation's records in our possession. If this information has changed, please advise us so we can update our records and prepare revised documents.

The OBCA requires that the board approval of the financial statements be evidenced by the signature of two of the directors at the foot of the balance sheet. If you have not yet received the financial statements from your accountants, please wait until you receive them before having the attached documents signed and returned.

The Corporation must file an annual income tax return with each of Canada Revenue Agency, the Ministry of Finance and each province in which it carries on business.

If the Director under the OBCA is notified by the Ministry of Finance that an OBCA corporation is in default in complying with the provisions of the *Corporations Tax Act*, the Director may give notice by registered mail to the corporation or by publication once in *The Ontario Gazette* that an order dissolving the corporation will be issued unless the corporation remedies its default within ninety days after giving of the notice. The implications of this are:

- Forfeiture of corporate assets to the Crown;

- Loss of limited liability and insurance coverage; and

- Inability to claim tax losses.

The Ontario government requires corporations with tax due to pay a late filing penalty of up to 17 per cent on the outstanding balance, escalating up to 50 per cent for repeat late non-filers. In addition, directors of corporations may be prosecuted for failure to file and fined $200 per day.

If you have any questions regarding the above please do not hesitate to contact either the undersigned or Jessie Bruton, Corporate Law Clerk, at 905-415-9999.

Yours truly,

Alan Hill

Encls.

FIGURE 12.3   CONTINUED

RESOLUTION OF THE BOARD OF DIRECTORS
OF
01111111 ONTARIO INC.
(the "Corporation")

FINANCIAL STATEMENTS

RESOLVED that the unaudited financial statements of the Corporation for the financial period ended April 30, 2004 are approved and the directors of the Corporation are authorized to sign the balance sheet on behalf of the board to evidence such approval.

THE UNDERSIGNED, being all of the directors of the Corporation, pass the foregoing resolution pursuant to the provisions of the *Business Corporations Act* (Ontario).

DATED the   day of   , 2004.

_____   _____
David Green   Carol Green

FIGURE 12.3 CONTINUED

RESOLUTIONS OF THE SOLE SHAREHOLDER
OF
01111111 ONTARIO INC.
(the "Corporation")

FINANCIAL STATEMENTS

RESOLVED, as an ordinary resolution, that the unaudited financial statements of the Corporation for the financial period ended April 30, 2004 are received.

ELECTION OF DIRECTORS

RESOLVED, as an ordinary resolution, that the following individuals are elected as the directors of the Corporation until the next annual meeting of the shareholders of the Corporation or until they otherwise cease to hold office as directors of the Corporation:

David Green
Carol Green

EXEMPTION FROM AUDIT REQUIREMENTS

WHEREAS the Corporation is not an offering corporation within the meaning of the *Business Corporations Act* (Ontario) (the "Act");

RESOLVED, as a unanimous resolution, that the Corporation be exempt from the requirements of the Act regarding the appointment and duties of an auditor for the financial period ending April 30, 2004.

APPOINTMENT OF ACCOUNTANT

RESOLVED, as an ordinary resolution, that ABC Accounting LLP is appointed the accountant of the Corporation until the close of the next annual meeting of the shareholders or it sooner ceases to hold office as such at a remuneration to be fixed by the directors, the directors being authorized to fix such remuneration.

CONFIRMATION OF PROCEEDINGS

RESOLVED, as a special resolution, that all by-laws resolutions, contracts, acts and proceedings of the board of directors of the Corporation enacted, passed, made, done or taken since the last annual meeting (or the last resolutions of the shareholders in lieu of the annual meeting) which are:

(a)   referred to or appear in or may be inferred from any resolution, minutes of meeting, financial statements, registers, records or reports concerning the Corporation; and

FIGURE 12.3 CONTINUED

(b) now or have been available to the shareholders,

are approved notwithstanding any defect in the procedure for calling or holding any meeting, in the procedure for appointing directors or in the qualification of any director of the Corporation.

THE UNDERSIGNED, being the sole shareholder of the Corporation entitled to vote thereon, passes the foregoing resolutions pursuant to the provisions of the *Business Corporations Act* (Ontario).

DATED the   day of   , 2004.

_____

David Green

FIGURE 12.3   CONTINUED

DIRECTOR'S CONSENT AND ACKNOWLEDGEMENT

TO: 01111111 ONTARIO INC.
(the "Corporation")

I, the undersigned, in accordance with the provisions of the *Business Corporations Act* (Ontario) (the "Act"):

(1)   Consent to act as a director of the Corporation, such consent to continue in effect unless revoked by instrument in writing delivered to the Corporation.

(2)   Acknowledge and declare that I am:

☐   a Canadian citizen ordinarily resident in Canada; **OR**

☐   a Canadian citizen <u>not</u> ordinarily resident in Canada who is a member of a prescribed class of persons (refer to Schedule A); **OR**

☐   a permanent resident within the meaning of the *Immigration Act* and ordinarily resident in Canada; **OR**

☐   none of the above

(3)   Undertake to advise the Corporation, in writing, forthwith after any change in citizenship, residence or status of lawful admission for permanent residence.

(4)   Acknowledge that:

a)   I am not under 18 years of age;

b)   I am not a person who has been found by a court in Canada or elsewhere to be of unsound mind; and

c)   I am not an undischarged bankrupt.

(5)   Consent to any director participating in a meeting of the directors or of a committee of directors by means of such telephone, electronic or other communication facilities as permit all persons participating in the meeting to communicate with each other simultaneously and instantaneously.

FIGURE 12.3   CONTINUED

(6)   Acknowledge that the Corporation will rely upon the foregoing consents and undertakings for the purpose of ensuring compliance by the Corporation with the provisions of the Act.

DATED the   day of   , 2004.

David Green
111 Red Street
White Port ON P3P 0P9

FIGURE 12.3 CONTINUED

SCHEDULE A

"Resident Canadian" Class of Persons Prescribed
Ont. Reg. 62, s. 26 made under the *Business Corporations Act* (Ontario) (the "Act")

For the purposes of clause (b) of the definition of "resident Canadian" in subsection 1(1) of the Act, the following classes of persons are prescribed:

1. Full-time employees of the Government of Canada, a province or a territory of Canada or of an agency of any such government or of a federal or provincial crown corporation.

2. Full-time employees of a body corporate,

    (i) of which more than 50 per cent of the voting securities are beneficially owned or over which control or direction is exercised by resident Canadians, or

    (ii) a majority of directors of which are resident Canadians,

    where the principal reason for the residence outside Canada is to act as such employees;

3. Full-time students at a university outside of Canada or at another educational institution outside of Canada recognized by the province.

4. Full-time employees of an international association or organization of which Canada is a member.

5. Persons who were, at the time of reaching their 60th birthday, ordinarily resident in Canada and have been resident outside of Canada since that time.

FIGURE 12.3 CONTINUED

DIRECTOR'S CONSENT AND ACKNOWLEDGEMENT

TO: **01111111 ONTARIO INC.**
(the "Corporation")

I, the undersigned, in accordance with the provisions of the *Business Corporations Act* (Ontario) (the "Act"):

(1)   Consent to act as a director of the Corporation, such consent to continue in effect unless revoked by instrument in writing delivered to the Corporation.

(2)   Acknowledge and declare that I am:

☐   a Canadian citizen ordinarily resident in Canada; **OR**

☐   a Canadian citizen <u>not</u> ordinarily resident in Canada who is a member of a prescribed class of persons (refer to Schedule A); **OR**

☐   a permanent resident within the meaning of the *Immigration Act* and ordinarily resident in Canada; **OR**

☐   none of the above

(3)   Undertake to advise the Corporation, in writing, forthwith after any change in citizenship, residence or status of lawful admission for permanent residence.

(4)   Acknowledge that:

a)   I am not under 18 years of age;

b)   I am not a person who has been found by a court in Canada or elsewhere to be of unsound mind; and

c)   I am not an undischarged bankrupt.

(5)   Consent to any director participating in a meeting of the directors or of a committee of directors by means of such telephone, electronic or other communication facilities as permit all persons participating in the meeting to communicate with each other simultaneously and instantaneously.

FIGURE 12.3   CONTINUED

(6)   Acknowledge that the Corporation will rely upon the foregoing consents and undertakings for the purpose of ensuring compliance by the Corporation with the provisions of the Act.

DATED the   day of   , 2004.

Carol Green
111 Red Street
White Port ON   P3P 0P9

FIGURE 12.3   CONTINUED

SCHEDULE A

"Resident Canadian" Class of Persons Prescribed
Ont. Reg. 62, s. 26 made under the *Business Corporations Act* (Ontario) (the "Act")

For the purposes of clause (b) of the definition of "resident Canadian" in subsection 1(1) of the Act, the following classes of persons are prescribed:

1.   Full-time employees of the Government of Canada, a province or a territory of Canada or of an agency of any such government or of a federal or provincial crown corporation.

2.   Full-time employees of a body corporate,

     (i)   of which more than 50 per cent of the voting securities are beneficially owned or over which control or direction is exercised by resident Canadians, or

     (ii)   a majority of directors of which are resident Canadians,

     where the principal reason for the residence outside Canada is to act as such employees;

3.   Full-time students at a university outside of Canada or at another educational institution outside of Canada recognized by the province.

4.   Full-time employees of an international association or organization of which Canada is a member.

5.   Persons who were, at the time of reaching their 60th birthday, ordinarily resident in Canada and have been resident outside of Canada since that time.

FIGURE 12.3   CONCLUDED

RESOLUTIONS OF THE BOARD OF DIRECTORS
OF
01111111 ONTARIO INC.
(the "Corporation")

APPOINTMENT OF OFFICERS

RESOLVED that the following individuals are appointed to the office or offices set opposite their respective names, to hold office at the pleasure of the board:

David Green	-	President
Carol Green	-	Secretary

LOCATION OF BOOKS AND RECORDS

RESOLVED that the Corporation maintains, at its registered office or at the offices of Thorn & Hill LLP, the records and registers specified in the *Business Corporations Act* (Ontario).

THE UNDERSIGNED, being all of the directors of the Corporation, pass the foregoing resolutions pursuant to the provisions of the *Business Corporations Act* (Ontario).

DATED the   day of   , 2005.

_____   _____
David Green   Carol Green

FIGURE 12.4 ONTARIO ANNUAL RETURN (EXTRACTS FROM CT23 SHORT-FORM CORPORATIONS TAX AND ANNUAL RETURN)

Ontario

Ministry of Finance
Corporations Tax Branch
PO Box 620
33 King Street West
Oshawa ON L1H 8E9

2003

CT23 Short-Form Corporations Tax and Annual Return *For taxation years commencing after September 30, 2001*

Corporations Tax Act - Ministry of Finance (MOF)
Corporations Information Act - Ministry of Consumer and Business Services (MCBS)
(formerly Ministry of Consumer and Commercial Relations)

This return is a combination of the Ministry of Finance (MOF) CT23 Short-Form Corporations Tax Return and the Ministry of Consumer and Business Services (MCBS) Annual Return. Page 1 is a common page required for both returns. For tax purposes, depending on which criteria the corporation satisfies, it must complete either the **Exempt from Filing (EFF)** declaration on page 2 or file the **CT23 Short-Form Return** on pages 3-6. **Corporations that do not meet the EFF criteria or the Short-Form criteria, must file the regular CT23 return.**

The Annual Return (common page 1 and MCBS Schedules A or K on pages 7 and 8) contains non-tax information collected under the authority of the *Corporations Information Act* for the purpose of maintaining a public database of corporate information. This return must be completed by Ontario share-capital corporations or Foreign-Business share-capital corporations that have an extra-provincial licence to operate in Ontario.

MCBS Annual Return Required? *(Not required if already filed or Annual Return exempt. Refer to Guide)* ☐ Yes ☐ No   **Page 1 of 8**

— Ministry Use —

Corporation's Legal Name *(including punctuation)*
01111111 Ontario Inc.

Ontario Corporations Tax Account No. (MOF)

Mailing Address
111 Red Street
White Port ON P3P 0P9

This CT23 Return covers the Taxation Year

Start | year | month | day

End | year | month | day

Has the mailing address changed since last filed CT23 Return? Yes ☐
Date of Change | year | month | day

Date of Incorporation or Amalgamation
year | month | day

Registered/Head Office Address
111 Red Street
White Port ON P3P 0P9

Ontario Corporation No. (MCBS)

Location of Books and Records
Thorn & Hill LLP
8476 Waterview Avenue
White Port ON P3Q 1R6

Canada Customs and Revenue Agency (formerly Revenue Canada) Business No.
If applicable, enter | **RC**

Name of person to contact regarding this CT23 Return
Jessie Bruton
Telephone No. **905-385-8374**
Fax No. **905-385-8300**

Jurisdiction Incorporated

Address of Principal Office in Ontario *(Extra-Provincial Corporations only)* (MCBS)

If not incorporated in Ontario, indicate the date Ontario business activity commenced and ceased:
Commenced | year | month | day

Former Corporation Name *(Extra-Provincial Corporations only)* **Not Applicable** [X] (MCBS)

Ceased | year | month | day

(Not Applicable) ☐

Information on Directors/Officers/Administrators must be completed on MCBS Schedule A or K as appropriate. If additional space is required for Schedule A, only this schedule may be photocopied. State number submitted (MCBS). ▶

No. of Schedule(s)
1

Preferred Language / *Langue de préférence*
English anglais ☐   French français ☐

Ministry Use

If there is **no change** to the Directors'/Officers'/Administrators' information previously submitted to MCBS, please check ☑ this box. Schedule(s) A and K are not required (MCBS). ▶ ☐ No Change

Certification (MCBS)

I certify that all information set out in the **Annual Return** is true, correct and complete.

Name of Authorized Person *(Print clearly or type in full)*
David Green

Title: [X] **D** Director   ☐ **O** Officer   ☐ **P** Other individual having knowledge of the affairs of the Corporation

Note: Sections 13 and 14 of the *Corporations Information Act* provide penalties for making false or misleading statements or omissions.

ISBN 0-7794-4471-X   © Queen's Printer for Ontario, 2003   1399D (2004-01)

FIGURE 12.4 CONCLUDED

Schedule A: Information on Ontario Corporations

(Corporations that are incorporated, continued or amalgamated under the
Ontario Business Corporations Act)

MCBS

Schedule A

Page 7 of 8

To submit additional Director or Officer Information, please photocopy this page and attach the completed schedules with your return.

Identification

Corporation's Legal Name *(including punctuation)* 01111111 Ontario Inc.	Ontario Corporation No. (MCBS) 0 1 1 1 1 1 1 1	Date of Incorporation or Amalgamation year 2 0 0 3 month 1 0 day 3 1

Director/Officer Information

Full Name and Address for Service:

Last Name Green	First Name David	Middle Name(s)

Street Number and Name 111 Red Street	Suite

City/Town/Village White Port	Province/State ON	Country Canada	Postal/Zip Code P3P 0P9

Director	**Officer**

Are you a Resident Canadian? *(Applies to directors of business corporations only)*

[X] Yes [ ] No

Date Elected
year 2 0 0 3 month 1 0 day 3 1

Date Ceased
year month day

Indicate the appointment period for each of the following:

Other Titles *(please specify)*:

	Date Appointed			Date Ceased		
	year	month	day	year	month	day
President	2 0 0 3	1 0	3 1			
Secretary						
Treasurer						
General Manager						
Other (specify)						

[ ] Chair
[ ] Chair Person
[ ] Chairman
[ ] Chairwoman
[ ] Vice-Chair
[ ] Vice-President
[ ] Assistant Secretary
[ ] Assistant Treasurer
[ ] Chief Manager
[ ] Executive Director
[ ] Managing Director
[ ] Chief Executive Officer
[ ] Chief Financial Officer
[ ] Chief Information Officer
[ ] Chief Operating Officer
[ ] Chief Administrative Officer
[ ] Comptroller
[ ] Authorized Signing Officer
[ ] Other (untitled)

Director/Officer Information

Full Name and Address for Service:

Last Name Green	First Name Carol	Middle Name(s)

Street Number and Name 111 Red Street	Suite

City/Town/Village White Port	Province/State ON	Country Canada	Postal/Zip Code P3P 0P9

Director	**Officer**

Are you a Resident Canadian? *(Applies to directors of business corporations only)*

[X] Yes [ ] No

Date Elected
year 2 0 0 3 month 1 0 day 3 1

Date Ceased
year month day

Indicate the appointment period for each of the following:

Other Titles *(please specify)*:

	Date Appointed			Date Ceased		
	year	month	day	year	month	day
President						
Secretary	2 0 0 3	1 0	3 1			
Treasurer						
General Manager						
Other (specify)						

[ ] Chair
[ ] Chair Person
[ ] Chairman
[ ] Chairwoman
[ ] Vice-Chair
[ ] Vice-President
[ ] Assistant Secretary
[ ] Assistant Treasurer
[ ] Chief Manager
[ ] Executive Director
[ ] Managing Director
[ ] Chief Executive Officer
[ ] Chief Financial Officer
[ ] Chief Information Officer
[ ] Chief Operating Officer
[ ] Chief Administrative Officer
[ ] Comptroller
[ ] Authorized Signing Officer
[ ] Other (untitled)

Note: Sections 13 and 14 of the *Corporations Information Act* provide penalties for making false or misleading statements or omissions.

1399D (2004-01)

CHAPTER 13

Corporate changes

CHAPTER OVERVIEW

This chapter considers the legal issues, procedures, and government filings affecting the basic changes in structure that a corporation may make throughout its history. These include changes made by resolution of the directors; changes made by resolution of the directors and subsequent filing of articles of amendment; changes made by special resolution of the shareholders, including the steps that need to be taken on the sale, lease, or exchange of all or substantially all of the property of a corporation; and the changes made by special resolution and filing articles of amendment. The chapter also discusses how shareholders who disagree with an action approved by a majority of shareholders can have their shares purchased back by the corporation for fair market value, and how any voting shareholder can make a proposal to amend the articles.

CHAPTER OBJECTIVES

After completing this chapter, you should be able to:

1. Recognize when and why corporate changes are required.

2. Identify the sections of the CBCA and the OBCA that apply to various corporate changes.

3. Describe the procedures to be followed to effect the changes.

4. Name the classes of shareholders entitled to vote on the changes.

5. Complete the documents required for the changes.

6. List the documents for filing with Corporations Canada and the Ontario Companies Branch to effect certain changes.

7. Distinguish when dissent rights will attach to changes.

8. Identify the differences between the procedures under the CBCA and the OBCA.

9. Understand when the federal Director and the Ontario Director will agree to issue a corrected certificate.

10. Discuss the procedures to be followed to have a corrected certificate issued by the federal Director and the Ontario Director.

INTRODUCTION

A corporation will make a number of different corporate legal changes throughout its history. The corporate statutes govern the procedures for most of the significant changes. Knowing when and how to make these changes is a fundamental part of maintaining the corporate records for a corporate client. Making changes accurately and thoroughly will save much rectification work at the time of conducting minute book due diligence.

In general, changes can be adopted by:

- a resolution of the directors,

- a resolution of the directors and filing of articles of amendment,

- a special resolution of the shareholders, or

- a special resolution of the shareholders and filing of articles of amendment.

CHANGES MADE BY RESOLUTION OF THE DIRECTORS

The passing of a directors' resolution can make simple corporate changes, but reference must be made to the relevant statute to determine any restrictions that may apply to the change. In addition, if the shareholders have entered into a unanimous shareholder agreement (USA) that restricts the powers of the directors, the changes approved by the directors must then be approved by the shareholders pursuant to their powers obtained under the USA.

Changes that can be effected by simple resolution of the directors include:

- a change of financial year-end;

- a bylaw amendment;

- a change of officers;

- a change in the street address of the registered office;

- an increase or decrease in the number of directors within the minimum and maximum number, if the directors are empowered by the shareholder to make such a change;

- a change in the location of the records office; and

- a change in the bank signing authority.

Change of financial year-end

The directors of a corporation usually determine the financial year-end either at the time of organization or within the first year of the corporation's existence. You should check the bylaws and any USA to confirm that the directors have the authority to change the year-end without shareholder approval. If they do, a change can be done by way of a directors' resolution. If the first financial year has ended, after the resolution is passed, the corporation should write to the Canada Revenue Agency (CRA), giving a sound business reason for the change and requesting approval.

Bylaw amendment (CBCA ss. 103(1)–(4); OBCA ss. 116(1)–(4))

If any of the provisions of the bylaws require change, subject to the articles, the bylaws, or a USA, the directors may amend a bylaw by passing a resolution and submitting the bylaw to the shareholders for confirmation at their next meeting. At the meeting, the shareholders may, by an ordinary resolution, confirm, reject, or amend the bylaw amendment. The amendment is effective from the date it is passed by the directors until it is confirmed, confirmed as amended, or rejected by the shareholders.

If the amendment is rejected by the shareholders, or if the directors do not submit the amendment to the shareholders as required, the amendment ceases to be effective. A subsequent resolution to amend a bylaw with a similar purpose is not effective until it is confirmed or confirmed as amended by the shareholders.

Change of officers

A corporation may wish to change its officers, perhaps as a result of employee promotions or changes in the employment roll. A change of officers can be done by obtaining a resignation from the individual for their existing position and then, subject to any provisions to the contrary in the bylaws or any USA, passing a directors' resolution to appoint a new officer. Since officers hold office at the pleasure of the board, the board can also pass a resolution to remove an officer.

There is no requirement for a federal corporation to file notice of a change of officers.

If the change of officers is being completed for an Ontario corporation, you must file a notice of change (Form 1) under the *Corporations Information Act* (CIA) with the Companies and Personal Property Security Branch of the Ontario Ministry of Consumer and Business Services ("Ontario Companies Branch"). You can file a notice by delivering or mailing a paper copy of the notice to the Ontario Companies Branch or by filing online with one of the ministry's service providers. Notice must be filed within 15 days of the change.

If a corporation has more than five corporate officers appointed, only the five most senior officers can be listed on the notice of change. The officers to list can be identified by your client or supervising lawyer.

The CIA requires a corporation to keep an up-to-date paper or electronic record of the prescribed information set out in returns and notices that the corporation has filed under the CIA. This record must be made available for examination by any shareholder, director, officer, or creditor of the corporation during its normal business hours at its registered office or principal place of business in Ontario.

When you change an officer, you should also review the signing authorities for cheques and other documents. If the person being replaced is listed as a signing authority, he or she should be removed and a new person appointed, if required. To appoint a new signing authority, the directors can pass a new bank resolution in the form required by the corporation's bank. In addition, a signature card with a sample signature and a list of directors and officers should be prepared on the bank's standard form, signed by a director or authorized officer of the corporation, and delivered to the bank.

Finally, the register of officers maintained in the corporation's minute book should be updated to reflect the changes that have been made.

Change in the street address of the registered office (CBCA s. 19; OBCA s. 14 and CIA s. 4)

If the street address of the registered office of a corporation is being changed to a new address within the same place or municipality stated in the articles, the directors may, subject to the provisions of any USA, pass a resolution stating the new address. You will then need to prepare and file a notice of change with the relevant government authority.

For a federal corporation, the notice of change is Form 3 under the CBCA, "Notice of Change of Registered Office." You can file by mail, by fax, or online. If you are filing a paper copy by mail, the form must be filed in duplicate. There is no fee for this filing. Notice must be filed within 15 days of the change.

For an Ontario corporation, the notice of change is Form 1 under the CIA, "Notice of Change." The notice can be filed by mail or electronically through one of the service providers.

There are other steps to consider when the registered office is changed:

1. Determine whether the corporation carries on business in any other jurisdiction. If it does, file the appropriate notice of change of registered office in that jurisdiction also, if required. For example, a CBCA corporation with a registered office in Ontario has to file Form 2 under the CIA.

2. Amend any *Personal Property Security Act* and business name filings, if applicable.

3. Advise, or remind the client to advise, all taxing authorities of the change of address.

Changes in the number of directors within the minimum and maximum (CBCA s. 106(8); OBCA ss. 125(3), 124(2))

The CBCA does not provide a procedure for fixing the number of directors within the minimum and maximum number set out in the articles. Sometimes, however, a provision is included in the articles or bylaws. When the number of directors of a federal corporation changes, the first thing you should do is check the articles, bylaws, or any USA to see whether any requirements need to be met.

Where an Ontario corporation has a floating number of directors in its articles, the shareholders may "empower" the directors to fix the number within the minimum and maximum number. If this has been done, you can expect to find in the minute book a special resolution of the shareholders "empowering" the directors to do so and, at some later stage or stages, a resolution or resolutions of the directors changing the number within the minimum and maximum provided in the articles.

Large or public companies often empower the directors to fix the number of directors within a minimum and maximum number in order to avoid having to hold a shareholders' meeting to change the number of directors.

Both the CBCA and the OBCA provide that directors, in addition to filling a vacancy, may appoint one or more additional directors to hold office for a term expiring not later than the close of the next annual meeting of shareholders, provided that the total number of directors appointed in this way does not exceed one-third of the number of directors elected at the previous annual meeting of shareholders. The articles of a CBCA corporation must authorize the directors to appoint additional directors (CBCA s. 106(8)).

A notice of change is required where there is a change in the number of directors.

For a federal corporation, the notice of change is Form 6 under the CBCA, "Notice of Change of Directors." You can file by mail, by fax, or online. If you are filing a paper copy by mail, the form must be filed in duplicate. There is no fee for this filing. Notice must be filed within 15 days of the change.

For an Ontario corporation, the notice of change is Form 1 under the CIA, "Notice of Change." The notice can be filed by mail or electronically through one of the service providers.

There are other steps to consider when directors change and or the number of directors changes, including:

1. Prepare a resignation for a resigning director. You should also check whether the director is an officer. If the director is an officer, query whether he or she will also resign as an officer.

2. Review the articles and bylaws to determine whether sections regarding quorum and residency need to be changed.

3. Prepare consents for a new director.

4. Consider whether the corporation carries on business in any other jurisdiction. If it does, file the appropriate notices of change.

5. Review bank signing and contract signing authorities. If a resigning director is named in person, make the appropriate changes.

6. Prepare a new list of directors and officers to be delivered to the corporation's bank.

7. Consider whether an indemnity is required for a new director (see chapter 4 for more indemnity provisions).

8. Consider whether any existing USA needs to be amended.

9. Update the directors' register in the minute book.

Change in the location of the records office

The directors, usually pursuant to a resolution passed as part of the organizational business, designate the place where the statutory corporate records of the corporation will be kept. Any change in this location must therefore be designated by a further resolution of the directors, subject to the provisions of any USA.

Change to bank signing authority

If a corporation decides to change its bank signing authorities, the directors, subject to the provisions of any USA, must pass a new resolution to approve the change and rescind any previous documents delivered to the bank. New specimen signatures will also be required. If a corporation changes its bank, a complete new set of banking documents will be required.

CHANGES MADE BY RESOLUTION OF THE DIRECTORS AND FILING OF ARTICLES OF AMENDMENT

Certain changes can be made by first passing a directors' resolution (subject to any USA) and then filing articles of amendment with the Director. These changes include change of a number name, changes with respect to designation, and the issue of series shares.

Change of number name (CBCA s. 173(3); OBCA s. 168(4))

Where a corporation has a number name, the directors may pass a resolution authorizing an amendment to its articles to change the name to a word name. All other procedures are identical to those discussed below, under the heading "Considerations for Specific Changes: Change of Name," except that a NUANS report, a name decision letter, or a consent to use of name is not required.

Series shares (CBCA ss. 27(1), (4); OBCA ss. 25(1)(b), (4))

The articles may authorize the directors to issue any class of shares in one or more series, to fix the number of shares in each series, and to determine the designations, rights, privileges, restrictions, and conditions attaching to the shares of each series.

Where the directors exercise this authority, they must first pass a resolution to designate series shares, then file articles of amendment. The shares come into existence on the effective date of the articles and can be issued after that date.

CHANGES MADE BY SPECIAL RESOLUTION

There are a number of changes that are required by the corporate statutes to be done by way of special resolution. As discussed in chapter 11, a special resolution is a resolution that is

- passed by at least two-thirds of the votes cast in respect of the resolution, or

- signed by all the shareholders who are entitled to vote on the resolution.

Under the OBCA, a shareholder's attorney authorized in writing can also sign a special resolution.

The changes that can be authorized by special resolution and that are discussed here include:

- a reduction in stated capital;

- an addition to stated capital;

- the sale, lease, or exchange of all or substantially all of the property of the corporation;

- an increase or decrease in the number of directors within the minimum and maximum number specified in the articles; and

- a change in the place or municipality of the registered office.

An important point to consider when shareholders pass resolutions is which shareholders are entitled to vote on the resolution. In general, only voting shareholders are entitled to vote on special resolutions, but in some circumstances non-voting shareholders also may have the right to vote on a change and to vote separately as a class. These circumstances are described below, as applicable.

Changes in stated capital

As discussed in chapter 5, both the CBCA (s. 26(1)) and the OBCA (s. 24(1)) require a corporation to maintain a "stated capital account" for each class of shares. When shares are issued, the full amount of the consideration received is added to the stated capital account for that class, subject to an exemption for non-arm's-length transactions. Where shares are issued for property or past service, the amount added to the stated capital account is the amount of consideration that would have been received if the shares had been issued for money. When a corporation issues shares in payment of a dividend, the amount to be added to the stated capital account is the declared amount of the dividend stated as an amount of money (CBCA 43(2); OBCA s. 38(2)).

Stated capital can be altered by a variety of means, including the above, upon the redemption or retraction of shares and purchase of its own shares by the corporation (see chapter 5), not all of which require a special resolution of the shareholders. A corporation can reduce its stated capital for any purpose by special resolution. Under the CBCA, if a corporation's stated capital is set out in the articles, a reduction or an increase in the stated capital requires the filing of articles of amendment, which must first be approved by special resolution (CBCA s. 173(1)(f)).

REDUCTION IN STATED CAPITAL (CBCA SS. 26(10), 38; OBCA SS. 24(9), 34)

A corporation can reduce its stated capital for any purpose by special resolution. However, where a reduction in stated capital would affect one class or series of shares differently from another class or series, the holders of the other class or series are entitled to vote separately as a class or series on the reduction, whether or not the shares otherwise carry the right to vote.

Note that the CBCA and the OBCA clearly state that no dissent rights arise on a reduction in stated capital. For a discussion of dissent rights, see chapter 5.

Under the CBCA, if a corporation's stated capital is set out in the articles, a reduction in the stated capital requires the filing of articles of amendment, which must first be approved by special resolution (CBCA s. 173(1)(f)).

There are several circumstances in which a corporation may want to reduce its stated capital:

1. to free up funds to be paid to shareholders by way of dividends;

2. to reduce or extinguish an amount unpaid on any share (generally applicable only to a corporation continuing from another jurisdiction that allows investors to purchase shares with partial payment);

3. to reduce the stated capital by an amount that is not represented by realizable assets (for example, goodwill or intellectual property, such as trademarks); and

4. to reduce the stated capital by an amount, no part of which will be distributed to shareholders (OBCA only); this would happen in relatively rare circumstances — for example, where the holders' adjusted cost base of the shares is less than the stated capital of those shares.

insolvent
being unable to pay one's liabilities as they become due, or having assets whose realizable value is less than the aggregate of one's liabilities

Generally, a corporation cannot reduce its stated capital if it is **insolvent** — that is, if there are reasonable grounds for believing that the corporation is, or would be after reducing its stated capital, unable to pay its liabilities as they become due; or the realizable value of the corporation's assets would, after a reduction, be less than the aggregate of its liabilities.

The one situation in which an insolvent corporation may reduce its stated capital is where the amount of the reduction is not represented by realizable assets.

ADDITION TO STATED CAPITAL (CBCA S. 26; OBCA S. 24)

A corporation may make an addition to its stated capital account from any amount credited to a retained earnings or other surplus account (a procedure referred to as "capitalizing surplus").

If a corporation proposes to add any amount to a stated capital account that it maintains for a class or series of shares, the addition to the stated capital account must be approved by special resolution if

1. the amount to be added

   a. was not received by the corporation as payment for the issue of shares, or

   b. was received by the corporation as consideration for the issue of shares but does not form part of the stated capital attributable to such shares; and

2. the corporation has outstanding shares of more than one class or series.

However, for an OBCA corporation, where an addition to stated capital affects one class or series of shares differently from another class or series, the holders of the other class or series are entitled to vote separately as a class or series, whether or not the shares otherwise carry the right to vote.

There are several circumstances in which a corporation may want to make an addition to its stated capital:

1. to ensure that stated capital and paid-up capital are equal;

2. to trigger a tax-free dividend to a parent corporation — for example, to take advantage of tax-free intercorporate dividends;

3. to strip out retained earnings (also known as "safe income"; a corporation may increase its stated capital to an amount that is the total amount that can be paid to a parent corporation without incurring a capital gain, and then reduce its stated capital by the safe income amount, with the result that the safe income passes to the parent tax-free); or

4. to increase the corporation's cost base prior to sale or to enable it to pay a safe income dividend.

An increase in stated capital may also occur in the following circumstances:

5. on an issuance of shares, the corporation must add to the appropriate stated capital account the full amount of the consideration it receives for the shares;

6. on a continuance under the CBCA or the OBCA;

7. where shares are issued in exchange for property of a person or corporation who is not at arm's length to the corporation, or under an amalgamation agreement or an arrangement, or where shares are received by shareholders of an amalgamating corporation who receive the shares in addition to or instead of securities of the amalgamated corporation, a corporation may add all or any portion of the consideration received for the shares to the appropriate stated capital account; and

8. where a corporation issues a stock dividend, the corporation must add the declared amount of the dividend in dollars (CBCA s. 43(2); OBCA s. 38(2)).

Sale, lease, or exchange of all or substantially all of the property of a corporation (CBCA ss. 189(3)–(8); OBCA ss. 184(3)–(8))

A sale, lease, or exchange of all or substantially all of the property of a corporation other than in the ordinary course of business of the corporation requires approval by a special resolution of the shareholders who are entitled to vote.

In a CBCA corporation, each share of the corporation carries the right to vote in respect of a sale, lease, or exchange. Where the transaction affects the shares of one class differently from the shares of another class, the holders of the other shares have the right to a separate vote on the transaction.

In an OBCA corporation, where the transaction affects one class or series of shares differently from another class or series of shares that carries the right to vote on the transaction, the holders of the first-mentioned class or series of shares are entitled to vote separately as a class or series, whether or not the shares otherwise carry the right to vote.

Under the CBCA and the OBCA, dissent rights arise on a sale, lease, or exchange of all or substantially all of the property of a corporation. A statement to this effect must be included in any notice of meeting at which such a transaction is to be voted on.

Increase or decrease in the number of directors (OBCA s. 125(3))

The OBCA states that where a corporation's articles provide for a minimum and maximum number of directors, the number of directors of the corporation is such number as is determined from time to time by special resolution, unless the shareholders have empowered the directors to determine the number.

If no special resolution is passed, the number of directors of the corporation is the number of directors named in the articles.

Every time there is a change in the number of directors within the minimum and maximum number, you must prepare a special resolution fixing the new number, or, if the directors are empowered to do so, they must pass a resolution.

Once this is done, you should consider the points outlined above, under the heading "Changes Made by Resolution of the Directors — Changes in the Number of Directors Within the Minimum and Maximum."

Change in the place or municipality of the registered office (OBCA s. 14(4))

An Ontario corporation can change the municipality of its registered office by passing a special resolution. Once this is done, you should follow the procedures outlined above, under the heading "Changes Made by Resolution of the Directors — Change in the Street Address of the Registered Office."

CHANGES MADE BY SPECIAL RESOLUTION AND FILING OF ARTICLES OF AMENDMENT (CBCA s. 173; OBCA s. 168)

The corporate statutes provide that certain fundamental changes have to be carried out by filing articles of amendment. These changes must first be approved by special resolution of the holders of each class or series of shares who are entitled to vote on the resolution. Where a separate vote for a class or series is authorized, these shareholders must also vote separately.

The passing of a special resolution and the filing of articles of amendment are required in order to:

1. change the corporation's name;

2. change the province in which the registered office is situated (CBCA only);

3. add, change, or remove any restriction on the business or businesses that the corporation may carry on and, under the OBCA, the powers the corporation may exercise;

4. change any maximum number of shares that the corporation is authorized to issue;

5. add, change, or remove any maximum number of shares that the corporation is authorized to issue or any maximum consideration for which any shares of the corporation are authorized to be issued (OBCA only);

6. create new classes of shares;

7. change the designation of all or any of the corporation's shares, and add, change, or remove any rights, privileges, restrictions, and conditions, including rights to accrued dividends, in respect of all or any of the corporation's shares, whether issued or unissued;

8. change the shares of any class or series, whether issued or unissued, into a different number of shares of the same class or series, or into the same or a different number of shares of other classes or series;

9. divide a class of shares, whether issued or unissued, into series and fix the number of shares in each series and the rights, privileges, restrictions, and conditions thereof;

10. authorize the directors to divide any class of unissued shares into series and fix the number of shares in each series and the rights, privileges, restrictions, and conditions thereof;

11. authorize the directors to change the rights, privileges, restrictions, and conditions attached to unissued shares of any series;

12. revoke, diminish, or enlarge any authority conferred under items 10 and 11;

13. increase or decrease the number of directors or the minimum or maximum number of directors (subject to CBCA ss. 107 and 112; OBCA ss. 120 and 125);

14. add, change, or remove restrictions on the issue, transfer, or ownership of shares; or

15. add, change, or remove any other provision that is permitted by law to be set out in the articles (OBCA only).

Procedure for making amendments to articles

To effect an amendment to the articles, the following steps must be taken:

1. passage of a special resolution by the shareholders who are entitled to vote;

2. preparation and filing of articles of amendment:

   a. for a CBCA corporation, preparation of articles of amendment (Form 4), in duplicate, to be signed by a director or authorized officer; or

   b. for an OBCA corporation, preparation of articles of amendment (Form 3), in duplicate, to be signed by a director or authorized officer.

Non-voting shareholders' right to vote on amendments and separate votes (CBCA s. 176; OBCA s. 170)

There are certain amendments on which shareholders have the right to vote separately as a class. A separate vote allows shareholders of one class, whose interests in an amendment may differ from the interests of shareholders of another class, to vote independently and without influence of the other shareholders. Shareholders may also vote separately as a series if an amendment affects the series of shares of a class differently from other shares of the same class. (However, shareholders may not vote separately where the directors have the power to designate a series.) This right to vote applies whether or not the shares otherwise carry the right to vote.

Holders of a class or series of shares are entitled to vote separately on a proposal to:

1. increase or decrease any maximum number of authorized shares of such class, or increase any maximum number of authorized shares of a class that has rights or privileges equal or superior to the shares of such class;

2. effect an exchange, reclassification, or cancellation of all or part of the shares of such class;

3. add, change, or remove the rights, privileges, restrictions, or conditions attached to the shares of such class, including

   a. remove or change prejudicially rights to accrued dividends or rights to cumulative dividends;

   b. add, remove, or change prejudicially redemption rights (under the CBCA) or sinking fund provisions (under the OBCA);

   c. reduce or remove a dividend preference or a liquidation preference; or

   d. add, remove, or change prejudicially conversion privileges, options, voting, transfer, or pre-emptive rights, or rights to acquire securities of a corporation (under the OBCA), or sinking fund provisions (under the CBCA);

4. increase (add to) the rights or privileges of any class of shares that has rights or privileges equal or superior to the shares of such class;

5. create a new class of shares equal or superior to the shares of such class;

6. make any class of shares that has rights or privileges inferior to the shares of such class equal or superior to the shares of such class;

7. effect an exchange or create a right of exchange of all or part of the shares of another class into the shares of such class;

8. constrain the issue, transfer, or ownership of the shares of such class or change or remove such constraint (CBCA only); or

9. add, remove, or change restrictions on the issue, transfer, or ownership of the shares of such class (OBCA only).

The articles may restrict the right to a separate vote on the matters listed in items 1, 2, and 5, in which case non-voting shares would not have a right to vote.

Consider the following example. An Ontario corporation has three classes of shares: common shares (voting), class A special shares (voting), and class B special shares (non-voting). The right to a separate vote is not restricted. An amendment is proposed to change the articles by creating a class of shares that have prior rights over the class A and B special shares and the common shares with respect to dividends.

1. The amendment must be approved by a special resolution of all the voting shareholders — that is, common shareholders and class A special shareholders (CBCA s. 173(1); OBCA s. 168(5)); if the resolution is not passed by all the classes entitled to vote, it does not become effective; and

2. Because the amendment would create a new class of shares that is superior to the existing classes of shares, the amendment must also be approved by a special resolution of the shareholders, each voting separately by class — that is, common shareholders, class A special shareholders, and class B special shareholders (CBCA ss. 176(1) and (6); OBCA ss. 170(1) and (3)).

Dissent rights (CBCA s. 190; OBCA s. 185)

If a corporation resolves to

1. amend its articles to add, remove, or change restrictions on the issue, transfer, or ownership of a class or series of shares; or

2. amend its articles to add, remove, or change any restriction upon the business or businesses that the corporation may carry on or upon the powers that the corporation may exercise,

any shareholder who is entitled to vote on the resolution may dissent. See chapter 5 for a discussion of dissent rights.

In addition, if a shareholder is entitled to a separate vote (under CBCA s. 176(1); OBCA s. 170(1)), he or she also has the right to dissent. However, the OBCA provides that the articles may restrict the dissent right of a holder of shares of a class where an amendment proposes to:

1. increase or decrease any maximum number of authorized shares of such class, or increase any maximum number of authorized shares of a class that has rights or privileges equal or superior to the shares of such class;

2. effect an exchange, reclassification, or cancellation of all or part of the shares of such class; or

3. create a new class of shares equal or superior to the shares of such class.

DIRECTOR OR SHAREHOLDER PROPOSAL FOR AMENDMENT (CBCA S. 175; OBCA S. 169)

The directors or any shareholder who is entitled to vote at an annual meeting of shareholders may make a proposal to amend the articles by following the procedures set out in CBCA s. 137 and OBCA s. 99. The notice of a meeting of shareholders at which a proposal to amend the articles is to be considered must set out the proposed amendment and, where applicable, state that dissenting shareholders are entitled to be paid the fair value of their shares.

Directors' right to revoke special resolution (CBCA s. 173(2); OBCA s. 168(3))

It may sometimes happen, after an amendment has been authorized by the shareholders, that a situation arises that would not be in the best interests of the corporation. For example, if a number of shareholders dissent on a resolution and demand payment for their shares, the financial position of the corporation could be seriously affected. Fortunately, there is a provision that allows the directors, if authorized by the shareholders in the special resolution authorizing the amendment, to revoke the resolution before it is acted on if they feel that doing so would be in the best interests of the corporation.

Filing articles of amendment

After an amendment is adopted, articles of amendment (CBCA Form 4; OBCA Form 3) should be completed, signed by a director or authorized officer of the corporation, and sent to the federal or Ontario Director.

Pursuant to a notice to client issued in December 1998, the federal Director has the right to refuse to endorse articles submitted to the Director if the corporation has not filed its annual returns.

OBCA proposed s. 274, if proclaimed in force, will provide that, notwithstanding any other provision in the OBCA, the Ontario Director shall not endorse a certificate if a corporation is in default of a filing requirement under the CIA or has any unpaid fees or penalties outstanding. As of the date of writing, the lieutenant governor has not proclaimed this section in force.

FEDERAL CORPORATIONS (CBCA S. 177(1))

Federal articles of amendment can be filed in one of three ways:

1. by delivering, in person or by mail, two copies of the articles, each bearing the original signature of a director or authorized officer, to the federal Director either at Corporations Canada or at one of the regional offices, together with the required fee made payable to the Receiver General for Canada;

2. by faxing a signed copy of the articles to Corporations Canada and providing for payment out of a deposit account maintained with the directorate; or

3. by electronic filing and payment of the filing fee by credit card.

Where hard copies of the articles are being filed, it is not mandatory to use the forms provided by Corporations Canada. However, the form must follow the same format, provide all the required information in legible printing and be set out on paper measuring 21.6 cm × 27.9 cm (8½ in. × 11 in.).

ONTARIO CORPORATIONS (OBCA S. 171)

At the time of writing, the only way to file articles of amendment in Ontario is to deliver two copies of the articles, each bearing the original signature of a director or authorized officer, to the Ontario Director either at the Ontario Companies Branch in Toronto (in person or by mail) or at one of the regional offices (in person). The required fee payable to the Minister of Finance should accompany the articles.

Issuance of certificate (CBCA ss. 178, 179, 262; OBCA ss. 172, 273)

On receipt of the articles of amendment, the Director will issue a certificate of amendment. The amendment becomes effective on the date shown in the certificate and the articles are amended accordingly.

An amendment to the articles does not affect an existing cause of action or claim or liability to prosecution in favour of or against the corporation or its directors or officers, or any civil, criminal, or administrative action or proceeding to which a corporation or its directors or officers is a party.

Restated articles (CBCA s. 180; OBCA s. 173)

If a corporation has made many changes to its articles, it may be difficult to determine the current provisions that apply. If the directors of the corporation feel it is necessary they may "restate" the articles of the corporation. To restate the articles, the corporation must file with the federal Director CBCA Form 7, Restated Articles of Incorporation, or with the Ontario Director OBCA Form 5, Restated Articles of Incorporation. The articles must correctly set out the corresponding provisions of the articles of incorporation as amended. Note that CBCA Form 7 provides that the articles of incorporation as previously amended must be set out "without substantive change." Despite this statement, it is generally accepted that restated articles "correctly set out the corresponding provisions of the articles of incorporation as amended." Once the restated articles are filed, the Director issues a restated certificate of incorporation and the restated articles of incorporation are effective on the date shown in the certificate. As well, the restated articles supersede the original articles of incorporation and all amendments thereto.

CONSIDERATIONS FOR SPECIFIC CHANGES
Change of name

There may be several different reasons to change the name of a corporation

- to change the name from a number name to a word name;

- to use a new name;

- to add a French or English form of the name; or

- to provide for the corporation to use its name in a different language.

An Ontario corporation cannot change its name if it is insolvent (OBCA s. 171(3)).

If the corporation's name is being changed from a number to a word, the directors themselves may pass a resolution approving the change (CBCA s. 173(3); OBCA s. 168(4)); the shareholders' approval is not then required.

For a federal corporation, if the sole purpose of filing articles of amendment is to change the corporation's name by the addition of an English or French form of the name, there is no fee for the issuance of a certificate of amendment.

DOCUMENTS REQUIRED FOR A FEDERAL CORPORATION

The following documents must be filed to change the name of a federal corporation:

1. a federal-biased NUANS report dated not more than 90 days prior to the date of filing;

2. a name decision letter (this is optional, but will ensure that your application is processed promptly);

3. CBCA, Form 4, Articles of Amendment, in duplicate, duly completed and bearing the original signature of a director or authorized officer;

4. any consents that are required for the use of the name; and

5. a filing fee payable to the Receiver General for Canada.

DOCUMENTS REQUIRED FOR AN ONTARIO CORPORATION

The following documents must be filed to change the name of an Ontario corporation:

1. an Ontario-biased NUANS report dated not more than 90 days prior to the date of filing;

2. OBCA Form 3, Articles of Amendment, in duplicate, duly completed and bearing the original signature of a director or authorized officer; if the corporation has a seal, the seal should be affixed to the articles next to the signature;

3. any consents that are required for the use of the name (these do not have to be filed with the Ontario Director but should be maintained with the corporation's records); and

4. a filing fee payable to the Minister of Finance.

OTHER CONSIDERATIONS ON A CHANGE OF NAME

1. After the certificate of amendment is issued, the corporation may need to adopt a new corporate seal (if any) and forms of share certificates in the new name. These changes can be done by resolution of the directors, subject to any restrictions in a USA.

2. Although it is not necessary, the old share certificates may be recalled and new ones issued reflecting the correct name of the corporation.

3. If the corporation carries on business in other jurisdictions, the appropriate documents must be filed in those jurisdictions.

4. The CRA, all other taxing authorities, and the corporation's bank should be notified of the change of name.

5. Other changes may need to be made — for example, trademarks, patents, title to real estate, contracts with service providers, and registered security interests. Bring all such changes to the attention of your client.

Change of registered office (CBCA only)

If a corporation wishes to move its registered office out of the province stated in its articles, the shareholders must first pass a special resolution and the corporation must file articles of amendment. The directors should then pass a resolution fixing the street address of the registered office. Form 3, Notice of Change, must be filed with Corporations Canada at the time of filing the articles of amendment.

The following documents must be filed with Corporations Canada:

1. CBCA Form 4, Articles of Amendment, in duplicate, each copy bearing the original signature of a director or authorized officer;

2. Form 3, Notice of Change of Registered Office, in duplicate, signed by a director or authorized officer or, if authorized by the directors, any individual who has the relevant knowledge of the corporation; and

3. a filing fee, payable to the Receiver General for Canada.

Change in the number of directors

There are three situations that may arise on a change of directors. First, you may wish to change a fixed number of directors; second, you may wish to change a floating number of directors; or third, you may wish to change either from a fixed to a floating number or from a floating to a fixed number of directors.

Note that cumulative voting requires that the number of directors be fixed. For a discussion of cumulative voting, see chapter 4.

To change the number of directors from that specified in the articles, the shareholders must first pass a special resolution and then file articles of amendment.

The documents for filing are:

1. for a federal corporation:

    a. CBCA Form 4, Articles of Amendment, in duplicate, signed by a director or authorized officer; and

    b. a filing fee payable to the Receiver General for Canada; and

2. for an Ontario corporation:

    a. OBCA Form 3, Articles of Amendment, in duplicate, signed by a director or authorized officer; and

    b. a filing fee payable to the Minister of Finance.

Changes to share capital and share transfer restrictions

There are several changes that a corporation may wish to make to its share capital or share transfer restrictions, and it will have to pass the appropriate special resolutions before filing the articles of amendment with the federal or Ontario Director. For example, a corporation may want to increase or decrease the number of authorized shares, or convert shares of one class into shares of another class.

The documents for filing are:

1. for a federal corporation

    a. CBCA Form 4, Articles of Amendment, in duplicate, signed by a director or authorized officer; and

    b. a filing fee payable to the Receiver General for Canada; and

2. for an Ontario corporation:

    a. OBCA Form 3, Articles of Amendment, in duplicate, signed by a director or authorized officer; and

    b. a filing fee payable to the Minister of Finance.

Other changes to articles

Changes may also be made to restrictions on business the corporation may carry on, or to any of the other provisions contained in the articles. Once again, to make the changes effective, the appropriate special resolutions must be passed and articles of amendment filed.

The documents for filing are:

1. for a federal corporation:

    a. CBCA Form 4, Articles of Amendment, in duplicate, signed by a director or authorized officer; and

    b. a filing fee payable to the Receiver General for Canada; and

2. for an Ontario corporation

    a. OBCA Form 3, Articles of Amendment, in duplicate, signed by a director or authorized officer; and

    b. a filing fee payable to the Minister of Finance.

CORRECTED CERTIFICATES

As careful as one may be, it is inevitable that mistakes happen. You may discover that you, your client, or someone else in your office has filed articles that contain an error. The error could be as simple as a typographic error in figures or a name, or as complex as the wrong redemption amount for a class of shares. Fortunately, the government recognizes that we are all human. Both the CBCA and the OBCA provide procedures for correcting a certificate that has been endorsed by the respective directors.

Legal issues to be considered

There are two main issues to be considered when correcting an error:

1. who may request the Director to correct an error; and

2. in the Director's opinion, whether the correction would prejudice any of the shareholders or creditors of the corporation.

Under CBCA s. 265(3), the corporation itself, or any other interested person, may ask the federal Director to make a correction to articles, a notice, a certificate, or other document. The term "interested person" is not defined in the CBCA, but it appears to include a representative of a corporation who may have been in a position to make a mistake in the documents, such as a lawyer.

The Ontario provisions are much narrower. Under OBCA s. 275(1), a corporation, its directors, or its shareholders may apply for a corrected certificate where a certificate has been endorsed or issued on articles or any other documents that contain an error.

The type of errors generally correctable include:

1. Errors that are obvious from reading the document or made by the Director, or a clerical error or provisions in the articles that do not conform to the statute.

Examples given in the Ontario Companies Branch Information Sheet on "Corrected Certificate" include:

a. an error in the name of the corporation (the name does not correspond to the NUANS report, its legal ending is omitted, it is missing a word, etc.);

b. a misquotation of the corporation number;

c. typographical errors, obvious spelling errors, or words that were clearly omitted from a sentence;

d. missing pages or clauses (where it is apparent that they are missing); and

e. anything that was clearly intended to be done at the time of the original application (as evidenced by the original resolution) — for example, the document does not make sense as it currently reads and it is clearly evident what was intended.

2. Errors that are not obvious.

The federal or Ontario Director has the power to analyze each situation on its own merits and to request whatever documentation the Director feels necessary to determine that the correction would not prejudice any of the shareholders or creditors of the corporation and that the correction reflects the original intention of the corporation or the incorporators, as the case may be.

A corrected document or certificate is generally dated with the same date as the document it replaces unless:

a. the correction is made with respect to the date of the document, in which case the document will bear the corrected date; or

b. the court decides otherwise.

If the federal Director thinks that a requested correction would prejudice the rights of the shareholders or creditors of a corporation, the person who wishes the correction may apply to the court for an order to correct the documents and determine the rights of the shareholders or creditors (CBCA s. 265(4)). In reviewing the required documentation, the Director will not correct errors in judgment unless the language used in the articles was not intended by the applicant.

Under the OBCA, a decision of the Ontario Director may be appealed to the Divisional Court (OBCA s. 275(4)).

Documentation for correction of CBCA certificates and articles

To correct an obvious error under the CBCA, you must return the original certificate and articles with duplicate replacement pages, if applicable, together with a written request for correction from the corporation or other interested person, and the applicable fee, payable to the Receiver General for Canada.

According to *Policy Statement 2.7* issued by Industry Canada on November 19, 2003, where the error relates to a corporate name, a statutory declaration of a director or officer must also be made. The declaration must state that, to the best of his or her knowledge after diligent inquiry, the corporation has not executed any security agreements or other documents using its incorrect name, and no filings have been made under any personal property security legislation in Canada against the incorrect corporate name.

Where the error is not obvious, however, the procedure for correcting it is more complicated. In this case, the Director has the sole discretion to correct a certificate. The following is a summary of Corporations Canada's guidelines to the minimum documentation that will be required:

1. a current certified copy of a directors' resolution that requests a correction and recites the matters listed below or, where no organizational meeting has been held, an affidavit of the incorporator, which requests a correction and recites the matters listed below:

   a. that an error was made, with an explanation of how it was made;

   b. that to remove the error by articles of amendment would cause undue hardship;

   c. that no shareholders or creditors would be adversely affected by the correction and that the correction reflects the original intention of the corporation;

   d. that (in a case of correction of the corporate name or the effective date) no use has been made of the incorrect name or effective date (if use has been made, further documentation will be required to establish lack of prejudice); and

   e. provide information regarding who the shareholders were before and after issue of the certificate and the number of shares they held before and after;

2. where the error was made not by the corporation itself but by its representative to whom it had given correct instructions, a statutory declaration of the representative indicating the instructions received and the reasons why those instructions were not reflected in the articles, or, where it is not possible to obtain this statutory declaration, a statutory declaration of an officer of the company explaining why it is not possible to obtain a statutory declaration, and reciting what instructions were given to the representative, and, if known to such person, the reason why those instructions were not reflected in the articles;

3. the original certificate, attached articles, together with corrected replacement pages, where applicable;

4. where the certificate to be corrected was issued over two years prior to the request for correction, a resolution of shareholders authorizing the correction (this is not strictly required by the federal Director);

5. a certified copy of the original special resolution that authorized the intended amendment (or other fundamental change) that was incorrectly reflected in the articles;

6. the applicable fee, which is equivalent to the fee paid for the original certificate being corrected, payable to the Receiver General for Canada (if the correction is for an error made solely within the federal Director's office, no fee is applicable);

7. where the error relates to a corporate name, a statutory declaration of a director or officer stating that, to the best of his or her knowledge after diligent inquiry, the corporation has not executed any security agreements or other documents using its incorrect name, and no filings have been made under any personal property security legislation in Canada against the incorrect corporate name; and

8. if deemed necessary by the Director, documents assuring that the correction will not prejudice shareholders or creditors of the corporation, and that the correction reflects the original intention of the corporation.

Documentation for correction of Ontario certificates

An application to the Ontario Director for a corrected certificate for a document filed under the OBCA must include the following:

1. the corrected articles or other document in duplicate, each bearing original signatures;

2. a certified copy of a resolution of the directors confirmed by the shareholders, authorizing the application for the corrected certificate; the resolution must state that the corporation waives any right to be heard by the Ontario Director under OBCA s. 275, and must be on $8^{1}/_{2} \times 11$-inch paper in accordance with the regulations;

3. the original articles or other documents as issued by the Ontario Companies Branch, bearing the original effective date;

4. a fee of $500, payable to the Minister of Finance;

5. a covering letter that lists a contact name, return address, and telephone number and that clearly outlines the nature of the error to be corrected; and

6. any supporting documents requested by the ministry, such as affidavits.

If the correction is material

If a correction made to any document is considered "material," notice of the correction will be published. If the correction is being made under the CBCA, it will be published "without delay" in a publication generally available to the public (CBCA s. 265(8)). Currently, this is the *Canada Corporations Bulletin*. If the correction is being made under the OBCA, it will be published in the *Ontario Gazette* (OBCA s. 275(3)).

KEY TERM

insolvent

REFERENCES

Statutes

Business Corporations Act (Ontario) (OBCA), RSO 1990, c. B.16, as amended.

Canada Business Corporations Act (CBCA), RSC 1985, c. C-44, as amended, and regulations.

Corporations Information Act (Ontario) (CIA), RSO 1990, c. C.39, as amended.

Income Tax Act (Canada) (ITA), RSC 1985, c. 1 (5th Supp.), as amended.

Personal Property Security Act (Ontario) (PPSA), RSO 1990, c. P.10, as amended.

Amendments

Industry Canada, Corporations Canada, *Canada Business Corporations Act Amendment Kit*, August 13, 1999.

Kingston, R.A., *Ontario Corporation Manual* (Toronto: Carswell, 1993–2003), 10-1 to 10-59.

Ontario Ministry of Consumer and Business Services, Companies and Personal Property Security Branch, *Information Sheets — Amendment (Business Corporations)* [BC-2], April 3, 2000.

Corrected certificates

Industry Canada, Corporations Canada, "Requests for Correction of CBCA Certificates," *Policy Statement 2.7*, November 19, 2003.

Ontario Ministry of Consumer and Business Services, Companies and Personal Property Security Branch, *Information Sheets — Corrected Certificate (Business Corporations)* [BC-6], April 3, 2000.

FORMS AND PRECEDENTS

Figure 13.1: Directors' resolution regarding change of financial year-end

Figure 13.2: Directors' resolution regarding change of officers

Figure 13.3: Shareholders' resolution changing number of directors within minimum and maximum in articles (CBCA) — for use if articles specify shareholders to determine number of directors

Figure 13.4: Special resolution and directors' resolution regarding change of registered office (OBCA)

Figure 13.5: Special resolution approving amendment

Figure 13.6: CBCA Form 4, articles of amendment

Figure 13.7: OBCA Form 3, articles of amendment

Figure 13.8: CBCA Form 7, restated articles of incorporation

Figure 13.9: OBCA Form 5, restated articles of incorporation

NOTE

1 OBCA Form 5, Restated Articles of Incorporation, in *Consolidated Ontario Business Corporations Act, Related Statutes and Regulations*, 25th ed. (Toronto: Carswell, 2002).

REVIEW QUESTIONS

1. What corporate steps are required to complete the following (include documents for filing, if any)?

    a. Birdbaths Limited wishes to change its financial year-end from January 31 to June 30.

    b. Cardinal Books Ltd. wishes to make major changes to its general bylaw.

    c. Aloha Inc. wishes to create and issue series 1 of its class A preference shares, which are issuable in series.

    d. Deadly Nightshade Corporation wishes to add April Showers as a new director and assistant secretary to its board. It currently has a floating number of directors provided for in its articles.

    e. Masterpiece Antiques Ltd., a federal corporation, has moved from Ottawa to Montreal and has to change its registered office.

    f. Cupcakes Ltd., an Ontario corporation, wishes to change its name to Delicious Bakeries Inc.

    g. Grass Mowers Inc. wants to change 1,000 of its issued and outstanding common shares into 500 class A voting common shares.

    h. The president of Trout Pond Limited has discovered a typographical error in the articles of amendment regarding the redemption price of the class A preference shares. The articles state that the redemption price is $2,000,000, but the price was intended to be $20.

2. List four corporate actions that give rise to shareholders' right of dissent.

3. Give two occasions when a class of non-voting shares becomes voting.

4. Name three changes that must be effected by special resolution.

5. If you are concerned that too many shareholders may dissent on an amendment, what could you advise your client to do?

6. Are the following statements true or false?

    a. If empowered by the shareholders, directors can fix the number of directors of an Ontario corporation between the minimum and maximum number provided in the articles.

    b. Directors can approve a change in the name of an Ontario corporation even if it is insolvent.

    c. Shareholders have a right to dissent if a corporation reduces its stated capital.

    d. A corporation cannot reduce its stated capital if it is insolvent.

    e. Directors can sell all of the assets of a corporation without the approval of the shareholders.

7. Describe the meaning of "restated articles." Explain when they would be required.

FIGURE 13.1   DIRECTORS' RESOLUTION REGARDING CHANGE OF FINANCIAL YEAR-END

RESOLUTION OF THE BOARD OF DIRECTORS

OF

CORPORATION NAME

(the "Corporation")

FINANCIAL YEAR END

WHEREAS the Corporation has obtained the consent of Canada Revenue Agency, to change the financial year end of the Corporation, a copy of which consent is attached hereto as Schedule A.

RESOLVED that the financial period of the Corporation which began on * shall terminate on * and thereafter the financial year end of the Corporation shall terminate on * in each year, unless further changed by resolution of the directors.

THE UNDERSIGNED, being the sole director of the Corporation, passes the foregoing resolution pursuant to the provisions of the *Canada Business Corporations Act / Business Corporations Act* (Ontario).

DATED as of the   day of   ,   .

_____

*

FIGURE 13.2 DIRECTORS' RESOLUTION REGARDING CHANGE OF OFFICERS

RESOLUTIONS OF THE BOARD OF DIRECTORS

OF

[NAME OF CORPORATION]
(the "Corporation")

ACCEPTING RESIGNATION OF OFFICER

RESOLVED that the resignation of [name of resigning officer] as an officer of the Corporation [set out specific offices if not resigning from all offices held] is accepted effective the   day of   , 200 .

APPOINTMENT OF OFFICER

RESOLVED that the following persons are appointed as officers of the Corporation, to hold the office shown opposite each respective name at the pleasure of the board:

Name	Office Held

CONFIRMATION OF CURRENT OFFICERS

RESOLVED that after giving effect to the above changes in officers, be and it is hereby confirmed that the following are the officers of the Corporation at [insert effective date]:

Name	Office Held

THE UNDERSIGNED, being all of the directors of the Corporation, pass the foregoing resolutions made pursuant to the provisions of the *Canada Business Corporations Act / Business Corporations Act* (Ontario).

DATED the   day of   , 200 .

_____   _____
[name of director]   [name of director]

RESOLUTIONS OF THE SHAREHOLDERS

OF

*

(the "Corporation")

NUMBER OF DIRECTORS

RESOLVED as an ordinary resolution, that until changed by further resolution in accordance with the articles, the number of directors of the Corporation shall be three (3) and the number of directors to be elected at the annual meeting of the shareholders shall be three (3).

ELECTION OF DIRECTORS

RESOLVED as an ordinary resolution that:

1.   *, * and * be and are hereby elected directors of the Corporation to hold office until the next annual meeting of the Corporation or until their successors have been duly elected or appointed.

2.   after giving effect to the above changes in directors, be and it is hereby confirmed that the following are the directors of the Corporation at the date hereof:

> *
> *
> *

THE UNDERSIGNED, being all the shareholders of the Corporation, pass the foregoing resolutions pursuant to the provisions of the *Canada Business Corporations Act*.

DATED the   day of   ,   .

SHAREHOLDER

By: _____
         Name:
         Title:

FIGURE 13.3   CONCLUDED

R E S I G N A T I O N

TO: *[NAME OF CORPORATION]*
               (the "Corporation")

AND TO: **THE SHAREHOLDERS THEREOF**

I hereby tender my resignation as a director of the Corporation, such resignation to become effective *[upon the election or appointment of my successor.] OR [insert effective date].*

DATED the_____day of _____, _____.

_____
                                                   [Name of Director]

SPECIAL RESOLUTION OF THE SHAREHOLDERS

OF

*

(the "Corporation")

CHANGE OF MUNICIPALITY OF REGISTERED OFFICE

RESOLVED, as a special resolution, that:

1.   The municipality in which the registered office of the Corporation is located is changed to the Regional Municipality of Peel, in the Province of Ontario; and

2.   Any director or officer is authorized and directed to do, execute and perform all acts, documents and instruments necessary or desirable to give full force and effect to the foregoing.

THE UNDERSIGNED, being all the shareholders of the Corporation, pass the foregoing special resolution pursuant to the provisions of the *Business Corporations Act* (Ontario).

DATED the   day of   , 2002.

NAME   OF   SHAREHOLDER CORPORATION

By: _____
        Name:
        Title:

FIGURE 13.4   CONCLUDED

RESOLUTIONS OF THE BOARD OF DIRECTORS

OF

*

(the "Corporation")

CHANGE OF REGISTERED OFFICE ADDRESS

RESOLVED that the address of the registered office of the Corporation within the Regional Municipality of Peel, in the Province of Ontario is:

*

LOCATION OF BOOKS AND RECORDS

RESOLVED that the Corporation maintain, at its registered office or at the offices of Miller Thomson LLP, the records and registers specified in the *Business Corporations Act* (Ontario).

THE UNDERSIGNED, being all of the directors of the Corporation, pass the foregoing resolutions pursuant to the provisions of the *Business Corporations Act* (Ontario).

DATED the   day of   ,   .

_____   _____
[Name of Director]   *[Name of Director]*

FIGURE 13.5 SPECIAL RESOLUTION APPROVING AMENDMENT

SPECIAL RESOLUTION OF THE SHAREHOLDERS

OF

[NAME OF CORPORATION]
(the "Corporation")

ARTICLES OF AMENDMENT

RESOLVED THAT:

1. The Corporation be and it is hereby authorized to make application for Articles of Amendment [give brief description of amendment — i.e., change in minimum and maximum number of directors, authorized share capital, etc.] substantially in the form of the Articles of Amendment attached to this resolution as Schedule A.

2. Any one of the directors or officers of the Corporation be and he or she is hereby authorized and directed, for and on behalf of the Corporation, to execute and deliver the Articles of Amendment in prescribed form to the Director appointed under the *Canada Business Corporations Act / Business Corporations Act* (Ontario) (the "Act"), whether under the corporate seal of the Corporation or otherwise, and to deliver all such other documents and to take all such further and other steps as may be necessary or desirable to give effect to the foregoing.

3. Upon articles of amendment becoming effective in accordance with the provisions of the Act, the articles of the Corporation are amended accordingly.

THE UNDERSIGNED, being all of the shareholders of the Corporation entitled to vote thereon, pass the foregoing special resolution pursuant to the *Canada Business Corporations Act / Business Corporations Act* (Ontario).

DATED the   day of   , 200 .

_____
*

FIGURE 13.6 CBCA FORM 4, ARTICLES OF AMENDMENT

 Industry Canada   Industrie Canada

Canada Business   Loi canadienne sur les
Corporations Act   sociétés par actions

**FORM 4
ARTICLES OF AMENDMENT
(SECTIONS 27 OR 177)**

**FORMULAIRE 4
CLAUSES MODIFICATRICES
(ARTICLES 27 OU 177)**

1 -- Name of the Corporation - Dénomination sociale de la société

2 -- Corporation No. - Nº de la société

3 -- The articles of the above-named corporation are amended as follows: Les statuts de la société mentionnée ci-dessus sont modifiés de la façon suivante :

Signature	Printed Name - Nom en lettres moulées	4 -- Capacity of - En qualité de	5 -- Tel. No. - Nº de tél.

FOR DEPARTMENTAL USE ONLY - À L'USAGE DU MINISTÈRE SEULEMENT

IC 3069 (2003/06)

Canada

FIGURE 13.6   CONCLUDED

Canada Business Corporations Act

Articles of Amendment
FORM 4
INSTRUCTIONS

General

If you require more information in order to complete Form 4, you may wish to consult the Amendment Kit.

You can file Form 4 through the Corporations Canada On-line Filing Centre at http://strategis.ic.gc.ca/corporations **or** you can send or fax the completed documents to the address provided below.

Prescribed Fees
Corporations Canada On-line Filing Centre, by mail or fax: $200

(1) Any change in the articles of the corporation must be made in accordance with section 27 or 177 of the Act. If an amendment involves a change of corporate name, the new name must comply with sections 10 and 12 of the Act. Articles of amendment must be accompanied by a Canada-biased NUANS search report dated not more than ninety (90) days prior to the receipt of the articles by the Director. On request, a number name may be assigned under subsection 11(2) of the Act, without a search.

(2) Each amendment must correspond to the paragraph and subparagraph references of the articles being amended.

Signature

(3) Indicate the capacity of the signing person. Form 4 must be signed by one of the following persons:

- a **director** of the corporation
- an **authorized officer** of the corporation

Other Notices
If applicable, the articles must be accompanied by a Notice of Change of Registered Office (Form 3) and Notice of Change of Directors (Form 6).

The completed document and fees payable to the Receiver General for Canada are to be sent to:

The Director, Canada Business Corporations Act
9th Floor, Jean Edmonds Tower, South
365 Laurier Ave. West
Ottawa, Ontario
K1A 0C8
or by facsimile at: (613) 941-0999
Inquiries: 1-866-333-5556

Loi canadienne sur les sociétés par actions

Clauses modificatrices
FORMULAIRE 4
INSTRUCTIONS

Généralités

Si vous désirez obtenir de plus amples informations afin de compléter le formulaire 4, veuillez consulter le Recueil d'information sur les modifications.

Vous pouvez déposer le formulaire 4 par l'entremise du Centre de dépôt des formulaires en ligne de Corporations Canada au http://strategis.ic.gc.ca/corporations **ou** encore envoyer ou télécopier le document complété à l'adresse indiquée au bas de cette page.

Droits
Centre de dépôt des formulaires en ligne, par la poste ou télécopieur : 200 $

(1) Toute modification apportée aux statuts de la société doit satisfaire aux exigences de l'article 27 ou 177 de la Loi. Dans les cas où la modification comporte un changement de dénomination sociale, la nouvelle dénomination sociale doit satisfaire aux exigences des articles 10 et 12 de la Loi. Les clauses modificatrices doivent être accompagnées d'un rapport de recherche NUANS couvrant le Canada, dont la date remonte à quatre-vingt-dix (90) jours ou moins avant la date de réception par le directeur des clauses modificatrices. Si un numéro matricule est demandé en guise de dénomination sociale, il peut être assigné, sans recherche préalable, en vertu du paragraphe 11(2) de la Loi.

(2) Chaque modification doit correspondre aux renvois des alinéas et sous-alinéas des statuts modifiés.

Signature

(3) Veuillez indiquer la qualité du signataire. Le formulaire 4 doit être signé par une des personnes suivantes :

- un **administrateur** de la société
- un **dirigeant autorisé** de la société

Autres avis
S'il y a lieu, les clauses doivent être accompagnées de l'avis de changement du siège social (formulaire 3) ou de l'avis de changement des administrateurs (formulaire 6).

Le document complété et les droits payables au Receveur général du Canada doivent être envoyés au :

Directeur, Loi canadienne sur les sociétés par actions
9ième étage, Tour Jean Edmonds, sud
365, av. Laurier ouest
Ottawa (Ontario)
K1A 0C8
ou par télécopieur : (613) 941-0999
Renseignements : 1-866-333-5556

FIGURE 13.7   OBCA FORM 3, ARTICLES OF AMENDMENT

1

For Ministry Use Only
À l'usage exclusif du ministère

Ontario Corporation Number
Numéro de la société en Ontario

ARTICLES OF AMENDMENT
STATUTS DE MODIFICATION

Form 3
Business
Corporations
Act

*Formule 3
Loi sur les
sociétés par
actions*

1.   The name of the corporation is: (Set out in BLOCK CAPITAL LETTERS)
Dénomination sociale actuelle de la société   (écrire en LETTRES MAJUSCULES SEULEMENT) :

2.   The name of the corporation is changed to (if applicable): (Set out in BLOCK CAPITAL LETTERS)
Nouvelle dénomination sociale de la société (s'il y a lieu)   (écrire en LETTRES MAJUSCULES SEULEMENT) :

3.   Date of incorporation/amalgamation:
Date de la constitution ou de la fusion :

(Year, Month, Day)
(année, mois, jour)

4.   **Complete only if there is a change in the number of directors or the minimum / maximum number of directors.**
Il faut remplir cette partie seulement si le nombre d'administrateurs ou si le nombre minimal ou maximal
d'administrateurs a changé.

Number of directors is/are: **or**   minimum and maximum number of directors is/are:
Nombre d'administrateurs :   **ou**   *nombres minimum et maximum d'administrateurs :*

Number   or   minimum   and   maximum
Nombre   ou   *minimum   et   maximum*

5.   The articles of the corporation are amended as follows:
Les statuts de la société sont modifiés de la façon suivante :

07119 (03/2003)

FIGURE 13.7 CONCLUDED

2

6. The amendment has been duly authorized as required by sections 168 and 170 (as applicable) of the *Business Corporations Act*.
    La modification a été dûment autorisée conformément aux articles 168 et 170 (selon le cas) de la Loi sur les sociétés par actions.

7. The resolution authorizing the amendment was approved by the shareholders/directors (as applicable) of the corporation on
    Les actionnaires ou les administrateurs (selon le cas) de la société ont approuvé la résolution autorisant la modification le

_____

(Year, Month, Day)
(année, mois, jour)

These articles are signed in duplicate.
Les présents statuts sont signés en double exemplaire.

_____

(Name of Corporation) (If the name is to be changed by these articles set out current name)
(Dénomination sociale de la société) (Si l'on demande un changement de nom, indiquer ci-dessus la dénomination sociale actuelle).

By/
Par :

_____   _____
(Signature)   **(Description of Office)**
(Signature)   *(Fonction)*

07119 (03/2003)

FIGURE 13.8   CBCA FORM 7, RESTATED ARTICLES OF INCORPORATION

Industry Canada Industrie Canada	FORM 7	FORMULAIRE 7
Canada Business Loi canadienne sur les	RESTATED ARTICLES OF	STATUTS CONSTITUTIFS
Corporations Act sociétés par actions	INCORPORATION	MIS À OUR
	(SECTION I)	(ARTICLE I)

1-- Name of the Corporation - Dénomination sociale de la société

Corporation No. - Nº de la société

2-- The province or territory in Canada where the registered office is situated

La province ou le territoire au Canada où est situé le siège social

3-- The classes and any maximum number of shares that the corporation is authorized to issue

Catégories et tout nombre maximal d'actions que la société est autorisée à émettre

4-- Restrictions, if any, on share transfers

Restrictions sur le transfert des actions, s'il y a lieu

5-- Number (or minimum and maximum number) of directors

Nombre (ou nombre minimal et maximal) d'administrateurs

6-- Restrictions, if any, on business the corporation may carry on

Limites imposées à l'activité commerciale de la société, s'il y a lieu

7-- Other provisions, if any

Autres dispositions, s'il y a lieu

These restated articles of incorporation correctly set out, without substantive change, the corresponding provisions of the articles of incorporation as amended and supersede the original articles of incorporation.

Cette mise à jour des statuts constitutifs démontre exactement, sans changement substantiel, les dispositions correspondantes des statuts constitutifs modifiés qui remplacent les statuts constitutifs originaux.

Signature	Printed Name - Nom en lettres moulées	8 -- Capacity of - En qualité de	9 -- Tel. No. - Nº de tél.

FOR DEPARTMENTAL USE ONLY - À L'USAGE DU MINISTÈRE SEULEMENT

IC 3167 (2003/08)

Canadä

FIGURE 13.8 CONCLUDED

Canada Business Corporations Act

Restated Articles of Incor oration
FORM 7
INSTRUCTIONS

Format

If you require more information in order to complete Form 7, you may wish to consult the Amendment Kit.

You must file Form 7 by sending or faxing the completed documents to the address provided below.

Prescribed Fees

By mail or fax: $50
Free, if issued with the Certificate of Amendment

General

Restated articles of incorporation shall set out without substantive change the Articles of Incorporation as previously amended.

Item I

Set out the full legal name of the corporation and the corporation number.

Item 2

Set out the name of the province or territory within Canada where the registered office is situated.

Item

Set out the details required by paragraph 6(1)(c) of the Act, including details of the rights, privileges, restrictions and conditions attached to each class of shares. All shares must be without nominal or par value and must comply with the provisions of Part V of the Act.

Item 4

If restrictions are to be placed on the right to transfer shares of the corporation, set out a statement to this effect and the nature of such restrictions.

Item

State the number of directors. If cumulative voting is permitted, the number of directors must be invariable otherwise it is permissible to specify a minimum and maximum number of directors.

Item

If restrictions are to be placed on the business the corporation may carry on, set out the restrictions.

Item 7

Set out any provisions permitted by the Act or Regulations to be set out in the by-laws of the corporation that are to form part of the article, including any pre-emptive rights or cumulative voting provisions.

Signature

Item

Indicate the capacity of the signing person. Form 7 must be signed by one of the following persons:

- a **director** of the corporation
- an **authorized officer** of the corporation

The completed document and fees payable to the Receiver General for Canada are to be sent to:

The Director, Canada Business Corporations Act
Jean Edmonds Towers, South
9th Floor
365 Laurier Ave. West
Ottawa, Ontario
K1A 0C8
or by facsimile at: (613) 941-0999
Inquiries: 1-866-333-5556

IC 3167 (2003/08) p.2

Loi canadienne sur les sociétés par actions

Statuts constitutifs mis   our
FORMULAIRE 7
INSTRUCTIONS

Présentation

Si vous désirez obtenir de plus amples informations afin de compléter le formulaire 7, veuillez consulter le Recueil d'information sur les modifications.

Vous devez déposer le formulaire 7 en envoyant ou en télécopiant le document complété à l'adresse indiquée au bas de cette page.

Droits a ables

Par la poste ou télécopieur : 50 $
 ratuit, s'il est délivré de concert avec un Certificat de modification

Généralités

Les statuts mis à jour doivent indiquer sans modification substantielle les statuts constitutifs modifiés au préalable.

Rubri ue I

Indiquer la dénomination sociale complète de la société et son numéro.

Rubri ue 2

Indiquer le nom de la province ou du territoire au Canada où le siège social est situé.

Rubri ue

Indiquer les détails requis par l'alinéa 6(1)(c) de la Loi, y compris les détails des droits, privilèges, restrictions et conditions assortis à chaque catégorie d'actions. Toutes les actions doivent être sans valeur nominale ou sans valeur au pair et doivent être conformes aux dispositions de la partie V de la Loi.

Rubri ue 4

Si le droit de transfert des actions de la société doit être restreint, inclure une déclaration à cet effet et indiquer la nature de ces restrictions.

Rubri ue

Indiquer le nombre d'administrateurs. Si un vote cumulatif est prévu, ce nombre doit être fixe autrement, il est permis de spécifier un nombre minimal et maximal d'administrateurs.

Rubri ue

Si des limites doivent être imposées à l'activité commerciale de la société, les indiquer.

Rubri ue 7

Indiquer les dispositions que la Loi ou le règlement permet d'énoncer dans les règlements administratifs de la société et qui doivent faire partie des statuts, y compris les dispositions relatives au vote cumulatif ou aux droits de préemption.

Signature

Rubri ue

Veuillez indiquer la qualité du signataire. Le formulaire 7 doit être signé par une des personnes suivantes :

- un **administrateur** de la société
- un **dirigeant autorisé** de la société

Le document complété et les droits payables au Receveur général du Canada doivent être envoyés au :

Directeur, Loi canadienne sur les sociétés par actions
Tours Jean Edmonds, sud
9ième étage
365, ave Laurier ouest
Ottawa (Ontario)
K1A 0C8
ou par télécopieur : (613) 941-0999
Renseignements : 1-866-333-5556

FIGURE 13.9   OBCA FORM 5, RESTATED ARTICLES OF INCORPORATION

Ontario Corporation Number
Numéro de la compagnie en Ontario   1.

RESTATED ARTICLES OF INCORPORATION
STATUTS MIS À JOUR

Form 5
Business
Corporations
Act

*Formule
numéro 5
Loi sur les
compagniess*

1. The name of the corporation is: *Dénomination sociale de la compagnie:*

2. Date of incorporation/amalgamation: *Date de la constitution ou de la fusion:*

(Day, Month, Year) / *(jour, mois, année)*

3. The address of the registered office is: *Adresse du siège social:*

(Street & Number, or R.R. Number & if Multi-Office Building give Room No.)
(Rue et numéro, ou numéro de la R.R. et, s'il s'agit édifice à bureaux, numéro du bureau)

(Postal Code/*Code postal*)

(Name of Municipality or Post Office)
(Nom de la municipalité ou du bureau de poste)

4. Number (or minimum and maximum number) of   *Nombre (ou nombres minimal et maximal)*
   directors is: *d'administrateurs:*

5. The director(s) is/are: *Administrateur(s):*

First name, initials and surname *Prénom, initiales et nom de famille*	Address for service, giving Street & No. or R.R. No., municipality and postal code *Domicile élu, y compris la rue et le numéro, le numéro de la R.R. ou le nom de la municipalité et le code postal*	Resident Canadian State Yes or No *Résident Canadien Oui/Non*

DSG 01/2000

FIGURE 13.9 CONTINUED

2.

6. Restrictions, if any, on business the corporation may carry on or on powers the corporation may exercise.

Limites, s'il y a lieu, imposées aux activités commerciales ou aux pouvoirs de la compagnie.

7. The classes and any maximum number of shares that the corporations is authorized to issue:

Catégories et nombre maximal, s'il y a lieu, d'actions que la compagnie est autorisée à émettre:

DSG 01/2000

FIGURE 13.9   CONTINUED

8. Rights, priviliges, restrictions and conditions (if any) attaching to each class of shares and directors authority with respect to any class of shares which may be issued in series:

Droits, privilèges, restrictions et conditions, s'il y a lieu, rattachés à chaque catégorie d'actions et pouvoirs des administrateurs relatifs à chaque catégorie d'actions qui peut être émise en série: 3.

DSG 01/2000

FIGURE 13.9   CONTINUED

9. The issue, transfer or ownership of shares is/is not restricted and the restrictions (if any) are as follows:

L'émission, le transfert ou la propriété d'actions est/n'est pas restreinte.   Les restrictions, s'il y a lieu, sont les suivantes: 4.

10. Other provisions, (if any):

Autres dispositions, s'il y a lieu:

DSG 01/2000

FIGURE 13.9   CONCLUDED

5.

11. These restated articles of incorporation correctly set out the corresponding provisions of the articles of incorporation as amended and supersede the original articles of incorporation and all the amendments thereto.

These articles are signed in duplicate.

Les présents statuts mis à jour énoncent correctement les dispositions correspondantes des statuts constitutifs telles qu'elles sont modifiées et remplacent les statuts constitutifs et les modifications qui y ont été apportées.

Les présents statuts sont signés en double exemplaire.

_____

(Name of Corporation)
(Dénomination sociale de la compagnie)

By/*Par:* _____

(Signature)   (Description of Office)
(Signature)   *(Fonction)*

DSG 01/2000

CHAPTER 14

Other changes

CHAPTER OVERVIEW

This chapter examines various fundamental changes undertaken by corporations, including continuances, revivals, and reorganizations. It explains each type of change, discusses the procedures required to implement the change, and lists the documents required to be filed with the respective government departments in order to effect the change. The chapter also briefly considers "arrangements."

CHAPTER OBJECTIVES

After completing this chapter, you should be able to:

1. Define continuance, revival, reorganization, and arrangement.

2. Identify when a corporation will have to continue, revive, and reorganize.

3. Recognize the legal issues involved in continuance and revival.

4. Compare the different procedures under the CBCA and the OBCA for continuance, revival, and reorganization.

5. List the documents required for continuance, import and export, articles of revival, and articles of reorganization for corporations governed by the CBCA and the OBCA.

CONTINUANCE

Continuance is a procedure contained in various corporate statutes, including the CBCA and OBCA, that allows a corporation governed by the laws of one jurisdiction to leave that jurisdiction ("export") and to continue and become governed by the laws of another jurisdiction ("import"). Continuance often happens as part of the restructuring of a corporation's affairs. For example, a corporation may wish to amalgamate with an affiliated corporation in another jurisdiction in order to improve its tax position, or a corporation may wish to continue into another jurisdiction in

continuance
a procedure that allows a corporation governed by the laws of one jurisdiction to leave that jurisdiction and to continue and become governed by the laws of another jurisdiction

order to take advantage of the provisions of the governing statute in the new jurisdiction, such as director residency requirements.

Generally, when a corporation continues, it "discontinues" in the original jurisdiction. The provincial statutes provide for notice of continuance to be given by the importing jurisdiction to the exporting jurisdiction, with two exceptions. British Columbia and Nova Scotia do not require that notice be given, though it is their practice to do so.

Continuance requires that there be appropriate provisions in the statutes of the exporting and importing jurisdictions. Canadian corporations — but not Quebec companies — can continue into other jurisdictions in Canada or elsewhere. Quebec's *Companies Act* does not provide for the import or export of corporations into or out of Quebec.

Continuance occurs in two stages:

1. The Director or Registrar in the exporting jurisdiction must authorize the continuance.

2. The continuing corporation must submit an application for continuance and the required supporting documentation to the importing jurisdiction and receive some type of certificate of continuance evidencing that the corporation is now subject to the laws of the new jurisdiction as if it had been incorporated in that jurisdiction. A certificate of discontinuance will be issued from the exporting jurisdiction upon satisfactory proof of the continuance into the importing jurisdiction.

The main concerns that have to be addressed on a continuance are:

- that it is legally possible;

- that it is properly authorized; and

- that the rights of shareholders and creditors will not be adversely affected.

Some Canadian jurisdictions have similar legislation that permits corporations to import and export and that contains similar provisions respecting shareholders' and creditors' rights. These jurisdictions are Alberta, British Columbia, Manitoba, New Brunswick, Newfoundland and Labrador, Nova Scotia, Ontario, Saskatchewan, and Yukon.

Where a corporation is continuing into or out of another jurisdiction in Canada or a foreign jurisdiction, further steps may have to be taken in order to obtain the consent of the jurisdiction.

Both Corporations Canada and the Ontario Companies and Personal Property Security Branch ("Ontario Companies Branch") have policy statements or information guides concerning continuance. These guides can be accessed online, and are also reprinted in some versions of the consolidated statutes.

Steps required to export

1. AUTHORIZING CONTINUANCE (CBCA S. 188; OBCA S. 181)

To continue a federal or Ontario corporation into another jurisdiction, the first step to take, once the concerns above have been satisfied, is to obtain the approval of the shareholders. This can be done either by holding a meeting of shareholders or by passing a written special resolution of the shareholders.

The CBCA provides that each share of a corporation carries the right to vote in respect of a continuance, whether or not it otherwise carries the right to vote (CBCA s. 188(4)). The OBCA, however, does not have a corresponding provision.

Neither the CBCA nor the OBCA allows a corporation to amend its original articles in its articles of continuance on an export. The authority to amend the original articles is found in the statute of the importing jurisdiction (CBCA s. 187(2); OBCA s. 180(3)).

If a corporation passes a resolution to be continued, a holder of shares of any class who is entitled to vote on the resolution may dissent (CBCA s. 190(1)(d); OBCA s. 185(1)(d)).

Both the CBCA and the OBCA allow the directors to abandon the application before the articles of continuance are filed if they are authorized to do so by the shareholders (CBCA s. 188(6); OBCA s. 181(4)). This provision is useful if a number of shareholders dissent and it is not in the best interests of the corporation at that time to pay them the fair market value of their shares.

A federal or Ontario corporation is prohibited from making an application to continue unless the laws in the importing jurisdiction provide in effect that:

1. the property of the corporation continues to be the property of the body corporate;

2. the body corporate continues to be liable for the obligations of the corporation;

3. an existing cause of action, claim, or liability to prosecution is unaffected;

4. a civil, criminal, or administrative action or proceeding pending by or against the corporation may be continued to be prosecuted by or against the body corporate; and

5. a conviction against the corporation may be enforced against the body corporate or a ruling, order, or judgment in favour of or against the corporation may be enforced by or against the body corporate (CBCA s. 187(7); OBCA s. 181(9)).

2. OBTAINING DIRECTOR'S APPROVAL TO EXPORT

Federal corporation

To export from the federal jurisdiction, a federal corporation must obtain a **letter of satisfaction** from the federal Director. A letter of satisfaction is a document issued by the federal Director that authorizes a corporation to continue. It is good for only 90 days after the date of issue. The letter is submitted to the authorities in the importing jurisdiction.

To apply for the letter of satisfaction, the following are required:

1. a $200 filing fee payable to the Receiver General for Canada;

2. the consent of the Minister of Finance where the *Investment Companies Act* applies to the corporation;

3. good standing under the CBCA (for example, all annual returns must be filed and the corporation must not be subject to a current investigation);

letter of satisfaction
a document issued by the federal Director, good for only 90 days, that authorizes a corporation to continue and that is submitted to the authorities in the importing jurisdiction

4. if the corporation is a federal corporation that is exporting to Alberta, British Columbia, Manitoba, New Brunswick, Newfoundland and Labrador, Nova Scotia, Ontario, Saskatchewan, or Yukon, a letter from a representative of the corporation stating that the necessary special resolution authorizing the export has been passed;

5. if the corporation is a federal corporation that is exporting to a jurisdiction other than those listed in item 4, the following documentation is required:

    a. an opinion from counsel in the importing jurisdiction that legislation of that jurisdiction

        i. permits the import of a federal corporation and

        ii. provides for the rights listed in CBCA s. 188(10),

    b. a copy of legislation of the importing jurisdiction;

    c. an affidavit of an authorized director or officer to the effect that

        i. shareholders and creditors will not be adversely affected by the export,

        ii. export has been authorized by a special resolution of the shareholders of the corporation, and

        iii. shareholders have been given full disclosure of the effect of the export on their rights and interests; and

    (the documentation in points b and c will be referred to Legal Services of the importing jurisdiction for an opinion)

    d. where there are dissenters to the export,

        i. an undertaking to honour the dissent right granted by CBCA s. 190 and, if necessary, to turn the matter over to Canadian courts for that purpose; and

        ii. a statement from a director that there are sufficient funds to pay dissenting shareholders and that arrangements have been made to ensure that those funds will be available to satisfy that claim.

The issue of a federal letter of satisfaction is at the discretion of the federal Director. The Director must be satisfied that the export is legally possible and duly authorized and will not adversely affect creditors or shareholders of the corporation.

The application for a letter of satisfaction can be made by submitting the required documents by mail or by fax to Corporations Canada in Ottawa. Processing time is generally around seven business days.

Once the letter of satisfaction is received, an application to continue in the importing jurisdiction can be made.

After the continuance has been completed in the importing jurisdiction, a certified or notarized copy of the document evidencing continuance must be filed with the federal Director. Even though some jurisdictions file this document automatically, the onus is on the applicant to ensure the federal Director receives it.

On receiving this document, the federal Director issues a certificate of discontinuance dated retroactively to the date of the effectiveness of the continuance and files notice in the *Canada Corporations Bulletin*.

Ontario corporation

To export from Ontario, an Ontario corporation must obtain the authorization of the Ontario Director. This is accomplished by completing and submitting OBCA Form 7, Application for Authorization To Continue in Another Jurisdiction, to the Director. The Director will endorse the application, and this document is submitted to the authorities in the importing jurisdiction. The authorization to continue in another jurisdiction expires six months after the date of endorsement.

To apply for an application for authorization to continue in another jurisdiction, the following documents must be filed with the Ontario Director:

1. OBCA Form 7, Application for Authorization To Continue in Another Jurisdiction, in duplicate, bearing the original signature of a director or authorized officer of the corporation;

2. good standing under the *Corporations Information Act* (CIA) (for example, the corporation must not be in default in filing any notices under the CIA);

3. no actions, suits, or proceedings pending against the corporation and no unsatisfied judgments or orders outstanding against the corporation, except those described in the application;

4. a consent letter from the Ministry of Finance, Corporations Tax Branch (Ontario) (the letter should be attached to Form 7 and is valid for a period of 60 days from the date of issuance);

5. a consent letter from the Ontario Securities Commission where the corporation is an offering corporation (the letter should be attached to Form 7);

6. a legal opinion (except in the case of continuance under the laws of another Canadian jurisdiction, including federal) to the effect that the laws of the other jurisdiction meet the requirements set out in OBCA s. 181(9); and

7. a filing fee payable to the Minister of Finance.

These documents must be submitted to the Ontario Companies Branch in person or by mail. If the application is delivered over the counter at the Ontario Companies Branch in Toronto, it is generally processed immediately; if the application is mailed, it is generally processed within two to four weeks. For an additional fee, the Ontario Companies Branch will provide an expedited service and will process the certificate and articles of continuance within 24 hours.

The Ontario Director will endorse the authorization if he or she is satisfied that the laws of the importing jurisdiction provide for the matters outlined in OBCA s. 181(9) (set out above).

Once a corporation has continued into another jurisdiction, it is required to file with the Ontario Companies Branch a copy of the continuation documents issued to it by the other jurisdiction within 60 days after the date of issuance.

The OBCA ceases to apply to the corporation on the date on which the corporation is continued under the laws of the importing jurisdiction.

Steps required for import

A corporation can apply to be continued federally or into Ontario if it appears to the Director in the importing jurisdiction that the corporation is authorized to do so by the laws of the exporting jurisdiction in which it was incorporated.

To import into a jurisdiction, a corporation must file articles of continuance with the Director in the importing jurisdiction. The articles must make any changes necessary to comply with the laws of the importing jurisdiction. The articles can also make any other changes to the articles of the corporation that are permitted by the importing jurisdiction, provided that the same shareholder approval has been obtained for the amendments as would have been required if the corporation was incorporated under the laws of the importing jurisdiction.

When the Director in the importing jurisdiction receives the required documents, the Director will issue a certificate of continuance and send a copy to the appropriate person in the exporting jurisdiction. On the effective date of the certificate:

1. the corporation becomes a corporation to which the relevant corporate statute applies as if it had been incorporated under that act;

2. the articles of continuance are deemed to be the articles of incorporation of the continued corporation; and

3. except for the purposes of the meeting of directors to organize the corporation, the certificate of continuance is deemed to be the certificate of incorporation of the continued corporation.

A continued corporation:

- possesses all the property, rights, privileges, and franchises and is subject to all the liabilities, including civil, criminal, and quasi-criminal, and all contracts, disabilities, and debts of the pre-continued corporation;

- a conviction against or a ruling, order, or judgment in favour of or against the pre-continued corporation may be enforced by or against the continued corporation; and

- the continued corporation shall be deemed to be the party plaintiff or the party defendant, as the case may be, in any civil action commenced by or against the pre-continued corporation.

DOCUMENTS FOR FILING

To obtain a certificate of continuance, a corporation must file the following.

Federal corporation

To obtain a certificate of continuance under the CBCA, a corporation must file the following:

1. except where the corporation is requesting a number name, a federal-biased NUANS report not more than 90 days old;

2. the name decision letter, if one was obtained;

3. CBCA Form 3, Notice of Registered Office, in duplicate, bearing the original signature of a director or authorized officer or, if authorized by the directors of

the corporation, any individual who has the relevant knowledge of the corporation;

4. CBCA Form 6, Notice of Directors, in duplicate, bearing the original signature of a director or authorized officer or, if authorized by the directors of the corporation, any individual who has the relevant knowledge of the corporation;

5. articles of continuance, in duplicate, bearing the original signature of a director or authorized officer;

6. authorization from the exporting jurisdiction; and

7. a filing fee payable to the Receiver General for Canada.

These documents can be delivered in person or faxed to Corporations Canada in Ottawa. Processing time is approximately six working days.

Ontario corporation

To obtain a certificate of continuance under the OBCA, a corporation must file the following:

1. except where the corporation is requesting a number name, an Ontario-biased NUANS report not more than 90 days old;

2. OBCA Form 6, Articles of Continuance, in duplicate, bearing the original signature of a director or authorized officer;

3. a letter of satisfaction, certificate of discontinuance, or other document issued by the appropriate officer of the incorporating jurisdiction that indicates that the corporation is authorized under the laws of that jurisdiction to apply for articles of continuance;

4. a copy of the incorporating document, together with all amendments made, certified by the appropriate official of the incorporating jurisdiction;

5. if the corporation was incorporated outside Canada, a legal opinion to the effect that the laws of the jurisdiction to which the corporation is subject authorize the corporation to apply for continuance;

6. a filing fee payable to the Minister of Finance; and

7. a cover letter giving a contact name, return address, and telephone number.

These documents can be delivered in person or mailed to the Ontario Companies Branch in Toronto. Processing time is 48 hours for hand-delivered documents or two to four weeks for mailed-in documents. Expedited processing of 24 hours is available upon payment of an additional fee.

The endorsement of the certificate of continuance is subject to the Ontario Director's discretion and may include such terms and limitations and conditions as the Ontario Director considers proper (OBCA s. 180(4)).

Post-continuance organization

Once a corporation has been continued, it is general practice to complete some form of post-continuance organization to bring the corporation into compliance with the laws of the new jurisdiction. Filings in other jurisdictions may also be required. Examples of items to be attended to are:

1. post-continuance organizational matters, including approval of new bylaws, approval of new forms of share certificates, and, if the jurisdiction of the corporation is indicated on its corporate seal, a new corporate seal;

2. confirmation that the exporting jurisdiction has received notification that the certificate of continuance has been issued and that a certificate of discontinuance has been issued;

3. if the corporation is continuing into Ontario, the filing of Form 1, Initial Return, under the CIA within 60 days after the date of continuation; and

4. notificaton of the continuance to all provinces in which the corporation is registered to carry on business.

REVIVAL

revival
the process of restoring a corporation that has been dissolved as if it had never been dissolved

If a corporation has been dissolved and an individual or a corporation has a legitimate interest in "reviving" the corporation both the CBCA and the OBCA provide a mechanism to do so. **Revival** is the process of restoring a corporation to its previous legal position in the same manner and to the same extent as if it had not been dissolved.

An "interested person" can make an application for revival to the federal or Ontario Director, who may in his or her discretion, on the terms and conditions that such Director sees fit to impose, revive the corporation. Upon revival, subject to the terms and conditions imposed by the Director and to the rights, if any, acquired by any person during the period of dissolution, the corporation will be deemed for all purposes to have never been dissolved.

It has always been clear from the legislation that the revived corporation is responsible for its acts, liable for its obligations, and entitled to the rights and privileges arising before its dissolution or arising after its revival. The main question usually asked when dealing with revival is whether a revival retroactively validates the activities and thus the obligations and rights that would otherwise have been incurred in the name of the corporation during the period from the time of its dissolution to the time of its revival.

Case law on this issue has been divided. However, recent amendments to the CBCA have clarified the answer and have made it clear that revival does retroactively validate a corporation's activities and obligations.

Process for revival of a federal corporation (CBCA s. 209)

A corporation can be revived if it was dissolved by any of the following methods:

1. under part XVIII, Liquidation and Dissolution, by:

    a. filing articles of dissolution voluntarily under CBCA s. 210 or 211;

    b. having its certificate of incorporation cancelled by the federal Director under CBCA s. 212 for cause, including:

i. not commencing business within three years after the date shown in its certificate of incorporation;

ii. not carrying on its business for three consecutive years;

iii. being in default for a period of one year in sending to the federal Director any fee, notice, or document required by the CBCA; and

iv. not having any directors or having a "deemed" director pursuant to CBCA s. 109(4);

2. by court order under CBCA s. 213 or 223; or

3. by the federal Director for not making an application to continue under the CBCA within the required time period.

WHO MAY MAKE APPLICATION FOR REVIVAL

Any "interested person" may apply to the Director for a certificate of revival for a dissolved corporation. Under CBCA s. 209(6), an "interested person" includes:

(a) a shareholder, a director, an officer, an employee and a creditor of the dissolved corporation;

(b) a person who has a contractual relationship with the dissolved corporation;

(c) a person who, although at the time of dissolution of the corporation was not a person described in paragraph (a), would be such a person if a certificate of revival is issued under this section; and

(d) a trustee in bankruptcy for the dissolved corporation.

The definition is not inclusive, and any person who has a legitimate economic or other interest in reviving a corporation should be entitled to apply.

The revival provisions of the CBCA do not apply to a corporation that is insolvent or bankrupt within the meaning of the *Bankruptcy and Insolvency Act* (Canada) (BIA). The onus is on the applicant to ensure that, at the time of issuance of the certificate of revival, the corporation is neither bankrupt nor insolvent within the meaning of the BIA.

DOCUMENTS REQUIRED FOR APPLICATION FOR REVIVAL

To revive a federal corporation, the interested person must file the following documents with the federal Director:

1. CBCA Form 15, Articles of Revival, in duplicate, bearing the original signature of the applicant, containing the same information as the original articles of the dissolved corporation, with some exceptions (generally, if any changes are required, they should be made by articles of amendment after the certificate of revival has been issued); exceptions include:

a. par value shares should be shown as having no par value;

b. the name of the corporation should not be confusing with a name acquired by another corporation between the date of dissolution and the date of revival; if another corporation has acquired the identical or a similar name, the revived corporation will be assigned a number name; after revival, the corporation may change its name in accordance with the CBCA;

2. a federal-biased NUANS report dated not more than 90 days prior to the submission of the application;

3. any outstanding fees not paid for filing the annual returns that would have been due ($40 per return or $20 if filed electronically), payable to the Receiver General for Canada; and

4. a filing fee payable to the Receiver General for Canada.

In addition, to ensure that the corporation is in good standing, at the time of revival, all outstanding annual returns that were due in the three-year period immediately preceding the revival and, for a distributing corporation, any outstanding financial statements that would be due in the two-year period immediately preceding the revival, if applicable, should be filed with the federal Director.

The registered office of the corporation must be the same as the registered office of the corporation prior to revival. Therefore, it is not necessary to file CBCA Form 3, Notice of Registered Office, with the application. If, however, the registered office does change, Form 3 can be filed concurrently with the application for revival.

Similarly, since the directors of the corporation must be the same as the directors of the corporation prior to revival, except as discussed below, it is not necessary to file CBCA Form 6, Notice of Directors, with the application.

If a director dies, becomes bankrupt, or has been found to be of unsound mind after the dissolution but before the revival, a notice of directors signed by the interested person should be filed. The notice can be filed concurrently with the application for revival.

ISSUANCE OF CERTIFICATE OF REVIVAL

CBCA s. 209(4) allows the federal Director to impose "reasonable terms" to a corporation's revival. According to the policy of the federal Director concerning revival, there is case law that suggests that the Director cannot refuse to issue a certificate of revival or to impose terms that are so onerous as to prevent the revival. The policy suggests that reasonable terms would include:

- allowing a corporation to file financial statements (where required for distributing corporations) within a stated time;

- allowing an interested person other than a director or officer of the dissolved corporation to file any necessary Form 6 and, further, to do so on the basis of knowledge, information, and belief;

- allowing a revived corporation to file annual returns and pay filing fees for not more than the three-year period preceding the revival;

- allowing changes to the articles where the articles of the dissolved corporation are inconsistent with the CBCA, such as where the pre-dissolution articles contain a reference to par value shares;

- where an applicant is not a director or officer of the dissolved corporation at the time of its dissolution, imposing a requirement that the applicant undertake reasonable steps to notify the corporation itself and the pre-dissolution directors, officers, and shareholders of the revival; and

- where the interested person was not a director or officer of the revived corporation at the time of its dissolution, requiring the applicant to take reasonable steps to send the original certificate of revival to a director or officer of the revived corporation (the federal Director will return the certificate of revival to the person making the application for revival).

APPEAL AGAINST A DECISION OF THE FEDERAL DIRECTOR

CBCA s. 246(f) allows a person who feels aggrieved by a decision of the federal Director to apply to a court for an order, including an order to require the federal Director to change the decision.

RETURN OF PROPERTY

CBCA s. 228(1) provides that property of a corporation that has not been disposed of at the date of its dissolution under the CBCA vests in Her Majesty in right of Canada ("the Crown").

Under CBCA s. 228(2), any property other than money that has not been disposed of and that vested in the Crown will be returned to the corporation. Any money that was received by the Crown and any amount received from the disposition of the property that was disposed of will be paid to the corporation out of the consolidated revenue fund.

Process for revival of an Ontario corporation (OBCA s. 241(5))

An Ontario corporation can be revived under OBCA s. 241(5) if it was dissolved by having its certificate of incorporation cancelled by the Ontario Director for:

1. non-compliance with the provisions of the Ontario *Corporations Tax Act*;

2. non-compliance with certain sections of the *Securities Act*;

3. failure to comply with a filing requirement under the CIA; and

4. failure to pay a fee under the OBCA.

If an Ontario corporation was voluntarily dissolved by way of filing articles of dissolution or cancelled by the Ontario Companies Branch for "sufficient cause" under OBCA s. 240, it may be revived only by a special act of the Legislature (a private member's bill). "Sufficient cause" with respect to cancellation of a certificate of incorporation includes:

- failure to have at least one director (for a non-offering corporation) or three directors (for an offering corporation);

- failure to meet the residency requirements for directors under the OBCA; and

- failure to make payment of any required fee under the OBCA.

If a corporation must be revived through a special act, the necessary information can be obtained from the Legislative Assembly of Ontario, Office of the Legislative Counsel, at 416-326-2841, or the Web site of the Legislative Assembly at http://www.ontla.on.ca/Committees/regulations.htm.

Upon revival, the corporation, subject to the terms and conditions imposed by the Ontario Director and to the rights, if any, acquired by any person during the period of dissolution, shall be deemed for all purposes to have never been dissolved. It is restored to its legal position, including all its property, rights, and privileges, and is subject to all its liabilities, contracts, and debts, as of the date of dissolution, in the same manner as if it had not been dissolved (OBCA s. 241(5)).

WHO MAY MAKE APPLICATION FOR REVIVAL

OBCA s. 241(5) provides that any "interested person" may, on the terms and conditions that the Ontario Director sees fit to impose, revive the corporation. Since March 27, 2000, a person who acquires an interest in a corporation after its dissolution may apply for its revival. Previously, persons were required to have had an interest in the corporation prior to its dissolution in order to apply for revival.

DOCUMENTS REQUIRED FOR APPLICATION FOR REVIVAL

To revive an Ontario corporation, the interested person must file the following documents with the Ontario Director:

1. OBCA Form 15, Articles of Revival, in duplicate, bearing the original signature of the applicant on both copies;

2. an Ontario-biased NUANS report (required only if the corporation is reviving under a name other than the name at dissolution or if at least 10 years have elapsed since the corporation was dissolved);

3. consent of the Corporations Tax Branch of the Ministry of Finance bearing an original signature, if the corporation was dissolved for failure to comply with the provisions of the *Corporations Tax Act* (to request consent, call the Corporations Tax Branch in Oshawa at 905-433-6500);

4. consent to the revival from the Office of the Public Guardian and Trustee (OPGT) if the OPGT is currently dealing with assets formerly owned by the dissolved corporation (for information, call the OPGT at 416-314-1963 or toll-free in Ontario at 1-800-366-0335);

5. any outstanding special notice/annual return filings and fees for the period 1992–1995 ($50 for each year not paid);

6. any annual returns outstanding since 2000;

7. a fee payable to the Minister of Finance (the revival fee was reinstated September 1, 1999); and

8. a cover letter giving a contact name, return address, and telephone number.

ISSUANCE OF CERTIFICATE OF REVIVAL

OBCA s. 241(7) authorizes the Ontario Director, upon receipt of articles of revival and any other prescribed documents, to endorse a certificate that constitutes the certificate of revival. The Director may also, in his or her discretion, impose any terms and conditions that he or she sees fit.

Upon revival, the corporation, subject to the terms and conditions imposed by the Ontario Director and to the rights, if any, acquired by any person during the period of dissolution, is deemed for all purposes to have never been dissolved.

APPEAL AGAINST A DECISION OF THE ONTARIO DIRECTOR

OBCA s. 252(1) allows a person aggrieved by a decision of the Ontario Director to appeal to the Divisional Court.

FORFEITURE OF UNDISPOSED PROPERTY

OBCA s. 244(1) provides that any property of a corporation that has not been disposed of at the date of its dissolution is immediately upon such dissolution forfeit to and vests in the Crown.

REORGANIZATION

A **reorganization** is a court order made under

reorganization
a court order made under the CBCA, the OBCA, or the *Bankruptcy and Insolvency Act* approving a proposal, which may include an amendment to a corporation's articles

1. CBCA s. 241 or OBCA s. 186 (where a complainant applies for a court order on the grounds that the corporation, the powers of the directors, or the business of the corporation has been carried on in a manner that is oppressive or unfairly prejudicial to or that unfairly disregards the interests of any security holder, creditor, director, or officer);

2. the *Bankruptcy and Insolvency Act* approving a proposal; or

3. any other act of Parliament that affects the rights of the corporation, its shareholders, and its creditors (limited in Ontario to the *Companies' Creditors Arrangement Act* (Canada) approving a proposal).

If a corporation is subject to such a court order, its articles may be amended by the order to effect any change that might lawfully be made under the amendment sections (CBCA s. 173; OBCA s. 168).

The court also has the power to:

1. authorize the issue of debt obligations of the corporation, whether or not convertible into shares of any class or having attached any rights or options to acquire shares of any class, and fix the terms thereof; and

2. appoint directors in place of or in addition to all or any of the directors then in office.

The reorganization remedy is most often ordered by a court in response to oppressive or prejudicial conduct against minority shareholders whose rights or interests are overlooked or disregarded by the actions of a corporation under the influence of dominant shareholders. Examples of oppressive actions include dominant shareholders appointing themselves officers of the corporation, thus eliminating any profits that might be released as dividends; the issue of shares to dominant shareholders on advantageous terms; or the repeated refusal to issue dividends on shares held by a minority group.

After a reorganization has been made, articles of reorganization are filed with the federal or Ontario Director, who endorses the articles with a certificate that constitutes the certificate of amendment. The articles are amended effective as of the date of the certificate in accordance with the contents of the articles of reorganization.

A shareholder is not entitled to dissent if an amendment to the articles is effected by way of reorganization.

Filing requirements for a federal corporation

To reorganize a federal corporation, the following documents must be filed with the federal Director:

1. CBCA Form 14, Articles of Reorganization, in duplicate, bearing the original signature on both copies of a director or authorized officer of the corporation or the court;

2. a copy of the court order;

3. if applicable, CBCA Form 3, Notice of Change of Registered Office, in duplicate, each copy bearing the original signature of a director or authorized officer or of any individual who has the relevant knowledge of the corporation and who is authorized by the directors to sign the document;

4. if applicable, CBCA Form 6, Notice of Change of Directors, in duplicate, each copy bearing the original signature of a director or authorized officer or of any individual who has the relevant knowledge of the corporation and who is authorized by the directors to sign the document;

5. if required, a Canada-biased NUANS report dated not more than 90 days prior to the receipt of the articles by the Director (a number name can be assigned upon request); and

6. a filing fee (by cheque) payable to the Receiver General for Canada.

Filing requirements for an Ontario corporation

To reorganize an Ontario corporation, the following documents must be filed with the Ontario Director:

1. OBCA Form 9, Articles of Reorganization, in duplicate, each copy bearing the original signature of a director or authorized officer of the corporation;

2. a certified copy of the order of the court;

3. if required, an Ontario-biased NUANS report dated not more than 90 days prior to the receipt of the articles by the Ontario Director (a number name can be assigned upon request); and

4. a filing fee (by cheque) payable to the Minister of Finance.

ARRANGEMENT

An **arrangement** is an agreement entered into by a corporation with its shareholders to effect a compromise or arrangement with respect to the rights of the shareholders that cause a corporation difficulty, financial or other. The provisions of the CBCA differ greatly from the provisions of the OBCA. Under the CBCA, the arrangement provisions are designed to be used only where it is not practicable for a corporation that is not insolvent to effect a fundamental change in the nature of an arrangement under any other provision of the CBCA. Under the OBCA, the arrangement provisions are designed to be an alternative procedure to the various procedures specified elsewhere in the OBCA.

Given the complexity of arrangements, we will not deal with them further here. The Canada and Ontario corporations manuals give good accounts of the procedures to follow with respect to filing articles of arrangement. In addition, Industry Canada and the Ontario Companies Branch have policy statements, concerning arrangements.

arrangement
an agreement entered into by a corporation with its shareholders to effect a compromise or arrangement with respect to the rights of the shareholders that cause the corporation difficulty, financial or other

KEY TERMS

arrangement

continuance

letter of satisfaction

reorganization

revival

REFERENCES

Statutes

Bankruptcy and Insolvency Act (Canada) (BIA), RSC 1985, c. B-3, as amended.

Business Corporations Act (Ontario) (OBCA), RSO 1990, c. B.16, as amended.

Canada Business Corporations Act (CBCA), RSC 1985, c. C-44, as amended.

Companies Act (Quebec), RSQ, c. C-38, as amended.

Companies' Creditors Arrangement Act (CBCA), RSC 1985, c. C-36, as amended.

Corporations Information Act (Ontario) (CIA), RSO 1990, c. C.39, as amended.

Corporations Tax Act (Ontario), RSO 1990, c. C.40, as amended.

Securities Act (Ontario), RSO 1990, c. S.5, as amended.

Continuance

Industry Canada, Corporations Canada, *Canada Business Corporations Act (Import) Kit*, dated January 29, 1999, published March 14, 2003.

Industry Canada, Corporations Canada, "Regarding 'Export' Transactions Under Section 188 of the CBCA," dated May 29, 2002, published March 12, 2003.

Kingston, R.A., *Ontario Corporation Manual* (Toronto: Carswell, 1993–2003), 10-53 to 10-59.

Ontario Ministry of Consumer and Business Services, Companies and Personal Property Security Branch, *Information Sheets — Authorization To Continue in Another Jurisdiction (Business Corporations)* [BC-4], January 19, 2001.

Ontario Ministry of Consumer and Business Services, Companies and Personal Property Security Branch, *Information Sheets — Continuance (Business Corporations)* [BC-5], April 3, 2000.

Revival

Industry Canada, Corporations Canada, *Canada Business Corporations Act Revival Kit*, April 1, 2001.

Industry Canada, Corporations Canada, "10.6 — Policy of the Director Concerning Revivals Under Section 209 of the Canada Business Corporations Act," September 4, 1997.

Ontario Ministry of Consumer and Business Services, Companies and Personal Property Security Branch, *Information Sheets — Revival (Business Corporations)* [BC-10], July 27, 2000.

Reorganization and arrangement

Industry Canada, Corporations Canada, "15.1 — Policy of the Director Concerning Arrangements Under Section 192 of the Canada Business Corporations Act," April 17, 1998.

Kingston, R.A., *Ontario Corporation Manual* (Toronto: Carswell, 1993–2003), 10-1 to 10-61.

Ontario Ministry of Consumer and Business Services, Companies and Personal Property Security Branch, *Information Sheets — Arrangement (Business Corporations)* [BC-10], April 3, 2000.

FORMS AND PRECEDENTS

Continuance

Revival

REVIEW QUESTIONS

Continuance

1. Explain the meaning of "continuance."

2. List the three main concerns of the Director when considering an application for continuance.

3. Assume that an Ontario corporation has three directors, and three classes of shares issued and outstanding: 100 common shares, 50 class A special shares with 10 votes per share, and 50 class B non-voting special shares. It decides to continue into the federal jurisdiction.

    a. Explain what must be done to authorize the continuance.

    b. Does each class of shares have dissent rights?

    c. Would your answers be different if the corporation were a federal corporation continuing into Ontario? Explain.

4. It is August 20 and your client, an Ontario corporation called The Perfect Peach Corporation, wishes to continue into the federal jurisdiction to amalgamate with a federal corporation on September 1. Prepare a list of the documents that are required to effect the continuance and indicate the processing time for the relevant steps.

Revival

5. List three circumstances under which a federal corporation could be revived.

6. Who can make an application for revival? Explain.

7. List the documents that are required for filing articles of revival under the CBCA and under the OBCA.

Reorganization

8. Explain the meaning of "reorganization."

9. List the documents that are required for filing articles of reorganization under the CBCA and under the OBCA.

Arrangement

10. Explain the meaning of "arrangement."

11. Explain when an arrangement might be used.

True or false

12. Are the following statements true or false?

    a. If the rights of the shareholders and creditors of an Ontario corporation are adversely affected on a continuance, the Ontario Director will authorize a corporation to continue out of Ontario.

    b. Under the CBCA, all shares carry the right to vote on a continuance, even if they are otherwise non-voting.

    c. A federal corporation that was cancelled because it had no directors cannot be revived.

    d. An "interested person" includes a creditor of the dissolved corporation.

    e. Revival retroactively validates the activities and thus the obligations and rights that would otherwise have been incurred in the name of the corporation during the period from the time of its dissolution to the time of its revival.

Case study 14.1: Continuance of an Ontario corporation under the CBCA

Jessie Bruton participates in a telephone conference call with Alan Hill of Thorn & Hill LLP and David Green of 01111111 Ontario Inc. Mr. Green has sold the property he bought in the name of 01111111 Ontario Inc. at a loss. He is now considering amalgamating the corporation with another corporation in his group of companies so that he can take advantage of the loss. He tells Jessie that this other corporation is a federal corporation. Jessie explains that before he can amalgamate, both corporations must be in the same jurisdiction. Since it is the other corporation that will continue to be active, Jessie suggests that they continue the Ontario corporation under the CBCA. Jessie explains the process to Mr. Green, and Alan Hill confirms that this would be the best procedure.

Jessie advises that it will take her a day to prepare the documents, a few days to obtain the Ontario Corporations Tax Branch consent, and another 48 hours to obtain the authorization from the Ontario Director to transfer out of Ontario, and that the date of continuance will be the date of filing the federal articles of continuance with the federal Director.

See figures 14.1 to 14.7 at the end of this chapter, which are prepared on the basis of the amended and restated rule 45-501 effective January 12, 2004.

FIGURE 14.1   SPECIAL RESOLUTION OF THE SOLE SHAREHOLDER (ONTARIO)

SPECIAL RESOLUTION OF THE SOLE SHAREHOLDER

OF

01111111 ONTARIO INC.
(the "Corporation")

CONTINUANCE UNDER THE LAWS OF CANADA

WHEREAS:

A. The Corporation was incorporated pursuant to the *Business Corporations Act* (Ontario) ("OBCA"), by Articles of Incorporation dated October 31, 2003 (herein referred to as the "Articles"); and

B. It is considered to be in the best interests of the Corporation that it be continued under the *Canada Business Corporations Act* (the "CBCA") pursuant to section 181 of the OBCA and section 187 of the CBCA;

NOW THEREFORE BE IT RESOLVED AS A SPECIAL RESOLUTION that:

1. The continuance of the Corporation under the CBCA is hereby authorized and approved;

2. The Corporation is hereby authorized to make application to the Director under the OBCA, pursuant to section 181 of the OBCA, for authorization to continue under the CBCA;

3. The Corporation be and it is hereby authorized to make application to the Director under the CBCA, pursuant to section 187 of the CBCA, for a certificate of continuance continuing the Corporation under the CBCA;

4. Subject to such continuance and without affecting the validity of the Corporation and existence of the Corporation by or under its Articles and of any act done thereunder, its Articles are amended to make all changes necessary to conform to the CBCA and by substituting for the provisions of its Articles the provisions set out in the Articles of Continuance attached hereto as Schedule A;

5. The directors of the Corporation are hereby authorized to abandon the application for continuance of the Corporation under the CBCA at any time without further approval of the shareholders of the Corporation; and

6. Any director or officer of the Corporation is hereby authorized to execute (whether under the corporate seal of the Corporation or otherwise) and deliver all such documents and to do all such other acts and things as such director or officer may determine to be necessary or advisable in connection with such continuance (including, without limitation, the execution and delivery of such articles of continuance and of certificates or other

FIGURE 14.1   CONCLUDED

assurances that such continuance will not adversely affect creditors or shareholders of the Corporation), the execution of any such document or the doing of any such other act or thing by any director or officer of the Corporation being conclusive evidence of such determination.

THE UNDERSIGNED, being the sole shareholder of the Corporation, hereby passes the foregoing special resolution pursuant to the provisions of the *Business Corporations Act* (Ontario).

DATED the 15th day of October, 2005.

_____
David Green

FIGURE 14.2 ONTARIO CORPORATIONS TAX CONSENT LETTER

Ministry of Finance
33 King Street West
Oshawa ON L1H 8H5
PO Box/CP 622
L1H 8H6

Ministère des Finances
33 rue King ouest
Oshawa ON L1H 8H5

Oshawa (905)433-5942
Toronto (416)920-9048 Ext. 5942
Ontario & Quebec 1-800-262-0784 Ext. 5942

November 15, 2003

Attention:

Alan Hill
Thorn & Hill
151 All Park Drive
Toronto, ON M7V 5K8

Dear Sir:

Re: 01111111 Ontario Inc.

        Consent — Transfer of Ontario
                Corporation

In accordance with the Business Corporations Act, we are pleased to advise you
that the Corporations Tax Branch of the Ministry of Finance consents to the
issuance of an instrument of continuation to 01111111 Ontario Inc., continuing the
company as if it were incorporated under the laws of the Government of Canada.

This consent is only valid for sixty days from the date of this letter and must
be filed within this specified period with the Companies Branch, Ministry of
Consumer and Business Services.

Please be advised that, if the corporation intends to continue to conduct
business in Ontario, it is required that the corporation file a Form 2 with the:

Ministry of Consumer and Business Services
Companies Branch
393 University Avenue, Suite 200
Toronto, ON M5G 2M2
(416)314-8880 or 1-800-361-3223

The Form 2 is available on the internet at:
http://www.cbs.gov.on.ca/mcbs/english/4VWQQC.htm

For your assistance, I have attached guidelines for Authorization to Continue
in Another Jurisdiction.

Yours truly,

Susan L. Loza

(Mrs.) Susan L. Loza
Tax Roll Administrator
Tax Roll Administration
Corporations Tax Branch

Encl.
/am

1757A (95-03)

FIGURE 14.3   OBCA FORM 7, APPLICATION FOR AUTHORIZATION TO CONTINUE IN ANOTHER JURISDICTION

For Ministry Use Only
À l'usage exclusif du ministère

Ontario Corporation Number
Numéro de la société en Ontario

1.

Form 7
Business
Corporations
Act

Formule 7
Loi sur les
sociétés par
actions

APPLICATION FOR AUTHORIZATION TO CONTINUE IN ANOTHER JURISDICTION
DEMANDE D'AUTORISATION DE MAINTIEN
SOUS LE RÉGIME D'UNE AUTORITÉ LÉGISLATIVE

1. The name of the corporation is: Dénomination sociale de la société:

| 0 | 1 | 1 | 1 | 1 | 1 | 1 | 1 | | O | N | T | A | R | I | O | | I | N | C | . | | | | | | | |

2. Date of incorporation/amalgamation: Date de la constitution ou de la fusion:

2003, 10, 31

(Year, Month, Day)
(année, mois, jour)

3. The corporation is/is not offering securities to the public within the meaning of subsection 1(6) of the Business Corporations Act.

La société offre/n'offre pas des valeurs au public au sens du paragraphe 1(6) de la Loi sur les sociétés par actions.

4. The corporation is not in default in filing notices and returns under the Corporations Information Act.

La société a déposé tous les avis requis par la Loi sur les renseignements exigés des personnes morales.

5. There are no actions, suits or proceedings pending against the corporation and no unsatisfied judgements or orders outstanding against the corporation, except as follows XXXXXX

Aucune action ni aucune instance n'est en cours contre la société et les jugements ou les ordonnances à l'encontre de la société ont été exécutés à l'exception de ce qui suit:

DSG 01/2000

FIGURE 14.3 CONCLUDED

2.

6. It is requested that the corporation be authorized under section 181 of the Business Corporations Act to apply to the proper officer for an instrument of continuance continuing the corporation as if it had been incorporated under the laws of

La société demande l'autorisation aux termes de l'article 181 de la Loi sur les sociétés par actions de s'adresser au fonctionnaire compétent pour obtenir un certificat de maintien la maintenant de la même façon que si elle avait été constituée en vertu des lois de/du

the Canada Business Corporations Act

7. The necessity therefore is as follows:
To amalgamate with a federal corporation.

La présente demande se fonde sur les motifs suivants:

8. The laws of the jurisdiction to which the corporation will apply for an instrument of continuance provide in effect that

Les lois de l'autorité législative à laquelle le société demandera un certificat de maintien prévoient ce qui suit:

(a) The property of the corporation continues to be the property of the body corporate;

(a) *les biens de la société deviennent les biens de la personne morale;*

(b) The body corporate continues to be liable for the obligations of the corporation;

(b) *la personne morale continue d'être tenue des obligations de la société;*

(c) An existing cause of action, claim or liability to prosecution is unaffected;

(c) *le maintien n'a pas de conséquence sur les causes d'action, les créances et les poursuites dont la sociétés est passible;*

(d) A civil, criminal, or administrative action or proceeding pending by or against the corporation may be continued to be prosecuted by or against the body corporate; and

(d) *les instances civiles, pénales ou administratives auxquelles la société est partie peuvent être continuées par la personne morale ou contre elle; et*

(e) A conviction against the corporation may be enforced against the body corporate or a ruling, order or judgement in favour of or against the corporation may be enforced by or against the body corporate.

(e) *les condamnations prononcées à l'encontre de la société sont susceptibles d'exécution à l'encontre de la personne morale et les ordonnances ou les jugements prononcés en faveur de la société ou contre elle sont susceptibles d'exécution par la personne morale ou contre elle.*

9. This application has been authorized by a special resolution.

La présente demande a été autorisée par résolution spéciale.

10. This application is accompanied by the consent of:

(a) The Corporations Tax Branch of the Ministry of Finance XXXX

XXXXXXXXXXXXXXXXXXXXXXXXXXXXXXXX

La présente demande est accompagnée du consentement:

(a) *d'une part, de la Direction de l'imposition des corporations du ministère des Finances;*

(b) *d'autre part, de la Commission des valeurs mobilières de l'Ontario.*

This application is signed in duplicate.

La présente demande est signée en double exemplaire.

DSG 01/2000

01111111 ONTARIO INC.
(Name of Corporation)
(Dénomination sociale de la société)

By/*Par:* _____
(Signature)
(Signature)

President
(Description of Office)
(Fonction)

FIGURE 14.4 CBCA FORM 11, ARTICLES OF CONTINUANCE

Industry Canada Industrie Canada	FORM 11 ARTICLES OF CONTINUANCE (SECTION 187)	FORMULAIRE 11 CLAUSES DE PROROGATION (ARTICLE 187)
Canada Business Loi canadienne sur les Corporations Act sociétés par actions		

1 -- Name of the Corporation	Dénomination sociale de la société	2 -- Taxation Year End Fin de l'année d'imposition
01111113 CANADA INC.		M D - J 1 ‚2 ‚ 3 ‚1

3 -- The province or territory in Canada where the registered office is to be situated   La province ou le territoire au Canada où se situera le siège social

Ontario

4 -- The classes and the maximum number of shares that the corporation is authorized to issue   Catégories et le nombre maximal d'actions que la société est autorisée à émettre

The Corporation is authorized to issue an unlimited number of shares.

5 -- Restrictions, if any, on share transfers   Restrictions sur le transfert des actions, s'il y a lieu

The annexed Schedule A is incorporated in this form.

6 -- Number (or minimum and maximum number) of directors   Nombre (ou nombre minimal et maximal) d'administrateurs

A minimum of one (1) director and a maximum of ten (10) directors.

7 -- Restrictions, if any, on business the corporation may carry   on   Limites imposées à l'activité commerciale de la société, s'il y a lieu

None.

8 -- (1) If change of name effected, previous name   (1) S'il y a changement de dénomination sociale, indiquer la dénomination sociale antérieure

Not Applicable

(2) Details of incorporation   (2) Détails de la constitution

Incorporated under the Business Corporations Act (Ontario) on October 31, 2003.

9 -- Other provisions, if any   Autres dispositions, s'il y a lieu

The annexed Schedule B is incorporated in this form.

Signature	Printed Name - Nom en lettres moulées	10 -- Capacity of - En qualité de Secretary	11 -- Tel. No. - N° de tél.

FOR DEPARTMENTAL USE ONLY - À L'USAGE DU MINISTÈRE SEULEMENT

IC 3247 (2003/06)

Canadä

FIGURE 14.4   CONTINUED

SCHEDULE A TO THE ARTICLES OF CONTINUANCE
OF
01111113 CANADA INC.

No shares shall be transferred without either:

(a)   the approval of the directors of the Corporation expressed by a resolution passed by the board of directors of the Corporation at a meeting of the directors or by an instrument or instruments in writing signed by a majority of the directors; or

(b)   the approval of the holders of a majority of the voting shares of the Corporation for the time being outstanding expressed by a resolution passed at a meeting of shareholders or by an instrument or instruments in writing signed by the holders of a majority of such shares.

FIGURE 14.4   CONTINUED

SCHEDULE B TO THE ARTICLES OF CONTINUANCE
OF
01111113 CANADA INC.

Other Provisions:

1.   The outstanding securities of the Corporation may be beneficially owned, directly or indirectly, by not more than 35 persons or companies, exclusive of:

(1)   persons or companies that are, or at the time they last acquired securities of the Corporation were, accredited investors as such term is defined in the Ontario Securities Commission ("OSC") Rule 45-501 Exempt Distributions as amended from time to time;

(2)   current or former directors or officers of the Corporation or of an affiliated entity of the Corporation; and

(3)   current or former employees of the Corporation or an affiliated entity of the Corporation, or current or former consultants as defined in MI 45-105, who in each case beneficially own only securities of the Corporation that were issued as compensation by, or under an incentive plan of, the Corporation or an affiliated entity of the Corporation;

provided that:

1.   two or more persons who are the joint registered holders of one or more securities of the Corporation are counted as one beneficial owner of those securities; and

2.   a corporation, partnership, trust or other entity is counted as one beneficial owner of securities of the Corporation unless the entity has been created or is being used primarily for the purpose of acquiring or holding securities of the Corporation, in which event each beneficial owner of an equity interest in the entity or each beneficiary of the entity, as the case may be, is counted as a separate beneficial owner of those securities of the Corporation.

2.   The Corporation has a lien on a share registered in the name of a shareholder or his legal representative for a debt of that shareholder to the Corporation.

3.   The number of directors of the Corporation shall be determined from time to time as follows:

(1)   where directors are to be elected at a meeting of shareholders, the number shall be determined by resolution of the board of directors and set out in the notice calling the meeting of shareholders; and

(2)   where directors are to be elected by way of a written resolution of shareholders, the number shall be set out in the resolution;

FIGURE 14.4 CONTINUED

provided that the number of directors may not be less than the minimum number nor more than the maximum number of directors set out in the articles.

4.   The directors of the Corporation, may, between annual meetings of shareholders of the Corporation, appoint one or more additional directors to serve until the next annual meeting, provided that the number of additional directors shall not at any time exceed one-third of the number of directors who held office at the expiration of the last annual meeting and provided further that the total number of directors of the Corporation after any such appointment shall not exceed the maximum number of directors permitted by the articles.

FIGURE 14.4 CONCLUDED

Canada Business Corporations Act

**Articles of Continuance
FORM 11
INSTRUCTIONS**

General

If you require more information in order to complete Form 11, you may wish to consult the Name Granting Compendium or the Name Granting Guidelines and the Continance (Import) Kit.

You can file Form 11 through the Corporations Canada On-line Filing Centre at http://strategis.ic.gc.ca/corporations **or** you can send or fax the completed documents to the address provided below.

Prescribed Fees

Corporations Canada On-line Filing Centre, by mail or fax: $200

Item 1

Set out the full legal name of the corporation which complies with sections 10 and 12 of the Act. Articles of continuance must be accompanied by a Canada-biased NUANS search report dated not more than ninety (90) days prior to the receipt of the articles by the Director. Upon request, a number name may be assigned under subsection 11(2) of the Act, without a search.

Item 2

Set out the taxation year end (day and month) of the corporation. The taxation year must be the same as the taxation year end pursuant to the *Income Tax Act.*

Item 3

Set out the name of the province or territory within Canada where the registered office is to be situated.

Item 4

Set out the details required by paragraph 6(1)(c) of the Act. Unless an exemption is obtained under subsection 187(11) of the Act, all shares must be without nominal or par value and must comply with Part V of the Act. Nominal or par value shares issued by a body corporate before continuance comply with the Act by virtue of subsection 24(2) and 187(8) and (9) of the Act. In the case of the application of subsection 187(11) of the Act, set out the maximum number of shares of a class or series as required by subsection 187(12) of the Act.

Item 5

If restrictions are to be placed on the right to transfer shares of the corporation, set out a statement to this effect and the nature of such restrictions.

Item 6

Set out the number of directors. If cumulative voting is permitted, the number of directors must be invariable; otherwise it is permissible to specify a minimum and maximum number of directors.

Item 7

If restrictions are to be placed on the business the corporation may carry on, set out the restrictions.

Item 8

1) Set out the previous name of the corporate body if a change of name is effected on continuance.
2) Set out the date of incorporation of the body corporate. If the body corporate has been subject to any previous continuance, set out the details of each such continuance, i.e., the date of continuance, any change of name at the time of continuance and the name and provision of the statute under which it was effected.

Item 9

Set out any provisions, permitted by the Act or Regulations to be set out in the by-laws of the corporation, that are to form part of the articles, including any pre-emptive rights or cumulative voting provisions.

Item 10

Indicate the capacity of the signing person. Form 11 must be signed by one of the following persons:

- a **director** of the corporation
- an **authorized officer** of the corporation

Other Documents

If the continuance is under subsection 187(1) of the Act, the articles of continuance must be accompanied by:
a) proof of authorization under the laws of the jurisdiction where the body corporate is incorporated; and
b) a Notice of Registered Office (Form 3) and a Notice of Directors (Form 6).

The completed documents and fees payable to the Receiver General for Canada are to be sent to:

The Director, Canada Business Corporations Act
Jean Edmonds Tower, South
9th Floor
365 Laurier Ave. West
Ottawa, Ontario K1A 0C8
or by facsimile at: (613) 941-0999
Inquiries: 1-866-333-5556

IC 3247 (2003/06) p.2

Loi canadienne sur les sociétés par actions

**Clauses de prorogation
FORMULAIRE 11
INSTRUCTIONS**

Généralités

Si vous désirez obtenir de plus amples informations afin de compléter le formulaire 11, veuillez consulter l'Énoncé d'octroi des dénominations ou les Lignes directrices pour l'octroi des dénominations ainsi que le Recueil d'information sur la prorogation-importation.

Vous pouvez déposer le formulaire 11 par l'entremise du Centre de dépôt des formulaires en ligne de Corporations Canada au http://strategis.ic.gc.ca/corporations **ou** encore envoyer ou télécopier le document complété à l'adresse indiquée au bas de cette page.

Droits

Centre de dépôt des formulaires en ligne, par la poste ou télécopieur : 200 $

Rubrique 1

Indiquer la dénomination sociale complète de la société, laquelle doit satisfaire aux exigences des articles 10 et 12 de la Loi. Les clauses de prorogation doivent être accompagnées d'un rapport de recherche NUANS couvrant le Canada, dont la date remonte à quatre-vingt-dix (90) jours ou moins avant la date de réception par le directeur des clauses de prorogation. Si un numéro matricule est demandé en guise de dénomination sociale, il peut être assigné, sans recherche préalable, en vertu du paragraphe 11(2) de la Loi.

Rubrique 2

Indiquer la date (jour et mois) de la fin de l'année d'imposition de la société. La date de fin d'année d'imposition doit être la même que celle en vertu de la *Loi de l'impôt sur le revenu.*

Rubrique 3

Indiquer le nom de la province ou du territoire au Canada où le siège social se situera.

Rubrique 4

Indiquer les détails requis par l'alinéa 6(1)(c) de la Loi. Sauf dans les cas où une dispense est accordée en vertu du paragraphe 187(11) de la Loi, toutes les actions doivent être sans valeur nominale ou sans valeur au pair et doivent se conformer à la partie V de la Loi. Les actions avec valeur au pair ou nominales émises par une personne morale avant sa prorogation sont conformes à la Loi en vertu des paragraphes 24(2) et 187(8) et (9) de la Loi. Si le paragraphe 187(11) de la Loi s'applique, indiquer le nombre maximal des actions d'une série ou catégorie requis par le paragraphe 187(12) de la Loi.

Rubrique 5

Si le droit de transfert des actions de la société doit être restreint, inclure une déclaration à cet effet et indiquer la nature de ces restrictions.

Rubrique 6

Indiquer le nombre des administrateurs. Si un vote cumulatif est prévu, ce nombre doit être fixe; autrement, il est permis de spécifier un nombre minimal et maximal d'administrateurs.

Rubrique 7

Indiquer les limites devant être imposées aux activités commerciales de la société.

Rubrique 8

1) Indiquer la dénomination sociale antérieure de la personne morale si un changement de dénomination sociale est effectué lors de la prorogation.
2) Indiquer la date de constitution de la personne morale. Si la personne morale a fait l'objet de toute prorogation antérieure, indiquer les détails de chacune d'elles, soit la date de prorogation, tout changement de dénomination sociale lors de la prorogation, ainsi que le nom et la disposition du texte de loi en vertu duquel elle a été opérée.

Rubrique 9

Indiquer les dispositions que la Loi ou le règlement permet d'énoncer dans les règlements administratifs de la société et qui doivent faire partie des statuts en incluant les dispositions relatives au vote cumulatif ou aux droits de préemption.

Rubrique 10

Veuillez indiquer la qualité du signataire. Le formulaire 11 doit être signé par une des personnes suivantes :

- un **administrateur** de la société
- un **dirigeant autorisé** de la société

Autres documents

Si la prorogation est effectuée en vertu du paragraphe 187(1) de la Loi, les clauses de prorogation doivent être accompagnées :
a) d'une preuve de l'autorisation en vertu de la Loi sous le régime de laquelle la personne morale est constituée; et
b) d'un avis de désignation du siège social (formulaire 3) et d'une liste des administrateurs (formulaire 6).

Les documents complétés et les droits payables au Receveur général du Canada doivent être envoyés au :

Directeur, Loi canadienne sur les sociétés par actions
Tour Jean Edmonds, sud
9ième étage
365, ave Laurier ouest
Ottawa (Ontario) K1A 0C8
ou par télécopieur : (613) 941-0999
Renseignements : 1-866-333-5556

FIGURE 14.5   CBCA FORM 3, NOTICE OF REGISTERED OFFICE

Industry Canada   Industrie Canada

Canada Business   Loi canadienne sur les
Corporations Act   sociétés par actions

FORM 3 **NOTICE OF REGISTERED OFFICE OR** **NOTICE OF C ANGE OF ADDRESS OF REGISTERED OFFICE** **(SECTION 19)**	**FORMULAIRE 3** **A IS DE D SIGNATION OU** **DE C ANGEMENT D'ADRESSE DU SIÈGE SOCIAL** **(ARTICLE 19)**

1 -- Name of the Corporation - Dénomination sociale de la société

01111113 Canada Inc.

2 -- Corporation No. - N° de la société

3 -- Street address of Registered Office - Adresse civique du siège social

111 Red Street
White Port, Ontario
P3P 0P9

(and mailing address, if different from that of registered office) - (si l'adresse postale diffère de celle du siège social)

CAUTION Address of registered office must be within the province or territory that is described in the Articles at Item 2; otherwise an amendment to the Articles
is required, using Form 4, in addition to this form (see paragraph 173(1) b) of the Act).
A IS L'adresse du siège social doit se situer dans les limites de la province ou du territoire indiqué dans les statuts à la rubrique 2. Sinon, il faut modifier les
statuts en déposant le formulaire 4, en plus du présent formulaire (voir l'alinéa 173(1) b) de la Loi).

4 -- Effective Date of Change - Date de prise d'effet

Not Applicable

5 -- Previous Address of Registered Office - Adresse précédente du siège social

Not Applicable

Signature	Printed Name - Nom en lettres moulées David Green	6 -- Capacity of - En qualité de Director and President	7 -- Tel. No. - N° de tél.

FOR DEPARTMENTAL USE ONLY - À L'USAGE DU MINISTÈRE SEULEMENT

IC 3420 (2003/06)

Canada

FIGURE 14.6 CBCA FORM 6, NOTICE OF DIRECTORS

 Industry Canada   Industrie Canada

Canada Business   Loi canadienne sur les
Corporations Act   sociétés par actions

FORM 6
NOTICE OF DIRECTORS
NOTICE OF C ANGE
OF DIRECTORS OR NOTICE OF
C ANGE OF ADDRESS OF A
PRESENT DIRECTOR
SECTIONS 106 AND 113(1)

FORMULAIRE 6
LISTE DES ADMINISTRATEURS
A IS DE C ANGEMENT
DES ADMINISTRATEURS OU A IS DE
C ANGEMENT D'ADRESSE D'UN
ADMINISTRATEUR ACTUEL
ARTICLES 106 ET 113(1)

1 -- Name of the Corporation - Dénomination sociale de la société	2 -- Corporation No. - N° de la société
01111113 Canada Inc.	

3 -- The following persons became directors of this corporation - Les personnes suivantes sont devenues administrateurs de la présente société

Name - Nom	Effective Date / Date d'entrée en vigueur	Residential Address - Adresse domiciliaire	Resident Canadian - Y/N / Résident canadien - O/N
Not Applicable			

4 -- The following persons ceased to be directors of this corporation - Les personnes suivantes ont cessé d'être administrateurs de la présente société

Name - Nom	Effective Date / Date d'entrée en vigueur	Residential Address - Adresse domiciliaire
Not Applicable		

5 -- The directors of this corporation now are - Les administrateurs de la présente société sont maintenant

Name - Nom	Residential Address - Adresse domiciliaire	Resident Canadian - Y/N / Résident canadien - O/N
David Green	111 Red Street / White Port, Ontario P3P 0P9	Yes
Carol Green	111 Red Street / White Port, Ontario P3P 0P9	Yes

6 -- Change of address of a present director - Changement d'adresse d'un administrateur actuel

Name - Nom	Effective Date / Date d'entrée en vigueur	Former Residential Address / Adresse domiciliaire précédente	New Residential Address / Nouvelle adresse résidentielle
Not Applicable			

Signature	Printed Name - Nom en lettres moulées	7 -- Capacity of - En qualité de	8 -- Tel. No. - N° de tél.
	David Green	Director and President	

FOR DEPARTMENTAL USE ONLY - À L'USAGE DU MINISTÈRE SEULEMENT

IC 3103 (2003/06)

Canada

FIGURE 14.7   CBCA FORM 15, ARTICLES OF REVIVAL

Industry Canada Industrie Canada	FORM 15
Canada Business Loi canadienne sur les	ARTICLES OF REVIVAL
Corporations Act sociétés par actions	(SECTION 209)

FORMULE 15
CLAUSES DE RECONSTITUTION
(ARTICLE 209)

---

1 -- Name of the Corporation · Dénomination sociale de la société | 2 -- Corporation No. - N° de la société

---

3 -- The province or territory in Canada where the registered office is situated · La province ou le territoire au Canada où se situe le siège social

---

4 -- The classes and any maximum number of shares that the corporation is authorized to issue · Catégories et le nombre maximal d'actions que la société est autorisée à émettre

---

5 -- Restrictions, if any, on share transfers · Restrictions sur le transfert des actions, s'il y a lieu

---

6 -- Number (or minimum and maximum number) of directors · Nombre (ou nombre minimal et maximal) d'administrateurs

---

7 -- Restrictions, if any, on the businesses the corporation may carry on · Limites imposées aux activités commerciales de la société, s'il y a lieu

---

8 -- (1) If change of name effected, previous name · (1) S'il y a changement de dénomination sociale, indiquer la dénomination sociale antérieure

(2) Details of incorporation · (2) Détails de la constitution

---

9 -- Other provisions, if any · Autres dispositions, s'il y a lieu

---

10 -- Reasons for dissolution · Raisons de la dissolution

---

11 -- Interest of applicant in revival of the dissolved corporation · Intérêt du demandeur dans la reconstitution de la société dissoute

---

Date	Signature	13 -- Address of applicant - Adresse du demandeur
For Departmental Use Only l'usage du ministère seulement Filed Déposée ►	Printed Name - Nom en lettres moulées	Canada

IC 3339 (2001/11)

FIGURE 14.7 CONCLUDED

Canada Business Corporations Act

Articles of Revival
FORM 15
INSTRUCTIONS

General

If you require more information in order to complete Form 15, you may wish to consult the Policy of the Director Concerning Revivals under section 209 and the Revival Kit of the *Canada Business Corporations Act*.

Item 1

Set out the full legal name of the corporation which complies with sections 10 and 12 of the Act. Articles of revival must be accompanied by a Canada-biased NUANS search report dated not more than ninety (90) days prior to the receipt of the articles by the Director. Upon request, a number name may be assigned under subsection 11(2) of the Act, without a search.

Item 2

If applicable, set out the corporation number.

Item 3

Set out the name of the province or territory within Canada where the registered office is situated.

Item 4

Set out the share structure of the corporation exactly as it was before dissolution, except that any shares previously with nominal or par value must now be without nominal or par value.

Item 5

No new restrictions may be placed on the right to transfer shares of the revived corporation.

Item 6

The number of directors must be the same as the number of directors of the dissolved corporation.

Item 7

Any restrictions to be placed on the business of the revived corporation must be identical to such restrictions or objects of the corporation before its dissolution.

Item 8

1) Set out the name of the dissolved corporation if a change of name is effected on revival.
2) Set out the date of incorporation of the dissolved corporation. If the dissolved corporation has been subject to any previous continuance or amalgamation, set out the details of each such continuance or amalgamation, i.e., the date, any change of name and the name and provision of the statute under which it was affected.

Item 9

No provisions may be added that were not included in the charter of the dissolved corporation.

Item 10

State the reasons why the dissolved corporation was dissolved, including specific references when applicable to the statutory provisions under which it was dissolved.

Item 11

State details of the applicant's interest in the dissolved corporation and why the applicant see s to have the corporation revived. According to s. 209(6) of the Act, the applicant must be an interested person which includes:

a) a shareholder, a director, an officer, an employee or a creditor of the dissolved corporation
b) a person who has a contractual relationship with the dissolved corporation
c) a person who was not a person described in paragraph (a) at the time of dissolution, but would be such a person if a certificate of revival is issued
d) a trustee in ban ruptcy for the dissolved corporation

Item 12

Set out the first given name, initial and family name of the applicant.

Item 13

Set out the business or residential address of the applicant.

The information you provide in this document is collected under the authority of the *Canada Business Corporations Act* and will be stored in personal information ban number IC/PPU-049. Personal information that you provide is protected under the provisions of the *Privacy Act*. owever, public disclosure pursuant to section 266 of the *Canada Business Corporations Act* is permitted under the *Privacy Act*.

Other Documents

If there has been no change in the directors or registered office of the Corporation during the period of dissolution, the applicant may, but is not required to, file Form 3 and Form 6.
Where changes have ta en place, Form 3 and Form 6 signed by a director or an authorized officer or an authorized agent should be filed.

The completed document and fees payable to the Receiver General for Canada are to be sent to:

The Director, Canada Business Corporations Act
Jean Edmonds Towers, South
9th Floor
365 Laurier Ave. West
Ottawa, Ontario K1A 0C8
or by facsimile at (613) 941-0999

Loi canadienne sur les sociétés par actions

Clauses de reconstitution
FORMULE 15
INSTRUCTIONS

Généralités

Si vous désirez obtenir de plus amples informations afin de compléter la formule 15, veuillez consulter la politique concernant les reconstitutions (a. 209) ainsi que les procédures pour les demandes de reconstitution en société.

Rubrique 1

Indiquer la dénomination sociale complète de la société, laquelle doit satisfaire aux exigences des articles 10 et 12 de la Loi. Les clauses de reconstitution doivent être accompagnées d'un rapport de recherche NUANS couvrant le Canada, dont la date remonte à quatre-vingt-dix (90) jours ou moins avant la date de réception par le directeur des clauses de reconstitution. Si un numéro matricule est demandé en guise de dénomination sociale, il peut être assigné, sans recherche préalable, en vertu du paragraphe 11(2) de la Loi.

Rubrique 2

S'il y a lieu, indiquer le numéro de la société.

Rubrique 3

Indiquer le nom de la province ou du territoire au Canada où le siège social se situe.

Rubrique 4

Indiquer la structure exacte du capital de la société avant la dissolution, sauf que toute action préalablement avec valeur nominale ou au pair doit dorénavant être sans valeur nominale ou au pair.

Rubrique 5

Aucune nouvelle limite ne doit être imposée sur le droit de transfert des actions de la société reconstituée.

Rubrique 6

Le nombre des administrateurs doit être le même que celui de la société dissoute.

Rubrique 7

Toute limite concernant les activités commerciales de la société reconstituée doit être identique aux limites ou aux objets de la société avant sa dissolution.

Rubrique 8

1) Indiquer la dénomination sociale de la société dissoute si un changement de dénomination sociale est effectué lors de la reconstitution.
2) Indiquer la date de constitution de la société dissoute. Si la société dissoute a fait l'objet d'une prorogation ou d'une fusion antérieure, indiquer les détails de chaque prorogation ou fusion, soit la date, tout changement de dénomination, ainsi que le nom et la disposition du texte de loi en vertu duquel elle a été opérée.

Rubrique 9

Aucune disposition ne peut être ajoutée à moins qu'elle ne soit déjà énoncée dans la charte de la société dissoute.

Rubrique 10

Donner les raisons pour lesquelles la société a été dissoute, notamment, le renvoi précis à la disposition statutaire en vertu de laquelle elle a été dissoute, s'il y a lieu.

Rubrique 11

Donner les détails de l'intérêt du demandeur dans la société dissoute et indiquer pourquoi il demande la reconstitution de la société. En vertu de l'article 209(6) de la Loi, le demandeur doit être un intéressé, ce qui s'entend:
a) d'un actionnaire, administrateur, dirigeant, employé ou créancier de la société dissoute
b) de toute personne ayant un lien contractual avec la société dissoute
c) de toute personne qui ou bien que non visée par l'alinéa a) à la date de la dissolution, le deviendrait si la société était reconstituée
d) du syndic de faillite de la société dissoute

Rubrique 12

Indiquer le prénom, les initiales et le nom de famille du demandeur.

Rubrique 13

Indiquer l'adresse d'affaires ou domiciliaire du demandeur.

Les renseignements que vous fournissez dans ce document sont recueillis en vertu de la *Loi canadienne sur les sociétés par actions*, et seront emmagasinés dans le fichier de renseignements personnels IC/PPU-049. Les renseignements personnels que vous fournissez sont protégés par les dispositions de la *Loi sur la protection des renseignements personnels*. Cependant, la divulgation au public selon les termes de l'article 266 de la *Loi canadienne sur les sociétés par actions* est permise en vertu de la *Loi sur la protection des renseignements personnels*.

Autres documents

Lorsque qu'aucun changement d'adresse du siège social ou changement des administrateurs n'est survenu, le demandeur peut, mais n'est pas requis de le faire, compléter les formule 3 et formule 6.
Lorsque des changements à l'adresse du siège social et/ou des changements d'administrateurs, les formule 3 et formule 6 doivent être complétées par un directeur, un dirigeant autorisé ou un agent autorisé.

Le document complété et les droits payables au receveur général du Canada doivent être envoyés au :

Directeur, Loi canadienne sur les sociétés par actions
Tours Jean Edmonds, sud
9ième étage
365, ave Laurier ouest
Ottawa (Ontario) K1A 0C8
ou par télécopieur ou (613) 941-0999

FIGURE 14.8 OBCA FORM 15, ARTICLES OF REVIVAL

For Ministry Use Only
À l'usage exclusif du ministère

Ontario Corporation Number
Numéro de la société en Ontario

ARTICLES OF REVIVAL
STATUTS DE RECONSTITUTION

Form 15
*Business
Corporations
Act*

*Formule 15
Loi sur les
sociétés par
actions*

1. Name of dissolved corporation: (Set out in BLOCK CAPITAL LETTERS)
   Dénomination sociale de la société dissoute (écrire en LETTRES MAJUSCULES SEULEMENT) :

2. The name under which the corporation is to be revived if other than name at dissolution:
   (Set out in BLOCK CAPITAL LETTERS)
   Dénomination sociale après la reconstitution si elle est différente de celle de la société lors de la dissolution
   (écrire en LETTRES MAJUSCULES SEULEMENT) :

3. Date of incorporation/amalgamation:
   Date de la constitution ou de la fusion :

4. Date of dissolution:
   Date de la dissolution :

Year *année*	Month *mois*	Day *jour*		Year *année*	Month *mois*	Day *jour*

5. The address of the registered office is:
   Adresse du siège social :

(Street & Number or R.R. Number & if Multi-Office Building give Room No. - *Post Office Box not acceptable*)
(Rue et numéro ou numéro de la R.R. et, s'il s'agit d'un édifice à bureaux, numéro du bureau - Case postale
non acceptée)

ONTARIO

(Name of Municipality or Post Office)
(Nom de la municipalité ou du bureau de poste)

Postal Code/
Code postal

07127 (03/2004)

FIGURE 14.8 CONCLUDED

2

6. **The following terms and conditions have been complied with:**
Les conditions suivantes ont été respectées :

   a) all outstanding notices and returns required to be filed by the corporation under the *Corporations Information Act* are attached except for any current outstanding annual return, which the corporation will file immediately upon revival.

   a) *Tous les avis et rapports en souffrance que la société doit déposer aux termes de la Loi sur les renseignements exigés des personnes morales sont joints aux statuts, sauf les rapports annuels courants éventuellement en souffrance, que la société déposera immédiatement après la reconstitution.*

   b) all documents required to be filed by the corporation under Ontario tax statutes have been filed and all defaults of the corporation under the tax statutes have been remedied.

   b) *Tous les documents exigés par les lois d'imposition de l'Ontario ont été déposés et toutes les omissions commises par la société à l'égard de ces lois ont été corrigées.*

   c) the consent of the Corporations Tax Branch of the Ministry of Finance to the requested revival (if applicable) is enclosed.

   c) *La Direction de l'imposition des compagnies du ministère des Finances a approuvé (le cas échéant) la reconstitution. Son consentement est annexé.*

   d) the consent of the Public Guardian & Trustee to the requested revival (if applicable) is attached.

   d) *Le Tuteur et curateur public a approuvé (le cas échéant) la reconstitution. Son consentement est annexé.*

   e) the consent of the Ontario Securities Commission to the requested revival (if applicable) is attached.

   e) *La Commission des valeurs mobilières de l'Ontario a approuvé (le cas échéant) la reconstitution. Son consentement est annexé.*

   f) all other defaults of the corporation to the date of dissolution have been remedied.

   f) *Toutes les omissions commises par la société avant la dissolution ont été corrigées.*

7. The interest of the applicant in the corporation is: (for example, director, officer, shareholder, creditor, estate trustee of shareholder)
   Indiquer l'intérêt de l'auteur de la demande dans la société (p. ex. : administrateur, dirigeant, actionnaire, créancier, exécuteur testamentaire d'un actionnaire, etc.) :

These articles are signed in duplicate.
Les présents statuts sont signés en double exemplaire.

First name, middle name, surname, **signature** and full address for service of applicant
*Auteur de la demande : prénom, 2ᵉ prénom, nom de famille, **signature** et adresse complète du domicile élu*

07127 (03/2004)

PART IV

Not-for-profit corporations

CHAPTER 15

Not-for-profit organizations, corporations, and charities

CHAPTER OBJECTIVES

After completing this chapter, you should be able to:

1. Understand the distinction between a non-charitable NPO and a registered charity.

2. Describe the procedure for incorporating an NPO in the federal and Ontario jurisdictions.

3. Understand the steps for applying for registration as a charity, and for maintaining compliance with reporting requirements with the Canada Revenue Agency and the Office of the Public Guardian and Trustee for the Province of Ontario.

4. List the ongoing reporting requirements of NPOs and registered charities generally.

5. Prepare organizational and annual proceedings for an NPO or a registered charity.

6. Identify the steps required to initiate various corporate changes in an NPO.

INTRODUCTION

A not-for-profit organization (NPO) is one that is formed "for the purpose of carrying on, without **pecuniary gain**, objects of a patriotic, charitable, philanthropic religious, professional, sporting or athletic character. In other words, not-for-profit corporations are engaged in activities that are of benefit to the community."[1] The exception to this is an NPO that is a **club**. In a club, members can ultimately share accumulated profits when the club is wound up and its remaining assets are distributed among its **members**.

This chapter discusses various types of NPOs; however, it will focus on NPOs that are corporations. When they are incorporated, NPOs are commonly referred

pecuniary gain
a gain that a person may have in a matter because of a likelihood or expectation of appreciable financial gain to that person or to another person with whom the person is associated

club
an organization or premises, typically a service (such as the Rotary Club) or social club, whose objectives are wholly or partly social in nature

members
the persons who elect directors of an NPO (like shareholders of a share capital corporation); members do not "own" an NPO, but they may, if authorized in the letters patent or bylaws of a non-charitable NPO, be entitled to receive the remaining assets of an NPO on windup or dissolution

to as not-for-profit corporations, non-profit corporations, non-share capital corporations, or corporations without share capital.

An incorporated NPO, though formed as a legal corporate entity like a share capital (or for-profit) corporation, is distinctly different. A **share capital corporation** is incorporated with the goal of making a profit for the benefit of its shareholders. In contrast, an NPO is not incorporated for a profit-making purpose, and its profits are not passed on to its members (other than in a club). It should also be noted that while it is technically possible to structure a share capital corporation as an NPO, it is uncommon to do so.

The incorporation of an NPO such as a trade association requires different consideration and, following incorporation, is subject to different reporting requirements from those of an NPO that is a **registered charity**.

LEGAL STRUCTURES

There are various legal structures or vehicles available for NPOs. This section provides a brief overview of non-corporate legal structures; the remainder of the chapter will focus on the corporation.

Trusts

A trust is created when one person or a group of persons holds legal title to property but another person or group of persons has the right to the enjoyment of that property or the right to benefit from that property. The trust may arise through:

- the words or acts of a person which indicate an intention to create a trust, or
- the law imposing a trust to ensure that equitable title to the property passes from one person to another.[2]

The legal instrument that creates a trust (such as a trust deed) sets out the objects or purposes of the trust and the duties of the trustees to make decisions based on those objects. The trustees have a fiduciary duty to carry out their duties with confidence, trust, honesty, and loyalty to the beneficiaries of the trust.

A trust is most often used among a small group of individuals for the administration of a fund for specific purposes. The "rules and regulations" of a trust can be set out like the bylaws of a corporation.

The advantage of using a trust is that the trustees and beneficiaries have greater flexibility in amending the purposes of the trust (if the trust deed provides for such amendments) than the directors and shareholders have in amending a corporation's articles. In addition, a trust has no filing or registration fees and, provided that it is not a charitable trust, no reporting requirements, other than those specified in the trust document.

A charitable trust may be established for a specific purpose, but the beneficiaries of the trust need not be identified by name. For example, a charitable trust could be set up to benefit the homeless. There are many charitable organizations or programs that may qualify to be a beneficiary of charitable funds from a trust. The trustees are bound by the trust document to ensure that the monies paid from the trust to the beneficiaries support the objects of the trust document.

Partnerships

A partnership exists when two or more organizations "share resources to reach a common goal." A partnership can be set up as a temporary measure for a specific project, or it can be intended to be permanent. A partnership really defines or identifies the relationship between two or more organizations.

The partnership arrangement may be informal or formal, and may be governed by a partnership agreement. It should be noted that the Ontario *Partnerships Act* does not apply to an NPO.

A partnership may be formed between or among other NPOs with similar objectives, to carry out a common project or to reach a common goal. A partnership may also be formed between an NPO and the private sector, or between an NPO and a government agency or program.

Unincorporated organizations

An organization or association can be created without incorporating. Its "governing document," if it has one, may be a memorandum of association or constitution of its members, which sets out its purpose and structure and acts as the contract and terms under which its members relate to each other. It may also have bylaws that support its purpose and govern its activities. In the absence of a governing document or bylaws, one would have to review the actual practices followed by the unincorporated organization, whether recorded in the minutes or by some other means, to "construct or reconstruct" its constitution.

The attributes of an unincorporated organization include:

1. It has no "legal status" other than its members. This may not be of concern in some cases, such as an organization that is formed for a limited time or for a single purpose. In other cases, the lack of legal status may give the impression that the organization has an "informal" structure, whether that is true or not, and could prevent the organization from doing some of the good and valuable work it was created to do.

2. An unincorporated organization cannot legally enter into or enforce contracts. It cannot sue or be sued in its own name, and any suit action has to be made or defended by its individual members or by representative action — that is, by one or more members on behalf of the entire membership.

3. Members of an unincorporated organization or association, like partners of a partnership, may be held personally liable for the debts or liabilities of the organization.

4. An unincorporated organization cannot hold real estate in its name, unless it is a religious organization governed by the Ontario *Religious Organizations' Lands Act*.

Incorporated organizations

An NPO may be incorporated either pursuant to a general corporate law statute or by special act of the federal Parliament or a provincial legislature. (However, this chapter does not consider special act companies other than in the context of continuation.)

An NPO is similar to a share capital corporation (a for-profit corporation) in many ways, including:

perpetual existence
existence with an indefinite
term ("forever")

1. it has **perpetual existence** (until it is voluntarily or involuntarily dissolved);

2. it exists separately from its members;

3. it may hold real estate in its own name;

4. it may contract in its own name, and therefore it may sue and be sued; and

5. in most cases, individual members of the NPO are exempt from personal liability for the corporation's debts pursuant to provisions contained in the statute under which it was created.

Table 15.1 shows the various types of NPOs, incorporated and unincorporated, non-charitable and charitable.

DIFFERENCES BETWEEN SHARE CAPITAL (FOR-PROFIT) CORPORATIONS AND NPOs

NPOs differ from share capital corporations in three respects:

1. NPOs are created without share capital, and have members, not shareholders.

2. If the activities of an NPO produce a profit on its operations, the members of the NPO do not personally benefit from that profit and all profit accrues to the NPO. In contrast, any profit in a share capital corporation accrues to the benefit of the corporation's shareholders.

3. NPOs are established for purposes other than the gain for their members; in other words, NPOs are not incorporated for the purpose of making a profit. While NPOs are "permitted" to make a profit, the profit must be used in support of the objects or purposes set out in their letters patent. Those objects can be charitable or non-charitable.

DIFFERENCES BETWEEN CHARITABLE AND NON-CHARITABLE NPOs

Registered charities (which may or may not be corporations) and NPOs (which may or may not be corporations) differ in a number of ways:

1. NPOs may not be registered as registered charities under the federal *Income Tax Act* (ITA). The ITA recognizes categories of charities that are eligible for exemption from income tax and that may be issued a charitable registration number.

2. A registered charity is an organization that operates for the benefit of the public and has been established for one of the following purposes:

    a. the relief of poverty;

    b. the advancement of religion;

TABLE 15.1 TYPES OF NOT-FOR-PROFIT ORGANIZATIONS: INCORPORATED AND UNINCORPORATED, NON-CHARITABLE AND CHARITABLE

	Non-charitable	Charitable	
		Not registered	Registered
Incorporated*	Canada	Canada	Canada
	Ontario	Ontario	Ontario
Unincorporated	Club/association	Non-registered trust	Registered trust
	Partnerships	Non-registered non-trust (association)	Registered non-trust (association)

* When incorporated, sometimes referred to as "non-share capital corporations," "societies," "not-for-profit corporations," or "non-profit corporations."

    c. the advancement of education; or

    d. other purposes beneficial to the community.

3. Charities may issue receipts to donors for income tax purposes, but NPOs may not.

ADVANTAGES AND DISADVANTAGES OF CHARITABLE REGISTRATION

Advantages

The advantages of charitable registration include:

1. the organization may issue income tax receipts to its donors;

2. the organization is exempt from taxation; and

3. the organization may more readily qualify for other benefits.

Disadvantages

The disadvantages of charitable registration include:

1. the organization must devote all of its resources to its charitable activities;

2. the organization must make annual filings with the CRA;

3. none of the property of the organization may be distributed to its members on dissolution or winding up of the organization.

INCOME TAX CONSIDERATIONS

Registered charities are automatically exempt from tax on their income. An NPO may be exempt from the payment of tax on its income if all of the following conditions are met:

1. it is not a charity in the opinion of the minister (that is, it is not registered as a charity);

2. it is organized exclusively for social welfare, civic improvement, pleasure, recreation, or any other purposes except profit;

3. it is in fact operated exclusively for one of the purposes just mentioned; and

4. no part of its income is paid, payable, or otherwise made available for the pecuniary benefit of any proprietor, member, or shareholder.

NPOs may, however, be subject to tax on their property income and on certain taxable capital. An NPO is required to file a non-profit organization information return (Form T1044, which must be filed within six months after its fiscal period) under the ITA[3] under the following conditions:

1. it receives more than $10,000 in interest, rent, or royalties;

2. it had more than $200,000 in assets at the end of the preceding fiscal year; or

3. it filed an information return in the preceding fiscal year.

A sample T1044 can be viewed online at http://www.cra-adrc.gc.ca/E/pbg/tf/t1044.

A registered charity must, within six months after its fiscal period, file a **registered charity information return** (on Form T3010A) with applicable schedules. A sample T3010A can be viewed online at http://www.cra.gc.ca/E/pbg/tf/t3010a.

registered charity information return (Form T3010)
the charity information return that must be filed with the CRA by every registered charity on an annual basis and within six months following the expiration of a registered charity's financial year

THE USES OF NPOs OR REGISTERED CHARITIES

An NPO or registered charity may be used as a vehicle for charitable or non-charitable purposes. A charitable corporation may be:

1. a charitable organization — that is, an organization that carries on its own charitable activities; or

2. a public or private foundation — that is, an organization that receives and uses funds to finance the charitable activities of another registered charity.

A non-charitable corporation may be:

1. a club of a social, service, or athletic nature, which may or may not have club premises; or

2. a trade or business association, ratepayers' association, community organization, or other general organization.

REGISTERED CHARITIES

Charitable organization

A charitable organization is one that carries on its own charitable activities (as opposed to one that funds the charitable activities of others). It may also make grants to other charities. "Charitable organization" is defined in s. 149.1(1) of the ITA as an organization, whether or not incorporated,

1. all of whose resources are devoted to charitable activities that it carries on;

2. none of whose income is payable to, or available for, the personal benefit of any proprietor, member, shareholder, trustee, or settlor of the organization;

3. more than 50 percent of whose directors, trustees, officers, or similar officials deal at arm's length with other directors, trustees, officers, or similar officials; and

4. where it is designated as a private foundation or public foundation under the Act, no more than 50 percent of its capital has been contributed by one person or by a group of persons who do not deal at arm's length with each other (for the purpose of this provision, "person" does not include the Crown, a province, a municipality, another registered charity that is not a private foundation, or a non-profit organization described in s. 149(1)(l).

Charitable foundation

"Charitable foundation" is defined in s. 149.1(1) of the ITA as "a corporation or trust that is constituted and operated exclusively for charitable purposes, no part of the income of which is payable to, or is otherwise available for, the personal benefit of any proprietor, member, shareholder, trustee or settlor thereof, and that is not a charitable organization." Charitable foundations can be either public or private foundations.

The distinction between public and private foundations under current legislation is set out below. Note, however, that pending amendments would, among other changes, replace the 50 percent of capital contribution test for both charitable organizations and public foundations with the requirement that a large donor be at arm's length with the recipient charity after the donation and not control the charity or any activity of the charity.

PUBLIC FOUNDATION

A public foundation is a widely controlled charity whose primary purpose is to fund other organizations that are qualified donees (defined below). It may also carry out some of its own activities. Less than 50 percent of its principal officers may be "related persons" (defined below). In addition, 50 percent of its funding must be received from donors who are not related persons. A public foundation can be established as either a trust or a corporation.

PRIVATE FOUNDATION

A private foundation is a closely controlled charitable entity that carries on its own activities or that funds other organizations that are qualified donees. At least 50 percent or more of its principal officers are related persons, or it receives more than 50 percent of its funding from one person or a group of related persons. A private foundation can be established as either a trust or a corporation. It is important to note that a private foundation may not carry on any business operations.

QUALIFIED DONEES

Under s. 149.1(1) of the ITA, a "qualified donee" is one of the following:

1. a registered Canadian charity;

2. a registered Canadian amateur athletic association;

3. a housing corporation resident in Canada that has been formed exclusively to provide low-cost housing for the aged;

4. a municipality in Canada;

5. the United Nations or an agency thereof;

6. a university outside Canada that is prescribed to be a university, the student body of which includes students from Canada;

7. a charitable organization outside Canada to which Her Majesty in right of Canada has made a gift in the year or in the 12-month period preceding the year; or

8. Her Majesty in right of Canada or a province.

RELATED PERSONS

Individuals can be related to each other by blood, marriage, common law marriage, or business relationship (for example, business partners or employer–employee). Individuals or groups can also be related to a corporation in which they have a controlling interest. Persons who are related to these individuals are also related to the corporation.

Application to the Canada Revenue Agency

Application for registration as a charity is completed on CRA Form T2050. A sample T2050 can be viewed online at http://www.cra.gc.ca/E/pbg/tf/t2050.

The information that must be included on the application is as follows:

1. the name and address of the applicant, as well as details of all addresses at which the applicant's activities will be carried out and where books and records are kept;

2. business numbers, if assigned;

3. a list of the applicant's directors or trustees, including their addresses, phone numbers, birth dates, and occupations;

4. details of incorporation (a copy of the charter documents);

5. information to designate the registered charity as a charitable organization, a public foundation, or a private foundation;

6. a detailed description of the programs or activities that the applicant will carry on in support of its objectives, including supplemental information such as newspaper clippings, minutes of meetings, videos, fundraising materials, pamphlets, brochures, or other information on the applicant that illustrates its work and purposes;

7. information on political activities, if any (applicants for registration are strongly advised to ensure that this question can be and is answered in the negative);

8. information on regular or occasional fundraising;

9. a detailed proposed budget for the first 12 months of operation;

10. if the applicant has been in operation for more than one year, a copy of its most recent financial statements;

11. copies of the following ancillary documentation:

    a. the parent organization's certificate, if applicable;

    b. governing documents;

    c. a certificate of good standing, if applicable; and

    d. the bylaws.

There is no fee for making an application for registration as a charity. Once the application is submitted, charitable registration can take many months. Certain foundations can be incorporated and registered as charities quickly; these foundations are based on pre-approved model objects and are limited to funding qualified donees.

APPLICATIONS BY TRUSTS

To be considered for registration as a charity with the CRA, a trust must ensure that its trust document contains the following fundamental items:

1. the effective date of the trust document;

2. the name of the trust;

3. the names of the original trustees;

4. the purpose for establishing the trust;

5. rules governing how trustees will administer funds received by the trust;

6. an assurance that all monies received by the trust will be used by the trustees solely for the purposes outlined in the trust document;

7. an ability to replace trustees; and

8. the signatures of at least three trustees.

Once charitable registration is granted, the charitable trust is required, like all other registered charities, to file a registered information return and public information return (on Form T3010A) to maintain its charitable status. It is also required to notify the CRA of any changes to the charitable trust document, including changes of trustees.

If the charitable trust is established in Ontario, it is required to notify the Office of the Public Guardian and Trustee for the Province of Ontario (PGT) of its existence in accordance with the requirements of the *Charities Accounting Act*. The charitable trust must also meet the ongoing reporting requirements of the PGT; it must report the names and addresses of its trustees, mailing address, names under which the charitable trust may operate, and all changes to that information.

APPLICATIONS BY UNINCORPORATED ASSOCIATIONS

To be considered for registration as a charity with the CRA, an unincorporated association must ensure that its memorandum of association or constitution includes at least the following:

1. the effective date of the document;

2. the name of the organization;

3. a summary of the association's objects or purposes;

4. an assurance that the organization has not been established and shall not carry on its activities for gain, and that all profits or accretions shall be used solely to promote its objects;

5. a summary of the association's structure (for directors, officers, etc.);

6. a procedure for replacing directors and officers; and

7. the signatures of least three principal officers.

The reporting requirements to any government agency that an unincorporated organization must meet are limited to those that registered charities must meet. These requirements would be similar to those for charitable trusts.

DECIDING TO INCORPORATE AND CHOOSING THE JURISDICTION

There are many factors to consider in choosing the jurisdiction of an NPO. These factors, which may make incorporation in one jurisdiction significantly more desirable than incorporation in another, are discussed below.

Exposure

An NPO that intends to carry on operations in many or all provinces or territories would likely prefer to incorporate federally. In contrast, an NPO with a narrower scope of operations would have no need to operate beyond its own municipal or provincial jurisdictions, and therefore provincial incorporation would be preferable.

Charitable status

Regardless of the parameters of operations, if an NPO intends to have charitable objects, it may be more prudent to incorporate federally. By doing so, the NPO can avoid having its application for incorporation reviewed by the PGT. While any registered charity operating in Ontario is required to comply with the reporting requirements of the PGT, a federally incorporated NPO with charitable status need only provide information to the PGT and is not required to submit charter documents for approval prior to proceeding. An NPO with charitable objects that incorporates in Ontario is required to submit its application for incorporation and any application for supplementary letters patent to the PGT for prior approval. This process carries with it a review fee (currently, $150). This approval also slows down the review process.

Timing of review

Federal NPOs are currently being reviewed by Corporations Canada, and letters patent issued within three to four weeks. In contrast, Ontario NPOs currently take six to eight weeks to incorporate; if charitable objects are desired, the PGT review time (which can be several weeks) is added to the Ontario processing time.

Bylaws

Federal NPOs are required to submit their bylaws for approval to Corporations Canada with their application for incorporation. Corporations Canada (through its **Not-for-Profit Policy Summary**) has adopted a form of model bylaw for convenience of use. In addition, law firms that have their own model bylaw can apply to Corporations Canada for a "model identifier number," which will identify a bylaw as having received pre-approval from Corporations Canada. When submitting a bylaw using that model identifier number, one need only cite differences in the bylaw submitted and the model.

Ontario NPOs are not required to submit bylaws to the Ontario Companies and Personal Property Security Branch of the Ministry of Consumer and Business Services ("the Ontario Companies Branch") either before or following incorporation as an NPO. However, an Ontario NPO that is applying for charitable status must submit its bylaws to the CRA (for information only, not for pre-approval).

In general, approval of bylaws of either a federal or Ontario NPO may also be subject to the requirements and to the approval of any other regulatory body by which the NPO is regulated.

Not-for-Profit Policy Summary
the summary published from time to time by Corporations Canada that outlines the requirements for incorporation under the *Canada Corporations Act*; it describes the process of application for incorporation and the framework for bylaws of a federal NPO, and addresses requests for ministerial approval to amend the bylaws of existing corporations

Conducting meetings of directors and members versus written resolutions

The boards of federal NPOs may not conduct business by way of written resolution, though previously they could. However, the current Not-for-Profit Policy Summary of Corporations Canada provides for certain circumstances under which written resolutions (or mail ballots) may be used. The bylaws of federal NPOs may provide that, where communication ability, security, and confidentiality can be assured, meetings of the board or members may be conducted by electronic communication. The parameters for such communication are set out in the policy summary of Corporations Canada.

It was previously the case that meetings of directors and members of Ontario NPOs could be conducted by way of written resolutions only in the first year of an NPO's existence. However, with the passage of amendments to Ontario's *Corporations Act* under **red tape reduction legislation**, the business of directors and members may now be conducted either by meeting or by **unanimous written resolution**. It is also interesting to note that the Ontario statute provides only for electronic meetings of a board of directors; there is no like provision for conducting meetings of members.

STATUTES

Canada Corporations Act

NPOs are incorporated under part II of the *Canada Corporations Act* (CCA) (ss. 153 to 157). The CCA contains far fewer provisions that apply to the powers and duties of members, directors, and officers than does the Ontario *Corporations Act*. The regulation of those powers is vested in the minister of industry by virtue of the requirement that the bylaws of a corporation, including any amendments and variations, must be approved by the minister prior to being effective. In addition, the policy summary of Corporations Canada provides certain parameters.

It should be noted that there are major changes proposed to the CCA that will make the statute much more like the *Canada Business Corporations Act*. This transition may make federal NPOs even more attractive. It could be that corporations existing under the current CCA will be required to continue under any new and highly modified statute, as they were required in the late 1970s when the *Canada Business Corporations Act* was introduced.

Ontario Corporations Act

NPOs are incorporated under part III of the Ontario *Corporations Act* (OCA) (ss. 117 to 133). Certain other sections of the CCA also apply to NPOs:

1. Sections 1 to 16 of part I and O. reg. 181 contain general provisions relating to, for example, the power of the minister, names, and the incorporation process.

2. The sections of part II referred to in s. 133 deal with incidental powers, borrowing, removal and payment of directors, establishment of executive committee, disclosure of directors, interests, indemnities to directors, places of meetings, proxies, meetings of members, audits and auditors, and amalgamation.

3. Sections 228 to 271 in part VI deal with windups of corporations.

4. Sections 272 to 335 in part VII contain general provisions relative to the routine corporate provisions.

PROCEDURE FOR INCORPORATING FEDERALLY

Industry Canada publishes an **information kit** that sets out the requirements, procedures, and precedents for incorporating in the federal jurisdiction. The kit can be a valuable resource, particularly for those not familiar with the process and documentation. It can be obtained online through links at http://strategis.ic.gc.ca.

While there are similarities in the considerations for the corporate framework of a federal NPO or registered charity and a federal non-charity, the procedures, documents, and government approvals are different.

information kit
a resource published by Corporations Canada that sets out the requirements, procedures, and precedents for incorporating in the federal jurisdiction

Name

Corporations Canada, the government agency with jurisdiction over corporations, has the power to determine whether or not a proposed name conforms to law. Unlike in Ontario, however, in the federal jurisdiction the proposed name of a federal NPO or registered charity may be pre-approved. Pre-approval is very helpful in ascertaining whether a name is available for use before all the documentation is prepared and executed.

The procedure for seeking such prior name approval is as follows:

1. Obtain a federal-biased NUANS name search report in the proposed name.

2. Forward the report (which can be done by fax) to Corporations Canada requesting name approval. It is helpful to include in the fax transmission a synopsis of the type of activity proposed to be carried on, as well as the details of any consents you would be able to provide, either for an individual whose name forms part of the proposed corporate name, or for similar corporations or trademark owners shown on the NUANS report.

3. Corporations Canada will consider the submission and provide you (by return fax) with its name decision letter. The letter is usually sent within one or two days after the request for approval is submitted. If the name decision is positive, you would submit the name decision as part of your submission of the application for incorporation. If the name decision is negative, Corporations Canada will indicate how you may be able to satisfy the directorate on the name, such as by adding a distinctive or descriptive element or by providing a consent.

In general, the name of a federal NPO must contain both a descriptive and a distinctive element. A descriptive element describes the nature of the main type of corporate activity. A distinctive element identifies and sets the corporate name apart from others. An example of a name that contains both a descriptive and a distinctive element is Pickering Rowing Club Inc. The word "Pickering" is the distinctive element, and the words "Rowing Club" constitute the descriptive element. In addition, the proposed name may not include the words "Limited" or "Ltd." However, the minister will accept the legal endings "Incorporated," "Inc.," "Corporation," or "Corp." There is no requirement that the name have a legal ending.

Application for incorporation: Requirements respecting applicants and first directors

There must be a minimum of three first directors on an application for incorporation. There is no requirement that a majority of the first directors be resident Canadians. The Not-for-Profit Policy Summary of Corporations Canada provides the following additional requirements respecting applicants and first directors:

> Where there are more than three applicants, only three of them are needed to constitute the first board of directors. However, more than three applicants may be first directors.
>
> Persons other than the applicants may be members of the board in addition to the three or more applicants, as long as the application states that the additional persons have consented to being directors.
>
> In the absence of specific legislative approval, federal Ministers or public servants cannot be applicants for the establishment of a not-for-profit corporation controlled by the federal government under the [*Canada Corporations Act*].

Application for incorporation: Required information

The application for incorporation, which is made on a pre-approved form of Corporations Canada must include the following information:

1. the proposed name of the NPO;

2. the names, addresses, and occupations of the individuals who are the applicants and first directors;

3. the objects or purposes of the proposed NPO;

4. a statement that the operations of the NPO may be carried on throughout Canada (and elsewhere if permitted by the laws of another jurisdiction);

5. the geographic location of the head office (no physical address is required);

6. a statement that the proposed bylaws of the proposed NPO are being filed with the application for incorporation;

7. a statement that the proposed NPO will be carried on without pecuniary gain for its members; and

8. the date and place of signing of the application, and the original signatures of the applicants for incorporation.

Objects clauses

objects
statements of the purposes and objectives of an NPO

The **objects** of a federal NPO or registered charity are statements of the purposes and objectives of an NPO. The objects should be set out in the application for incorporation, and should be broad enough yet defined enough to accurately reflect the NPOs intended operations. The guidelines of the PGT for objects are useful for a federal NPO that will be a registered charity and operate in Ontario, even though pre-approval by the PGT is not required.

Sample object clauses for a registered charity are as follows (in this example, for a private foundation):

The objects of the Corporation are:

1. To receive and maintain a fund or funds and to apply all or part of the principal and income therefrom, from time to time, to charitable organizations that are qualified donees under the *Income Tax Act* (Canada) [and that are engaged in the field of _____].

Power clauses

A federal NPO that will make application for registration as a registered charity should include **charitable power clauses** in its application for incorporation. Sample power clauses are as follows:

charitable power clauses clauses inserted in an application for incorporation or application for supplementary letters patent that empower an NPO to do specific acts

For the further attainment of the above objects, the Corporation shall have the following powers:

1. Subject to any applicable provincial or federal law and subject to the foregoing objects of the Corporation, to acquire, solicit or receive by purchase, lease, contract, donation, legacy, gift, loan, grant, bequest or otherwise, any kind of real or personal property, either as an annual or other contribution or as an addition to the fund or funds of the Corporation;

2. To hold, mortgage, sell or convert any of the real or personal property from time to time owned by the Corporation for the charitable purposes aforesaid;

3. To invest and re-invest the funds of the Corporation in such manner as determined by the Board of Directors, and in making such investments, the Board of Directors shall not be limited to investments authorized by law for Trustees, provided such investments are reasonable, prudent and sagacious under the circumstances and do not constitute, either directly or indirectly, a conflict of interest;

4. To exercise all voting rights and to authorize and direct the execution and delivery of proxies in connection with any shares or obligations in any company or corporation owned by the Corporation;

5. Subject to any applicable provincial or federal law, in connection with any company or corporation in which the Corporation may at any time hold shares or obligations, to take up the proportion of any increased capital to which as holders of such shares or obligations it may be entitled and to purchase any additional shares or obligations in such company or corporation; to join any plan for the reconstruction and reorganization of such company or corporation or for the amalgamation of such company or corporation or for the sale of the assets of such company or corporation or any part thereof and, in pursuance of such plan, to accept any shares or obligations in lieu of or in exchange for the shares or obligations held by the Corporation in such company or corporation; to enter into any pooling or other agreement in connection with the shares or obligations held by the Corporation in such company or corporation and, in case of the sale thereof, to give any options considered advisable; to give consent to the creation of any mortgage, lien or indebtedness by any company or corporation whose shares or obligations are held by the Corporation; to retain as an investment for such length of time as may be considered advisable any shares or obligations acquired by the Corporation through the exercise of the objects of the Corporation;

6. To employ and pay such assistants, clerks, agents, representatives and employees and to procure, equip and maintain such offices and other facilities

and to incur such reasonable expenses as may be necessary, provided that the Corporation shall not hire its directors as paid assistants, clerks, agents, representatives and employees;

7. To enter into and carry out agreements, contracts and undertakings incidental thereto; and

8. To do all such other things as are incidental or conducive to the attainment of the above objects.

PGT approval for charities

A federal NPO that will operate in Ontario and apply for registration as a registered charity is not required to submit its application for incorporation to the PGT for approval before the application is considered by Corporations Canada. After it is incorporated and registered as a charity, however, the federal NPO must submit certain documentation to the PGT to allow it to set up its file. The federal registered charity is also required to comply with the ongoing reporting requirements of the PGT.

Statutory declaration

The application for incorporation must be supplemented with a **statutory declaration** of one of the applicants for incorporation. This declaration confirms the following:

1. that the individual is one of the applicants for incorporation and has knowledge of the matters connected with the proposed NPO;

2. that each applicant for incorporation is at least 18 years of age and is capable of contracting under law;

3. that the proposed name of the NPO is not objectionable on any public grounds and that it is not the same as that of an existing entity so as to be likely to deceive; and

4. that no public or private interest will be prejudicially affected by the incorporation of the NPO.

Bylaws

The bylaws of a proposed federal NPO must be submitted to Corporations Canada with the application for incorporation. Because the NPO has not yet been created, the bylaws do not have to be (and should not be) signed. However, they should accurately reflect the proposed governance structure of the NPO and should also be in compliance with both the CCA and the Not-for-Profit Policy Summary of Corporations Canada.

Any subsequent amendments to the bylaws of a federal NPO, once passed by the directors and confirmed by the members, must be submitted to Corporations Canada for ministerial approval before they can become effective.

There are many considerations in the preparation of bylaws, whether the NPO is incorporated in Ontario or federally. These considerations are summarized below.

MEMBERS

1. Who is eligible to be a member?

2. May corporations apply for membership?

3. Will there be one or several classes of voting and non-voting members?

4. What is the number of votes for each class of voting members?

5. Are there other criteria for membership classes — for example, may each class elect a certain number of directors?

6. Does the corporation want to be able to charge a membership fee?

7. If there is a fee, when must a member pay it in order to remain in good standing?

8. For those members who are also directors, is there a desire to have persons admitted as members automatically and without further formality upon their becoming directors?

9. Should there be a membership committee?

10. Should new members be admitted by the board or the remaining members?

11. Does membership need to be confirmed at the next general meeting of members?

12. Will there be delegates?

13. Are memberships transferable?

14. Under what circumstances can a membership be terminated?

15. For those members who are also directors, is there a desire to have membership terminated automatically upon their ceasing to be directors?

16. What is the procedure for withdrawing from membership?

17. Should there be the power to authorize rules for membership in the bylaws?

MEETINGS OF MEMBERS

1. What is the quorum for a meeting of members?

2. Where shall the meetings be held (at the head office or at another location determined by the directors)?

3. How much notice is required for meetings of members?

4. Which officers have the authority to call a general meeting of members?

5. What percentage of members can requisition a meeting of members?

6. Can the members transact business that is not included in the notice of the meeting?

VOTING AT MEETINGS OF MEMBERS

1. Should the bylaws permit proxy votes and, if so, how many proxy votes may each member hold?

2. Can members appoint non-members to be their proxy?

3. Is voting done by a show of hands or by secret ballot?

4. Can members vote by mail?

5. Who is the chair of the annual meeting? Who serves as the chair in the usual chair's absence? Does the chair have a second or casting vote?

6. What percentage of votes is required to carry a motion (other than a special resolution)?

BOARD OF DIRECTORS

1. Do members have to elect directors from among themselves, or can non-members be elected as long as they become members within 10 days of election?

2. Are there other criteria for the board — for example, do directors have to be members of a particular organization?

3. Will there be *ex officio* directors? If so, will they have the right to vote?

4. How are the directors to be elected — for example, by a certain number per membership class, through a slate put forward by a nominating committee, by regional representation, or otherwise?

5. What is the term of office for directors?

6. Can directors be re-elected to hold consecutive terms?

7. Are there rotating terms for directors? If so, how many vacancies each year will there be and what is the length of the rotating terms?

8. How does a director resign — that is, to whom does a director give notice?

9. How is a director removed — that is, by remaining directors or by members?

10. How are vacancies in the board filled? For example, if directors are removed by members, are vacancies filled by members? If a vacancy occurs through resignation or statutory removal, is the vacancy filled by the remaining directors for the balance of the unexpired term?

MEETINGS OF THE BOARD OF DIRECTORS

1. What constitutes a quorum at directors' meetings?

2. Where should board meetings be held?

3. Should there be regular meetings specified in the bylaws or are meetings convened at the discretion of the board?

4. How much notice is required for director meetings?

5. What form should the notice take — telephone, facsimile, hand-delivered notice, registered mail?

6. Who has the authority to call board meetings?

OFFICERS OF THE CORPORATION

1. Which officers will be appointed or elected and what are the duties of each office? Should there be an executive director, chair, president, vice-president, secretary, treasurer, others?

2. Who appoints the officers — the directors or the members? Do officers have the power to appoint other officers?

3. Can one person hold more than one office?

4. Is remuneration permitted for officers?

5. What is the length of term of office?

6. How can officers be removed?

7. What events cause automatic removal of officers?

8. How does an officer resign?

9. Will there be any *ex officio* officers?

CONTRACTING POWERS OF OFFICERS

1. Which officers have the authority to sign contracts on behalf of the corporation?

2. Is there any limit on any contract that one or more officers can sign?

STANDING COMMITTEES

1. Does the corporation wish to establish **standing committees**, such as:

   a. executive;

   b. nominating;

   c. advisory;

   d. membership;

   e. finance;

   f. personnel;

   g. programs;

   h. strategic planning?

2. What is the mandate of each committee?

3. What are the rules of procedure?

4. Who sits on each committee?

standing committee
committee that is permanent during the existence of an NPO

Indemnification of directors and officers

Confirm that indemnification by the corporation extends to both directors and officers.

Special approvals

Depending on the intended operations of a federal NPO or registered charity that operates in Ontario, the NPO may be subject to other regulatory approvals and compliance. Therefore, the considerations shown for special approvals by an Ontario NPO set out in the next section under the heading "Special approvals" would also apply to a federal NPO.

Summary

For convenience of review, table 15.2 summarizes the steps for incorporating a federal NPO.

PROCEDURE FOR INCORPORATING IN ONTARIO

The considerations and procedures for incorporating an Ontario NPO or registered charity are summarized below.

Name

Unlike share capital corporations, which can be incorporated with any name chosen by the principals (other than names specifically prohibited by law), with the principals assuming the risk and responsibility for the name conforming to law, the name of an Ontario NPO is subject to the approval of the minister. The OCA and its regulations provide the guidelines and prohibitions respecting names.

As with a federal NPO, the name of an Ontario NPO should not be too general and must contain both a descriptive and a distinctive element. There are certain exceptions to this rule, which are set out in the OCA and its regulations.

The OCA and its regulations also prohibit the use of certain words or expressions, such as:

1. "Amalgamated," unless the NPO is a corporation resulting from an amalgamation;

2. "College," unless the Ministry of Education consents to its use;

3. "Housing," unless the NPO is owned by, sponsored by, or connected with the federal or Ontario government or a municipal Ontario government;

4. "Royal," when used as an adjective, unless the consent of the Crown as been obtained through the Secretary of State;

5. numerals indicating the year of incorporation, unless the NPO is a successor corporation, the name of which is the same as or similar to the proposed corporation, or is the year of amalgamation of the NPO; and

6. any word or expression that would lead to the inference that the corporation is a business corporation.

TABLE 15.2 STEPS FOR INCORPORATING A FEDERAL NPO

Step	Comment
Search desired name	• proposed name should contain a descriptive and distinctive element; • once name search conducted, search report is submitted by fax to Industry Canada for name decision on availability; • decision usually provided within 24 hours

Application for incorporation	• minimum of three applicants required;
	
	• full name, address, and occupation required for each first director;
	
	• no Canadian residency requirements for directors;
	
	• the following additional information to be set out in application:
	
	  ❑ objects (in infinitive form);
	
	  ❑ charitable powers, if applicable;
	
	  ❑ statement re carrying out operations in Canada or elsewhere;
	
	  ❑ statement that bylaws submitted with application;
	
	  ❑ statement re operations of NPO are without gain for members;
	
	  ❑ geographic location of head office (no street address);
	
	  ❑ recipient of assets on dissolution;

Statutory declaration	• to be completed by one applicant and sworn before a commissioner of oaths
Consents	• any required consents of individuals whose name forms part of corporate name or names of similar organizations or corporations
General bylaw	• standard bylaw can be used as a starting point, with any customized provisions required
Submission of above documents to Corporations Canada for issue of letters patent	Cover letter should include: • executed application for incorporation, in duplicate; • one unsigned copy of bylaw; • statutory declaration, in duplicate; • name search report (not more than 90 days old); • copy of name decision letter; • any required consents; • street address of head office; • filing fee. Once filed with Industry Canada, the application for incorporation usually takes three to four weeks to process. The date of the letters patent will be the date of receipt of the incorporation package by Corporations Canada.

It is important to note that any legal ending used for an Ontario NPO may not include the words "Limited" or "Ltd." However, the minister will accept the legal endings "Incorporated," "Inc.," "Corporation," or "Corp." There is no requirement that the name have a legal ending.

Once the name has been chosen, a NUANS name search report must be obtained and submitted (with a currency date of less than 90 days) with the application for incorporation. The minister will rule on the availability of the name as part of the processing of the application.

Where the proposed name is similar to the name of an existing person, corporation, or organization, the application for incorporation should be supplemented with the written consent of the person, corporation, or organization to the use of the name. Without such consent, the proposed name may be rejected as being unacceptable.

Application for incorporation

As with a federal NPO, the application for incorporation for an Ontario NPO must be made by a minimum of three persons, who as applicants are also the first directors. There is no requirement that a majority of those persons be resident Canadians. The application is made on Form 2 under the OCA and must include the following information:

1. the proposed name of the NPO;

2. the address of the NPO's head office;

3. the full names and address for service of the applicants and first directors;

4. the objects for which the NPO is incorporated; and

5. the special provisions governing the NPO.

The application for incorporation must be submitted with original signatures, in duplicate, together with the NUANS name search report, any required consents, and the required filing fee (currently, $155). If the NPO will apply for registration as a charity, the application must first be submitted to the PGT for approval, together with the review fee ($150).

Objects clauses

As with a federal NPO, the objects of an Ontario NPO or registered charity are statements of its purposes and objectives. The objects must be broad enough yet specific enough to encompass the NPO's intended operations. The Ontario Companies Branch and the PGT in their publication *Not-for-Profit Incorporator's Handbook* state that the objects should not simply be an enumeration of the proposed activities and/or aims of the NPO. They advise that the statement of objects be kept brief and sufficiently specific so as to avoid ambiguity, but remain broad enough to provide flexibility.

The handbook contains several suggested objects for various types of NPOs and proposed registered charities and is a useful tool in drafting the objects clauses.

Power clauses

Section 23 of the OCA contains the details of the powers possessed by an NPO; therefore, none of those powers need to be repeated or mirrored in an application for incorporation. However, there are certain powers that do not appear in s. 23 and that are particularly relevant to NPO making an application for charitable registration, such as the power of the directors to invest and deal with funds of the NPO not required for the objects of the NPO in the manner in which they see fit. Therefore, when incorporating a registered charity, those special power clauses should also be set out in the application for incorporation. The following is sample language for power clauses to be included in an application for incorporation of a proposed NPO that will apply as a charity:

> For the above objects, and as incidental and ancillary thereto, to exercise any of the powers as prescribed by the *Corporations Act* (Ontario), or by any other statutes or laws from time to time applicable, except where such power is limited by these letters patent or the statute or common law relating to charities including, but not limited to the following:
>
> 1. To solicit and receive donations, gifts, legacies and bequests for use in promoting the objects of and carrying on the work of the Corporation, and to enter into agreements, contracts and undertakings incidental thereto;
>
> 2. To acquire, by purchase, contract, donation, legacy, gift, grant, bequest or otherwise, any personal property and to enter into and carry out any agreements, contracts or undertakings incidental thereto, and to sell, dispose of and convey the same, or any part thereof, as may be considered advisable;
>
> 3. To acquire by purchase, lease, devise, gift, or otherwise, real property, and to hold such real property or interest therein necessary for the actual use and occupation of the Corporation or for carrying on its charitable undertaking, and, when no longer so necessary to sell, dispose of and convey the same or any part thereof;
>
> 4. To accumulate from time to time part of the fund or funds of the Corporation and income therefrom subject to any statutes or laws from time to time applicable;
>
> 5. To invest and re-invest the funds of the Corporation in such manner as determined by the Board of Directors, and in making such investments, the Board of Directors shall not be subject to the *Trustee Act*, but provided that such investments are reasonable, prudent and sagacious under the circumstances and do not constitute, either directly or indirectly, a conflict of interest.

Special provisions

The application for incorporation should also set out the following certain special provisions (those that should be included for a charity have been highlighted in italics):

> 1. The corporation shall be carried on without the purpose of gain for its members and any profits or their accretions to the corporation shall be used in promoting its objects.
>
> 2. *The corporation shall be subject to the Charities Accounting Act (Ontario) and the Charitable Gifts Act (Ontario).*

3. The directors shall serve as such without remuneration and no director shall directly or indirectly receive any profit from their positions as such, provided that directors may be paid reasonable expenses incurred by them in the performance of their duties.

4. The borrowing power of the corporation pursuant to any bylaw passed and confirmed in accordance with s. 59 of the *Corporations Act* (Ontario) shall be limited to borrowing money for current operating expenses, provided that the borrowing power of the corporation shall not be so limited if it borrows on the security of real or personal property.

5. *If it is made to appear to the satisfaction of the Minister, upon report of the Office of the Public Guardian and Trustee, that the Corporation has failed to comply with any of the provisions of the Charities Accounting Act (Ontario) or the Charitable Gifts Act (Ontario), the Minister may authorize an inquiry for the purpose of determining whether or not there is sufficient cause for the Lieutenant Governor to make an Order under s. 317(1) of the Corporations Act to cancel the Letters Patent of the Corporation and declare it to be dissolved.*

6. Upon the dissolution of the Corporation and after payment of all debts and liabilities, its remaining property shall be distributed or disposed of to *qualified donees who are charities registered under the Income Tax Act (Canada), in Canada.*

Note that this last paragraph should be altered for either an NPO or a registered charity and should include the recipient of the remaining assets of the NPO.

PGT approval for charities

An Ontario NPO that will apply for registration as a charity must submit its application for incorporation to the PGT for approval before the application is considered by the Ontario Companies Branch.

This PGT review is subject to a review fee, which is currently $150. Once the PGT has reviewed, approved, and stamped an application for incorporation, the PGT's office will submit the application for incorporation to the Ontario Companies Branch for processing, provided that the ministry's required filing fee for issue of the letters patent is included with the application. The filing fee is currently $155.

Special approvals

The NPO or registered charity, depending on its intended operations, may be subject to other regulatory approvals and compliance.

Table 15.3 is a partial list of circumstances under which consultation with regulating bodies is recommended. These ministries should be consulted in the incorporation process, and may have their own regulations and policies on incorporation (including choosing a name), organization, maintenance, and ongoing reporting requirements.

TABLE 15.3 MINISTRIES TO CONSULT FOR PROPOSED UNDERTAKINGS

Proposed undertaking of NPO	Ministry to consult
To provide home for the poor and the aged	Ministry of Community, Family and Children's Services and the Ministry of Municipal Affairs and Housing
To operate a kindergarten or nursery school, home for children, or a daycare centre	Ministry of Community, Family and Children's Services
To provide health care services or to engage in related activities or if the NPO is to be an association of health care professionals	Ministry of Health and Long-Term Care
To provide cultural or citizenship programs	Ministry of Culture
To provide education or training programs	Ministry of Education and Ministry of Training, Colleges and Universities
To provide prisoner rehabilitation services	Ministry of Public Safety and Security
To be a charity	Office of the Public Guardian and Trustee (Ministry of the Attorney General) and the Charities Directorate of the Canada Customs and Revenue Agency
To be an association of professionals, such as architects or engineers	Ontario Association of Architects Association of Professional Engineers of Ontario

Submission of documents

The following documents must be submitted to incorporate an Ontario NPO:

1. the executed application for incorporation, in duplicate, originally signed by all applicants for incorporation;

2. an Ontario-biased NUANS name search report not more than 90 days old;

3. any required consents respecting the use of the name; and

4. the applicable filing fee.

A proposed Ontario NPO that will apply for registration as a charity must first submit the application for incorporation and accompanying documents to the PGT for review and approval, together with the PGT's review fee. As noted above, the submission to the PGT may also include the filing fees for the Ontario Companies Branch. If those fees are included, the PGT, when it issues its approval, will submit the application for incorporation directly to the Ontario Companies Branch for review.

Processing time

An application for incorporation is typically processed by the Ontario Companies Branch in six to eight weeks. Any prior approval by the PGT generally also takes several weeks. The date of the issue of the letters patent will be, unless a future date is otherwise requested, the date of receipt of the application by the Ontario Companies Branch. Note that it is possible to obtain expedited review by the Ontario Companies Branch within seven working days. Expedited service carries an additional fee (currently, $100). It is not possible to expedite the PGT review by paying an additional fee. A request for expedited review should be included in the cover letter to the PGT and will be considered on a case-by-case basis. If there is a valid reason for expedited review (that is, if the public would benefit from it), the PGT will expedite its review.

ORGANIZATION: FEDERAL OR ONTARIO NPO OR REGISTERED CHARITY

There are few differences between jurisdictions with regard to the steps to be taken to organize a federal or Ontario NPO or proposed registered charity. The differences are as follows:

- A federal NPO is not required to file an initial government filing in its home jurisdiction. A federal NPO that will carry on its operations in Ontario must file a Form 2 Initial Notice within 60 days of incorporation, as well as a Form 2 Notice of Change within 15 days of a change of information, pursuant to the Ontario *Corporations Information Act*.

- The directors and members of an Ontario NPO may choose to organize themselves by calling and holding meetings, or by passing their organizational proceedings by written resolution. In contrast, a federal NPO may not use written resolutions to deal with matters required by the CCA to be dealt with at a members' meeting, and may not use written resolutions to replace a directors' meeting.

- An Ontario NPO must file a Form 1 Initial Notice within 60 days of incorporation, as well as a Form 1 Notice of Change within 15 days of a change of information, pursuant to the Ontario *Corporations Information Act*.

Table 15.4 sets out the required organizational proceedings as if they are conducted by meeting, as well as distinctions between a federal NPO and an Ontario NPO. Note that the organizational proceedings do not include the information required to make an application for registration as a charity, which is set out above, under the heading "Application to Canada Revenue Agency."

NOTIFYING THE PGT AND THE CRA OF INCORPORATION AND ORGANIZATION

For federal and Ontario NPOs that have applied for and been issued charitable registration, it is important to remember that the PGT and the CRA must be kept informed of a registered charity's corporate structure and of changes to that structure. Following the organization of a charity, it is advisable to send to both the PGT and the CRA a package containing the following documentation and information (to the extent that it reflects any change):

TABLE 15.4 REQUIRED ORGANIZATIONAL PROCEEDINGS FOR FEDERAL AND ONTARIO NPOs

Step	Comment
Obtain corporate supplies	Order a minute book in which the constating documents and all corporate proceedings will be kept. Order corporate seal.
Organizational proceedings of the board	The first directors call and hold a special meeting of the board, at which resolutions are passed to accomplish the following: • approval of bylaw no. 1; • approval of form of corporate seal; • admission of members; • appointment of officers; • approval of banking documents; • if applicable, establishment of any committees; • if applicable, authorize or ratify the application for charitable registration
Applications for membership	To be completed by any person, firm, corporation, etc., whose application for membership requires submission and approval by the board of directors. For federal NPOs, such application for membership can include the authority for the members to conduct meetings by electronic conference.
Organizational proceedings of the members	The members call and hold a general meeting of members, at which resolutions are passed to accomplish the following: • confirmation of bylaw no. 1; • if applicable, acceptance of resignation of first directors; • election of permanent directors; • appointment of auditor
Consents to act as directors	• to be signed by all permanent directors (including first directors who will remain on the board); • consent should include a consent to meetings by electronic conference
Banking documents	• to establish corporate bank account and provide for signing authority on bank account
Form 1 initial notice (for Ontario NPOs only)	• to be filed within 60 days of incorporation; • form 1 in the same format as that for a share capital corporation, except is designated in box provided as an NPO
Form 2 Initial Notice (for federal NPOs only)	• to register the corporation to carry on its operations in Ontario; • principal place of business (if any) in Ontario required; otherwise, use lawyers' office address; • name and address of chief manager, if any (optional)
Extra-provincial registration	• to be filed in any province or territory in which the NPO carries on its operations (other than in Ontario)

1. a copy of the issued letters patent (if they have not already been provided);

2. a copy of the executed bylaws;

3. a list of the names and addresses of each of the permanent directors and officers;

4. a list of the mailing address of the registered charity, and all addresses at which the registered charity carries on its operations; and

5. the details of any business names under which the registered charity carries on operations.

EXTRA-PROVINCIAL REGISTRATION

In most provinces and territories, an NPO is required to register extra-provincially/territorially before or within a certain period of time after it commences carrying on operations in the province or territory. (An extra-provincial corporation is defined as a corporation incorporated otherwise than by or under an act of the legislature of a given province or territory.)

Although a federal NPO may be required to register in certain provinces and territories, failure to do so will not impair its rights in a province or territory. Federal corporations enjoy special constitutional status: legislation preventing federal corporations that have not been registered or licensed from resorting to the provincial courts for the enforcement of contracts made in pursuance of their powers is *ultra vires*. However, federal NPOs are subject to provincial laws of general application — for example, in respect of holding lands, liability for taxes, and the regulation of contracts.

The appendix to this chapter provides information on provinces and territories in which an NPO is required to register extra-provincially. Note that the information is based on information gathered from corporate registries and research of the applicable statutes. Before providing information to clients, be sure to obtain legal advice from agents in the province or territory with respect to the type of business carried on and whether or not an NPO is considered to be carrying on business for registration purposes.

Federal corporations have the capacity to carry on business, conduct their affairs, and exercise their power in any jurisdiction outside Canada to the extent that the laws of the jurisdiction permit (s. 15(3) of the *Canada Business Corporations Act*). However, federal NPOs are subject to provincial laws of general application — for example, in respect of holding lands, liability for taxes, and the regulation of contracts.

ANNUAL MEETINGS AND GOVERNMENT FILINGS: FEDERAL AND ONTARIO NPOs OR REGISTERED CHARITIES

As with the organization of federal and Ontario NPOs or registered charities, the annual maintenance of federal and Ontario NPOs or registered charities are similar in many ways. The primary difference, once again, lies in the ability of an Ontario NPO to conduct its corporate proceedings by way of written resolution.

The other differences arise from the actual structure of each corporation (through its bylaws) and from each corporation's filing requirements, which vary on the basis of its jurisdiction of incorporation and the other jurisdictions under which it may carry on operations.

For the purpose of setting out the requirements for annual proceedings in this chapter, the example of meetings has been used. Table 15.5 summarizes the steps to be taken to maintain the corporate records and comply with the government filing requirements of a federal or Ontario NPO or registered charity.

FUNDAMENTAL CHANGES: FEDERAL NPOs

Bylaws

As noted above, the bylaws of a federal NPO, once they have been passed by the directors and confirmed by the members, must be submitted to the Minister of Industry for ministerial approval before they can be considered effective.

Procedure for amending bylaws

Before submitting any bylaw amendments, and particularly if the amended bylaw repeals prior bylaws, it is important (but not mandatory) to complete and submit an Industry Canada checklist that sets out where all required bylaw provisions can be found. This checklist will greatly accelerate the ministerial review process. A sample checklist can be found on Industry Canada's Web site.

A request for ministerial approval of bylaw amendments of an NPO must include the following:

1. a letter specifying:

    a. the exact changes that have been made to the existing bylaws (with section references — this can be shown in the checklist referred to above);

    b. the date on which the amendments were sanctioned by the members in accordance with the existing bylaws;

    c. a request for ministerial approval; and

2. a consolidation of the existing bylaws where a number of amendments have been made to the provisions that are not being amended again.

There is no filing fee for requesting ministerial approval.

Once ministerial approval has been granted, the minister will issue a letter verifying approval of the bylaws on a specified effective date, which will be the date that Corporations Canada received the request for approval.

Change in number of directors

The information kit published by Corporations Canada provides that there must be either a fixed number of directors, no fewer than three, or a floating number of directors between three and a specified maximum, or a determinable formula having a minimum of three directors.

TABLE 15.5 STEPS FOR MAINTAINING CORPORATE RECORDS AND COMPLYING WITH FILING REQUIREMENTS FOR FEDERAL AND ONTARIO NPOs

Step	Comment
Annual and general meeting	An annual meeting is required to be conducted within 18 months following incorporation and every 15 months thereafter, and should be held within six months of financial year-end. An annual meeting is generally composed of a series of three meetings, as follows (minimum requirements shown only): Directors • to approve financial statements, and authorize them to be laid before the annual meeting Members • to receive financial statements; • to elect directors for ensuing year (or as required pursuant to bylaws); • to appoint auditors; • to approve prior acts of directors and officers Directors • to elect and/or appoint officers • to appoint committee members, if applicable
Annual summary (for federal NPOs)	• to be filed by June 1 of each year, containing information as of March 31 of that year
Annual return (for Ontario NPOs)	• to be filed within 60 days of the anniversary date of incorporation/amalgamation
Form 2 notice of change in Ontario	• to be filed within 15 days of a change in previously filed information
Extra-provincial annual return	• to be filed annually in any jurisdiction (other than Ontario) in which the corporation carries on its operations; • timing for filing of return varies in each jurisdiction
CRA charity information return (Form T3010A) (for registered charities)	• to be filed annually with the CRA within six months of financial year-end
CRA and PGT	• file notification of any changes to information from previous year relative to charter documents, bylaws, directors and officers, mailing address or principal place of business, or business names
CRA information return (Form T1044) (for NPOs)	• if the corporation meets Form T1044 tests, to be filed annually with the CRA within six months of financial year-end
T2 or T3 returns (for NPOs)	• to be filed annually with the CRA within six months of a financial year-end

In the case of an NPO that has a floating number of directors, and presuming that the bylaws are silent on the method of changing the number, a resolution of the members fixing the number of directors within the minimum and maximum number of directors is sufficient to fix the number of directors. There is no requirement to file a notice of this resolution with any governmental authority.

In the case of an NPO that has a fixed number of directors, any change in the number of directors must be accomplished by bylaw amendment. Once the amended bylaw has been passed, it must be sent to Industry Canada for ministerial approval.

Procedure for changing a fixed number of directors

1. Pass a bylaw in prescribed form by the directors and members of the NPO.

2. Send a letter to Industry Canada requesting ministerial approval. There is no fee for obtaining ministerial approval.

3. If the NPO is a registered charity, file notice of the change in the directors with the CRA. If the registered charity also carries on its operations in Ontario, notice of the change of directors must be filed with the PGT.

Change of head office (s. 24 of the CCA)

The corporation information kit provides that an NPO may by bylaw, sanctioned by at least two-thirds of the votes cast at a special general meeting, change the place where the head office is to be situated.

A copy of the bylaw certified under the seal of the NPO must be filed with the minister. A notice of the bylaw must be published in the *Canada Gazette*. A covering letter indicating a street address for the head office must also be submitted.

Note that a change of street address within the same municipality of the head office does not require a bylaw amendment. This type of amendment can be authorized by a board resolution changing the street address of the head office. The change must be indicated on the annual summary filed each year by June 1. In the meantime, a letter to Corporations Canada providing the new address is sufficient.

Procedure for changing the head office

1. Pass a bylaw changing the location of the head office.

2. Publish notice of the change of head office in the *Canada Gazette*.

3. If the NPO is registered to carry on business in Ontario, file a form 2 Notice of Change with the Ontario Companies Branch.

4. If the NPO is a registered charity, file notice of the change of head office with the CRA and the PGT.

Application for supplementary letters patent

The corporation information kit provides that in order to amend the provisions of letters patent — for example, name, objects, and other provisions — one must apply for supplementary letters patent.

Supplementary letters patent must be authorized by bylaw, sanctioned by two-thirds of the votes cast at a special general meeting of members called for that purpose, to extend, reduce, or amend its objects or change its name.

Supplementary letters patent take effect from their date of issuance.

Notice of the issuance of supplementary letters patent will be published in the *Canada Gazette*.

Procedure for application for supplementary letters patent

1. Pass a bylaw authorizing the changes to the charter and the application for supplementary letters patent.

2. Prepare an application for supplementary letters patent.

3. Prepare a statutory declaration of a person with full knowledge of the facts surrounding the application, in a form like that contained in the corporation information kit.

4. If the name of the corporation is being changed, obtain a federal-biased NUANS name search report.

5. File all applicable documents with Corporations Canada.

6. If the NPO is a registered charity, file a copy of the issued supplementary letters patent with the CRA and the PGT.

Amalgamation

The amalgamation provisions of the CCA do not apply to NPOs incorporated under part II of that act.

Continuation of special act companies

A special act company without share capital that wishes to amend its charter may do so either by having Parliament pass an amending statute, or by applying for continuation under part II of the CCA, pursuant to s. 159, during which process the corporation is entitled to "limit or extend its powers" and "change its corporate name." Once the new corporation is continued under part II, it is entitled to change any part of its charter or bylaws in accordance with the provisions of the CCA.

Note that there is no provision under the CCA for exporting a part II corporation to a provincial jurisdiction, nor for importing a provincial corporation to come under part II of the CCA.

Procedure for continuation

1. Prepare an application for continuation.

2. Obtain an affidavit or statutory declaration of an officer, sworn before a commissioner for taking oaths, certifying that:

   a. the facts in the application are true;

   b. the NPO is currently carrying on its affairs; and

   c. the resolution authorizing the continuation was duly passed.

3. Make two certified copies of the directors' resolution, duly confirmed by two-thirds of the members, or a resolution originating with the members, passed by a two-thirds vote.

4. Amend the NPOs bylaws to comply with the requirements of s. 155(2) of the CCA, or provide Corporations Canada a notice to the effect that the bylaws will be so amended at the next meeting of members.

5. File a copy of the incorporating statute and any amending statutes.

6. Submit the filing fee (currently, $200) payable to the Receiver General for Canada.

7. Obtain a federal-biased NUANS name search report not more than 90 days old.

8. If the NPO is a registered charity, notify the CRA and the PGT.

Surrender of charter (s. 32 of the CCA)

The corporation information kit provides that the procedure for making application for surrender of charter (dissolution) of a federal NPO is as follows:

1. Prepare an application for surrender of charter.

2. Pass a bylaw authorizing the surrender. Note that certified copies of the bylaw must be filed with the documentation, indicating the date it was passed by the members.

3. Obtain a certificate or statement of an officer attesting to the due passage of the bylaw.

4. Obtain an affidavit or statutory declaration of an officer certifying that the facts mentioned in the application are true.

5. Obtain an officer's statement, certifying:

   a. that the NPO has no assets; or

   b. if the NPO had assets, that they have been

      i. rateably divided among the members, or

      ii. distributed among other corporations in Canada with the same or similar objects or among other recognized registered charities in Canada; and

   c. that the NPO has no debts, liabilities, or other obligations, or that the debts, liabilities, or obligations have been duly provided for or protected or that the creditors or other persons with interests in such debts, liabilities, or other obligations consent to the surrender of charter.

6. The original letters patent (and supplementary letters patent, if any) must accompany the documentation. If those documents have been lost, an affidavit attesting to that fact is required.

FUNDAMENTAL CHANGES: ONTARIO NPOs
Change of directors

Section 285(1) of the OCA provides that a corporation may, by special resolution, increase or decrease the number of its directors.

PROCEDURE FOR CHANGING THE NUMBER OF DIRECTORS

1. Pass a special resolution. A special resolution is defined in the OCA as a resolution passed by the directors and confirmed with or without variation by at least two-thirds of the votes cast at a general meeting of the members of the corporation duly called for that purpose, or, in lieu of such confirmation, by the consent in writing of all of the members entitled to vote at such a meeting.

2. File a Form 1 Notice of Change with the Ontario Companies Branch respecting the changes in the directors.

3. If the NPO is a registered charity, file notice of the change in the directors with the CRA and the PGT.

Changing head office

Section 277 of the OCA provides as follows:

> 277(1) Subject to subsection (2), a corporation shall at all times have its head office in the place in Ontario where the letters patent provide that the head office is to be situate.
>
> (2) A corporation may by special resolution change the location of its head office to another place in Ontario.
>
> (3) Where the location of the head office of a corporation is changed by reason only of the annexation or amalgamation of the place in which the head office is situate to or with another municipality, such change does not constitute and has never constituted a change within the meaning of subsection (2).

Procedure for changing the head office

1. Pass a special resolution (as defined above).

2. Pass a directors' resolution fixing the address of the head office within the new geographic location.

3. File a Form 1 Notice of Change with the Ontario Companies Branch respecting the change of head office.

4. If the NPO is a registered charity, file a notice of the change of head office with the CRA and the PGT.

Application for supplementary letters patent

Section 131 of the OCA provides, in part, as follows:

> 131(1) A corporation may apply to the Lieutenant Governor for the issue of supplementary letters patent,

(a) extending, limiting or otherwise varying its objects;

(b) changing its name;

(c) varying any provision in its letters patent or prior supplementary letters patent;

(d) providing for any matter or thing in respect of which provision may be made in letters patent under this Act;

(e) converting it into a company;

(f) converting it into a corporation, with or without share capital.

(2) An application under subsection (1) shall be authorized by a special resolution. ...

(6) This section does not apply to a corporation incorporated by special Act, except that a corporation incorporated by special Act may apply under this section for the issue of supplementary letters patent changing its name.

Note that with respect to members' approval in registered charities, s. 133(2) of the OCA provides as follows:

133(2) Despite subsection (1), in the case of a corporation to which this Part applies, the objects of which are exclusively for charitable purposes, it is sufficient notice of any meeting of the members of the corporation if notice is given by publication at least once a week for two consecutive weeks next preceding the meeting in a newspaper or newspapers circulated in the municipality or municipalities in which the majority of the members of the corporation reside as shown by their addresses on the books of the corporation.

Procedure for application for supplementary letters patent

1. Pass a special resolution (as defined above).

2. Prepare an application for supplementary letters patent on Form 3.

3. If the name of the NPO is being changed, obtain an Ontario-biased NUANS name search report.

4. If the NPO is a registered charity, file the application for supplementary letters patent with the PGT for approval, with applicable filing fees, which, if desired, can include the review fees of the Ontario Companies Branch.

5. If the NPO is a registered charity, forward copies of the issued supplementary letters patent to the CRA and the PGT.

Passage of bylaw amendments

Section 129 of the OCA provides as follows:

129(1) The directors of a corporation may pass bylaws not contrary to this Act or to the letters patent or supplementary letters patent to regulate,

(a) the admission of persons and unincorporated associations as members and as members by virtue of their office and the qualification of and the conditions of membership;

(b) the fees and dues of members;

(c) the issue of membership cards and certificates;

(d) the suspension and termination of memberships by the corporation and by the member;

(e) the transfer of memberships;

(f) the qualification of and the remuneration of the directors and the directors by virtue of their office, if any;

(g) the time for and the manner of election of directors;

(h) the appointment, remuneration, function, duties and removal of agents, officers and employees of the corporation and the security, if any, to be given by them to it;

(i) the time and place and the notice to be given for the holding of meetings of the members and of the board of directors, the quorum at meetings of members, the requirement as to proxies, and the procedure in all things at members' meetings and at meetings of the board of directors;

(j) the conduct in all other particulars of the affairs of the corporation.

(2) A bylaw passed under subsection (1) and a repeal, amendment or re-enactment thereof, unless in the meantime confirmed at a general meeting of the members duly called for that purpose, is effective only until the next annual meeting of members unless confirmed thereat, and, in default of confirmation thereat, ceases to have effect at and from that time, and in that case no new bylaw of the same or like substance has any effect until confirmed at a general meeting of the members.

(3) The members may at the general meeting or the annual meeting mentioned in subsection (2) confirm, reject, amend or otherwise deal with any bylaw passed by the directors and submitted to the meeting for confirmation, but no act done or right acquired under any such bylaw is prejudicially affected by any such rejection, amendment or other dealing.

Procedure for bylaw amendments

1. Prepare a bylaw amendment in a similar form to that of a new bylaw, setting out the sections of the original bylaw to be deleted and amended. If a former bylaw of the corporation is to be repealed, the details of the repeal should be set out in the amended bylaw.

2. Pass a resolution of the board of directors passing the bylaw amendment.

3. Pass a resolution of the members confirming the bylaw amendment, which confirmation is to take place no later than the next annual meeting of members.

4. If the corporation is a registered charity, file a copy of the bylaw amendment with the CRA and the PGT.

Amalgamation

Section 113 of the OCA is applicable to NPOs, and provides as follows:

113(1) Any two or more companies, including a holding and subsidiary company, having the same or similar objects, may amalgamate and continue as one company.

(2) The companies proposing to amalgamate may enter into an agreement for the amalgamation prescribing the terms and conditions of the amalgamation, the

mode of carrying the amalgamation into effect and stating the name of the amalgamated company, the names and address for service of each of the first directors of the company and how and when the subsequent directors are to be elected with such other details as may be necessary to perfect the amalgamation and to provide for the subsequent management and working of the amalgamated company, the authorized capital of the amalgamated company and the manner of converting the authorized capital of each of the companies into that of the amalgamated company.

(3) The agreement shall be submitted to the shareholders of each of the amalgamating companies at general meetings thereof called for the purpose of considering the agreement, and, if two-thirds of the votes cast at each such meeting are in favour of the adoption of the agreement, that fact shall be certified upon the agreement by the secretary of each of the amalgamating companies.

(4) If the agreement is adopted in accordance with subsection (3), the amalgamating companies may jointly apply to the Lieutenant Governor for letters patent confirming the agreement and amalgamating the companies so applying, and on and from the date of the letters patent such companies are amalgamated and are continued as one company by the name in the letters patent provided, and the amalgamated company possesses all the property, rights, privileges and franchises and is subject to all liabilities, contracts, disabilities and debts of each of the amalgamating companies.

Procedures for amalgamation

1. Prepare an amalgamation agreement.

2. Prepare letters patent of amalgamation on Form 11.

3. If neither of the bylaws of the amalgamating corporations are to be adopted as part of the amalgamation process, prepare a general form of bylaw for the amalgamated corporation.

4. Prepare a resolution of the board of directors (by properly called and held meeting or by written resolution) of each amalgamating corporation to approve the amalgamation agreement and the application for letters patent of amalgamation and, if applicable, the bylaws to be adopted by the amalgamated corporation.

5. Prepare a resolution of the members (by properly called and held meeting or by written resolution) of each amalgamating corporation to approve the amalgamation agreement and the application for letters patent of amalgamation and, if applicable, the bylaws to be adopted by the amalgamated corporation.

6. Prepare a solvency certificate of each amalgamating corporation to be made by an officer of each amalgamating corporation.

7. Prepare a certificate of the secretary of each amalgamating corporation, certifying the adoption of the amalgamation agreement.

8. Ensure that all due diligence issues respecting each amalgamating corporation have been conducted, that all corporate records of each amalgamating corporation are up to date, and that all directors, officers, and members have been duly elected, appointed, or admitted, as applicable.

If the due diligence is being conducted by either amalgamating corporation and not by the law firm acting for either amalgamating corporation or the amalgamated corporation, consideration should be given to obtaining a certificate of the secretary of each amalgamating corporation confirming the conduct of all due diligence steps, including governmental filings, and verification of all directors, officers, and members.

9. If the NPO is a registered charity, submit all amalgamation documents to the PGT for approval, together with the applicable filing fees, which, if desired, can include the review fees of the Ontario Companies Branch.

10. If the NPO is a registered charity, forward copies of the issued letters patent of amalgamation to the CRA and the PGT. The submission fee to the CRA should request the transfer of one of the charitable registration numbers of the amalgamating corporations to the amalgamated corporation and the termination of the other charitable registration number.

Continuation into Ontario

Section 312 of the OCA provides as follows:

> 312(1) A corporation incorporated otherwise than by letters patent and being at the time of its application a subsisting corporation may apply for letters patent under this Act, and the Lieutenant Governor may issue letters patent continuing it as if it had been incorporated under this Act.
>
> (2) Where a corporation applies for the issue of letters patent under subsection (1), the Lieutenant Governor may, by the letters patent, limit or extend the powers of the corporation, name its directors and change its corporate name, as the applicant desires.
>
> (3) A corporation incorporated under the laws of any jurisdiction other than Ontario may, if it appears to the Lieutenant Governor to be thereunto authorized by the laws of the jurisdiction in which it was incorporated, apply to the Lieutenant Governor for letters patent continuing it as if it had been incorporated under this Act, and the Lieutenant Governor may issue letters patent on application supported by such material as appears satisfactory and such letters patent may be issued on such terms and subject to such limitations and conditions and contain such provisions as appear to the Lieutenant Governor to be fit and proper.

Continuation out of Ontario

Section 313 of the OCA provides, in part, as follows:

> 313(1) A corporation incorporated under the laws of Ontario ... may, if authorized by a special resolution, by the Minister and by the laws of any other jurisdiction in Canada, apply to the proper officer of that other jurisdiction for an instrument of continuation continuing the corporation as if it had been incorporated under the laws of that other jurisdiction. ...
>
> (2) The corporation shall file with the Minister a notice of the issue of the instrument of continuation and on and after the date of the filing of such instrument this Act ceases to apply to that corporation.

Procedure for continuation into Ontario

1. Prepare an application for continuation on Form 12.1.

2. Prepare a members' resolution consistent with the requirements of the exporting jurisdiction authorizing the continuance and providing for any changes in the corporate structure of the corporation. A certified copy of this resolution should be submitted with the application for continuation.

3. Obtain an Ontario-biased NUANS name search report respecting the name of the NPO to be continued.

4. If the NPO is a registered charity, submit the continuation documents to the PGT with applicable filing fees, which, if desired, can include the review fees of the Ontario Companies Branch.

5. If the NPO is a registered charity, forward copies of the issued certificate and letters patent of continuation to the CRA and the PGT.

Surrender of charter

Section 319 of the OCA provides, in part, as follows:

> 319(1) The charter of a corporation incorporated by letters patent may be surrendered if the corporation proves to the satisfaction of the Lieutenant Governor,
>> (a) that the surrender of its charter has been authorized,
>>> (i) by a majority of the votes cast at a meeting of its shareholders or members duly called for that purpose or by such other vote as the letters patent or supplementary letters patent of the corporation provide, or
>>> (ii) by the consent in writing of all the shareholders or members entitled to vote at such meeting;
>> (b) that it has parted with its property by distributing it rateably among its shareholders or members according to their rights and interests in the corporation;
>> (c) that it has no debts, obligations or liabilities or its debts, obligations or liabilities have been duly provided for or protected or its creditors or other persons having interests in its debts, obligations or liabilities consent;
>> (d) that there are no proceedings pending in any court against it.
> (2) The Lieutenant Governor, upon due compliance with this section, may by order accept the surrender of the charter and declare the corporation to be dissolved on such date as the order may fix.

Note that ss. 319(2), (3), (4), (5), (6), and (7) relate to matters where a corporation surrenders its charter. If a creditor is unknown or his or her whereabouts are unknown, the NPO may, by agreement with the PGT, pay to the PGT an amount equal to the amount of the debt due to the creditor to be held in trust for the creditor. The OCA should be reviewed for these ancillary provisions.

Procedure for surrender of charter

1. Prepare an application for surrender of charter on Form 9.

2. Prepare a certified copy of the extract from the minutes or resolution of the directors and members indicating approval of the application.

3. Obtain a tax clearance certificate from the CRA.

4. If the NPO is a registered charity, apply to the CRA for revocation of the corporation's charitable registration under s. 149.1(1)(f) of the *Income Tax Act*.

5. If the NPO is a registered charity, submit all documents to the PGT, with applicable filing fees, which, if desired, can include the review fees of the Ontario Companies Branch. Note that the PGT will provide a letter confirming compliance with the *Charities Accounting Act* and consenting to the surrender of charter. Also note that the original charter documents must be submitted with this package to the Ontario Companies Branch. If the original charter documents have been lost, submit an affidavit of an officer or director to that effect and an undertaking by the officer or director to return the documents to the minister if they are found.

6. If the NPO is a registered charity, forward copies of the issued order surrendering the charter to the CRA and to PGT. Note that there is a statutory requirement for all books and records of the NPO to be kept for a minimum of six years.

Revival after charter cancelled for failure to file returns

Section 317(10) of the OCA provides as follows:

> 317(10) Where a corporation has been dissolved under subsection (9) [cancellation for default of a filing requirement under the *Corporations Information Act*] or any predecessor thereof, the Lieutenant Governor, on the application of any interested person, may in his or her discretion by order, on such terms and conditions as he or she sees fit to impose, revive the corporation, and thereupon the corporation shall, subject to the terms and conditions of the order and to any rights acquired by any person after its dissolution, be restored to its legal position, including all its property, rights, privileges and franchises, and be subject to all its liabilities, contracts, disabilities and debts, as at the date of its dissolution, in the same manner and to the same extent as if it had not been dissolved.

Procedure for revival of an Ontario NPO

1. Prepare an application for revival on Form 10.

2. Prepare all outstanding filings under the Ontario *Corporations Information Act*.

3. Obtain the consent of the Corporations Tax Branch of the Ministry of Finance;

4. If the NPO is a registered charity, obtain the consent of the CRA and, if required, the PGT.

5. If the NPO is a registered charity, file copies of the letters patent of revival with the CRA and the PGT.

SUPERVISION OF CHARITIES OPERATING IN ONTARIO BY THE PGT

The Charities Accounting Act

The *Charities Accounting Act* requires that any person who is an executor or trustee of a will or trust that has been established for a religious, educational, charitable, or public purpose and any corporation established for such a purpose must file a notice with the PGT and with the beneficiary of the will or trust.

The PGT has general reporting requirements that are provided to a charity upon its incorporation. Currently, those reporting requirements, in appendix F of the *Not-for-Profit Incorporator's Handbook*, are to provide the PGT with the following information on an ongoing basis:

1.
   a. A copy of the document establishing or governing the charity or charitable fund (e.g. corporate charter, trust, will, constitution) and of each document that has made any change thereto.

   b. For the future, a copy of all documents making or recording further changes, as those changes occur.

2. The street and mailing addresses of the charity or charitable fund, and the names and the street and mailing address of its trustees, directors and officers.

   a. for each of its last three financial years (or since its establishment, if established less than three years ago), and

   b. for the future, as this information changes.

3. All legal and popular or common names or acronyms by which the charity or charitable fund:

   a. has been or is known or identified, and

   b. in the future, becomes known or identified.

4. The registration number assigned by [the CRA] for charitable donation tax-credit purposes. If a registration number has not been assigned, or has been or subsequently is revoked, provide an explanation.

The Charitable Gifts Act

The *Charitable Gifts Act* sets out the limits for persons and others carrying on a religious, educational, or charitable purpose on the holding of business interests that may have been bequeathed as a charitable gift. The Act also provides that:

1. if a registered charity owns more than 10 percent of a business, it must sell its interest within seven years, or apply to the court for an extension of the deadlines; and

2. if a registered charity owns more than 50 percent of a business, it must report the profits to the PGT annually for supervision of their distribution.

KEY TERMS

charitable power clauses

club

information kit

members

Not-for-Profit Policy Summary

objects

pecuniary gain

red tape reduction legislation

registered charity

registered charity information return (Form T3010A)

share capital corporation

standing committee

statutory declaration

unanimous written resolution

REFERENCES

Bourgeois, Donald J., *Charitable and Non-Profit Organizations* (Markham, ON: Butterworths Canada, 1990).

Burke-Robertson and Drache, *Non-Share Capital Corporations* (Toronto: Carswell) (looseleaf).

Canada Business Corporations Act, RSC 1985, c. C-44, as amended.

Canada Corporations Act, RSC 1970, c. C-32, as amended.

Canadian Bar Association — Ontario, "Non-Share Capital Corporations: A Guide to Securing Letters Patent," seminar, April 19, 1991.

Charitable Gifts Act, RSO 1990, c. C.8, as amended.

Charities Accounting Act, RSO 1990, c. C.10, as amended.

Corporations Act, RSO 1990, c. C.38, as amended.

Corporations Information Act, RSO 1990, c. C.39, as amended.

Income Tax Act, RSC 1985, c. 1 (5th Supp.), as amended.

Industry Canada, Corporations Canada, "Not-for-Profit Information Kit"; available online at http://strategis.ic.gc.ca.

Industry Canada, Corporations Canada, "Not-for-Profit Policy Summary"; available online at http://strategis.ic.gc.ca.

Law Society of Upper Canada, "Fundamentals of Non-Profit Organizations and Charities," Continuing Legal Education seminar, June 13, 1995.

Miller Thomson LLP, *Charities and Not-for-Profit Newsletter*, various issues.

Ontario, Ministry of Consumer and Business Services, Companies and Personal Property Security Branch, and the Office of the Public Guardian and Trustee, Charitable Property Division, *Not-for-Profit Incorporator's Handbook*; available online at http://www.attorneygeneral.jus.gov.on.ca/english/family/pgt/nfpinc/default.asp.

Partnerships Act, RSO 1990, c. P.5, as amended.

Religious Organizations' Lands Act, RSO 1990, c. R.23, as amended.

Trustee Act, RSO 1990, c. T.23, as amended.

FORMS AND PRECEDENTS

Figure 15.1: Form 2, *Ontario Corporations Act*, application for incorporation of corporation without share capital

Figure 15.2: Form 2, *Ontario Corporations Information Act*, initial return/notice of change by extra-provincial corporation

Figure 15.3: Form 1, *Ontario Corporations Information Act*, initial return/notice of change by Ontario corporation

Figure 15.4: Form 3, *Ontario Corporations Act*, application for supplementary letters patent

Figure 15.5: Form 11, *Ontario Corporations Act*, application for letters patent of amalgamation

Figure 15.6: Form 12.1, *Ontario Corporations Act*, application for continuation

Figure 15.7: Form 9, *Ontario Corporations Act*, application for surrender of charter/termination of corporate existence

Figure 15.8: Form 10, *Ontario Corporations Act*, application for revival of corporation

NOTES

1 Ontario, Ministry of Consumer and Business Services, Companies and Personal Property Security Branch, and the Office of the Public Guardian and Trustee, Charitable Property Division, *Not-for-Profit Incorporator's Handbook*, section 1.4; available online at http://www.attorneygeneral.jus.gov.on.ca/english/family/pgt/nfpinc/default.asp.

2 Donald J. Bourgeois, *The Law of Charitable and Non-Profit Organizations* (Markham, ON: Butterworths Canada, 1990), 18.

3 Incorporated NPOs must file T2 corporate tax returns (which can be marked "Non-Profit Organization"). See Canada Revenue Agency, *Interpretation Bulletin* IT-496R, "Non-Profit Organizations," August 2, 2001.

REVIEW QUESTIONS
True or false

Are the following statements true or false?

1. A not-for-profit partnership is subject to the provisions of the *Partnerships Act* (Ontario).

2. A service club that is an unincorporated organization can hold real estate in its name.

3. An NPO that is a registered charity is required to donate all its resources to its charitable activities.

4. A charitable organization is one that receives and uses its funds to fund the activities of other charities.

5. When forwarding an application for registration as a charity to the CRA, an NPO is required to provide copies of its bylaws.

6. An Ontario NPO is required to submit its bylaws for approval with its application for incorporation.

7. Ontario NPOs are entitled to conduct their proceedings by written resolution.

8. A statutory declaration, signed by one of the applicants, must be submitted with an application for incorporation of an Ontario NPO.

9. A federal NPO must have a majority of resident Canadians as directors.

10. A federal NPO is required to obtain an extra-provincial licence if it carries on its operations in Ontario.

11. An annual summary for a federal NPO must be filed within six months of the NPO's financial year-end.

12. A federal NPO is required to submit any amendments to its bylaws to the minister of industry for approval.

13. An application for surrender of charter by an Ontario NPO with charitable status must be submitted to the PGT for approval.

14. A federal NPO may amalgamate with another federal NPO.

15. A trade association is required to comply with the reporting requirements of the PGT.

Questions

1. Name three different legal structures and provide a brief description of each.

2. Name three similarities and three differences between an NPO and a share capital corporation.

3. Name three differences between a non-charitable NPO and a registered charity.

4. Describe the difference between a public foundation and a private foundation.

5. Define "qualified donee" under the *Income Tax Act*.

6. Describe the procedure for incorporating a federal NPO.

7. Describe the procedure for organizing an Ontario NPO.

8. Set out the minimum requirements for holding an annual meeting of an Ontario NPO.

9. Describe the procedure for a federal NPO to change the number of its directors from a fixed number.

10. Describe the procedure for an Ontario NPO to make an application for supplementary letters patent to change its name.

11. Describe the procedure for a federal NPO to amalgamate with another federal NPO.

12. Describe the procedure for a special act company to continue under part II of the *Canada Corporations Act*.

13. Set out the requirements for passing amendments to an Ontario NPO's bylaw.

14. Describe the procedure to revive an Ontario NPO.

15. List the general reporting requirements of the PGT.

APPENDIX EXTRA-PROVINCIAL REGISTRATION OF NPOs

Province and timing for registration	Definition of carrying on business	Consequences of not registering
British Columbia *Society Act*, RSBC 1996, c. 43 Part 8 – Extraprovincial Societies • registration not mandatory	Note: The British Columbia Corporate Registry advises that NPOs are not required to register extra-provincially. They may be required to register if they own a vehicle or property; otherwise, they can function without registration. "Extra-provincial society" means a society or association, incorporated or otherwise, formed outside British Columbia, and includes a branch of that society or association, but does not include a society or association, incorporated or otherwise, formed to acquire profit or gain or that has capital divided into shares. s. 76(6) Unless the Registrar otherwise orders, the limitations, prohibitions and conditions applicable to incorporation of societies under s. 2 apply to the registration of an extraprovincial society. s. 2(1) A society **may** be incorporated under this Act for any lawful purpose or purposes such as national, patriotic, religious, philanthropic, charitable, provident, scientific, fraternal, benevolent, artistic, educational, social, professional, agricultural, sporting or other useful purposes, but not for any of the following: (a) the operation of a boarding home, orphanage or other institution for minors, or the supplying of any other form of care for minors without the written consent of the director designated under the *Child, Family and Community Service Act* for the purposes of this section; (b) the ownership, management or operation of a hospital without the written consent of the Minister of Health; (c) the ownership, management or operation of a social club without the written consent of the Minister; (d) the purpose of paying benefits or rendering services as described in s. 14 without the written consent of the Superintendent of Financial Institutions; (e) any purpose without the consent of an existing society should the Registrar require it; (f) the purpose of carrying on a business, trade, industry or profession for profit or gain. (2) Carrying on a business, trade, industry or profession as an incident to the purposes of a society is not prohibited by this section, but a society must not distribute any gain, profit or dividend or otherwise dispose of its assets to a member of the society without receiving full and valuable consideration except during winding up or on dissolution and then only as permitted by this Act. s. 75(1) states "an extraprovincial society **may** apply for registration under this Act." s. 75(2) The registrar may require an extraprovincial society that carries on operations in British Columbia, other than an extraprovincial society that is authorized to carry on insurance business under the *Financial Institutions Act*, to apply for registration under this Act, and that society must, unless registration is granted, cease to operate in British Columbia, and the registrar must set the date after which it must cease to operate. s. 75(3) An extraprovincial society whose purposes include carrying on a social club must not be registered without the written consent of the minister, and every branch of that society must, if the registrar so requires, apply for separate registration and consent. Registrar tel. no.: 250-356-8673	s. 81 An extraprovincial society that is not registered as required by this Act is not capable of (a) maintaining a proceeding in a court in British Columbia in respect of a contract made in whole or in part in British Columbia in the course of or in connection with its operation, or (b) acquiring or holding land or an interest in land in British Columbia or registering title to land under the *Land Title Act*. *Penalty* There is no penalty for non-registration.

Province and timing for registration	Definition of carrying on business	Consequences of not registering
Alberta *Business Corporations Act*, RSA 2000, c. B-9 Part 21 • register within 30 days	Note: Although the Registry would not confirm, it was indicated that soliciting business or charitable funds by mail may be covered under s. 277(1)(d) below. s. 277(1) For the purposes of this Part, an extra-provincial corporation carries on business in Alberta if: (a) its name, or any name under which it carries on business, is listed in a telephone directory for any part of Alberta, (b) its name, or any name under which it carries on business, appears or is announced in any advertisement in which an address in Alberta is given for the extra-provincial corporation, (c) it has a resident agent or representative or a warehouse, office or place of business in Alberta, (d) it solicits business in Alberta, (e) it is the owner of any estate or interest in land in Alberta, (f) it is licensed or registered or required to be licensed or registered under any Act of Alberta entitling it to do business, (g) it is, in respect of a public vehicle as defined in the *Motor Transport Act*, the holder of a certificate of registration under the *Motor Vehicle Administration Act*, unless it neither picks up nor delivers goods or passengers in Alberta, (h) it is the holder of a certificate issued by the Alberta Motor Transport Board, unless it neither picks up nor delivers goods or passengers in Alberta, or (i) it otherwise carries on business in Alberta. (2) The Registrar may exempt an extra-provincial corporation from the payment of fees under this Part if the Registrar is satisfied that it does not carry on business for the purpose of gain. Alberta Corporate Registry tel. no.: 780-427-2311	s. 294 No act of an extra-provincial corporation, including any transfer of property to or by an extra-provincial corporation, is invalid by reason only (a) that the act or transfer is contrary to or not authorized by its charter or internal regulations or any law of the jurisdiction in which it is incorporated, or (b) that the extra-provincial corporation was not then registered. s. 295(1) An extra-provincial corporation while unregistered is not capable of commencing or maintaining any action or other proceeding in any court in Alberta in respect of any contract made in the course of carrying on business in Alberta while it was unregistered. s. 295(2) If an extra-provincial corporation was not registered at the time it commenced an action or proceeding referred to in subsection (1) but becomes registered afterward, the action or proceeding may be maintained as if it had been registered before the commencement of the action or proceeding. *Penalty* s. 296 A person who contravenes this Part is guilty of an offence and liable to a fine of not more than $5000.

Province and timing for registration	Definition of carrying on business	Consequences of not registering
Saskatchewan *The Non-Profit Corporations Act*, SS 1995, c. N-4.2, as amended Part III • time required to register not specified in the Act	Note: Corporations Branch confirmed that soliciting charitable funds by mail would be considered carrying on business pursuant to s. 2(1)(a). s. 252 An extra-provincial corporation may apply for registration pursuant to this Part. s. 2(1) Activities respecting a charitable corporation or a membership corporation, includes: (a) any conduct of the corporation to further its charitable or membership purposes; and (b) any business carried on by the corporation. Carrying on business or activities is not more particularly defined; however, s. 253 provides that the Director may refuse registration of an extra-provincial corporation where: (a) pursuant to the laws of the jurisdiction where it is incorporated, the extra-provincial corporation may pay dividends to its members; (b) the activities of the corporation are not of a benevolent, religious, charitable, philanthropic, education, agricultural, scientific, artistic, social, professional, fraternal, sporting, athletic or similar purpose; or (c) the name of the corporation is for any reason objectionable. Corporations Branch tel. no.: 306-787-2962	s. 276(1) A corporation that is not registered under this Act is not capable of commencing or maintaining any action or other proceeding in a court respecting a contract made in whole or in part in Saskatchewan in the course of, or in connection with, its activities. s. 276(3) No provision of this section applies to a Canada corporation or to a corporation registered pursuant to *The Business Corporations Act*. s. 277 Where a corporation was not registered but becomes registered pursuant to this Act, any action or proceeding mentioned in subsection 276(1) may be maintained as if the extra-provincial corporation had been registered before the institution of the action or proceeding. *Penalty* s. 281 Any person who, without reasonable cause, contravenes a provision of this Act or the regulations for which no punishment is provided is guilty of an offence and liable on summary conviction to a fine of not more than $500.

Province and timing for registration	Definition of carrying on business	Consequences of not registering
Manitoba *The Corporations Act,* RSM 1987, c. C225, as amended • register prior to commencing business • federal corporations must register within 30 days of commencing business (s. 187(3))	NPOs are governed by the same rules and regulations as share capital corporations. Note: The Manitoba Corporate Registry indicated that soliciting charitable funds by mail is considered carrying on business pursuant to s. 2.187(2)(e). s. 187(1) This part, except where it is expressly provided, applies to every body corporate carrying on its business or undertaking in Manitoba, other than a body corporate licensed under the *Insurance Act* as an insurer or a body corporate created solely for religious purposes. s. 187(2) A body corporate is deemed to be carrying on business in Manitoba if: (a) it has a resident agent or representative, or a warehouse, office or place of business in Manitoba; (b) its name or any name under which it carries on business, together with an address for the body corporate in Manitoba, is listed in a Manitoba telephone directory; (c) its name or any name under which it carries on business, together with an address for the body corporate in Manitoba, is included in any advertisement advertising the business or any product of the body corporate; (d) it is the registered owner of real property situate in Manitoba; or (e) it otherwise carries on its business or undertaking in Manitoba. Corporations Branch tel. no.: 204-945-2500	s. 197(1) An extra-provincial body corporate is not capable of commencing or maintaining any action or other proceeding in a court in respect of a contract made in whole or in part in the province, in the course of, or in connection with, the business or undertaking carried on by it, without being registered under the provisions of this Part. s. 197(3) The registration of a body corporate is deemed to authorize all previous acts of the body corporate and is construed as if the certificate of registration or supplementary certificate of registration had been granted before the body corporate commenced to carry on its business or undertaking in the Province, except for the purpose of a prosecution for an offence under this Part. *Penalty* s. 187(5) Every body corporate that carries on its business or undertaking in the province without being registered, and every director and officer of the body corporate, and every representative or agent acting in any capacity for the body corporate so carrying on its business or undertaking is respectively guilty of an offence and is liable to a penalty of $50 for every day the business or undertaking is so carried on.
Ontario *Corporations Act,* RSO 1990, c. 38, as amended	The Companies Branch of the Ministry of Consumer and Business Services confirmed there is no mechanism in the *Corporations Act* providing for the extra-provincial registration of NPOs; therefore, there is no penalty for non-registration. A form 2 initial notice must be filed under the *Corporations Information Act,* RSO 1990, c. C.39, as amended, within 60 days after the date the corporation begins to carry on business in Ontario (s. 3); an Ontario corporation number will be assigned, but this is not a licence. In order to bring or maintain an action, it would be advisable to register a new NPO under the *Corporations Act,* but a lawyer should be consulted with respect to this issue.	

APPENDIX CONTINUED

Province and timing for registration	Definition of carrying on business	Consequences of not registering
Quebec *An Act Respecting the Legal Publicity of Sole Proprietorships, Partnerships and Legal Persons*, RSQ. c. P-45, as amended • register no later than 60 days after the date on which it commences business (s. 9)	NPOs are governed by the same rules and regulations as share capital corporations. Note: The code "APE" in s. 2 of the form "Legal Person" for registration of the corporation is marked to identify the corporation as a non-share corporation. Soliciting charitable donations by mail is considered to be carrying on business in the province of Quebec. The corporation would also be required to have an agent in the province of Quebec. s. 2(3) every natural person operating a sole proprietorship in Quebec, whether or not it is a commercial enterprise under a name which does not include the person's surname; s. 2(5) every legal person established for a private interest not constituted in Quebec, but domiciled in Quebec, which carries on an activity in Quebec, including the operation of an enterprise, or possesses an immovable real right, other than a prior claim or hypothec, in Quebec. Quebec Registry tel. no.: 418-643-3625	s. 100 Where a person or partnership subject to the requirement of registration has not registered, the examination of an application presented by that person or partnership before a court or a body exercising judicial or quasi judicial functions may be suspended until registration is effected, where so requested by an interested person before the hearing. ss.101, 102, 103, 104, 105 and 106 provide that an offence is any of failing to register within prescribed time, failure to file annual declaration, or an amending declaration. *Penalty* s. 107 Every person guilty of an offence is liable to a fine of not less than $200 and not more than $2,000. For a second or subsequent offence, the fines are doubled.

Province and timing for registration	Definition of carrying on business	Consequences of not registering
New Brunswick *Business Corporations Act*, SNB 1981, c. B-9.1, as amended Part XVII • register within 30 days of commencing business (s. 196)	Note: The Corporations Branch indicated that soliciting charitable donations by mail would likely be considered carrying on business; but that is a matter of legal interpretation. It advises that the corporation should apply for exemption pursuant to s. 194(3). NPOs are governed by the same rules and regulations as share capital corporations; however, s. 194(3) provides that the Director may exempt an extra-provincial corporation from the operation of this part except s. 194(4) if he is satisfied that it does not carry on business for the purpose of gain. Note: Corporate Affairs confirms that an NPO is required to apply for the exemption by submitting a letter stating that the corporation does not carry on business for gain, provide a photocopy of all charter documents from home jurisdiction, forms 25 and 25.1, and $100. Annual returns must be filed; because there are no prescribed forms, a copy of the annual return from the home jurisdiction is acceptable. s. 194(1) For the purposes of this Part, an extra-provincial corporation carries on business in New Brunswick if (a) its name, or any name under which it carries on business, appears or is announced in any advertisement in which an address in New Brunswick is given for the extra-provincial corporation; (b) it has a resident agent or representative or a warehouse, office or place of business in New Brunswick; (c) it solicits business in New Brunswick; (d) it is the owner of any estate or interest in land in New Brunswick; (e) it is licensed or registered or required to be licensed or registered under any Act of New Brunswick entitling it to do business; (f) it is the holder of a certificate of registration under the *Motor Vehicle Act*; (g) it is the holder of a licence issued under the *Motor Carrier Act*; or (h) it otherwise carries on business in New Brunswick. s. 194(2) Where an extra-provincial corporation has its name or any name under which it carries on business listed in a telephone directory for any part of New Brunswick, that corporation shall be deemed, in the absence of evidence to the contrary, to be carrying on business in New Brunswick. s. 194(2.1) An extra-provincial corporation is not carrying on business in New Brunswick by reason only that it is a general or limited partner in a limited partnership or an extra-provincial limited partnership that has filed a declaration under the *Limited Partnership Act*. Pursuant to s. 195(1), s. 11.1 of the General Regulation under the *Business Corporations Act*, NB Reg 81-147, as amended, provides that an extra-provincial corporation incorporated under the laws of the province of Nova Scotia is exempted from part XVII of the Act. New Brunswick Corporate Affairs tel. no.: 506-453-2703	s. 211 No act of an extra-provincial corporation, including any transfer of property to or by an extra-provincial corporation, is invalid by reason only (a) that the act or transfer is contrary to or not authorized by its charter or internal regulations or any law of the jurisdiction in which it is incorporated, or (b) that the extra-provincial corporation was not then registered. s. 213(1) An extra-provincial corporation, while unregistered, is not capable of commencing or maintaining any action or other proceeding in any court in New Brunswick in respect of any contract made in the course of carrying on business in New Brunswick while it was unregistered or otherwise in violation of this Part. s. 213(2) If an extra-provincial corporation is not registered at the time it commences an action or proceeding referred to in subsection (1) but becomes registered afterward, the action or proceeding may be maintained as if it was registered before the commencement of the action or proceeding. s. 213(3) This section does not apply to an extra-provincial corporation incorporated under the laws of Canada. *Penalty* s. 214(1) An extra-provincial corporation who fails to comply with this Part commits an offence and is liable on a summary conviction to a fine of not more than five thousand dollars and in default of payment is liable to levy by distress and sale in accordance with section 35 of the *Summary Convictions Act*. s. 214(2) Whether or not the extra-provincial corporation has been prosecuted or convicted, any director or officer of the extra-provincial corporation who knowingly authorizes, permits or acquiesces in such failure commits an offence and is liable on a summary conviction to a fine not exceeding five thousand dollars or to imprisonment for a term not exceeding six months or to both and in default of payment of a fine is liable to imprisonment in accordance with subsection 31(3) of the *Summary Convictions Act*.

Province and timing for registration	Definition of carrying on business	Consequences of not registering
Nova Scotia	There is no requirement to extra-provincially register an NPO in Nova Scotia. The Registry's office advises that if the NPO was required to bring or maintain an action in Nova Scotia, they would have to register under the *Corporations Registration Act*. Registry of Joint Stock Companies tel. no.: 902-424-7770	
Prince Edward Island *Licensing Act*, RSPEI 1988, c. L-11, as amended • register within 30 days (s. 6(2))	NPOs are governed by the same rules and regulations as share capital corporations. Note: Soliciting charitable donations by mail is considered to be carrying on business. s. 1(e) "doing business," or the expression "carrying on business," means the transaction of any of the ordinary business of a corporation or person, including franchises, whether or not by means of an employee or an agent and whether or not the corporation or person has a resident agent or representative or a warehouse, office or place of business in the province. s. 3(1) The following corporations and persons are required to be licensed under this Act: (a) all railway express companies doing business within this province; (b) all banks, finance companies, loan companies or trust companies doing business within this province; (c) every telegraph or other corporation working a telegraph, telex or other similar method of communication for the use of the public within this province; (d) every corporation or person operating a chain store and every corporation or person operating a branch chain wholesale store, and each branch of such corporation doing business in this province over and above the number of one; (e) each corporation or person operating a branch chain theatre and each branch of such corporation doing business in this province over and above the number one; (f) every electric light company and electric power company doing business in this province and each branch of such corporation, doing business in this province over and above the number of one; (g) the Island Telephone Company Limited; (h) all oil and gas companies carrying on the business in this province of wholesale gasoline; (i) all corporations or persons not ordinarily resident in the province carrying on any construction trade in the province and employing therein one or more persons but the Lieutenant Governor in Council may reduce the license fee payable by any such corporation or person if it would appear to impose an undue hardship in proportion to the small amount of business transacted by the Company; (j) all other persons not hereinbefore specified who are not ordinarily resident in the province and whose chief place of business is located outside of the province, and who carry on business in the province; (k) all franchisees carrying on business in the province, and each branch of each franchise operated by the franchisee; (l) all other companies and corporations not hereinbefore specified which, not being incorporated under the laws of this province, and having their head office or chief place of business located outside of this province, carry on business in Prince Edward Island. Registry tel. no.: 902-368-4550	s. 6(2) Any corporation or person who is required by this Act to obtain a licence and who neglects, omits or fails to do so for a period of one month, or whose licence stands revoked for a period of one month, in addition to liability for payment of the licence fee, is liable to a penalty not exceeding $100 and costs, recoverable on summary conviction or by suite in a court of competent jurisdiction; a similar penalty is recoverable for each successive month during which the omission or revocation is continued. s. 7 Unless and until a corporation holds a licence that is in force, it shall not be capable of bringing or maintaining any action, suit or other proceeding in any court in Prince Edward Island in respect to any contract made in whole or in part in Prince Edward Island in connection with any part of its business done or carried on in Prince Edward Island while it did not hold a licence that was in force; but this section does not apply to any company incorporated by or under the authority of an Act of the Parliament of Canada, or by or under the authority of an Act of the Legislature of Prince Edward Island.

Province and timing for registration	Definition of carrying on business	Consequences of not registering
Newfoundland *Corporations Act*, RSN 1990, c. C-36, as amended • register prior to commencing business (s. 433)	NPOs are governed by the same rules and regulations as share capital corporations. Note: The Registrar's Office states that soliciting charitable donations by mail is considered carrying on business. s. 431(2) For the purposes of this Part, an extra-provincial company is carrying on an undertaking in the province where (a) it holds title to land in the province or has an interest otherwise than by way of security in land; (b) it maintains an office, warehouse or place of business in the province; (c) it is licensed or registered or required to be licensed or registered under a law of the province that entitles it to do business or to sell securities of its own issue; (d) it is the holder of a certificate of registration issued under the *Highway Traffic Act* respecting a public service vehicle; or (e) in another manner it carries on an undertaking in the province. s. 431(3) For the purposes of subsection (2), where an extra-provincial company is listed with a number under the name of the extra-provincial company in a telephone directory published by a telephone company for use in this province, that extra-provincial company is presumed, in the absence of proof to the contrary, to be carrying on an undertaking in this province. Registry tel. no.: 709-729-3316	s. 452(1) An extra-provincial company, other than a federal company, that is not registered under this Act may not maintain an action, suit or other proceeding in a court in the province in respect of a contract made in whole or in part within the province in the course of or in connection with the carrying on of an undertaking by the company in the province. (2) Notwithstanding subsection (1), where an extra-provincial company, other than a federal company, described in that subsection becomes registered under this Act or has its registration restored, the company may then maintain an action, suit or other proceeding in respect of the contract described in subsection (1) as though it had never been disabled under that subsection whether or not the contract was made or proceeding instituted by the company before the date the company was registered or had its registration restored.
Yukon	There is no requirement for an NPO to extra-territorially register in the Yukon. However, if applying for a grant from the Yukon government, you will be required to register as a new NPO under the *Societies Act*. The *Societies Act* does not provide for extra-territorial registration. An NPO can extra-provincially register under the *Business Corporations Act* and be subject to the provisions contained; however, it would not be classified as a society. Justice Services Division Corporate Affairs tel. no.: 867-667-5811	

Province and timing for registration	Definition of carrying on business	Consequences of not registering
Northwest Territories *Business Corporations Act*, SNWT 1996, c. 19 • register within 30 days (s. 281(1))	NPOs are governed by the same rules and regulations as share capital corporations. The Corporate Registry confirmed that soliciting charitable donations by mail is considered to be carrying on business. s. 279 An extra-territorial corporation carries on business in the Northwest Territories if: (a) its name, or any name under which it carries on business or operations, is listed in a telephone directory for any part of the Northwest Territories; (b) its name, or any name under which it carries on business or operations, appears or is announced in any advertisement in which an address in the Northwest Territories is given for the extra-territorial corporation; (c) it has a resident agent or representative or a warehouse, office or place of business or operations in the Northwest Territories; (d) it solicits business in the Northwest Territories; (e) it is the owner of any estate or interest in land in the Northwest Territories; (f) it is licensed or registered or required to be licensed or registered under any Act of the Northwest Territories entitling it to do business or carry on operations; (g) it otherwise carries on business or operations in the Northwest Territories. Companies Registry tel. no.: 877-743-3303	s. 298(1) While it is unregistered, an extra-territorial corporation is not capable of commencing or maintaining any action or other proceeding in any court in the Northwest Territories in respect of any contract made in the course of carrying on business in the Northwest Territories while it was unregistered. s. 298(2) If an extra-territorial corporation was not registered at the time it commenced an action or proceeding referred to in subsection (1) but subsequently becomes registered, the action or proceeding may be maintained as if the extra-territorial corporation had been registered before the commencement of the action or proceeding. *Penalty* s. 299 A person who contravenes any provision of this Part is guilty of an offence and liable on summary conviction to a fine not exceeding $10,000.
Nunavut *Business Corporations Act*, SNWT 1998, c. 34 • register within 30 days (s. 281)	NPOs are subject to the requirements of the *Business Corporations Act* with a reduced registration fee of $100. The Legal Registries Office confirmed that soliciting donations by mail is considered carrying on business. Note: The *Societies Act* applies only to corporations incorporated in Nunavut. s. 279 Its name, or any name under which it carries on business or any operations, is listed in a telephone directory for any part of Nunavut; (a) its name, or any name under which it carries on business or operations, appears or is announced in any advertisement in which an address in Nunavut is given for the extra-territorial corporation; (b) it has a resident agent or representative or a warehouse, office or place of business or operations in Nunavut; (c) it solicits business in Nunavut; (d) it is the owner of any estate or interest in land in Nunavut; (e) it is licensed or registered or required to be licensed or registered under any Act of Nunavut entitling it to do business or carry on operations; (f) It otherwise carries on business or operations in Nunavut. Nunavut Regional Office tel. no.: 867-975-6190	s. 298(1) While it is unregistered, an extra-territorial corporation is not capable of commencing or maintaining any action or other proceeding in any court in Nunavut in respect of any contract made in the course of carrying on business in Nunavut while it was unregistered. s. 298(2) If an extra-territorial corporation was not registered at the time it commenced an action or proceeding referred to in subsection (1) but subsequently becomes registered, the action or proceeding may be maintained as if the extra-territorial corporation had been registered before the commencement of the action or proceeding. *Penalty* s. 299 A person who contravenes any provision of this Part is guilty of an offence and liable on summary conviction to a fine not exceeding $10,000.

 Ontario

Ministry of
Consumer and
Business Services

Companies and Personal   393 University Ave Suite 200
Property Security Branch   Toronto ON M5G 2M2

**Application for Incorporation of a
Corporation without Share Capital
Form 2**
Corporations Act

INSTRUCTIONS FOR COMPLETING APPLICATION FORM

FEE

$155.00   BY MAIL - Cheque or money order payable to the Minister of Finance.
IN PERSON - If you are delivering the application in person, you can
also pay by cash, Visa, MasterCard, American Express or debit card.
The address for personal delivery is 375 University Ave., 2nd floor, Toronto.
Please note these documents are **not** checked while you wait, they
take several weeks to process.

**There will be a service charge payable for any cheque returned
as non-negotiable by a bank or financial institution.**

DOCUMENTS REQUIRED

1. Application for Incorporation of a Corporation without Share Capital, Form 2, as prescribed by the Ontario Regulations under the *Corporations Act*, completed in duplicate and bearing original signatures on both copies.

2. An original, Ontario-biased NUANS name search report for the proposed name of the corporation. The search report must be submitted with the application within 90 days of the production of the report.

3. A covering letter, setting out the name, address and telephone number of the person or firm to whom the Letters Patent, or any correspondence, should be mailed.

4. If the proposed name of the corporation is similar to the name of an existing corporation, organization, registered business or includes the name of a person, Companies and Personal Property Security Branch may require consent to the use of the proposed name from the corporation, organization, business or individual.

APPEARANCE OF DOCUMENTS

The Application for Incorporation, and any supporting documents must be typewritten, or if completed by hand, printed in CAPITAL letters in black ink. All documents must be legible and suitable for microfilming.

Forms, extra pages and any supporting documents, must be printed on one side of good quality white bond paper 8 ½" by 11". Facsimile (Fax) applications, or supporting documents, cannot be accepted in lieu of original copies.

Pages are numbered 1 through 4; applications with missing pages cannot be accepted. If additional pages are required due to lack of space, they *should be numbered the same as the original page with the addition of letters of the alphabet to indicate sequence. For example, supplementary pages for the objects Item 4 on page 2, would be numbered 2A, 2B, etc. Do not attach schedules to the form. The last page should be the signing page.*

CORPORATE NAME

Prior to completing the form, the applicants should determine if the proposed corporate name is available for use. To do this they must obtain, from a name search company, an Ontario-biased NUANS name search report for the name under which the corporation is to be incorporated.

Name search companies are listed in the Yellow Pages of the telephone directory under "Searchers of Records". The original, five-page name search report should be submitted with the application. The name set out in the application must be exactly the same as the name set out in the name search report. Reports received more than 90 days from the date they were produced will not be accepted and a new report will be required.

07109 (03/2003)

FIGURE 15.1 CONTINUED

The Ministry will determine whether a proposed corporation name is acceptable. A name that is identical to another corporation or that contravenes the *Corporations Act or Regulations* will not be approved. If the proposed name is similar to that of an existing corporation, organization, business, or the name contains the nam of an individual, the consent of the existing corporation, organization, business or the individual may be required. The name must reflect the objects of the corporation and should not be too general in character. It should contain a distinctive element and a descriptive element, for example:

HAPPY TIME *DAYCARE CENTRE*
(Distinctive) (*Descriptive*)

The name may include the word "Incorporated", "Incorporée" or "Corporation" or the corresponding abbreviations, but it is not required. A corporation without share capital cannot have "Limited", "Limitée" or the corresponding abbreviations as part of the name.

APPLICATION

Item 1 Set out the name of the corporation in block capital letters starting on the first line in the first box on the left with one letter per box and one empty box for a space. Punctuation marks are entered in separate boxes. Complete one line before starting in the first box of the next line. The name entered must be exactly the same as that on the name search report.

H	A	P	P	Y	T	I	M	E		R	E	C	R	E	A	T	I	O	N		A	N	D		D	A	Y	C	A
R	E		C	E	N	T	R	E		I	N	C	.																

Item 2 Set out the full address of the head office of the corporation, including the postal code. (If the address is a multi-office building, include the room or suite number). A post office box or *general delivery* is not acceptable for the address. The head office must be in Ontario.

Item 3 Set out the full name and address for service of all persons who are to be first directors of the corporation. The address should be in full, including postal code and room or suite number if applicable. A post office box or general delivery is not acceptable. *There must be at least three directors.* All of the directors must also be applicants under Item 6.

Item 4 Set out the objects of the corporation. The objects should be a concise statement of the ultimate purpose of the corporation. First describe the principal object, or primary undertaking of the corporation. Then set out the secondary objects, if any. It is advisable to keep the objects short but broad in nature. They should however, be sufficiently specific so as to avoid misinterpretation. You will find examples of these clauses in the Not-For-Profit Incorporator's Handbook (see the end of these instructions for information on obtaining this Handbook). Note that the objects of a corporation without share capital cannot contain a clause contrary to Section 126 of the *Corporations Act*, which states that a corporation shall be carried on without the purpose of gain for its members.

Item 5 In this item, you may include special provisions or ancillary powers of the corporation. For a non-profit **non-charitable** corporation the only special provision that **must be** set out is the "No Gain for Members" clause which is pre-printed on the form. However, you may include other provisions such as providing that on dissolution of the corporation and after payment of all debts and liabilities, any remaining property shall be distributed or disposed of to charities. For more information refer to the Not-for-Profit Incorporator's Handbook.

Ancillary powers are also listed under this item. There is usually no need to set out ancillary powers as all corporations without share capital automatically acquire ancillary or supplementary powers (Section 23(1)(a) to (p) and (s) to (v) of the *Corporations Act*) unless withheld in the Letters Patent or Supplementary Letters Patent.

Charities must include certain special provisions. For a list of the standard objects, special provisions and powers for **charities** contact Companies and Personal Property Security Branch or the Office of the Public Guardian & Trustee website listed at the end of these instructions.

FIGURE 15.1 CONTINUED

Item 6 Set out the full name, and the address for service of each of the applicants. All of the directors listed in Item 3 must be included as applicants.

EXECUTION

Both copies of the form must be signed by each of the applicants. The signatures must be original signatures. Photocopies will not be accepted.

CHARITABLE CORPORATIONS

To incorporate a charity you can use either pre-approved (standard) objects and special provisions or if none of the pre-approved objects accurately describe the objects of the organization you can draft your own objects (non-standard):

Pre-approved objects (standard)
The standard objects and special provisions are clauses that have been approved by the Office of the Public Guardian and Trustee. Applications for Incorporation using the pre-approved objects and special provisions should be sent directly to the Ministry of Consumer and Business Services (the address is listed at the end of this form). As the Office of the Public Guardian and Trustee do not review these corporations, the only fee payable will be the incorporation fee. See the end of these instructions for information on obtaining a list of the pre-approved objects and special provisions. You cannot add extra objects or change the wording of the standard objects.

Objects that have not been pre-approved (non-standard)
If the corporation uses non-standard objects or special provisions they must be reviewed and approved by the Office of the Public Guardian & Trustee. There is a fee for this review, which must be paid, as well as the incorporation fee. The application, supporting documents and both fees should be sent to the Office of the Public Guardian and Trustee for review (the address is listed at the end of this form). The approval for a charity is not a guarantee that the Letters Patent will be issued. After the objects have been reviewed and approved by the Office of the Public Guardian and Trustee they will forward the application directly to the Companies and Personal Property Security Branch. If the application and supporting documents are complete and comply with the *Corporations Act* the Letters Patent will be issued.

Not-for-Profit incorporation forms and the bulletin listing the pre-approved charitable objects are available from the Ministry of Consumer and Business Services. The completed forms for not-for-profit corporations and charitable not-for-profit corporations that are using the standard objects should be sent, together with the name search, any supporting documents and incorporation fee, to:

Ministry of Consumer and Business Services
Companies and Personal Property Security Branch
393 University Ave., Suite 200
Toronto ON M5G 2M2
Tel: (416) 314-8880 or in Ontario toll free 1-800-361-3223

Applications for charitable corporations that are not using the pre-approved objects should be filed together with the name search, any supporting documents, the incorporation fee and the fee for review, with the Office of the Public Guardian and Trustee:

Office of the Public Guardian & Trustee
Charitable Property Program
595 Bay Street, Suite 800
Toronto ON M5G 2M6
Tel: (416) 326-1963 or in Ontario toll free 1-800-366-0335
Website: http://www.attorneygeneral.jus.gov.on.ca/english/family/pgt/

NOT-FOR-PROFIT INCORPORATOR'S HANDBOOK

The Not-For-Profit Incorporator's Handbook contains general information as well as precedent clauses for objects and special provisions for both non-profit **non-charitable** corporations, and the pre-approved objects and provisions for non-profit **charitable** corporations. The Handbook may be purchased in person at Companies and Personal Property Security Branch or at the government bookstore.

Bookstore (Walk in Service)
Main Floor, 880 Bay St
Toronto ON M7A 1N8

Publications Ontario (Mail Order)
50 Grosvenor St.,
Toronto ON M7A 1N8

The Handbook is also available on the Office of the Public Guardian & Trustee website (see above).
To order publications, mail-order inquiries - general inquiry (416) 326-5300 or in Ontario toll free at 1-800-668-9938
Website: www.publications.gov.on.ca

07109 (03/2003)

FIGURE 15.1   CONTINUED

This space is for
Ministry Use Only
Espace réservé à
l'usage exclusif
du ministère

Ontario Corporation Number
Numéro de la société en Ontario

1.

Form 2
**Corporations
Act**

Formule 2
**Loi sur les
personnes
morales**

APPLICATION FOR INCORPORATION OF A CORPORATION WITHOUT SHARE CAPITAL
REQUÊTE EN CONSTITUTION D'UNE PERSONNE MORALE SANS CAPITAL-ACTIONS

1.   The name of the corporation is: (Set out in BLOCK CAPITAL LETTERS)
     Dénomination sociale de la société : (Écrire en LETTRES MAJUSCULES SEULEMENT)

2.   The address of the head office of the corporation is:
     Adresse du siège social:

     (Street & Number or R.R. Number & if Multi-Office Building give Room No.)
     (Rue et numéro ou numéro de la R.R. et, s'il s'agit d'un édifice à bureaux, numéro du bureau)

     Ontario

     (Name of Municipality or Post Office)   (Postal Code)
     (Nom de la municipalité ou du bureau de poste)   *(Code postal)*

3.   The applicants who are to be the first directors of the corporation are:
     Requérants appelés à devenir les premiers administrateurs de la personne morale :

First name, middle names and surname *Prénom, autres Prénoms et nom de famille*	Address for service, giving Street & No. or R.R. No., Municipality, Province, Country and Postal Code *Domicile élu, y compris la rue et le numéro, le numéro de la R.R. ou le nom de la municipalité, la province, le pays et le code postal*

07109 (03/2003)

FIGURE 15.1   CONTINUED

2.

4.   The objects for which the corporation is incorporated are:
     Objets pour lesquels la personne morale est constituée:

07109 (03/2003)

FIGURE 15.1 CONTINUED

3.

5. The special provisions are:
   Dispositions particulières:

   The corporation shall be carried on without the purpose of gain for its members, and any profits or other accretions to the corporation shall be used in promoting its objects.

   La personne morale doit exercer ses activités sans rechercher de gain pécuniaire pour ses membres, et tout bénéfice ou tout accroissement de l'actif de la personne morale doit être utilisé pour promouvoir ses objets.

07109 (03/2003)

FIGURE 15.1   CONCLUDED

6. The names and address for service of the applicants: 4.
    Nom et prénoms et domicile élu des requérants :

First name, middle names and surname *Prénom, autres Prénoms et nom de famille*	Address for service, giving Street & No. or R.R. No., Municipality, Province, Country and Postal Code *Domicile élu, y compris la rue et le numéro, le numéro de la R.R. ou le nom de la municipalité, la province, le pays et le code postal*

This application is executed in duplicate.
La présente requête est faite en double exemplaire.

Signatures of applicants
Signature des requérants

07109 (03/2003)

 **Ontario**

Ministry of
Consumer and
Business Services

Companies and Personal
Property Security Branch

393 University Ave, Suite 200
Toronto ON M5G 2M2

FORM 2
Initial Return/Notice of Change
by an Extra Provincial Corporation

Corporations Information Act

Instructions for Completion

The attached form is to be used by a corporation that is incorporated, continued or amalgamated **in a jurisdiction other than Ontario:**

OR

(A) as an Initial Return to be filed within 60 days of the date of commencing business activity in Ontario;

(B) as a Notice of Change to be filed within 15 days after the change or changes take place in the information previously filed.

A duplicate copy of this return/notice must be kept at the corporation's registered office or principal place of business in Ontario and must be available for examination.

Please type or print all information **in block capital letters using black ink.**

All items on Form 2, page 1 and page 2 must be completed in full, unless otherwise indicated.

Documents filed with the Companies and Personal Property Security Branch must be neat, legible and suitable for microfilming. Documents that do not conform to this standard will be returned to the corporation.

All **dates** must be completed using the following numeric format:

January 3, 1999 would be:

Year	Month	Day
1999	01	03

Addresses must be completed in full, including the street number and name, the city or town and the unit or suite number, if applicable. The province or state, country and postal code must be included when required. **Do not use abbreviations for provinces, states or countries. Post office box numbers cannot be used.**
Please note that any handwriting or typing outside the designated boxes will be ignored; it is not part of the approved form.

FEE

There is no fee for the filing of an initial return or notice of change.

PENALTIES

Sections 13 and 14 of the **Corporations Information Act** provide penalties for contravening the Act or Regulations.

Section 18(1) of the Act provides that a corporation that is in default of a requirement under this Act to file a return/ notice or that has unpaid fees or penalties is not capable of maintaining a proceeding in a court in Ontario in respect of the business carried on by the corporation except with leave of the court.

07201 (02/2002)

FIGURE 15.2 CONTINUED

COMPLETION OF PAGE 1

Item 1:   **Initial Return/Notice of Change by a business corporation/not-for-profit corporation:**
Indicate whether an extra-provincial corporation is filing an Initial Return or a Notice of Change by placing an **X** in the appropriate box. (Choose **one** box only.)

Item 2:   **Ontario Corporation Number:**
Insert the Ontario Corporation Number. This number appears in the top right corner of the Extra-Provincial Licence issued to the corporation.
If the corporation does not require a licence, the number will be assigned upon filing the Initial Return.

Item 3:   **Date of Incorporation or Amalgamation:**
Insert the full date of incorporation or amalgamation, whichever is the most recent.
Where an amalgamation has taken place since last filing, please submit a photocopy of the Certificate of Amalgamation with Form 2.

Item 4:   **Corporation Name:**
Insert the name of the corporation, including punctuation and spacing.

Item 5:   **Address of Registered or Head Office.**
Do not leave this blank.
Complete the full address of the Registered or Head Office. Post Office box numbers cannot be used. A street address or lot and concession number is required.

Item 6:   **Address of Principal Office in Ontario:**
If the address is the same as the address of the Registered or Head Office, place an **X** in the box provided.
If this item is not applicable, place an **X** in the box provided.
If the address of the principal office is different from the address of the registered or head office, complete this item in full.

Item 7:   **Language of Preference:**
Specify whether you prefer to receive correspondence from Companies and Personal Property Security Branch in English or French.

Item 8:   **Former Corporation Name:**
Insert the most recent former name of the corporation, including spacing and punctuation.

Item 9:   **Date Commenced Business Activity in Ontario:**
Insert the date the corporation commenced business activity in Ontario.

Item 10:   **Date Ceased Carrying on Business Activity in Ontario:**
Insert the complete date on which the corporation ceased carrying on business activity in Ontario.
If not applicable, place an **X** in the box provided.

Item 11:   **Jurisdiction of Incorporation, Amalgamation or Continuation:**
The jurisdiction of incorporation, continuation or amalgamation (whichever is most recent) must be indicated by placing an **X** in the appropriate box. If the jurisdiction is one other than those listed, set out the name of the jurisdiction in full in the space provided.

COMPLETION OF PAGE 2

Complete the Ontario Corporation Number and the Date of Incorporation or Amalgamation (whichever is most recent).

Item 12:   **Name and office address of the Chief Officer/Manager in Ontario:**
If this item is not applicable to your corporation, place an **X** in the box provided.
If applicable, complete the name in full, providing the last name, first name, and middle name/initials. Complete the full office address of the Chief Officer/Manager in Ontario.

Date Effective:
Insert the date the Chief Officer/Manager in Ontario assumed his/her position.

Date Ceased:
Insert the date the Chief Officer/Manager in Ontario ceased to hold his/her position.
If the date ceased has been completed, the date the Chief Officer/Manager assumed his/her position must also be completed.

Item 13:   **Name and office address of Agent for Service in Ontario:**
If the corporation is incorporated outside of Canada, an agent for service is required.
If the requirement for an agent for service is not applicable, place an **X** in the box provided.
If Item 14 is applicable, indicate if the agent is an individual or a corporation with its registered office address in Ontario. If the agent is an individual, complete section (a) his/her last name, first name, middle name/initials and section (c) full address.

If the agent is a corporation, complete section (b) the Ontario Corporation Number and the full Corporation name, including punctuation and spacing, and section (c) full address.

Please Note: For a foreign corporation, (business corporation incorporated or continued under the laws of a jurisdiction outside of Canada), to change information about an Agent for Service, a completed Form 2, Revised Appointment of Agent for Service under the Extra-Provincial Corporations Act (Ontario) must accompany the document you are presently completing.

Not for-for-Profit corporations incorporated outside of Canada do not require an Agent for Service and therefore a Revised Appointment of Agent for Service is not required for these corporations.

Item 14:   **Person Authorizing Filing:**
Print the name of the person authorizing this filing. This must be a director, officer or other individual having knowledge of the affairs of the corporation. The name of the individual must be completed in the box provided and an **X** must be placed in the appropriate box to indicate whether the individual is a director, officer or other individual having knowledge of the affairs of the corporation.

The completed form must be mailed or delivered to:
Ministry of Consumer and Business Services
Companies and Personal Property Security Branch
393 University Avenue Suite 200
Toronto ON M5G 2M2

07201 (02/2002)

FIGURE 15.2 CONTINUED

Form 2 - Extra Provincial Corporations / Formule 2 - Personnes morales extra-provinciales — Initial Return/Notice of Change / Corporations Information Act (Ontario).

07201 (02/2002)

FIGURE 15.2   CONCLUDED

FORM 2 - EXTRA PROVINCIAL CORPORATIONS/
FORMULE 2 - PERSONNES MORALES EXTRA-PROVINCIALES

Page 2/Page 2

Please type or print all information in block capital letters using black ink.
Prière de dactylographier les renseignements ou de les écrire en caractères d'imprimerie à l'encre noire.

FOR MINISTRY USE ONLY À L'USAGE DU MINISTÈRE SEULEMENT	Ontario Corporation Number/ Numéro matricule de la personne morale en Ontario	Date of Incorporation or Amalgamation Date de constitution ou fusion Year/Année Month/Mois Day/Jour	For Ministry Use Only À l'usage du ministère seulement

12. Name and Office Address of the Chief Officer/Manager in Ontario/
Nom et adresse du bureau du directeur général/gérant en Ontario

☐ Not Applicable/Ne s'applique pas

Last Name/Nom de famille   First Name/Prénom   Middle Name/Autres prénoms

Street Number/Numéro civique

Street Name/Nom de la rue

Street Name (cont'd)/Nom de la rue (suite)   Suite/Bureau

City/Town/Ville   **ONTARIO, CANADA**   Postal Code/Code postal

Date Effective
Date d'entrée en vigueur   Year/Année Month/Mois Day/Jour

Date Ceased
Date de cessation
des fonctions   Year/Année Month/Mois Day/Jour

13. Name and Office Address of Agent for Service in Ontario - Check One box
Nom et adresse du bureau du mandataire aux fins de signification en Ontario. Cocher la case pertinente.

☐ Not Applicable/Ne s'applique pas

Only applies to foreign business corporations
S'applique seulement aux personnes morales étrangères

a) ☐ Individual or   b) ☐ Corporation
un particulier ou   une personne morale
Complete appropriate sections below/Remplir les parties pertinentes ci-dessous.

a) Individual Name/Nom du particulier

Last Name/Nom de famille   First Name/Prénom   Middle Name/Autres prénoms

b) Ontario Corporation Number/Numéro matricule de la personne morale en Ontario

Corporation Name including punctuation/Raison sociale, y compris la ponctuation

c) Address/Adresse

c/o / a/s

Street No./N° civique   Street Name/Nom de la rue   Suite/Bureau

Street Name (cont'd)/Nom de la rue (suite)   City/Town/Ville

ONTARIO, CANADA   Postal Code/Code postal

14. (Print or type name in full of the person authorizing filing./ Dactylographier ou inscrire le prénom et le nom en caractères d'imprimerie de la personne qui authorise l'enregistrement.

Check appropriate box /
Cocher la case pertinente

D) ☐ Director/Administrateur

I /
Je

O) ☐ Officer/Dirigeant

certify that the information set out herein, is true and correct.
atteste que les renseignements précités sont véridiques et exacts.

P) ☐ Other individual having knowledge of the affairs of the Corporation/Autre personne ayant connaissance des activités de la personne morale

NOTE/REMARQUE: Section 13 and 14 of the **Corporations Information Act** provide penalties for making false or misleading statements, or omissions.
Les articles 13 et 14 de la **Loi sur les renseignements exigés des personnes morales** prévoient des peines en cas de déclaration fausse ou trompeuse, ou d'omission.

This information is being collected under the authority of The Corporations Information Act for the purpose of maintaining a public data base of corporate information. /
La Loi sur les renseignements exigés des personnes morales autorise la collecte de ces renseignements pour constituer une banque de données accessible au public.

FOR MINISTRY USE ONLY/À L'USAGE DU MINISTÈRE   ☐ See deficiency letter enclosed/Voir l'avis d'insuffisance ci-joint

07201 (02/2002)

FIGURE 15.3   FORM 1, ONTARIO CORPORATIONS INFORMATION ACT, INITIAL RETURN/NOTICE OF CHANGE BY ONTARIO CORPORATION

 **Ontario**

Ministry of Consumer and Business Services	Companies and Personal Property Security Branch	393 University Ave, Suite 200 Toronto ON M5G 2M2

FORM 1
Initial Return/Notice of Change
by an Ontario Corporation

Corporations Information Act

Instructions for Completion

The attached form is to be used by a corporation that is incorporated, continued or amalgamated in Ontario:

OR

(A) as an Initial Return to be filed within 60 days of the date of incorporation, continuation or amalgamation;

(B) as a Notice of Change that must be filed within 15 days after the change or changes take place in the information previously filed.

It is not necessary to file a notice of change in respect of a director's retirement and subsequent re-election for consecutive terms of office.

A duplicate copy of the return/notice must be kept at the Corporation's registered/head office in Ontario and must be available for examination.

Please type or print all information in block capital letters using black ink.

Only information completed within the input boxes will be captured and reflected in the Public Record.

All items on Form 1 and Schedule A must be completed in full, unless otherwise indicated.

Documents filed with the Companies and Personal Property Security Branch must be legible. Documents that do not conform to this standard will be returned to the corporation.

All **dates** must be completed using the following numeric format:
For example:

December 3, 2001 would be:

Year	Month	Day
2001	12	03

Addresses must be completed in full, including the street number and name, the city or town and the unit or suite number, if applicable. The province or state, country and postal code must be included when required. **Do not use abbreviations for provinces, states or countries. Post office box numbers cannot be used.**
Please note that any handwriting or typing outside the designated boxes will be ignored because it is not part of the approved form.

FEE

There is no fee for the filing of an initial return or notice of change.

PENALTIES

Sections 13 and 14 of the **Corporations Information Act** provide penalties for contravening the Act or Regulations.

Section 18(1) of the Act provides that a corporation that is in default of a requirement under this Act to file a return/notice or that has unpaid fees or penalties is not capable of maintaining a proceeding in a court in Ontario in respect of the business carried on by the corporation except with leave of the court.

07200 (03/2002)

FIGURE 15.3 CONTINUED

COMPLETION OF FORM 1

Item 1: **Initial Return/Notice of Change:**
Indicate whether a business corporation or not-for-profit corporation is filing an initial return or a notice of change by placing an **X** in the appropriate box. (Choose **one** box only.)

Item 2: **Ontario Corporation Number:**
Insert the Ontario Corporation Number. This number appears in the top right corner of your Certificate of Incorporation /Continuation or Amalgamation or your Letters Patent.

Item 3: **Date of Incorporation or Amalgamation:**
Insert the full date of incorporation or amalgamation, whichever applies.

Item 4: **Corporation Name:**
Insert the name of the corporation, including all punctuation and correct spacing.

Item 5: **Address of Registered or Head Office in Ontario:**
Complete the full address of the Registered or Head Office in Ontario. Post office box numbers cannot be used. A street address or lot and concession number is required.

Item 6: **Mailing Address:**
Do not leave this item blank.
If the address is the same as the registered or head office address, place an **X** in the box provided.
If the address is different from the registered or head office in Ontario, you must set out the address in full.
If you do not wish to set out a mailing address, place an **X** in the "Not Applicable" box.

Item 7: **Language of Preference:**
Specify whether you prefer to receive correspondence from Companies and Personal Property Security Branch in English or French.

Item 8: **Number of Schedule A(s) submitted:**
Schedule A must be submitted with your form. Specify the number of Schedule A(s) you are submitting.
NOTE:
A blank Schedule A may be photocopied if required.

Item 9: **Person Authorizing Filing:**
Print the name of the person authorizing the filing. This must be a director, officer or other individual having knowledge of the affairs of the corporation. The name of the individual must be completed in the box provided and an **X** must be placed in the appropriate box to indicate whether the individual is a director, officer or other individual having knowledge of the affairs of the corporation.

07200 (03/2002)

FIGURE 15.3   CONTINUED

COMPLETION OF SCHEDULE A

Complete all applicable items on Schedule A in full, including the Ontario Corporation Number and Date of Incorporation or Amalgamation.

Schedule A must report all information pertaining to directors and the five most senior officers of the corporation and must include all changes that have taken place since the filing of the initial return, special notice, annual return or most recent notice of change.

One director/senior officer information section must be completed for each individual who is a director and/or senior officer of the corporation.

There must be a minimum of one director in a non-offering business corporation and a minimum of three directors in a not-for-profit corporation or an offering business corporation.

Not-for-profit corporations must also have a minimum of two senior officers, namely a president and a secretary, plus three directors.

DIRECTOR/OFFICER INFORMATION

The following two sections must be completed for each individual:

NAME
Complete the name in full, providing last, first, and middle name or initials.

ADDRESS
A full address for service is required for the individual. A box number is not acceptable.

Director Information

If the individual is a director, the next three sections must be completed.

Resident Canadian
This information is required for directors of business corporations only.

Specify whether the individual is a Resident Canadian by checking **yes** or **no**.

Date Elected
Complete the date on which the individual became a director.

Date Ceased
Insert the date the director ceased to hold his/her position.

If the date ceased has been completed, the date the director assumed his/her position must also be completed.

Officer Information

If the individual is one of the five most senior officers, the next two sections must be completed:

Date Officer Appointed
Complete the date the individual was appointed as a senior officer under the appropriate title(s).
If the senior officer is not the president, secretary, treasurer or general manager, select the appropriate position(s) from the pre-printed « **Other Titles** » list and include the proper date appointed.

Date Officer Ceased
Insert the date the senior officer ceased to hold his/her position, or
Insert the date an officer ceased to be one of the five most senior officers (as applicable).

If the date ceased has been completed, the date the officer assumed his/her position must also be completed.

The completed form must be mailed or delivered to:

> Ministry of Consumer and Business Services
> Companies and Personal Property Security Branch
> 393 University Ave, Suite 200
> Toronto ON M5G 2M2

07200 (03/2002)

FIGURE 15.3   CONTINUED

(v) **Ontario**   Ministry of
Consumer and
Business Services

Ministère des Services
aux consommateurs
et aux entreprises

Companies and Personal
Property Security Branch
393 University Ave Suite 200
Toronto ON M5G 2M2

Direction des compagnies
et des sûretés mobilières
393 av., University, bureau 200
Toronto ON M5G 2M2

| For Ministry Use Only |
| À l'usage du ministère seulement |
| Page/Page 1   **of/de** _____ |

Form 1 - Ontario Corporation
Formule 1 - Personnes morales de l'Ontario

Initial Return/Notice of Change/
Rapport initial/Avis de modification
Corporations Information Act/*Loi sur les*
renseignements exigés des personnes morales

1.		Notice of Change
		Initial Return Avis de
		Rapport initial modification
Business Corporation/		
Société par actions		
Not-For-Profit Corporation/		
Personne morale sans but		
lucratif		

Please type or print all information in block capital letters using black ink.
Prière de dactylographier les renseignements ou de les écrire en caractères d'imprimerie à l'encre noire.

2.	Ontario Corporation Number	3.	Date of Incorporation or Amalgamation/	For Ministry Use Only
	Numéro matricule de la personne		Date de constitution ou fusion	À l'usage du ministère seulement
	morale en Ontario		Year/Année Month/Mois Day/Jour	

4.   Corporation Name Including Punctuation/Raison sociale de la personne morale, y compris la ponctuation

5. Address of Registered or Head Office/Adresse du siège social

c/o / a/s

Street No./Nº civique   Street Name/Nom de la rue   Suite/Bureau

Street Name (cont'd)/Nom de la rue (suite)

City/Town/Ville   **ONTARIO, CANADA**

Postal Code/Code postal

For Ministry Use Only/
À l'usage du ministère seulement

6. Mailing Address/Adresse postale

☐ Same as Registered or Head Office/
Même que siège social

☐ Not Applicable/
Ne s'applique pas

Street No./Nº civique

Street Name/Nom de la rue   Suite/Bureau

Street Name (cont'd)/Nom de la rue (suite)

City/Town/Ville

Province, State/Province, État   Country/Pays   Postal Code/Code postal

7. Language of Preference/Langue préférée   English - Anglais ☐   French - Français ☐

8. **Information on Directors/Officers must be completed on Schedule A as requested.** If additional space is required, photocopy Schedule A./**Les renseignements sur les administrateurs ou les dirigeants doivent être fournis dans l'Annexe A, tel que demandé.** Si vous avez besoin de plus d'espace, vous pouvez photocopier l'Annexe A.

Number of Schedule A(s) submitted/Nombre d'Annexes A présentées   (At least one Schedule A must be submitted/Au moins une
Annexe A doit être présentée)

9.

I/Je

(Print or type name in full of the person authorizing filing / Dactylographier ou inscrire le prénom et le
nom en caractères d'imprimerie de la personne qui autorise l'enregistrement)

certify that the information set out herein, is true and correct.
atteste que les renseignements précités sont véridiques et exacts.

Check appropriate box
Cocher la case pertinente

D) ☐   Director/Administrateur

O) ☐   Officer /Dirigeant

P) ☐   Other individual having knowledge of the
affairs of the Corporation/Autre personne
ayant connaissance des activités de la
personne morale

NOTE/REMARQUE : Sections 13 and 14 of the **Corporations Information Act** provide penalties for making false or misleading statements or omissions. Les articles 13 et 14 de la *Loi sur*
les renseignements exigés des personnes morales prévoient des peines en cas de déclaration fausse ou trompeuse, ou d'omission.

07200 (03/2002)

FIGURE 15.3   CONTINUED

Form 1 - Ontario Corporation/Formule 1 - Personnes morales de l'Ontario
Schedule A/Annexe A

For Ministry Use Only
À l'usage du ministère seulement
Page/Page _____ **of/de** _____

Please type or print all information in block capital letters using black ink.
Prière de dactylographier les renseignements ou de les écrire en caractères d'imprimerie à l'encre noire.

Ontario Corporation Number
Numéro matricule de la personne morale en Ontario

Date of Incorporation or Amalgamation
Date de constitution ou fusion
Year/Année Month/Mois Day/Jour

DIRECTOR / OFFICER INFORMATION - RENSEIGNEMENTS RELATIFS AUX ADMINISTRATEURS/DIRIGEANTS
Full Name and Address for Service/Nom et domicile élu

Last Name/Nom de famille   First Name/Prénom   Middle Names/Autres prénoms

Street Number/Numéro civique   Suite/Bureau

Street Name/Nom de la rue

Street Name (cont'd)/Nom de la rue (suite)

City/Town/Ville

Province, State/Province, État   Country/Pays   Postal Code/Code postal

*OTHER TITLES (Please Specify)
*AUTRES TITRES (Veuillez préciser)
Chair / Président du conseil
Chair Person / Président du conseil
Chairman / Président du conseil
Chairwoman / Présidente du conseil
Vice-Chair / Vice-président du conseil
Vice-President / Vice-président
Assistant Secretary / Secrétaire adjoint
Assistant Treasurer / Trésorier adjoint
Chief Manager / Directeur exécutif
Executive Director / Directeur administratif
Managing Director / Administrateur délégué
Chief Executive Officer / Directeur général
Chief Financial Officer / Agent en chef des finances
Chief Information Officer / Directeur général de l'information
Chief Operating Officer / Administrateur en chef des opérations
Chief Administrative Officer / Directeur général de l'administration
Comptroller / Contrôleur
Authorized Signing Officer / Signataire autorisé
Other (Untitled) / Autre (sans titre)

Director Information/Renseignements relatifs aux administrateurs

Resident Canadian/   YES/OUI   NO/NON   (Resident Canadian applies to directors of business corporations only.)/
Résident canadien   (Résident canadien ne s'applique qu'aux administrateurs de sociétés par actions)

Date Elected/   Year/Année Month/Mois Day/Jour   Date Ceased/   Year/Année Month/Mois Day/Jour
Date d'élection   Date de cessation

Officer Information/Renseignements relatifs aux dirigeants

	PRESIDENT/PRÉSIDENT			SECRETARY/SECRÉTAIRE			TREASURER/TRÉSORIER			GENERAL MANAGER/ DIRECTEUR GÉNÉRAL			OTHER/AUTRE		
	Year/Année	Month/Mois	Day/Jour	Year/Année	Month/Mois	Day/Jour	Year/Année	Month/Mois	Day/Jour	Year/Année	Month/Mois	Day/Jour	Year/Année	Month/Mois	Day/Jour
Date Appointed/ Date de nomination															
Date Ceased/ Date de cessation															

DIRECTOR / OFFICER INFORMATION - RENSEIGNEMENTS RELATIFS AUX ADMINISTRATEURS/DIRIGEANTS
Full Name and Address for Service/Nom et domicile élu

Last Name/Nom de famille   First Name/Prénom   Middle Names/Autres prénoms

Street Number/Numéro civique   Suite/Bureau

Street Name/Nom de la rue

Street Name (cont'd)/Nom de la rue (suite)

City/Town/Ville

Province, State/Province, État   Country/Pays   Postal Code/Code postal

*OTHER TITLES (Please Specify)
*AUTRES TITRES (Veuillez préciser)
Chair / Président du conseil
Chair Person / Président du conseil
Chairman / Président du conseil
Chairwoman / Présidente du conseil
Vice-Chair / Vice-président du conseil
Vice-President / Vice-président
Assistant Secretary / Secrétaire adjoint
Assistant Treasurer / Trésorier adjoint
Chief Manager / Directeur exécutif
Executive Director / Directeur administratif
Managing Director / Administrateur délégué
Chief Executive Officer / Directeur général
Chief Financial Officer / Agent en chef des finances
Chief Information Officer / Directeur général de l'information
Chief Operating Officer / Administrateur en chef des opérations
Chief Administrative Officer / Directeur général de l'administration
Comptroller / Contrôleur
Authorized Signing Officer / Signataire autorisé
Other (Untitled) / Autre (sans titre)

Director Information/Renseignements relatifs aux administrateurs

Resident Canadian/   YES/OUI   NO/NON   (Resident Canadian applies to directors of business corporations only.)/
Résident canadien   (Résident canadien ne s'applique qu'aux administrateurs de sociétés par actions)

Date Elected/   Year/Année Month/Mois Day/Jour   Date Ceased/   Year/Année Month/Mois Day/Jour
Date d'élection   Date de cessation

Officer Information/Renseignements relatifs aux dirigeants

	PRESIDENT/PRÉSIDENT			SECRETARY/SECRÉTAIRE			TREASURER/TRÉSORIER			GENERAL MANAGER/ DIRECTEUR GÉNÉRAL			OTHER/AUTRE		
	Year/Année	Month/Mois	Day/Jour	Year/Année	Month/Mois	Day/Jour	Year/Année	Month/Mois	Day/Jour	Year/Année	Month/Mois	Day/Jour	Year/Année	Month/Mois	Day/Jour
Date Appointed/ Date de nomination															
Date Ceased/ Date de cessation															

07200 (03/2002)

FIGURE 15.3   CONCLUDED

This information is being collected under the authority of The Corporations Information Act for the purpose of maintaining a public database of corporate information.

La *Loi sur les renseignements exigés des personnes morales* autorise la collecte de ces renseignements pour constituer une banque de données accessible au public.

The completed form must be mailed or delivered to:
        Ministry of Consumer and Business Services
        Companies and Personal
        Property Security Branch
        393 University Ave, Suite 200
        Toronto ON M5G 2M2

La formule dûment remplie doit être envoyée par la poste ou livrée à l'adresse suivante :
        Ministère des Services aux consommateurs et aux entreprises
        Direction des compagnies
        et des sûretés mobilières
        393, av. University, bureau 200
        Toronto (Ontario) M5G 2M2

FIGURE 15.4   FORM 3, ONTARIO CORPORATIONS ACT, APPLICATION FOR SUPPLEMENTARY LETTERS PATENT

 **Ontario**

Ministry of
Consumer and
Business Services

Companies and Personal
Property Security Branch
393 University Ave Suite 200
Toronto ON M5G 2M2

**Application For
Supplementary Letters Patent
Form 3**
Corporations Act

INSTRUCTIONS FOR COMPLETING

A corporation may apply for Supplementary Letters Patent to change its name, to amend the objects or provisions set out in the original Letters Patent or an earlier Supplementary Letters Patent or any other matter set out in Section 131 of the *Corporations Act*. Applications should be mailed or delivered to the address listed above. ***Please note these documents are reviewed by the Companies and Personal Property Security Branch (CPPSB) and take several weeks to process***.

FEE

$130   **BY MAIL** - Cheque or money order payable to the Minister of Finance.
IN PERSON - If you are delivering the application in person, you can also pay by cash, Visa, MasterCard, American Express or debit card. If the corporation is a charity there is an additional fee for review by the Public Guardian and Trustee. (See below, "Charities")

There will be a service charge payable for any cheque returned as non-negotiable by a bank or financial institution.

DOCUMENTS REQUIRED

1. Application for Supplementary Letters Patent (Form 3, under the *Corporations Act*) completed in duplicate with original signatures on both copies.

2. A covering letter, setting out the name, address and telephone number of the person or firm to whom the Supplementary Letters Patent, or any correspondence, should be mailed.

3. *If the application is being made to change the name of the corporation, an original, Ontario-biased NUANS name search report, dated not more than 90 days before the submission of the application, is required for the proposed name.*

4. *If the proposed name is similar to the name of a known corporation, association, partnership, individual, or business, or contains the family name of an individual the CPPSB may require consent in writing to the use of the proposed name from the individual or the existing entity. CPPSB may require that the existing entity dissolve or change its name before issuing the Supplementary Letters Patent.*

APPEARANCE OF DOCUMENTS

The Application for Supplementary Letters Patent and any supporting documents must be typewritten, or if completed by hand, printed in BLOCK CAPITAL letters in black ink. All documents must be legible and suitable for microfilming.

Forms, extra pages and any supporting documents must be printed on one side of good quality white bond paper 8½" by 11". Pages are numbered 1 and 2; applications with missing pages cannot be accepted. If additional pages are required due to lack of space, they should be numbered the same as the original page with the addition of letters of the alphabet to indicate sequence. For example, supplementary pages for item 5 on page 1 would be numbered 1A, 1B, etc. Do not attach schedules to the form. The last page must be the signing page.

NAME CHANGE

For a name change request, the Companies and Personal Property Security Branch requires an original Ontario-biased NUANS search for the proposed new name. The NUANS name search must be obtained from a private name search company and cannot be dated more than 90 days before the submission of the application. For example, applications submitted on November 28th could be accompanied by a NUANS name search report dated as early as August 30th, but not dated earlier. If the report is dated earlier, a new report will be required. Name search companies are listed in the Yellow Pages under the heading "Searchers of Records". The name set out in the application must be exactly the same as the name set out in the name search report.

07108 (12/2003)

FIGURE 15.4   CONTINUED

The Ministry will not grant a name that is identical to another corporation or that contravenes the *Corporations Act* or Regulations. If the proposed name is similar to that of a known corporation, association, partnership, individual or business, or contains the family name of an individual, the consent in writing of the existing corporation, association, partnership, individual or business may be required or CPPSB may require that the existing entity dissolve or change its name. The name must reflect the objects of the corporation and should not be too general in character or imply the corporation is a business corporation. It should contain a distinctive element and a descriptive element, for example:

WESTWAY ROAD COMMUNITY CENTRE
(Distinctive)   (Descriptive)

The name may include the word "Incorporated" or "Corporation" or the corresponding abbreviations, but it is not required. A corporation without share capital cannot have "Limited", "Limitée" or the corresponding abbreviations as part of the name.

In the case of an application for a name change, subsection 19(2) of Regulation 181 under the *Corporations Act* requires that the Application for Supplementary Letters Patent contain a statement that the corporation is not insolvent within the meaning of subsection 19 (4) of Regulation 181. This statement should be included under item 5 on the form. (see below, "item 5")

APPLICATION

ITEM 1   Set out the current name of the corporation in BLOCK CAPITAL letters starting on the first line in the first box on the left, with one letter per box and one empty box for a space. Punctuation marks are entered in separate boxes. Complete one line before starting in the first box of the next line. The name entered must be exactly the same as it appeared on the original Letters Patent or if there has been a name change, the most recent Supplementary Letters Patent changing the name.

H	A	P	P	Y		T	I	M	E		R	E	C	R	E	A	T	I	O	N		A	N	D		D	A	Y		C	A
R	E		C	E	N	T	R	E		I	N	C	.																		

ITEM 2   If this is an application for a name change, set out the new name in BLOCK CAPITAL letters starting on the first line in the first box on the left, with one letter per box and one empty box for a space. Punctuation marks are entered in separate boxes. Complete one line before starting in the first box of the next line. The name entered must be exactly the same as that on the NUANS name search report submitted with the application. **If the name is not to be changed, leave this item blank.**

ITEM 3   Set out the date of incorporation or amalgamation of the corporation.

ITEM 4   Set out the date the resolution authorizing the application for Supplementary Letters Patent was approved by the members/shareholders of the corporation.

ITEM 5   This item must contain an extract from the Resolution passed by the corporation setting out the change, or changes, which are to be made to the original, or previously amended, Letters Patent of the corporation. The application should clearly set out in what way the existing Letters Patent would be changed. For example:

"RESOLVED that the corporation apply for Supplementary Letters Patent

To delete object 4(a) from the original Letters Patent which reads
   (a) To promote the sport of soccer for children aged 15 and under.
      and replace it with the following:
   (a) To promote the sport of soccer for children and adults.

To change the objects of the corporation by adding the following paragraph after object (c),
   (d) To arrange soccer competitions and social functions for the members of the corporation.

To change the name of the corporation from:
   West Bay Youth Soccer Club
to
   West Bay Soccer Club"

FIGURE 15.4   CONTINUED

If the application includes a proposed new name (as shown in item 5 on the previous page), the following statement must be included in item 5,

"The corporation is not insolvent within the meaning of subsection 19(4) of Ontario Regulation 181."

EXECUTION Both copies of the application must be signed by two officers, two directors or one officer and one director of the corporation. The signatures must be original signatures. Photocopies of signatures will not be accepted. Also set out the office of each person who signs (e.g., President, Director, Secretary). The current name of the corporation should be set out above the signatures. If the corporation has a seal it should be affixed to both copies of the form beside the signatures. Under the *Corporations Act* the corporation may have a seal but it is not required.

CHARITABLE CORPORATIONS

Applications for Supplementary Letters Patent to change the objects or provisions of a charitable corporation must be reviewed and approved by the office of the Public Guardian and Trustee. This would also apply to a not-for-profit, non-charitable corporation that was applying to change its objects to those of a charity.

If the applicant is filing an application for Supplementary Letters Patent only to change the corporate name, the application should be sent directly to Companies and Personal Property Security Branch, as the Public Guardian and Trustee does not have to approve the new name.

The Public Guardian and Trustee charges a fee of $150.00 to review the new objects and/or provisions of the corporation. Both the fee for the Public Guardian and Trustee and the $130.00 filing fee for Companies and Personal Property Security Branch should be sent with the completed application to the Office of the Public Guardian and Trustee. Both fees should be paid by a single cheque in the amount of $280.00 payable to the "Public Guardian and Trustee". After the application has been reviewed and approved as a charity the Public Guardian and Trustee will forward the forms, filing fee and name search (if applicable) to the Companies and Personal Property Security Branch. If the application and supporting documents are complete and comply with the *Corporations Act*, the Supplementary Letters Patent will be issued.

Applications to amend the objects or provisions of a **charity** should be mailed to:

> The Ministry of the Attorney General
> Office of the Public Guardian and Trustee
> Charitable Property Program
> 595 Bay Street, Suite 800
> Toronto ON M5G 2M6
>
> Phone: (416) 326-1963 or toll free 1-800-366-0335
> Internet: *www.attorneygeneral.jus.gov.on.ca*

Applications for non-profit **non-charitable** corporations or charitable corporations that are only changing the name of the corporation, should be mailed in duplicate together with the name search (if applicable), any supporting documents and fee of $130.00, to:

> Ministry of Consumer and Business Services
> Companies and Personal Property Security Branch
> 393 University Ave., Suite 200
> Toronto ON M5G 2M2
> Tel: (416) 314-8880 or in Ontario toll free 1-800-361-3223

FIGURE 15.4   CONTINUED

For Ministry Use Only
À l'usage exclusif du ministère

| Ontario Corporation Number | 1 |
| *Numéro de la société en Ontario* | |

Form 3
Corporations Act

Formule 3
Loi sur les personnes morales

APPLICATION FOR SUPPLEMENTARY LETTERS PATENT
REQUÊTE EN VUE D'OBTENIR DES LETTRES PATENTES SUPPLÉMENTAIRES

1. Name of the applicant corporation: (Set out in BLOCK CAPITAL LETTERS)
    Dénomination sociale de la personne morale : (écrire en LETTRES MAJUSCULES SEULEMENT)

2. The name of the corporation is changed to (if applicable): (Set out in BLOCK CAPITAL LETTERS)
    La dénomination sociale de la personne morale devient (le cas échéant) : (écrire en LETTRES MAJUSCULES SEULEMENT)

3. Date of incorporation/amalgamation:
    Date de la constitution ou de la fusion   _____
    　　　　　　　　　　　　　　　　　　　　　Year/Année　　　Month/Mois　　　Day/Jour

4. The resolution authorizing this application was confirmed by
    the shareholders/members of the corporation on:
    La résolution autorisant la présente requête a été ratifiée
    par les actionnaires ou membres de la personne morale le : _____
    　　　　　　　　　　　　　　　　　　　　　　　　Year/Année　　　Month/Mois　　　Day/Jour

    under section 34 or 131 of the *Corporations Act.*
    aux termes de l'article 34 ou 131 de la Loi sur les personnes morales.

5. The corporation applies for the issue of supplementary letters patent to provide as follows:
    La personne morale demande la délivrance de lettres patentes supplémentaires qui prévoient ce qui suit :

07108 (12/2003)

FIGURE 15.4   CONCLUDED

2

This application is executed in duplicate
La présente requête est faite en double exemplaire.

Current Name of Corporation
Dénomination sociale actuelle de la personne morale

By
Par :

| Signature | Description of Office |
| *Signature* | *Fonction* |

| Signature | Description of Office |
| *Signature* | *Fonction* |

FIGURE 15.5   FORM 11, ONTARIO CORPORATIONS ACT, APPLICATION FOR LETTERS PATENT OF AMALGAMATION

Ministry of
Consumer and
Business Services

Companies and Personal
Property Security Branch
393 University Ave Suite 200
Toronto ON M5G 2M2

**Application for Letters Patent
of Amalgamation
Form 11
Corporations Act
Instructions for Completing**

FEE

For fee payable refer to Regulations made under the **Corporations Act.** If you do not have a copy of the Regulations on hand, you may obtain information regarding fees payable under the **Corporations Act** by phoning, in Toronto 314-8880, or Toll free 1-800-361-3223. Cheques or Money Orders are to be made payable to the Minister of Finance. Where a cheque is tendered as payment, the name of the corporation should be written on the front of the cheque. Do not send cash through the mail.
There will be a service charge payable for any cheque returned as non-negotiable by a Bank or Financial Institution.

FORMAT

The application must be submitted **in duplicate** on Form 11 as prescribed in Ontario Regulations made under the **Corporations Act.** Applications which do not conform to Form 11 cannot be accepted, and will be returned to the applicant(s)/agent who submitted the application.

APPEARANCE OF DOCUMENTS

Applications, and any supporting documents, which are to be filed with the Ministry must be typewritten, or, if completed by hand printed in BLOCK CAPITAL letters in black ink. Applications, and supporting documents, must be legible and compatible with the microfilming process.

Forms, and any supporting documents or extra pages, must be printed on one side of good quality white bond paper 8 1/2" by 11", or the metric equivalent. Facsimile (Fax) applications or supporting documents cannot be accepted in lieu of original copies.

PAGES

Pages are numbered 1 through 3 and should remain in that order. Applications with missing pages cannot be accepted. If additional pages are required due to lack of space, they must be the same size as all other pages, must have a margin of 30mm. or 1 1/4" on the left hand side, and must be numbered the same as the original page with letter(s) of the alphabet indicating sequence. e.g. 1A,1B etc.

CORPORATE NAME

If the name of the **amalgamated corporation** is not to be the same as one of the amalgamating corporations the application must be accompanied by a name search report for the "new" name of the amalgamated corporation.
Applicants must obtain an "Ontario biased" name search report for the name under which the applicant corporations are to be amalgamated. Name search reports are obtainable from name search corporations. These corporations are listed in the Yellow Pages of the telephone directory under the heading "Searchers of Records".
The name search report must be submitted with the application for amalgamation and must be dated no more than 90 days from the date of production of the report.
An original name search report, and not a photocopy, must be submitted. Reports dated more than 90 days from the date of production of the report will not be accepted and a new report will be required.
An amalgamated corporation may have a name the same as one of the amalgamating corporations, **except where the name is an Ontario Corporation Number name.**

FIGURE 15.5   CONTINUED

APPLICATION

Item 1   The name of the **amalgamated corporation** must be set out in this item. The name must be set out in BLOCK CAPITAL letters in the squares provided and must commence on the first line of the "grid" in the first square. Each square of the "grid" represents a letter of the alphabet, a punctuation mark or other mark permitted by the Regulations to the **Corporations Act** as forming part of a corporate name, or a space. If there is not sufficient space on the first line of the "grid" for the name, continue onto the second line and so on. (See example below.)

H	A	P	P	Y		T	I	M	E		R	E	C	R	E	A	T	I	O	N		A	N	D		D	A	Y		C	A
R	E		C	E	N	T	R	E		I	N	C	.																		

Item 3   Set out the names of the **amalgamating corporations**, their Ontario corporation numbers and the full date(s), day, month and year, on which the amalgamation agreement was approved by the shareholders/members of each of the amalgamating corporations.

Item 4   Set out the full address of the head office of the amalgamated corporation, including the postal code. (If the address is a multi-office building, include Room or Suite number.) A post office box is not an acceptable head office address.

Item 5   Set out the full names, including all given names, of the persons who are to be directors of the amalgamated corporation. Set out the address for service, including the postal code, of each of the persons who are to be directors of the amalgamated corporation. (Include Room or Suite number, if applicable.)

Item 6   A copy of the amalgamation agreement **must form part of the application** and must not be submitted as a separate Schedule to the application. Pages of the agreement should be numbered 2A, 2B, etc.

EXECUTION

Both copies of the application must be signed by two officers or one officer and one director of each of the amalgamating corporations. The signatures must be original signatures. Applications containing photocopied signatures will not be accepted.

The application, in duplicate together with the applicable fee, NUANS name search report (if applicable), and any supporting documents should be mailed, or delivered to:

Ministry of Consumer and Business Services
Registration Division
Companies and Personal Property Security Branch
393 University Ave Suite 200
Toronto ON M5G 2M2

FIGURE 15.5   CONTINUED

This space is for
Ministry Use Only
Espace réservé à l'usage
exclusif du ministère

Ontario Corporation Number
Numéro de la personne morale en Ontario

APPLICATION FOR LETTERS PATENT OF AMALGAMATION
REQUÊTE EN VUE D'OBTENIR DES LETTRES PATENTES DE FUSION

1. Name of the amalgamated corporation:/Dénomination sociale de la personne morale issue de la fusion :

2. The amalgamation agreement has been duly approved as required by subsection 113(3) of the **Corporations Act.**
   La convention de fusion a été dûment approuvée conformément au paragraphe 113(3) de la **Loi sur les personne morales.**

3. The names of the amalgamating corporations and the dates on which the amalgamation agreement was approved by the shareholders/members of each of the amalgamating corporations are:
   La dénomination sociale des personnes morales qui fusionnent et la date à laquelle la convention de fusion a été approuvée par les actionnaires ou membres de chaque personne morale qui fusionne sont les suivantes:

Name of corporation Dénomination sociale de la personne morale	Ontario Corporation Number Numéro de la personne morale en Ontario	Date of shareholders/Members approval Date de l'approbation par les actionnaires ou membres

07063 (01/2002)

FIGURE 15.5   CONTINUED

2.

4.   The address of the head office of the amalgamated corporation is:
Adresse du siège social de la personne morale issue de la fusion :

_____

(Street & No., or R.R. No., or Lot & Concession No., or Lot & Plan No., Post Office Box No. not acceptable; if Multi-Office Building give Room No.)
(Rue et numéro, ou R.R. et numéro, ou numéro de lot et de concession, ou numéro de lot et de plan; numéro de boîte postale inacceptable; s'il s'agit d'un édifice à bureaux, numéro du bureau)

_____ | | | | | | |

(Name of Municipality)   (Postal Code/Code postal)
(Nom de la municipalité)

5.   The persons who are to be directors of the amalgamated coporation are:
Les personnes appelée à devenir les administrateurs de la personne morale issue la fusion sont :

Name in full, including all given names Nom et prénoms au complet	Address for service giving Street & No., or R.R. No., or Lot & Concession No., or Lot & Plan No., and Postal Code (Post Office Box No. not acceptable) Domicile élu y compris la rue et le numéro, ou la R.R. et le numéro, ou le numéro de lot et de concession, ou le numéro de lot et de plan, ainsi que le code postal (numéro de boîte postale inacceptable)

6.   The following is a copy of the amalgamation agreement duly certified under corporate seal by the secretary of each of the amalgamating corporations:
Copie de la convention de fusin dûment certifiée et revêtue du sceau de la personne morale par le secrétaire de chacune des personnes morales qui fusionnent :

07063 (01/2002)

FIGURE 15.5   CONCLUDED

3.

The corporations named below apply jointly for letters patent confirming the agreement and amalgamating the said corporations.
Les personnes morales nommées ci-dessous demandent conjointement des lettres patentes confirmant la convention et les fusionnant.

This application is executed in duplicate./La présente requête est faite en double exemplaire.

Names and seals of the amalgamating corporations and signatures and descriptions
of office of their proper officers.
Dénomination sociale et sceau des personnes morales qui fusionnent, signature et fonction
de leurs dirigeants régulièrement désignés.

07063 (01/2002)

FIGURE 15.6 FORM 12.1, ONTARIO CORPORATIONS ACT, APPLICATION FOR CONTINUATION

Ontario	Ministry of Consumer and Business Services	Companies and Personal Property Security Branch 393 University Ave Suite 200 Toronto ON M5G 2M2

Application For Continuation
Form 12.1
Corporations Act
Instructions For Completing

THIS APPLICATION APPLIES ONLY TO THOSE CORPORATIONS INCORPORATED IN ONTARIO UNDER AN ACT OTHER THAN THE CORPORATIONS ACT

FEE $155.00

For fee payable refer to Regulations made under the **Corporations Act.** If you do not have a copy of the Regulations on hand, you may obtain information regarding fees payable under the **Corporations Act** by phoning, in Toronto (416) 314-8880, or Toll free I-800-361-3223. Cheques or Money Orders are to be made payable to the Minister of Finance. Where a cheque is tendered as payment, the name of the corporation should be written on the front of the cheque. Do not send cash through the mail. **There will be a service charge payable for any cheque returned as non-negotiable by a Bank or Financial Institution.**

FORMAT

The application must be submitted **in duplicate** on Form 12.1 as prescribed in Ontario Regulations made under the **Corporations Act.** Applications which do not conform to Form 12.1 cannot be accepted, and will be returned to the applicant(s)/agent who submitted the application.

APPEARANCE OF DOCUMENTS

Applications, and any supporting documents, which are to be filed with the Ministry must be typewritten, or, if completed by hand, printed in BLOCK CAPITAL letters in black ink. Applications, and any supporting documents, must be legible and compatible with the microfilming process.

Forms, and any supporting documents or extra pages, must be printed on one side of good quality white bond paper 8 I/2' by 11" or the metric equivalent. Facsimile (Fax) applications or supporting documents cannot be accepted in lieu of original copies.

PAGES

Pages are numbered 1 through 5 and should remain in that order. Applications with missing pages cannot be accepted. If additional pages are required due to lack of space, they must be the same size as all other pages, must have a margin of 1,1/4" on the left hand side, and must be numbered the same as the original page with letter(s) of the alphabet indicating sequence. e.g. 1 A, 1 B, etc.

CORPORATE NAME

If the corporation is to be continued under a corporate name **other than** its name, at the time of submission of this application the applicants should determine if the name is available for use. To do this the applicants must obtain, from a name search company, an "Ontario biased" name search report for the name under which the corporation is to be continued.
Name search corporations are listed in the Yellow Pages of the telephone directory under the heading "Searchers of Records".
The name search report must be submitted with the application for continuation and must be dated no more than 90 days from the date of production of the report. The name set out in the application for continuation must be exactly the same as the name set out in the name search report.
An original name search report, and not a photocopy, must be submitted. Reports dated more than 90 days from the production of the report will not be accepted and a new report will be required.
The Ministry will determine whether the name is available for use. Names that contravene the **Corporations Act** or Regulations will not be approved for use. If the name under which the corporation proposes to continue is similar to an existing corporate name, or the name contains the name of an individual, the consent of the existing corporation, or the individual, may be required to be submitted with the application.

An "Ontario biased" name search report is not required if the only change to the name of the corporation applying for continuation is the deletion of the legal element, e.g Limited, Incorporated or Corporation or the corresponding abbreviations thereof.

APPLICATION

Item 1 The current name of the applicant corporation must be set out in this item. The name must be set out in.BLOCK CAPITAL letters in the squares provided and must commence on the first line of the "grid" in the first square. Each square of the "grid" represents a letter of the alphabet, a punctuation mark or other mark permitted by the Regulations

07111 (06/2002)

FIGURE 15.6   CONTINUED

to the **Corporations Act** as forming part of the corporate name, or a space. If there is not sufficient space on the first line of the "grid" for the name, continue onto the second line and so on. (See example below.)

H	A	P	P	Y		T	I	M	E		R	E	C	R	E	A	T	I	O	N		A	N	D		D	A	Y		C	A
R	E		C	E	N	T	R	E		I	N	C	.																		

Item 2   This item must be completed if the corporation is to be continued under a name other than its current corporate name. A name search report must accompany the application if the name under which the corporation is to be continued is different from the current name of the corporation.
The procedure for obtaining .a name search report is as set out under the heading "Corporate Name" in these instructions.

Where the only difference in the name is the deletion of the legal element i.e. Limited, Corporation or Incorporated, or the corresponding abbreviation thereof, then a name search report is not required.

If the current name of the corporation is an Ontario Corporation Number name, e.g. 123456 Ontario Limited, the corporation cannot continue as a non-profit corporation under the Corporations Act under a "number name". The applicants for continuation will have to choose a new corporate name and will have to submit a name search report for the new name of the corporation.

Item 3   State the full date of incorporation/amalgamation of the corporation. (Day, Month and Year.)

Item 4   Set out the full address of the head office of the corporation, including postal code. (If the address is a multi-office building, include Room or Suite number.) A post office box is not an acceptable head office address.

Item 5   Set out the number of directors of the corporation. There must be a minimum of three directors set out in this item. Section **283(2)** of the **Corporations Act** states that the board of directors of a corporation shall consist of a fixed number of directors **not fewer than three.**

If the board of directors of the corporation consists at present of fewer than three directors then new directors must be appointed prior to completion of the application.

Item 6   The names, in full, address for service including postal codes, must be set out in this item.
A post office box is not an acceptable residence address.

Item 7   Set out the objects of the corporation in this item.

Item 8   Set out any special Provisions in this item. If none, state "Nil", "None" or "N/A".

Item 9   The date on which the shareholders/members of the corporation approved the making of the application must be set out in this item. (Day, Month and Year.)

The application must be accompanied by a certified copy of the shareholders/members resolution or an extract from the minutes of the general meeting of the shareholders/members indicating unanimous approval of the application.

EXECUTION

Both copies of the application must be signed by two officers, or one officer and one director of the corporation. Signatures must be originals on both copies of the application. Applications with photocopied signatures will not be accepted.

The name of the corporation must be set out above the signatures.

The corporate seal, if the Act under which the corporation was incorporated requires corporations to adopt a corporate seal, musi be affixed to both copies of the application.

07111 (06/2002)

FIGURE 15.6 CONTINUED

SUPPORTING DOCUMENTS

The application must be accompanied by:

An "Ontario biased" name search report only if the applicant corporation is to be continued under a corporate name other than its name at the time of submission of the application.

A name search report **is not** required if the only change to the corporate name is the deletion of the legal element, e.g. Limited, Incorporated or Corporation, or the corresponding abbreviation thereof. The name search report must be submitted within 90 days of production of the report.

A certified copy of a shareholders/members resolution or an extract from the minutes of a general meeting of the sharehlders/members indicating unanimous approval to the application for continuation. The resolution must also provide for the cancellation of all shares of the corporation, where applicable, upon issuance of the Letters Patent of Continuation.

The application, in duplicate, accompanied by the applicable fee, NUANS name search (if applicable) and supporting documents should be mailed or delivered to:

Ministry of Consumer and Business Services
Companies and Personal Property Branch
393 University Avenue, Suite 200
Toronto ON M5G 2M2

FIGURE 15.6 CONTINUED

1.

Ontario Corporation Number
Numéro de la personne morale en Ontario

Form 12.1
Corporations Act

Formule 12.1
Loi sur les personnes morales

APPLICATION FOR CONTINUATION
REQUÊTE EN VUE DU MAINTIEN DE LA PERSONNE MORALE

1. The name of the corporation is:
   Dénomination sociale de la personne morale :

2. The corporation is to be continued under the name (if different from 1):
   La personne morale sera maintenue sous le dénomination sociale de (si elle diffère de 1) :

3. Date of incorporation/amalgamation:
   Date de la constitution ou de la fusion :

   _____

   (day/jour, month/mois, year/année)

4. The address of the head office is:
   L'adresse du siège social est :

   _____
   (Street & Number., or R.R. No., or Lot & Concession No., or Lot & Plan No., Post Office Box No. not acceptable;
   if Multi-Office Building give Room No.)
   (Rue et numéro, ou R.R. et numéro, ou numéro de lot et de concession, ou numéro de lot et de plan; numéro de boîte postale inacceptable;
   s'il s'agit d'un édifice à bureaux, numéro du bureau)

   _____

   (Name of Municipality)   (Postal Code
   (Nom de la municipalité)   Code postal)

FIGURE 15.6 CONTINUED

2.

5. The number of directors is:
    Les administrateurs sont au nombre de :

6. The directors of the corporation are:
    Nom des administrateurs de la personne morale :

Name in full, including all given names Nom et prénoms au complet	Address for service, giving Street & No., or R.R. No.or Lot & Concession No., or Lot & Plan No., and Postal Code (Post Office Box No. not acceptable) Domicile élu y compris la rue et le numéro, ou la R.R. et le numéro, ou le numéro de lot et de concession, ou le numéro de lot et de plan, ainsi que le code postal (Numéro de boîte postale inacceptable)

FIGURE 15.6   CONTINUED

3.

7.   The objects of the corporation which is continued are to be:
     Objets de la personne morale qui est maintenue :

FIGURE 15.6 CONTINUED

4.

8. Special provisions (if any) are:
    Dispositions particulières (s'il y a lieu) :

07111 (06/2002)

FIGURE 15.6 CONCLUDED

5.

9. The continuation of the corporation has been properly authorized on
   Le maintien de la personne morale a été dûment autorisé le

   _____
   (day/jour, month/mois, year/année)

10. The corporation is to be continued under section 312 of the *Corporations Act* to the same extent as if it had been incorporated under this Act.

    La personne morale sera maintenue en vertu de l'article 312 de la *Loi sur les personnes morales* comme si elle avait été constituée en vertu de cette loi.

This application is executed in duplicate.
La présente requête est faite en double exemplaire.

_____
Name of corporation
Nom de Dénomination sociale de la personne morale

By:
Par : _____
Signature and Discription of Office
Signature et fonction du titre

(corporate seal)
(sceau de la personne morale)

_____
Signature and Discription of Office
Signature et fonction du titre

FIGURE 15.7 FORM 9, ONTARIO CORPORATIONS ACT, APPLICATION FOR SURRENDER OF CHARTER/ TERMINATION OF CORPORATE EXISTENCE

 **Ontario**   Ministry of Consumer and Business Services

Companies and Personal Property Security Branch
393 University Ave Suite 200
Toronto ON M5G 2M2

**Application for surrender of charter/ termination of corporate existence
Form 9
Corporations Act
Instructions for Completing**

FEE

NO FEE REQUIRED

FORMAT

The application must be submitted **in duplicate** on Form 9 as prescribed in Ontario Regulations made under the **Corporations Act**. Applications which do not conform to Form 9 cannot be accepted, and will be returned to the applicant(s)/agent who submitted the application.

APPEARANCE OF DOCUMENTS

Applications, and any supporting documents, which are to be filed with the Ministry must be typewritten, or, if completed by hand, printed in BLOCK CAPITAL letters in black ink. Applications, and supporting documents, must be legible and compatible with the microfilming process.

Forms, and any supporting documents or extra pages, must be printed on one side of good quality white bond paper 8 1/2" by 11", or the metric equivalent. Facsimile (Fax) applications or supporting documents cannot be accepted in lieu of original copies.

PAGES

Pages are numbered 1 and 2. Applications with missing pages cannot be accepted.

SUPPORTING DOCUMENTS

An application for surrender/termination of corporate existence must be accompanied by:

a)   in the case of a company with share capital, the consent of the Corporations Tax Branch of the Ministry of Finance; and

b)   in the case of a company with share capital that is a reporting issuer under the Securities Act, a consent from the Ontario Securities Commission.

APPLICATION

Item 1   The current name of the corporation must be set out in BLOCK CAPITAL letters in the squares provided and must commence on the first line of the "grid" in the first square. Each square of the "grid" represents a letter of the alphabet, a punctuation mark or other mark permitted by Regulations to the **Corporations Act** as forming part of a corporate name, or a space. If there is not sufficient space on the first line of the "grid" for the name, continue onto the second line and so on. (See example below.)

H	A	P	P	Y		T	I	M	E		R	E	C	R	E	A	T	I	O	N		A	N	D		D	A	Y		C	A
R	E		C	E	N	T	R	E		I	N	C	.																		

Item 2   State the full date of incorporation/amalgamation of the corporation. (Year, Month and Day).

Item 4   Delete those sentences which **do not apply.** Leave only (a), only (b) or only (c).

EXECUTION

Both copies of the application must be signed by two officers, two directors or one officer and one director of the corporation. Applications containing photocopied signatures will not be accepted.

The name of the corporation must be set out above the signatures.

The application (in duplicate) should be mailed or delivered to:

Ministry of Consumer & Business Services
Companies and Personal Property Security Branch
393 University Avenue Suite 200
Toronto ON M5G 2M2

07070 (01/2002)

FIGURE 15.7 CONTINUED

This space is for Ministry
Use Only
Espace réservé à l'usage
exclusif du ministère

Insert Ontario Corporation Number
Insérer le numéro de la
personne morale en Ontario

1.

Form 9
Corporations
Act

Formule 9
Loi sur les
personnes
morales

APPLICATION FOR SURRENDER OF CHARTER/TERMINATION OF CORPORATE EXISTENCE
REQUÊTE EN ABANDON DE CHARTE OU EN VUE DE METTRE FIN À L'EXISTENCE
DE LA PERSONNE MORALE

1. Name of the applicant corporation/Dénomination sociale de la personne morale requérante :

2. Date of incorporation/amalgamation/Date de la constitution ou de la fusion :

_____
(year/année   month/mois   day/jour)

3. The surrender of charter/termination of corporate existence has been duly authorized under clause 319 (1) (a) of the **Corporations Act.**

L'abandon de la charte ou la fin de l'existence de la personne morale a été dûment autorisé aux termes de l'alinéa 319 (1) (a) de la **Loi sur les personne morales.**

4. The corporation/La personne morale :
   (a) has no debts, obligations or liabilities;
       n'a ni dettes, ni obligations, ni engagements;
   (b) has duly provided for or protected its debts, obligations or liabilities in accordance with subsection 319 (1) of the **Corporations Act;**
       a dûment pourvu à ses dettes, obligations ou engagements, ou les a protégés, conformément au paragraphe 319 (1) de la **Loi sur les personnes morales;**
   (c) has obtained consent to its dissolution from its creditors or other persons having interests in its debts, obligations or liabilities.
       a obtenu le consentement à sa dissolution de ses créanciers ou des autres personnes ayant des intérêts dans ses dettes, obligations ou engagements.

5. The corporation has parted with its property by distributing it rateably among its shareholders or members according to their rights and interests in the corporation.
   La personne morale s'est départie de ses biens en les répartissant entre ses actionnaires ou ses membres au prorata de leurs droits et intérêts dans la personne morale.

6. The corporation has filed all notices and returns required under the **Corporations Information Act.**
   La personne morale a déposé tous les avis et déclarations exigés par la **Loi sur les renseignements exigés des personnes morales;**

7. There are no proceedings pending in any court against the corporation.
   Il n'y a contre la personne morale aucune instance judiciaire en cours.

07070(01/2002)

FIGURE 15.7 CONCLUDED

2.

8. The corporation has complied with the requirements of the **Corporations Act** and the conditions contained in the letters patent or by-laws of the corporation precedent to the delivery of this application for the surrender of its charter/ termination of corporate existence.

La personne morale s'est conformée à toutes les exigences de la **Loi sur les personnes morales** et aux conditions contenues dans ses lettres patentes ou ses règlements administratifs préalablement à la remise de la présente requête en abandon de charte ou en vue de mettre fin à son existence.

This application is executed in duplicate. / La présente requête est faite en double exemplaire.

_____
(Name of corporation/Dénomination sociale de la personne morale)

By/Par: _____
(Signature/Signature)   (Description of Office/Fonction)

_____
(Signature/Signature)   (Description of Office/Fonction)

07070 (01/2002)

FIGURE 15.8 FORM 10, ONTARIO CORPORATIONS ACT, APPLICATION FOR REVIVAL
OF CORPORATION

Ontario

Ministry of	Companies Branch
Consumer and	393 University Ave Suite 200
Commercial Relations	Toronto ON M5G 2M2

**Application for Revival
of a Corporation
Form 10
Corporations Act
Instructions for completing**

FEE

For fee payable refer to Regulations made under the **Corporations Act**. If you do not have a copy of the Regulations on hand, you may obtain information regarding fees payable under the **Corporations Act** by phoning, in Toronto 314-8880, or Toll free 1-800-361-3223. Cheques or Money Orders are to be made payable to the Minister of Finance. Where a cheque is tendered as payment, the name of the corporation must be written on the front of the cheque. Do not send cash through the mail. **There will be a service charge payable for any cheques returned as non-negotiable by a Bank or Financial Institution.**

FORMAT OF DOCUMENTS

When forwarding Applications for Revival please enclose a covering letter which sets out the name of the firm and /or the name of the individual submitting the Articles, as well as a return address and a telephone number. This will facilitate the processing of the document should a question arise as to the content of the Application for Revival.

The application must be submitted in duplicate on Form 10 as prescribed in Ontario Regulations made under the **Corporations Act**. Applications which do not conform to Form 10 cannot be accepted, and will be returned to the applicant(s)/agent who submitted the application.

APPEARANCE OF DOCUMENTS

Applications, and any supporting documents, which are to be filed with the Ministry must be typewritten, or, if completed by hand printed in BLOCK CAPITAL letters in black ink. Applications, and supporting documents, must be legible and compatible with the microfilming process.

Forms, and any supporting documents or extra pages, must be printed on one side of good quality bond paper 8 1/2" by 11", or the metric equivalent. Facsimile (Fax) applications or supporting documents cannot be accepted in lieu of original copies.

PAGES

Pages are numbered 1 and 2. Applications with missing pages cannot be accepted. If additional pages are required due to lack of space they must be the same size as all the other pages, must have a margin of 30 mm. or 1 1/4" on the left hand side, and must be numbered the same as the original page with letter of the alphabet indicating sequence. e.g. 1A, 1B etc.

APPLICATION

Item 1   The name of the reviving corporation, at dissolution, must be set out in this item. The name must be set out in BLOCK CAPITAL letters in the squares provided and must commence on the first line of the "grid" in the first square. Each square of the "grid" represents a letter of the alphabet, a punctuation mark or other mark permitted by the Regulations of the Corporations Act as forming part of the corporate name, or a space. If there is not sufficient space on the first line of the "grid" for the name, continue onto the second line and so on. (See Example below.)

07106 (08/98)

FIGURE 15.8   CONTINUED

Item 2	If the corporation is to be revived under a name other than its name at dissolution set out the "new" name in this item. If this item is not applicable please leave it blank.

Applicants must obtain an "Ontario biased" name search report produced by the NUANS system, for the new name under which the corporation is to be revived. Name search reports are obtainable from name search corporations. These corporations are listed in the Yellow Pages under the heading "Searchers of Records". The name search report must be submitted with the application for revival and must be dated no more than 90 days prior to the date of submission of the report. An original name search report and not a photocopy must be submitted.

Item 3   State the date of incorporation/amalgamation of the corporation. (Year, Month and Day)

Item 4   State the date of dissolution of the corporation. (Year, Month, Day)

Item 5   Set out the full mailing address, including postal code, for mailing Notices and Returns under the **Corporations Information Act**. (If the address is a multi-office building include Room or Suite number.) A post office box is not an acceptable mailing address. If there is no street and number assigned then set out a Lot and Concession number.

Item 6

a)   All Notices and Returns under the **Corporations Information Act** must be filed and all defaults of the corporation up to the date of dissolution must be remedied.

b)   A letter from the Public Trustee, if applicable, stating that the Public Trustee has no objection to the requested revival must be filed with the application.

c)   Where the revival is sought for a company **with share capital** the consent of the Corporations Tax Branch of the Ministry of Finance must accompany the application. In the case of a corporation **without share capital** the consent is not required and clause (c) of Item 6 should be deleted.

d)   All documents required to be filed by the corporation under Ontario tax statutes must be filed and all defaults remedied, (If applicable).

Item 7   State briefly, the interest the applicant had in the corporation immediately before its dissolution. (e.g. member, officer, creditor etc.)

Item 8   State the reason(s) for requesting the revival of the corporation. e.g. To continue to carry out the objectives of the corporation.

EXECUTION

Set out the full name of the applicant. Both copies of the application must be **manually** signed.
Applications containing photocopied signatures will not be accepted.

The application, in duplicate, and supporting documents. if applicable, may be mailed or delivered to:

> Ministry of Consumer and Commercial Relations
> Companies Branch
> 393 University Ave. Suite 200
> Toronto ON M5G 2M2

FIGURE 15.8 CONTINUED

This space is for
Ministry Use Only
Espace réservé à l'usage
exclusif du ministère

Insert Ontario Corporation Number
Insérer le numéro de la
personne morale en Ontario

1.

APPLICATION FOR REVIVAL OF CORPORATION
REQUÊTE EN RECONSTITUTION DE LA PERSONNE MORALE

Form 10
Corporations Act

Formule 10
Loi sur les personnes morales

1. Name of dissolved corporation/Dénomination sociale de la personne morale dissoute :

2. The corporation is to be revived under the name (if different from 1):
La personne morale sera reconstituée sous la dénomination sociale de (si elle diffère de 1) :

3. Date of incorporation/amalgamation:
Date de la constitution ou de la fusion:

4. Date of dissolution:
Date de la dissolution:

(year/année)　month/mois　day/jour)　　(year/année)　month/mois　day/jour)

5. The address for the head office is/Adresse du siège social :

(Street & No., or R.R. No., or Lot & Concession No., or Lot & Plan no.; Post Office Box No. not acceptable;
if Multi-Office Building give Room No.)
(Rue et numéro ou, R.R. et numéro, ou numéro de lot et de concession, ou numéro de lot et de plan; numéro de boîte postale inacceptable;
s'il s'agit d'un édifice à bureaux, numéro du bureau)

(Name of Municipality)
(Nom de la municipalité)

(Postal Code/Code postal)

07106(08/98)

FIGURE 15.8 CONCLUDED

2.

6. The following terms and conditions have been complied with:

    (a) all notices and returns required to be filed by the corporation under the **Corporations Information Act** have been filed and all other defaults of the corporation to the date of dissolution have been remedied.

    (b) the consent of the Public Trustee to the requested revival (if applicable) accompanies this application.

    (c) the consent of the Corporations Tax Branch of the Ministry of Finance (if applicable) accompanies this application.

    (d) all documents required to be filed by the corporation under Ontario tax statutes have been filed and all defaults of the corporation under the tax statutes have been remedied (if applicable).

7. Immediately before dissolution the interest of the applicant in the corporation was:

8. The reasons for requesting revival of the corporation are:

9. It is requested that the corporation be revived under the provisions of subsection 317(10) of the **Corporations Act.**

This application is executed in duplicate.

Full name and signature of the applicant

Les conditions suivantes ont été observées :

(a) tous les avis exigés par la **Loi sur les renseignements exigés des personnes morales** ont été déposés et toutes autres omissions de la personne morale à la date de la dissolution ont été corrigées.

(b) le consentement du curateur public à la reconstitution de la personne morale (le cas échéant) est joint à la présente requête.

(c) le consentement de la Direction de l'imposition des corporations du ministère des Finances (le cas échéant) est joint à la présente requête.

(d) tous les documents exigés par les lois d'imposition de l'Ontario ont été déposés et toutes les omissions commises par la personne morale à l'égard de ces lois ont été corrigées (le cas échéant).

Immédiatement avant la dissolution l'intérêt du requérant dans la personne morale était le suivant :

La reconstitution de la personne morale est demandée pour les motifs suivants :

La reconstitution de la personne morale est demandée aux termes du paragraphe 317(10) de la **Loi sur les personnes morales.**

La présente requête est faite en double exemplaire.

Nom au complet et signature du requérant

07106(08/98)

Glossary

agent for service an individual or a corporation whose responsibilities are to be available to receive service of documents on an extra-provincially registered corporation and to pass these documents on as quickly as possible to the principal

annual meeting a meeting of shareholders held to consider the minutes of the previous meeting; receive the directors' annual report, the financial statements, and the auditor's report; elect directors; appoint auditors; and conduct any further business properly brought before the meeting

appraisal rights a shareholder remedy where a dissenting shareholder may require a corporation to purchase its shares upon the shareholder's complying with the requirements set out in the statutes

arrangement an agreement entered into by a corporation with its shareholders to effect a compromise or arrangement with respect to the rights of the shareholders that cause the corporation difficulty, financial or other

articles of incorporation a document filed with the appropriate government authority that provides for incorporation as of right, provided that the required steps are followed

bylaws regulations made by a corporation to govern its internal affairs

casting vote a vote that decides between two equal parties, especially when used by the chair of a meeting

charitable power clauses clauses inserted in an application for incorporation or application for supplementary letters patent that empower an NPO to do specific acts

club an organization or premises, typically a service (such as the Rotary Club) or social club, whose objectives are wholly or partly social in nature

co-operative a type of member-owned organization in which people with common interests and goals join forces to advance a cause such as providing housing assistance or promoting the interests of workers

co-ownership a number of persons holding title to some property — generally real property — where the parties' interests remain separate and they are free to dispose of their interest without the consent of the other co-owners, subject to any agreement the parties may have entered into

coined word   a word that has been created and is unrelated to any other word

common law   the body of recognized legal principles that is derived from case law and judicial precedent

common shares   shares that entitle their owners to participate fully in the corporation and to receive dividends and any remaining property of the corporation available for distribution on its dissolution or windup

condominium   a method of land ownership in which the entire property is owned by a corporation, which is in turn owned by the owners of individual units within the condominium; ownership of units is registered separately from ownership of the complex as a whole

continuance   a procedure that allows a corporation governed by the laws of one jurisdiction to leave that jurisdiction and to continue and become governed by the laws of another jurisdiction

corporation profile report   a report produced by the Ontario Companies Branch that displays current information on the public record about a corporation, including all directors, officers, and registered office, as well as some historical information, such as amalgamation and name history

corporation   an entity with a separate legal identity from that of its principals, which is brought into existence by filing a document under the appropriate statute or special statute of the jurisdiction in which the corporation carries on business

cumulative voting   a right sometimes given to shareholders whereby every shareholder entitled to elect directors can cast a number of votes equal to the number of votes attached to that shareholder's shares multiplied by the number of directors to be elected; in some cases, the shareholder may cast all his or her votes in favour of one candidate or distribute the votes among the candidates in any manner he or she sees fit

derivative action   a shareholder remedy where a complainant may apply to the court for permission to bring an action on behalf of the corporation or to intervene in an action to which the corporation is a party, for the purpose of prosecuting, defending, or discontinuing the action on behalf of the corporation

designated partner   a partner in a partnership with more than 10 partners and a principal place of business in Ontario who submits a form on behalf of the partnership for registration under the *Business Names Act*

directors   individuals responsible for managing the business and affairs of a corporation for the benefit of the shareholders

domain name   an address for individuals and businesses on the World Wide Web

electronic meeting   a meeting conducted by telephonic or other electronic means that allows all participants in the meeting to communicate fully

ex officio   by virtue of office — a person holding office who becomes a director because he or she holds that office

extra-provincial limited liability company an unincorporated association, other than a partnership, formed under the laws of another jurisdiction that grants to each of the members limited liability with respect to the liabilities of the association

extra-provincial limited partnership in Ontario, a limited partnership organized under the laws of a jursidiction other than Ontario

fixed board a board of directors of a corporation that has a set number of directors determined in the articles

floating board a board of directors of a corporation that has a minimum and maximum number of directors determined in the articles

franchise an arrangement formed by a written agreement whereby one person — the franchisor — grants a right to another person — the franchisee — to use a trademark or trade name in connection with the supply of goods or services by the franchisee and requires the franchisee to conduct its business in accordance with operating methods and procedures developed and controlled by the franchisor

general partnership a partnership in which each partner is liable for the debts and other obligations of all partners to an unlimited degree

information kit a resource published by Corporations Canada that sets out the requirements, procedures, and precedents for incorporating in the federal jurisdiction

insolvent being unable to pay one's liabilities as they become due, or having assets whose realizable value is less than the aggregate of one's liabilities

issued capital number of shares issued and outstanding in the capital of the corporation

joint stock company a company created by statute whose members traded on the capital of all other members

joint venture a commercial business activity carried on by two or more parties for a common purpose in compliance with established terms and conditions

legend conspicuous notice on a share certificate to ensure that the transferee is bound by the terms of the document, notice of which is being given

letter of satisfaction a document issued by the federal Director, good for only 90 days, that authorizes a corporation to continue and that is submitted to the authorities in the importing jurisdiction

letters patent a document issued by the Crown through its representative to create a commercial entity

licence a contractual arrangement whereby the owner of certain property such as a trademark, copyright, or patent — the licensor — grants to another person — the licensee — the right to use such property for a royalty fee

limited liability corporation (LLC)   an alternative to a traditional corporation, general partnership, and limited partnership; like a general partnership, an LLC has the advantage of flowthrough taxation — that is, the LLC's profits and losses flow through to the LLC members — and flexibility in management and other matters; like a corporation, an LLC has limited liability for its investing members or shareholders

limited liability partnership   a partnership in which each partner is jointly and severally liable for all the debts and obligations of the partnership except for liabilities arising from professional negligence, which remain those of the partner whose acts or omissions or whose subordinates' acts or omissions resulted in the professional liability

limited partnership   a partnership in which there are one or more general partners who are liable for the debts and other obligations of the other partners to an unlimited degree and one or more limited partners whose liability is limited to the amount that such limited partner has contributed to the partnership business

master business licence (MBL)   a licence issued by the Ministry of Consumer and Business Services upon registration of a sole proprietorship, partnership, limited partnership, or business name that can be used as proof of business name registration at financial institutions and to facilitate any other business-related registration with the Ontario government

members   the persons who elect directors of an NPO (like shareholders of a share capital corporation); members do not "own" an NPO, but they may, if authorized in the letters patent or bylaws of a non-charitable NPO, be entitled to receive the remaining assets of an NPO on windup or dissolution

memorandum of association   a document filed with an appropriate government department to bring a company into existence

minute book   a book in which the corporate records of a corporation are maintained

non-offering corporation   a corporation that does not offer its shares for sale to the public

Not-for-Profit Policy Summary   the summary published from time to time by Corporations Canada that outlines the requirements for incorporation under the *Canada Corporations Act*; it describes the process of application for incorporation and the framework for bylaws of a federal NPO, and addresses requests for ministerial approval to amend the bylaws of existing corporations

NUANS system   a computerized search system that compares a proposed corporate name or trademark with databases of existing names or trademarks

objects   statements of the purposes and objectives of an NPO

offering corporation   a corporation that offers its shares for sale to the public

officers   individuals who manage a corporation's day-to-day activities under the supervision of the directors

Ontario Business Information System (ONBIS)   an electronic database of information on companies, sole proprietorships, partnerships, limited partnerships, and business names registered in Ontario, maintained by the Ontario Companies Branch

oppression remedy   a shareholder remedy where a complainant may apply to the court for an order to rectify the matters complained of; the complainant must satisfy the court that the specified concerns are oppressive or unfairly prejudicial to, or that they unfairly disregard the interests of, a security holder, creditor, director, or officer of the corporation

option   a right to acquire securities of a corporation on specified conditions and prices at specified times

ordinary resolution   a resolution that is passed by at least a majority of the votes cast

par value   an arbitrary sum prescribed in the corporation's articles, which was the minimum amount for which a share could be issued

partnership   the relation that subsists between persons carrying on a business in common with a view to profit

passing off   a common law tort whereby one person carries on a business under a name that tends to mislead the public into thinking that the business is being carried on by another person

pecuniary gain   a gain that a person may have in a matter because of a likelihood or expectation of appreciable financial gain to that person or to another person with whom the person is associated

perpetual existence   existence with an indefinite term ("forever")

post-incorporation organization   the passage of certain resolutions and the preparation of certain documents to set the corporation up to be in a legal position to do business

pre-emptive rights   any further issue of shares must first be offered to the existing shareholders of the same or another class or series of shares on such terms as are provided in the articles or USA before being offered to others

pre-incorporation contract   a written or oral contract entered into by a person on behalf of a corporation to be incorporated

preferred shares (or preference shares)   shares that have priority over other classes of shares

proxy   a document by which a shareholder appoints a "proxyholder" or one or more alternate "proxyholders," who need not be shareholders, as the shareholder's nominee to attend and act at the meeting in the manner, to the extent, and with the authority conferred by the proxy

quorum   the minimum number of directors, shareholders, or members, as applicable, that must be present at a meeting to constitute a valid meeting

record date (for shareholders entitled to receive notice of meetings) a date fixed in advance by the directors for the purpose of determining which shareholders are entitled to receive notice of a meeting of shareholders

red tape reduction legislation a series of Ontario statutes intended to simplify the administration of several statutes

registered charity an organization, whether incorporated or not, that has been established for one or more charitable purposes and registered as a charity with the CRA

registered charity information return (Form T3010A) the charity information return that must be filed with the CRA by every registered charity on an annual basis and within six months following the expiration of a registered charity's financial year

reorganization a court order made under the CBCA, the OBCA, or the *Bankruptcy and Insolvency Act* approving a proposal, which may include an amendment to a corporation's articles

resident Canadian defined under the CBCA and the OBCA variously but essentially as an individual who is a Canadian citizen ordinarily resident in Canada, a Canadian citizen not ordinarily resident in Canada who is a member of a prescribed class of persons, or a permanent resident of Canada within the meaning of the federal *Immigration Act* and ordinarily resident in Canada

revival the process of restoring a corporation that has been dissolved as if it had never been dissolved

secondary meaning when applied to a corporate name, a meaning that has acquired distinctiveness through use over a period of time

series a subdivision of shares within a class of shares

share capital corporation a corporation that has been incorporated for profit and issues shares

shareholders the "owners" of a corporation who elect the directors

shares a percentage of the ownership of a corporation that entitles its holder to certain rights in the corporation

sole proprietorship the carrying on of business for profit by an individual without other owners

special act corporation or company a corporation formed by a special statute passed by Parliament to undertake special projects

special business business conducted at a meeting of shareholders other than consideration of the minutes of an earlier meeting, the financial statements and auditor's report, election of directors, and reappointment of the incumbent auditor

special resolution a resolution that is passed by at least two-thirds of the votes cast in respect of the resolution, or that is consented to in writing by all the shareholders who are entitled to vote on the resolution

special shares   shares that have rights, privileges, restrictions, and conditions that do not apply to common shares

staggered term   a varied period of time for which directors are elected

standing committee   committee that is permanent during the existence of an NPO

statutory declaration   a sworn declaration (like an affidavit) made by an applicant for incorporation of a federal NPO

Strategis   an information site and online database of resources for businesses, operated by Corporations Canada

term   when applied to the election of directors, the period of time for which the director is elected to act as a director

trademark   a word, symbol, or design, or a combination of these, used to identify wares, goods, or services of one business and differentiate them from those of others

unanimous shareholder agreement (USA)   a written agreement among all of the shareholders of a corporation or among all of the shareholders and a person who is not a shareholder (for example, a director), or a declaration made by the sole beneficial shareholder, that restricts in whole or in part the powers of the directors to manage the business and affairs of the corporation

unanimous written resolution   a resolution that is passed by all of the directors or members of an NPO

unincorporated association   an association of persons carrying on a not-for-profit activity without the protection of incorporation

warrant   a certificate or other document issued by a corporation as evidence of conversion privileges or options or rights to acquire securities of the corporation

Index